Catharine Arnold read English at Cambridge University and holds a further degree in psychology. Catharine's previous books include the novel *Lost Time* and the acclaimed *Necropolis: London and Its Dead*, *Bedlam: London and Its Mad*, and *City of Sin: London and Its Vices*, also available from Simon & Schuster.

Praise for *Underworld London*:

'Catharine Arnold has assembled a history of British crimes to chill the blood but also titillate the reader' *Mail on Sunday*

'Arnold has already published four excellent social histories of sex, madness, debauchery and death in the capital and maintains her usual high standard here, never flinching from grisly facts' Press Association

Praise for *Necropolis*:

'*Necropolis* is deeply pleasing: it satisfies the desire for wayward knowledge, being a compendium of death in all its forms while at the same time providing entertainment of the most garish and exquisite kind ... It is a Baedeker of the dead' Peter Ackroyd, *The Times*

Praise for *Bedlam*:

'Finely written and colourful' *Independent*

Praise for *City of Sin*:

'Fascinating and colourful' *Observer*

'Arnold ... is a delightful travelling companion through the centuries of the city of sin' Jeanette Winterson, *The Times*

UNDERWORLD LONDON

*Crime and Punishment
in the Capital City*

CATHARINE ARNOLD

SIMON &
SCHUSTER

London · New York · Sydney · Toronto · New Delhi

A CBS COMPANY

First published in Great Britain by Simon & Schuster UK Ltd, 2012
This paperback edition published by Simon & Schuster UK Ltd, 2013
A CBS COMPANY

3 5 7 9 10 8 6 4 2

Simon & Schuster UK Ltd
1st Floor
222 Gray's Inn Road
London
WC1X 8HB

www.simonandschuster.co.uk

Simon & Schuster Australia, Sydney
Simon & Schuster India, New Delhi

A CIP catalogue record for this book is available
from the British Library

Paperback ISBN: 978-1-47114-194-2
Ebook ISBN: 978-0-85720-117-1

Typeset by M Rules
Printed and bound by CPI Group (UK) Ltd, Croydon, CR0 4YY

For my husband

Till a' the seas gang dry, my dear,
And the rocks melt wi' the sun:
I will luve thee still, my dear,
While the sands o' life shall run.

Robbie Burns

Contents

Acknowledgements

With grateful thanks to Cambridge University Library; the Hallward Library at the University of Nottingham; my agent, Charlie Viney; my editor, Kerri Sharp; Dr Simon Lee Price for his generous and helpful comments; Sue Stephens and Rory Scarfe at Simon & Schuster; Brian Catling for allowing me to share the inscription from his beautiful memorial at Tower Green; Paul Willetts; Lucille Venn; and most of all my wonderful family.

'Many cart-loads of our fellow-creatures are once in six weeks carried to slaughter.'

Henry Fielding, 1751

'The following malefactors were executed at Tyburn – John Kelly, for robbing Edward Adamson in a public street of sixpence and one farthing.'

Gentleman's Magazine, 7 March 1783

'It is frequently said by the prisoners of Newgate that the crimes of which they have been guilty are as nothing when compared with the crimes of Government towards themselves: that they have only been thieves, but that their governors have been murderers.'

Mrs Elizabeth Fry, prison reformer, 1818

Introduction

Imagine that you are standing at Marble Arch today, looking east, down the vista of eight hundred years. Picture an innumerable procession of men and women advancing from the mist, walking to their deaths from the Tower of London or Newgate Gaol to the bloody field of Tyburn. Historians can only surmise the number of those who suffered violent death here, but a modest estimate would put the figure at around 50,000. This black parade is composed of all sorts and conditions of men, from aristocrats to artisans, priests to petty thieves, and notorious murderers to young boys who have stolen a few pennies. Learned scholars and priests rub shoulders with illiterate thugs. Highwaymen swagger in their finery while fraudulent clerks twitch nervously. There are women here, too: an unrepentant murderess resplendent in black satin and an innocent maiden in her white bridal gown. Alongside them stride rebels and martyrs whose only crime was to refuse to renounce their cherished beliefs at the bidding of a tyrant.

Tyburn's dead travel along this Via Dolorosa in different ways. Some are bound with rope, tied to a horse and dragged five miles from the Tower. The majority ride in horse-drawn carts, alongside their coffins. This is, for the most part, a nameless, unrecorded crowd. Over the centuries, only the occasional figure emerges here and there from the anonymous throng. It is just for a few decades in the history of Tyburn that we will see certain characters from this procession clearly, and in detail. Mainly they pass in faceless batches of ten, fifteen, twenty: laughing boys; women with babies at the breast; men and women drunk, cursing, crying, praying. Some of the women will be burnt alive. Of the men, all will hang, but some will be cut down, still conscious, and forced to watch as they are disembowelled and their entrails burnt before their very eyes. A few will be hanged in chains or placed in a gibbet until the flesh rots from their bones. Alongside these unfortunates march the spectators, the family and friends of the dead, and those who consider public executions to be first-rate entertainment. For centuries, hangings were holidays, offering all the fun of the Tyburn fair. The crowd gorged on gingerbread, roast pork and beer, before shouting 'Hats off!' and craning to see the condemned men kicking their way to death at the end of a short rope.

Barbaric by modern standards, public executions were a common sight up until 1868. In 1660, the diarist Samuel Pepys went to see Major-General Harrison hanged, drawn and quartered, and observed that he looked as cheerful as any man could in that condition. 'He was presently cut down, and his head and his heart shown to the people, at which there was great shouts of joy.' Pepys also witnessed the hanging of Colonel John Turner for burglary in 1664. After paying a shilling to watch, Pepys stood on the wheel of a cart, 'in great pain', as Turner tried to delay his death by delivering speech after speech. Turner was eventually hanged, 'flung off the ladder in his cloak' and Pepys went home to dinner 'all in a sweat'. Pepys also saw a number of gibbets. During a country ride, he and a female companion 'rode under the man that hangs upon Shooter's Hill; and a filthy sight it was to see how his flesh is shrunk to his bones'.

The 1752 Murder Act allowed judges to make an example of murderers by ordering that their corpses should be displayed on a gibbet. Thus, in the 1770s, up to one hundred gibbets stood on Hounslow Heath, so that, according to the poet Robert Southey, 'from whatever quarter the wind blew, it brought with it a cadaverous and pestilential odour'. The Sunday after the highwayman Lewis Avershaw was gibbeted on Wimbledon Common in 1795, the city was deserted as Londoners flocked to view the corpse. For months after, this grisly spectacle was a popular outing.

Taking Tyburn and the history and abolition of capital punishment as its major theme, this book visits the major landmarks of London's underworld. In the course of this journey, I introduce the reader to Newgate Gaol, described by the barrister Henry Fielding as 'London's prototype of Hell', and its equally famous neighbour, the venerable Old Bailey. There is the chance to canter across the moonlit Common with the highwaymen, learn the secrets of top pickpockets in the Victorian West End, and venture into the dark and deadly territory of Whitechapel on the trail of Jack the Ripper. From time to time, the narrative will be interrupted, just as London has been, by insurrection, from the Gordon Riots of 1780 which saw Newgate Gaol burnt to the ground, to the disturbances of August 2011.

The horrific history of capital punishment includes an extraordinary cast of characters, from the celebrated Newgate escapee Jack Sheppard to the evil thief-taker Jonathan Wild, from the mild-mannered Doctor Crippen to the glittering ash-blonde Ruth Ellis, the last woman to be hanged. This tour of the capital's underworld is not for the faint-hearted. Beneath the veneer of sophistication and culture lurks a lawless London, a substratum of passion, darkness and despair. The legacy of this lingers on in the incipient melancholy of the London street, the abiding sense of mystery and unsolved crimes, of footsteps echoing in the distance, the flick of a cape, the discovery of a battered corpse lying in a pool of blood. Murderers cast a long shadow. Even today, serving police officers post in chat rooms, speculating on the true identity of Jack the Ripper and other unsolved crimes. Who can forget the image of Lady Lucan, staggering out of her Belgravia home with a massive head wound, after her husband Lord Lucan had apparently murdered their nanny, Sandra Rivett, mistaking her for his wife? Or the glittering, violent career of the Kray twins – local heroes, celebrity socialites and ruthless murderers?

Everyone in London has their own tale to tell of near-misses and narrow escapes. When the estate agent, Suzy Lamplugh, went missing in 1986, her car was found outside the house where I lived. My flatmate, who knew Suzy from the West London social scene, took it personally. I also recall the sense of outrage when the television presenter Jill Dando was shot dead on her own doorstep, just a street away from ours.

My own interest in crime began early, after I raced through the original Sherlock Holmes stories then read my way through my parents' extensive collection of Penguin thrillers. Rather more unsuitably, I picked up Colin Wilson's *Encyclopaedia of Murder* at the age of twelve and scared the life out of myself. To my mother's horror, I was transfixed by this graphic catalogue of true-life crime, but my interest was creative and forensic rather than ghoulish. I was intrigued not only by crime itself, but by the killers' motivations, and the strong conviction that above all the victims should not be forgotten. Years later, after exploring the darkest aspects of London's history, this fascination still endures. The distinguished advocate Sir Edward Marshall Hall once said that when defending a client, and bringing the details of the case alive, he set out 'to create an atmosphere out of the vivid, living dream of someone else's life'. If I have managed to do this in *Underworld London: Crime and Punishment in the Capital City*, then I shall have succeeded.

1

CITY OF GALLOWS

Roots of the Tyburn Tree

The shadow of the noose looms large over London's history. Nowhere more so than at Tyburn, that desolate space beyond the city walls, where rebels, criminals and martyrs have been executed from time immemorial, as merciless governments strove to preserve an iron grip upon the populace. In the earliest years, offenders were hanged from the branches of the elm trees, until the development of purpose-built gallows, consisting of simple wooden structures with a transverse beam, from which the unfortunate prisoners dangled at the end of a very short rope.

Today, Marble Arch, surrounded by an endless flow of traffic, marks the spot where once the gallows stood. Eight hundred years ago, this windswept plain was silent, apart from the rustle of the elm trees and the caw of the carrion crow. Tyburn was located three miles north west of London for a reason. While the sight of a hanged man was believed to represent an effective deterrent, no citizen wanted to live alongside the reek of putrefaction. Tyburn also had its gibbets, metal cages in which the corpses of the hanged were displayed and left to rot. The mediaeval historian Matthew Paris recorded seeing two prisoners gibbeted, one already dead, the other still alive, condemned to die of exposure and starvation. Between executions, foxes, birds and badgers feasted on the 'friendless bodies of unburied men'[1] and scattered their remains across the heath.

On 6 April 1196, the stillness was shattered by the arrival of a roaring mob, and the pounding of hooves as a horse appeared in a cloud of dust over the horizon, dragging behind it the body of a man. This was the scene as William Fitzosbert, alias 'Longbeard', arrived at Tyburn to be executed for treason, the most grievous crime in the land. Plotting to overthrow the king and the state could only be punishable by death, and death of the most horrific and undignified kind. The sentence consisted of drawing, hanging and quartering, a barbaric practice which involved being dragged or 'drawn' to the gallows, then 'hanged by the neck and let down alive' before being disembowelled (another form of 'drawing' when the intestines were 'drawn' from the body), burnt alive, beheaded, and hacked into four parts or 'quarters'. Finally, the mutilated head and 'quarters' were put on display in prominent positions, such as Tower Bridge or the Temple Bar, *pour décourager les autres.*

Fitzosbert had already been stripped to the waist, bound hand and foot with rope, tied to the tail of a horse, and then 'drawn' or dragged from the Tower of London, a distance of over five miles. Many prisoners died of 'drawing' long before they reached the gallows.

As Fitzosbert was untied and hurled at the foot of the gallows, where a thick chain was placed around his neck preparatory to hanging, he must have reflected on the unhappy series of events that had brought him to this pass. For Fitzosbert had been a privileged man, even if the 'Fitz' in his name denotes that he was a 'bastard', born out of wedlock, to the affluent Osbert family. Fitzosbert, who was raised by his older brother and followed him into the family tailoring business, should have led a long and uneventful life, without troubling the history books. But Fitzosbert was the original bearded agitator.[2] Despite the Norman fashion for a clean shave and cropped hair, Fitzosbert had retained the waist-length beard he had grown when serving on the Third Crusade. Indeed, Fitzosbert's beard became a symbol of political resistance as he encouraged his Saxon supporters to follow his example, making them as unlike the Norman ruling class as possible.

Fitzosbert prided himself on challenging the authorities, denouncing the government from St Paul's Cross, a prototype of Speakers' Corner located in the precincts of St Paul's Cathedral, where craftsmen and labourers flocked to hear him.[3] Fitzosbert's moment of glory finally arrived as a result of the imposition of a tax to secure the release of King Richard I, who had been kidnapped by Duke Leopold of Austria on his return from the Crusades. The Duke demanded £100,000 (around £20 million today) for his release. 'Some citizens claimed, with considerable justification, that the Mayor and Corporation of London had assessed themselves and their friends lightly for the tax and passed the greater part of the burden on to their poorer neighbours.'[4] In a bid to stop the tax, Fitzosbert sailed to France, where the king was held hostage, and explained his grievance to the king in person. Richard gave him assurances that he and his fellow Londoners would not be heavily taxed to raise funds for the ransom. Fitzosbert returned to London, where the authorities were waiting for him. A well-loved demagogue of the people he may have been, but Fitzosbert was not so popular with the Mayor of London and his aldermen, who were terrified that Fitzosbert would incite a tax riot. The government, headed by the Justiciar Hubert Walter in the absence of

Richard I, shared their fears. Apprehensive that trouble in the City might spread to the outlying countryside, the authorities decided to move against him.

Barricading himself into his headquarters with a band of loyal supporters, Fitzosbert prepared for a long siege. But the authorities surrounded him, fearing that London would go up in flames. During the fighting that ensued, Fitzosbert killed one of the king's men. Fitzosbert might have seized this opportunity to parade through London with a dripping sword, followed by hundreds of rebels. Instead, he was so horrified by the fact that he had killed a man that he fled to the nearby church of St Mary-le-Bow for sanctuary. Many of his supporters deserted him, and a mere nine men and his 'concubine' accompanied him into the church where he prepared to wait it out. Hubert Walter, the Justiciar, was faced with a dilemma. Should he defy ecclesiastical law and send in his men to arrest Fitzosbert and his supporters, with the attendant violence and possible killing, on holy ground? Or should he play a waiting game, until Fitzosbert ran out of food and ammunition and gave himself up?

The resourceful Hubert Walter formulated a plan. He ignored the time-honoured right of sanctuary and instructed his men to kindle a fire around the walls of the church. Coughing and spluttering, with streaming eyes, Fitzosbert and his followers were forced to abandon their sanctuary or choke to death on the fumes. One long-term consequence of this tactic was that the tower of St Mary-le-Bow collapsed in 1271, as a result of the fires lit to smoke Fitzosbert out.[5] As they emerged into Bow Lane, Fitzosbert was attacked and wounded by the son of the man he had killed. Fitzosbert and his men were arrested, and Fitzosbert was tied up, fastened to a horse's tail and dragged to the Tower to await trial for treason and the inevitable sentence of death.

And so Fitzosbert found himself at Tyburn, standing with

a chain around his neck, awaiting the remainder of his sentence, which entailed being 'hanged by the neck and let down alive', then disembowelled while still conscious. He would then be faced with the grisly prospect of watching his own intestines burnt in front of him, before his head was cut off.

There are conflicting accounts as to how Fitzosbert responded to his final ordeal. Over one thousand years later, historians cannot agree on the exact circumstances of his death. According to the thirteenth-century Benedictine monk, Matthew Paris, a massive crowd turned out to pay their last respects to this people's champion who had incited riots against an unfair tax. The Elizabethan historian John Stow, however, wrote that Fitzosbert died ignobly, blaspheming Christ, and calling 'upon the devil to help and deliver him. Such was the end of this deceiver, a man of an evil life, a secret murderer, a filthy fornicator, a polluter of concubines, and a false accuser of his elder brother, who had in his youth brought him up in learning and done many things for his preferment.'[6]

Whatever the truth of his final moments, Fitzosbert's execution was notable for two reasons. His death was the first recorded execution for treason at Tyburn, and it was also the first occasion upon which a victim of Tyburn had become a martyr. According to Matthew Paris, after Fitzosbert had been hanged in chains, his gibbet was carried off and treated as a holy relic by his supporters. 'Men scooped the earth from the spot where [the gibbet] had stood. The chains which had held his decomposing body were claimed to have miraculous powers.'[7] Fitzosbert was vindicated, having 'died a shameful death for upholding the cause of truth and the poor'.

Fitzosbert's status as a secular martyr did not prove popular with the authorities. The pilgrims who came to worship at Fitzosbert's 'shrine' were driven away by Hubert the Justiciar, who had instigated the action against him. But

Fitzosbert had his posthumous revenge. Two years later (1198), the monks of Canterbury complained to the Pope about Hubert's conduct, claiming that he had violated the peace of the church of St Mary-le-Bow by forcing out Fitzosbert and his supporters. In response, the Pope put pressure on Richard I and Hubert was dismissed from his post as Justiciar.[8]

Fitzosbert's status and crime made him eminent enough to enter the record books, while the thousands of humble thieves who perished at Tyburn were regarded as so unexceptional that they did not deserve a mention. Hanging had been introduced by the Anglo-Saxons during the fifth century as a punishment for murder, theft and treason. While William I repealed the death penalty, it was reinstated by Henry I in 1108. As Fitzosbert's fate demonstrates, hanging served as a means of social and political control. According to the great Edwardian historian of Tyburn, Alfred Marks, 'the country swarmed with courts of inferior jurisdiction, each with the power to hang thieves'.[9] The law of the day had nothing to do with dispensing justice, and existed merely to defend property, which was regarded as more valuable than human life. The right to erect a gallows was granted to some surprising places, including monasteries. Despite the fact that England was nominally a Christian country, the church had no reservations about capital punishment, with St Paul and Thomas Aquinas enlisted in its defence.[10] The treatment of criminals was governed not by the compassionate doctrines of the New Testament, but by the implacable concepts of the Old. Wrongdoers were publically punished, so that their agonies would be witnessed by as many people as possible, both for the retributive satisfaction and the deterrent effect.[11]

Although the priesthood were forbidden to shed blood, they were not banned from requesting their bailiffs to hang criminals. The Abbot of Westminster owned sixteen gallows in Middlesex in 1281, and the practice extended to convents. Geoffrey Chaucer's tender-hearted prioress, Madame Eglantyne, who was said to weep at the sight of a mouse caught in a trap, would nevertheless have had a gallows on her property, upon which, at the hands of her bailiff, she would have hanged thieves.[12]

The gallows was a familiar sight throughout the land. One popular anecdote tells of a foreign traveller, who, having survived shipwreck, scrambled ashore on the English coast and found himself gazing up at what appeared to be a massive shrine. Crossing himself he fell to his knees, grateful to have arrived in a Christian country. But the structure he was kneeling before was in fact a gallows.[13]

The very first recorded execution at Tyburn was that of John Senex, in 1177. Senex, a nobleman, had been the ringleader of a gang that perpetrated a series of burglaries on private houses in London. By 1236, when Henry III had ordered the King's Gallows to be erected at Tyburn, it had become the place for men of rank to be executed, usually for treason. A notable case was that of William Marsh, who was not only drawn and hanged but quartered. Marsh, son of the viceroy of Ireland, was accused in 1235 of murdering Henry Clement, a messenger who interceded between the Irish and the king. Although he protested his innocence, Marsh was already under suspicion for the attempted assassination of the king. His assets were seized and he went on the run, eventually joining a gang of brigands on the island of Lundy, off the English south-west coast. Turning to a life of piracy, Marsh gave himself up to plunder and rape, as he and his gang descended suddenly on parties of unsuspecting travellers. Henry III put a price on Marsh's head, and he was eventually betrayed by his comrades and ambushed by the king's men, who brought him back to London and threw him into the Tower in 1242,[14] with instructions that he 'should be safely contained in the direst and most secure prison in that fortress, and so loaded with irons' that there could be no risk of his escaping.[15]

On 25 July Marsh and sixteen of his henchmen went on trial at Westminster and were condemned to death by the king with immediate effect. Marsh was drawn from Westminster to Tyburn, and hanged from a gibbet. When his body was stiff it was cut down and disembowelled, and the bowels were at once burnt on the spot. And then, according to the chronicler, 'the miserable body was divided into four parts, which were sent to four of the chief cities, so that this lamentable spectacle might inspire fear in all beholders'.[16]

Some fifty years later, the execution of Sir Thomas De Turberville for treason on 6 October 1295 is notable for the degree of humiliation the prisoner endured as he travelled to

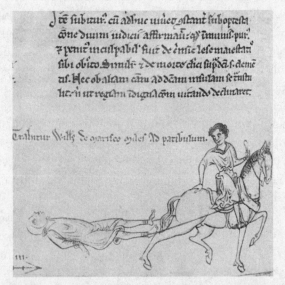

Execution for Treason: William Marsh is dragged to Tyburn gallows, where he will be hanged and eviscerated. 1242.

his death. De Turberville had been captured during the war with France and released on condition that he became a spy and conspired with the French to invade England and support the cause of William Wallace, the Scottish patriot. Detected in the act of writing to the Provost of Paris, De Turberville was tried and condemned. The unusual manner of his execution was described as follows. 'He came from the Tower, mounted on a poor hack, and shod with white shoes, his being covered with a hood, and his feet tied beneath the horse's belly, and his hands tied before him.'[17] Riding alongside De Turberville were six torturers dressed up as devils, who hit him with cudgels and taunted him. Sitting on the horse with De Turberville was the hangman himself, grasping the horse's bridle. De Turberville was led through London to Westminster Hall in this manner, where Sir Robert Brabazun pronounced judgement upon him, sentencing him to be drawn and hanged, 'and that he should hang so long as anything should be left whole of him'.[18] De Turberville was drawn on a fresh ox hide from Westminster to Cheapside, and then to Tyburn. The purpose of the ox hide was not humanitarian. Instead, this method was adopted so that the prisoner would not die before reaching the gallows.

De Turberville's death was barbaric, even by the standards of the day. The fate that awaited William Wallace, the Scottish patriot, was even worse. Wallace (1272–1305) went on trial at Westminster Hall in 1305, although the trial itself was a travesty, and Wallace was forced to wear a crown of laurels as a mockery. He was condemned to be hanged and drawn for his 'robberies, homicides and felonies', and, 'as an outlaw beheaded, and afterwards for your burning churches and relics your heart, liver, lungs, and entrails from which your wicked thoughts come shall be burned . . .'[19] Wallace's execution included one refinement. 'The Man of Belial', as the chroniclers refer to him, was hanged on a very high gallows, specially built for the occasion, let down alive, then disembowelled before being beheaded and then undergoing the further indignity of ementulation or *abscisis genitalibus*.[20] In other words, Wallace's genitals were cut off his body and burnt.[21] Finally, because all Wallace's 'sedition, depredations, fires and homicides were not only against the King, but against the people of England and Scotland', Wallace's head was placed upon Drawbridge Gate on London Bridge, where it could clearly be seen by travellers on land and water, and his quarters were hung in gibbets at Newcastle, Berwick, Stirling and Perth, 'to the terror of all who pass by'.[22] A year later, on 7 September, the head of Simon Fraser, another Scots rebel, was placed on Drawbridge Gate alongside that of his leader.

Brutal and barbaric as these methods of execution may appear to the modern reader, they were consequence of an unstable political climate. And as kings were believed to be divinely appointed, treason was regarded as a crime against God. They are perfect examples of the punishment being designed to fit the crime. But while the majority of convicted criminals awaited a predictable fate on the gallows, early records also yield some curious anecdotes, such as the fate of the ringleader of the first great robbery in the annals of London crime, and his cruel and unusual – but very apposite – punishment.

In 1303 the biggest robbery for six centuries was carried out in London, the amount involved being £100,000, or £20,000,000 in today's currency. The target for the robbery was the palace of King Edward I, which at that period was located next to Westminster Abbey and housed the king's treasury. In addition to valuable ceremonial regalia, there were funds amounting to £100,000, destined to finance Edward's ongoing war with Scotland. When Edward I left Westminster for Scotland on 14 March 1303, a gang of thieves broke into the treasury, scaled a ladder by the Palace gate, broke open the refectory door, and 'carried off a considerable amount of silver plate', as well as jewels and coins.[23] When officers arrived to investigate they found broken boxes, scattered jewels and the king's signet ring, bearing the privy seal, rolling about on the floor. There was no sign of the treasure.

As soon as the robbery had been discovered, forty-one friars and thirty-four monks were rounded up and sent to the Tower of London. It soon emerged that this audacious robbery was the earliest 'project crime' in London, an inside job plotted by William the Sacrist, the churchwarden, and Richard de Podlicote, keeper of the Palace of Westminster, and both their servants.[24]

Months earlier, the monks had planted a crop of hemp in the cemetery plot in the cloisters, creating a thick bed of vegetation. It was here that they stashed their ill-gotten gains, which were later removed by another monk, Alexander of Pershore. Alexander placed the treasure in baskets, and rowed off with it to King's (now Westminster) Bridge. Eventually, ten monks and one cleric were arraigned but they refused to be tried by secular judges. They were remanded to the Tower, but the secular judges 'condemned the Sacrist of Westminster for receiving and concealing jewels of our lord the king',[25] There is no record of the sentence handed down to Richard de Podlicote or William the Sacrist. Indeed, there was not a word as to their fate for centuries.

It was not until 1863, when the architect Sir Gilbert Scott was working on the restoration of St Margaret's, Westminster, that he became fascinated by the discovery that certain doors giving access to the king's treasury appeared to be covered, inside and out, with skin. Scott submitted a sample to an eminent scientist of the day, a Mr Quekett of the Royal College of Surgeons, who, Scott regretted to tell us, pronounced it to be human skin. There had been vague anecdotes about these doors having been covered with 'the skins of Danes' at some grisly point in the abbey's history, but Dean Stanley (the dean of Westminster Abbey) stated that the skin was that of 'a fair-haired, ruddy-complexioned man' and concluded that this was all that remained of William the Sacrist. Scott concluded that the human skins were 'those of persons executed for sacrilege, intended as a means of terrifying less hardened depredators'. A cruel and unusual punishment indeed.[26] The fate of Sir Richard, meanwhile, remains a mystery.

The gallows at Tyburn did not stand idle over the following century. While hundreds, if not thousands, of unrecorded executions took place on this spot, the next notable victim was Roger Mortimer, Baron of Wigmore and Earl of March and effectively king of England for three years between 1327 and 1330.

In February 1327 the unscrupulous and ambitious Mortimer had joined forces with Queen Isabella to depose and murder her husband, Edward II. Isabella, living up to her name as 'the she-wolf of France', proved as ruthless as Mortimer. More than anything, Isabella wanted to see her husband dead so that she could rule in his stead, with Mortimer at her side. Edward II, a flamboyant homosexual with little interest in government, was murdered at Berkeley Castle on the orders of Mortimer, in a particularly grisly fashion – suffocated with a mattress while a red-hot poker was rammed up his anus. By 1329, Isabella's son, Edward, had formed a powerful alliance to overthrow Mortimer, and Mortimer was eventually seized at Nottingham Castle, brought to London and committed to the Tower. On 29 November, Mortimer was condemned to death at Westminster, in the presence of the entire parliament. Despite pleas from Queen Isabella to her son to spare Mortimer's life, Mortimer was drawn to Tyburn, 'and there hanged on the common Gallowes'.[27] Mortimer was left to hang for two days before his body was cut down and buried in Greyfriars Church.

The execution of an innocent man or woman is one of the

most grievous consequences of capital punishment. One of the earliest examples of a miscarriage of justice was recorded in the *Chronicle of the Grey Friars* in 1386. It concerns the landlord of the Cock in Cheapside, who was 'mortheryd in hys bedde be nyght'.[28] The victim's wife was found guilty of killing her husband and sentenced to the mandatory punishment for husband murder or 'petty treason', which was to be burnt to death at Smithfield. Three of the servants, who were implicated in the murder, were drawn and hanged at Tyburn. According to Marks, this was a terrible judicial error. The landlord's wife was innocent, and the actual perpetrator was a thief who 'came in at a gutter window' in the night and who later confessed to the murder when he was at the gallows, waiting to be hanged for another crime.[29]

One of the most extraordinary cases – which led to its protagonists' deaths at Tyburn and Smithfield respectively – came in 1441, when Roger Bolingbroke, an astrologer and magician, was charged with attempting to kill King Henry VI by sorcery, at the instigation of Eleanor Cobham, Duchess of Gloucester. Eleanor's intention was to see Henry VI dead so that her own husband, the Duke of Gloucester, could take the throne. The plotters set about their nefarious task with the aid of Margery Gourdemaine, 'the Witch of Eye' (Ebury, a village near Westminster), and Canon Thomas Southwell of St Stephen's Chapel, Westminster. While Margery worked on her magic potions, Southwell attempted to 'consume the kings person by way of Negromancie' by saying black masses in Hornsey Park, and Bolingbroke sat in a special chair decorated with magical symbols and willed the king to die.

Despite the fact that these spells were manifestly unsuccessful, Bolingbroke and Southwell were arrested and charged with treason, while Dame Eleanor fled into sanctuary at Westminster, which was taken to be an admission of guilt. Thomas Southwell boasted that he would never live long enough to be executed, and indeed, he was found dead in the Tower. The trial of the remaining three plotters at the Guildhall features in Shakespeare's *Henry VI Pt 2*, with their sentences providing some insight into the way that social class affected punishment. While 'the witch in Smithfield shall be strangled on the gallows', Dame Eleanor escapes capital punishment on the grounds that she is 'more nobly born', but she is condemned to spend the rest of her life 'in banishment' on the Isle of Man.[30] The reference to the witch being strangled on the gallows alludes to the practice of garrotting the more fortunate prisoners before the fire was lit, so that they would be dead before the flames consumed them. Bolingbroke, being a nobleman, was drawn from the Tower to Tyburn where he was hanged and quartered, proclaiming his innocence with his dying breath and begging for God's mercy.

Bolingbroke and his comrades suffered the predictable fate for conspiracy and witchcraft. While Margery was consigned to the flames for 'witchcraft', a specious crime for which thousands of women were murdered over the centuries, Bolingbroke met his death at Tyburn, like so many men before him. Far more rare are references to the death of women at Tyburn, as the following intriguing entry in the *Chronicle of the Grey Friars* reveals:

> **1523.** And this yere in Feuerelle [February] the xxth [20th] day was the lady Alys Hungrford was lede from the Tower vn-to Holborne, and there put in-to a carte at the churchyerde with one of hare seruanttes, and so carred vn-to Tyborne, and there bothe hongyd, and she burryd at the Grayfreeres in the nether end of the myddes of the churche on the northe syde.[31]

Upon reading this one immediately wonders who this mysterious lady could have been, and what she could have done to deserve such a fate. Stow provides some clues in *A Survey of London,* in which the great historian refers to a monument in Greyfriars Church commemorating one 'Alice Lat Hungerford, hanged at Tiborne for murdering her husband'. The Victorian antiquarian John Hardy became so fascinated with this case that he decided to investigate the fate of 'Lady Alice' more closely. Hardy concluded that whatever the lady's motive for murdering her husband, it seemed unlikely to have been greed. An inventory of her assets, which were forfeit to the Crown, included an extraordinary collection of valuable property including plate, jewels and sumptuous hangings.

Hardy published his findings in *The Antiquary* in December 1888. He revealed that the lady's name was not Alice at all, but Agnes, and she had married Sir Edward Hungerford in 1518. Sir Edward's family seat was Farleigh Castle, near Bath, and he owned a magnificent house in London, while the name lives on in Hungerford Stairs, by the Thames, and Hungerford Bridge. In December 1521, Sir Edward made a will in favour of his wife. When he died six weeks later on 24 January 1522, he freely bequeathed the residue of his estate to Agnes, including all goods, jewels, plate, harnesses 'and all other moveables [furniture] whatsoever they be'.[32] One wonders why Agnes would want to kill such a generous husband, a man considerate enough to leave her such wealth, when she already enjoyed a lavish lifestyle as his wife while he was alive?

The answer is simple. The husband who died, and who Agnes was accused of murdering, was not Sir Edward Hungerford. It emerged that Agnes had been married before, to a John Cotell of Somerset. Digging through the court records, John Hardy discovered that on 25 August 1522, two yeomen appeared in court in the county of Somerset charged with murdering Cotell three years previously on the orders of Agnes Hungerford. These two men, William Matthew and William Ignes, both from Wiltshire, were indicted for attacking Cotell at

Farleigh Castle. The pair set upon Cotell and 'then and there feloniously did throttle, suffocate, and strangle' him with his own scarf. In order to dispose of Cotell's body, they placed it in the kitchen furnace, where it was consumed by fire.[33]

This case raises many questions. Agnes obviously had a considerable position of power at the castle. Burning one's first husband's body in the kitchen fire was guaranteed to set tongues wagging among the staff. How had John Cotell come to be at the castle? Had he heard that Agnes had married again, and come to Farleigh Castle demanding an explanation, or threatening to blackmail her for bigamy? Or had young Agnes, employed upon the estate, caught the eye of rich old Sir Edward, who had arranged to have Cotell murdered so that he could marry Agnes? Was Sir Edward ruthlessly securing the hand of an attractive but innocent young woman, or was she herself complicit in her first husband's murder? The fact remains that for three years nothing was said about the death of Agnes' first husband, though there must have been gossip and speculation. Perhaps the powerful Sir Edward protected her while he was still alive. It was just seven months after he died that Agnes went on trial for 'petty treason', the murder of her first husband. Agnes was subsequently charged with providing shelter, comfort and aid to her servants, and all three were hanged at Tyburn on 20 February 1523.

Whilst Tyburn had become infamous as an execution ground for criminals and traitors, another faction to be put to death here were the religious dissenters. The first religious martyrs were the Jews, during the thirteenth century. Jewish immigration to England came with William I, when he brought Jews over after the Conquest on the grounds of financial expediency. Although the Christians were forbidden by canon law to practice usury, the Jews suffered no restrictions. Banned from entering medicine or the law, money lending was the only profession open to them. But as they prospered, the Jews endured terrible hatred from the gentiles. In 1189, a series of riots saw the entire Jewish population of London fleeing for protection to the Tower.[34] In 1255, eighteen Jews were accused of the ritual murder of a seven-year-old boy, Hugh of Lincoln. This 'blood libel', which was nothing more than anti-Semitic propaganda, saw the eighteen men hanged at the Tower.

In 1275, Edward I's Jewish Statute insisted that the Jews abandoned usury and learned a trade. Unable to practise as moneylenders, many Jews turned to a form of forgery known as 'clipping the coin'. This consisted of filing the edges off legitimate coins and melting them down to produce higher-denomination counterfeit money. The Jews became so proficient at 'clipping the coin' that there were fears that the entire financial system would collapse. However, they paid dearly for their skill. As the king controlled the Royal Mint, and therefore all the money in England, 'clipping the coin' constituted a form of treason. As a result, in November 1278, the entire Jewish population of England, around 600 people, was rounded up, charged with fraud and taken to the Tower.[35] Two hundred and eight Jews of both sexes were hanged, many at Tyburn. Those who survived were banished by King Edward in 1290.

The next persecuted minority consisted of the Lollards. This group (the word 'Lollard' derives from the Dutch, *lollen,* to 'mutter') were precursors of the Protestants. They followed the preaching John Wycliffe (c.1320–84), a priest and teacher who helped translate the Bible into English and criticized the authority of the Pope, who promptly launched a Papal Bull against him. The Lollards were regarded as heretics on the grounds that they disregarded the sacraments and encouraged the laity to preach, and they represented such a threat to the established church that, in 1401, an act was introduced entitled *De Haeretico Comburendo* or 'On the Burning of Heretics'.

This act permitted sheriffs and Justices of the Peace to burn suspected heretics to death. This punishment gave rise to the popular misconception that the name 'Tyburn' derived from the fate of the Lollards, as in the observation that: 'Tieburne, some will have it so called from Tie and Burne, because the poor Lollards for whom this instrument was first set up, had their necks tied to the beame, and their lower parts burnt in the fire'.[36] In fact, many Lollards also perished at Smithfield, and the name 'Tyburn' derives from the Saxon 'Teo-burna' or 'Two Brooks', referring to the two streams that converged at this location.[37]

The third category of martyrs to die at Tyburn were the Roman Catholics, executed upon the orders of King Henry VIII following the Reformation of 1534, when Henry severed relations with the Pope of Rome and appointed himself Defender of the Faith and head of the Anglican church in England. Among the unfortunate was one Elizabeth Barton (1506–34), later christened 'the Holy Maid of Kent'. Elizabeth, a nun, suffered from *petite mal,* a mild form of epilepsy, and was credited with seeing visions during her trances. In 1534, Elizabeth prophesied that if Henry VIII married Anne Boleyn, the 'Bullen whore', he would no longer be king of England and would die shortly afterwards. As a result of this prediction, Elizabeth Barton was arrested for treason, imprisoned in the Tower, and hanged at Tyburn on 20 April.[38] Elizabeth's head was later placed upon a spike on London Bridge, making her the only woman to be granted that grisly distinction.

As for the king, he survived for another fifteen years, during which he continued to stamp out support for the Roman Catholic cause with a series of high-profile executions at Tyburn. One of the most graphic instances was the execution of three Carthusian priors. On 4 May 1535, Father Robert Lawrence, prior of Beauvale, Father Augustine Webster, prior of Axholem, and Father John Houghton, prior of the Charterhouse in London, were dragged from Newgate to Tyburn. Father Houghton was cut down while still breathing and dragged to one side, where his garments were torn from his body and his genitals sliced off and roasted on a spit in front of him. Despite the fact that he was being disembowelled and his entrails burnt in a brazier, Father Houghton 'bore himself with more than human endurance, most patiently', to the astonishment of the crowd. Even as his heart was being torn out, the Father turned to his executioner and enquired, 'Sweet

Executions at Tyburn, c. 1607. Criminals, traitors and martyrs met a grisly end at this infamous execution ground.

Jesu, what will you do with my heart?'[39] These were his final words. His head was cut off, his body quartered, and his right arm was taken back to the Charterhouse where it was nailed to the door as an horrific warning. The remains of his fellow Carthusians were thrown into cauldrons and parboiled, and later displayed in different parts of London. In all, 105 Catholic martyrs died at Tyburn. Many were subsequently canonized, and they are commemorated at Tyburn Convent. This Benedictine convent, founded in 1901, stands on the spot where so many met their deaths, known and unknown.

This completes the first visit to Tyburn. Now it is time to travel to another sinister landmark on the historical map of London. To the Tower, that great castle of darkness from which so few escaped with their lives.

CASTLE OF DARKNESS

*Torture and Death in the
Tower of London*

No history of crime and punishment in London would be complete without a visit to the Tower. This magnificent edifice has reared above the city since 1079, serving as a terrible warning to those who challenge the authority of the crown. Five miles from Tyburn, the Tower dominates the south-east stretch of old London Wall, forming another landmark on the city's bloody map. For generations, the Tower represented law and order, an important visual reminder in the years before the existence of a standing army and a professional police force. A royal palace, a fortress and a prison, the Tower exuded a powerful mystique that fascinated and repelled.

This chapter is the story of murder most royal, of the famous and infamous who spent their last days here. The prisoners in the Tower were men and women of the highest rank, who met their fate on Tower Green, or Tower Hill. Then there were those who spoke out against monstrous tyranny, and endured agonies of torture before being dragged to Tyburn and Smithfield. To step inside these high walls on a cold, grey morning, with the mist rising from the river, is to feel the shades of the prison house closing around one and to understand how those two words, 'the Tower', could strike fear into the bravest heart.

As any modern visitor soon realizes, the Tower of London consists not of one tower, but of many, gradually added over the centuries as the Tower expanded into its various roles as palace, royal mint and prison. The oldest tower was 'the White Tower', so called because it was painted white in the thirteenth century. The White Tower was erected upon the site of an existing Roman fortification, chosen for its elevated, well-drained position above the tidal River Thames, and protected by the massive defensive wall which the Romans had built to protect Londinium. Beginning work under the guidance of Gundulf, Bishop of Rochester in 1077, the Normans exploited this existing fortification and created additional walls to enclose the site. Within the site, they built the White Tower, an immense, square castle with turrets 36 x 32.5 m (118 x 106 ft) across and, on the south side (where the ground is lowest), 27.5 m (90 ft) tall. The second largest structure of its type known to have been built, the White Tower is still remarkably well preserved and remains the most complete eleventh-century palace in Europe.

Slammed down upon the London skyline in 1079 like a massive fist, the Tower demonstrated the power and might of the new Norman government, and it served three purposes. As a palace, with state rooms, lodgings, a chapel, kitchens and even a latrine, it was fit for a king. But the Tower was also a fortress, with a moat surrounding it, an entrance well above ground and walls up to 4 m (15 ft) thick, making it virtually impregnable.[1] And as the Normans struggled to control England and her unruly cousins in Scotland and Wales, the Tower performed another role: it operated as a prison for men or women of rank. The prisoners fell into three categories: powerful men who had offended the king, prisoners of war, detained awaiting ransom, and potential troublemakers whose continued liberty was undesirable for political reasons.[2]

The first prisoner in the Tower to appear upon the records was Bishop Ranulf Flambard (1060–1128), chief tax collector under William Rufus. When William died, his brother Henry I incarcerated Flambard in 1100 on the grounds of extortion, a move calculated to win favour with the barons.[3] The conditions in which the bishop was held were not uncongenial; he was allowed his own servants and could use his ill-gotten gains to purchase food and drink, which were brought in to him by collaborators.

The bishop could also afford to purchase his freedom. A rope was smuggled into the Tower in a butt of wine, and a horse stood ready beneath the wall. On 2 February 1120 the bishop threw a feast for his jailors, ensured that they were hopelessly drunk, then slipped away to another room where he tied up the rope, squeezed his bloated body out through the window, and made his way to freedom, becoming not only the first recorded prisoner at the Tower, but the first man to escape from the fortress too. The bishop evidently led a charmed life; after taking refuge in France, he made his peace with Henry I and returned to England, where he was restored to his bishopric and died peacefully in 1128.

In 1244, Gruffydd ap Llewlyn, a Welsh rebel imprisoned by Henry III, attempted to emulate the bishop's death-defying feat. Despite being kept in reasonable conditions, enjoying good food and regular visits from his wife, Llewlyn decided after two and a half years of imprisonment that he would try to escape by a similar method, knotting together his sheets, bedcovers and every hanging he could find to make a rope.

Unlike the bishop, Llewlyn did not climb out of a window.

Instead, he went up on to the roof of the White Tower, fastened one end of his improvized rope to the parapet and began to lower himself over the side. He had scarcely started when the rope gave way and he plummeted ninety feet to his death. According to a contemporary writer, 'his head and neck were crushed between his shoulders, a most horrid spectacle'.[4]

Another famous escapee was Sir John Oldcastle, the first prisoner to be held in the Tower for religious dissent. Sir John, who was the model for Shakespeare's Falstaff, was revealed to be a Lollard when some of his old books were found in a second-hand shop in Paternoster Row. King Henry V, Sir John's former boon companion, risked his own reputation to protect his old friend, but as Sir John refused to deny his beliefs, he was inevitably gaoled. He managed to escape from the Tower on 19 October 1413, with the help of his co-religionists, but instead of fleeing abroad, Sir John squandered his opportunity for freedom by mounting an ambitious coup against his former protector, Henry V. The plot hinged on Sir John and his comrades gaining access to the king disguised as a company of entertainers on Twelfth Night. Characteristically brave but reckless, this plan was soon foiled and Sir John was recaptured and hanged at St Giles's Fields. According to John Foxe, writing in his *Book of Martyrs,* Sir John made a good end:

> He was brought out of the Tower with his arms bound behind him, having a very cheerful countenance. Then he was laid upon a hurdle, as though he had been a most heinous traitor to the Crown, and so drawn forth into St Giles Field, where they had set up a new pair of gallows.

After praying to God to forgive his enemies, and exhorting the huge crowd to follow the scriptures, 'he was hanged up there by the middle in chains of iron, and so consumed alive in the fire, praising the name of God so long as his life lasted'.[5]

The Tower had always been a place of terror, but it was towards the end of the fifteenth century that the fortress really developed its bloodstained reputation, as a result of the bitter family feud between the two factions of the Plantagenet family, commonly known as the 'Wars of the Roses'. The first victim of the power struggle between the two houses of York and Lancaster was Henry VI. When Edward IV seized power from Henry in 1461, Henry and his queen, Margaret, fled into Scotland. But they were recaptured four years later and Henry was confined to the Wakefield Tower. Gentle, ascetic Henry, with his religious fervour and scholarly ways (he was responsible for founding Eton College and King's College, Cambridge), had never been an effective ruler. Long considered to be insane, his symptoms consistent with a modern diagnosis of schizophrenia, Henry adapted to imprisonment better than many, and there is no suggestion that he was subjected to a particularly Spartan regime. If Henry was seen shuffling unshaven in ragged garments, this was more likely to have been a consequence of his austere lifestyle rather than a form of punishment.

The deposed Henry VI was permitted to attend Mass every day in the Wakefield Tower, to receive visitors, to study and to read. He appeared to be relieved that he no longer had to deal with the burdens of office. Edward IV, for his part, had no interest to serve by ill-treating the former king. However, in 1470, after a successful coup by the Duke of Warwick, 'the Kingmaker', and Edward's younger brother, the Duke of Clarence (both former supporters of Edward who had switched sides), Henry was briefly restored to the throne after being paraded through the streets from the Tower to St Paul's before his applauding subjects.

Edward IV soon regained the upper hand, however, and Henry was sent back to the Tower where, on 21 May 1471, he was found dead in the oratory of the Wakefield Tower, 'stykked with a dagger' while he knelt at prayer, according to Polydore Vergil, Henry VII's official historian.[6] Vergil attributed the crime to Edward's youngest brother, Richard, Duke of Gloucester, the first in a grisly series of charges laid against the future King Richard III as he carved his bloody path towards the throne.

The next victim was George, Duke of Clarence, brother of Edward IV. Although Clarence had supported the coup of 1470 that had briefly restored Henry VI to the throne, Edward had forgiven him, and continued to tolerate Clarence despite the fact that Clarence resented Edward's power and influence, insulted Edward's queen, Elizabeth Woodville, and continued to plot against him. Edward's generosity finally reached its limit in 1477, when he summoned Clarence to Westminster and had him arrested for treason and sent to the Tower. There he was detained for seven months while Edward waited for some sign of remorse from his weak and disloyal brother.

But Clarence remained defiant, and was condemned to death by the House of Lords in 1478, who ruled that he should be executed privately in the Tower. According to Polydore Vergil, Clarence was drowned in a butt of Malmsey wine, which seems an extraordinary method of execution. One explanation could be that Clarence's body was removed from the Tower in a barrel of wine after his death; another is that Clarence, a notorious drunkard, had asked to be despatched in this fashion with characteristic bravado.

William Shakespeare, upholding the Tudor view of history, accused Richard, Duke of Gloucester, later Richard III, of murdering Clarence. But, it has to be said, that although Clarence left the world in an unconventional manner, his execution had been authorized by Parliament and was perfectly legal, if shrouded in secrecy.[7] It is a similar veil of secrecy that surrounds the disappearance of the sons of Edward IV, the little princes Edward and Richard, who were sent to the Tower in 1483.

Edward IV died suddenly on 9 April 1483, and was immediately succeeded by his twelve-year-old son, Edward. However, Richard Duke of Gloucester, Edward IV's brother, swiftly seized control. Edward's widow, Elizabeth Woodville, fled into sanctuary at Westminster Abbey, and Richard appointed himself Protector.

Fearing that her son would not inherit the throne, Elizabeth Woodville plotted with William Hastings, the Lord Chamberlain, to overthrow Richard. But Richard, who by this stage was referring to himself as 'the Protector', learned of the conspiracy and summoned Hastings and his confederates Lord Stanley, Bishop Morton and the Archbishop of York to the Tower. Assuming that they had been summoned to a meeting of the Privy Council, the four men appeared promptly, only to be arrested on the orders of the Protector. Stanley, Morton and the Archbishop were immediately imprisoned in the Tower, but Hastings suffered a different fate. As Richard commented tersely that he could not sit down to dinner 'until he had seen his head', Hastings was led out on to Tower Green. A priest was sent for so that Hastings could make his final confession, and then, a piece of timber for repair work being conveniently to hand, Hastings laid down his neck and was beheaded, the first person to be executed on Tower Green.[8]

Having set a brutal example by executing Hastings, Richard the Protector promptly claimed the throne on the grounds that Edward IV's marriage to Elizabeth Woodville had been bigamous and that Edward's sons, who were living in the Tower in its capacity as a Royal Palace, were therefore bastards. While Richard appointed himself King Richard III, twelve-year-old Prince Edward and nine-year-old Prince Richard remained in the Tower, ostensibly for their own protection. From this point, their fate becomes a matter of conjecture. At the end of 1483, an Italian visitor who had been in London during that year noted that after Hastings had been removed, all the deposed young king's servants were denied access to him. He and his brother retreated into the inner apartments of the Tower and their appearances at the windows became rarer and rarer, day by day, until they ceased to be seen altogether. A doctor from Strasbourg reported that the young king, like a victim prepared for sacrifice, sought remission of his sins by daily confession and penance, because he believed that death was facing him:

> I have seen many men burst forth into tears and lamenta-
> tion when mention was made of him after his removal
> from men's sight; and already there was a suspicion that he
> had been done away with. Whether, however, he has been
> done away with, and by what manner of death, so far I
> have not at all discovered.[9]

The 'inner apartments' are probably a reference to the White Tower, an area of the Tower to which few had access. Given the fate of Henry VI twelve years earlier, it is understandable that the populace would fear for the young princes. Rumours were circulating in the taverns of London that the princes were dead from July onwards, when an attempt to overthrow Richard, place Elizabeth Woodville upon the throne and rescue the little princes met with failure. By October, the general assumption was that they had been murdered and their remains interred somewhere in the Tower.[10] But who knew where the bodies were buried?

In 1674, some 191 years later, a complex of mediaeval buildings along the front of the White Tower was demolished. Part of this complex consisted of a stair turret giving access to the original entrance. Ten feet below the foundations of this stair-case the workmen found a wooden chest containing the skeletons of 'two striplings', or young male children. These were assumed to be the remains of the princes, and buried in Westminster Abbey.

In 1933 the bones were examined by forensic experts, who concluded that the remains were those of the princes. Subsequent doubts have been raised but it is unlikely that the bodies of any other children would have been concealed in such a fashion at about the same time that the boys disappeared.

If the princes in the Tower were murdered, then by whom, and upon whose orders? The evidence is wholly circumstantial. Henry VII claimed to have received a confession from one of Richard III's trusted aides, Sir James Tyrell, before the latter was executed for treason in 1502. This flimsy claim was seized upon by pro-Tudor propagandists Sir Thomas More and Polydore Vergil, who were intent upon casting Richard III as the villain of the piece.

Later historians, eager to make the case for Richard III as a much-maligned monarch, attributed the murders to the Duke of Buckingham, a loyal supporter of Richard III who later deserted him; other writers claimed that the princes had been murdered on the orders of Henry Tudor, later Henry VII, as a method of discrediting Richard and removing any opposition to Henry's claim to the throne.

We shall never know the fate of the little princes, or who was responsible for their deaths. The Tower will never reveal this particular dark secret. But had the princes survived, they would almost certainly have endured the brief lives and early deaths experienced by their cousins. From 1483 onwards, the Tower's history becomes stained with tragedy, 'when the prisons were constantly filled and the scaffold deluged with blood'.[11]

This is the period when the ranks of servants at the Tower included jailers, torturers and an executioner, when all the terrible machinery of so-called justice could be made ready at a moment's notice, and when the steps of Traitors' Gate were worn down by the feet of those who climbed them. It was here that Henry Tudor, once he had defeated Richard III at the Battle of Bosworth Field in 1485, held court, and filled the Tower's prisons with his enemies, real and imaginary.[12]

In his position as founder of the new Tudor dynasty, Henry VII was confronted with a succession of rebels and pretenders to the throne. One such was Lambert Simnel, c. 1477–1525, who impersonated the Earl of Warwick and led a rebellion against Henry VII until the genuine Earl of Warwick was produced (while Simnel was parading around the country claiming to be him, the genuine Earl of Warwick had been imprisoned in the Tower). Simnel actually received a lenient sentence, being set to work in the royal kitchens – Henry VII shrewdly realizing that humiliation was more effective than martyrdom.

This tactic did not extend to the unfortunate Perkin Warbeck (c.1474–99), a young man 'of visage beautiful, of countenance demure, of will subtle',[13] who claimed to be Richard, Duke of York, the younger of the missing princes. Warbeck claimed that he had been spirited out of the country in 1483, and a young stable lad had taken his place, while he had been raised anonymously in France as 'Perkin'.

Henry VII could not suffer the young man to live. If Warbeck were to be the son of Edward IV, last of the Plantagenets, he represented a threat to the newly established Tudor throne. Even as a pretender, Perkin Warbeck was capable of summoning sufficient support to destabilize the monarchy and seize power. Warbeck was arrested and taken to the Tower of London before being drawn to Tyburn along with his supporters. Lost king or no, Warbeck made a good death of it, according to the Tudor historian Edward Hall, who tells us in his *Chronicle* of 1542 that 'Perykn standing on a little skaffolde, read his confession, and took it on hys death to be true ... asked the king forgiveness and dyed patiently.'[14]

The horrors which resulted from Henry VII's battle to enforce his position as monarch were as nothing compared with his son's reign of terror. Henry VIII's escalating rage and syphilitic paranoia guaranteed a death sentence for any man or woman who thwarted him, either on the grounds of religious convictions or treason. Many of these individuals met their deaths on Tower Hill, an execution ground established by Edward IV when he had built a permanent gallows on this former rubbish tip. This desolate spot, a 'liberty' or open space outside the Tower and beyond the jurisdiction of the Mayor and Aldermen, became one of the most grisly locations in London, where those who had defied the king met their deaths in an appalling public spectacle.

Among those made an example of under Henry VIII's regime were the Duke of Buckingham, who had a plausible case for opposing Henry's monarchy, and Sir Thomas More, the statesman and theologian who could not bring himself to support Henry's Reformation of the Church. When Sir Thomas mounted the scaffold in 1553, his parting words were: 'See me safe up, for my coming down I can shift for myself.'[15] Thomas Cromwell, Henry's secretary, fell out of favour in 1540, following Henry's disastrous marriage to Anne of Cleves, which Cromwell had brokered. Cromwell went to his death on Tower Hill on 28 July, to die horribly at the hands of a 'ragged, butcherly miser, which very ungodly performed the office'.[16]

Tower Green, by contrast, was a relatively private execution site. Tower Green lies next to the chapel of St Peter ad Vincula, and was where Lord Hastings had been summarily executed on the orders of Richard III. Tower Green was the execution site of Henry VIII's second wife, Anne Boleyn, beheaded for treason on the grounds of adultery in 1536. Despite her youth and innocence, Anne went to her death with impeccable poise, even joking to her executioner that his task would not take long as she had 'a little neck'. Executioners could by no means be relied upon to despatch their victims swiftly, but Anne seems to have been fortunate in her headsman, an experienced man brought over from France, who severed her head from her little neck with one blow of his sword.

Margaret Pole, Countess of Salisbury, did not demonstrate such commendable *sang froid* when she was put to death for treason in 1541. Although Margaret was the last member of the Plantagenet family, at seventy-one years old she scarcely represented a threat. Indeed, Henry's decision to have her executed rather than permanently imprisoned in the Tower gives some indication of his deranged mental state. The countess was a formidable woman who refused point blank to lie down with her head on the block, protesting that 'so should traitors do, and I am none!'[17] Instead of submitting to the headsman's axe, Margaret ran around the scaffold shrieking, dodging the executioner's blows, until, in a barbaric and shameful display, she was eventually hacked to death.

Henry VIII's fifth wife, Katherine Howard (born c. 1525), died on Tower Green in 1542, after Henry had discovered her affairs with the courtiers Francis Dereham and George Culpepper. It is said that Henry was so infuriated when he learnt of his wife's exploits that he would have run her through with his sword himself had he not been restrained by his aides. Katherine demonstrated a certain degree of bravado. So determined was she to appear at her best on the scaffold, that she demanded that an executioner's block be brought to her cell, so that she could perfect the appropriate pose. Katherine might not have been able to choose her executioner, but is said to have handed the headsman her golden chain with a request for an easy death. Katherine was buried in St Peter's ad Vincula, next to Anne Boleyn.

During their periods of imprisonment, state prisoners such as Anne Boleyn, Sir Thomas More and Thomas Cromwell experienced reasonably comfortable conditions. The Tower was luxurious compared with prisons such as Newgate and the Fleet. Eminent prisoners were permitted food, books, wine and adequate clothing, and it was customary for female prisoners to be accompanied by their ladies in waiting and servants. However, there was a far more disturbing aspect to life in the Tower if one refused to confess to one's crimes: torture.

Although England had its own form of brutality in the form of drawing, hanging, quartering and burning at the stake, and although prison conditions were barbaric for the common man, torture as such was rare, compared with conditions on the Continent. In 1215, Magna Carta had established that: 'No freeman shall be taken or imprisoned, or deceased or outlawed or exiled, *or in any way destroyed* [tortured] ... except by the lawful judgement of his peers or by the law of the land.'[18] However, torture could be condoned in exceptional circumstances, although these cases were rare, as permission had to be obtained from the Privy Council.

The existence of a torture chamber at the Tower of London is a powerful myth, derived from authors such as Harrison Ainsworth, who claimed in his novel *The Tower of London* (1840) that the torture chamber was located in the Constable Tower and consisted of a dank underground room filled with an impressive array of thumbscrews, gauntlets, collars, pincers, saws, chains and a rack. This was an exaggeration: there was no torture chamber as such. Instead, most instruments of torture were portable, and could be carried to the individual cells of those unfortunate prisoners upon whom they were employed. No ingenuity was spared in the creation of these barbaric instruments, many of which were named in honour of their sadist inventors.

Take, for instance, 'Skeffington's Gyves' or 'the Scavenger's Daughter', devized by Leonard Skeffington, the Lieutenant of the Tower during the 1530s. The 'Scavenger's Daughter' was 'in all respects the opposite of the rack, for while that draws apart the joints by the feet and hands tied, this, on the contrary constricts and binds into a ball'.[19] The device consisted of two iron bars that pressed the lower legs against the thighs and the thighs against the belly, so that the prisoner was effectively squashed inside a cage fastened with clamps, which could be tightened or released according to the whims of the torturer. This piece of apparatus was 'more dreadful and more complete than the rack' because the body was so cruelly bent that in some cases blood exuded from the tips of the hands and feet, or in other cases the pressure was such that the ribs burst and blood was expelled from the prisoner's mouth and nostrils.[20]

Then there was the rack, also known as 'the Duke of Exeter's Daughter' after Henry Holland, Fourth Duke of Exeter, who was credited with inventing it.[21] First mentioned 1446, the rack consisted of an open rectangular wooden frame, about seven feet long, raised about one to three feet from the floor on four or six legs. The victim was laid on the floor immediately beneath the framework and secured with ropes around his wrists and ankles to the windlass mechanisms at each of the narrow ends of the frame. Levels inserted into the sockets on the windlasses were then operated by jailors in opposite directions by means of which the prisoner was raised from the floor until level with the frame. At this stage, the sheer weight of the body simply induced pain to all four limbs; but any subsequent movement of the windlass levers would start to strain heavily on the shoulder and hip sockets until, as Thomas Norton, the Elizabethan rack-master was proud to boast when racking the Jesuit priest Alexander Briant in 1581, 'the prisoner was stretched twelve inches taller than God had created him'.[22]

Another method of torture consisted of manacles, which were fitted around the wrists, like modern handcuffs, but were much heavier. The method consisted of hanging the prisoner by the wrists from a beam, so that they stretched under their own weight. Another Jesuit priest, John Gerard, underwent such treatment in 1597, and remained permanently crippled from its effects.[23] Remarkably, Father Gerard nevertheless survived and went on to become one of the few prisoners to escape from the Tower, making his getaway in a boat with the help of his warder, Bennett.

While there was no specific torture chamber, certain dungeons served as instruments of torture in their own right. These included rat-infested caverns that filled with water when the Thames reached high tide, or Little Ease, a chamber in the cellar of the White Tower which was so small that the occupant could neither stand up to full height or lie down full length. As a place of punishment it could be made available on the orders of the Lieutenant and did not require permission from the Privy Council. Also in the White Tower was 'the Pit', a subterranean dungeon twenty feet deep and entirely without light, which may have been the remains of the old Norman well and into which prisoners could be hurled as into an oubliette.[24]

Under Henry VIII, torture was justified in the interests of national security. A staunch supporter of Rome before he chose to reform the Church, Henry VIII began his reign persecuting Protestants, such as the Lollards, and ended it with the Dissolution of the Monasteries and the extermination of the Roman Catholics. During the Reformation, any person who clung to their Roman Catholic faith and did not accept King Henry as the head of the Protestant church in England was considered to be committing treason. On these grounds, the Tower was constantly filled with prisoners, and the soil beneath the scaffold on Tower Hill was dyed with the richest and best blood in the land.[25] Notable victims included Robert Dalyvell, racked on the suspicion of being a Papist spy, and eventually released – but only after his ears had been cut off[26] – and Abbot Thomas Marshall of Colchester, who was arrested and interrogated for opposing Henry's marriage to Anne Boleyn.

Protestants might also find themselves accused of treason. One such, in 1546, was Anne Askew, an outspoken gentlewoman from Lincolnshire who had become good friends with Henry's sixth wife, Catherine Parr, and sympathized with Catherine's Protestant beliefs. Two courtiers, Archbishop Gardiner and the Duke of Norfolk, seized on Anne as a means of discrediting Catherine Parr for their own purposes, and had Anne arrested as a heretic, condemned to death by burning and sent to the Tower.

The intention was to frighten Anne into giving damning evidence against Catherine. Anne was questioned for hours by the Lord Chancellor, Thomas Wriothesley, and the Chancellor, Richard Rich, but refused to bear false witness against Catherine or recant her Protestant sympathies. In a desperate bid to scare Anne into a false confession, they sent for the lieutenant of the Tower, Sir Anthony Knyvett, and asked him to have the rack prepared in the basement of the White Tower. The racking of a woman was unprecedented, and Sir Anthony was assured that Anne would require no more than a light 'pinching' to make her talk.[27]

But Sir Anthony was wrong. Anne Askew was born to the role of martyr, and endured patiently as she was stretched on the rack and the screw was turned. Wriothesley and Rich resumed their interrogation, but still she said nothing. Further pressure was applied, but Anne still refused to discredit Queen Catherine or renounce her beliefs. When Sir Anthony demanded that Anne be released, the Chancellor told him not to interfere. Sir Anthony pointed out that what they were doing was illegal, and carried out without the consent of the Privy Council. Wriothesley ordered him to continue with the torture, in the king's name. When Sir Anthony refused, Wriothesley and Rich took off their gowns, rolled up their sleeves and continued with the racking themselves, while Anne prayed quietly and patiently, and 'abode their tyranny, till her bones and joints were almost plucked asunder'.[28]

When Anne was eventually released, she fainted, and never regained the full use of her limbs. As soon as he left the White Tower, Sir Anthony hurried to see the king at Westminster and told him what had happened. Although Henry's response is not on record, we do know that within days the attempt to discredit Catherine Parr had collapsed, and she was not quietly executed on Tower Green. Anne Askew saw her martyrdom through to the bitter end. Refusing to recant, so badly crippled that she could not walk, Anne was carried to Smithfield in a chair, where she was burnt to death.[29]

Henry VIII's reign of terror was continued by 'Bloody' Mary Tudor (1516–58), a fanatical devotee of the Roman Catholic Church, who rejected Henry's break with Rome and was eager to make England a Catholic country once again. A weak and unstable monarch, Mary was easily led by her councillors, who manipulated her to their own ends and persuaded her to sign the warrant for the execution of her rival, Lady Jane Grey. Although very much in keeping with the Tudor tradition of eliminating all opposition, this was a brutal and unnecessary gesture, as the sixteen-year-old Jane was no more than a political pawn, placed upon the throne for a mere nine days in July 1553, following an unsuccessful coup. A show of mercy would have brought dividends to Mary, and she did offer Jane a fragile opportunity of survival if she agreed to convert to Roman Catholicism. But Jane refused to abandon her Protestant faith, and Mary was convinced by

Archbishop Gardiner that it would be best to execute Jane and Jane's young husband, the Earl of Dudley.[30]

Execution day dawned on the morning of 12 February 1554, leaving Jane and her husband with no doubt as to the outcome of events. On execution days, prisoners and staff alike heard the carpenters hard at work, the noise of their saws rasping through the wood and their hammers echoing about the surrounding buildings as they nailed the planks to the posts. As Jane watched from her prison cell, her husband was led away through the gateway of the Bloody Tower.

Some time later, a cart returned through the archway, bearing the body of her husband, and his head, wrapped in a cloth. Soon afterwards, Jane herself went to the scaffold, accompanied

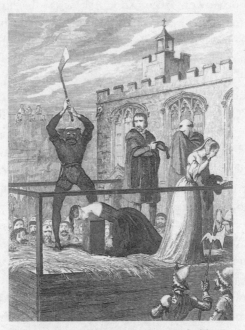

*The execution of Lady Jane Grey at the Tower
of London, as envisaged by Cruikshank.*

42

by her weeping ladies-in-waiting and a Catholic priest, John Feckenham, who had made a last, unsuccessful bid to convert Jane to the Church of Rome. Jane was poised and calm until the last moment, when, blindfolded, she was unable to find the block, and stumbled about, crying out pitifully, 'Where is it? What shall I do? What shall I do?' It fell to Father Feckenham to guide Jane and help her to retain her dignity to the end.[31]

Weeks later, on 18 March, another young princess arrived at the Tower. As the 21-year-old Elizabeth Tudor stepped out of the boat and on to the steps of Traitors' Gate, making the same journey as her mother, Anne Boleyn, had done nineteen years earlier, it must have seemed to Elizabeth that she would soon join her illustrious predecessors on the scaffold. But within four years Queen Mary was dead and, in November of 1558, Elizabeth was crowned Queen of England. When she returned to the Tower as queen, Elizabeth touched the ground and said, 'Some have fallen from being princes of this land to be prisoners in this place. I am raised from being prisoner in this place to be the prince of this land. That dejection was a work of God's justice; this advancement is a work of His mercy.'[32]

Not only did Elizabeth I prove to be one of the few prisoners of the Tower to survive the experience, she consigned her enemies to the Tower in her turn. In 1586, Anthony Babington (1561–86) was seized and consigned to the Tower for his part in the eponymous plot that intended to assassinate the queen and replace her with Mary, Queen of Scots. Babington and his co-conspirators were subsequently hanged, drawn and quartered at Lincoln's Inn Fields in scenes considered disturbing even by hardened execution-goers.

Queen Elizabeth's sometime favourite, Sir Walter Raleigh (1554–1618), was twice sentenced to the Tower. In 1592 the queen had him imprisoned for six weeks for his affair with one of her ladies-in-waiting, Elizabeth Throgmorton. Raleigh was released in September but Elizabeth Throgmorton was held until the end of the year to ensure Raleigh's compliance.[33] In 1603 Elizabeth's successor, James I, sent Raleigh back to the Tower, on a charge of plotting an assassination attempt. Elizabeth Throgmorton, now Raleigh's wife, accompanied him in his imprisonment, where the conditions for an aristocratic family were tolerable enough and Raleigh remained productive. He wrote his *History of the World* (eventually published in 1628) and fathered a son, Carew, born in the Tower in 1604. Briefly released to lead an expedition into Venezuela, Raleigh could not escape his fate. Executed at Westminster when he returned to England, he died as bravely as he had lived. His last words, as he laid his head upon the block and the executioner raised the axe, were: 'Strike man, strike!'[34]

Every prisoner of consequence carved their names upon the walls of the Tower. Today, some of these inscriptions are still visible, serving as a lasting memorial. The Beauchamp Tower, where Philip Howard, Earl of Arundel, was held in 1572 before being beheaded for aspiring to marry Mary, Queen of Scots, includes the inscriptions *Dolor Patientia Vincitur* [Patience Will Triumph Over Sadness].[35] In the same tower appears an inscription from an Irishman, Thomas Miagh, tortured for spying in 1580. Having endured the horrors of Skeffington's Daughter and the rack, Miagh carved his own epitaph:

> Thomas Miagh which liethe here alone
> That fayne wold from hence begon
> By torture straunge mi trovth was tryed
> Yet of my libertie denied.[36]

Hugh Draper, imprisoned on charges of sorcery, left an elaborate carving and inscription on the wall of the Salt Tower in 1561, while on 10 September 1571 Charles Bailly offered the observation: 'Be friend to one. Be ennemye to none. The most unhappy man in the world is he that is not patient in adversities: For men are not killed with the adversities they have, but with the impatience they suffer.'[37]

Occasionally the mood of resignation breaks down, as in this anonymous carving, where a prisoner recorded that he had been: 'Close prisoner 8 months, 22 wekes, 224 dayes, 5376 houres'.[38]

On Tower Green, where once the headsman's axe rested in readiness upon the block, there is now a simple memorial to the prisoners who died at the Tower. Designed by the artist Brian Catling, this sculpture consists of two glass discs, one atop the other, with a glass pillow resting in the centre. Engraved around the upper disc is an epigraph in the spirit of those earlier inscriptions, carved upon the walls of the Tower during the desperate hours:

> Gentle visitor, pause awhile,
> Where you stand death cut away the light of many days,
> Here jewelled names were broken from the vivid thread
> of life,
> May they rest in peace while we walk the generations
> around their strife
> And courage under these restless skies.[39]

After taking a moment or two to pause and reflect on those who died here, it is time to move on, and travel up the Thames to the City, the mighty heart of London.

3

FRATERNITY OF
VAGABONDS

London, Den of Thieves

Imagine, for a moment, flying over Jacobean London, from
the bustling shops of Cheapside to the brothels of Petticoat
Lane, then on to Whitechapel, to drink beer with Dutch
sailors. Soar across the city, looking down over Billingsgate
Market at its squabbling fishwives, and pampered aristocrats
gorging on claret and oysters. And finally flutter down to the
Strand, to witness the fops parading in their finery and the
lawyers strutting up from Westminster Hall, clutching their
wealthy clients like ivy clinging to a tree. Such was Ben
Jonson's invitation to his audience in *The Devil Is an Ass* (1616)
and Jonson knew his city better than most. As well as chron-
icling its nefarious underworld in a series of dramas, this
playwright was a convicted criminal who had narrowly
escaped the gallows after killing a man in a sword fight.
Jonson owed his freedom to 'benefit of clergy', which stipulated that anyone literate enough to recite an excerpt from the

Bible was technically a priest and therefore immune to prosecution. This convenient legal loophole later became known as the 'neck verse'.

Jonson had first-hand experience of London's teeming lowlife of cheats, cutpurses, cony-catchers, roaring girls, pickpockets, counterfeit cranks, disgraced soldiers, thieves and whores, who spilled like human vermin through the chinks and gulleys between the cramped and narrow houses, to prey upon the law-abiding with a dazzling array of tricks and scams.

The glittering panoply of criminal behaviour at this period is a drama in itself, with its protagonists ranging from the elegant gentleman thief to the roughest, stinking lowlife, and locations extending from the hallowed precincts of St Paul's Cathedral to the bawdy anarchy of St Bartholomew's Fair, right up to the grim portals of Newgate Gaol which loomed nearby and marked the penultimate stage on the one-way journey to the execution grounds of Tyburn and Smithfield. This turbulent period is one of the most exciting, for it is at this point that the foundations of London's underworld were laid down for centuries to come.

Long before Jonson and his fellow writers, Green, Dekker and Nashe classified the knaves and villains, counterfeit cranks (fake invalids) and pedlars who flicker through their plays and pamphlets, London had developed an infamous reputation. The city had already become notorious as the crime-ridden capital of a blighted land, a reputation that had developed over previous centuries. As early as 1497, a Venetian diplomat had written home to his masters observing that no other nation in the world had as many thieves and robbers as England and that London was the worst place of all.[1] 'Few venture to go alone in the country, excepting in the middle of the day, and fewer still in towns at night, and least of all in London,' he wrote.[2] By 1516, Sir Thomas More noted that it had become commonplace to see twenty thieves hanged upon a single gibbet, while the breakdown of the old feudal system following Henry VIII's Dissolution of the Monasteries in 1536 brought thousands of uprooted labourers to the city, desperate for work, only to be sucked into a life of crime. As the Elizabethan historian William Harrison later recorded in his *Description of England* (1577), 'because they will not begge, some of them doeth steale, and then they be hanged'.[3]

The government had responded to the increase in crime by introducing draconian legislation. By 1540, during the reign of Henry VIII, crimes which carried the death penalty had risen from the original three (theft, murder and treason) to eleven: high treason including counterfeiting, petty treason, murder, rape, piracy, arson of a dwelling house or barn, highway robbery, embezzlement, horse theft, robbing churches and robbing a person in a dwelling house. In 1547, Edward VI's 'Act for the Punishment of Vagabonds' made it an offence to be a vagrant. Any unemployed man found wandering about was liable to be branded on the forehead with the mark of slavery and even subjected to having a ring of iron put about his neck, arm or leg.

Before this, another class of outsiders had already been persecuted under the 'Act Concerning Egyptians' (1530). The 'Egyptians' or gypsies had arrived in England during the reign of Henry VIII. This nomadic people constituted a 'spectacular class of vagrants, at once exotic and familiar, spectacular and outlandish with their faces painted red or yellow, fantastic costumes made up of embroidered turbans and brightly coloured scarves and clothes composed of shreds and patches, with bells tinkling around their ankles'.[4] Known as 'the offspring of Ptolemy' and the 'Moon Men', the gypsies were believed to be descendants of the ancient Egyptians, something they actively encouraged as Egypt was believed to be the land of all that was magical and mystical. They travelled from shire to shire reading palms and telling fortunes, and their reputation for supernatural powers provided some protection against persecution.[5] Such protection was needed, given that the Act Concerning Egyptians described them as 'wretched, wandering wily vagabonds' who committed 'many and heinous felonies and robberies to the great hurt and deceit of the people'.[6]

The Act, designed to expel all gypsies from England, seize their assets and bar further immigration, was ultimately unsuccessful, and the gypsies remained, leaving an ineradicable impression on two aspects of London life: underworld slang and place names. Existing thieves' cant mixed with Romany to produce a secret language, with terms such as *darkmans* (nighttime), *crackmans* (hedge), *figure caster* (astrologer), *greenmans* (fields), *merripen* (life and death), and *Romeville* (London) designed to confuse the outsider. And the old Romany names lingered on to mark the spot where their caravans had rested, such as Herne Hill and Gypsy Hill.

The law of the land was savage, and yet such was the desperation of the criminal underclass that the threat of execution was no deterrent. In a city of wealth beyond the dreams of avarice, crime flourished. And in noisy, dirty, dangerous London, where the rich and poor lived side by side, and where poverty and injustice rubbed shoulders with privilege, a bold new species was born. The urban criminal, characterized by a rebellious streak and contempt for authority.

London may have been the largest city in Europe but it was small by modern standards. Lying within the protective embrace of its ancient Roman walls, late sixteenth-century London was equivalent in scale to the 'Square Mile' of the City of London today. The wall still surrounded London on three sides, with the Thames marking the fourth boundary. Citizens and visitors made their entrances and their exits through the vast wooden gates of Aldersgate, Cripplegate, Moorgate and Bishopsgate, which were ceremoniously locked every evening. From dusk onwards, the streets were patrolled by the 'Bellman' or night watchman, equipped with a lantern, a dog, and a pike, whose task it was to call out the hour and warn residents to lock up their houses and protect themselves against fire and theft. Inside the city, the two main thoroughfares consisted of the Strand, lined with the mansions of the rich – such as Somerset House, Arundel House and Leicester House – and Cheapside, which was a broad street flanked by the handsome black and white half-timbered houses of affluent merchants. There were no other streets as such, merely narrow alleyways winding between overcrowded wooden houses, built so close together that, if he were so minded, a man leaning out of the upper window of one might reach over and shake hands across the divide with his neighbour. At ground level, the tapering thoroughfares were filled with rotting vegetables, animal carcasses, and the slops from chamber pots, tossed unceremoniously from bedroom casements.

Beyond the city walls, Hampstead and Highgate were still remote villages and Tyburn, with its gallows as a dreadful landmark, was the first stop on the road to Oxford, hence its modern name of Oxford Street. Moorfields, now the site of the Museum of London, was an open stretch of land where washerwomen spread out their sheets to dry. And through all this ran the River Thames, like a silver ribbon, busy with all manner of craft, from the modest boats of watermen, who ferried passengers back and forth from north to south bank, with their cries of 'Eastward Ho!' and 'Westward Ho!' to the royal barges shuttling between the Tower and the palaces of Whitehall and Hampton Court.

The responsibility for maintaining law and order within the city of London itself lay with the 'constables' of 'the watch', ordinary men who were co-opted into policing the city on an annual basis. Essentially, the city was 'policed by consent'.[7] When the shout of 'Stop! Thief!' went up, all able-bodied citizens were expected to join in a 'hue and cry' until the miscreant had either been arrested, and taken before the local Justice of the Peace, or had high-tailed it into one of the teetering rookeries where ne'er-do-wells would go to lay low until the pursuit had died down.

This somewhat arbitrary approach to policing London met with varying degrees of success. Certain parts of the city became 'no-go' areas controlled by a criminal underworld with its own security system and intelligence network, which was more sophisticated than the amateur police force or 'watch' intended to protect the city.[8] Amongst other activities, providing refuge for a man on the run became a vital function of the underworld underground. A thief fleeing for his life, with a hue and cry in hot pursuit, would always find shelter in the maze of winding lanes behind St Martin's Church or the ruins of the Savoy hospital, or take refuge in Damnation Alley, Devil's Gap or the exotically named 'Bermudas', the area now known as King's Cross.

The most notorious no-go area consisted of 'Alsatia', which lay between Whitefriars, a former Carmelite friary, and Carmelite Street, with the Thames to the south and Fleet Street to the north. This ancient citadel of vice and crime operated as a sanctuary on the grounds that it was a former monastery and therefore exempt from the jurisdiction of the City of London. As a result, it became a criminal ghetto. According to the historian Thomas Babington Macaulay, at any attempt to extradite a criminal, 'Bullies with swords and cudgels, termagant hags with spits and broomsticks poured forth by the hundred and the intruder was lucky if he escaped back to Fleet Street, hustled, stripped and jumped upon.'[9]

The failure of the authorities to control crime inside the city was compounded by the fact that they had no jurisdiction over crime outside the city. Districts such as Islington to the north, and Southwark, on the south bank of the Thames, accordingly became notorious dens of vice, swarming with taverns, bear gardens and brothels. London's criminal classes gravitated to these areas, living on their wits and emerging betimes to avail themselves of the glittering prospects. While criminality had always existed in London, the increased density of population meant greater opportunities for the urban rogue, with thieves thronging the alehouses and colluding with the landlords to relieve the unwary traveller of their worldly goods, and innkeepers encouraging professional thieves to use their premises, and 'fencing' (selling on) stolen goods. And so organized crime was born.

One good example of this was a notorious criminal known as 'the King of Cutpurses', Laurence Pickering, who held weekly thieves' kitchens at his home in Kent Street, Hackney, where robbers could swap tips, plan robberies and discuss which members of the watch were most likely to take a backhander. Like many a successful villain, Pickering was formidably well connected, possessing a reliable source in the form of his ostensibly respectable brother-in-law, William Bull, the Tyburn hangman.[10]

Stealing was a skill that had to be learned, and to this end many a prototype of Dickens' Fagin set up his own training school for pickpockets. Writing in 1585, William Fleetwood, Recorder of the City of London, described the activities of one 'Wotton', who had been a prosperous merchant but had fallen upon hard times. Wotton took on an alehouse in Billingsgate, to make ends meet, and when the alehouse was closed down by the authorities, he decided to open a school for thieves. Wotton invited all the best cutpurses in London to his alehouse, to provide professional training for aspiring young thieves. The instruction technique was as follows: two pieces of equipment were hung up, consisting of a pocket, and a purse. The pocket held a selection of counters, and was hung about with little bells, similar to the bells on hawks' feet. The purse, also decorated with bells, held silver coins. Any lad who could extract a counter from the pocket without ringing the bells was awarded the title of 'Public Foister', and if he could remove a coin from the purse without any noise from the bells, he was made a 'Junior Nipper'.

Other accomplishments learned at Wotton's academy included 'shaving' (which meant stealing a small item such as a sword or a silver spoon) and 'lifting' (robbing a shop, a term still in circulation today), a task best achieved with the collusion of two other thieves, one of whom would be wearing a heavy cloak which could be cast over the coveted objects. Aspiring criminals could also learn how to become a 'curber', with the aid of a long hook that folded down to resemble a walking stick, and which could be used to pull items of clothing from open windows. Small boys frequently started their careers as 'divers', wriggling through windows and passing objects down to their gaffers. An invaluable accomplice in these circumstances was a sympathetic serving wench, who could be prevailed upon to leave a window open for her 'hooker' and his 'diver'. If such inside help was not available, criminals trained in the 'black art' of picking locks would be called upon.[11]

Thieves newly graduated from this academy of crime had numerous opportunities to perfect their skills in Elizabethan London. The broad expanses of Cheapside and the Strand were thronged with affluent visitors, belts groaning with full purses, their persons adorned with flamboyant velvet cloaks, feathered hats and jewelled daggers, while the plethora of attractions provided many an opportunity to take advantage of an unfortunate traveller. Modern readers may be surprised to learn that the first of these 'crime hot-spots' was none other than St Paul's Cathedral, which by the reign of Elizabeth had become less a hallowed place of worship than a byword for iniquity. The cathedral dated from 1300 and consisted of a massive Norman cathedral, with a wooden spire, 160 metres (520 feet) high, which was struck by lightning in 1561. This wooden spire subsequently proved to be the downfall of the building during the Great Fire of 1666, when it was burnt to the ground. Standing at the western end of Cheapside and covering over twelve acres, St Paul's was already in an advanced state of disrepair by the age of Elizabeth I, thanks to the depredations of Henry VIII's assault on religious institutions, but the cathedral was still a major landmark in Elizabethan London, a tourist attraction, shopping centre and entertainment complex all rolled into one, operating rather as Covent Garden Piazza does today. And, like the Piazza, St Paul's attracted every type of con-artist, rogue and beggar in the city.

While preachers, rebels and self-appointed dissidents flocked to harangue the crowds at the outdoor pulpit of St Paul's Cross, the nave of the cathedral operated like a street market. Following the Dissolution of the Monasteries, the chantries and chapels had been given over to booksellers and printers, who published Protestant tracts, ballads, and broadsides. While tobacconists offered the intriguing tawny-brown weed from the New World to the curious, prostitutes plied their trade and unemployed servants perused the 'wanted' notices pinned on the cathedral doors.

St Paul's even operated as a horse fair, with all the dubious associations of financial double-dealing, conspiracy, brawls and even murder. Thomas Dekker exposed the chicanery of the second-hand horse trade in his *Lanthorn and Candlelight* (1608). A glossy-coated animal, he warned, had probably been painted to disguise the fact that it had been stolen, while sickness, such as the glanders, characterized by a runny nose, could be concealed by tickling the horse's nostrils with a feather dipped in mustard, which would prove so irritating that the horse would stand with its head held up for hours at a time. Lameness could be disguised by removing one shoe, and blaming the disability on the fact that the horse was missing a shoe, while a slow-moving animal could be systematically beaten for days so that its skin became so sensitive that the slightest tap would be sufficient to send it galloping away like Bucephalus with a young Alexander the Great upon his back.[12]

St Paul's Walk, the central aisle of the cathedral, was crammed with men and women from all walks of life, and every part of the country. With its vast confusion of people and stacks of fallen masonry, it resembled nothing so much as the Tower of Babel. Crushed together within this heaving, breathing mass one might meet the knight, the gallant, the upstart, the gentleman, the clown, the captain, the lawyer, the usurer, the citizen, the bankrupt, the scholar, the beggar, the idiot, the ruffian, the cheater, the puritan and the cut-throat. It was inevitably a magnet for 'nips' and 'foists' and 'cony-catchers' to hunt down their 'gulls'.

In an era when dress really did maketh the man, potential victims were easy to spot. The most obvious 'marks' were the ostentatiously wealthy, dressed in silk, gold and jewels and attended by three or four servants. A classic case concerns that of a magnificently clad country squire, who had come up to London to look for a wife, and who had invested the equivalent of £5,000 in a heavy gold chain so that he looked suitably prosperous. As he arrived at St Paul's, this splendid chain immediately attracted the attention of a gang, who formed a plan on the spot. The first thief, pretending to be an innocent well-wisher, advised the old gentleman that his chain made him vulnerable, and that he should take it off and hide it away at once, to avoid the possibility of being mugged. The gentleman did as he was instructed, telling the well-wisher that he would put the chain in the sleeve of his coat, as nobody would even consider looking for it there. Shortly afterwards, the old gentleman was making his way through St Paul's Walk when a fight broke out in front of him between two scruffy young men. When the old gentleman bravely attempted to do his civic duty and intervene, both men fled. But just as they ran off, a third party tripped the old gentleman up from behind, toppling him to the ground. As the old gentleman came to his senses and was helped to his feet, by yet another accomplice, he put his hand in his sleeve and discovered that his precious chain was gone. The old gentleman had been the victim of a formidably organized robbery.[13]

Another vulnerable group consisted of the naïve young country gentlemen sent up to London to study law at the Inns of Court. These 'gulls' were easily identified by their coats of homespun russet (coarse red cloth, the Tudor equivalent of tweeds), and their expressions of wide-eyed wonder as they gazed around the bustling environs of St Paul's. For an experienced cutpurse working alone, it was a simple matter to turn a young law student into a victim of crime as he paused to listen to divine service or devoutly bent his knee in prayer. Another effective strategy consisted of the thief collapsing at the feet of his prospect and cutting his purse strings when he bent down to help.[14]

Soft-hearted young men might also fall prey to the 'whip-jacks', vagrants who told hard-luck stories, claiming they had been left destitute after their house burnt down or they had lost everything in a shipwreck. Asking for a handout after such invented catastrophe was known as a 'demand for a glimmer'.[15] New young arrivals were also fair game for professional gamblers or 'courtesy men', who would lure them into a card game, allow them to win, praising their skill at gambling, and then rob them blind with the aid of false dice, designed to eliminate the element of chance in the game.

'Fullams' were loaded with lead to make them heavier, while 'bristles' had a hair set into one side, meaning that they would only land in certain positions. Sleight of hand also played a part here, with cunning gamesters stacking the cards in their own favour, with doctored packs designed to fall in a certain way. Many false dice and dodgy playing cards were manufactured in prisons, with the King's Bench and the Marshalsea providing the finest examples of workmanship.[16]

Any public gathering offered rich pickings for London's lowlife. The law courts themselves, where thieves and robbers went on trial for their offences, were not exempt. As the spectators concentrated on the technicalities of the trial, nimble-fingered 'nips' and 'foists' worked the crowd, escaping with purses and handkerchiefs even as the judge laid down the death sentence.[17]

Another common ploy was for a gang to team up with a street singer, who, between belting out ballads and broadsides, would entreat the crowd to protect their possessions. As people's hands instinctively flew to their pockets, sharp-eyed thieves quickly noted exactly where their valuables were stowed, 'either in sleeve, hose or at girdle, to know whether they be safe or no'.[18]

Not every visitor to London was quite as naïve as the old gentleman with his gold chain, or the country bumpkin still wet behind the ears. The educated, sceptical victim required a different approach, and it was here that another species of criminal came into his own. This individual was the cony-catcher, who, with his elegant clothes and urbane manner, possessed a devastating mixture of plausibility and insight into human nature. The cony-catcher was generally well educated – a university man. He might have expected to find preferment (gain a fellowship) at his college, or be taken on as the private secretary to a courtier. But, with no inheritance or appropriate employment, he was thrown back upon his own resources, with nothing to rely upon but his quick wits and social accomplishments. This young man (for they were, most of them, young, cony-catching not being an occupation in which one could expect to grow old) was the original 'gentleman thief' or 'Volpone', the 'urban fox' from Jonson's play of the same name. Slinking through the dangerous streets of Elizabethan London and lying in wait for their prey, these sharp professionals would watch their victims leaving Westminster Hall after a banquet, or roam up and down St Paul's, Fleet Street, Holborn, and the Strand, dressed like honest gentlemen, 'or good fellows, with a smooth face, as if butter would not melt in their mouths'.[19]

Cony-catchers did not get rich underestimating human frailty. They understood that every man had his weakness, with sentimentality, lust and hate being the uppermost. In the dusty precincts of St Paul's, a shrewd cony-catcher would instruct his sidekick to reel in the punters with the Elizabethan equivalent of dirty postcards, in the form of French illustrations to Aretino's erotic sonnets. Intrigued by this merchandise, unsuspecting men were issued an invitation to a brothel, with the bawds splitting the proceeds with the cony-catcher and the unfortunate punter ending up robbed and beaten in a back alley.[20]

In a credulous age, when educated men might pose as doctors or even magicians, it was easy for cony-catchers to pose as quacks and charlatans. They offered charms to win over the objects of unrequited love, or potions to destroy a man's enemies. They sold rings which they swore blind incorporated such a 'quaint device' that a wench only had to slip it on her finger and she would have no choice but to follow her suitor up and down the street.[21] Those tormented by a rival could purchase a 'burning glass', which, if they stood upon the roof of St Paul's and aimed it at their enemy, would cast the sun upon his face with such force that he would be struck dead more violently than if he had been hit by a bolt of lightning. If this did not have the desired effect, then there was even an early prototype of the letter bomb, which consisted of 'a letter full of needles, which shall be laid after such a mathematical order, that when he opens it to whom it is sent, they all spring up and fly into his body as forcibly as if they had been blown with gunpowder'.[22] With his cynical ability to read his victim's baser desires and his smooth, plausible manner, the experienced cony-catcher was in many ways a more fearsome adversary for an unwary traveller – the enemy disguised as a friend.

At the beginning of this chapter the reader was invited to imagine flying over London, taking a bird's eye view of the nefarious city with Ben Jonson as guide. Now, at the end of this journey, it is time to land at Smithfield, a ten-acre stretch of wasteland just outside the city wall. On its margins stood Newgate Gaol, St Bartholomew's Church, St Bartholomew's Hospital and the Charterhouse, and the lanes between these august institutions were crammed with pens full of livestock, for sale at the cattle market.

Smithfield is best known as the site of Bartholomew Fair, celebrated by Jonson in his play of the same name from 1614. This annual extravaganza of debauchery, dating back to 1133, was the only real city fair in Elizabethan England and reflected the noisy, chaotic life of Londoners at the time. The authorities greeted Bartholomew Fair with much the same horror that the residents of Notting Hill used to respond to the August Carnival, with real anxiety at the prospect of lawlessness and anarchy. The event offered endless opportunities for cutpurses, cony-catchers and mountebanks, and was almost impossible to police as it took place upon the 'liberty' of St Bartholomew's, land which belonged to the church before the Reformation but which was now beyond the City's jurisdiction.

Opening upon St Bartholomew's Day, 24 August, the fair took place during the 'dog-days', when Sirius, the dog star, was ascendant in the heavens, and believed to cause mad behaviour in dogs and people. Bartholomew Fair was ostensibly a trade fair for cloth merchants, though by Jonson's time it had expanded to provide every form of entertainment, from freaks of nature such as a bull with five legs and two pizzles, to a black wolf, a team of dogs performing a Morris dance, and a hare that played the tabor, thumping away on the drum with its powerful back legs. Then there were the viciously satirical puppet shows, the origins of our modern Punch and Judy, to be enjoyed while munching on roast pork, gingerbread and hot pies, all washed down with ale. Enjoyment came with the tag of *caveat emptor* or 'buyer beware'. Those 'golden' rings were made of brass and would turn your finger green in a week, while even the beer frequently contained unappealing additives such as spiders and snails.[23]

The fair was opened by the Lord Mayor of London every year, after he had taken a cup of sack (fortified wine) with the governor of Newgate. A German visitor, Paul Hentzner, recalled watching the fair being opened in 1600. The Lord Mayor, clad in his scarlet robes and golden chain, rode out of the city accompanied by twelve aldermen, and took up a position near one of the tents to watch members of the crowd engage in a wrestling match, with money for the winners being awarded by the magistrates. After this, a sack of live rabbits was released into the crowd, eagerly pursued by a number of boys, trying to catch them while making as much noise as possible. Hentzner and his friends became so absorbed in the scene that it was not until afterwards that one colleague, Dr Tobias Salander, realized he had been robbed of a purse containing nine crowns by an Englishman who had been standing close by.[24]

Given the gleeful lawlessness of the occasion, the authorities made some effort to impose order on the proceedings in the form of a 'fair court'. This was known as the court of 'Pie Powder', a corruption of *pedes pulverosi* or *pieds poudrés,* a reference to the 'dusty feet' of itinerant pedlars, but the court frequently proved ineffectual. Jonson depicted this court as presided over by Adam Overdo, a well-intentioned Justice of the Peace who attempts to fight crime by patrolling the fair in disguise. Overdo tracks down tricksters such as Joan Trash, the gingerbread woman, whose wares are composed of stale bread, rotten eggs and old honey. But Overdo himself is taken in, by Ezekiel Edgeworth, a bright young gentleman who turns out to be a cutpurse. Meanwhile, Overdo's own wife, who has been tricked into prostitution, is brought before him in a state of intoxication. Other recognizable London characters include Ursula the Pig Woman who sells roast pork and bottled beer from her booth, which doubles as a brothel, 'Punk Alice', a prostitute, and 'Zeal of the Land Busy', a Puritanical prig who denounces Bartholomew Fair as 'the shop of Satan'. For all his preaching, Busy is eventually revealed as a randy hypocrite who has consumed two entire roast pigs.[25]

The exuberant lawlessness of Bartholomew Fair represented just one aspect of Smithfield. This 'field of smiths, the grove of hobby horses and trinkets' as Jonson described in *Bartholomew Fair* had another, darker aspect. Jonson's audience knew that this foul stretch of wasteland had a far more sinister side. It was here that rebel Wat Tyler was stabbed to death by the Mayor of London, William Walworth, in 1381. By the Tudor period, Smithfield had become another of London's chief execution sites. In terms of the number who died there, it was the equal of Tyburn, and Newgate Gaol had become death row for heretics.

Henry VIII, a staunch supporter of Rome before he chose to reform the Church, began his reign persecuting those who preached against the Catholic faith and ended it with the Dissolution of the Monasteries and execution of the monks. While Henry VIII's most famous victims were, of course, Sir Thomas More and John Fisher, Bishop of Rochester, these were just two notables from a long list of martyrs. Among them was Richard Byfield, who was imprisoned for supporting Protestant doctrine. In 1532, he was led out to Smithfield to be burnt as a heretic. Although Byfield showed great courage and dignity, and 'went to the fire in his apparel manfully and joyfully', it took him over thirty minutes to die, 'for lack of a speedy fire'.[26] A similar fate awaited John Frith, a Cambridge man who had already fallen foul of the authorities for his support of Martin Luther. When Frith made the short walk from Newgate to Smithfield on 4 July 1533, he was accompanied by a naïve young tailor named Andrew Hewitt, who had fallen in with Frith and found himself convicted of heresy. Hewitt was tied up alongside Frith in order to balance the stake. Although the executioners had been at work since daybreak preparing the fire, a strong wind persistently flattened the flames, and both men died a protracted and agonizing death. To the end, Frith retained his dignity, and his calm voice could be heard attempting to reassure Hewitt above the crackle of the flames as poor Hewitt screamed in agony. An even more appalling fate awaited John Forest, a former chaplain to Catherine of Aragon. In 1538, after refusing to acknowledge Henry VIII as supreme head of the church, Forest was roasted to death at Smithfield, in a cage placed over a log fire. It took him two hours to die.[27] It was at Smithfield that 289 Protestants were burnt at the stake on the orders of Queen Mary, thanks to the zeal of Mary's ruthless enforcer, Bishop 'Bloody' Bonner, described by John Foxe in his *Book of Martyrs* (1563) as 'this cannibal in three years space three hundred martyrs slew, they were his food, he loved so blood, he spared none he knew.'[28]

More unusual crimes were dealt with by special legislation. Such was the fate of Richard Rouse, a cook accused of attempting to poison his master, John Fisher, the Bishop of Rochester. Rouse achieved the rare distinction of having an Act of Parliament passed against him in 1531. The story of Rouse's cruel and unusual punishment is told in the Act, 22 Henry VIII (1530–1), C9. On 17 February, during the seventeenth year of Henry's reign, Rouse, late of Rochester in the county of Kent, otherwise known as Richard Cook, 'of his moste wyked and dampnable dysposicyon' cast poison into a pot of porridge while it stood in the kitchen of his master, the Bishop of Rochester. Rouse was presumably motivated by religious hatred, as the bishop was a convinced Roman Catholic. But since the porridge was intended for the bishop's family, the entire household was poisoned. Sixteen people suffered severe poisoning, while Benett Curwen, a local gentleman, Alyce Tryppytt, a widow, and several paupers who had visited in search of alms actually died. As for the bishop, he had been too busy to eat all day and escaped entirely. Rouse was charged with high treason, a crime that parliament ordained should carry the most severe punishment. On 5 April 1531 a massive crowd gathered at Smithfield as Rouse was placed in an iron cauldron of cold water over a fire. As the cauldron heated up, Rouse was slowly and excruciatingly boiled to death.[29]

Newgate Gaol had seen all this, gazing down implacably over the burning heretics and revelling fairgoers alike. It is to Newgate, the next dark landmark on the map of criminal London, that I now turn.

SHADES OF THE
PRISON HOUSE

*From Newgate Gaol
to the Old Bailey*

By the reign of Queen Elizabeth I (1558–1603), London had eighteen prisons within the space of a square mile, of which the most infamous was undoubtedly Newgate Gaol, already a den of iniquity. An entry in an ancient book at the Guildhall refers to the 'foul, heinous jail of Newgate',[1] while by the Tudor period the gaol had become notorious as 'an abode of woe, a hotbed of vice and a school of crime'.[2] Beside Newgate sat the sessions house of the Old Bailey, dating from 1539 and so named because it was built upon the old fortified city wall. These two institutions, prison and court-house, would represent London's criminal justice system for centuries to come. In terms of human misery, Newgate had the same ghastly significance as Tyburn and Smithfield, while at the Old Bailey, ostensibly the repository of justice, thousands of prisoners became victims of the 'brutal methods of English criminal law' and the 'callous customs' of the period.[3]

While Newgate was London's most famous prison, many other prisons proved its equal in sheer human misery. The Clink, the Fleet, Bridewell and the Marshalsea loom large in the topography of London's underworld, and this chapter will explore them in all their horror and degradation. The high number of prisons in London was a result of the city's swelling population and the rising crime rate, and reflected the fact that London had been at the heart of the British legal system from Norman times. The great institutions of the legal profession were developed here, including the Houses of Parliament, the Royal Courts of Justice, the specific London courts in the form of Guildhall and the Lord Mayor's Court at Mansion House, as well as the Inns of Court where lawyers lived, trained and practised their profession.

English law had been influenced by two other legal systems, first that of the Roman invaders and subsequently French law as practised by the Normans. The law also operated in conjunction with the ecclesiastical authorities. 'The law was thought to have mystical significance' with judges regarded as 'priests of the law' and all judicial sentences as 'the judgement of God'.[4]

The earliest trials consisted of ordeals, such as trial by water. This involved throwing the accused into deep water. If he floated, without swimming, he was guilty, but if he drowned he was judged innocent. A variation of this practice consisted of plunging the arm of the accused into boiling water. Innocence or guilt was then determined by the condition of the wound. Trials by ordeal ceased in 1215 after Pope Innocent III declared that ordeals were not a demonstration of God's judgement. In the same year, clause 39 of the Magna Carta stated that: 'No freeman shall be taken, imprisoned, outlawed, banished or in any way destroyed [tortured], nor will we proceed to prosecute him, except by the lawful judgement of his peers and by the law of the land.'[5]

Being tried by one's peers was a new concept, but this clause helped pave the way for the first trials by jury four years later in 1219. Instead of being tried by ordeal, the prisoner was given the opportunity to be judged by their neighbours, local men of some standing in their community. In criminal trials they were known as 'local accusers'. Over the centuries, it was the jurors, and not the judges, who would decide the fate of the prisoner by returning the verdict of 'guilty' or 'not guilty'. In 1367 it was decided that the jury should consist of twelve men, and their decision or verdict had to be unanimous. As will become evident in subsequent chapters of this book, jury trials were frequently unsatisfactory, and subject to the capricious whims of powerful and often ruthless judges. Trials were very swift; evidence usually took the form of confessions, often extracted under torture, and juries frequently convicted on the basis of confessions.[6]

By the thirteenth century a prisoner or 'litigant' was permitted to appoint a legal representative, an agent or 'attorney'. As the law became more complex, the attorney required an increasingly complex body of knowledge; these men were often clerks of the court who acted for litigants in return for payment; they often possessed particular skills of advocacy or pleading or detailed knowledge of particular areas of the law. However only a wealthy person could afford to hire an attorney; the majority of common men and women had no such recourse, and were left to conduct their own defence, reliant on the character witnesses of friends and neighbours.

Although the former royal palace of Bridewell had been opened as a house of correction for vagabonds and whores in the sixteenth century, prisons were not designed for the rehabilitation of offenders. Nor was any distinction made between those remanded in custody awaiting trial and convicted prisoners awaiting execution. Instead, the prisons of London served to incarcerate anyone who had offended the authorities. Gaoling for debt had been common since the twelfth century. Hapless individuals, who would never satisfy their creditors, were locked up together with their entire families. In a microcosm of chaotic London, debtors, dissenters and dissidents were detained alongside rapists and murderers. And since prisons were run as businesses, the only class distinction once you were inside was how much 'garnish' you could offer your gaoler in return for provisions. Such was the corruption of the day that many guilty prisoners bribed their gaolers and delighted in an endless supply of roast meat and wine, while thousands of innocent captives languished in appalling conditions.

For an imaginative tour of London's prisons during the Tudor and Jacobean period, the 'water poet' John Taylor (1578–1653) serves as a useful guide. A prolific pamphleteer and waterman, also known as 'the Sculler', Taylor has been dismissed in some quarters as a 'literary bargee', but he spent forty years on the river and acquired an in-depth knowledge of London and its multifarious residents. In 1623, Taylor published a satirical survey of London's prisons entitled *The Praise and Virtue of a Jail and Jailers*, describing the horrors of the city's gaols and their wretched inhabitants:

> In London, and within a mile I ween [calculate]
> There are of jails or prisons full eighteen,
> And sixty whipping-posts, and stocks and cages,
> Where sin with shame and sorrow hath due wages ...[7]

Like the mythical Charon ferrying the dead across the Styx to Hades, Taylor regales his listeners with tales of London's darkest dungeons, providing a dour running commentary above the creak and splash of the oars as he rows along the Thames from the comparative serenity of the Gatehouse at

Westminster Abbey, where Sir Walter Raleigh spent his last night on earth, to the full horror of Newgate.

The Gatehouse, which strictly speaking falls outside the remit of the 'Square Mile', dates from 1370. The Gatehouse was built over two gates at right angles to each other, at Westminster Abbey. One gate looked north and included the Bishop of London's prison for convicted clerics, whilst the other looked west and included a gaol for lay offenders. Chiefly used for high-status prisoners such as royalty or prisoners of war, it offered 'good lodging-rooms and diet', which must have been some consolation to Sir Walter Raleigh in 1618, as he awaited his execution in Old Palace Yard.

Next on the itinerary is Bridewell, where, according to Taylor, 'Idleness and lechery is vext: for vagabonds and runa-gates [rogues] / For whores and idle knaves and suchlike mates.'[8] Bridewell was not intended to be a prison. Originally, Henry VIII had built a palace at Bridewell, at the spot where the Fleet River flowed into the Thames, in 1515, but the palace was little used. In 1553, Henry's son Edward VI granted the palace to the Corporation of the City of London to use as a House of Correction, designed to punish wrongdoers and teach beggars and vagrants the error of their ways. The opening ceremony on 16 December 1556 consisted of a woman being publically whipped, and then placed in a pillory at Cheapside, for the crime of abandoning her baby on the street.

The next stop on this grisly tour is the 'Compters', of which there were three in London: the Poultry Compter, taking its name from the Cheapside street market specializing in fowl, the Borough Compter, originally built within the precincts of the parish church of St Margaret's, Southwark, and mostly intended for debtors and petty offenders, and the Wood Street Compter. The term 'compter' derives from the 'counting' or keeping of official records, and Compters were sheriff's prisons, for all offenders against the City's laws. According to

Taylor, 'The Counter in the Poultry is so old / That it in history is not enrolled.'[9] The Poultry Compter actually dated back to the fourteenth century, was rebuilt in 1615, and enjoyed a particularly gruesome reputation, with its inhabitants described as 'ill-looking vermin, with long, rusty beards, swaddled up in rags'.[10]

The Wood Street Compter dated from 1555, taking in prisoners from the former Bread Street Compter, which had been closed down by the authorities in 1550. The Keeper of Bread Street Compter, Richard Husband, had been jailed briefly in Newgate for cruelty, but returned to his old ways when he was released, letting out his cells as cheap overnight accommodation for thieves and prostitutes. The historian John Stow, who was on the jury that tried Husband, observed at the time that gaolers such as Husband 'will deal hardly with pitiful prisoners'.[11]

One of the best accounts of prison life in Jacobean London was published by William Fennor, an Anglo-Dutch writer and rogue, whose pamphlet of 1617 recounts his experiences as a prisoner at Wood Street Compter. As Fennor tells it, he was walking down the street one autumn evening in 1616, when a merchant accidentally ran into him and knocked him into the gutter. Fennor was enraged and struck the merchant over the head with his sword. It was a blow that should have stunned an ox, but this tough tradesman was made of sterner stuff. He shrugged off Fennor's assault and ran away, while Fennor was arrested by a pair of constables and dragged off to Wood Street Compter.

Once he arrived, Fennor was offered three different types of accommodation, depending on how much money or 'garnish' he was prepared to pay to his keepers.[12] The choice consisted of the Master's Side, the Knight's Side, or a destination referred to ominously as the Hole. Flush with cash, Fennor opted for the Master's Side. Once his name had been entered on the prison register or 'black book', Fennor was conducted through a series of locked gates, and had to pay a shilling each time to the turnkey until he reached the Master's Side, where he had to produce another two shillings to gain entry, or forfeit his hat and cloak. Having spent the best part of ten shillings, Fennor was eventually conducted to a narrow cell festooned with cobwebs, lit by a guttering stub of candle. His bedding consisted of a straw mattress and dirty sheets, but at least there was the prospect of dinner to come, with claret, ale and even tobacco. However, these luxuries came at a price. As he sat down to eat, Fennor was informed that on this occasion he was not only expected to pay for his own dinner, but everyone else's, including all the prisoners on the Master's Side, and the keepers, right down to the vintner's boy who poured the wine.

For those who could afford to lodge on the Master's Side, conditions were relatively comfortable. A knight or wealthy yeoman who could afford to pay a weekly charge of ten shillings could enjoy beef on the bone, roasted veal, capon (chicken), claret and unlimited bread. On 'fish days', when notional fasting was observed for religious purposes, the wealthy prisoner still received two bowls of butter and three or four generous dishes of fresh fish. He could dine alone or with his friends, and be waited on hand and foot. After dinner, a further helping of 'garnish' ensured the prisoner would not be locked in his cell for the night. Instead, he could entertain his friends or enjoy a whore, brought in from a local brothel at his request. Gambling was so widespread that the Fleet Prison even had its own bowling alley.

Fennor remained on the Master's Side for three or four weeks, but, given that he needed to fork out 'garnish' on a regular basis, he soon ran short of funds and was transferred to the Knight's Side. Conditions here were tolerable, and a reasonable meal could be had for fivepence a time, but Fennor still had to pay for everything, from a cup of wine to a breath of fresh air. As shortage of funds dictated that Fennor's cell was located next to the stinking 'jakes' or latrine, regular access to an open window was a necessity.[13]

Happily for Fennor, he was released before he ran out of money altogether and could be consigned to the third and worst form of accommodation, known as the Hole. Here prisoners endured conditions of the most abject wretchedness, and up to fifty distressed inmates slept on bare boards, famished and 'languishing in great need, cold and misery'.[14]

Conditions were no better at the Poultry Compter, where the Hole was less than twenty feet square, but inhabited by over forty prisoners. Thomas Dekker, who spent seven years at the Poultry Compter for debt, recalled the pandemonium caused by snoring bedfellows and bellowing gaolers while drunken singing and laughter emanated from the Master's Side. Dekker's hair turned completely white while he was doing his time there.

Even if prisoners could endure the hardship and deprivation of the Hole, they were still likely to starve to death. With no funds set aside to provide food and drink, the prisoners were wholly dependent on charity or leftovers from the food confiscated from traders who had been caught giving short measure. Religious orders offered bread and meat, but the keepers inevitably took the choicest cuts, leaving the prisoners the remains – unsavoury scraps that had passed through unwashed fingers and been licked and rejected by dogs. Charitable donations, such as the £20 a year bequeathed by Robert Dowe in 1612, which was intended to pay off prisoners' debts, were pocketed by the keepers, while friends and relatives were reduced to tossing money through the bars of the Hole so that the prisoners could stretch their arms out through the gratings to buy food direct from the street vendors. When a prisoner died, the keepers' greed knew no bounds. According to Fennor, the Wood Street keepers were so rapacious that they refused to release one body for burial unless they received a handsome payment from the prisoner's relatives.

According to Taylor the Water Poet, the Fleet Prison dates from 'Richard's Reign the First', specifically 1197. The Fleet Prison was located on what is now Farringdon Street, and named after the Fleet River, which subsequently gave its name to Fleet Street. The Fleet was built on an island formed by the Fleet River and ditches, and by the fourteenth century these ditches were full of foul, stagnant water. In its early years, the Fleet was used for those in contempt of the Royal Courts, and, in Tudor and Stuart times, those convicted in the Court of Star Chamber. Distinguished prisoners included the Earl of Surrey in 1543 and William Herbert, Earl of Pembroke, in 1601. Conditions were tolerable for wealthy prisoners. As well as decent food, tobacco and whores, there was a tap room, racquet games in the courtyard and even a bowling alley.[15]

The Clink, 'where handsome lodgings be' as Taylor ironically comments, was of course anything but handsome. The prison's very name became synonymous with incarceration, the 'clink' referring to the rattle of the prisoners' chains. The Clink was the oldest prison in London, dating back to Saxon times when it originated in cells beneath the Bishop of Winchester's palace in Southwark. The Bishop's Palace was burnt down during the peasants' revolt of 1381, and in the rebuild that followed the men's prison was transferred to a vault underneath the palace's great hall. While gratings at street level allowed ventilation and enabled the prisoners to stretch out their hands for alms, the vaults were often flooded when the Thames reached high tide, and there was no latrine.

Although the majority of the Clink's population consisted of prostitutes and drunks, actors and writers joined their ranks with the development of the Bankside theatres. On more than one occasion the entire cast of one theatre was 'thrust into the Clink for acting obscenely',[16] while in 1554 the aristocrat Sir Francis Wyatt was committed to the Clink after an unsuccessful attempt to depose Queen Mary. Of London's other prisons, John Taylor refers to a 'hole or den for men' at St Katherine's Dock, a prison in East Smithfield which was little better, a 'gaol for heretics' at Three Cranes, Blackfriars, and two other gaols at Whitechapel and Finsbury. But these institutions pale into insignificance as John Taylor takes his leave at the final destination of this tour, described by the chronicler Raphael Holinshed as the 'most ugly and loathsome prison' of Newgate.

Originally taking its name from 'New Gate', one of the gates in the massive fortified wall that surrounded London, Newgate had been a gatehouse gaol since the reign of King John.[17] Five storeys tall and measuring 25 x 15 m (85 x 50 feet), it was an imposing building, with room for around 150 prisoners, although occupation was normally closer to 250.

Conditions had been dismal from the earliest years. In 1218, John's successor, Henry III, wrote to the sheriffs of London, 'commanding them to repair the jail of Newgate for the safe-keeping of his prisoners' and offering to contribute to the expense.[18] The repairs were clearly inadequate as by 1253 Henry III sent the city sheriffs to the Tower of London for a month because they had allowed a prisoner to escape from Newgate who had killed the queen's cousin.[19]

Since Newgate accommodated so many desperate criminals, many of whom were destined for execution, the escape rate was high. Methods varied from climbing out through the roof, rushing the gates or blowing a hole through the walls. In 1456, a crowd of prisoners crawled out onto the leads (roof tops) and held the sheriffs and keepers at bay until they were surrounded by a crack squad of constables and forced to give themselves up. Escape was relatively easy because the fabric of Newgate was in a constant state of disrepair – the walls were so weak and crumbling that they provided very little security.[20]

By 1341 the prospect of the gaol was already enough to inspire terror. The prison had become a repository for every class of offender, and King Edward III complained to the Mayor of London that the jail was 'so full of prisoners that they are continually dying of hunger and oppression'.[21] Newgate, like Tyburn, also provided the authorities with the opportunity to discourage potential malefactors with grisly exhibitions of justice in action. For example, on 10 July 1345, Sir John of Shoreditch, a member of the King's Household, was suffocated by four of his servants at his house in Ware. The servants confessed and were convicted of 'petty treason', the crime of killing their masters. Just eight days after the murder, on 18 July, they were drawn, hanged and quartered and their heads set up on poles at Newgate.[22]

Men were sent to Newgate for comparatively trivial offences. In 1287 Roger le Skirmisour was sent to Newgate for running a fencing school, which had been forbidden as it was thought to encourage sword fights. Even speaking your mind could land you in this most dismal of prisons. In December 1371 Nicolas Mollere, a smith, was sent to Newgate until such time as the sheriffs saw fit to release him for the offence of 'circulating lies'. Mollere, who was sentenced to the pillory, had claimed that Newgate was to be closed and all the prisoners sent to the Tower of London.[23] In 1378, a parish clerk was incarcerated for insinuating that John of Gaunt had Lollard sympathies.[24] Other offences which could land one in Newgate included cheating at dice, highway robbery and 'nightwalking', being out after the official curfew of nine o'clock.

Conditions became so overcrowded at Newgate that in

1382 Ludgate Prison was opened for 'respectable' criminals such as debtors or tradesmen convicted of fraud. However, Ludgate was closed in 1419 and its unfortunate denizens transferred to Newgate, where sixty of them promptly succumbed to 'brain fever', probably typhus, which would have flourished in Newgate's filthy conditions.

Newgate had reached such a distressing state by 1421 that Sir Richard Whittington, legendary Mayor of London, reopened Ludgate Prison and left a substantial part of his estate to rebuild Newgate when he died in 1423. Work started almost immediately and the new prison, which was completed within a few years, stretched up from the Old Bailey in a northerly direction, forming an arch over Newgate Street. It was a much larger building than its predecessor, with a central hall, a chapel, day and night wards, and separate quarters for women. There were the inevitable dungeons, and more comfortable rooms for those prisoners who could afford to pay for them. Some effort was made to segregate the debtors and minor offenders from the more serious criminals, and in 1435, Thomas Knolleys, a grocer who had been Mayor of London in 1400, paid for the installation and upkeep of a water supply, and 'caused sweet water to be conveyed to the gates of Newgate and Ludgate for the relief of the prisoners there'.[25]

Despite these improvements, Newgate continued to be a byword for iniquity. One of its most ghoulish features was 'Jack Ketch's Kitchen', named after the legendary hangman. All the reassuring associations of the word 'kitchen' disappear when one learns what happened in there. This chamber was known as 'Jack Ketch's Kitchen' because 'it is the place in which that honest fellow boils the quarters of such men as have been executed for treason'. According to one eyewitness:

When we first came into Newgate, there lay (in a little by-place like a closet in the room where we were lodged), the quartered bodies of three men who had been executed some days before for a real or pretended plot, and the reason why their quarters lay there so long was that the relatives were all that while petitioning to have leave to bury them; which at length, with much ado, was obtained for the quarters but not for the heads, which were ordered to be set up in some part of the City. I saw the heads when they were brought up to be boiled; the hangman fetched them in a dirty dust basket, out of some by-place, and setting them down among the felons he and they made sport with them. They took them by the hair, flouting, jeering and laughing at them; and then, giving them ill-names, boxed them on the ears and cheeks. Which done the Hangman put them into his kettle, and parboiled them with Bay-salt and Cummin-seed, – that to keep them from putrefaction, and this to keep off the fowls from seizing on them. The whole sight (as well as that of the bloody quarters first and this of the heads afterwards) was both frightful and loathsome, and begat an abhorrence in my nature.[26]

In keeping with its barbaric reputation, Newgate endured a succession of cruel and sadistic gaolers. The records reveal a list of brutal administrators, beginning in 1290 with a keeper who was hanged for murdering a prisoner. In 1330 Edmund le Lorimer, Keeper of Newgate, was sent to the Fleet prison for torturing and blackmailing prisoners, loading them mercilessly with irons and subjecting them to excessive fees.[27] A few years later, one of his successors was dismissed for confining minor offenders in the dungeons and torturing them until they had given large sums of money. In 1447 the keeper, James Manning, left the corpse of one prisoner in the street outside his gaol, 'causing a nuisance and great danger to the King who was passing there'. Manning refused to remove the body and, following an exchange of 'shameful words' between Manning and the king's messenger, Manning and his wife were both jailed.[28] After one keeper was imprisoned for raping female prisoners, the Court of Aldermen set up a board of visitors who were instructed to make regular inspections of the jail.

Despite these measures, Newgate continued to be a byword for infamy, notorious for its appalling keepers. One such was Andrew Alexander, appointed during the reign of Henry VIII and obnoxious even by the standards of his day. Alexander charged 'garnish' to have chains and fetters removed, and anyone who could not pay him was consigned to the Hole. Alexander was particularly sadistic towards martyrs, and once left eleven monks chained, standing up, until they starved to death. When John Rogers, vicar of St Sepulchre's, was awaiting execution at Smithfield and wanted to share his food with his fellow prisoners, Alexander intervened and took it for himself. According to John Foxe in his *Book of Martyrs,* Alexander suffered divine retribution. In 1554, 'Alexander, the severe keeper of Newgate, died miserably, swelling to a prodigious size, and became so inwardly putrid that none could come near him.'[29]

It is from around this period, under Mary Tudor, that references to the sinister 'Black Dog of Newgate' start to appear, although the legend itself is much older. This terrifying and mythical beast appears to have emerged during the reign of Henry III, when London had been hit by a famine. The prisoners, already deprived of food, suffered more harshly than most.

When a portly German scholar was detained in Newgate on charges of sorcery, the prisoners could not contain themselves. They fell on the man, killed him, cooked him and ate him, pronouncing him to be 'good meat'. However, the prisoners soon regretted their actions. Shortly after the scholar had been killed and eaten, a hideous black dog – with eyes of fire and jowls dripping with blood – appeared in the dead of night and proceeded to exact a terrifying revenge. Some hapless prisoners were torn limb from limb by the ferocious beast, as their anguished screams echoed through the gaol, striking terror into the very souls of the other inmates. Others simply died of fright, when they heard its ghostly panting and its heavy paws padding towards them across the cold, stone floors. Those who survived the first nights of its lust for vengeance became so terrified that they killed their guards and escaped. But no matter how far they travelled, the beast hunted them down one by one.

Only when the murder of its master, the sorcerer, had been fully avenged did the Black Dog return to the prison's foetid dungeons, where it became a hideous harbinger of death, always appearing on the eve of executions or the night before a felon breathed his last. References to the Black Dog appeared for centuries afterwards, with chilling descriptions of a shapeless, black form seen slithering along the wall of Amen Court, near St Paul's Cathedral, then sliding down into the courtyard and melting away, its appearances accompanied by the sound of dragging footsteps and a nauseating stench, like the smell of death. It fell to one prisoner, Luke Hutton, to immortalize the beast in 1596. Hutton wrote about the Black Dog while he was imprisoned at Newgate, describing a shape-shifting monster that was sometimes gaoler, sometimes coney-catcher. At first the creature appeared in the shape of a man, but then transformed himself into a coal-black Cerberus (the dog at the gates of Hades), with eyes like torches, poisonous breath and smoking nostrils:

> His countenance ghastly, fearefull, grim, and pale,
> His foamy mouth still gaping for his prey:
> With Tigers teeth he spares none to assail,
> His lippes Hell gates, ore-painted with decay:

His tongue the Clapper, sounding wofull knell,
Tolling poore men to ring a peale in Hell.[30]

It was always said that the Black Dog appeared on the eve of one's execution: a sighting of this dismal creature meant that you were as good as dead. Whether Hutton chose to memorialize the creature in a final bid to gain immortality or actually saw it is a matter for speculation. But one thing is for certain: whether Hutton saw the dog or not, he was a marked man. The 'neck-verse', normally guaranteed to secure release for an educated man, did not save Hutton from the gallows. Although he was released from Newgate, Hutton was subsequently hanged at York in 1598. Hutton, who had abandoned writing for a more lucrative career as a robber, was typical of a new breed of criminal, many of whom would end up in Newgate en route to Tyburn. These characters, some of the most famous criminals in the history of London, were the highwaymen.

STAND AND DELIVER!

The Golden Age of Highway Robbery

As the trees rapidly disappeared behind them, the riders galloped across a broad tract of wasteland, interspersed with ditches and fences, over which their horses bounded as if well accustomed. At that moment, what with the fresh air, the fitful moonlight now breaking broadly out, now lost in a rolling cloud, the exciting exercise, and that racy and dancing stir of the blood, we cannot ignore the fascination of that lawless life. A fascination so great, that when one of the most noted gentlemen highwaymen of the day stood upon the scaffold with the rope about his neck, and the priest exhorted him to repent of his ill-spent life, the reply was defiant. 'Ill-spent, you dog! –'Gad! (smacking his lips) it was delicious!'[1]

This description, drawn from the 1830 novel *Paul Clifford* by Edward Bulwer-Lytton, epitomizes the romantic appeal of the highwayman, that swashbuckling, debonair character who has haunted popular culture for three centuries, but whose origins are lost in the mists of time. The earliest high-waymen were semi-mythical men such as Hereward the Wake who led a resistance movement against the Normans, and the legendary Robin Hood, the rebel nobleman banished to the greenwood by a savage king. Closer to our own times, the notorious figures of Claude Du Vall, Plunkett and MacLaine and Dick Turpin come bounding into view. These 'high Tobys' (robbers on horseback) were the most glamorous of English villains, celebrated in their day for their defiant courage and romantic appeal, living like legends and dying like heroes.

This chapter ventures out from the heart of London to the fringes of the underworld, to the shady groves where the robbers lie in wait, ready to ambush the stagecoaches of wealthy travellers and the post-chaises that delivered the mail. For centuries, London had been framed by woodland, and any person brave enough to risk the open road did so in the knowledge that mortal danger haunted the wayside. Travellers heading for the Great North Road had to traverse the wilds of Hampstead and Highgate. Bearing east meant riding through the gloomy depths of Epping Forest whilst the Dover Road took one through the aptly named Shooter's Hill. The route of the Great West Road to Bath and Exeter took a hazardous course across the leafy commons of Putney and Hounslow. Even within twelve miles of London, the roads were treacherous, their muddy surfaces full of potholes, while deep ditches ran either side. Every traveller had cause to dread the rustle of leaves as a masked gunman emerged from the undergrowth and levelled his pistol with that terrifying command: *'Stand and deliver – your money or your life!'*

The archetypal highwayman was the dispossessed aristocrat, turning his military skills to useful account as a courtly armed robber. Following the Reformation, many gentlemen lost their family estates and turned to robbery to survive. One of the earliest documented highwaymen was Gamaliel Ratsey (d. 1605), a gentleman's son from Lincolnshire. Name-checked by Ben Jonson in *The Alchemist*,[2] Ratsey was one of the first high-waymen to exhibit a whimsical, humorous approach to his calling. When it emerged that one of his victims was an undergraduate from Cambridge, he demanded a speech in Latin. Holding up an actor in Norwich, Ratsey asked him to perform a scene from *Hamlet*. Most significant of all, in the best Robin Hood tradition, Ratsey robbed only the rich. Ratsey's social conscience did not, alas, endear him to the judiciary. Betrayed by one of his colleagues, he was hanged in 1605.

A near-contemporary of Ratsey, John Clavell (1601–43), was more fortunate. From a distinguished Dorset family, he attended Brasenose College, Oxford, but not for long. He was sent down for stealing the silver, became a career criminal and was sentenced to death for robbery. It was only due to the intervention of his father that he was pardoned, and married an Irish heiress.[3]

The actual term 'highwaymen' entered the language in 1617, when William Fennor complained that Newmarket Heath and Royston Downs were so infested with highway-men that the poor were unable to make their way home without being robbed.[4] Just as the Restoration had produced an early wave of gentleman thieves, the English Civil War (1642–9) saw the beginning of 'the golden age of highway rob-bery'. Royalist officers who had lost their estates to the Commonwealth put their skills of horsemanship and combat to the service of crime, leading gangs of robbers eighty strong through the chaos and anarchy of war-torn England. Among the most celebrated was Captain Philip Stafford (1622–49), one such Royalist officer whose estates had been sequestered. Stafford possessed many of the essential criteria for being a romantic highwayman; a dispossessed gentleman with an army background, he was a notorious jewel thief and seducer of women. Stafford was eventually arrested and sentenced to hang at Reading, setting an example of the heroic death that would be imitated for years to come. Defiant to the last, Stafford dressed in his finest clothes and, when the cart paused at a tavern on its way to the gallows, he took a pint of wine and laughingly told the innkeeper that he would pay for it on his way back. His funeral was attended by several fashionable people, including society ladies who wept copiously.[5]

Another legendary highwayman was Captain James Hind. Although not a gentleman by birth, Hind had a long and distinguished army career, fighting alongside Charles I, before turning to robbery during the Commonwealth. When he was tried by the Council of State in 1651, Hind admitted to being a highwayman, but it was for his Royalist sentiments rather than his crimes that he was subsequently drawn, hanged and quartered for high treason. Accounts of his exploits continued to be printed a century after his death.

Stafford and Hind fade into insignificance, however, compared with Claude Du Vall, the epitome of the romantic highwayman whose reputation was much embellished after death. So much so, indeed, that it is now difficult to separate the fact from the fiction. Alfred Marks, author of *Tyburn Tree,* observed that 'there have been other highwaymen before Duval [sic] and he was succeeded by others. But the great merit of Duval is that he gave a tone and dignity to the profession which it never wholly lost'.[6] This 'prince of highwaymen' was born in Normandy in 1643 and arrived in England during the Restoration as a footman to the Duke of Richmond. The Restoration of Charles II in 1660 ushered in a period of wild extravagance, and Du Vall soon proved himself as proficient in drunkenness and debauchery as his masters. Running out of money, he took to the road, operating between Islington and Highgate, north of London. Du Vall soon became one of the most famous highwaymen of his day, an imaginative and resourceful robber, as this anecdote demonstrates.

One evening, Du Vall arrived at the Crown Inn, Beaconsfield, to find celebrations in full swing. There had been a fair on the common that day, and now the young people were making merry in one room, while a haggard old farmer sat next door, nursing a tankard. He had sold several animals that day and his takings sat in a bag at his feet. Du Vall plied him with wine and encouraged him to join in the dancing, while he watched his bag. Gingerly, the old fellow climbed to his feet and went into the other room. Du Vall, meanwhile, did a deal with one of the grooms, offering him two guineas to assist with a robbery. Together, the two men seized a large mastiff dog and dressed it up in a cowhide, fastening the horns directly over the beast's forehead. With the help of a ladder, the pair managed to drag the unfortunate dog onto the roof and let it down the chimney, into the room where the party was going on. The scene may be imagined. Pandemonium broke out as the massive dog emerged howling from the fireplace: tables went over, drinks were spilt, a violin was smashed to pieces as the partygoers stampeded in all directions, convinced that the devil himself had come for them. Meanwhile, Du Vall slipped away under cover of the chaos, and was on the road to London, £100 the richer. By this time the ostler had released his dog from its disguise, none the worse for the experience. When they realized that the farmer's bag of money was gone, the assembled company came to the only conclusion that made sense: the devil had vanished into thin air, taking with him the money, as a punishment for the farmer's covetousness.[7]

Du Vall's most famous characteristic was his 'gallantry' towards the ladies. One evening, having learned that a knight and his lady were travelling through Holloway with £400 in their coach, Du Vall overtook them on the road with four or five accomplices. As the couple spotted several horsemen riding backwards and forwards beside the coach, they realized that they were about to be robbed. At this point the young lady, who was a spirited woman, pulled out her flageolet and began to play. Taking the hint, Du Vall took out a flageolet of his own and picked up the tune, riding along to the coach door. 'Sir,' he said to the knight, 'your lady plays excellently, and I make no doubt but she dances as well. Will you please to step out of the coach and let me have the honour to dance one courant with her on the heath?' 'I dare not deny anything, sir,' the knight readily replied, 'to a gentleman of your quality and good behaviour.' Immediately the footman opened the door and the knight emerged. Du Vall leapt off his horse and handed the lady down from the coach. Although he wore heavy French riding boots, Du Vall moved as gracefully as the best dancing master in London. As soon as the dance was over, Du Vall handed the lady politely back into the coach, but not before he had asked her husband to pay for the music. The knight took the hint and handed over £100, before the parties politely wished each other good night.[8]

Du Vall soon had a huge price on his head and escaped to France, where he might have lived on into a healthy old age, gambling and seducing to his heart's content. However, bravado dictated that he return to England, where he was arrested, drunk, at the Hole-in-the-Wall pub in Chandos Street. He was promptly committed to Newgate and condemned to death.

On 21 January 1670, Du Vall rode to the gallows. Hundreds of women, from great ladies to street prostitutes, witnessed his execution and then attended his funeral in Covent Garden, where he was buried under a white marble stone, bearing his coat of arms and the following epitaph:

Here lies Du Vall, reader, if male thou art,
Look to thy purse; if female, to thy heart.
Much havoc hath he made of both; for all
Men he made stand, and women he made fall.
The second conqueror of the Norman race,
Knights to his arms did yield, and ladies to his face.
Old Tyburn's glory, England's bravest thief,
Du Vall the ladies' joy! Du Vall the ladies' grief.[9]

Given his aristocratic connections and lack of violence, it is perhaps surprising that Du Vall did not receive a pardon. But, whatever his personal appeal, Du Vall's actions represented a real threat and the government could not be seen to condone his flamboyant flouting of authority. Highway robbery had increased steeply during the reign of Charles II, with a series of royal proclamations for the arrest of highwaymen being issued from 1668 onwards. Further proclamations followed in 1677, 1679–80, 1681, and 1682–3. In 1684 and 1684–5, more proclamations were issued, followed in 1687 by an Order in Council, which would pave the way for the Highwayman Act of 1694. A new proclamation came in 1690, with another notable execution when the notorious highwayman William Davis, commonly known as 'the Golden Farmer', was hanged in Fleet Street and his remains subsequently hung in chains on Bagshott Heath.

Endless proclamations failed to serve as an effective deterrent. In December 1691, sixteen highwaymen plundered £2,500 of the king's money from the Worcester stagecoach, and, in 1692, seven highwaymen robbed the Manchester carrier of £15,000 of royal treasure. In a more unusual form of robbery, one gang even stole an heiress. On 7 November 1691, Sir John Jonston and his gang kidnapped Mistress Mary Wharton, who was only thirteen years old and worth £1500 a year. The girl was bundled into a coach and carried off. When

Mary returned home a week later, she said that she had been married, against her consent, to a Captain Campbell, the brother of Lord Argyle. A proclamation went out ordering the arrest of the gang, and a week later Sir John was captured and committed to Newgate. On 23 December, he went up to Tyburn in a mourning coach and was executed. The final reference to Mistress Wharton appears three months later. '1692. March 19. On Thursday last Colonel Byerley was married to Mrs. Wharton, stole formerly by Campbell.'[10] Let us hope for her sake that this time she was happy.

After outrages such as this, the new monarch, William III, had no option but to take the toughest line against highwaymen, as the case of 'Captain' James Whitney illustrates. Whitney (b. 1660) was a man of humble origins who had promoted himself to the rank of captain. Intelligent and brave, Whitney commanded the respect of his gang, which roamed the countryside around his native Reading. But Whitney was inevitably a thorn in the side of the authorities and by 1692 there was a price on his head. On 20 December that year Whitney offered to bring in thirty horses with as many stout men if the king would grant him a royal pardon. The king refused, and Whitney was subsequently arrested in Bishopsgate, after being followed home to his lodgings by a Mr Hill. Whitney did not give in without a fight; he stabbed Hill with a bayonet, although the wound was not mortal, and defended himself for an hour before being arrested. Whitney was taken to Newgate and closely guarded, his legs weighed down with 40 lb of iron weights. Far from downcast, Whitney petitioned the king for a pardon, and ordered a rich embroidered suit and hat, worth £100, for his journey to the scaffold. Sentenced to death, Whitney was carted to Tyburn on 28 January 1693, only to be reprieved, and brought back to Newgate with a rope still around his neck, followed by a vast crowd of people. From Newgate, Whitney went by sedan chair to Whitehall, where he claimed that he knew of a plot to assassinate the king, and would reveal the names of the conspirators in return for a pardon. But in the end, it made no difference. Whitney was executed on 1 February at Porter's Block, near Cow Cross in Smithfield. 'He seemed to die very penitent,' wrote one chronicler, 'was an hour and halfe in the cart before turn'd off.' Perhaps he was waiting for another reprieve.[11]

The rise in highway robbery had caused such outrage that in 1694 the Highwayman Act was ushered in, raising the reward for capturing a highwayman from £20 to £40 per head. Villains were actively encouraged to impeach or 'peach' on their partners-in-crime, informing on them to the 'thief-takers' or bounty hunters who roamed the country, searching for wanted men. As highwaymen tended by nature to be boastful, gregarious and given to holding forth about their exploits while in their cups, arrests were easily made and thief-takers flourished. However, some prisoners were more recalcitrant, and for those who refused to inform or confess, torture remained the order of the day.

In February 1721, William Spiggot and Thomas Phillips were indicted at the Old Bailey for committing several highway robberies, but they refused to plead unless the goods taken off them when they were arrested were returned. As this was directly contrary to the Highwayman Act, the Court informed them that their demand could not be complied with. Spiggot still refused to plead guilty, and so the judge ordered that he should be sent to the Press Room at Newgate, to undergo *peine forte et dure* or 'pressing', a form of legally sanctioned torture, 'and shall there be laid on the bare ground without any litter, straw, or other covering, and without any garment about him except something about his middle. He shall lie upon his back, his head shall be covered and his feet shall be bare. One of his arms shall be drawn with a cord to the side of the room, and the other arm to the other side, and his legs shall be served in the like manner. Then there shall be laid upon his body as much iron or stone as he can bear, and more.'[12] This barbaric treatment, coupled with a diet of barley bread and stagnant water on alternate days, was designed to eke a confession or death.

When the prisoners arrived back at Newgate, Phillips had scarcely entered the Press Room before he agreed to return to the bar and plead guilty, but Spiggott continued to be obstinate and was put under the press. 'He bore three hundred and fifty pounds weight for half an hour, but then fifty more being

The torture of William Spiggot by 'peine forte et dure'
(pressing) in the Press Room at Newgate Gaol. 1721.

added, he begged that he might be carried back to plead, which favour was granted.'[13]

Before he was taken out of the press, Spiggot had fallen into 'a kind of slumber' and had hardly any sense of pain left. After his ordeal, Spiggot was very faint and almost speechless for two days. Eventually, he told the Ordinary of Newgate that his chief reason for enduring the press had been so that nobody might reproach his children by telling them their father had been hanged. But hanged he was, along with Phillips, at Tyburn on 23 February.

In an another bid to prevent highway robbery, and the poaching of deer and cattle, the government ushered in the 'Black Act' of 1723, which made it a capital offence to ride out with one's features concealed by a mask, or a kerchief tied over the face. Despite this threat, the following decades became the golden age of highway robbery, with the high-waymen becoming celebrities, feted and pampered by fashionable society hostesses. 'Tales of their cunning and generosity were in the mouths of everybody, and a noted thief was a kind of hero.'[14] Indeed, for many, the prospect of dying young served to enhance the romantic appeal. The brave and the reckless concluded that there was nothing to being hanged apart from 'a wry neck and a wet pair of breeches'.[15]

Whether they were gentlemen turned thieves, or ordinary men aspiring to the role of gentleman by becoming highway-men, highway robbers certainly enjoyed a distinctive status in eighteenth-century London. Their 'wanted' posters became pin-ups; Moll Hackabout, the anti-heroine of Hogarth's *Harlot's Progress* (1732), sports a picture of a famous highway-man on the wall of her Covent Garden bedchamber. This fictional character is one of the most famous highwaymen of all, the infamous but irresistible Macheath, protagonist of *The*

Beggar's Opera, a topical satire by John Gay and John Rich. This 'Newgate pastoral' proved such a rip-roaring success when it first appeared in 1728 that it was universally agreed to have made 'Gay rich and Rich gay'. A parody of the overblown Italian operas popular at the time, set among the thieves and whores of Newgate, it featured the villainous but sexually compelling Macheath and his evil nemesis Peachum, based on the thief-taker Jonathan Wild. The fictional Macheath rapidly became the inspiration for real-life outlaws, who whistled his songs as they polished their pistols before 'going upon the Common'.

Macheath cast a long shadow. Decades later, in 1763, James Boswell tells of picking up a couple of girls on Covent Garden Piazza, and taking them to a private room in a tavern where a bottle of sherry was swiftly placed before them. 'I surveyed my seraglio and found them both good subjects for amorous play,' he wrote. 'I toyed with them and drank about and sung "Youth's the Season" [the song Macheath sings with his whores] and then thought myself Captain Macheath; and then I solaced my existence with them, one after the other, according to their seniority.'[16]

English travellers became so habituated to the constant threat of highway robbery that it was commonplace to carry ten guineas or so in a special pocket, which could be handed over when they were waylaid. According to one French visitor, the Abbe Le Blanc, the English took a pragmatic attitude to highway robbery and were almost proud of the robbers' exploits. Le Blanc relates the experience of an 'M. C.', who was ambushed near Cambridge by 'the celebrated Turpin'. When M. C. failed to 'stand and deliver', despite threats, the celebrated Turpin fired a pistol at him, but missed. Fearing a second shot, M. C. handed over his money, his watch and his snuff-box, leaving him just two shillings. Before he departed, Turpin asked M. C. to give his word of honour that he would not inform upon him or cause the justices to pursue him. When M. C. agreed, they parted politely.

Subsequently, M. C. ran into Turpin at the races, and he kept his word. He did not allow Turpin to be arrested, and, in return, Turpin gave him a good betting tip. M. C. accepted this with good grace and subsequently won. Whereupon Turpin, impressed with M. C.'s generous behaviour, paid back the money he had stolen and even expressed regret that, because of the trifling matter of the robbery, he did not feel that they could drink together.[17]

The legendary Dick Turpin was the most famous of all highwaymen, although he lays least claim to the title, having been a ruthless criminal who turned to the highway late in life, after an extensive career as an armed robber. Born in Essex in 1705, Turpin was apprenticed to a butcher but never completed his training. With his heavy-set build and brutal, pockmarked features, he was marked out early on as a man of violence.

After being caught out stealing his neighbour's cattle and selling the meat at market, Turpin went on the run and teamed up with William Gregory's Essex Gang. From their base in Epping Forest, the Essex Gang carried out a series of brutal armed robberies, targeting lonely farmhouses occupied by the frail and elderly. At Loughton in Essex they broke into the home of an elderly lady and Turpin had her thrown onto the fire when she would not reveal the whereabouts of her cash. In agony, she was forced to reveal the hiding place, and the gang escaped with over £400. In another robbery, a Mr Mason, the keeper of Epping Forest, was beaten unconscious and the gang escaped with 120 guineas that had been hidden in a punchbowl. Mr Mason's daughter, meanwhile, had a lucky escape. When she heard the gang breaking in through the front door, she ran out of the back door and hid in the pigsty.

The gang's most brutal robbery took place at the home of a Mr Lawrence at Edgware, near Stanmore, on 4 Februrary 1735. Turpin's gang descended on the house at seven in the evening. When Mr Lawrence refused to tell the gang where the money was, Turpin pistol-whipped him on the bare buttocks, and dragged him around the house by his nose, and threw a kettle of water over him. William Gregory found the maid-servant hiding in the dairy, dragged her upstairs and raped her.

Once news of this particularly atrocious robbery reached the authorities a £50 reward was slapped on Turpin's head and a pardon was promised to anyone who informed on him. But this made no difference to the robbers, who continued their devastation as before, and, flushed with success, seemed to defy the law. After further robberies and the violent beating of a householder and her maid, the price on Turpin's head went up to £100. Two of the gang were arrested, tried, convicted and hanged at Tyburn, and their bodies hung in chains to rot.

Turpin fled north to Yorkshire, where he reinvented himself as 'John Palmer', a hunting, shooting, fishing country gent. He ran a horse-stealing operation on the side, and would perhaps have remained undetected had it not been for his poor impulse control. One afternoon, on the way back from a shoot, Turpin gratuitously blew the head off a neighbour's cockerel. This random act of violence proved to be his downfall. When the cockerel's furious owner tracked Turpin down, his true identity was revealed, and he was exposed as a thief and a killer. Sentenced to hang at York, Turpin redeemed himself with the courage shown at his execution. Before the hangman could complete his work, Turpin kicked away the ladder and leapt to his death.

Richard Bayes, an opportunistic hack, promptly rushed out a memoir of Turpin, portraying him as a hero in the mould of Claude Du Vall. Almost a century later, William Harrison

Ainsworth glamorized Turpin in *Rookwood* (1834) and provided Turpin with a mare, 'Black Bess', which carried him on a two-hundred-mile ride from London to York before collapsing and dying from her ordeal. Turpin never possessed such a magnificent beast. The story of 'Black Bess' derived from folklore about a highwayman and his loyal animal, perpetuated by Daniel Defoe. But the story took hold, transforming Turpin's reputation from that of pockmarked armed robber into a sympathetic anti-hero.

While Turpin represented the dark side of 'the gentleman of the road', James MacLaine (d. 1750) was one of the last embodiments of the gallant highwayman. Descended from a reputable Scottish family, young MacLaine was extravagant, gambling his way through his own fortune and that of his wife, a young heiress. Destitute after his wife died, MacLaine became so despondent he consulted an Irish apothecary named Plunkett for a pick-me-up. Plunkett soon realized that MacLaine was a valuable ally, handsome and fit, although something of a coward. Plunkett, for his part, was totally fearless and handy with a gun. Plunkett suggested they take to the road, and after a solemn agreement to abide by each other in all adventures, and to share their profits to the last shilling, the pair ventured out together.[18]

On their first *sortie* Plunkett and MacLaine held up a farmer on Hounslow Heath, taking £60 off him. As they both had extravagant tastes, this money was soon gone, and so they headed for the St Albans Road. Seeing a stagecoach coming towards them, the pair agreed to ride up to the carriage on opposite sides. But MacLaine hesitated, frightened, and when Plunkett finally ordered the driver to stop, MacLaine demanded money from the passengers with the utmost trepidation. When they got back to London, Plunkett accused him of being a coward, and told him that he was unfit to be a highwayman. This made such an impact on MacLaine that he rode out alone, robbed a gentleman of a large sum and returned and shared it with his companion.

Shortly afterwards, Plunkett and MacLaine robbed Sir Horace Walpole, the prominent author and MP, in Hyde Park. MacLaine's pistol went off, although Walpole was unscathed. When MacLaine read about the attack in the press, and realized who his distinguished victim had been, he penned an open letter to the *Daily Advertiser*, apologizing to Walpole and assuring him that the gunfire had been entirely accidental and that it was 'by no means Design'd Either to hurt or frighten you for tho' we are Reduced by the misfortunes of the world and obliged to have Recourse to this method of getting money Yet we have Humanity Enough not to take any bodys life where there is Not a Nessecety for it'.[19]

MacLaine even offered to return Walpole's valuables in exchange for forty guineas, rather than fencing them elsewhere, an offer that Walpole subsequently accepted. By this point, MacLaine had become quite the dashing young blade, posing as an Irish aristocrat to avoid inconvenient questions regarding the source of his wealth. Gracious and charming, he seemed destined to make a good marriage. But then, on the night of 26 June 1750, the pair overreached themselves.

Riding out together beyond Hounslow, Plunkett and MacLaine met the Earl of Eglinton in a post-chaise. MacLaine, going towards the coachman, commanded him to stop, but placed himself in a direct line in front of the driver, in case his lordship attempted to shoot him with a blunderbuss, for he was certain that the peer would not fire so as to endanger the life of the coachman. In the meantime, Plunkett forced a pistol through the glass at the back of the carriage, and threatened to shoot him unless his lordship threw away the blunderbuss. Eglinton realized that resistance was futile, and gave in, allowing himself to be robbed. Once the carriage had moved on, MacLaine retrieved the blunderbuss, which had fallen to the ground, and a frock coat.

A few days later, MacLaine tried to sell the frock coat to a tailor, a Mr Loader of Monmouth Street. Loader recognized the garments from a description circulated in a broadsheet, and followed MacLaine back to his lodgings with a constable; there, they found Lord Eglinton's stolen blunderbuss. MacLaine's arrest and trial caused a sensation. He was so popular in high

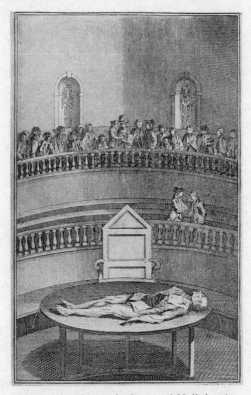

An anatomy class at the Surgeons' Hall showing the dissection of a hanged man. Under the Murder Act, the bodies of felons were donated to medical students.

society that many people sprang to his defence, and Lord Eglinton refused to give evidence against him in court. According to Horace Walpole, 'the first Sunday after his trial three thousand people went to see him. He fainted away twice with the heat of his cell.'[20] According to the *Newgate Calendar,* MacLaine was a model prisoner, but his courage deserted him at the end. Arriving at Tyburn, he looked sadly up at the gallows, and with a heartfelt sigh exclaimed: 'O Jesus!'

Under the provisions of the Murder Act 1752, MacLaine's body was handed over to the College of Surgeons for anatomy practice. His skeleton appears in the fourth plate of Hogarth's *Stages of Cruelty* showing an anatomy demonstration at the Surgeons' Hall.

Although the *Gentleman's Magazine* was complaining, in 1774, that highway robbery seemed to have become a recognized form of outdoor sport for young men, the 'profession' was actually falling into decline by the end of the eighteenth century.[21] This was largely thanks to the astonishing developments brought in by the Bow Street magistrates Henry and John Fielding, whose achievements will be discussed in a later chapter. For the time being, though, let me return to those gallant figures riding through the dusk at the beginning of the chapter. I left one of the 'noted gentleman highwayman of the day' standing on the gallows with the noose around his neck, and being urged, by the minister, to repent of his ill-spent life.

'Ill-spent, you dog! – Gad! (smacking his lips) it was delicious!'

'Fie! fie!' replies the priest. 'Raise your thoughts to Heaven!'

The gentleman highwayman is having none of this. In the face of death his last words are: 'But a canter across the Common–oh!'

His soul, we are told, 'cantered off to eternity'.[22]

6

THE BLACK PARADE

The Road to Tyburn

On the night before they died, Newgate's condemned prisoners were issued with a stern exhortation. The bellman patrolled the streets outside the gaol intoning this grim reminder of their fate:

> All you that in the condemned hold do lie
> Prepare you, for tomorrow you shall die ...
> And when St Sepulchre's bell tomorrow tolls
> The Lord above have mercy on your souls.[1]

After a sleepless night, riddled with desperate plans of escape and hopeless prayers for reprieve, the prisoners were bombarded by the noise of the bells of St Sepulchre's, which were only rung on hanging days, tolling out across the neighbourhood to remind one and all that death was imminent. The sound of the bells was met with 'dismal groaning and crying' from the condemned cells, swiftly followed by uproar, with fellow prisoners displaying their sympathy by weeping bitterly, cheering, cursing, and a few, a very few, praying.[2] The condemned men and women were about to embark on the three-mile journey from Newgate Gaol to Tyburn, along a route that twisted like a black ribbon through the streets of London.

Eight times a year, prisoners made this grim pilgrimage, witnessed by thousands of spectators wedged fast into every rooftop, window frame, balcony and tree. The horse-drawn carts were followed by a massive crowd which wove its way through the streets in a macabre carnival, growing ever greater, gathering into itself the young and the old, the rich, the poor, the halt and the lame until it became a many-headed monster, 100,000 strong, weaving drunkenly but defiantly to the gallows.

Without much provocation, the crowd was capable of shape-shifting into 'the mob', a large and powerful entity described by the novelist Henry Fielding as 'the fourth estate', prefiguring its modern meaning.[3] Public executions might have been designed to demonstrate the terrible power of the king, but when the mob turned out authority was mocked and criminals frequently transformed into heroes.[4] This noisy, anarchic crowd provided some comfort for the prisoners, even as the deafening roars drowned out the educated tones of the Ordinary as he urged his doomed flock to repent. And the many-headed monster could demonstrate sympathy, too, when needed. In 1777, while one Joseph Harris, a fifteen-year-old burglar, sat weeping in his cart, the crowd walked to the gallows alongside him, in silent commiseration.

This chapter returns to Tyburn, which has changed little since our first visit, in 1196. A permanent gallows, the infamous triple tree, had been erected in 1571. Since then, Tyburn had become the principal execution site in London. In the eighteenth century alone, 6,000 prisoners were sentenced to death at the Old Bailey. Of these, 1,600 were hanged (the remainder were either pardoned or transported to the penal colonies of the New World). The majority of those who died perished at Tyburn. This chapter follows in the footsteps of the crowd that accompanied the condemned on their last journey. It pays its final respects, and salutes the courage or considers the evil deeds of Tyburn's notorious dead.

The journey begins at Newgate, where conditions had not significantly improved since the Tudor period. Rebuilt after the Great Fire of 1666 to hold around 300 prisoners, Newgate's population was now closer to 800, with debtors' children adding to the ranks of miscreants, robbers and murderers. Wealthy criminals with access to funds could still enjoy reasonable conditions on the Master's Side, where their 'garnish' purchased food, wine and even feather beds. They were permitted to stroll in the Press Yard and receive visitors in the Stone Kitchen, where well-wishers might be entertained with wine from 2s. or brandy at 4d. a bottle. For the poor, the situation on the Common Side was as dire as ever. The cells had no heat or light, and were riddled with vermin; cockroaches crunched beneath the foot with every step. Newgate Gaol was so dark that 'links' or torches burnt all day, thickening the already foetid air with tallow fat and smoke. 'Gaol fever' or typhus flourished in these insanitary conditions; during one outbreak in 1750, which spread from the gaol to the neighbouring Old Bailey, forty-three people died, including two judges and the Lord Mayor of London. Little wonder that Daniel Defoe, who had been a prisoner there himself, described Newgate Gaol as 'an Emblem of Hell' in *Moll Flanders* (1722).[5]

Defoe's novel testified to the public fascination with Newgate, which had developed its own macabre charisma composed of 'the mesmerism of depravity and the morbid fascination of the gibbet'. Throngs of sightseers assembled daily outside the massive gates, just watching and waiting and seeping up the malevolent atmosphere of the gaol.[6] The criminals themselves had become celebrities, stars of ballads and broadsheets, leading Horace Walpole to despair of 'the ridiculous rage there is of going to Newgate and the prints that are published of the malefactors, and the memoirs of their lives'.[7]

The most famous example was Jack Sheppard, a true son of Newgate whose story illustrates the black parade from gaol to gallows like no other. Jack Sheppard was a young burglar whose *pièce de résistance* was not stealing, but escaping. Jack Sheppard features prominently in this chapter, but the stories of other felons, from the most prolific to the hapless, are intertwined with his. Like the carts that rumbled out of the Press Yard on hanging days, bearing a miscellany of offenders from devil-may-care highwaymen to forlorn young pickpockets, this chapter carries the last sightings of a motley crew, from much-loved Jack Sheppard to the despised 'Thief-Taker General of England' Jonathan Wild.

A carpenter's son from Spitalfields, Sheppard intended to follow the same trade as his father before falling into bad company with 'Edgworth Bess', a handsome receiver from Drury Lane. Sheppard absconded from his master and took on a different type of apprenticeship with the robber Joseph Blake, also known as 'Blueskin' on account of his swarthy complexion. First arrested in August 1723, Sheppard was imprisoned in St Giles's Roundhouse but managed to escape through the roof. Shortly afterwards, he was arrested again, along with Edgworth Bess, whilst trying to steal a gentleman's pocket watch in Leicester Square. The couple were remanded at the New Prison in Clerkenwell awaiting trial, only to make spectacular escape by securing a sheet to the bars of their cell window, climbing down twenty-five feet to the ground, and then scaling the twenty-two-foot high doors by hanging on to the locks and bolts. This exploit made Sheppard particularly popular with women, as he could so easily have left Bess to her fate.

Sheppard was back in gaol by 30 August, sentenced to death for housebreaking. Committed to the condemned hold at Newgate, he managed to escape through a hatch in the door, aided and abetted by Edgworth Bess. After going on the run, Sheppard was recaptured a week later in Finchley. By this time, the keeper of Newgate had learnt from his mistakes. Sheppard was incarcerated in a strong room known as 'the Castle', loaded with irons and chained to the floor. Over the following days, dozens of sightseers trooped in to pay tribute to the famous thief. James Thornhill (father-in-law of William Hogarth) drew his portrait and his memoirs were ghost written by his publisher, John Applebee. Sheppard entertained his visitors with a rich stream of anecdotes, pausing only to beg visiting aristocrats to petition the king for a pardon.[8]

At some stage of the proceedings, a helpful visitor dropped a tiny nail. This was all Sheppard needed to work on the great 'horse padlock' that shackled him to the floor, and he whittled away at his manacles while the keepers' backs were turned, waiting for his moment. Sheppard's chance came on the afternoon of Wednesday 14 October. Blueskin had been arrested by the thief-taker Jonathan Wild, and put on trial at the Old Bailey. Condemned to death, Blueskin asked to speak to Wild in confidence, begging him to get his sentence commuted to transportation. When Wild told him this was impossible, Blueskin grabbed Wild by the neck and slashed his throat. Wild would have died instantly had it not been for his thick muslin stock; as it was, he suffered severe injuries.

In the pandemonium that followed, the guard on Sheppard was dropped, leaving him free to escape. With windows opening onto a sheer drop, and the door of his cell locked,

*The villain Blueskin attacks Thief-Taker General Jonathan Wild
outside the Old Bailey after being condemned to death.*

Sheppard's only recourse was to the fireplace. He was not the
first to attempt this hazardous form of exit; rumours abounded
that desperate men had tried to escape from Newgate through
the labyrinth of chimneys, and had been trapped, suffocated
and killed in the attempt. But Sheppard kept his nerve and
crawled upwards through choking clouds of dust, emerging at
last into the room above his cell.

But Sheppard was far from free. Over the following hours,
he systematically picked his way through a series of heavily
locked chambers, until he emerged onto the leads. Springing
across to the roof of a neighbouring house, Sheppard sneaked

into an attic bedroom and lay low, until the family had settled down for the evening and he could creep downstairs. Just as he was setting foot on the top step, the clink of his chains gave him away. The mistress of the house cried out, alarmed: 'What's that?' 'It's only the dog,' replied her husband, reassuringly, and Sheppard stole past the door and escaped into the street, a free man once again.[9]

But not for long. Unable to resist the opportunity to boast about his exploits, he was recaptured a week later, drunk in an alehouse, and taken back to Newgate. And yet even when execution day dawned, on 16 November 1724, Sheppard had not given up hope. Alerted by his bravado, a young under-sheriff named Watson decided to search him before the cart left the Press Yard. Sheppard had concealed a penknife in his coat pocket, intending to cut through the ropes which bound him and escape into the crowd at a suitable moment.

Eventually the procession set off, with Sheppard seated on his own coffin, a halter around his neck and his arms tightly bound. Two officers sat either side of him, and the cart was flanked by horse-guards. These in turn were surrounded by javelin-men walking four abreast and constables of the watch securing the perimeter. Outside St Sepulchre's, the cart paused so that the sexton might exhort everyone present to pray for the poor sinners; his sentiments were almost drowned out by the noise of the crowd – the shrieks, yells, groans and cheers – as the guards struggled to clear the way. Over 100,000 people had turned out to follow Jack Sheppard to Tyburn, and the route was jammed in every direction. As the cart made its ponderous way down Snow Hill and crossed the Fleet Ditch by a stone bridge, every window, from ground floor to garret, was filled with spectators, while more were crowded onto the roofs, all calling out encouragement and expressions of sympathy. Young girls in pretty dresses and prostitutes in their finest gowns strewed his path with flowers and pelted him with bouquets. As the procession toiled slowly up Holborn Hill, a dreadful scream rang out. It was Edgworth Bess, come to witness Sheppard's last journey; with the scream she fainted dead away, but was caught by a group of well-wishers.

At St Giles, the procession halted outside the Crown Inn, so that the condemned man might enjoy his last refreshment on earth. The soldiers and javelin-men dismounted and drank too, while Sheppard was offered 'the St Giles's bowl', full of ale, which he downed in one, much to the delight of the crowd. The tradition of the St Giles's stop was a merciful one, allowing many a prisoner to go almost unconscious to the gallows.

The journey resumed and entered its final stages along Tyburn Road, with the crowd filling the street from side to side and the windows and rooftops black with sightseers, and out into open country. The crowd dispersed across the fields, leaping over, sometimes running through, the hedges, rushing towards the gallows as fast as their legs could carry them. As the cart arrived at the foot of the gallows, the crowd emitted a collective gasp of anticipation. Sheppard, from his position in the cart, had his back to the infamous 'triple tree', the triangular gallows standing eighteen foot high, but he would have seen a sea of heads, and the crowd milling around the scaffold in a frenzy of expectation. Tyburn Fair, a 'free market for outlaws, whores, and rogues of the meaner sort',[10] was in full swing, with buxom women elbowing their way through the crowd, baskets of gingerbread and meat pies on their arms; others carried frothing tankards of ale, while another category offered simply themselves. Child pickpockets scampered through the melee, while thugs and rogues scuffled in the dust. The more discerning visitor could avoid the contamination of *hoi polloi* by purchasing a 'Tyburn ticket', which bought him a ring-side seat in 'Tyburn pews', erected near the gallows.

Sheppard had visited Tyburn in the past, but as a spectator, not as the main event. Now, taking in this tumultuous scene, he remained calm, aware that he still had the opportunity to cheat death. It would not have been the first time. In 1705, a housebreaker named Smith was cut down after being reprieved. Smith had been hanging for seven minutes but was revived after a bronchotomy and made a full recovery.[11] In 1651, one Anne Greene was executed in Oxford for killing her newborn child, although it was doubtful whether the child had actually been born alive. After hanging for half an hour, Anne was cut down and found to be unconscious but still living. Dr Petty, the Oxford professor of anatomy, revived her, and within a month Anne had made a full recovery. She went off to her friends in the country, taking her coffin with her.[12]

Sheppard was convinced that he too could make a great escape. As he stood in the cart with the noose around his neck and the clergyman encouraging him to say his final prayers, Sheppard's eyes searched the crowd for his publisher, John Applebee, who had planned in advance to cut Sheppard down the instant he was hanged and whisk him away. A surgeon had been retained, ready to resuscitate him. Before Sheppard could spy Applebee, the hood was placed over his head, and the crowd roared 'Hats off!', not from respect but so that their headgear would not spoil the view. There was a sudden dreadful silence, like the calm before a thunderstorm, as a constable struck the horse's flank a sharp blow, the cart moved towards the fatal tree and Sheppard was 'turned off'. After a collective intake of breath, the crowd emitted a blood-curdling shriek, as Sheppard was launched into the air and left dangling. But instead of his neck being broken, as intended, he was choking to death on the end of the rope. Twitching and circling in the death throes, 'stretched', 'nubbed', 'dancing the Tyburn jig'. This sight proved too much for Sheppard's family, who rushed forwards and grabbed his short legs, wet with urine, trying to break his neck and put him out of his misery.

When Applebee and his men eventually fought their way forward and tried to cut Sheppard down, they were mistaken for body snatchers and a dreadful tug-of-war ensued. Matters were made worse by hordes of trophy hunters. Some jostled forward to clip a lock of Sheppard's hair or pluck a ring from his finger, while superstitious gamblers tried to grasp fibres from the rope, believing it would bring luck at the gaming tables. Then came the sick, the maimed and the diseased, eager to touch the body of the hanged man with its miraculous properties. During this struggle, the unfortunate Sheppard expired. Eventually, his body was cut down and taken to the Barley Mow pub in Long Acre, for the wake, and he was buried in the churchyard of St Martin-in-the-Fields.

Despite his grisly last moments, Jack Sheppard died a hero, and his legend lived on. A century later, the social investigator Henry Mayhew noted that, among the London poor, children were more familiar with the adventures of Jack Sheppard than they were with the Bible. Newgate ballads and broadsheets were handed down from one generation to another, the story becoming increasingly embellished with the retelling. But if Sheppard was a hero, his story also had to have a villain, and that villain was Jonathan Wild, the self-styled 'Thief-Taker General of England and Ireland', who followed Sheppard to the gallows six months later.

'Thief-takers' were effectively bounty hunters, tracking down criminals in exchange for rewards. Escalating levels of crime had led to the government offering substantial rewards for the arrest and conviction of serious criminals, such as highwaymen and coiners. In addition, many victims of crime would offer rewards for the return of their stolen goods. The advent of daily newspapers meant that information about these rewards was circulated on a regular basis. Jonathan Wild had thoroughly developed all aspects of the thief-taker's trade and dominated London's criminal underworld in the early 1720s. By arresting Jack Sheppard and the villainous Blueskin, he was much praised for making the streets of London safe for the emerging middle classes, and by 1723 he was petitioning the Lord Mayor to give him the Freedom of the City of London.

But Wild was himself a crook. Totally corrupt, he had been committed to the Wood Street Compter in 1704, which had proved to be the making of him. In this academy of crime, Wild built up the extensive web of criminal contacts who were to provide his substantial income for the next twenty years, and met his match in the form of Mary Milliner, a prostitute and receiver. The pair set up home together when they were released in 1708, and Wild went into business in Newtoner's Lane, Covent Garden, where he effectively devised a new method of organized crime: Wild's 'corporation of thieves' employing legions of criminals, from highwaymen to pick-pockets. Specialist teams robbed shops and churches, while protection rackets extorted payment from taverns, inns and brothels. Even highwaymen had to pay protection money, or risk being captured. Wild preferred to recruit convicts who had illegally returned to England after being transported, since they could not give evidence against him if they were caught. Wild had complete and utter power over them, because if they rebelled, he could hang them. At the height of his career, Wild offered immunity to his henchmen in return for absolute loyalty.

Criminals sneaked into Wild's offices with details of robberies and stolen goods. For a fee, Wild reunited the victims of robberies with their stolen property while gaining vital information that would allow his men to organize another robbery. Wild even engaged craftsmen to remove the hallmarks or owners' names from the watches, rings, silver plate and other valuables so that they could be sold on without being traced. This system worked flawlessly until 1717, when the Solicitor General, Sir William Thompson, ushered in an Act of Parliament which made it a capital offence to take a reward under the pretence of assisting the owner to recover their stolen goods. 'Jonathan Wild's Act', as it became known, was designed to put an end to at least one aspect of Wild's nefarious business. Wild was ultimately caught out when, in 1725, he was paid by the owner for the return of some lace that Wild had arranged to have stolen, worth just £40. Wild was arrested and went on trial at the Old Bailey. Despite the fact that his reputation was in tatters as crime after crime was revealed, Wild conducted his own defence and pleaded for clemency on the grounds that he had sent at least sixty criminals to the gallows and secured the imprisonment and transportation of many more. But Sir William Thompson, who was sitting as judge, sentenced Wild to death on 17 May 1725.

Wild was taken to Newgate, where news reached him that Mary Milliner had attempted to kill herself, but failed. Wild was a broken man. On 24 May, the night before he was due to hang, Wild took an overdose of laudanum, but not a sufficient quantity to end his life; and when his fellow prisoners saw that he had attempted to dodge the gallows, they dragged him to his feet and walked him up and down until he had regained consciousness and vomited. By the time Wild entered the cart in the Press Yard, he was deathly pale and almost unconscious, which was perhaps just as well, considering the reception he received from the mob. Not for Wild the paths strewn with flowers and genial condolences that met young Jack Sheppard. 'The populace treated this offender with remarkable severity,' noted *The Newgate Calendar*, 'execrating him as the most consummate villain that had ever disgraced human nature,' and pelting the semi-comatose Wild with sticks and stones, excrement, dead dogs and cats. 'Rough music' (pots and pans beaten with sticks), whistles and catcalls accompanied him on the journey to Tyburn, where he appeared to have revived.

When the executioner allowed Wild time to sit in the cart and compose himself, and prepared to hang a coiner, Ralph Harpham, first, the crowd went mad. They threatened to attack the executioner if he delayed any longer. Judging it prudent to comply, the hangman cut Harpham down and turned his attention to Wild, at which the clamour ceased.[13] Wild's body was cut down quickly before the surgeons' men could seize it and buried in St Pancras Churchyard. A few days later the coffin was dug up, and found later in Kentish Town. His body had disappeared. An unidentified body washed up on the banks of the Thames near Whitehall soon afterwards, and the extremely hairy chest led some to believe that it was Wild. An ignoble fate indeed for the former 'Thief-Taker General of England and Ireland' and a suitable reminder as to how the mighty are fallen.

So far, this narrative has concentrated on the men who were hanged at Tyburn. But women too were subject to the death penalty. Between 1703 and 1772, ninety-two of the 1,242 people hanged in London were female. The lower numbers testify to the fact that fewer women than men become involved in criminal activity, but the harsh sentencing of the era reflects the fact that those women who fell from grace were treated with equal, if not greater, severity than their male counterparts.

In 1726, Catherine Hayes was executed at Tyburn for the murder of her husband. While this was a grim enough occurrence, it was scarcely unusual. Murder carried the death penalty, and the murder of one's husband was classified as 'petty treason', the husband at that time standing in relation to his wife as the king did to his subjects. But the appalling reality of this sentence was, of course, that the punishment for treason consisted of more than a trip to the gallows. In the case of a man, it meant that the prisoner was drawn, hanged and quartered. Since quartering was regarded as an inappropriate punishment for a woman, involving as it did a display of nudity, the sentence for a woman convicted of treason was to be burnt at the stake.

The mysterious sequence of events that ended with Catherine Hayes' execution began on 5 March 1726. As dawn broke over Westminster, a severed head was discovered floating in the dock near the Horse Ferry. The head was that of a man, aged around thirty, with brown curly hair; his skull had been fractured in two places, and there was a large cut on his cheek. A bloodstained bucket was found nearby, and a number of bargees said that they had seen a couple of ruffians bring the bucket to the waterside, throw the head into the dock and run away. Despite an extensive search, the constables of the watch could not find a body. There was only one solution. The head was placed on a wooden pole in St Margaret's churchyard, in the hope that someone would identify it. After two false leads, when it was believed the head had been that of a gang member murdered by his accomplices, and when a woman came forward claiming it was that of her husband (it wasn't; he was alive and well and living in Deptford), the constables had a breakthrough on 26 March when a headless corpse was discovered in a pond near Tyburn Road. According to *Mist's Weekly Journal,* the body was 'much mangled and bruised'.[14] Not only did *Mist's* identify the corpse as that of one John Hayes, but they also had a scoop. Hayes' wife had been arrested for murder, along with her lover, and committed to Newgate.

By 2 April 1726, Catherine Hayes, a shopkeeper, had confessed to the murder of her husband, aided and abetted by not one but two lovers: Thomas Wood, a butcher, and Thomas Billings, a tailor, who were both also sent to Newgate. Wood and Billings claimed that the murder had been instigated by Catherine, who had offered them to kill her husband. The men had challenged John Hayes to a drinking contest, and when he slumped unconscious to the floor, they smashed his head in with an axe. The plan was to remove the body in a trunk, but when the trunk proved too small for the purpose, they dismembered his body, put the head in a bucket and removed his remains under cover of darkness.

Thus far, the case seemed a typical if lurid example of murder, driven by the traditional motives of love, lust and lucre. The fact that Hayes had not one but two lovers to assist her added a little spice, but then the *Mist's Weekly Journal* revealed on 9 April that Thomas 'William Billings, the person that beat out Mr Hayes's brains with a hatchet,' was not only Catherine's young lover but her illegitimate son.[15] Now the heady mix of greed and desire was swelled by incest. It emerged that Thomas Billings was Catherine's long-lost son, conceived when Catherine was in service to Hayes' father in Worcestershire. Thomas had come to lodge with Catherine and her husband John in London, and their relationship had subsequently developed. In the sensational language of the tabloid press, 'Billings was her own son, got by Mr. Hayes's father ... So that Billings murdered his own brother, assisted in quartering him, and then lay with his own mother, while his brother's mangled limbs were under the bed.'[16]

Catherine denied any part in the murder of her husband, although she claimed that he had been abusive, beating and starving her. This might have met with a sympathetic reception had not Catherine developed a reputation as a harridan, with endless witnesses prepared to testify to her hatred of John Hayes and her constant desire to kill him off like an unruly dog. On 30 April, all three were sentenced to death at the Old Bailey, with Catherine facing the traditional punishment of being burnt at the stake – but with an exquisite refinement. In order to 'strike a proper terror in the spectators of so horrid a crime', she was to be burnt alive, 'without the indulgence of being first strangled, as has been customary in like cases'.[17] When the sentence was handed down, Hayes collapsed in the dock and fainted clean away.

On 14 May 1726, Catherine Hayes stood in the Press Yard of Newgate ready to join the traditional convey of death. Three carts left Newgate that morning. In the first cart were three 'sodomites' whose crime was considered so heinous that they took precedence over the usual aristocrats of the gallows, the highwaymen in the second cart. In the third cart stood Catherine Hayes' son, Thomas Billings, with three burglars. Thomas Wood had died of gaol fever ten days earlier. The journey was briefly enlivened when two of the highwaymen, John Map and Henry Vigus, made a bid to escape, but they were seized immediately.

Catherine Hayes did not travel to Tyburn by cart. Instead, she was drawn to Tyburn on a hurdle, where she endured the additional torture of watching her own son hanged before her eyes. She did not live to see his remains cut down and hung in a gibbet on the Paddington Road.[18]

Enticed by watching a woman burn, an even greater crowd than normal had assembled. Additional 'Tyburn pews', which had been shoddily erected nearby, collapsed under the combined weight of over 150 spectators, killing around a dozen people. Some parts of the platform remained standing, and the mob gathered on it in large numbers, but after about half an hour, this too gave way, and several more people were hurt.[19]

After order had been restored, Hayes was fastened to the stake by an iron collar around her neck, and an iron chain around her body. There was also a halter around her neck, which the executioner could have pulled tight if he wanted to end her suffering. The kindling was placed around her, and lit with a torch, as Hayes begged, for Christ's sake, to be strangled. The executioner relented, and tried to pull the halter tight; but the flames were so fierce that they burnt his hands, and he lost his grip. Hayes uttered three dreadful shrieks as the flames engulfed her on all sides. In a final attempt to put her out of her misery, the executioner threw a piece of timber

Catherine Hayes is burnt to death at Tyburn for 'petty treason' after conspiring to murder her husband.

at her, which fractured her skull and dashed her brains out. In three or four hours she was burnt to ashes.[20]

When another female killer, Sarah Malcolm, was accused in 1733, she suffered a similar level of vilification, even though the evidence linking her to the Inns of Court murders was largely circumstantial.

Born in County Durham in 1710, Sarah Malcolm was raised in Ireland. She was an educated woman, from a respectable family, but when her father moved to London, Sarah's life began to unravel. She fell in with a disreputable woman named Mrs Mary Tracey, and Mary's brothers, James and William Alexander. After a spell as a barmaid at the Black Horse in Temple Bar, Sarah became a laundress at the Inner Temple Inns of Court. Sarah's clients included Mrs Lydia Duncomb, a wealthy old lady, Mrs Duncomb's invalid companion, Mrs Harrison, and their young servant girl, Ann.

At midday on 5 February 1733, Mrs Duncomb's neighbour, Mrs Love, arrived for lunch. Receiving no reply, and worried that some harm had come to the old lady, Mrs Love and another neighbour, Mrs Rhymer, persuaded a young laundress to climb into Mrs Duncomb's chambers from a neighbouring garret, and help them gain admittance. This was a precarious enterprise as the chambers were on the fourth storey, but the girl agreed. When the door was finally opened, the first object that the horrified neighbours set eyes upon was: 'the poor unhappy young Maid murder'd! inhumanly murder'd! and lying weltring in her own Blood, and her Throat cut from Ear to Ear!' The tragic spectacle did not end here. They then found Mrs Duncomb strangled in her bed, and her good friend murdered in the same manner. Three hundred pounds' worth of money, plate and jewellery was missing, including a silver tankard.[21]

News of a brutal triple murder at the heart of the legal establishment caused consternation. The very nature of living in the Inns of Court involved trust, with the tenants obliged to entrust their keys, their property and even their lives to others. Collective suspicion fell immediately upon the servants. The following day, Sarah Malcolm's landlord approached the watch and said that he had found a bloodstained shirt and apron, and a silver tankard, hidden in Sarah's commode. Sarah was arrested, along with Mary Tracey and the two Alexander brothers.

Sarah Malcolm was indicted for the murders and the robbery, but was tried for murder only, at the Old Bailey on 23 February 1733. Sarah mounted her own defence, admitting to participation in the robbery, which in itself brought a capital sentence, but denying any knowledge of or part in the murder of the three women. Sarah claimed that the blood on her clothes was menstrual blood, and not that of the victim Ann Price, and the tankard had belonged to her father. The blood on the tankard came from a cut on her finger. But the jury found Sarah guilty of murder in just fifteen minutes and she was sentenced to death.

In Newgate, 'the Irish laundress' became a celebrity criminal, visited by William Hogarth among others. Hogarth, who painted Sarah's portrait, had no doubt as to her guilt, and said he found her 'capable of any wickedness'.[22] Sarah maintained her innocence and showed tremendous courage at her impending fate, but she was particularly distressed that she would not be executed at Tyburn. Instead of dying among strangers, Sarah was hanged in Fleet Street, near the Temple Gate. Following her execution, the other three suspects, Mary Tracey and the Alexander brothers, were released without charge. Dreadful as Sarah's fate was, she escaped a worse death. Had she been an indentured servant to Mrs Duncomb, her mistress's murder would have been classified as petty treason, for which the sentence was being burnt to death.

If gender was not a sufficient cause for leniency in sentencing then neither was social rank. In an earlier age, it seems unlikely that Laurence Shirley, Earl Ferrers, would have been executed in 1760 for killing a faithful family servant, John Johnson. In days gone by, perhaps this aristocrat, who had the blood of the Plantagenets running in his veins, would have escaped justice and the fatality passed off as a tragic accident. But with the 1752 Murder Act designed to 'put down murder', justice had to be seen to be done, to the highest as well as to the lowest in the land.

A violent drunk with a reputation for cruelty, Earl Ferrers once beat a footman to a pulp for serving him bad oysters. The attack was so severe that the man was rendered incontinent for years afterwards. Ferrers' treatment of his wife was so abominable that she sued him for divorce, an almost inconceivably elaborate procedure in those days that required an Act of Parliament. When Lady Ferrers demanded half of his estate, at Staunton Harold, Leicestershire, John Johnson, the Ferrers' trusted retainer, was appointed to administer Lady Ferrers' affairs. Ferrers took an acute dislike to Johnson, denouncing him as a swindler. Matters came to a head one afternoon when Ferrers summoned Johnson to Staunton Harold Hall, ordered him to kneel, and shot him. Johnson died the following morning, and a drunken Ferrers, armed with a blunderbuss and a brace of pistols, was captured by one of his tenants. Far from being frightened, the young man, a collier named Curtis, quietly talked the earl down and persuaded him to give himself up.

Ferrers was driven to London in his landau under an armed guard. As an aristocrat, he was spared the horrors of Newgate and committed to the Tower, where he boasted that, if executed, he would at least be despatched with a sword like his ancestor, Robert Devereux, the Earl of Essex (1567–1601). When Ferrers went on trial at the House of Lords on 16 April 1760, he put in a plea of insanity, but this failed to convince his fellow peers, and Ferrers eventually confessed that he had been reduced to attempting to prove himself a lunatic in order that he might not be regarded a murderer. The greatest shock came when the death sentence was passed and Ferrers was informed that he would be hanged at Tyburn, like a common criminal.

Ferrers' last journey was spectacular, with the disgraced earl appearing in the white silk suit, richly embroidered with silver, which he had worn to his wedding. He travelled to the gallows in his own landau, preceded by a body of horse guards and mourning coaches crammed with aristocratic friends and civic dignitaries. The procession moved so slowly that the journey from the Tower to Tyburn took two and three-quarter hours, but Ferrers remained quite calm, remarking that the journey was worse than death itself and he supposed so large a mob had gathered because the people had never seen a lord hanged before. The traditional stop at St Giles was denied to him, on the grounds that to pause for a glass of wine would delay the proceedings even further.

When the landau arrived at Tyburn, Ferrers maintained his composure. As a concession to his noble birth, the gallows had been decorated with black mourning cloth and a special scaffold had been built, described by Horace Walpole as 'a newly-invented stage, to be struck from under him'.[23] Ferrers was to experience the latest innovation in the executioner's art: a trapdoor designed to make death instantaneous by ensuring that his neck was broken by the fall. After reciting the Lord's Prayer with the chaplain, Ferrers prepared to submit to his fate. As a peer, he was entitled to be hanged with a silk rope, though whether this was the case is a matter for conjecture.

What is not a matter for conjecture, sadly, is what happened next. Instead of falling open at the moment of execution, the trapdoor remained steadfastly shut. In Walpole's words, 'As the machine was new, they were not ready at it; his toes touched it, and he suffered a little, having had time by their bungling to raise his cap.'[24] Far from being launched into eternity, the earl was left to dangle; he even freed a hand and managed to pull off the hood covering his face. Swiftly, the executioner drew Ferrers' hood down again, and the bystanders pulled at his legs, 'so that he was soon out of pain, and quite dead in four minutes'.[25] The body was left to hang for a full hour, before being taken to Surgeons' Hall to be anatomized. According to Walpole, the mob tore the black fabric off the gallows for use as relics, but 'the universal crowd behaved with great decency and admiration'.[26]

Many of the anecdotes that emerge from this period in London's history of crime appear bleakly comic. Such was the fate of Hannah Dagoe, an Irish woman sentenced to death for robbing her employer in 1763. Hannah, who had stripped her mistress's house of its possessions, was sentenced to death at the Old Bailey. A strong, masculine woman with a filthy temper, Hannah was the terror of her fellow prisoners, and actually stabbed one of the men who had given evidence against her. Hannah's stubborn streak of defiance really began to assert itself during her journey to Tyburn. Showing little concern for her impending fate, Hannah ignored the Roman Catholic priest who was trying to administer the Last Rites, wriggled free of her bonds and began to strip off her clothes, much to the delight of the mob, which cheered her on. Eager to cheat the hangman of one of his perks, the garments of the deceased, Hannah removed one item after another and flung them into the crowd. By the time the procession arrived at the scaffold, Hannah was virtually naked. As her cart was drawn under the gallows, Hannah seized the executioner and punched him so hard that he nearly fell over. Eventually, after a struggle, the hangman got his noose around Hannah's neck, but she was determined to deny him his moment of triumph. Before the signal was given, she threw herself out of the cart so violently that she broke her neck and died instantly.

By contrast, the crimes of Elizabeth Brownrigg were so shocking that the midwife had become a universal hate-figure by the time of her execution at Tyburn in 1767. Even by the standards of the day, the vicious treatment Brownrigg dispensed to her young charges made a powerful impression on the public, and the response to her crimes was one of universal loathing.

Brownrigg had not always been a cruel, sadistic woman. Originally, she had a reputation for being skilful and humane to the women in her care. When she approached the Foundling Hospital and asked to take on young girls as apprentices, the trustees were happy to comply. But it later emerged that she treated these girls with unimaginable cruelty. They were stripped naked, horsewhipped, forced to sleep in the coal-hole and sexually exploited by the men of the family. One girl escaped and complained to the hospital, but no further action was taken until another girl, fourteen-year-old Mary Clifford, was rescued after a neighbour found her emaciated and bleeding in the yard. When Mary died of her injuries, Mr and Mrs Brownrigg and their son went on trial for murder. Only Elizabeth Brownrigg was found guilty of the 'wilful murder' of her apprentice although it was established that at times other members of the family had joined in the beatings. No adequate explanation has ever been given for Elizabeth Brownrigg's sadistic impulses. The *Gentleman's Magazine* published a full account showing the 'hole' in which the girls were confined, and the kitchen in which one of the girls is shown tied to a beam to be flogged.

Brownrigg was executed on 14 September and her body carried to Surgeons' Hall to be anatomized. Afterwards, 'her skeleton has since been exposed in the niche opposite the first door of the Surgeons' Theatre, that the heinousness of her cruelty may make the more lasting impression on the minds of the spectators'.[27]

In stark contrast, Mary Jones, executed in 1771, was clasped to the collective bosom of the Tyburn crowd and embraced like a martyr. Mary Jones was between nineteen and twenty-six years old and happily married when her husband was press-ganged and forced to join the navy. Mary was left with no money, no food, no home, and two small children. Refusing to turn to prostitution, Mary, who had been honest all her short life, attempted to steal some muslin from a draper's shop on Ludgate Hill. Arrested before she had completed the theft, Mary was taken to court, and, as it was her first offence, she might well have been pardoned. But, when Mary received the guilty verdict, she lost her temper, and turned on the judge and jury, accusing them of being 'a lot of old fogrums!'[28] This outburst cost Mary her life, although her neighbours from Red Lion Street, Whitechapel, rallied to her defence with a petition. A pardon denied, Mary set out on the cart from Newgate with one of her children still at her breast, and 'met death with amazing fortitude'. Sir William Meredith, one of the earliest campaigners for the abolition of capital punishment, later observed that 'I do not believe that a fouler murder was ever committed against law, than the murder of this woman by law.'[29]

Mary, and many others like her, was a victim of 'the Bloody Code', one of the most savage systems of laws and punishments ever devised. Under the Bloody Code, the number of capital offences in England had risen from fifty in 1688 to 160 by 1765. Theft of any item worth more than a shilling (twelve pence in today's currency) carried the death sentence. Hence the observation that one 'might as well be hanged for stealing a sheep as for a lamb'. As the government's attempts to enforce the rule of law became increasingly brutal, even those guilty of what we would now term 'white-collar crimes' were not exempt. In 1776, the Perreau twins, Robert and Daniel, who ran an upmarket apothecary's shop in Golden Square, forged documents to obtain a bank loan. Although it was suggested at their trial that the forgery was actually carried out by Robert's mistress, a Mrs Rudd, the twins were found guilty and sentenced to hang. A petition signed by seventy-eight influential tradesmen, bankers and merchants was not sufficient to convince the king that the sentence should be commuted to transportation and the twins went to Tyburn. In death, they were not divided: the young men fell from the gallows with their four hands clasped together.[30]

Even men in holy orders were not exempt, and the days of being acquitted with a recital of the 'neck verse' were long since over. In 1777, Dr William Dodd, a popular clergyman, found himself on the scaffold for the crime of forgery. Dodd had been one of the king's chaplains and a fashionable young preacher before falling into debt. At some point, his situation became so desperate that 'he even descended so low as to become the editor of a newspaper'. Dodd fell even lower: he forged the signature of his patron, Lord Chesterfield, to a cheque for £4,200. The forgery was discovered, and Dodd made partial repayment and guaranteed to pay back the remainder. When Dodd was sentenced to death on 26 May 1777, he delivered a rousing speech, written for him by his supporter, Dr Samuel Johnson. Johnson subsequently claimed the eloquence was all Dodd's own. 'Depend upon it, Sir, when a man knows he is to be hanged in a fortnight, it concentrates his mind wonderfully.'[31]

Everything possible was done to save him. Newspapers were full of letters and editorials voicing support for him, and a petition, twenty-three pages long, was sent to the king. The king agonized over the sentence, before concluding: 'If I pardon Dodd, I shall have murdered the Perreaus.'[32] On

June 27 the fatal procession set out from Newgate, followed by 'perhaps the greatest concourse of people ever drawn together by a like spectacle'.[33]

The last hanging at Tyburn took place in 1783, but not as a result of penal reform or enlightened attitudes towards capital punishment. Instead, public executions were moved to the exterior of Newgate Gaol as a concession to genteel sensibilities. The authorities had been attempting to move the gallows from Tyburn for decades. Back in 1719, one writer noted that: 'the famous and ancient Engine of Justice called Tyburn is going to be demolished' and moved to Stamford Hill, 'the Reason given is said to be, because of the great Buildings that are going to be erected in Maribone-Fields'.[34] This came to nothing, but as the impressive Palladian mansions spread west from Mayfair towards Hyde Park Corner, it became obvious that the last thing the fashionable new residents wanted to see was an unruly drunken mob fighting and cheering its way towards the gallows. The last man to hang at Tyburn was John Austin, who had been convicted the preceding Saturday of robbing and wounding John Spicer. According to the chronicles, Austin behaved with great composure, requesting the populace to pray for his departing soul. Austin 'died hard': 'The noose of the halter having slipped to the back part of his neck, it was longer than usual before he was dead.'[35]

Transferring public executions to Newgate meant the end of the processions that had been a feature of London's life for six hundred years. Many people, including Dr Johnson, did not approve. 'All the business of the world is to be done in a new way,' he blustered. 'Tyburn itself is not safe from the fury of innovation!' When told that this represented an improvement, Johnson replied, 'No, Sir, it is not an improvement: they object that the old method drew together a number of spectators. Sir, executions are intended to draw spectators. If they do not draw spectators, they don't answer their purpose. The old method was the most satisfactory to all parties: the public was gratified by a procession: the criminal was supported by it. Why is all this to be swept away?'[36]

'All this' was not swept away. Although the gallows at Tyburn was demolished, public executions continued to enthral Londoners for almost another century, drawing massive crowds, and the appetite to witness capital punishment continued unabated. The judiciary continued to inflict the Bloody Code upon those who offended against the law, while a new development meant that the gallows was never short of victims. This was the founding of London's professional police force, bringing with it two memorable names which would dominate the landscape of crime for generations to come: Bow Street and Scotland Yard.

7

THE LONG ARM
OF THE LAW

From Bow Street to Scotland Yard

The story of London and crime so far has concentrated on villains, prisons and executions. Now, moving through the eighteenth century, we arrive at the first great landmarks of law enforcement: Bow Street Magistrates' Court, with its famed Bow Street Runners, and Scotland Yard, home of the Metropolitan Police. This chapter traces the evolution of London's crime-fighting force, from De Veil's Covent Garden mansion to the founding of the Metropolitan Police.

These institutions did not spring, fully formed, into being. Instead, these legendary crime-fighting bodies emerged gradually from the barely suppressed anarchy of Hanoverian London. First Thomas De Veil founded Bow Street Magistrates' Court, and then the Fielding brothers created its eponymous 'Runners'. Towards the end of the eighteenth century, the visionary reformer Patrick Colquhoun lobbied for the establishment of a professional, city-wide police force, but it would not be until 1829, after the Bow Street Runners foiled the Cato Street conspiracy, that Sir Robert Peel's Metropolitan Police was finally unleashed against London's 'dangerous classes'.

Thomas De Veil (1684–1746) was Bow Street's presiding genius. A former army officer turned magistrate, De Veil had only to look out of the windows of his house at 4 Bow Street to witness the groundswell of felony that lapped about its walls. De Veil's house was set on the borders of Covent Garden, the fashionable hub of vice from which taverns, theatres, coffee houses and brothels radiated outwards like the spokes on a wheel. Every other house in the street was a gin shop or a brothel, and within a short walk of Inigo Jones' magnificent piazza stood the stinking tenements and thieves' kitchens of Seven Dials.

Chaotic, violent Hanoverian London was almost impossible to police. The writer Fanny Burney complained that she could not take a walk before breakfast 'because of the danger of robbers' and dusk was generally known as 'the footpad hour'.[1] The teeming rookeries of Seven Dials and Saffron Hill were villains' strongholds, a labyrinth of secret passageways riddled with booby traps. Any constable of the watch foolhardy enough to give chase into the tottering ruins might find himself stumbling headfirst into a cesspool or set upon by an army of thugs. Drink had always played a prominent part in the underworld, but now the traditional flagons of ale and sack had been forsaken and London was floating on a tide of gin, the cheap but potent liquor sold at 15,000 drinking establishments throughout the city, where the public could be 'drunk for one penny and dead drunk for tuppence'.[2] Once they had recovered, drinkers had to go and find the wherewithal to do it all again, which inevitably meant crime.

Such law enforcement as there was consisted of parish constables, and 'Charlies', a corps of night watchmen introduced by Charles II. Positioned in little sentry boxes by the side of the road, the elderly and infirm Charlies attracted much ridicule, particularly from the Mohocks, upper-class hooligans who delighted in rolling the sentry boxes over, with the Charlies still inside.[3]

Given the failure of the watchmen and the unreliability of volunteer constables, parishes began to hire paid constables instead, but many such constables developed too close a relationship with the underworld they were supposed to police, and were prone to corruption.

If the constables did succeed in making an arrest, the felon was taken before a magistrate or 'Justice of the Peace' who would then pass sentence or, if the crime was serious enough, remand them in custody until they could be tried at the Old Bailey.

As the authorities came to understand that London required a more efficient method of dealing with crime, 'rotation offices' or magistrates' courts opened in the capital. These were offices where Londoners could be certain to find a magistrate at fixed hours. Anyone witnessing a felony was legally obliged to apprehend those responsible for the crime, and to notify a constable or Justice of the Peace if they heard that a crime had taken place.

Unfortunately, Justices of the Peace could prove to be as venal as the offenders who appeared before them and were often men of corrupt morals, incapable of inspiring respect and quite indifferent about the efficiency of their subordinates. While there was no shortage of reputable country gentlemen in the shires, content to serve as Justices of the Peace without financial gain, in London the duties of a magistrate were so much more arduous that the candidates were seldom men of distinction and frequently people whose motive was to exploit rather than serve the public. Although the justices were not paid, they were entitled to certain fees, and many were referred to scathingly as 'trading justices' who lived on their expenses.[4]

Sir Thomas De Veil joined the ranks of the magistrates in 1739, and opened his own magistrates' court at 4 Bow Street in 1740. A former army officer from a Huguenot family, De Veil was an authoritative, energetic and intelligent man, who had previously dispensed legal advice from an obscure corner of Whitehall known as 'Scotland Yard'. As befitted a former army officer, De Veil was not lacking in physical courage. He survived at least one murder attempt after breaking up a criminal gang, and faced down a violent rabble that tried to torch Bow Street during a gin riot in 1743. De Veil had been involved in the legislation to curb the consumption of gin by imposing a massive 5 per cent increase in duty, which earned him the undying hatred of the London mob. De Veil was immortalized in a ballad as a hero who 'cool and dauntless saw the Bow Street fray, and taught rebellious lackeys to obey'.[5]

However, for all his hatred of gin, De Veil was no stranger to the bottle himself, as illustrated by Hogarth in *Night* (1738). Hogarth, who despised De Veil for being a Freemason and a hypocrite, depicted the magistrate being escorted home from his Masonic lodge so hopelessly drunk that he was oblivious to the chamber pot being tipped over his head or the gin riots raging in the background. De Veil's other appetites included 'a most irregular passion for the fair sex'. He kept a small room directly behind the bench for swift couplings between cases, and, according to his obituary in the *Gentleman's Magazine,* 'he served himself by means of his office with a variety of women'.[6] If an attractive young woman appeared in the dock, De Veil would ask in a kindly way if her lodging was far from Bow Street, and if a sedan chair might halt outside without suspicion. On hearing a positive response, De Veil would drop the charges.[7]

Following the death of De Veil in 1746 a magistrate named John Poulson held office until 1748, when the Bow Street practice was taken over by a barrister named Henry Fielding, an attractive and gregarious man, 'overflowing with wit, mirth and good humour'.[8] Today, Henry Fielding is best remembered as the author of hearty picaresque novels such as *Joseph Andrews* (1742) and *Tom Jones* (1751) but at the time he was better known as a satirist. In *Jonathan Wild* (1743), Fielding drew a sardonic parallel between the disgraced thief-taker and the notoriously corrupt prime minister, Robert Walpole. Jonathan Wild proved to be more than a literary inspiration. Fielding, who had attended Wild's hanging in 1725, was determined to reform the climate of sleaze that had allowed Wild to flourish and the culture of fear that left private individuals afraid to come forward as prosecutors, meaning that no proceedings could be taken against the criminal.

Henry Fielding was appointed to the bench on 25 October 1748; six weeks later, he was dispensing justice in Bow Street. Living with him at the same house was his half-brother, John Fielding, who had been blinded after a naval accident at the age of nineteen. Despite his blindness, John Fielding was also a respected magistrate, known as 'the blind beak of Bow Street' because he could recognize over 3,000 individual criminals by the sound of their voices. John Fielding's original and witty personality used to attract audiences to listen to his examinations of prisoners, and the figure of the blind magistrate, with a bandage over his eyes and a cane in his hand to wave before him when he left the bench, came to be as familiar to high society as it was to the poor wretches who appeared before him.[9]

To be a magistrate in eighteenth-century London was no easy task. The Fieldings handled up to fifty hearings a week, and attended frequent all-night sittings, in the foetid, soot-blackened courtroom. On one occasion, forty-five people were arrested following a raid on a casino in the Strand, all of whom had to be committed immediately.[10] Henry Fielding's new career offered little in the way of financial recompense in return for the long hours. Although his fees were supposed to amount to some £1,000 a year, much of this had to go to his clerk. However, between the two of them, the brothers made the name Fielding synonymous with peacekeeping for a generation of Londoners, and ushered in a number of innovations that played a vital part in the development of criminal intelligence.[11]

The first of these innovations was an effective weapon against the highwaymen who laid siege to the carriages, post chaises and mail coaches travelling in and out of London. Henry Fielding enlisted the support of twenty country gentlemen with houses within twenty miles of the capital. These individuals were asked to donate two guineas to a common pool and to send Fielding a messenger on horseback with written details of any crime committed in his area, including, if possible, an accurate description of the thief and the horse he was riding, together with the name of the victim. On his way to London, the messenger was to warn all innkeepers, stable boys and turnpike keepers against harbouring the fugitive, supplying him with a horse or letting him pass. The messenger was to return with a note from the magistrates proving that he had performed his task, and for this he was paid out of the pool. The information and description of the highwayman was then published in the *Public Advertiser* (the forerunner of the *Police Gazette)* and, with its pictures of known offenders, constituted an early form of the criminal records department. Even if the highwayman got safely away to London, he was at the mercy of the thief-takers. And, since highwaymen tended to be flamboyant young men, prone to bragging about their exploits in the taverns, it was only a matter of time before they were identified and arrested. The result of Fielding's scheme was the 'Mounted Patrol', which reduced the rate of highway robbery in three months. Unfortunately, soon after Fielding's death, the Mounted Patrol was disbanded, and highwaymen immediately took to the road again. It was not until 1806 that the Mounted Patrol was revived, eventually becoming the mounted division of the Metropolitan Police.[12]

The Fieldings believed that they could deter criminals by increasing the certainty that they would be detected and prosecuted, and that by supervizing their activities, they could improve the reputation of thief-takers, who they believed were essential in the fight against crime. These officers, who liked to refer to themselves as 'principal officers' of Bow Street, were more commonly known as 'the Bow Street Runners', although Londoners also, in a more irreverent fashion, referred to them as the 'Robin Redbreasts' or the 'Raw Lobsters' on account of their distinctive red waistcoats.

Alongside the problem of widespread criminality, another form of lawlessness threatened the capital in the form of civil unrest. During the eighteenth century London saw three serious disturbances of this kind: the riots which broke out after the 1736 Gin Act, the Spitalfields Riots of 1765 and the Gordon Riots of 1780. Existing legislation in the form of the Riot Act (1715) meant that magistrates could order 'riotous assemblies' of more than twelve people to disperse within the hour or be charged with capital felony. Dispersing the crowd became the responsibility of the army, but the troops were placed in an unenviable position. A soldier who overreacted and opened fire on the mob, killing or seriously injuring a rioter, faced a court martial, as did the magistrate.

Reluctance to invoke the Riot Act in June 1780 led to shocking scenes when the Gordon Riots raged through London for days. Over 400 people were killed, the Bank of England was attacked, and 150 houses and shops were destroyed, causing £70,000-worth of damage to property (£6.5 million at today's prices) and £30,000-worth of personal injury claims (c. £3 million

Newgate Gaol in flames during the Gordon Riots.

today). Events culminated with the destruction of Newgate Gaol by fire and the release of its prisoners.

Events had unfolded peacefully at first, with little indication of the anarchy that would follow. On 2 June 1780, Lord George Gordon (1751–93), leader of the 'Protestant Association', arrived in London with his band of 40,000 supporters, to petition Parliament against the 1778 Catholic Relief Act. Gordon and his followers feared that, given sufficient power, the country's Roman Catholic community would overthrow the crown and put the country under the control of the Pope, hence their blue cockades and slogan of 'No Popery!' After their bid to overthrow the bill was dismissed by MPs, the protest started to get out of hand. Ranks swelled by another 20,000 people, ranging from ruffians and apprentices to prostitutes and anonymous 'gentlemen' who may well have been *agents provocateurs,* the rioters rampaged through London, raiding and burning Roman Catholic churches and businesses in Holborn, Covent Garden and Leicester Square. The mansions of Tory aristocrats such as Sir George Savile, a Papist sympathizer, were destroyed. Fearing for their lives, even the Jewish merchants deemed it expedient to hang out 'No Popery!' signs.

After three of Gordon's men were arrested and taken before the aged Sir John Fielding, Bow Street Magistrates' Court was attacked. According to a Bow Street Runner named Macmanus, the mob arrived at around nine, armed with clubs and shouting 'Damn you! We will have it down!'[13] The Runners chained and bolted the doors behind them and escaped through the back. Some hours later, Macmanus returned, armed with a pistol, to discover the windows broken, the wooden shutters and wainscoting torn down and fires in the street where the mob had set fire to the furniture. Meanwhile, the landlord of the Brown Bear, opposite, was trying to placate the rioters with free gin, but the liquor only served to intensify their rage. Although all the goods and chattels were taken out and burnt, 4 Bow Street was not destroyed beyond repair.[14]

At around eight o'clock on the evening of 6 June, a mob rampaged down Holborn bellowing 'Ahoy for Newgate!' and converged on the house of the keeper, Mr Richard Akerman, clamouring for the release of the three prisoners who had been arrested on 2 June, the day the riots broke out. Akerman and his family were forced to flee to safety across the rooftops, after which Akerman demanded that the Lord Mayor, Richard Kennett, read the Riot Act and send in the troops, but the magistrates refused, fearing that such an action would further inflame the mob. In the meantime, Newgate Gaol went up in flames, accompanied by the screams of terrified prisoners. The rioters quickly set about freeing them, breaking down doors and leading them out, still in their chains.

Spurred on by the symbolic gesture of destroying London's Bastille, the rioters smashed open the gates of the New Prison and Clerkenwell Bridewell, burned down the Fleet and the King's Bench, and attacked the Bank of England and the Houses of Parliament. At this point, realizing that the riots were becoming uncontrollable, the Lord Mayor called out the City Militia and the Honourable Artillery Company and gave the order to fire. About 10,000 troops descended on the rioters, killing over 300 and arresting 450. Twenty-five rioters were hanged, the majority of them less than eighteen years old. Horace Walpole observed bitterly that 'the bulk of the criminals are so young that half a dozen schoolmasters might have quashed the insurrection'.[15]

In the following days, many of the prisoners who had been freed from Newgate gave themselves up, tired, hungry and destitute. They were confined to the Compters, while plans went ahead for the complete reconstruction of Newgate Gaol. Lord George Gordon, who had instigated the riots, was arrested and detained in the Tower of London, before going on trial for treason. Gordon was acquitted but ironically he ended his days in Newgate in 1793, after being sentenced on a charge of seditious libel.

It took three years to assess the full impact of the Gordon Riots upon London. The damage to property ran into billions by today's standards, and the majority of the victims were the landed gentry, manufacturers and tradespeople. As insurance companies examined their policies to see if they could avoid paying out for 'civil commotion', well-to-do Londoners came to realize that the ancient parochial system of peace-keeping would always be ineffectual in dealing with violent and widespread disorder.[16] If the army was powerless to stop riots, and the constables of the watch were useless, there was only one solution. What was needed was a professional police force to act in collaboration with existing constables and watchmen to prevent crime and to 'put down' such acts of sedition before they became so destructive and dangerous. In 1785 the government attempted to pass a bill creating paid police commissioners throughout the metropolis. Their task would be to supervize a professional police force in London. The bill failed because the Lord Mayor opposed any infringement of his jurisdiction in the City of London and the magistrates saw police commissioners as a threat to their authority.

In 1797 the magistrate and statistician Patrick Colquhoun (1745–1820) argued the case for a professional force. 'It is an honourable profession to repel by force the enemies of the State. Why should it not be equally so to resist and to conquer these domestic invaders of property, and destroyers of lives who are constantly in a state of criminal warfare?' he demanded.[17] Colquhoun's detractors argued that a paid force would be regarded as 'anathema to the vast majority of the population', conjuring up the vision of governmental repression and a quite unwarranted interference with the liberties of the subject. Conversely, there was also a very real anxiety that, in the wrong hands, a professional police force would not serve the ends of the establishment but would be used against them, in a repetition of 'The Terror' when scores of people were seized and executed by the secret police in post-revolutionary France.[18]

Undeterred, Colquhoun persisted with his campaign and in 1798 he collaborated with a group of docklands merchants to form the Thames River Police, to protect the valuable cargoes coming in to the Pool of London, and opened the world's first police station, at Wapping. But it would take a sensational series of murders, an audacious assassination attempt and another riot before a city-wide force could come into being.

*

By 1811, the Ratcliffe Highway, near Wapping, was one of the worst streets in London – a dirty, dusty thoroughfare on the shore of the Thames, lined with taverns, brothels and cheap hotels. Close at hand was the grim spectacle of Executioner's Dock, where pirates and all manner of seafaring villains had undergone the traditional punishment of being chained to a post and left to drown. Shoehorned in between these dens of iniquity were the shabby genteel – the grocers, bakers, fish-mongers and tailors who struggled to make an honest living amid the depravity. Timothy Marr, who had opened a draper's shop at 29 Ratcliffe Highway, was a typical resident. A former merchant seaman who had served on the *Dover Castle* between 1808 and 1811, Marr lived behind his shop with his young wife, Celia, and their three-month-old son. Marr's apprentice, James Gowan, aged thirteen, and a servant girl, Margaret Jewell, also lived at number twenty-nine.

At midnight on Saturday, 7 December 1811, Marr finally shut up shop for the evening and instructed young Margaret to go out and buy oysters. When Margaret returned half an hour later, the shop was in darkness and she could not get in. After the watchman had hammered on the door to no avail, a neighbour, a Mr Murray, offered to investigate. When he walked round to the rear of the house, he found the back door wide open. Raising his candle, Murray encountered a scene of horror. The apprentice, James Gowan, lay dead, his head smashed in so violently that the walls were spattered with his blood and brains. Near Gowan was the body of young Celia Marr, blood seeping from her battered skull. Murray wrenched open the front door and raised the alarm with a cry of 'Murder! Murder! Come and see what murder is here!' By this time a small crowd had gathered in the street outside and as someone held up a lantern, the body of Timothy Marr was discovered, also battered to death. Margaret Jewell had been reduced to hysterics, and it fell to another woman to shriek: 'Where's the baby?' They found the child still in his cradle.

His throat had been cut and his head almost severed from his body.

When Charles Horton, of the Thames Police Office at Wapping, arrived to investigate, he found a ripping chisel at the scene, but it appeared to be perfectly clean. The actual murder weapon, a 'maul' or shipwright's hammer, was discovered upstairs, covered in blood and hair, and engraved with the initials 'J. P.' The discovery of two sets of bloody footprints, leading away from the back door, suggested that the perpetrators had been interrupted attempting a robbery. Marr's savings, £152, were still intact in a drawer, and he had £5 on his body when he died.[19]

As news of the terrible events spread throughout the East End, the street outside was crammed with sightseers, eager to satisfy their ghoulish curiosity. The bodies went on display as was the custom, and the Marrs were subsequently buried in a single grave at St George's-in-the-East, the church where only two months earlier young Timothy Marr had been christened.

Panic gripped the neighbourhood and a reward of five hundred guineas was offered for apprehending the killer. This was an unprecedented sum in an age when a working man was lucky to earn more than £1 a week. The incentive worked: the landlord of the Pear Tree public house, Robert Vermilloe, came forward to identify the owner of the maul as John Petersen, a merchant seaman and one of his lodgers. Vermilloe was in Newgate Gaol for debt, and must have welcomed the opportunity to claim the reward money. Another resident, Cornelius Hart, claimed ownership of the ripping chisel, saying he must have mislaid it when visiting Marr.

Before the Thames Police Office could act on this information, Wapping was shaken by another gruesome multiple murder. On 19 December a watchman patrolling New Gravel Lane was astonished to witness a half-naked man scrambling out of an upstairs window at the King's Arms Tavern shouting, 'Murder! Murder!'[20]

When the watchman and constables from the Thames Police Office forced their way into the King's Arms they discovered the body of the publican, John Williamson, hanging from a ladder in the cellar and the bodies of his wife, Elizabeth, and their servant, Bridget Harrington, in the kitchen. All three had been brutally battered and their throats had been cut. The murderer appeared to have escaped across open land at the rear of the premises, with Williamson's watch and other valuables. Apart from the lodger who had climbed out of the window, the only other survivor was Kitty Stillwell, the Williamsons' fourteen-year-old granddaughter, who had slept through the entire incident.

Wapping was again thrown into a state of panic, and several arrests were made. These included another resident of the Pear Tree, a sailor named John Williams. Williams was arrested on 21 December after a tip-off from Vermilloe, who stated that Williams had served with Marr on the *Dover Castle* and had a grievance against him. A ladies' man with no previous history of violence, Williams was an unlikely suspect for seven of the most brutal murders in London. The evidence against him was entirely circumstantial, consisting of the fact that the shirt he was wearing was torn and bloody, and that he was carrying an unusual amount of money. However, Williams was remanded in custody to Cold Bath Fields prison, and scheduled to appear at Shadwell Magistrates' Court on 27 December. In a shocking twist, a constable arrived on the morning of 27 December to inform the court that Williams had hanged himself in his cell.[21]

After a swift conferral, the magistrates decided to go ahead and hear the evidence of the other witnesses and by the end of the day had concluded that Williams had been the murderer and had acted alone. All of the evidence that pointed towards others being involved seems to have been conveniently ignored. That evening the Shadwell magistrates informed the Home Secretary, Mr Robert Ryder, that John Williams had murdered the Marr family and the Williamson family and had cheated the hangman by taking his own life in prison rather than face the consequences.

The Home Secretary accepted this verdict and decided to conclude the whole ghastly business by having Williams' body paraded through Wapping to prove that he no longer represented a threat. To avoid any danger of rioting, the Thames Police, the Bow Street Mounted Patrol, local constables and the watchmen were ordered to oversee the event. On New Year's Eve 1811, at half past ten in the morning, the procession set off from St George's Watch House, with Williams' body propped up on the back of a cart. The maul and the ripping chisel with which he had apparently committed the murders were displayed beside his head, while a wooden stake lay at his feet. As a crowd some 10,000-strong looked on, the procession wound down the Ratcliffe Highway, and halted outside the Marrs' shop, where a constable turned Williams' head so that he appeared to be gazing at the ghosts of his victims. A similar vigil was held outside the King's Arms, before the procession made its way along Ratcliffe Highway, up to the crossroads where Cannon Street meets Cable Street, where Williams' body was thrown into a narrow grave and the stake was driven through his heart, hammered in with the bloodstained maul. At that moment, the crowd, hitherto peaceful, let out a stream of shouting and curses.

Williams made a convenient scapegoat, offering the authorities the opportunity to reassure Londoners that law and order had been restored. But the circumstances surrounding his death remain mysterious. Witnesses from Cold Bath Fields prison said that on the night before he hanged himself, Williams did not appear to be distressed. Indeed, he was looking forward to

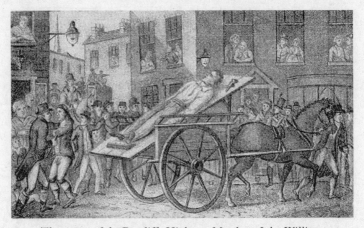

The corpse of the Ratcliffe Highway Murderer John Williams
is paraded down the Ratcliffe Highway before being buried
with a stake through his heart.

a visit from his fellow lodgers at the Pear Tree, Cornelius Hart and John Petersen, who seemed very concerned for his welfare. It is also curious that given Williams was in manacles, he actually managed to hang himself from a beam in his cell.

The temptation to speculate as to the real course of events is difficult to resist. In their case study, *The Maul and the Pear Tree,* the distinguished crime writer P. D. James and the police historian T. A. Critchley concluded that Williams had become involved in the robberies through the influence of his shady fellow lodgers, and then been silenced to prevent him from incriminating them. This made Williams himself the eighth victim of the Ratcliffe Highway murderers, his death representing an attempt to silence him and prevent him from incriminating other gang members.[22]

The horror and outrage generated by the Ratcliffe Highway murders contributed to the demand for a city-wide police force, although there were still libertarian protests from the House of Lords. For instance, in a high-handed dismissal of the murdered proletariat, Lord Dudley reflected, 'Although they have an admirable police force in Paris, they pay dear for it. I had rather half a dozen people's throats were cut every few years in the Ratcliffe Highway than be subject to domiciliary visits, spies and the rest of Fouché's contrivances.'[23]

Fouché's contrivances would become indispensible over the following decades. By 1820, an unpopular Tory government under Lord Liverpool was facing potential anarchy, fuelled by widespread resentment of the Corn Laws, which had caused soaring food prices and famine. Disillusioned veterans, unemployed after the end of the Napoleonic Wars, proved fertile recruits to radicalism, and the authorities struggled to maintain order. A political meeting at Spa Fields in the East End descended into a riot in 1817 with twelve men killed by troops. In 1819, a rally at St Peter's Fields, Manchester, developed into the Peterloo Massacre when troops killed fifteen people during a cavalry charge. As political tensions escalated with the death of King George III in January 1820, the radicals saw the opportunity to seize power.

Following the teachings of Thomas Spence (1750–1814), radical groups consisted of individual cells rather than an overall organization. One such cell consisted of Arthur Thistlewood (1774–1820), a veteran of Spa Fields and Peterloo, and his comrades William Davidson, son of the Attorney General of Jamaica and a black slave, and James Ings, Richard Tidd and John Brunt. In 1820 a new recruit arrived in the form of George Edwards, a stonemason from Eton, who swiftly impressed them with his radical spirit. On the evening of 22 February, Edwards pointed to a notice in the *New Times* newspaper stating that the Prime Minister, Lord Liverpool, intended to dine with Lord Harrowby in Grosvenor Square, along with his cabinet. Edwards suggested that this represented the ideal opportunity to overthrow the government. A plan was swiftly formed to storm the house, murder every member of the Cabinet, and behead Lord Castlereagh, who was particularly vilified. Castlereagh's head was to be displayed on a spike on Westminster Bridge, and the ultimate aim was to seize the Bank of England and proclaim a provisional government.[24]

The following evening, 23 February, Thistlewood's gang of around twenty-three men assembled in a hayloft in Cato Street off Edgware Road, a short distance away from Grosvenor Square. The gang had stockpiled guns, swords, cutlasses, home-made hand-grenades about the size of oranges and even an improvized explosive device in the form of a 14 lb bomb with an attached fuse. As they made the final preparations, the conspirators had no idea that they were already surrounded. A detachment of the Coldstream Guards was heading towards Cato Street, whilst a squad of twelve Bow Street Runners led by veteran Runner George Ruthven had already surrounded the hayloft. Without waiting for reinforcements, Ruthven started his assault by scrambling up the single ladder to the hayloft. Startled, Thistlewood realized he had been betrayed and responded with a volley of gunfire. Shooting at one Runner, Westcot, he missed his target. Three bullets whistled through Wescot's hat but he was unharmed. Bow Street Runner Richard Smithers was not so fortunate. Thistlewood ran him through with his sword, inflicting fatal injuries, before escaping through a window. When the Coldstream Guards arrived they mounted a full-scale assault on the hayloft, overpowering the conspirators. Thistlewood and three others were arrested later that same night.[25]

When the conspirators went on trial for treason at the Old Bailey on 28 March, George Edwards was revealed as a police spy who had infiltrated the cell on the orders of his brother, a Bow Street Runner, and incited the conspirators to murder.

On Edwards' evidence, the conspirators were convicted. When sentences were passed, five of the conspirators were sentenced to transportation. Thistlewood, Davidson, Ings, Brunt and Tidd received the death sentence for treason, while George Edwards, his cover blown, embarked for Australia and was never heard of again.

The death penalty for treason stated that: 'Your heads shall be severed from your bodies and your bodies divided into four quarters to be disposed of as His Majesty shall think fit.' In previous years, the obvious place for such an execution would have been Tyburn. But now public executions had moved to Newgate Gaol, and it was here, early on the morning of 1 May 1820, that the gallows were erected outside the Debtors' Door, and festooned with black fabric. Barriers went up thirty yards from the gallows, manned by dozens of soldiers and constables. A headsman's block and sawdust sprinkled liberally on the ground signified that the outcome of this execution would be particularly gruesome.[26] A massive crowd had already gathered. Ringside views, from windows overlooking the scaffold, had sold for exorbitant sums. The square tower of St Sepulchre's was packed, and the iron railings collapsed from the pressure and gave way, taking down sixteen people with it. By seven o'clock, magistrates ordered the Riot Act to be read, threatening the onlookers that if they did not behave in an orderly fashion, the army would be sent in. The Home Secretary, Lord Sidmouth, had to dispense with the tradition of drawing the conspirators to the scaffold on hurdles, in case they were seized by the crowd and rioting broke out.[27]

According to John Hobhouse, a government minister who observed the executions, 'the men died like heroes'.[28] Ings turned to Tidd and said gruffly, 'Come on, my old cock, keep up your spirits, it all will soon be over,' and began singing 'Death or Liberty' at the top of his voice. At this point Thistlewood, whose patience was understandably at its limit, turned to Ings and said wearily, 'Be quiet, Ings; we can die without all this noise.' Even Tidd wanted to leave something for posterity. His last words, as the noose was placed around his neck, were: 'Let it be known that I die an enemy to all tyrants!'

The executioner spent a long time tying up the prisoners. During this operation a dead silence prevailed among the crowd, but the moment the trapdoor opened, 'the general feeling was manifested by deep sighs and groans'. Thistlewood, Davidson and Tidd expired without putting up a struggle but Ings died hard, with the executioner's assistants pulling at his legs. So did Brunt, whose horrifyingly contorted face showed that he was suffering 'the most excruciating torture'.[29]

After half an hour the bodies were cut down and placed in coffins, and the executioner informed the sheriff that the time had come to carry out the next part of the sentence, upon which point a grotesque figure wearing a mask and dressed like a sailor sprang up through the trapdoor armed with a butcher's knife. He dragged Thistlewood's body back out of its coffin, up to the block and cut off his head. More deeply moved by the indignity to the dead than the sufferings of the living, the crowd erupted into roars of outrage. The executioner held up the dripping head, crying three times: 'This is the head of Arthur Thistlewood, a traitor!' as the crowd hissed and groaned. The other four bodies were also decapitated and the heads placed in the coffins. The executioner accidentally dropped the last head, Brunt's, and the crowd shrieked. By this stage in the proceedings, there was so much blood on the scaffold that it looked like a slaughterhouse. The quartering of the bodies was, mercifully, omitted.[30]

The skill with which the bodies were decapitated led some of Thistlewood's supporters to suspect that the executioner had been the surgeon Thomas Wakeley. That night, Wakeley's house was set on fire, and the surgeon severely injured. But

The decapitated body of Arthur Thistlewood, ringleader of the Cato Street Conspiracy, executed for treason at Newgate in 1820.

Wakeley survived the experience and went on to become a leading surgeon and the founder of *The Lancet*.

If the Cato Street Conspiracy had not been reason enough to lobby for an organized professional force, then the riots following the funeral of Queen Caroline the following year represented conclusive evidence. Queen Caroline, estranged wife of the Prince Regent, had not always been popular. However, the British public loathed the Prince Regent even more than they disliked Queen Caroline, and the tipping point came when the Prince publically humiliated the Queen by refusing to allow her into Westminster Abbey to attend his coronation in 1820. After the Queen died of peritonitis on 7 August 1821, there was such a public demonstration of grief that it was feared her funeral procession on 18 August might degenerate into a riot.

To prevent this outcome, Lord Liverpool ruled that the funeral procession taking the Queen's body to Harwich for burial in Germany would bypass the capital. But the Queen's loyal subjects had other ideas, determined that the cortège would pass through central London. By six o'clock in the morning a vast crowd had assembled at Hyde Park Corner, desperate to join the procession. By nine-thirty, the cortège arrived at Kensington Palace accompanied by a Guard of Honour, and then turned towards Hyde Park, preparing to travel north, up Park Lane and out of London. When the cortège arrived in Hyde Park at noon, vast numbers of people on foot and on horseback surged forward, intent on blocking the Cumberland Gate leading to Park Lane and forcing the cortège to take a different route. The Guards galloped through Hyde Park in a bid to reach Cumberland Gate before the crowd did, during which stones and mud were thrown at the military. A magistrate who was present sanctioned the use of armed force, and the soldiers fired their pistols into the unarmed crowd. 'Screams of terror were heard in every direction,' as forty or fifty shots rang out, and two people were killed. As the rain fell in torrents, the cortège was eventually forced through the city by the crowds.[31] Following this debacle it became clear to the authorities that an organized professional police force was essential if such scenes were not to be repeated at a later date.

In 1829 the Home Secretary, Sir Robert Peel, finally saw through the Act that created the Metropolitan Police. The new recruits went on parade for the first time on 26 September 1829 in the grounds of the Foundling Hospital in Holborn. The old system of constables and Charlies was replaced with 3,000 constables wearing blue coats, trousers and top hats. They were supervized by two commissioners, Sir Charles Rowan, a former army officer, and Richard Mayne, a barrister, who were both sworn in as Justices of the

Peace. Many of the police officers were former soldiers, but they were not allowed to carry arms. Instead they were equipped with truncheons, and instantly nicknamed 'Bobbies' and 'Peelers' after Sir Robert Peel. The headquarters of this new force was in the very same Whitehall backwater where Sir Thomas De Veil had set up an office back in the 1730s: Scotland Yard, a name that was to become synonymous with the detection and prevention of crime. As the following chapter reveals, the growth of the Victorian underworld over the following decades meant that the 'Old Bill' had their work cut out for them.

DARKEST LONDON

The Victorian Underworld

In the year 1850, Henry Mayhew made an intrepid ascent above London in a hot-air balloon. From his vantage point in the creaking basket, buffeted by the wind, the social reformer gazed down upon the monster city, which had grown out of all proportion over the previous decades. A time-traveller from an earlier era would have recognized the tiny outlines of the ancient walled city and the fortress of the Tower, but this square mile formed but the nucleus of the Leviathan metropolis which had sprawled out in all directions, swallowing up parish after parish and clusters of suburban villages and hamlets. Bow, Islington, Hampstead, Paddington, Kensington and Chelsea, and the towns of Westminster and Southwark had all disappeared into its gaping maw until London covered some 261 square miles of ground and contained three million citizens, a larger number of people than were to be found congregated in any other city in the world. Indeed, as one French commentator observed, London by this period was not so much a city as a province, covered by houses.[1]

A dense canopy of smoke lay across the scene, making it almost impossible to tell where the city began and where it ended. The buildings stretched not only to the horizon on either side, but far away into the distance, where, owing to the coming shades of evening and the dense fumes from the million chimneys, the town seemed to blend into the sky, making earth indistinguishable from heaven. Millions of roofs extended like a dingy red sea, rising up one after the other till the eye grew wearied with following them. Here and there appeared little green patches of parks, and the principal squares, and the fog of smoke that overshadowed the giant town was pierced with a thousand steeples and pin-like factory chimneys.[2]

Henry Mayhew had become an authority on the teeming life that filled the massive, vibrant city streets beneath him. In the course of researching his *London Labour and the London Poor*, Mayhew had interviewed scores of costermongers, flower sellers, street sweepers and hawkers, the dust and chaff who just scraped by, earning a crust on the grimy margins of London life. And Mayhew had also encountered the vast contingent of 'those that will not work', an entire alternative society composed of 'the dangerous classes', ranging from debonair gentlemen jewel thieves and beautiful courtesans to desperate mudlarks, children or old women who waded barefoot onto the Thames mudflats at low tide to pick up lumps of coal which they could sell for a halfpenny.

As London had expanded across the map like a blot of Indian ink, so too had its underworld, producing thousands of rogues and reprobates, tramps and beggars, fortune-tellers, dog-stealers, prigs (thieves), area-sneaks (opportunistic burglars), smashers or *shofulmen* (counterfeiters), broadsmen (card-sharps), bug-hunters (robbers of drunks), dragsmen (thieves who stole from carriages), hoisters (shoplifters), maltoolers (pickpockets who worked the omnibuses), *speelers* (gamblers), rampsmen (footpads), bogus wounded soldiers, sham shipwrecked sailors, 'epileptics' who faked fits of convulsions by chewing soap, and an entire cast of idlers, vagabonds and dissolute persons. All human life was here, from the *gonophs* (child thieves) to the swell mob (elite pickpockets), from the portico thieves and cat burglars to the card-sharps and cracksmen (safe-breakers), the aristocrats of the underworld. Every single one of these pursued their shadowy calling under the constant fear of the policeman's hand on the shoulder, followed by arrest and imprisonment. And yet, reared on the legends of Dick Turpin and Jack Sheppard, the dangerous classes preferred 'a short life but a merry one' to dull respectability or the workhouse. In this chapter, we meet the denizens of the Victorian underworld, and also visit 'the underworld of the underworld', the prisons to which so many felons were condemned.

Although the methodology of Henry Mayhew's 'cyclopaedia' is idiosyncratic by the standards of modern social scientists, his interviews with pickpockets and prostitutes provide fascinating insights into his age. Mayhew serves as a useful guide through the dark regions of criminal London. So too does Charles Dickens, for although his plots were outrageously contrived, Dickens' reporter's eye ensured that his details of dress, location and speech rang true. None more so than in *Oliver Twist* (1838), in which his eponymous hero arrives in the big city after being taken up by another young boy known as 'the Dodger'. As they descended from Islington turnpike down into Angel and then past Sadler's Wells theatre and into the slums of Saffron Hill, Oliver concluded that 'a dirtier or more wretched place he had never seen. The street was very narrow and muddy, and the air was impregnated with filthy odours. There were a good many small shops; but the only stock in trade appeared to be heaps of children, who, even at that time of night, were crawling in and out at the doors, or screaming from the inside.'[3] The only places that seemed to prosper were the pubs, which seemed full of brawling Irishmen. In narrow alleyways and yards, drunken men and women were positively wallowing in filth. And from several of the doorways, ugly, hulking men were cautiously emerging, looking as if they were up to no good.

Oliver Twist, a child whose very surname suggested that he was born to hang, soon found himself apprenticed to a life of crime by Fagin, who lived with his gang of youngsters in Field Lane, Holborn. Fagin was a viciously anti-Semitic caricature of Isaac 'Ikey' Solomons (d. 1850), a notorious receiver who was transported in 1831. It is in Fagin's teeming rookery that Oliver acquires the skills that will equip him for a criminal career, many of which have changed little since 'Wotton' set up his school for apprentice pickpockets in the London of 1585. The training session began with Fagin playing the part of a wealthy old gentleman, loaded with bounty, from the snuff-box and wallet in his trousers to the pocket-watch hanging from his waistcoat and the diamond pin stuck into his shirt. As Fagin parades across the room, pretending to stop and look into imaginary shop windows, the Dodger and another boy, Charley Bates, follow him. Whenever Fagin glances around nervously, slapping his pockets to make sure his possessions are still intact, the boys hide, only to re-emerge once Fagin resumes his stately progress. Eventually, in the time-honoured fashion, it is time for the boys to make their move:

At last, the Dodger trod upon his toes, or ran upon his boot accidentally, while Charley Bates stumbled up against him behind; and in that one moment they took from him, with the most extraordinary rapidity, snuff-box, note-case, watch-guard, chain, shirt-pin, pocket-handkerchief, even the spectacle-case. If the old gentleman felt a hand in any one of his pockets, he cried out where it was; and then the game began all over again.[4]

This 'game' was popular all over London, as boys as young as five or six were trained up to be gonophs by a 'kidsman' or thief trainer. The majority of these ragged urchins were the neglected offspring of costermongers or Irish immigrants from the slums of Westminster and Seven Dials. At all times of year, from the summer dusk to the foggy November evening, they were to be seen swarming barefoot across Blackfriars Bridge, London Bridge, Drury Lane, and Bishopsgate, on their way to pick the pocket tails of gentlemen.

Fagin was a benevolent kidsman compared with his real-life counterparts. One police officer, giving evidence against a receiver at Middlesex Sessions in 1850 testified that he had seen apprentice gonophs knocked down and kicked for 'not having exhibited the requisite amount of tact and ingenuity'.[5]

Oliver Twist embarks on his career as a 'gonoph' or child pickpocket.

Children made ideal thieves because they were treated with comparative leniency by the magistrates. The lack of a comprehensive criminal records system allowed many youngsters to provide false names and addresses and claim to be younger than their years. The vision of a small child pitifully protesting his innocence, his head scarcely visible above the dock, was guaranteed to pluck at the heartstrings. But as well as stealing, gonophs were exploited in another, profoundly disturbing fashion. The censorship laws of the day prevented Dickens from spelling out to his readers exactly what he meant, but many of these young boys also worked as child prostitutes. Brothels offering the sexual services of children were a grim fact of life in Victorian London. A resourceful kidsman would see no distinction between sending his lads off to pick pockets or pimping them out to wealthy perverts who could later be blackmailed on account of their peccadilloes.

The gonophs had their counterparts in the 'mudlarks' of the River Thames. Mostly aged between four and fifteen, this unique class of boys and girls confined their attention to stealing from the ships, barges and other vessels moored along the 367 wharfs of the Thames, including Shadwell and Wapping, Bankside and Borough, Waterloo Bridge, and the Temple and St Paul's Wharf. As soon as the tide was out, they appeared, and stayed on the muddy banks of the river until the tide came back in. Lumps of coal and coke that had fallen from the barges were an obvious target, but the most enterprising paired up, with one clambering onto a vessel and throwing down plunder to his companion. The coal was sold on in the street for a few halfpence, and arrests were frequent. After a short sentence of two or three weeks, the children were back. Occasionally, they were joined by robust older women; one in particular was often to be seen picking coal from the mud outside Wapping Police Office, and then parading around the neighbourhood with a bag of coal on her head.[6]

A more audacious breed of mudlarks sailed the Thames in decrepit little boats, boarding empty barges laden with coffee, sugar, rice, and other goods, and stealing anything they could lay their hands on. If pursued by the police, they took to the water like rats, splashing through the mud. Generally expert swimmers, their ages ranged from twelve to sixteen. Many of these strong, healthy boys were orphans, who slept in the barges at night, covering themselves with old sacks and tarpaulins. When one inspector from the Thames Marine Police found two little boys of nine and eleven who had been living in an old barge in Bermondsey for six months he took them before a magistrate to see if they could be provided for. The magistrate sent them to a workhouse for shelter, but they soon ran away, back to the river.[7]

As for the gonophs on dry land, the boldest and most determined rose to the top of their profession. Ten years on from being a ragged little boy, stealing a silk handkerchief from a gentleman's pocket, the skilful thief or 'buzzer' had joined the ranks of the 'swell mob', promenading around the Bank of England or strolling arm-in-arm along Cheapside with his handsome companion.[8] Henry Mayhew spotted just such a pair as he was being shown around Fleet Street one day by a police officer. As Mayhew watched, two tall, 'gentlemanly' men crossed the road outside St Clement Dane's church and entered a restaurant. 'They were wearing suits of superfine black cloth, cut in a fashionable style. They entered an elegant dining room and sat down to a costly meal with wine.' Mayhew was astonished when the police officer told him that these men were pickpockets.[9]

These 'swells' operated across London, in crowded streets, at railway stations, on omnibuses and steamboats, pursuing their trade in the Strand, Fleet Street, Holborn and Whitehall, out on all public occasions looking for plunder.[10] Expensively dressed, so that they could mingle undetected with their wealthy victims, these pickpockets travelled in first-class railway carriages to race meetings at Ascot and Epsom, often luring their fellow passengers into rigged card games during the journey, leaving their victims fleeced and robbed but too embarrassed to report the crime. Women particularly excelled at the new crime of 'portmanteau robbery'; dressed as respectable widows in heavy mourning garments, they hovered in railway station waiting rooms, biding their time until a passenger's attention was distracted, upon which they would pick up his suitcase and silently steal away. The swell mob mixed with the sightseers at Crystal Palace or the Zoological Gardens, and attended the theatre, the opera and other fashionable places of amusement. When 'the female Blondin' tiptoed precariously along the high wire at Cremorne Gardens, the buzzers were there, ready to take advantage as the audience craned their heads back to admire her performance.

Once business was concluded for the day, the swell mob retired to quiet, respectable homes in Islington, Hoxton or Lambeth, where they were careful to avoid drawing attention to themselves, and ready to move at a moment's notice if they were being observed by the police. To relax and unwind, the buzzer and his girl would head to the 'flash houses', the underworld pubs of King's Cross, Stepney and Whitechapel. Dressed up to the nines in flamboyant gowns and expensive (stolen) jewellery, the girls might have passed for ladies until they opened their mouths. The Rose and Crown in Seven Dials was a typical flash house, patronized by all members of the light-fingered gentry. In the tap room you could listen to Black Charlie, the fiddler, with ten or twelve lads and lasses enjoying a dance, and singing and smoking over glasses of gin and water, all seemingly free from care. The cheeks might turn pale when a policeman opened the door and glanced round the room, but when he departed the merriment would be resumed with vigour.[11]

But for all its rewards, buzzing was a young man's game, and by the age of twenty-five most swells had seen better days. As the effects of alcohol and imprisonment took their toll, the smartest swells changed tack and became receivers or kidsmen. Others slipped into destitution, their courage spent and their souls sapped. Henry Mayhew interviewed just such a young man, who I shall refer to as 'Edward'. Edward was 'rather melancholy and crushed in spirit, the result of repeated imprisonments, and the anxiety and suspense connected with his wild criminal life'. Edward's girl was in prison, and he was living in a seedy lodging-house in the West End. Handsome if weary, with a moustache and beard and dark, penetrating eyes, Edward was also intelligent and literate, having read Thomas Paine, Dickens and Bulwer-Lytton amongst others. Edward's story is a familiar one, but Mayhew's narrative renders it compelling.[12]

Like Oliver Twist, Edward was a runaway. A minister's son from Shropshire, he had left home at the age of nine following a bitter quarrel with his father. Edward had soon spent the four pounds he had stolen from his mother's purse and in a matter of weeks he was utterly destitute. Eventually, he 'palled up' with a gang of boys who lived in the arches underneath the Adelphi theatre and stole handkerchiefs for their master, 'Larry'. Handkerchief theft was a specialist trade with its own vocabulary, the handkerchiefs given names as beautiful and evocative as those of butterflies: the blue silk *watersman*, the green and white *randlesman*, and the yellow and white *fancy yellow*. The most sought after was the black silk mourning handkerchief, known as the *black fogle*.[13] The embroidered initials of the original owner were skilfully unpicked, and the handkerchiefs sold on.

Larry took an instant liking to Edward, immediately spotting his potential. Smart and well-spoken, Edward could pass without comment among the gentry, and soon showed outstanding prowess as a gonoph. Larry was so proud of his new acquisition that he invited other receivers to come and watch him in action, with a view to selling him to the highest bidder. But before this could happen, Edward was arrested and spent three months in Westminster Bridewell.

When he emerged, Edward found a reception committee waiting for him in the form of a gang from Whitechapel. Taken in, Edward was washed and fed, and within days had acquired his specialist training as a 'tooler' or a 'fine-wirer', picking the pockets of ladies. Dressed up in the full mourning of a middle-class child, Edward mingled with the crowds in St Paul's churchyard. And despite further sojourns in gaol, Edward flourished. By the age of thirteen he had a mistress and a luxurious lifestyle that more than compensated for the constant risk of being caught.

But as he matured, Edward's distinctive good looks became a burden; readily identifiable, he had lost that anonymity which is vital to the professional thief. It was time to move into a different field, and so he teamed up with a gang of burglars. The plan was to rob a building in the City, on the understanding that it would be empty on the day of the raid. But the gang, badly organized and inept, had been misinformed, and the robbery was already in progress when an irate employee discovered the men and sounded the alarm. As Edward ran for his life, a public-spirited bystander overheard the cries of 'Stop! Thief!' and adroitly tripped him up with his umbrella, sending Edward crashing to the ground. Edward received eighteen months in Holloway – a comparatively light sentence – but the 'silent system', under which he was forbidden to talk to his fellow prisoners, reduced him to a breakdown.

By the time he spoke to Mayhew, Edward had lost his nerve; his reputation had been damaged by the botched robbery, his mental and physical health were in decline and he was reduced to selling broadsheets in the street, the only job he could be trusted with. Edward's one consolation was his girl, and he believed relationships were stronger between thieves than between a law-abiding man and wife. 'It gives a zest to us in our criminal life, that we do not know how long we may be at liberty to enjoy ourselves. This strengthens the attachment between pickpockets and their women, who, I believe, have a stronger liking to each other, in many cases, than married people.'[14]

One reason for Edward's decline was his decision to move from one criminal speciality to another. While buzzers were highly regarded for their manual dexterity, the burglar's craft demanded a combination of stamina, athleticism and brutality, which Edward was quite incapable of. Prepared to resort to violence if necessary, the burglar carried a cosh as well as a jemmy. The character of Bill Sikes, who tried to employ Oliver as a 'snakesman' in an ill-fated robbery, was the stereotypical Victorian burglar – violent and aggressive, with his broad, heavy features, three weeks' growth of beard and black eye. In fact, there were as many different types of burglars as there were types of houses. The 'area sneaks' slipped down the steps into the 'areas' or basements of large houses, rattling door handles or testing windows; 'portico thieves' were more daring, climbing in over balconies and window ledges, often while the family was dining downstairs. Many burglars worked in cahoots with the domestic staff, investing time in chatting up a maidservant who could leave a door unlocked in return for proceeds from the robbery. The most daring dressed and spoke like landed gentry, and rented houses in Mayfair or St John's Wood. Insinuating themselves with their neighbours, they made a note of their movements and when the quality had left town for their country estates, they drove round in a smart carriage, systematically ransacked the house and trotted smartly away, with the swag concealed in a special compartment underneath the seat.

Burglars, like buzzers, generally served an apprenticeship. A promising lad would enter the trade early in life as a snakesman, slipping through the narrowest of windows to steal or unfasten the doors for his masters. Agile young chimney sweeps were particularly favoured, and the most famous 'climbing boy' was a lad called Henry Williams, who managed to escape from the Press Yard of Newgate in 1836 after being sentenced to death for burglary. Although the fifty-foot-high walls, topped with *chevaux de frise* (fearsome curved spikes), made escape well-nigh impossible, Williams, a former chimney sweep, managed to scale the wall behind the water cistern in the corner of the Press Yard. He achieved this extraordinary feat by removing his boots, pressing his back against one wall and bracing his bare feet against the opposite wall, clawing his way up with his hands and toes. Eventually, he was at a level with the water cistern, and managed to clamber on top of it and drag himself along the wall, dangling from the spikes. From there, Williams leapt nine feet onto a nearby rooftop and emerged into an adjacent property, dazed and bleeding. When Williams staggered in, he pleaded with the horrified residents to let him go, and they agreed not to raise the alarm. The tide of public opinion was turning against hanging people for burglary, and Williams disappeared into the streets surrounding the gaol.[15]

The Victorians were great innovators, quick to take advantage of all the latest developments, and Victorian criminals proved no different. The Victorian robber was no longer the flamboyant highwayman, mounted on his 'Black Bess' with a brace of pistols in his belt. Instead of ambushing stagecoaches, he robbed the express trains, despite the fact that these iron horses sped through the countryside at sixty miles an hour. This is how the Great Victorian Train Robbery was accomplished, when £12,000-worth of gold bullion (£809,417 at today's prices) was stolen from a moving train. For sheer planning and audacity, this was one of the crimes of the century.[16]

Around the time of the Crimean War (1853–6), numerous shipments of gold were sent from London to Paris for the British army. This was a regular enough occurrence to catch the attention of criminal gangs, such as the one led by a man called Edward Pierce who had a criminal record and had worked in a betting shop. Pierce teamed up with William Tester, a clerk from the traffic department of South Eastern Railways, and Robert Agar, a skilled safecracker. The gang doubtless had other accomplices who may not have been fully aware of the extent of the plan.

The gold bullion was packed in sealed iron-bound boxes which were placed inside steel safes. They were then loaded onto the passenger train from London to Folkestone. At Folkestone harbour they were transferred to the Boulogne steam packet. The railway officials clearly believed that the heavy modern safes constituted security enough. The consignments travelled in the guard's van along with other luggage, and the guard did not leave the van once the train was moving. The safes had heavy double locks that required two keys to open them; and there were two sets of keys, one held by the traffic superintendent in London, the other at Folkestone.

The robbery took over a year of planning. First, the gang needed an insider, in the form of a guard called Burgess, who sometimes worked on this route. They also needed duplicates of the two sets of keys. This was made more difficult by the fact that the keys were not kept together, and the regulations in the London office were strict. The gang's chance came when the safes were temporarily withdrawn and sent to the manufacturer, Chubb, for a service. Tester, the traffic clerk from South Eastern Railways, managed to get hold of one key for long enough for Agar to take a wax impression.

Meanwhile, Pierce had been keeping the traffic department at Folkestone under surveillance. His opportunity came when the office was briefly empty and he slipped in, found the second key in an unlocked cupboard, stole it, took it to Agar to take an impression and returned it to its rightful place without anybody noticing.

The safes had finely tuned mechanisms, and it was unlikely that they could be opened with crudely copied keys. However, the gang soon found a loophole. Passengers were permitted to travel in the guard's van if they were looking after a valuable item – a painting, perhaps, or an animal. Burgess, the guard who had been bribed to participate in the plot, allowed Agar to accompany him when he was carrying a consignment of bullion. This gave Agar the opportunity to try out his keys on the safes, tinkering with them until they worked perfectly. The time had come.

On 15 May 1855, Agar and Pierce travelled first class to Folkestone, equipped with a number of bags. If these bags seemed particularly heavy when the porters heaved them into the first-class compartment, it was because they were full of small-shot, sewn into the linings. Pierce took a seat but Agar waited until the train was moving and climbed into the guard's van. Burgess was on board, along with three safes. Agar unlocked the first safe, opened a bullion box, removed the gold and substituted lead shot. He refastened the box, locked the safe, and put the gold in his bag. As the train arrived at Redhill station, Tester appeared and collected the bag containing the gold, while Pierce joined Agar in the guard's van. During the rest of the journey, the men plundered the other two safes, removed the contents, substituted the lead and locked the safes. When the train arrived at Folkestone and the safes were being unloaded, they hid at the back of the van. Once the coast was clear, they got off the train and headed for Dover. They had already obtained tickets for the Dover–Ostend crossing and passed themselves off as travellers from the Continent.

The robbery did not come to light until the safes arrived in France. Alerted by a discrepancy in the weight of the safes, the authorities opened the safes and found that they were filled not with gold but with lead. This dramatic discovery made sensational newspaper headlines as the authorities assumed that the robbery had taken place at source, and the men who had packed the gold must be the culprits. It took eighteen months of bungled arrests and fruitless inquiries before the police got a lead, and this was purely by chance, when Agar was arrested for forging a cheque and imprisoned in Newgate. Agar had a child with his mistress, and wanted to give her some of the proceeds of the robbery. Pierce, who was in charge of the gold, was reluctant, either because he wanted to cheat Agar or did not want the woman to know about the money. But Agar's mistress had some knowledge of the robbery and once she found out that Pierce would not let her have the money, she turned Queen's Evidence. Agar, who was awaiting transportation, did the same. Pierce, Tester and Burgess were arrested and sentenced to long prison terms. Despite an almost faultless plan, the robbers had fallen prey to that most unpredictable factor, human nature. Even if Agar's desire to do the decent thing by his mistress and provide for his child had not given the game away, the woman's anger at Pierce's greed had been the final straw.

For those who were apprehended, arrested, tried and convicted, conditions in gaol remained as variable as ever. Wealthy and influential prisoners could still bribe their keepers with a little 'garnish', ensuring soft treatment. When Captain George Chesterton became governor of Cold Bath Fields prison in Islington in 1829, he was appalled to discover that as well as deriving a handsome secondary income from the sale of liquor, tobacco and food, the gaolers also rented out rooms in the attic on weekday afternoons where male and female prisoners could enjoy sexual congress.[17] The sneaking suspicion that conditions in gaol were cushy for many professional criminals is demonstrated in this extract from *Punch* magazine, where 'Toby Cracksman' writes to 'Bill Sikes' from Newgate, reassuring him that the old 'stone-jug' (prison):

> Is still the same snug, free-and-easy old hole,
> Where MACHEATH met his *blowens* [whores] and
>   WYLDE floor'd his bowl.
> In a ward with one's *pals*, not locked up in a cell,
> To an old hand like me it's a *fam'ly-hotel*.

This poem satirically promotes the popular misconception of Newgate as a villains' paradise, where the warders do as they are instructed, and at 'darkmans' (night-time) the prisoners run the place as they please. The poem concludes with a hearty prayer that:

> Long over Newgit their Worships may rule,
> As the *High-toby, mob, crack and screeve* [forgers] model-
>   school;
> For if Guv'ment was here, not the Aldermen's Bench,
> Newgit soon' 'ud be bad as '*the Pent*' or '*the Tench*'.[18]

The 'Pent' and the 'Tench' are references to Pentonville prison (opened 1842) and the Millbank Penitentiary (1816), which were among the first truly modern prisons. As a result of the work of the reformer John Howard, the political philosopher Jeremy Bentham and the philanthropist Elizabeth Fry, the legislature had come to understand that it was no longer acceptable to lock offenders up and throw away the key. Instead, the new wave of prison buildings were designed to provide the opportunity for repentance, sober reflection and the acquisition of a legitimate trade to equip former prisoners for life on the outside. Or such was the intention. Despite the recognition of the need for reform, progress was slow, with the penal system remaining a random hotchpotch of institutions with little coherent policy over the successive decades.

The beginning of an improvement in prison conditions owes much to the pioneering approach of John Howard (1726–90). Appointed High Sheriff of Bedfordshire in 1773, Howard was appalled by the conditions under which prisoners were held at Bedford Assizes, and horrified to discover that gaolers derived their only income from 'garnish'. A frail but determined man, driven by his Calvinist faith and reforming zeal, Howard undertook an inspection of the nation's prisons, at a risk to his own health. During this thankless task, he wrote, the disgusting reek of prison effluvia clung to his clothes. Howard stank so much after one prison visit that he had to abandon travelling by coach, even with the windows down, and took to travelling on horseback instead. [19] The pages of his notebook reeked to such an extent that he could not read them straight away but had to fumigate the book for an hour or two first, by placing it in front of the fire.[20] In 1777, prompted by 'the sorrows of the sufferers, and love of my country', Howard published *The State of the Prisons in England and Wales,* which incited outrage among philanthropists and reformers and marked the beginnings of the penal reform movement with which his name is still associated. Among Howard's most far-sighted recommendations were separate wings for younger prisoners, to prevent them mixing with hardened criminals in an 'academy of crime', separate quarters for female prisoners, an apothecary and a prison infirmary.[21] These improvements were gradually introduced over the following decades, but life in gaol was harsh for the majority, many of whom remained at the mercy of sadistic governors and warders who compelled them to perform strenuous and ultimately pointless tasks designed to crush mind, body and spirit.

When Millbank Prison or the 'National Penitentiary' opened in 1821, it was the biggest prison in England. Initially, Millbank was intended to hold all those prisoners who had been sentenced to transportation as they awaited their passage to the penal colonies of the New World. Built on a marshy site on the north bank of the Thames, Millbank or 'the Tench' was a unique structure, inspired by the theories of the Utilitarian philosopher Jeremy Bentham (1748–1832). Bentham had devised a 'Panopticon' or 'Inspection House' for prisoners in 1791, derived from a concept by his brother, the naval architect Samuel Bentham. The fundamental principle behind the Panopticon was that the prisoner was forever under surveillance but would see nothing of his watcher, or his fellow inmates. The original Panopticon consisted of a circular building, with the prisoners' cells side-by-side all round the circumference. The inspector's lodge was positioned at the centre. The cells were so completely divided from each other that no prisoner could see or communicate with his neighbours. Each cell had a window in its outer wall and in place of a fourth wall was a large iron grille containing a door. The lighting was to be arranged so that the inspector could watch all the prisoners from his lodge, but remain invisible to them.

The 'invisible omniscience' of the warder represented a method of obtaining control over prisoners' minds. Conscious that they were continually being watched, the prisoners had no option but to obey. The sensation of being under observation rendered manacles unnecessary, and any attempt at riot or a gaolbreak became impossible because the prisoners were so isolated. Bentham's theory was essentially the first example of what the French philosopher Michel Foucault later defined as 'social surveillance', the concept that by being watched, or suspecting that they were being watched, prisoners were frightened into compliance, and reluctant to reoffend.[22]

The original Panopticon never left the drawing board. Much to Bentham's disgust, his plans were eventually discarded in favour of a design by Robert Smirke. While Smirke's design was slightly different from Bentham's, taking the form of a six-pointed star with the chapel at its centre and each of its six separate radiating wings being three storeys high, Bentham's central premise remained. Each of the 1,000 cells contained a water closet, a hand basin, a hammock and a loom. On arrival, the prisoners were shut up alone for the first five days to reflect on their situation. Thereafter, they had to spend the first six months of their sentence alone in their cells, where they worked at tasks such as picking oakum. The prisoner was presented with a quantity of old rope cut into lengths, each of which had to be unravelled down to its thinnest strands. At the end of the day, the pile of rope was collected by a warder and weighed; if it did not reach the target weight prescribed by the prison governor, the prisoner was disciplined.[23]

Sundays were devoted to worship and meditation. Disciplinary offences were punished by a spell in a 'refractory cell' or 'solitary' for hours or even days at a time. According to one warder, this was a dreadful experience. 'It's impossible to describe the darkness; it's pitch black; no dungeon was ever so dark.'[24] The environment at Millbank was dreadful in another way, too. Located on the marshy banks of the Thames, it became a breeding ground for regular outbreaks of cholera.

From Millbank, male convicts progressed to Pentonville or the prison ships known as 'the hulks', decommissioned warships moored in the Thames and used as floating prisons. The first hulk was the *Justicia*, anchored in the Thames off Greenwich in 1776. By 1841, there were nine hulks holding 3,500 convicts moored in the Thames and at Plymouth,

Portsmouth, Sheerness, Chatham Bermuda and Gibraltar. Conditions were appalling, with prisoners suffering scurvy, typhus or dysentery and frequent outbreaks of cholera. Writing in 1841, one commentator said that the shirts of the prisoners, hung out on the rigging, were so black with vermin that the linen appeared to have been sprinkled over with pepper.[25]

Convicts went on shore to work at 'hard labour', breaking stones and cleaning sewers. Many convicts worked on the construction of the new London docks.[26] When Pentonville or 'the Pent' opened in 1842, Millbank became an ordinary prison and increased its capacity to about 1,500 prisoners, who shared their cells. Inmates were only held for a few months before their transfer to other prisons, so around 4,000 to 5,000 passed through its gates every year. It became a military prison in 1870 and closed in 1890.

Pentonville, which still operates as a prison, opened on Caledonian Road, Islington, in 1842, and was originally designed to hold convicts prior to transportation. In the course of researching their book on prisons, Henry Mayhew and his colleague John Binny watched a party of prisoners arriving at Pentonville from Millbank in 1862:

> The miserable wretches were chained together by the wrists in lines. Some were habited in the ordinary light, snuff-brown convict suits, and others wore grey jackets, all having Scotch caps and small bundles of Bibles and hymn-books tied in handkerchiefs under their arms. Jackets, trousers, caps and grey stocking were all marked with red stripes.[27]

Pentonville had been designed as a 'convict academy' where specially selected prisoners would undergo a period of moral instruction before transportation; they would also learn a trade that would provide them with a livelihood in exile once

Exercise yard at Pentonville, 1840. Note the prisoners' hoods and masks, designed to humiliate and break the spirit.

they had completed their sentence. The regime was a notoriously harsh one. Anonymity was imposed, and the prisoner was addressed only by the number of his cell, which was displayed on a brass badge pinned to his chest. Whenever he left his cell, he was required to wear a brown cloth cap with a mask that completely covered his face. One visitor to Pentonville remarked on the prisoners' eerie appearance:

> For the eyes glistening through the apertures in the mask give the notion of a spirit peeping out from behind it, so that there is something positively terrible in the idea that these are men whose crimes have caused their features to be hidden from the world.[28]

Mayhew and Binny described the gaol as 'a kind of penal purgatory where men are submitted to the chastisement of separate confinement so as to fit them for the afterstate'.[29]

To enforce discipline and prepare them for manual work in the colonies, prisoners were subjected to a regime of hard labour. In theory, hard labour served to train the flabby and feckless into a useful workforce. In practice, many of the tasks that the prisoners performed were backbreaking and soul-destroying, such as the treadmill, the crank and the shot drill.

The treadmill consisted of a large cylinder with steps on the outside. As prisoners stepped onto it, the treadmill would begin to turn and the prisoner would have to climb onto the next step, then continue climbing in order to remain upright. Sessions lasted three or four hours a day, with over 340 prisoners on the treadmills at one time, and although the treadmills were lined up side by side, prisoners were forbidden to talk to each other. Caroline Fox, a reformer who visited Coldbath Fields in 1842, observed the female prisoners on the treadmills and wrote that 'it was sad to see the poor

The treadmill at Coldbath Fields, c. 1870. An exercise in futility with prisoners toiling forever upwards, forbidden to speak to each other.

exhausted women ever toiling upward without a chance of progress'.[30]

Another meaningless task consisted of 'the crank', which a prisoner could use alone in his or her cell. This consisted of a narrow drum, placed on legs, with a long handle on one side, which on being turned caused a series of cups or scoops in the interior to revolve. At the lower part of the interior of the machine was a thick layer of sand, which the cups, as they came round, scooped up and carried to the top of the wheel, where they upturned and emptied themselves, along the same principle as a dredging machine. A dial-plate, fixed in front of the iron drum, showed how many revolutions the machine had made. This tedious task was known among inmates as 'grinding the wind'.[31]

Perhaps most soul-destroying of all was shot-drill, compulsory for all male prisoners who were not excused on medical grounds. After watching a session of shot-drill, Henry Mayhew declared that 'it was impossible to imagine anything more ingeniously useless than this form of hard labour'. Shot drill took place in the open, with the prisoners ranged on three sides of the exercise yard with the warder at the centre. At one end of the line of prisoners a number of cannon balls were piled into a pyramid. When the warder gave the command, the three men closest to the pyramid each picked up a cannon ball and placed it on the ground at their feet. On another word of command, they lifted the balls and passed them to the men alongside, who in their turn placed the balls at their own feet. The process was repeated, with the balls passing down the ranks in continuous succession, until they were eventually built up into another pyramid by the men in the last three lines. When all the cannon balls had been stacked in their new position, the operation was reversed and began all over again. The sessions lasted for over an hour every afternoon, and by the end of it the men were visibly distressed.[32]

Despite being subjected to these sadistic regimes, the prisoners continued to defy the silent system and insisted on communicating with one another even while being punished. In 1836, prison inspectors at Coldbath Fields recorded no less than 5,138 punishments for talking and swearing, with prisoners talking even when engaged on the treadmills. Despite the fact that 'turnkeys' or warders were stationed at each treadmill, the prisoners constantly spoke to each other; if reprimanded, they resorted to a form of sign language, indicating with their fingers what crime they had committed, and how long they were in for. Ever resourceful, prisoners succeeded in communicating through the wink of an eye, a cough, or a sneeze.[33] Mayhew and Binny, in the course of their investigations, observed that the silent system was ultimately doomed, since the convicts who had been subjected to the discipline of Millbank and Pentonville were then sent to the hulks, where they were brought into contact with offenders who had undergone no discipline whatsoever. 'All the care which has been taken at Pentonville and at Millbank to prevent the men talking together, and associating with one another, is thrown away.'[34] The silent system was eventually abandoned in 1854.

Toby Cracksman's 'Newgit' continued to occupy its minatory position in London's underworld well into the Victorian era. With its fortress-like appearance, *chevaux de frise* and high walls, Newgate had become London's high-security prison, generally used to hold prisoners awaiting trial at the Old Bailey. Thanks to the reforms led by the Quaker philanthropist Elizabeth Fry (1780–1845), improved conditions meant that prisoners could now expect regular meals, clean cells, and a laundry. Female prisoners in particular benefitted from Fry's innovations, which included education, child welfare and a modest uniform with a cap and apron.

Nevertheless, Newgate could not shake off its vestigial air of melancholy. Mayhew and Binny noted that the women's cells were 'more gloomy and lonely in appearance than [those] in any other prison we have visited – partly caused by the overhanging clouds of smoke which loom over the City, and partly by the sombre lofty surrounding walls of the prison'.[35] The investigators watched a party of felons in the exercise yard, marching around in their own 'miserable, poverty-stricken attire', including one youth in shabby black, who was charged with attempted suicide, and a pale-faced, knock-kneed youth 'with a very sinister look' who was on a fraud charge. Mayhew ends his deliberations by observing that on the whole, 'most of the prisoners were ordinary-looking people, charged with common offences,' a timely reminder of the banal reality of criminal life for the majority of offenders.[36] Stripped of bravado and camaraderie, the bold denizens of the Victorian underworld were more like Edward, the failed burglar, than Bill Sikes.

Unlike his real-life counterparts, Oliver Twist the gonoph did not die upon the gallows. Instead, the foundling was traced by his long-lost aunt and adopted by a kindly old gentleman. Even the Dodger was spared, sentenced to transportation rather than hanging. Fagin, the kidsman, was not so fortunate, and his fate reflected the grim reality of the Victorian penal system. In his most compelling depiction of Newgate, Dickens described the scene when Oliver visited his old master in the condemned cell on the eve of his execution, and Fagin's last night of torment behind the 'dreadful walls of Newgate, which have hidden so much misery and such unspeakable anguish'.[37] The tiny condemned cell itself, just nine by six feet, had changed little since this description by John Howard in 1777:

The doors are four inches thick. The strong stone wall is lined all round each cell with planks studded with broad-headed nails. I was told by those who attended them, that criminals who had an air of boldness during their trial and appeared quite unconcerned at the pronouncing of sentence upon them, were struck with horror and shed tears when brought to these darksome, solitary abodes.

This is certainly the case with Fagin, who has gone out of his mind with despair. After a distressing encounter, Oliver and his guardian left the prison as preparations were being made for the old kidsman's execution. The space before the Debtors' Door had been cleared, and a few strong barriers, painted black, had already been thrown across the road to break the pressure of the expected crowd. There was the sound of men's voices, mingled with the noise of hammering and the throwing down of boards. They were building the scaffold. By the time Oliver and his guardian emerged, shaken, with Fagin's howls of anguish ringing in their ears, it was daybreak. A vast crowd had already assembled. Neighbouring windows were crammed with onlookers, smoking and playing cards to pass the time. The crowd was quarrelling, joking, pushing against the barriers. 'Everything told of life and animation but one dark cluster of objects in the centre of all – the black stage, the cross-beam, the rope, and all the hideous apparatus of death.'[38]

This 'hideous apparatus of death', and its many victims, will be the theme of the following chapter.

THE HIDEOUS
APPARATUS
OF DEATH

*Murder and Execution
in Victorian London*

Over the centuries, Tyburn gallows and Newgate Gaol had become two of the most sinister landmarks in the history of London and crime. With the removal of the gallows from Tyburn to Newgate in 1783, the execution ground and the prison had converged to form a single 'prototype of Hell'. With the Old Bailey standing guard alongside, Newgate reared above the stinking carcasses and filth of Smithfield Market in all its evil glory, striking fear and awe into everyone who saw it.

The smouldering shell of Newgate had been rebuilt in 1780, after the Gordon Riots. Designed in the Palladian style, the new prison cost £50,000 and was intended as a fitting companion to the Old Bailey, also recently rebuilt. Improved conditions included separate accommodation for debtors, male and female wings, a chapel and infirmary. However nothing could disguise the purpose for which this institution had been conceived, and the new prison, with its massive blank walls and entrances decorated with shackles, resembled nothing so much as a giant mausoleum. The old condemned cells had survived the fire, and the architect, George Dance (1741–1825), retained these. A subterranean passageway known as Birdcage Walk or Dead Man's Walk was constructed, through which prisoners were led from the condemned cells to the Press Yard. This dismal thoroughfare had been built over the burial ground, so that prisoners walked to their deaths over the mortal remains of previous inmates, whose corpses had been stripped naked and buried in lime. The walls of Dead Man's Walk told their own story, etched with the initials of former prisoners, the dark history of Newgate carved into the stones.

It was from Dead Man's Walk that the condemned prisoners made their way to the 'New Drop', the trapdoor method of execution first used in 1760 which had now become established as the most efficient way to ensure a quickly broken neck.[1] The gallows measured around eight to ten feet across, depending on the number of prisoners to be hanged, and the trapdoor was held in place by several levers which, when operated by hand, would draw back the bolts. In what was to become a familiar weekly ritual, the portable gallows was rolled out in front of the Debtors' Door of Newgate on Sunday evenings, in preparation for the Monday hanging day. With the scaffold draped in black cloth, and the bells of St Sepulchre's tolling solemnly throughout the execution, the sheriffs intended to create a sober, elegiac mood, a world away from the raucous Bacchanalia of Tyburn.

But, given the sensational nature of public executions, this was not the case. After the very first execution outside Newgate on 3 December 1783, when ten men were hanged, outraged householders were begging the sheriffs to reinstate the gallows at Tyburn. Executions outside their own front doors, in the middle of London, were too close for comfort, evoking the spirit of an earlier, brutal age.

One particular episode lingered in the collective memory: the burning to death of a woman for coining. In 1788, the execution of Phoebe Harris was attended by 'a great concourse of people'.[2] As Phoebe emerged from Newgate, she appeared 'languid and terrified, and trembled greatly as she advanced to the stake'. Phoebe was hanged for half an hour before two cart-loads of faggots were piled around her and lit. The fire was still smouldering four hours afterwards. A year later, Catherine Murphy proved to be the last victim of this barbaric practice, which was abolished in 1790.

As a method of execution, the New Drop was far from foolproof. In 1789, as William Skitch, a burglar, was being hanged, the rope broke and he fell through the trapdoor to the ground. Amid the consternation, Skitch cheekily turned to the crowd and commented: 'Good people, be not hurried. I can wait a little!'[3] Skitch had (quite literally) fallen foul of the prevailing practice, which was to measure the rope in accordance with the prisoner's height, and not his weight. Although Skitch's execution contained an element of black comedy, the fate of many other prisoners was grotesque. Once the noose had been placed around the prisoner's neck, only two inches or so of rope were left to suspend them over a three-foot drop. One development, ushered in by the sheriff, Peter Laurie, consisted of a scaffold beam with adjustable chains. This meant that the prisoner no longer had to go to the gallows with his rope wound around his waist. But even this refinement could not diminish what Laurie referred to as the 'barbarous feelings' of the execution procedure.[4] The combination of a short rope and a short drop meant that most prisoners died of asphyxiation due to the constriction of the windpipe, and were left to kick convulsively. It was not an easy way to die; the majority of prisoners would have been conscious, for a moment or two, that they were hanging, and further humiliation included the involuntary expulsion of urine and faeces, while men often experienced erection and ejaculation.

Relocating the gallows to Newgate did not improve crowd safety. In 1807, over 40,000 people turned out to watch the execution of John Holloway and Owen Haggerty, convicted of a murder which had been committed five years earlier. Their accomplice, Benjamin Hanfield, had turned King's Evidence in return for a pardon. Both men went to the gallows protesting their innocence. A pie stall collapsed and in the ensuing commotion, over thirty people were crushed to death, while around seventy were injured. Fearing for her baby's life, a young woman handed over her baby before being trampled, and the baby was tossed like a ball from hand to hand until it was in a safe position away from the crowd. 'This dreadful scene continued for some time,' declared the Annual Register. 'The shrieks of the dying men, women and children were terrific beyond description, and could only be equalled by the horror of the event.'[5]

Far from being the solemn spectacle that the authorities had intended, executions at Newgate swiftly proved as lurid as anything witnessed at Tyburn. Dr Johnson might have lamented the fact that the crowd had been deprived of a procession, but it could still enjoy the drama of a good hanging, particularly if an attractive young woman was involved. Such was the case of Eliza Fenning.

Eliza Fenning went on trial at the Old Bailey on 5 April 1815, charged with attempted murder.[6] Eliza had only been in service to Robert Turner and his family at 68 Chancery Lane for a few weeks when the incident took place. On the night of Tuesday, 21 March 1815, Robert Turner and his wife

Charlotte were joined for dinner by Mr Haldebart Turner, Robert's father. Upstairs, the family sat down to a dinner of beef stew with dumplings, while down in the kitchen Eliza and the other servants ate the same meal. Almost immediately the entire household, including Eliza, was seized with vomiting and excruciating pain. While the most likely cause was a bout of food poisoning, stemming from a combination of Eliza's inexperience and contaminated meat, Robert Turner had another theory. Claiming that a packet of arsenic, kept to control vermin, had recently disappeared from his desk, he accused Eliza of lacing the dumplings with arsenic in a bid to poison the entire family. This allegation was supported by the surgeon who was called out to the Turners later that night. When the surgeon, Mr John Marshall, gave evidence during Eliza's trial, he maintained that Mr Turner had shown him a dish in which the dumplings had been prepared. When tested, it contained traces of arsenic. This was the extent of the prosecution case.

Few individuals could afford to hire a barrister in those days, and Eliza was forced to conduct her own defence. Naïve and inexperienced, her only recourse was to plead her innocence; if there had been something wrong with the dumplings, she argued, then that fault lay with the ingredients. Eliza had been very happy in service at the Turners' house, and had no motive to kill them. She even provided four glowing character references, testifying to her good reputation. Unfortunately these references were undermined by Mrs Turner, who accused Eliza of having an affair with an apprentice, despite the fact that she was engaged to be married.

At this point, the Recorder, Sir John Silvester, might have intervened. Sir John, or 'Black Jack', was known to be a legendary lecher, who would demonstrate leniency towards pretty young defendants if they responded to his amorous advances.[7] Eliza did not, and when the jury returned a guilty verdict, he sentenced her to hang. Eliza collapsed in a fit of hysteria and had to be carried out screaming.

The following day there was a public outcry at the severity of Eliza's sentence and the demand that it be commutated to transportation. As Eliza languished in the condemned cell at Newgate, she was visited by William Hone (1780–1842), a radical author who was convinced of her innocence.[8] Hone swiftly became obsessed with Eliza and founded a newspaper, *The Traveller,* to campaign for her release. Hone even moved out of the family home into a shabby little room opposite the prison so that he could spend more time with Eliza, and wrote a book about the case that was to become a classic of investigative journalism. Demolishing the prosecution case against Eliza, Hone suggested that Robert Turner, a mentally unstable man who had frequently threatened suicide, had tried to murder his own family and placed the blame on Eliza when the attempt went wrong.

Young, pretty and ostensibly innocent, Eliza swiftly became a *cause célèbre,* her popularity boosted by an engraving of her reading the Bible in Newgate. This image, by Robert Cruickshank, emphasized her attractive face and full breasts, turning her into 'an icon of wronged womanhood'.[9] But it was all in vain. At eight o'clock on the morning of 26 July, Eliza was escorted from her cell and down Dead Man's Walk to the Press Yard, to face a crowd of 45,000 people. She wore the white muslin gown that had been laid aside for her wedding, a white muslin cap bound with a white satin ribbon, and pale lilac boots, laced in front. When the Ordinary, Reverend Cotton, asked if she had anything to say in her last moments, Eliza paused, then said: 'Before the just and Almighty God, and by the faith of the Holy Sacrament I have taken, I am innocent of the offence with which I am charged. My innocence will be manifested in the course of the day.' Maintaining her composure, Eliza mounted the scaffold. A scarf was placed over her face, and she began to pray fervently before Oldfield, the hangman, gave the signal to open the trapdoor. She moved once, and was cut down after an hour.

When Eliza's parents claimed the body, they had to pay her execution bill of 14 shillings and 6 pence.[10] Eliza's body went on display at her parents' home in Eagle Street, Red Lion Square, as was the custom after death. According to witnesses, she lay in her coffin as if in a sweet sleep and her body was not seen to change colour within three days of her execution. As the victim of a miscarriage of justice, Eliza had been elevated to the sainthood.

The process of beatification continued with Eliza's funeral procession on 31 July. With a coffin carried by six female pall-bearers dressed in white, a mounted escort and hundreds of mourners following the coffin, it became one of the most notable funeral processions of the nineteenth century. 'Many thousands accompanied the procession, and the windows, and even the tops of the houses, as it passed were thronged with spectators. The whole proceeded in a regular manner until it reached the burying-ground of St George the Martyr. The number of persons assembled in and about the churchyard was estimated at ten thousand.'[11] Eliza's funeral was followed by riots that night, and several nights after; and an angry mob attacked the Turners' house in Chancery Lane.

Charles Dickens, who was to become a notable campaigner against capital punishment, had his own theory surrounding events at the Turner residence. Dickens argued that the apprentice had poisoned the family, after falling out with Eliza, and that he was 'more convinced of anything in my life' that Eliza was innocent.[12]

The outrage sparked by Eliza Fenning's death marked the beginning of a growing unease with public execution and even with capital punishment itself. Further misgivings emerged after the peculiarly unpleasant hanging of Charles

White outside Newgate in 1823. White, a bookseller, had torched his shop when bankruptcy threatened in order to claim the insurance. As arson constituted a capital offence, he was sentenced to hang. The night before his execution, White made several attempts to kill himself, and on the gallows he lashed out at the executioner, John Foxon, kicking him and struggling to free himself from his ropes. The hood covering White's face became loose and, seeing the chance of freedom, White hurled himself forward as the trapdoor flew open and balanced precariously on the edge. As the crowd roared its approval, White struggled with Foxon until the executioner eventually hurled him through the trapdoor, and two assistants dragged at his legs. White's face as he died would have been visible for all to see, the livid, swollen face with its contorted features and distended tongue, the eyes swollen and popping out of their cavities, the bloody froth or mucus seeping out of the mouth and nostrils.[13]

When John Foxon died in 1829, William Calcraft was appointed Executioner to the City of London at the rate of a guinea a week, plus another guinea for each execution he performed. Calcraft had previously been employed to flog juvenile offenders, but after being required to conduct a hanging at Lincoln in an emergency he had found his vocation, and was also retained at Horsemonger Gaol at the rate of another guinea a week. Described as a 'mild-mannered man of simple tastes, much given to angling in the New River', Calcraft was also fond of breeding rabbits.[14] But he hanged people like dogs and enjoyed entertaining the crowds with his antics, which included leaping onto the back of the prisoner as he fell through the trapdoor or disappearing into the pit beneath the gallows to pull on the prisoner's legs.

In 1831 Calcraft officiated at the hanging of John Bishop and Thomas Head, who went to the gallows after confessing to suffocating an Italian boy, intending to sell his cadaver to the surgeons for anatomy practice. The 'Italian' boy, who actually came from Lincolnshire, was one of three victims; the other two being another boy and an elderly woman. Bishop and Head's technique consisted of rendering their victims unconscious with laudanum and rum and then drowning them in the well behind Bishop's house, by lowering them down head first with a rope tied to their feet. The pair were nicknamed 'the Burkers' after William Burke and William Hare, the notorious murderers who scandalized Scottish society by intoxicating and smothering seventeen victims in Edinburgh in 1827–8, in order to sell the corpses for dissection at the University.

Outraged by 'the Burkers'' crime, a huge and angry crowd turned out to watch these child killers being executed, and despite the efforts of the New Police, barriers were broken down and three people trampled to death as the mob surged forward, intent on tearing Bishop and Head limb from limb.

A shocking murder and a sensational trial were guaranteed to draw a massive crowd outside Newgate. One of the largest ever assembled, numbering over 100,000 people, converged on Newgate for the hanging of James Greenacre on 2 May 1837. The newspapers, which fed a grisly fascination with murder, had dubbed this crime 'the Edgware Road Murder', and the mystery had begun months earlier, on 28 December 1836.

On that cold, blustery morning, George Bond, a bricklayer, had been walking to work when he passed Canterbury Villas, a newly completed terrace just off Edgware Road. Intrigued to see a flagstone propped up against one of the walls with a large bundle tucked away underneath it, Bond rolled away the flagstone to discover that a pool of frozen blood had congealed around the object. Bond called his gaffer and a workmate and together they unwrapped the package, which contained the headless torso of a woman, about fifty years of age. The head had been crudely severed from the trunk, with the neck having been partly sawn through and partly broken off; and the legs had been chopped off in a similar way. An inquest was held on Saturday 31 December, at the White Lion Inn, Edgware Road, when the jury returned a verdict of 'Wilful murder against some person or persons unknown' and the body was buried.

On 6 January 1837, the lock-keeper was summoned to the Ben Jonson Lock on the Regent's Canal in Stepney. One of the lock gates was blocked and would not open properly. The reason soon became evident. The lock gate was blocked by a woman's head. The headless torso was exhumed and Mr Girdwood, the local surgeon, confirmed that the head and the torso were part of the same body. But the corpse had yet to be identified, and there were no clues as to the murderer. Girdwood accordingly preserved the head in medical alcohol and retained it for further examination.

Meanwhile, the mystery surrounding the case grew deeper every day. Police enquiries met with no success until 2 February, when James Page, a labourer, was cutting osiers in Mr Tenpenny's reed bed off Coldharbour Lane, between Camberwell and Brixton. As he stepped over a ditch, Page spotted a large bundle partly immersed in the water. When he picked the bundle up, the toes of a human foot emerged from the end. Shocked, Page shouted for his workmates, and when they opened the package they found it contained a pair of human legs. When the legs were examined by Mr Girdwood, they proved to be part of the same body which had been discovered in the Edgware Road. The sack, which had originally belonged to a potato merchant and still had his name on it, was traced to a Mr Greenacre, of Kennington.

On 20 March, a Mr Gay of Goodge Street requested permission to view the remains. Mr Gay, a stockbroker, was concerned about the disappearance of his sister, Hannah Brown, who had left home on Christmas Eve and had never been seen again. As soon as he laid eyes on the preserved head, Mr Gay confirmed that it was indeed the head of the unfortunate Miss Brown. Mr Gay told the police that Hannah had announced that she was engaged and left her lodgings near Middlesex Hospital on Christmas Eve, to prepare for her impending nuptials the following Monday. Hannah's 'intended' lived in Camberwell, and his name was James Greenacre.

Marylebone Police Office immediately issued a warrant for Greenacre's arrest, and on 24 March 1837, Inspector Feltham and a police constable from L division raided Greenacre's small house at St Alban's Place, Kennington Road, where they found Greenacre in bed with his common-law wife, Sarah Gale. At first Greenacre denied all knowledge of Hannah Brown but then admitted that he had been planning to marry her, and that she had disappeared the night before the wedding. Once the couple had got dressed, Greenacre commented that the police were lucky to have come that night, since they were sailing for America in the morning. The number of trunks and suitcases, packed and labelled, seemed to bear this out. But an examination of the contents revealed important evidence. Many of the items in the trunks belonged to Hannah Brown; but alongside these, the police discovered the remains of an old cotton dress that exactly matched the pieces of fabric the body had been wrapped in when it was first discovered off Edgware Road.

On 10 April 1837 Greenacre and Gale went on trial at the Old Bailey. The courtroom was packed. Greenacre was charged with wilful murder while Gale was accused of being an accessory after the fact, consorting, aiding and assisting her fellow prisoner. In the course of the proceedings, Greenacre was unmasked as a bigamist who had been married at least four times. His victims had been wealthy older women and he had helped himself to their fortunes, a simple task in the days before the Married Women's Property Act of 1839.

In his desire to absolve Sarah Gale of all blame for the murder, Greenacre claimed that, during a quarrel, Hannah had fallen off her chair and died as a result of hitting her head on the floor. Rather than try to explain her accidental death, Greenacre admitted that he had dismembered the corpse and disposed of the body. Although Greenacre's account of events was sketchy, it appeared that he had travelled by omnibus from Camberwell to Mile End carrying Hannah's head in his lap, wrapped in a cotton handkerchief. Returning home, he took the legs down to the reed bed at five o'clock the following morning, and finally set out to dispose of the torso. It was too heavy to carry, so he placed it on a carrier's cart and walked alongside it until they reached Elephant and Castle. When a passer-by asked what was in the sack, Greenacre became nervous, and completed the journey with his grisly bundle by cab to Edgware Road.

Greenacre's defence that Hannah had died accidentally was smashed to pieces by the prosecution. It was pointed out that Hannah had been killed by a blow to the head with a stick, and that the force of the blow had been so severe that it had put her eye out. Greenacre then admitted that he had accidentally swung round with a silk-weaving roller, which had hit her. It took the jury just fifteen minutes to reach a guilty verdict. Greenacre was sentenced to death, while Sarah Gale was ordered to be transported for the rest of her natural life.[15]

The sensational details of Greenacre's crime guaranteed the massive crowd at Newgate, which gathered the night before his execution. In addition to the usual hanging-fair attractions of pies and prostitutes, rooms with a view of the gallows went on hire for £12 a time. A boy was almost crushed to death, and only survived because he was snatched up and passed over the heads of the crowd.[16]

Greenacre protested his innocence to the end. In a letter to his children, he warned them to profit by his example and never to panic if they were present at fatal accidents, which, it seemed, ran in the family, such as the incident when their uncle had apparently killed their grandmother, and 'shot off your Aunt Mary's hand!' Greenacre brusquely brushed off the Ordinary who wanted to pray with him before he died, but when it came to mounting the scaffold, 'he was totally unmanned'; his bravado had deserted him and, unable to speak, he had to be supported up the steps, otherwise he would have fallen over.[17] As he stumbled towards the gallows, Greenacre's appearance was greeted with a storm of hisses and boos, and cheers that could be heard several streets away as he dropped to his death. The *Weekly Chronicle* for 7 May 1837 described the strange, celebratory spectacle thus:

> As the body hung quivering in mortal agonies, the eyes of the assembled thousands were riveted upon the swaying corpse with a kind of satisfaction . . . the crowd seemed as if they never could satisfy themselves with gazing at the hanging murderer. The women were, if possible, more ruthless than the men.[18]

While the crowds seemed to enjoy such outrageous spectacles as never before, opposition to public executions was growing, fuelled by reformers and polemicists. In 1840, Charles Dickens invited his friend William Thackeray to witness the hanging of François Courvoisier outside Newgate. Dickens was then a journalist, and saw Thackeray, a barrister as well as a fellow writer, as a possible recruit to the abolitionist cause. Courvoisier had been sentenced to death for killing his master, Lord William Russell, motivated apparently by robbery.

The gallows might have been moved from Tyburn to Newgate but the crowd had not changed. Around 600 people crammed into the narrow street between the gaol and St Sepulchre's. Entire families had arrived, with picnic hampers, for a day out, eager to spot the celebrities, the actresses, statesmen and aristocrats who had paid upwards of £10 for a good spot on a balcony or at a window. Among the day-trippers, drunks and prostitutes, Dickens did not see 'one token in all the immense crowd of any one emotion suitable to the occasion; nothing but ribaldry, levity, drunkenness and flaunting vice in fifty other shapes'.[19]

As Courvoisier mounted the gallows, Thackeray observed that the condemned man 'turned his head here and there and looked about him for a while with a wild, imploring look. His mouth was contracted into a sort of pitiful smile.' The writer found himself unable to forget the troubling scene:

> For the last fourteen days, so salutary has the impression of this butchery been upon me, I have had the man's face continually before my eyes; I can see Mr Ketch [William Calcraft] at this moment, with an easy air, taking his rope from his pocket; I feel myself shamed and degraded at the brutal curiosity that took me to that brutal sight ... I have been abetting an act of frightful wickedness and violence and I pray that it may soon be out of the power of any man in England to witness such a hideous and degrading sight.[20]

It was to be another eighteen years before Thackeray's prayers were answered and capital punishment was hidden from the vulgar gaze, locked away behind the walls of Newgate in an execution shed.

Meanwhile, the gallows failed to act as a deterrent to London's criminals. As the capital was shaken by a succession of gruesome murders, it was becoming evident that the police required a dedicated team of professional detectives to run the perpetrators to ground. Whilst surviving members of the Bow

Street Runners had acted in this capacity up until 1839, taking on cases for anyone who would pay their expenses, the 'New Police' had no organized criminal investigation department. The need for such a body of men was thrown starkly into focus by the case of Daniel Good in April 1842.

On 11 April 1842, PC William Gardner was called to investigate the theft of a pair of trousers from a pawnbroker's shop in Wandsworth High Street. The suspect was Daniel Good, who worked as a coachman in Roehampton. PC Gardner went to Good's employer's house, arrested him, and began a thorough search of the premises. When they reached the stables, Good threw himself against the stable door and refused to let anyone inside. A neighbour was summoned to stand guard over Good, while PC Gardner searched the stable. Lifting his lantern, PC Gardner saw what appeared to be a plucked goose stashed behind a bale of hay. And then, with an exclamation of 'My God!' he realized that it was the body of a woman.

Meanwhile, Good seized his opportunity, locking the policeman and the neighbour in the stable and making his escape. It was fifteen minutes before they were released, and the police could do no more than track Good's footprints across the field towards Putney. After this, the trail went cold.

A surgeon's assistant was summoned who confirmed that the body was that of a pregnant woman in her mid-twenties, and that she had been dismembered with a sharp saw. A horrible smell drew them to the tack room, where they found the charred remains of her head and limbs, and an axe and saw stained with blood. Further enquiries revealed that the body was that of Jane Jones, Good's estranged wife. Good had a reputation as a ladies' man who had enjoyed a string of affairs. He was currently engaged to a young woman named Susan Butcher who lived in Woolwich. It was four hours or so before Good's details were circulated.

Over the next few days, nine divisions of the Metropolitan Police became involved in the chase for Daniel Good. In the days before telephones, the Metropolitan Police operated a system of 'route papers' which consisted of officers from neighbouring divisions meeting at pre-arranged points and exchanging messages and papers for other parts of London. Good always seemed to be a day or so ahead of the pursuing police, and this was reported in great detail by a critical press. Good was at large after having been arrested; there was a hue and cry all over the country and the very people who had been vociferous in opposing the establishment of the police were now accusing them of inefficiency. And yet, despite the defective communication system of the time, the police did their best.

D Division, for instance, learnt that Good had a ten-year-old son who lived with his aunt, Molly Good, off Manchester Square, but when they called in the afternoon, their suspect had left an hour or so earlier. A cab driver came forward to say that he had driven Good to Manchester Square and commented on his fare's nervousness and pallor. Good had merely retorted that he was recovering from a heavy drinking session the night before. It later emerged that Good returned to his wife's lodgings, told her landlady that Jane had been offered a job in Roehampton, and sold her mangle and bedding. Some of her clothes, which she had worn on the day of her murder, he gave to his fiancée, Susan Butcher.

Inspector Nicholas Pearce, assisted by Sergeant Stephen Thornton, both of whom were later to be among the original select band of six officers appointed for detective duties, took up the case and followed Good's trail from Spitalfields to Deptford, and then to Bromley where they could find no other clues. Two weeks later, Good was traced to Tonbridge where he was working as a bricklayer's labourer. One of his work mates, Thomas Rose, was a former police officer who recognized him and told the local police. Good was arrested and denied his identity, until it was observed that he had combed his hair over the bald spot which might have helped distinguish him.

Eventually, Good admitted his identity, but then claimed that his estranged wife had killed herself and a friend had recommended that he conceal the body. However, medical evidence quite clearly demonstrated that Jane Good had not cut her own throat. Good protested his innocence to the end, although he did break down in the dock when his own son entered the witness box to testify against him. Good was found guilty of murder and was hanged at Newgate on 23 May 1842, unaware that he had unwittingly contributed to the Metropolitan Police improving their crime-fighting performance by introducing specialist detectives.

A few days after Good's execution it was announced that a Criminal Investigation Department consisting of two inspectors and six sergeants would be attached to Scotland Yard for the investigation of crimes committed in the Metropolitan area. At first, because these officers were not specialists, the CID was not particularly successful. However, as public servants rather than private detectives, the CID team could investigate crimes straight away, rather than waiting for their expenses to be guaranteed.[21] Although slow to gather momentum, the formation of such a team was to be vindicated seven years later in the case of 'the Bermondsey Horror', when new methods secured the arrest and conviction of Frederick and Maria Manning.

Born Maria de Roux in 1821, Maria Manning was a handsome, raven-haired but somewhat plump young woman who arrived in London in 1846, as maid to Lady Blantyre, daughter of the Duchess of Sutherland. Shallow and materialistic, Maria was enraptured by her glamorous new surroundings and swiftly came to feel at home among the trappings of wealth. So much so that soon being a lady's maid was not enough for her. Maria wanted to be a lady herself. For this, she required a rich husband, and at first Patrick O'Connor, a customs officer at London docks, seemed to fit the bill. True, O'Connor was fifty years old and with a weakness for drink, but he also had substantial savings.

However, O'Connor had competition in the form of Frederick Manning, a railway guard on the Great Western. Frederick was poor, but handsome, and he told Maria that he expected to inherit a small fortune. Maria and Frederick were married at St James's, Piccadilly, a fashionable West End church, in May 1847, and the couple moved to a house in Minerva Place, Bermondsey. Within weeks, Maria's dreams of a life of leisure were dashed. The money was running out, and she discovered that Frederick had been lying about his promised inheritance. After an abortive attempt at running a pub in Taunton, the pair returned to London and Maria picked up her relationship with O'Connor, visiting his lodgings in the Mile End Road. Frederick, still smitten with Maria, condoned the affair, as he realized that the wealthy O'Connor represented the solution to all their problems.

On the evening of 7 August 1849, the Mannings invited O'Connor to dine at Minerva Place. O'Connor duly arrived, with some misgivings; he was a hypochondriac and the cholera outbreak in Bermondsey made him reluctant to visit. But Maria plied her lover with brandy, assuring him that the spirit provided great protection against infection. Under the influence of drink, O'Connor was persuaded to sign away a number of railway shares to the couple. The Mannings might have achieved more had it not been for the presence of a Mr Walsh, visiting their lodger. As it was, Frederick Manning escorted O'Connor safely home. Flushed with excitement, Maria realized that the dream was within her grasp. The following day, she invited O'Connor round again, teasing him with the suggestion that they would have dinner *à deux*. On the way home, she purchased some quicklime and a shovel, and dug a grave under the kitchen floor.

That night, when O'Connor arrived at Minerva Place, Maria suggested that he might like to smarten himself up, as the lodger was expecting his sister to call. She led him down to the basement kitchen, and as he bent over the sink, reached up and stretched her arm affectionately around his neck. As O'Connor turned to reciprocate, she shot him in the head with a pistol. But the wound was not fatal. As Frederick Manning came downstairs, he found O'Connor collapsed on the floor, writhing in agony. Manning battered him to death with a ripping chisel, justifying his actions later on with the laconic remark that 'I never really liked him.' The couple buried the body under the kitchen floor and covered it with quicklime.

The following evening, two of O'Connor's friends arrived at the Mannings' home. They knew that he had been invited for dinner there, and had become concerned when he did not arrive at work the following day. Maria told them that although O'Connor had dined with them on 7 August, he had never arrived for dinner the following evening. Rattled by these visitors, who Maria strongly suspected were detectives, the couple argued before agreeing to run away. Next morning, Maria sent Frederick off to find a furniture dealer so that they could sell off their possessions, while she cleaned up the murder scene. As soon as Frederick had left the house, Maria invited a twelve-year-old match seller in from the street and offered him five pennies to wash the kitchen down. The lad readily agreed, and Maria hurried out to O'Connor's lodgings, where she blagged her way into his room, and stole cash, two gold watches and more railway shares. By the time Frederick returned home, Maria was in a cab to King's Cross Station and the match seller had absconded with an egg, a razor, a purse and a pair of Maria's stockings. Frederick took one look at the house, panicked, and fled to Jersey.

By this time, O'Connor's friends had reported him missing, and shared their suspicions about the Mannings. When the police arrived at Minerva Place, one officer noticed that the mortar between two of the flagstones in the kitchen was still damp. The flagstones were raised and O'Connor's battered body was found lying underneath. This was clearly a case for Scotland Yard. Superintendent Hayes launched a manhunt for the couple, and the cabbie who had driven Maria to King's Cross came forward. When Hayes discovered that Maria had bought a ticket for Edinburgh he telegraphed his Scottish colleagues only to be told that Maria had already been arrested. She had been caught trying to sell the railway shares to a firm of stockbrokers, who realized that the shares had been stolen and were suspicious of her French accent. Maria was brought back to London and charged with murder. Frederick was arrested a week later in Jersey, where he had been recognized by an acquaintance who had read about the murder in the papers.

When the Mannings went on trial at the Old Bailey on 25 October 1849, they both attempted to blame each other for the crime. It took the jury just forty-five minutes to pronounce them guilty, at which point Maria lost the icy composure which she had displayed throughout the trial. Picking up the bundles of herbs which were traditionally strewn around the courtroom to ward off gaol fever, she threw them at the judge, screaming, 'You have treated me like a wild beast of the forest!' and continued to rant and rave as the judge sentenced her to death. Maria was placed on suicide watch, with three female warders in her cell at all times. Despite this, she attempted to strangle herself and slashed her windpipe with her own fingernails.[22]

The night before the Mannings' execution, a crowd began

to gather outside Horsemonger Gaol. Charles Dickens arrived at midnight, and his blood ran cold when he heard 'the shrillness of the cries and howls' raised by the boys and girls who had already found good vantage points. As the night went on, there was screeching and laughing, and a parody of a minstrel song in which *'Mrs Manning!'* had been substituted for *'Oh Susannah!'*

By dawn the crowd numbered 50,000, with 1,000 police officers struggling to maintain order. Dickens described the scene as an audience of thieves, prostitutes and vagabonds, delighting in offensive behaviour of every kind, jostling, fighting and whooping with indecent delight when fainting women were dragged out of the crowd by the police with their dresses disordered.

Inside the gaol, Maria struggled to maintain her composure. Taken to the chapel for the final sacraments, she nearly fainted as her arms and legs were being tied up. Maria only revived when Calcraft the hangman offered a slug of his brandy. Holding her nerve, Maria produced a black silk handkerchief for a blindfold, and a black lace veil to cover her face. Leaving the chapel by Dead Man's Walk, she walked over what was to be her own grave, just as she had walked over the grave of her victim. As Maria stepped out boldly towards her doom, Frederick Manning was scarcely capable of tottering to the scaffold.

Calcraft enjoyed his work that morning, with an approach characterized by 'unseemly briskness, jokes, oaths, and brandy'. Frederick Manning was hanged first, and he died instantly. Maria took longer to die; according to Dickens, she kicked and struggled for some minutes. Dickens was haunted, for years afterwards, by the vision of those two dangling forms: 'The man's limp, loose suit of clothes as if the man had gone out of them; the woman's fine shape, so elaborately corseted and artfully dressed, that it was unchanged in its trim appearance as it slowly swung from side to side.'[23] Maria had chosen to wear a gown of black satin, the most fashionable material of the time, for her execution. Inevitably, this fabric was tainted by association, and Maria's epitaph became 'the woman who murdered black satin'.

Dickens immortalized Maria as the murderous French maid Hortense in *Bleak House,* with her 'flashing eyes' and 'tigress mouth'; on a practical level, the author's distaste for the scenes at the Mannings' execution inspired him to write to *The Times* calling for an end to public executions. *The Thunderer* responded with an editorial stating that 'the mystery of private executions would be intolerable', as the public needed to see that murderers really had been hanged. In reply, Dickens suggested that a special 'witness jury' of twenty-four people drawn from all backgrounds should be summoned to attend private executions.[24]

Popular opposition to public hangings was gathering momentum. In 1840 a radical MP, William Ewart, had unsuccessfully attempted to get the death penalty abolished; a secondary campaign to abolish public executions gained widespread support from MPs and writers. A House of Commons Select Committee in 1856 recommended that all executions take place in private, but this motion was thrown out by the House of Lords. However, further support for private executions developed after appalling scenes at the hanging of William Bousfield in 1856.

Facing financial ruin, Bousfield had murdered his wife, two daughters aged six and four and his baby in a fit of despair before giving himself up to the police. The night before his execution, Bousfield had attempted to kill himself by throwing himself in the fire in his cell. Discovered in time, Bousfield had to be carried to the scaffold, wrapped in bandages.[25]

The hangman, William Calcraft, mounted the scaffold nervously. An attractive man during his youth, he had become scowling and surly, with shabby black attire and unruly hair. Over the years Calcraft had developed a reputation for incompetence, having been described in one newspaper as 'the public strangler', and on this occasion he was worse than usual. After hanging several Irish republicans he had received death threats, and was terrified of being shot as he stood on the gallows. Calcraft therefore drew the bolt swiftly to release the trapdoor and rushed back into Newgate before he could be picked off by a sniper's bullet.

Bousfield plunged through the trapdoor immediately – but then, to the utter astonishment of the crowd, drew himself up again and put his feet against the sides of the drop. A warden pushed him off the platform, but once again Bousfield scrambled back up. Eventually, after four attempts, Calcraft reappeared and leapt into the dark pit beneath the scaffold, where he dragged on the prisoner's legs until he died.

Such appalling scenes eventually led credence to the abolition of public executions, and in 1864 a Royal Commission on Capital Punishment recommended that in future all executions should be carried out inside a prison, 'under such regulations as might be considered necessary to prevent abuses, and to satisfy the public that the law has been complied with'.[26] A Bill to abolish public executions received its first reading in March 1866 and became law in the summer of 1868.

The last public execution to take place at Newgate was that of Michael Barrett on 26 May 1868. Barrett was a twenty-seven-year-old Irish Republican or 'Fenian' who had blown up Clerkenwell House of Detention in an effort to free some of his comrades, incarcerated there following an armed robbery. The massive explosion brought down the prison wall and blew up a terrace of houses nearby, killing six people and injuring over fifty, and inciting public outrage against the Irish. Karl Marx, who was living in London at the time, rightly predicted that the London working class, who had previously been sympathetic towards the Irish nationalists, 'will be made wild and driven into the arms of a reactionary government. One cannot expect the London proletarians to allow themselves to be blown up in honour of Fenian emissaries.'[27]

Fuelled by hatred, and intrigued by rumours of the death threats against William Calcraft, a massive crowd turned out to watch Barrett's execution. To the evident satisfaction of the crowd, Michael Barrett 'died hard'. The *Daily Telegraph* and *Daily News* referred to his 'protruding tongue and swollen distorted features discernible under their thin white cotton covering, as if they were part of some hideous masquerading'.[28] When he was taken down from the scaffold his red hair and beard had, it was said, turned black.

The majority would have been unaware that this was the last public execution they would ever see. Following the new legislation, a gallows shed was built in the Press Yard, adjacent to the chapel. Prisoners arrived from the condemned cells through Dead Man's Walk. It was first used on 8 September 1868, when Alexander Mackay, an eighteen-year-old waiter in a coffee house, was hanged for murdering his employer's wife.

Public executions had been a familiar feature of London life for centuries; generations of Londoners had witnessed at least one hanging and learned the sordid details of many more. Yet hanging had failed to act as an effective deterrent. It would remain to be seen whether hiding executions away would increase the mystique of the procedure. In the meantime, London's fascination with brutal murder continued, as the city became the setting for the crime of the century: the Whitechapel Murders, and the mysterious killer commonly referred to as 'Jack the Ripper'.

10

FROM HELL!

*A Murder Guide to
Victorian London*

Murder, the unique crime, exercised a powerful fascination upon the Victorian imagination, from the courtroom to the gallows. The publishing industry responded to the demand at every level, from court reports in *The Times* to the lurid drawings in the *Illustrated Police News*, an early tabloid. The names of certain cases resonate to this day, while others are forgotten. The Whitechapel murders sent a collective shudder throughout the metropolis and across the globe, and yet Harriet Lane and Kate Webster are little more than faded names from yellowed press cuttings. When these sources had been exhausted, thrill-seekers could turn to the 'sensation novels', mystery stories published in serial form, with each episode leaving readers desperate for more. Wilkie Collins (1824–89) was the greatest exponent of this genre. *The Moonstone* (1868), conceived in a fog of opium and brandy, proved such a runaway success that readers were queuing outside the publisher's offices in

Wellington Street for each new instalment. Between episodes, Collins' legions of fans could follow the real-life cases, which I revisit now, in this tour around some of the most notorious murder cases from Victorian London.

The murder of Harriet Lane in 1875 was one of the most lurid cases of the time, remarkable even by Victorian standards for its sheer gruesomeness. By the time it reached the Old Bailey, the case contained many of the key elements of the sensation novel, including a mutilated corpse, a chorus girl and a cigar-chomping villain.

The story began one Saturday night in September 1875, as a young man was spotted chasing a four-wheeler as it bowled along Whitechapel Road. 'Stop! Police!' he was shouting, to anyone who would listen. As his cries fell upon deaf ears, the young man went on running, chasing the cab over London Bridge as it headed towards Southwark. It was only when the vehicle stopped near the Hen and Chickens public house on Borough High Street, that the youth, by the name of Albert Stokes, managed to flag down two police officers. He begged them to search the vehicle. Despite outraged protests from the passengers, a bearded middle-aged man and an attractive young woman, police constables 48 and 290 wrenched open the door of cab number 8505 and promptly turned away vomiting, met by an overwhelming stench.

The cab was ordered to Southwark police station, where it was found to contain two parcels wrapped in canvas. The smallest parcel contained the decomposed trunk of a woman, while the second, which was larger, contained her head, arms and legs. The victim's auburn hair, with a distinctive fringe or 'bang' was partially burnt off and her eyes had decomposed The remains were taken to St Saviour's mortuary, and the male passenger, whose name was Henry Wainwright, was arrested along with his companion, Alice Day, a chorus girl.

Alice Day, who barely knew Henry Wainwright, was released without charge. But Wainwright, a brash East End entrepreneur, aged forty-three, was charged with murder.[1]

Once he had recovered his composure, young Albert Stokes told police that he had been passing through the Whitechapel Road when Alice Day had accosted him and asked him to help her move some parcels from a warehouse in Vine Court, just off Whitechapel Road. Wainwright, Stokes' former employer, had then appeared in a four-wheeler and asked the driver to wait while he went to fetch some luggage. When he went into the warehouse, Stokes was horrified to see two bloodstained bundles standing in the corner. From one of the bundles protruded a mutilated hand. The stench was appalling, and at first Stokes refused to help, but Wainwright offered him an impressive tip, so Stokes helped Wainwright load the bundles into his cab and resolved to chase after it and inform the police.

A post mortem conducted the following day showed that the corpse was that of a woman of about twenty-four, who had been dead for around one year. The body had been buried in a shallow grave, probably under a wall or floor. Although internal decomposition had taken place, the corpse had been preserved by the action of the quicklime that had been liberally sprinkled all over it. The murderer had failed to realize that while dry quicklime will destroy, wet quicklime preserves. The moisture in the soil had formed a chemical reaction with the quicklime that had served to embalm the corpse so that the cause of death was still immediately evident. The victim had been shot in the head, and her throat had been slashed. The corpse had then been disinterred and an attempt had been made to burn it. When this had ended in failure, it had been dismembered, presumably with a view to dumping the remains.

Next day, Chief Inspector James McDonald of H Division

led the search of Wainwright's warehouse. The police found a new spade and a hatchet, alongside a broken silk umbrella and a velvet hair band. Led by the smell of decomposition to a space beneath the floorboards, they discovered a jet button, a kneecap, and a human tooth.[2]

In an effort to identify the corpse, the remains went on display in a glass-topped coffin at the Southwark dead house, and within days a grieving family came forward to claim it. A Mr Lane approached the police saying that he had not seen his daughter Harriet, a milliner, for over a year. Relations had become strained when Harriet had become the mistress of a married man in 1872, and proceeded to bear him two children. When the relationship faltered, Harriet had begun drinking heavily, and complaining that her lover never gave her enough money to feed and clothe the children. Subsequently, Mr Lane received a letter saying that Harriet had married another man, her lover's brother, and fled abroad, and that her father must on no account come looking for her. Desperate to find her, Harriet's family hired a private detective, but Harriet had vanished without a trace.

Now the sensational newspaper coverage of the case had brought them forward, and they endured the horrific ordeal of identifying Harriet's body. When the chief inspector asked Mr Lane the name of Harriet's erstwhile lover, the father of her children, he could have predicted the response. 'Wainwright,' said Mr Lane, bitterly. 'Henry Wainwright.'

When Henry Wainwright went on trial for Harriet's murder at the Old Bailey, it emerged that by 1874 Wainwright had tired of Harriet, having become exasperated by her demands for money. Witnesses testified to the fact that Wainwright was often overheard saying that he wanted rid of Harriet. He even attempted to palm her off on his brother, Thomas, who went on trial alongside him, but this proved unsuccessful. At some point that year, Harriet was murdered and buried in Wainwright's warehouse. After constant complaints from the neighbours about the smell of his drains, Wainwright had scattered chloride of lime over the corpse. But instead of destroying the body, this substance had effectively embalmed it. A year later, Wainwright's business collapsed and he was forced to give up the warehouse and move to cheaper premises across the river in Borough High Street. Harriet's body stank so badly that he had to take her with him.[3]

Sentenced to death, Wainwright showed no remorse. He spent his last night on earth smoking cigars and boasting to the Newgate turnkeys about his sexual exploits. Around 100

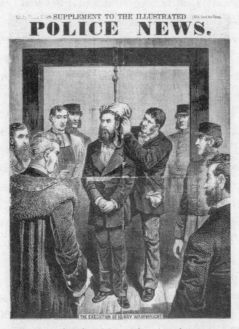

The Illustrated Police News *showing the unrepentant*
Henry Wainwright sneering from the gallows.
'You curs! Come to see a man die, have you!'

people were invited to witness his execution inside Newgate Gaol, and when he saw them, Wainwright turned on the spectators and sneered: 'You curs! Come to see a man die, have you!'[4] The scene, showing Wainwright unrepentant on the scaffold as the hangman prepared to put the hood over his head, was a front page special in the *Illustrated Police News*.

Lurid as it was, this publication and others like it did much to enhance the reputation of the police. While the traditional distrust for authority lingered in the Londoner's character, the detection and arrest of killers such as Wainwright marked the beginnings of tolerance, and even respect. There was some comfort to be derived from the knowledge that, if one were murdered in one's bed, then certain dour-faced men in bowler hats would almost certainly catch the murderer. The 'men from the Yard' or 'the detective force' as the Criminal Intelligence Department was originally known, had become a source of fascination. As the century progressed, Scotland Yard had developed from a small tract of land behind Whitehall to an ugly but imposing fortress built of granite quarried by the convicts at Dartmoor. The Yard looked like a prison but was the heart of the British police system, 'the centre of a mighty spider's web, which widens in a series of rings that are bound together in an eccentric and (often to the criminal) unexpected fashion, and extend to the utmost limit of the London district' and beyond.[5] Scotland Yard had begun to develop its own mystique.

In fiction, police detectives such as Dickens' Inspector Bucket and Wilkie Collins' Sergeant Cuff were portrayed as intelligent, tenacious men of the highest integrity. Dickens in particular had been highly impressed by the detective squad from Scotland Yard, 'forever on the watch, with their wits stretched to the utmost,' playing their games of chess with live pieces.[6] The world's pre-eminent fictional detective made his debut in 1887, when Arthur Conan Doyle published *A Study in Scarlet*. From his rooms at 221b Baker Street, the formidable investigator solved intricate mysteries and developed into a complex and compelling creation, with his first-class mind, low boredom threshold and recreational drug habit. The success of Sherlock Holmes demonstrated the 'lure of the detective' and the continuing mystique of 'the greatest hunter of all, the hunter of men'.[7] Holmes was, however, a fictional creation, and his cases, with their intriguing titles such as 'The Speckled Band' and 'The Engineer's Thumb', were beautifully constructed intellectual puzzles, far removed from the grim reality of late Victorian London.

Maria Manning, who featured in an earlier chapter, was the most notorious female murderer of the Victorian period, but by no means the only one. Although only 10 to 15 per cent of murders are committed by women, the majority of which constitute self-defence against an abusive partner,[8] Victorian London nevertheless produced some chilling examples of female killers. Three sensational cases of female murderers caught the public imagination during this period. The first took place in the unlikely environs of Park Lane in April 1872, at the residence of Madame Riel, a retired actress and the mistress of Lord Lucan, the general who had ordered the charge of the Light Brigade during the Crimean War. On the morning of 8 April 1872, Madame Riel's body was discovered in the pantry. She had been strangled, and the rope was still around her neck, with a deep indention beneath the ear where the slipknot had been tightened.

Suspicion immediately fell upon the Belgian cook, Marguerite Dixblanc, who been overheard quarrelling with her employer the previous day. Madame Riel had dismissed Dixblanc with just a week's wages and in return it appeared that Dixblanc, a powerfully built veteran of the Paris commune, had rifled the safe and fled to France. Dixblanc was arrested, extradited and sentenced to death, but when her former colleagues testified to Madame Riel's appalling treatment of her, Dixblanc was pardoned and given a custodial sentence. While the crime stoked the fears of the nervous middle classes that docile domestics might become cold-blooded murderers, Dixblanc was exonerated in the curious chauvinism of the times, on the grounds that her victim was also a 'foreigner' and a courtesan at that.[9]

Dixblanc's crime pales into insignificance compared with the exploits of another homicidal servant, Kate Webster. In 1879, Webster was hired by the elderly Julia Thomas, a wealthy widow of 2 Vine Cottages, Park Road, Richmond, but Mrs Thomas soon regretted her decision. On more than one occasion, Mrs Thomas confided to her friends that she found the high and mighty Miss Webster downright frightening, particularly during her drunken rages. Webster, meanwhile, had found an admirer in the form of John Church, the proprietor of the Rising Sun public house. Then the neighbours noted the absence of Mrs Thomas, and, more alarmingly, the sight of Webster, dressed in her mistress's gowns, striding boldly into a local shop and attempting to sell off Mrs Thomas's jewellery.

The following day, Webster invited Church round to Vine Cottages to buy the furniture. He stayed the night. The neighbours went to the police with their suspicions and the next day Vine Cottages was raided. An axe and fragments of charred bones were discovered in the kitchen. The copper, which would normally have been used to wash laundry, contained a scummy ring of fat. Mrs Thomas was nowhere to be seen, but within days a human foot was washed up in Twickenham, and a torso, believed to be that of the employer, was found in a hatbox at Barnes. Kate Webster had ensured her place in the murderers' hall of fame by attacking her mistress with the axe, hacking the corpse to pieces, and boiling down the remains in the copper, removing the bones. Most grisly of all was the fate of the fat. Webster had scooped the fat from the copper and sold it around the neighbourhood as dripping. One street urchin even claimed Webster had offered him a bowl of dripping as an act of charity.

Webster, who had fled home to Ireland, was arrested, tried and hanged by William Marwood, Calcraft's successor, at Wandsworth.[10] In a bizarre footnote, in 2010 Julia Thomas's skull was unearthed in the garden of the broadcaster and naturalist Sir David Attenborough. A team of builders discovered the skull when they were excavating foundations for an extension, at the spot where the Rising Sun once stood. In July 2011, the West London coroner Alison Thompson formally identified the skull as belonging to Julia Thomas and recorded a verdict of unlawful killing.[11]

Kate Webster – the killer servant who murdered her mistress and boiled up the body on the stove.

Horror rather than sympathy attended the conviction of Kate Webster. While the murder served as a terrifying reminder to all potential employers to check the references of domestic staff, the famous waxwork museum Madame Tussaud's was swift to exploit its potential. A disturbing wax effigy of Kate Webster, with minatory eyes, went on display in the 'Chamber of Horrors', which had been a crowd-pleasing feature of the museum since the 1840s.

The third instance of 'woman beware woman' is the most distressing of all. The abiding image of this case consists of one dark, unsettling vignette. It was an autumn night in October 1890, as Mary Pearcey steered a heavy black perambulator through the chilly streets of Camden Town, along Ivor Street, up to Chalk Farm, and then west to Maida Vale. A young woman wheeling a pram should be one of the most familiar and reassuring sights in the world, but something about this picture was unsettling. The big black perambulator with its looming hood was so heavy that she could scarcely push it uphill. The coachwork was collapsing under the weight of its sinister burden.

The perambulator did indeed hold a baby, eight-month-old Phoebe Hogg. But in addition it contained the baby's mother, a woman of thirty-one, also named Phoebe. Both were dead. The mother had been battered with a poker, and her throat cut so violently that the head was almost severed from the neck. The baby had been smothered by her own mother's corpse. Pearcey dumped the mother's body at Crossfield Road, and the baby at Cock and Hoop Field. She left the blood-stained pram at Hamilton Terrace, and went home to Ivor Street, to the house paid for by her lover, Charles Crichton. Although Crichton paid the rent, Pearcey also received visits from another long-time lover, Thomas Hogg, a furniture remover from Haverstock Hill. A year previously Hogg had married Phoebe, but continued to see Pearcey, and even had his own key. This arrangement proved satisfactory at first, but soon Pearcey became resentful, especially once Phoebe had given birth to a daughter and Hogg began paying more attention to his new family. One afternoon in October, Pearcey invited Phoebe and her daughter round to tea, attacked the mother with a poker, slit her throat and piled her into the pram.

A day later, the police came for Pearcey. She did not resist arrest, but instead sat at the piano in her bloodstained clothes, humming to herself and ignoring their questions. Finally, when one officer asked why there were bloodstains all over the walls, Pearcey replied, over and over again, that she had been 'killing mice, killing mice, killing mice!' Pearcey, who suffered from epilepsy and depression, was clearly mentally ill, but public outrage at the murder of baby Phoebe ensured that she was bound for the gallows.

During her custody, Pearcey waited every day for Hogg to visit her, convinced that now Phoebe was gone they could be together. The fact that Hogg would never forgive her for murdering his baby daughter never seemed to occur to her. Three hundred people gathered outside Newgate Gaol when Pearcey was executed on 23 December and cheers went up when the black flag was raised. Pearcey was subsequently demonized, and there was even lurid speculation to the effect that she had been 'Jill the Ripper', perpetrator of the Whitechapel murders.[12]

There have always been unsolved murders in London. The perpetrator of 'the Waterloo Bridge Mystery', when a carpet-bag containing a woman's torso was found floating down the Thames in 1857, escaped detection.[13] The deaths of so many prostitutes went unreported that it was impossible to calculate how many of these unfortunate women had not committed suicide but become the victims of a serial killer. They were nobody's daughter, nobody's wife. But it is the Whitechapel

Murders, perpetrated by a killer referring to himself as 'Jack the Ripper', which remain the greatest series of unsolved murders in London's history. The case contained many of the elements of the sensation novel, including the distinctive locale, the wretched female victims and the perception of the murderer as a sinister foreign gentleman.

When Whitechapel police were called out to a body on the morning of 31 August 1888, they had no conception of the horrors to come. Domestic tragedies and attacks on prostitutes were a sadly familiar part of 'the job', and there was no reason to believe that this case would be any different. The police had been summoned after a driver from Pickford's removals spotted a woman's body lying in Buck's Row, just off Whitechapel Road, yards from the London Hospital. Assuming that she was either dead drunk or dead, the driver and his mate had walked over to investigate, only to discover that the victim's throat had been cut, almost severing the head from the body. At the mortuary, one officer, an Inspector Spratley, casually turned up the victim's clothes and saw that the lower part of her abdomen had been ripped open. The injuries were 'the work of a madman' according to one officer, while the police surgeon, Dr Ralph Llewellyn, had never seen a more horrible case. 'She was ripped open just as you see a dead calf at a butcher's shop. The murder was done by someone very handy with the knife.'[14]

After the victim had been identified as Mary Ann Nicholls, the police were left with no idea as to a motive. With the local division out of its depth, Chief Inspector Frederick Abbeline, who had extensive experience of Whitechapel, was seconded from Scotland Yard to head up the case.

A week later, on 8 September, the corpse of Annie Chapman was found in a passage leading to a lodging house at 29 Hanbury Street, Spitalfields. Annie's body was discovered at six o'clock in the morning by a fellow lodger, John Davies, who lived on the top floor. He called across to some workmen, saying that a woman had clearly been murdered. 'Her clothes were thrown back, but her face was visible,' said James Kent, another eyewitness. 'Her apron seemed to be thrown back over her clothes ... it seemed as if her inside had been pulled from her, and thrown at her. It was lying over her left shoulder.'[15]

At this point, rumours began to circulate to the effect that John Pizer, a local tradesman, was the murderer. This was based on a rumour that a man in a leather apron, carrying a knife, had been seen at both crime scenes, and Pizer fitted this description. As a Jew, Pizer was also a convenient scapegoat for locals eager to pin the killings on a 'foreigner'. Pizer was arrested but released once he had satisfied the police that he had no connection with the killings.

On 27 September 1888, the Central News Agency received a letter that was subsequently forwarded to the Metropolitan Police. 'Dear Boss,' the letter began, 'I am down on whores and I shant quit ripping them till I do get buckled ... ' The letter was signed 'Jack the Ripper'. A day later, the body of Swedish 'Long Liz' Stride was discovered in an alley off Henriques Street. Liz's throat had been cut and she had died of massive blood loss, but there were no mutilations to the abdomen, suggesting that her killer was disturbed during the attack. Three-quarters of an hour later, the body of Catherine Eddowes was found in Mitre Square in the City of London: her throat had been cut and a major part of her uterus, and her left kidney, had been removed.

On 1 October, a postcard was sent to the police written in red ink. In this, the writer referred to himself as 'saucy Jack' and referred to 'the double event' before signing off as Jack the Ripper once more.[16]

The press seized on the gruesome potential of 'Jack the Ripper' and the murders inevitably became a source of public fascination. *Reynold's Weekly Newspaper* ran with a piece of doggerel to the effect that 'Murder is stalking red handed 'mid the homes of the weary poor,' while newsboys ran up and down the streets crying: 'Latest Hawful Horror. A woman cut in pieces! Speshul!'[17]

Meanwhile, Chief Inspector Abbeline, in an early form of criminal profiling, had noted the similarity between the victims: all prostitutes, all of middle years and medium height, all with missing teeth. 'Jack' was murdering the same woman over and over again, but why? As the chief inspector tried to find a motive, vigilantes were taking the law into their own hands and targeting Jewish immigrants, in an updated version of the blood libel, with cries of 'It was a Jew wot did it!' and 'No Englishman did it!' Racist outbursts were further fuelled by a mysterious piece of graffiti that appeared on Goulston Street, Whitechapel, where Eddowes' body had been found. In chalk, it read: 'The Juwes are The men that Will not be Blamed for nothing,' which was either a message from the murderer, an anti-Semitic statement or an enigmatic reference to an item of Freemasons' regalia, the 'juwes'.[18]

The discovery of a female torso in the cellars of the new police building under construction at Whitehall added to the air of horror on 2 October 1888, while a deluge of copycat 'Jack the Ripper' letters overstretched police resources. Then on 16 October 1888, George Lusk, Chairman of the Whitechapel Vigilance Committee, which had been set up to crack down on prostitution in the neighbourhood, received half a human kidney in a cardboard box through the post, accompanied by a letter scrawled in a spidery hand, addressed 'From Hell' and concluding: 'Catch me when you can Mishter Lusk.' The writer claimed to have fried and eaten the other half of the 'kidne' [sic], which was 'very nise'. The shaken Lusk took both kidney and letter to the police. While the police surgeon suggested it was probably a hoax by a medical student, others believed it was part of Eddowes' missing organ.[19]

On Friday 9 November the body of Mary Jane Kelly was discovered in her room at 13 Miller's Court, off Dorset Street, Spitalfields, the same street where Annie Chapman had been murdered four months earlier. Mary Jane had been murdered with such ferocity that it beggared description. Her throat had been severed down to the spine, and her abdomen virtually emptied of its organs. Her heart was missing and she was so horribly mutilated as to be virtually unrecognizable. It was impossible for the police to enter the room without slipping on her blood and flesh. The Ripper's latest atrocity led to the resignation of the Metropolitan Commissioner of Police, Sir Charles Warren.[20]

The Whitechapel murders dominated the newspapers from Europe to the Americas, and there was increasing pressure on the police to make an arrest. An image of the killer had taken shape in the popular imagination, a vision of a genteel man dressed in black and carrying a doctor's bag. In response, the police made a number of arrests ranging from doctors and tradesmen to sailors and tramps, but lacked sufficient evidence to charge. Those questioned included Aaron Kosminski, Montague Druitt, and Dr Francis J. Tumblety.

Kosminski, a poor Polish Jew resident in Whitechapel, was arrested on the orders of Sir Melville Macnaghten, Assistant Commissioner at Scotland Yard. Released for lack of evidence, Kosminski ended his days in Colney Hatch mental asylum.

When Montague Druitt (1857–88) drowned himself in the Thames and the killings stopped, Macnaghten concluded that he had been the perpetrator. A barrister with medical training, Druitt had the knowledge of anatomy to carry out such hideous crimes, and he was also, according to his family, 'sexually insane'. Druitt, a product of Winchester and New College, Oxford, was an amateur cricketer of national standing and a member of the MCC, with good prospects as a barrister. However, after being dismissed from his post as a master at a minor public school, Druitt's body was found floating in the Thames on 31 December 1888. Druitt's dismissal may have resulted from the school's discovery of his homosexuality (then a criminal offence), while a family history of severe depression may have contributed to his taking his own life. Although Druitt's death offered a convenient solution to the riddle of the Ripper, this unfortunate young man appears to have been an unlikely candidate for the role of serial killer.[21]

Francis Tumblety was an American 'quack' aged fifty-six and regarded as a very strong suspect by Detective Chief Inspector John Littlechild, a former head of the Special Branch. Tumblety, who specialized in selling spurious herbal remedies, had been arrested for gross indecency (homosexual activity) in November 1888, and fled the country soon afterwards, having obtained bail at a very high price.[22]

A more compelling suspect was Severin Klosovski, commonly known as George Chapman, who had arrived in England in 1888 and worked as a barber in Whitechapel. Apprenticed to a surgeon, Chapman never took his degree, preferring instead to run a pub. When Chapman was arrested in 1905 and charged with poisoning three of his wives, Inspector Abbeline, now retired, commented to the arresting officer, 'You've caught the Ripper, then?' But this seems unlikely. Chapman poisoned his wives because he became tired of them, rather than butchering prostitutes.[23]

One killer claimed, with his dying breath, that he had indeed been Jack the Ripper, and in many ways he fitted the profile. Dr Thomas Cream (1850–92) was an abortionist, who accidentally killed two patients with overdoses of chloroform, but escaped prosecution for lack of sufficient evidence. Fleeing to America, he had an affair with the wife of a patient, and was imprisoned when her husband died from an overdose of strychnine. As well as having the requisite medical training,

Cream satisfied the criteria in another respect. A sexual sadist, his particular fetish was to hire prostitutes and issue them with 'lucky pills' intended to pep them up, issuing strict instructions that they take these only after he had left. The pills were lethal and the poor women died in agony. Cream enjoyed playing cat and mouse games with the police, writing to them in the guise of a private detective with teasing fragments of 'evidence' but was eventually caught after one of his victims took her pep pill to the police. As he was about to be hanged at Newgate in 1892, Cream boasted that he had indeed been Jack the Ripper. Unfortunately, this proved impossible. Cream had been in gaol in Canada when the Whitechapel murders were committed.[24]

After the Kelly murder, and many more abortive arrests, the panic began to die down. In early 1889 Inspector Abbeline was transferred to other duties and the inquiry was handed over to Inspector Henry Moore. His last extant report on the murders is dated 1896, when another 'Jack the Ripper' letter was received. There were brief flurries of press activity and wild suggestions that the 'Ripper' had returned on the occasions of subsequent murders. The last serious suspect was Tom Sadler, a sailor who was arrested in 1891 for the murder of a prostitute, Frances Coles. When they tracked Sadler down to the Phoenix public house in Smithfield, the police were convinced that they had got their man. Sadler, a violent drunk with a history of assaulting women, fitted their profile. But when Sadler went on trial for murder, the jury remained unconvinced of his guilt and Sadler walked free.[25]

Theories as to the Ripper's true identity circulate to this day. The more bizarre explanations included one from the *British Medical Journal* suggesting that the atrocities might have been committed by a ruthless but enterprising gang of 'Burkers' eager to sell wombs to medical students, another accusing Freemasons of being the perpetrators, or even one suggesting it was the Duke of Clarence, the younger son of Queen Victoria who was rumoured to be insane.[26]

The lack of sexual activity at the crime scene prompted speculation that the killer had been a woman, an abortionist so incompetent that she had mutilated her patients to destroy the evidence of illegal terminations. A similar theory pointed the finger at Amelia Dyer, the baby farmer hanged in 1896 for murdering dozens of illegitimate babies entrusted to her care, suggesting that she had killed the mothers before they could expose her as a child murderer.

What is obvious is the fact that the police were at no stage in a position to prove a case against anyone, and it is highly unlikely a positive case will ever be proved. If the police were in this position between 1888 and 1891, then what hope for the enthusiastic modern investigator?

The enduring fascination of this case has attracted retired and serving police officers, writers and film-makers for over a century. There will never be a conclusive explanation but the case of 'Jack the Ripper' grips the popular imagination to this day, and makes armchair detectives of us all. Meanwhile, reality and art have combined to create a nightmare vision of Victorian London, a city haunted by imaginary sleuths and actual murderers, a fantasy world in which the fictional Sherlock Holmes pursues the real Jack the Ripper through foggy streets and narrow alleyways forever.

This London was already becoming history. In the dying days of the old century, as Queen Victoria's life slipped away with the years, a new age of crime and punishment beckoned from the future. Even those ancient bastions of crime and punishment, Newgate Gaol and the Old Bailey, would not escape unscathed.

11

CRIMES PASSIONNELS, FEMMES FATALES

Drama at the Old Bailey

On 15 August 1902, at a quarter past three in the afternoon, a piece of stone about the size of a man's foot fell from the wall of Newgate Gaol, just below the statue of Liberty. A hand grasping a chisel emerged and worked away at the hole, as a small crowd gathered to watch the operation. The old pigeons, 'rough and grimy as the prison itself compared with the other flocks in London, fluttered about the statue, evidently talking over the event with much excitement'.[1] But this was no gaol break, no last-minute escape from the gallows. Nor was it the desperate work of rioters, eager to free their comrades. This was the end of Newgate.

After a damning report by Sir Herbert Gladstone's investigative committee in the 1880s, the authorities had reached for the black cap and condemned Newgate to death. The gaol itself was being executed, taken apart, brick by brick. In its place would stand the most famous court in the land, the Old

Bailey, rebuilt at a cost of £392,277 and topped by the formidable bronze statue of Lady Justice, bearing the scales and sword.

Once the demolition work was underway, the governors began to sell off the fixtures and fittings of the old gaol. On 7 February 1903, a sale of relics drew crowds of the curious to gather within Newgate's gloomy precincts. The flagstaff, upon which the black flag used to be flown after an execution, fetched eleven and a half guineas. Equipment from the execution shed went for £5 15s., while souvenir hunters snatched up the death masks of hanged prisoners for £5 each.[2] Piles of official documents, faded and age-worn, were strewn about the rooms. These were records of indictments and sentences and shipments of convicts. They were bought up in their hundreds by second-hand book dealers, aware that there must be something of value in these old accounts of sin and suffering, the endless lists of half-forgotten names recorded in faded copperplate.[3]

Newgate Gaol shortly before demolition in 1904. Many of the massive slab stones went into the rebuilding of the Old Bailey on the same spot.

The demolition work was finally completed in 1904. It had been a laborious task, as the massive stones of the outer wall were several feet thick and weighed around five tons each. Many of these stones were subsequently used in the construction of the new building, an essential replacement for the cramped, ill-ventilated and stuffy courthouse of old. The Old Bailey, which was officially opened by King Edward VII on 27 February 1907, was an iconic monument to justice, a public arena in which some of the most dramatic trials of the twentieth century would be played out. Among these were some of the last examples of the Great English Murder, including that of Dr Crippen, Edith Thompson and Frederick Bywaters and the mysterious Madame Fahmy. Uxoricide and *crimes passionnels* made for dramatic courtroom scenes, filled the public gallery and kept the crime reporters in business.

The major players in these trials were not only the miserable defendants in the dock, but the barristers or King's Counsel who appeared for the prosecution and the defence, and upon whose soaring rhetoric and dazzling charisma their lives depended. The most famous KC of his day, Sir Edward Marshall Hall, was a past master of this art. In 1894, he defended Marie Herrmann, an Austrian prostitute charged with murdering one of her clients. In his closing speech for the defence, he turned to the jury, tears streaming down his face, and declared: 'Women are what men made them. Even this woman was at one time a beautiful and innocent child. Look at her, gentlemen of the jury, look at her! God never gave her a chance. Won't you?'[4] In a satisfactory conclusion to this display of oratory, Marie Herrmann was convicted of manslaughter, and received six years' penal servitude instead of a death sentence. Marshall Hall compared his profession with acting, apart from the fact that he had to write his own lines and conjure up his own *mise en scène*. 'Out of the vivid, living dream of somebody else's life, I have to create an atmosphere; for that is advocacy.'[5]

The public fascination with a nice juicy murder remained undiminished, particularly if those on trial were hitherto 'respectable' men and women who had succumbed to their passion. As George Orwell noted in his perceptive essay on *The Decline of the English Murder,* one of the remarkable factors in these cases is that the perpetrators were from the middle classes, and that the essential motive for killing was to maintain respectability, by obtaining money and marrying their mistress or lover. Another characteristic of a good murder trial was the unmasking of the criminal by some astonishing twist of fate that would have been discarded as outrageous by any crime novelist, such as Dr Crippen fleeing across the Atlantic with his mistress disguised as a boy.[6]

In the modern world of no-contest divorce and serial monogamy, it is impossible to imagine the crushing yoke imposed by 'respectability' a century earlier, and the tensions that led to the domestic murder. London in the 1900s was a city between two worlds, one dying, one struggling to be born. Victorian morality lingered on, in a gas-lit, sepia-tinted world of poverty and narrow horizons. Simultaneously, London existed as a glittering modern metropolis, where intrepid young women took on office jobs, applied to university and even marched for the vote. Many Londoners, confronted with this brave new world, yearned only for 'respectability'. Paradise was a red-brick villa in Camden Town for £50 a year, the respectable surburbia of H. G. Wells' daydreaming clerks or the social-climbing Charles Pooter in *The Diary of a Nobody.* But a few men and women led lives of quiet desperation. This was the world of keeping up appearances while living beyond your means, despising your spouse but relying on their income, biting back the acid reflux of sexual frustration and thwarted ambition and the abiding conviction that you deserved better. This was the world in which divorce spelt scandal and financial suicide, the world where an unhappy marriage was like being handcuffed to a rotting corpse and murderous thoughts flourished behind the Nottingham Lace curtains. This was the world where marriage could be murder. This was the world of Dr Crippen.

Certain names continue to chill the reader years after the event with which they are associated, and Crippen is one of those. Up until the 1940s, 'Crippen!' was a vernacular expression of horror, swearing without the profanity, and therefore safe enough to be common currency. The mild-mannered poisoner from Camden Town had been immortalized in schoolgirl slang. His crime had put him among the immortals, alongside Jack Sheppard, Dick Turpin and Jack the Ripper. The name itself seemed evil, with its nuances of criminal, ripper and *cripes!* Crippen was even celebrated in a second-rate music hall as a 'naughty boy', an illustration of the cognitive dissonance which allows the public to relish the criminal.[7] The Crippen case was notable for another reason, in that it combined the dogged persistence of old-school Scotland Yard sleuthing with developments in forensic science, and it was the first murder case in which a suspect was arrested at sea, following a telegram.

Dr Hawley Harvey Crippen, his full name reflecting the aspirations of his lower-middle-class parents, was an American homeopathic doctor who arrived in London with his second wife, Cora, in 1900. Unqualified to practise in England, Crippen worked in a dentistry practice in New Oxford Street and acted as an agent for Dr Munyon's, a patent medicine firm. The couple rented rooms off Tottenham Court Road before taking a lease on 39 Hilldrop Crescent in September 1905. The house, an imposing villa in a tree-lined street in Camden Town, had a rent of £58 10s. a year. As Crippen only earned a modest £3 per week, some of this cost was borne by Cora.

The Crippens were an odd couple. Photographs show Dr

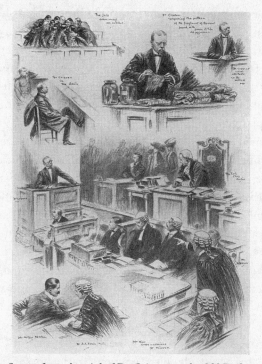

Scenes from the trial of Dr Crippen at the Old Bailey,
1910, 'the most sensational trial for many years'.

Crippen as an unprepossessing figure, just five foot three inches tall, with gold-rimmed spectacles and a sandy moustache. Cora was a vivacious New Yorker, several years his junior. With her dyed auburn hair and expensive jewellery, she cut a striking figure in suburban north London. With a determination that far outstripped her talent, Cora worked the music halls as the singer 'Belle Elmore' and aimed to become a star. Cora also had a series of lovers, including a former boxer who performed as a 'one-man band', while Crippen spent stolen afternoons in cheap hotels with his secretary, Ethel Le Neve.[8]

By December 1909, Cora had told Crippen that she knew about his affair with Ethel, and threatened to leave him, taking their life savings with her. As this sum amounted to around £600 (nearly £600,000 today), she effectively signed her own death warrant when she sent a notice of withdrawal to the bank on 15 December. To keep up appearances, the Crippens spent Christmas together. On 31 January 1910, they entertained the Martinettis, friends of Cora, for an evening of whist. The last guest departed at around one o'clock in the morning, and Cora was never seen again.

Some weeks later, Mrs Martinetti received a note addressed to her colleagues in the Music Hall Ladies Guild. Purporting to be from Cora, it stated that she had returned to America to care for a sick relative, but expected to come back to England before long. The letter was not written in Cora's hand, so Mrs Martinetti called on Crippen and asked after Cora's welfare. Crippen broke the news that Cora had died of influenza while nursing her aunt, and been buried in Los Angeles.

Meanwhile, Le Neve had moved into Hilldrop Crescent and was living openly with Crippen. To the horror of Cora's friends, she was spotted dressed in Cora's clothes and jewellery. Mrs Martinetti's suspicions were dismissed by the police but when another of Cora's friends, John Nash, returned from the United States saying that he could find no trace of her, Chief Inspector Walter Dew interviewed Crippen at his practice and ordered a search of the house. Crippen's status as a doctor and his impressive residence seemed to convince the police that he must be innocent. After a cursory inspection, the police left.[9]

But the visit from Chief Inspector Dew had been enough to rattle Crippen. Panicking, he and Le Neve fled to Belgium, where they boarded the SS *Montrose*, a Canadian Pacific liner bound for Quebec. On hearing that Crippen had disappeared, Chief Inspector Dew authorized another search of Hilldrop

Crescent on 13 July and discovered the rotting remains of a human torso hidden beneath the kitchen floor. Once the search team had revived themselves with the aid of Crippen's brandy, they observed that the corpse was wrapped in a pyjama jacket, and a hair curler with strands of dyed red hair lay nearby. The body had been buried in quicklime, but, as in the case of Henry Wainwright in 1875, the effect of the lime had been to preserve the remains. The head and limbs were never found. The celebrated pathologist Sir Bernard Spilsbury, a pioneer of forensic science, conducted the post mortem and noted an operation scar four inches long on the lower abdomen and 2.7 grains of hyoscine in the bloodstream. Although it was impossible to identify the gender of the body, Spilsbury concluded that the abdominal scar was consistent with an operation Cora had undergone some years earlier, to remove her ovaries.[10]

Meanwhile, the captain of the SS *Montrose*, Captain Henry Kendell, had become intrigued by the curious behaviour of two passengers in the first-class saloon, a middle-aged man and his young son. Captain Kendell noted that the 'boy's' trousers were splitting at the seams and held together with safety pins, and that he had very feminine table manners. Before the Canadian Pacific liner steamed out of range of the land-based transmitters, Captain Kendell sent a wireless telegram to Scotland Yard. It was the first occasion in which a telegram had been used to catch a murderer.

Have strong suspicions that Crippen London cellar murderer and accomplice are among saloon passengers. Moustache taken off growing beard. Accomplice dressed as boy. Manner and build undoubtedly a girl.[11]

Chief Inspector Dew, who already faced criticism for failing to investigate Cora's disappearance earlier, now faced a race against time. If Crippen succeeded in getting from Canada to his home soil of the United States, an international arrest warrant and extradition procedures would be required to bring him to trial in the United Kingdom. Canada, as a dominion, was still under British legal jurisdiction and so an arrest had to be made as soon as possible. Dew boarded a White Star liner, the SS *Laurentic*, which arrived in Quebec ahead of the SS *Montrose*, and contacted the Canadian police. As the Montrose entered the mouth of the St Lawrence River, Dew boarded the liner disguised as one of the pilots who would guide the liner up the inland waterway. As a courtesy to his first-class passenger, Captain Kendell invited Crippen on deck to meet the pilots. At which point Dew removed his cap with a 'Good morning, Dr Crippen, do you know me? I'm Chief Inspector Dew from Scotland Yard.' A shocked Crippen replied: 'Thank God it's over. The suspense has been too great. I couldn't stand it any longer,' and held out his wrists for the handcuffs. Crippen and Le Neve were arrested and taken back to England on the SS *Megantic*. Jeering crowds awaited the couple when the ship docked at Liverpool, and there was another hostile reception committee when their train arrived at Euston Station.[12]

The lovers went on trial separately at the Old Bailey. Le Neve, an accessory after the fact, was fortunate enough to be acquitted. Crippen, charged with the murder of his wife, claimed that Cora had fled abroad with a lover, Bruce Miller, and that the remains in the cellar must have been buried by a previous resident before the Crippens moved in on 21 September 1905. In his capacity as an expert witness, pathologist Sir Bernard Spilsbury replied that this would have been impossible. In one of the most chilling exhibits to grace the Old Bailey, the sliver of Cora's skin bearing the scar was passed around the jury on a soup plate.

The prosecution then produced a damning piece of

evidence. In January 1910, Crippen had ordered five grains of hyoscine hydrobromide at Lewis and Burrow's chemists in New Oxford Street. This had been such a large quantity that they had to place a special order with the wholesalers, but given Crippen's medical credentials no objection was made to the purchase. Crippen collected the order on 19 January 1910.

Hyoscine had a number of applications. It could be used for pain relief and as a sedative, but proved fatal in large doses. Cora had been described as having a nervous disposition, and Crippen may well have been administering hyoscine to his wife as a herbal tonic. Edward Marshall Hall, who had initially been instructed to represent Crippen, suggested that this was his best defence. Crippen could plead guilty to administering an accidental overdose, and panicking when he realized that he had killed his wife. But Crippen rejected this plea and Marshall Hall rejected the brief.

It took the jury just twenty-seven minutes to find Crippen guilty of murder. He was hanged at Pentonville on 23 November 1910 and buried in the prison grounds. His last request was to be buried with a picture of Ethel Le Neve. On the same day, Ethel emigrated to the United States to start a new life, but she later returned to London, married a clerk and settled down to comfortable obscurity in Croydon, dying in hospital at the age of eighty-four. The house at 39 Hilldrop Crescent was destroyed by enemy action during World War Two, taking its secrets to the grave.[13]

If you were a woman going on trial for murder, good character and the right appearance played a critical part in your defence. In a world where Edwardian standards of female behaviour still prevailed, the dress and deportment of a female defendant carried as much weight as hard evidence. Such was the fate of Edith Thompson, when she went on trial at the Old Bailey in 1922, accused of the murder of her husband.

On 3 October 1922, Edith and Percy Thompson had been making their way home to Ilford after a night 'Up West'. They had been to see *The Dippers* at the Criterion Theatre, Piccadilly.[14] The Thompsons appeared to be a happy couple, rich and successful by Ilford standards. Mr Thompson, at thirty-three, was dull but reliable, while Edith, a former buyer for a fabric importer, was clever and smart, her business trips to Paris reflected in her stylish, chic appearance. As the couple was walking along Belgrave Road, a young man sprang out of the bushes and attacked Mr Thompson. Edith shrieked, '*No! Don't! Don't do it!*' but the young man produced a knife and stabbed her husband to death. When their neighbours ran outside to help, Edith was discovered sobbing over her husband's body, saying again and again, 'Why did he do it? I never wanted him to!' As the police arrived and Edith was led away, she was overheard murmuring darkly, 'They'll blame me for this!'[15]

By the time the police arrived, Percy Thompson was dead, Edith had become hysterical and the killer had fled. Eventually, at the police station, Edith composed herself sufficiently to reveal that she recognized the killer as Frederick Bywaters. It was then that Edith made a fatal mistake. Convinced that she was a witness to the murder, and not an accomplice, Edith confessed that Bywaters had been her lover. The police arrested Bywaters, and when they discovered a box of love letters from Edith, they arrested her too. Despite the fact that Edith had not been actively engaged in the assault, the letters were enough for the prosecution to accuse Edith Thompson and Frederick Bywaters of 'joint enterprise', a term which indicated that if two people wanted a third party dead, and if one of those two people acted, both were equally guilty of murder.

Edith Thompson and Freddy Bywaters went on trial together at the Old Bailey on 6 December 1922. Bywaters had co-operated with the police, surrendering the murder weapon and maintaining that Edith had not been involved. However, when Edith's love letters were produced, the evidence appeared to be damning. In letter after letter, inspired by the romantic novels to which she was hopelessly addicted, Edith described her passionate love for Bywaters and the lengths to which she would go to be rid of Percy. Edith wrote that she had laced his mashed potatoes with ground glass on one occasion, and on another, she had tried to poison him with enough arsenic to kill an elephant, apparently at Bywaters' insistence. But Percy had survived with no obvious ill effects, and so in other letters Edith begged Bywaters to 'do something desperate!'[16]

Edith's counsel, Sir Henry Curtis-Bennett KC, built his case for the defence on his client's physical attractiveness and compelling personality, telling the jury that while writing the letters Edith had believed herself to be bathed in the 'glamorous aura of a great love'. Edith revelled in the attention. Finding herself in the most desperate of circumstances, she was at last where she had always wanted to be: centre stage. But then Edith had to take the greatest risk of all. After her counsel's glowing encomium, Edith had to go into the witness box herself.

It was a disaster. Curtis-Bennett pleaded with Edith not to testify, later telling a journalist:

> She spoiled her chances by her evidence and by her demeanour. I had a perfect answer to everything which I am sure would have won an acquittal if she had not been a witness. She was a vain woman and an obstinate one. She had an idea that she could carry the jury. Also she realized the enormous public interest, and decided to play up to it by entering the witness box. Her imagination was highly developed, but it failed to show her the mistake she was making.[17]

If Edith had entered the witness box playing the role of repentant, grieving widow, modestly dressed in mourning black, with a handkerchief to her eyes, she might indeed have carried the jury. Instead, Edith made a dreadful impression. She succeeded in being both maudlin and flirtatious, constantly contradicted herself, and claimed that all the references to poisoning her husband were invented to impress Bywaters. Sir Bernard Spilsbury, the Home Office pathologist, had testified to the effect that he had found no trace of poisoning during Percy Thompson's post mortem. But as if her affair with Bywaters was not enough to damn Edith in the eyes of the jury, her letters also contained graphic references to an abortion, a procedure then both illegal and viewed as morally repugnant. As the prosecution caught Edith out in lie after lie, her arrogance and vanity destroyed any chance of acquittal.

Bywaters maintained that Edith was completely innocent, since he had no intention of murdering Percy Thompson. In Bywaters' version of events, he lay in wait for the couple, intending to challenge Percy Thompson to a fight that went tragically wrong. Bywaters stuck to his story doggedly, claiming that he had never believed Edith would harm her husband but that she had a vivid imagination and her letters saw her acting out a role. Mr Justice Shearman, summing up, described the letters as 'full of the outpourings of a silly but at the same time, a wicked affection',[18] but instructed the jury not to convict Edith Thompson unless they were completely satisfied that both parties agreed that Percy Thompson should be murdered, and that 'she knew that he was going to do it, and directed him to do it, and by arrangement between them he was doing it'.[19]

The jury took just over two hours to find Edith Thompson and Freddy Bywaters guilty of murder. When the verdict was declared, Bywaters shouted out that Edith was innocent, while she succumbed to a fit of hysterics. Both parties lodged appeals but these were dismissed.

Until Edith was sentenced, she had fared badly in the popular press as an adulteress who had undergone an abortion and plotted to kill her husband. Once the death sentence had been imposed, the public attitude swiftly changed. A petition with almost one million signatures went to the Home Secretary, William Bridgeman, pleading for a reprieve. Overnight, Edith had been exonerated as a silly fantasist but nothing more, while there was admiration of Bywaters' protective attitude and enduring loyalty. Edith Thompson also attracted sympathy because the notion of hanging a woman had become distasteful. No woman had been executed in Britain since the double hanging of the baby farmers Amelia Sach and Annie Walters in 1903. Edith believed that it was only a matter of time before she was reprieved. When she was finally given the date for her execution, Edith suffered a complete breakdown and spent her last days crying and screaming, unable to eat or sleep.

On the morning of 9 January 1923, at nine o'clock, the lovers were executed simultaneously just half a mile apart. Edith Thompson died at Holloway, and Bywaters was hanged at Pentonville. Bywaters died bravely, hanged by William Willis, and protesting Edith's innocence to the last. Edith Thompson had become so distressed by the morning of her execution that she had to be heavily sedated. According to Edith's executioner, John Ellis, she had to be carried from the condemned cell by two warders and held upright on the gallows while Ellis completed the formalities.

As the trapdoor sprang open, and Edith Thompson plunged to her death, witnesses were horrified to observe blood gushing out between her legs. Edith, possibly pregnant, had suffered a massive haemorrhage. And yet she had refused to 'plead her belly', to use the archaic phrase, when pregnancy would have brought certain reprieve. Following this particularly horrific execution, several of the prison officers took early retirement. The hangman, John Ellis, retired in 1923 and committed suicide in 1931. As a consequence of Edith Thompson's execution, women condemned to the gallows were obliged to wear reinforced canvas knickers, in an attempt to prevent a repeat of such harrowing scenes.

Edith Thompson was buried within the precincts of Holloway and later reburied at Brookwood Cemetery in 1970, following building work at the prison. Edith was buried alongside the baby farmers Amelia Sach and Annie Walters, and her tombstone bears the epitaph: 'Sleep on beloved. Her death was a legal formality.'[20]

Edith Thompson's KC, Curtis-Bennett, was haunted for the rest of his life by his failure to save her from the gallows. Curtis-Bennett always maintained that Edith had 'paid the extreme penalty for her immorality'.[21] However, one of Curtis-Bennett's last remarks reveals the terrible irony of the entire case. 'Was it not proved that she had *posed* to him [Bywaters] as a woman capable of doing anything – even murder – to keep his love? She had to: Bywaters wanted to get away from her.'[22] Indeed he did. A series of letters between 20 June and 12 September 1922 shows Bywaters trying to break off the relationship. Had Bywaters been sufficiently strong enough to distance himself from Edith, both the lovers might have escaped the noose.

Social status and wealth appear to have been as vital an attribute to a successful court case as good counsel. Compare the fate of Edith Thompson with that of Madame Marguerite Fahmy, accused of shooting her husband, Prince Ali Fahmy Bey, at the Savoy Hotel.

The Savoy was one of the most expensive and exclusive hotels in London. Famous guests included Fred Astaire, and, as befitted the hotel where Oscar Wilde had once entertained his rent-boys, a blind eyed was turned to indiscretion. However, even the urbane patrons of the Savoy were taken aback by events on 10 July 1923. As the night porter was making his rounds at about 2 a.m., he heard three gunshots ring out in quick succession. As he raced into the luxury suite, he witnessed a beautiful, dark-haired woman in an evening gown throwing a gun to the floor, while the body of a young man was slumped against a wall, blood and brains oozing from a wound to his temple. Falling to her knees, the woman whimpered, *'Qu'est-ce que j'ai fait, mon cher?'* ('What have I done, my dear?') over and over again.[23]

The woman was Marguerite Fahmy and her victim was her 23-year-old husband, Prince Ali Fahmy Bey, an Egyptian national. The couple had met in Paris a year earlier, when Fahmy was just twenty-two. Marguerite, ten years older, had been regarded as a gold-digger by Fahmy's family and friends, but they had married in Egypt and Marguerite had even converted to Islam.

The shooting did not come as a surprise to the staff of the Savoy. Ever since they had arrived on 1 July, Marguerite and the prince had been embroiled in a series of bitter public rows. Witnesses testified to seeing the prince with scratches on his face, while Marguerite appeared with a bruised face, the marks inadequately covered with cosmetics. The previous evening, they had returned to the Savoy for supper after a performance of *The Merry Widow* at Daly's Theatre. There had been a terrible quarrel, during which Marguerite seized a wine bottle and threatened to smash it over her husband's head. With the help of the head waiter, the couple eventually settled down, and went off to the ballroom to listen to the band. Refusing to dance with her husband, Marguerite went off to bed.[24]

London had been sweltering under a heat wave for days

and that night the weather broke with a violent thunderstorm. Despite the appalling conditions, and deaf to the protests of his personal secretary, Said Enani, Prince Fahmy had jumped into a cab outside the Savoy and ordered the driver to take him to Piccadilly. When he eventually returned, there was another violent argument, the prince was shot dead and Marguerite was discovered holding a smoking gun.

The case was sensational. The murder of royalty, albeit foreign royalty, in a five-star hotel was enough to guarantee a packed gallery at the Old Bailey. When it emerged that the prince was apparently a sexual pervert who indulged in 'Oriental practices' the public was queuing up outside. Many of these were young women of barely eighteen. Edward Marshall Hall, appearing for the defence, glanced up at the gallery and warned them that if they chose to hear this case, they must take the consequences.[25] Nobody left.

Marshall Hall's strategy consisted of a plea of accidental killing. Marguerite had not intended to kill the prince, he argued. Instead, she had threatened to shoot herself and the gun had gone off accidentally during the ensuing struggle. A cynic might question whether anybody could be the victim of such extremely bad luck. Yet it was difficult to imagine that a woman who had never handled a gun before could blow a man's brains out with almost professional skill.

But Marshall Hall had an additional argument, which consisted of Marguerite's sickening catalogue of abuse at the hands of the prince. This took the form of a prolonged character assassination of the dead man, portraying him as a monster of sexual depravity. The prince had 'abnormal tendencies and he never treated Madame normally', he told the jury. Medical evidence testified to the effect that Marguerite had called the Savoy's doctor and complained of anal injuries caused by 'unnatural intercourse'. The resulting pain was so severe that she needed an operation.[26]

When Marguerite went into the witness box, she described a disturbing scene during which she had been seated 'in a state of undress' when she had noticed a strange noise and pulled aside the hangings to discover one of her husband's manservants spying on her. In response to Marguerite's horrified scream, her husband had just laughed and told her: 'He is nobody. He does not count. But he has the right to come here or anywhere you may go and tell me what you are doing.' Turning to the jury, Marshall Hall commented, 'We in this country put our women on a pedestal: in Egypt they have not the same views.'[27] In a parting shot, Marshall Hall suggested that there had been a homosexual relationship between the prince and his secretary, Said Enani.

'These things are horrible,' observed the judge, in his summing up. 'They are disgusting. How anyone could listen to these things who is not bound to listen to them passes comprehension.' The jury found Marguerite not guilty of murder or manslaughter in less than an hour.[28]

The world's press reported the case with undisguised glee, with headlines such as *Why They Forgave the Princess for Killing Her Husband*, and *Jury Unable to Convict the Unhappy Beauty After Hearing Her Tell How Prince Fahmy Bey's Black Spies Invaded Even the Privacy of Her Bridal Boudoir*.[29] While the French press wondered why English law did not have a defence of *crime passionnel,* the British press enjoyed portraying Marguerite as less than innocent. The prosecution had not been permitted to cross-examine Marguerite. If he had, the jury would have discovered that Marguerite had been a high-class prostitute, and a private detective hired by the prosecution claimed that her husband was not the only one in the marriage to enjoy same-sex relationships.

After the verdict, Marguerite left for Paris, where she found out that she had no claim to her late husband's fortune as he had left no will. After a failed attempt to convince her husband's family that she had given birth to a son, Marguerite became a laughing stock and withdrew from Parisian society. But she owed her life to Marshall Hall. The KC had used every theatrical device at his disposal, even appealing to the jury's latent racism and homophobia to ensure that she was acquitted. It had been a barnstorming performance.[30]

A similar case was heard at the Old Bailey in 1932, in which the socialite Elvira Barney was accused of shooting her lover, Scott Stephen, after a quarrel at her Belgravia home. On the advice of her counsel, Patrick Hastings, Elvira claimed that she had been trying to kill herself and that Stephen had been fatally injured as he tried to wrestle the weapon out of her hands. Hastings argued that the pistol had a hair-trigger, and the gun had gone off accidentally. The defence was successful: Elvira was acquitted.

Following the trials of Marguerite Fahmy and Elvira Barney, it seemed unlikely that any other woman would face execution for murder. Sadly, the fate of Ruth Ellis would subsequently challenge this assumption. In the meantime, let us leave the theatre of the courtroom, the 'little O' of the Old Bailey, and investigate the tide of crime lapping against its walls.

EAST END BOYS

The Origins of London's Gangland

The roots of London's 'gangland' have always been a rich source of myth and speculation. Ruled by 'diamond geezers' and 'hard bastards', it has been portrayed as a brutal, dangerous world in which domination was established by violence and neighbourhoods were carved up between rival villains. We have glimpsed the origins of this underworld in previous chapters, emerging like the points of jagged rocks from a stormy sea – the teeming slums of Seven Dials and Saffron Hill, the dangerous thoroughfare of Ratcliffe Highway, the foggy alleys of the East End. Victorian reformers attempted to sweep all this away with a rigorous combination of slum clearance, street lighting and the thin blue line of the Metropolitan Police. The rookeries were torn down and gas lamps glowed in the shadows, but this proved no match for the entrenched lawlessness of London's underworld, as family gangs marked out the city for their own.

By the Edwardian era, the East End was governed by gangs characterized by ethnic and national identity. There were

Irish gangs, Jewish gangs and Italian gangs, confirming the public prejudice that 'dangerous foreigners' were responsible for the majority of crime, as well as home-grown gangs in the form of the Elephant Boys, from Elephant and Castle, and the Titanics from Hoxton. From time to time, rival gangs from other cities would attempt to muscle in, such as Birmingham's Brummagen Boys, led by exiled East Ender Billy Kimber, and the Leeds gang. During this period, London's gangland had the aura of the Wild West about it, with a series of shoot-outs and gun fights. In the glittering gin-palaces mirrors were smashed, hapless thugs were punched across counters and optics were shot out as simmering vendettas erupted into bar-room brawls. But the villains still had their standards. Guns were commonplace but knives were considered unsporting. Top East End 'face' Arthur Harding boasted, 'As an Englishman, I would never use a knife.'[1]

Harding had been born into poverty in 1886, and received his first sentence in 1902, when he was sentenced to twelve months' penal servitude for helping 'One-Eyed Charlie' steal a bale of rags worth eighteen shillings from a cart. After three months in Wormwood Scrubs, Harding went to a Borstal, a specialist prison for young delinquents that had just been introduced that year. This proved the making of him. 'Borstal made me fitter, stronger, taller and when I went back to my old associates I found I was something of a hero.'[2] Harding's biggest rival was Isaac 'Ikey' Bogard, a pimp or *shundicknick*, also known as 'the Coon' on account of his dark complexion. As if to accentuate the frontier town atmosphere of the East End, Bogard affected an American accent, wore a Stetson and leather chaps and carried a gun.

The hostility between Harding and Bogard lasted for years. In 1903 Bogard conspired to have Harding murdered, but the plot failed. The feud culminated at Christmas 1907 in 'the

Vendetta Affair', after a fight over a woman led to a show-down in the Bluecoat Boy in Bishopsgate. Each gang was a dozen strong. Bogard offered Harding a drink. Harding promptly flung it back in his face and then followed it up with the glass. 'The Coon had a face like the map of England,' Harding gloated afterwards.[3] Harding's language, so offensive to the modern reader, did not merely reflect the prejudices of the times. Harding was a racist and subsequently an associate of Oswald Mosley.

Bogard and his gang were up in Old Street Police Court a few days later, and Bogard asked for police protection. He was justified, as Harding and his men attempted to shoot the Bogard gang as they left the court. This had the effect of intimidating any witnesses to the attack in the Bluecoat Boy, and the case collapsed. The landlord was so frightened that he refused to give evidence and retired to Southend, where his pub became a popular retreat for gangland types.

Considering that he had attempted to murder Bogard, Harding received a remarkably light sentence of just three years for affray and possessing a firearm in a court of law. Summing up, Mr Justice Avory commented that it was unacceptable for part of London to be 'infested by a number of criminal ruffians armed with revolvers', and recommended 'remedial legislation' to tackle gangsters. Such legislation was badly needed. Within a month of leaving gaol, Harding was back to his old ways.[4] But 'Ikey' Bogard took a different path. When the First World War came along, he enlisted and emerged with a Military Medal, and ended his days as a bookmaker in Wandsworth. By going straight, or reasonably straight, Bogard was something of an anomaly in post-World War I London.

By 1920, the city was in the grip of a crime wave, caused by one of the greatest innovations of the twentieth century, the motor car. Luxury cars left unattended in busy streets were stolen, used to execute a crime and then swiftly abandoned. Impossible to catch, high on excitement, this new breed of armed robbers became increasingly daring. In their stolen vehicles they could cover a considerable distance, with the result that householders in town and country alike were terrorized by masked burglars. Post offices were raided day and night, and female clerks held up at gunpoint. Cashiers, carrying the day's takings to the bank, were knocked down and robbed in broad daylight, while the actual banks were held up at gunpoint. Handbags were ripped from the arms of defenceless women, and West End jewellers were forced to fit metal grilles across the windows to guard against smash and grab. Safe-crackers, meanwhile, found it comparatively easy to transport their heavy oxy-acetylene cutting apparatus by car. Motorists were hijacked and threatened with death if they resisted, and garages pillaged for petrol, oil and cash. The police officers who attempted to intervene were shot with automatic pistols and in some cases murdered. As Detective Inspector Hambrook observed, for all practical purposes, there was no mobile police force at all, 'and criminals snapped their fingers at our impotent efforts to catch them'.[5]

A crime wave of this magnitude deserved a swift response, and it arrived in 1920 in the form of the Flying Squad. The Flying Squad began life as a mobile undercover patrol in 1919. It consisted of a covered wagon, with detectives hidden beneath the tarpaulin in the back, which patrolled the streets on the lookout for known criminals or 'faces'. In 1920, the squad bought two Crossley motor vehicles from the Royal Flying Corps. The Crossleys were unwieldy vehicles compared with the luxury motors favoured by villains. They had thin wheels and tyres, no front brakes and a top speed of 40 m.p.h. One patrolled the streets north of the Thames, and the other south of the river. The *Daily Mail's* crime reporter, G. T.

Crook, is credited with inventing the name 'the Flying Squad', which swiftly passed into Cockney rhyming slang as 'Sweeney Todd' or simply 'the Sweeney'. By 1923, a mobile receiver was fitted to the top of one of the Crossleys, linked to a radio at Scotland Yard. This rudimentary system allowed the Crossleys to receive radio signals while on the move. The heavy wireless antennae looked like bedsteads and made the Crossleys even more difficult to manoeuvre, but the benefits outweighed the disadvantages. According to Flying Squad veteran Inspector 'Nutty' Sharpe: 'What a change that little transmitter wrought in the business of catching crooks. One day the tenders were patrolling blind to what might be happening in the next street. The next, cruise where they might, they were in receipt instantaneously of whatever helpful information found its way into every department of the Metropolitan Police.'[6]

The Flying Squad faced one of its greatest challenges when faced with the formidable team of John 'Ruby' Sparks and Lillian Goldstein. Born in Bermondsey, Sparks was the son of a receiver and a bare-knuckle fighter. Sparks started young, working for a gang of mail robbers who would hide him in a hamper in the guard's van. Once the train was moving, Sparks would leap out and scarper with anything he could lay his hands on. The nickname Ruby derived from the fact that he had once stolen some rubies from a maharaja but had been told they were worthless by an incompetent fence. It was only after he had handed them out like sweeties that one of his acquaintances told him the hoard had been worth thousands of pounds.

Becoming a cat burglar in 1923, Sparks teamed up with Lillian Goldstein, who drove a Mercedes and was believed to have been the brains behind a series of daring country-house robberies. Lillian Goldstein, with her flapper bob and cheeky red beret, had started life as a nice Jewish girl from Wembley, but the rebellious streak had set in early. After a 'wide boy' broke her heart, Lillian abandoned her career as a dressmaker and worked briefly as a prostitute, servicing clients in the back of taxis as they drove round Hyde Park. After a brief gaol sentence Lillian threw in her lot with Sparks and found her true vocation as a getaway driver, keeping the engine running as Sparks slipped into deserted country houses and seized the valuables.

Inspector Nutty Sharpe displayed grudging respect for Lillian. 'She could whiz that great long tourer about with the skill of an artist,' he recalled. 'Her trouble was that she ought to have been a boy.'[7]

This dramatic existence came to an abrupt conclusion in 1927 when the couple was arrested. Sparks received three years in Strangeways, but Lillian was cleared. In 1940, the couple was briefly reunited, when Lillian hid Sparks in her Wembley home after he was on the run from Dartmoor. Lillian got six months for hiding Sparks but only served three weeks, as her willingness to harbour him was interpreted as evidence of her feminine nature. By this time, Lillian had clearly learned her lesson. After leaving prison, when Sparks approached her to take part in another raid which would involve throwing ammonia in a victim's face, she broke up with him for good, telling Sparks, 'I've had enough of this bandit queen lark!'[8] Sparks eventually abandoned the bandit game himself, setting up as a newsagent in Chalk Farm and regretting, in his memoirs, that he had not gone straight years earlier.

Ruby Sparks and Lillian Goldstein operated within the tradition of London crime. The Georgian highwaymen and the swaggering cracksmen of the Victorian era would have recognized the couple's athletic bravado and ruthless ambition, and understood Lillian's pragmatic decision to quit when it all got too much. Sparks and Goldstein emerged as sympathetic figures. 'They're a colourfully rascally lot, these wide 'uns!' as Inspector Nutty Sharpe observed.[9] But it is at this point that a darker element enters the picture. This is the shadowy world of illicit drugs.

In historical terms, legislation regarding the sale of drugs is comparatively recent. Until the Poisons and Pharmacy Act of 1908, 'dangerous' drugs were freely available. Opium, imported from India and China, was a universal sedative. Laudanum, a mixture of alcohol and opium, was a general specific against all ills, from teething to cramps and melancholia. Cannabis constituted a vital ingredient in cough syrup, while cocaine was valued for its uplifting properties. Ernest Shackleton took 'Forced March' cocaine tablets to Antarctica in 1909, as did Captain Scott a year later on his ill-fated journey to the South Pole.[10] Until the Defence of the Realm Act was imposed in 1916, chemists were still selling sheets impregnated with cocaine and opium to send to 'friends at the Front'.

The first stirrings of modern anxiety about drug abuse resulted in the International Opium Convention 1912 (the Hague Convention), which recommended limiting the manufacture, trade and use of opiates to medical purposes, closing opium dens, penalizing unauthorized possession of opiates and prohibiting their sale to unauthorized persons. When this was implemented in the Dangerous Drugs Act 1920, with subsequent legislation in 1925, drugs which had been a common feature of daily life became controlled substances and, with a few strokes of the pen, recreational drug use was criminalized. The impact of this legislation reverberated through London's underworld, from the flappers of Mayfair to the Chinese immigrants of the East End, and created a new breed of criminal: the drug dealer. It also created a new class of victims, the celebrity drug addict or 'dope fiend'. The first of these was Billie Carleton, an attractive young actress. On the night of 28 November 1918, Billie Carleton had a starring role in the Victory Ball at the Albert Hall, appearing in an 'extraordinary and daring costume which consisted almost entirely of transparent black georgette'.[11]

Billie's performance was a triumph, but the following morning she was found dead in bed at the Savoy Hotel. She was only twenty-two years old. A small gold box containing cocaine stood on her bedside table and at the inquest it was suggested that she had died of 'cocaine poisoning', although this is extremely rare and it is more likely that she choked. As the sordid details of Billie's brief life emerged, it was revealed that she was a heavy user of opium and cocaine, and had three 'protectors'. There were two older men who supported her financially and paid for her permanent suite at the Savoy and a third gentleman, a dress designer named Reggie de Veulle, who supplied her with the drugs he purchased from Lau Ping You, a Chinese man from Limehouse, and his Scottish wife Ada.

De Veulle's past as a drug dealer emerged when he went on trial at the Old Bailey charged with manslaughter and conspiracy to supply cocaine. In court, it was revealed that de Veulle had been involved in a previous homosexual blackmail case and with a headline that read *An Opium Circle – Chinaman's Wife Sent to Prison – High Priestess of Unholy Rites*, *The Times* reported that both de Veulle and Carleton had been at an all-night 'orgy' in a Mayfair flat where the women wore flimsy négligées and the men dressed in silk pyjamas while smoking opium.

Billie emerged from the case as a tragic victim, and was described by the *Daily Sketch* newspaper on 14 January 1919 as an innocent girl possessed of 'a certain frail beauty of that perishable, moth-like substance that does not last long in the wear and tear of this rough-and-ready world'. Ada was sentenced to five months' hard labour, her husband escaped with just a ten-pound fine while, despite the judge's direction, the jury acquitted Carleton's friend Reggie de Veulle of her manslaughter. He admitted, however, to supplying Carleton cocaine and was imprisoned for eight months.

A media frenzy followed, with the *Daily Express* warning readers that 'You will find the woman dope fiend in Chelsea, in Mayfair and Maida Vale. An obscure traffic is pursued in certain doubtful teashops,' while the *Daily Mail* asserted that 'Men do not as a rule take to drugs, unless there is a hereditary influence, but women are more temperamentally attracted.' Questions in the House of Commons called for drug dealers to be flogged and all Chinese to be deported, while the press insisted that there was a strong relationship between drug use and the so-called 'white slave trade' in which white women were lured into prostitution after becoming hooked on drugs.[12]

Opium dens had been a fixture of East End life for decades. Opium smoking had been introduced by Chinese immigrants and was popular with Lascars (East India Company sailors), prostitutes and drifters as well as appealing to aristocrats and bohemians. Until the Defence of the Realm Act, the practice was regarded as the Chinese prerogative. One policeman commented, 'They don't care for no drink, and seem to live without eating so far as I know. It's their opium at night they likes; and you'll find half-a-dozen on 'em in one bed at Yahee's, a-smoking and sleeping away like so many lime-kilns and dormice!'[13]

There were relatively low numbers of Chinese people in London during the early twentieth century but they had become associated with the popular myths of the evil genius Fu Man Chu and there was general prejudice against the Chinese. When, four years after the death of Billie Carleton, Freda Kempton died after an overdose of cocaine, the Chinese were again held responsible.

Freda was a 'dance instructress' – her task being to dance with any man who paid. She worked at Dalton's in Leicester Square, owned by the 'Queen of Clubs', Kate Meyrick, a resilient Irishwoman who had turned to club management to pay the school fees after Mr Meyrick had deserted her and their six children. Frequently raided by the police for infringing licensing laws, Dalton's had a secret exit enabling peers of the realm and high court judges to make a swift exit when the Old Bill arrived.[14]

At Freda's inquest, it emerged that on the night of her death she had been dancing with 'Brilliant Chang', a Chinese restaurateur. Brilliant Chang was a small, elegant man, handsome in a lean, ascetic way, who dressed in fur-collared coats and suede shoes. Women found him extraordinarily attractive, but his

Brilliant Chang, London's first celebrity
drug dealer, in 1924. Chang's Chinese restaurant
was condemned as 'a den of iniquity'.

good looks were turned against him by a Fleet Street determined to demonize him as a corrupter of women. According to the *World Pictorial News* he 'dispensed Chinese delicacies and the drugs and vices of the Orient' from his restaurant and his obsession with women required him to be paid 'in kind'. When women agreed to sleep with him, then apparently, 'The flame of evil passion burned more brightly within and he hugged himself with unholy glee!'[15]

At Freda's inquest, Brilliant Chang denied all knowledge of the cocaine. The coroner accepted this, but the press and police were determined to portray Chang as a villain and a series of raids forced him to close his restaurant and move to premises in Limehouse Causeway. In 1924, the police raided his flat and discovered a wrap of cocaine beneath a floorboard. This was all the evidence they needed to arrest the man behind 40 per cent of London's cocaine trade.

During Chang's trial, the press had a field day. The *World Pictorial News* told of girls visiting the 'den of iniquity' above the restaurant, where half a dozen women joined him for 'drug-fuelled orgies'. If drug-taking itself was not sufficient grounds for vilification, the notion that white women were being corrupted by a 'dangerous foreigner' appealed to popular bigotry.

Chang was gaoled for eighteen months in 1924 and then deported. Scores of women turned up at the Royal Albert Dock to see his ship sail. His subsequent life was the subject of wild speculation with some reports claiming he had become a successful drug dealer in Switzerland, and others maintaining he had died in penury. The *Daily Telegraph*'s Stanley Firmin insisted that Chang had gone blind and ended his days working in a kitchen garden. It was left to that keen student of human nature, Inspector Nutty Sharpe, to provide a decent epitaph. Believing that Chang had been framed, Sharpe concluded, 'The Chinaman is a pretty honourable fellow.'[16]

Another police officer, the legendary 'Fabian of the Yard',

Robert Fabian, had plenty to say about London's drug dealers. In his memoirs, he described the first time he set eyes on Eddie Manning. It was his first week in uniform, and he was in the 'mixed-up backyard of Soho', escorted by an old-timer who was due for retirement. Manning was 'a tall slim negro, superbly well dressed in a tightly tailored black overcoat with velvet collar and homburg hat, and cigar in his big teeth'. As Fabian described it:

> 'That's "Eddie the Villain",' says the old timer. 'If you get an urge to talk to him, don't. If he wants to give you a cig-arette, refuse it. Never take a drink with him; never go to his place if you want information. Scrub him out of your life – he's the worst man in London ... Some well-known men and women have died at his place under drugs or some other diabolical practice.'[17]

Eddie Manning certainly had form. In 1920 he had shot three men in Cambridge Circus after they had insulted his girlfriend, and was gaoled for sixteen months. In 1922 an ex-serviceman called Eric Goodwin died of a heroin overdose at Manning's house. Manning was arrested in Primrose Hill, carrying a silver-topped cane with a secret compartment for stashing drugs. According to Robert Fabian, Manning held 'dope-parties' all over London, offering injections of cocaine at ten shillings a time. He had a strong-arm gang of black and white henchmen and a sideline as a pimp. After being gaoled for drugs offences, which prompted predictably racist headlines about the 'evil negro', Manning turned to receiving stolen goods. He was arrested again after receiving luggage worth £1,500 stolen from Lady Diana Cooper and died in Parkhurst in 1931.[18]

While the drug trade was lucrative, it would be decades before it dominated the London underworld as it does today. By far

the most profitable area of crime in the early twentieth century was gambling, either the off-street variety in clubs or
spielers, or racecourse betting with bookmakers or 'turf
accountants', who took bets from punters on the 'runners'.
Bookies' activities were controlled by the Jockey Club, under
a strict code of conduct. (High-street betting shops would not
come into being until 1963, after a change in legislation.)
According to the East End criminal Arthur Harding, 'The
racecourse business was a profitable one. When a gang went to
a racecourse like Brighton they could clear £4,000 or £5,000
easy. At Epsom, on Derby Day, it could be £15,000 or
£20,000.'[19]

Bookies, with their massive quantities of cash, were vulnerable and racetrack gangs operated by offering bookies
protection from other gangs in return for a cut of the proceeds. Bookies were charged for the chalk they used on their
blackboards, showing the odds, the stools they stood on, and
even the sponging down of their boards between races. They
were also expected to keep the punters talking so that the
pickpockets could set to work, the 'dips' described by DS
Charles Vanstone as 'feral, shifty little men' who darted about
all over the place. Bookies were also expected to contribute to
funds for the distressed wives of gangsters who had recently
been gaoled. Young lads started in the business sponging
down the boards for the bookies. It was the first job for an
eight-year-old lad called Frankie Fraser, better known subsequently as 'Mad' Frankie Fraser.[20]

From 1910, Billy Kimber and his Brummagen Boys controlled the racetracks at Newbury, Epsom, Alexandra Park,
Earls Park and Kempton Park. Kimber's rivals were the
Italian gangs, the Sabinis and the Cortesis, the Titanics from
the East End, the Elephant Boys from south London, and the
Leeds gang. Hammers, hatchets, guns and coshes were
common weapons, but racetrack gangs particularly favoured

razors, which were silent but deadly and could be concealed in a lapel of a jacket or the peak of a cap. Slashings were commonplace and one bookie was killed at Sandown Park. There were also several mass brawls, such as the Battle of Epsom in 1921 when the Brummagen Boys and the Leeds mob decided to take on the Italian gangs. But the Brummagen Boys ambushed the Leeds mob by mistake and there was a pitched battle lasting ten minutes before it became obvious that they were attacking the wrong opponents. In the subsequent court case, twenty-three men were convicted.

'The Italians' consisted of two powerful families, the Sabinis, who boasted that they were descended from the Sabine tribe, and the Cortesis. The Sabinis lived in Saffron Hill, which had become known as 'Little Italy', as an Italian community had been there since the 1840s. The Sabini gang consisted of Charles 'Darby' Sabini, Joe, Fred, George and Harry Boy Sabini. Darby took on the role of Mafia Godfather, dispensing justice, resolving internal conflicts and protecting the honour of young women, such as a barmaid whose dress had been pulled off her by a local yob. The Sabinis possessed a daunting reputation; they would stand side-on at racetracks so that the bookmakers could see the hammers in their pockets.

The Sabinis' biggest rivals were the Cortesi gang, and matters came to a head in November 1922, in an incident remembered as the Battle of the Frattelanza Club. According to Louisa Doralli, daughter of the club's manager, the Cortesi gang, comprising Gus, Paul and George Cortesi, Harry 'Frenchie' and Alexander Tomaso Cortesi, a.k.a. Sandy Rice, had arrived at the club intending to attack the Sabinis. When Frenchie pulled a gun, Louisa grabbed him, assuming that he would not shoot a woman, but Frenchie wrenched the gun out of her grasp and all hell broke loose. Gus Cortesi hit Darby Sabini with a lemonade bottle and fired at him, but the bullet went out of the window.

Frenchie went on the run and the *Daily Express* circulated a description of him: 'He walks with a Charlie Chaplin step, the result of a combination of flat feet and knock knees but he is able to disguise not only his walk but his features.'[21] George, Paul and Tomaso Cortesi were cleared but Gus and Frenchie were gaoled for three years. The incident provoked a great deal of anti-Italian feeling. At the trial Mr Justice Darling warned the Sabinis and the Cortesis that if there were further trouble in the 'Italian colony', those responsible would be deported.

Darby Sabini moved to Brighton and took up permanent residence at the Grand Hotel, where, by corrupting police officers and intimidating witnesses, he assured the success of his next venture. He imported over 300 henchmen from Sicily as enforcers. Then, teaming up with the London gang known as the Yiddishers, and a Jewish bookmaker called Alf Solomons, Darby Sabini decided to challenge Billy Kimber's supremacy of the racetrack syndicate, by launching their Bookmakers and Backers Racehorse Protection Society. The end result was a bloody confrontation later known as the Battle of Lewes in 1936, when Alf Solomons and his clerk, Mark Frater, were attacked by a gang of around thirty anti-Sabini Londoners, mainly from Hoxton and Hackney. Frater was hit with a hatchet by gang member James 'Spinky' Spink, but his bowler hat deflected the impact of the blow. Sixteen of the men involved in the fight were later gaoled, and 'Spinky' became the inspiration for the gangster Pinky Brown in Graham Greene's *Brighton Rock*.

But Darby Sabini was losing control. He sued a newspaper for libel after an unflattering profile, and was then declared bankrupt. With the declaration of war in 1939, many Italians, including several of Darby's brothers, were interned as enemy aliens. The final straw came when Darby's beloved son was killed on active service with the RAF. Immortalized as the gangster Colleoni in *Brighton Rock*, Darby Sabini died in 1950, a broken man.

Rounding up the Italian gangsters was just one consequence of a war that was to change London, and its underworld, forever. As the Luftwaffe bombers wreaked destruction on the East End, the villains grew tougher than ever. It was a classic case of Nietzsche's maxim that whatever doesn't kill you, makes you stronger. The 'hard bastards' called up for military service returned leaner and fitter, equipped with professional weapons training and skills that would prove indispensable in the age of armed robbery, while the 'diamond geezers' took over the black market and traded in everything from ration books to silk stockings. Meanwhile the Metropolitan Police, numbers depleted by the call-up, struggled to maintain law and order. London became an 'unreal city', gripped by a climate of fear.

LONDON MONSTERS

Killers in the Smoke

Wartime London was known as 'the Smoke' and no name could have been more appropriate for this sinister shadowland. Coal dust and gas and the fumes of millions of cigarettes hovered over London in a permanent fog. It was easy to become disorientated in a city where familiar landmarks had been blotted out, road signs had been painted out to confuse the enemy and residential streets had been reduced to blackened bombsites. This twilight world of shifting allegiances and smudged identities proved the ideal climate for identity crime. In the Smoke, a conman with forged papers might masquerade as a military hero, while a bachelor with twinkling eyes could prise his victims from their fortunes. In this twilight realm, a sexual predator roamed free, his despicable crimes hidden behind an alias. The Smoke was a psychopath's playground, where appearances were deceptive, and nothing was what it seemed.

This was the backdrop against which a handsome US serviceman stepped into the Black and White Cafe,

Hammersmith, on the afternoon of 3 October 1944. When his eyes met those of a beautiful blonde girl, he introduced himself, in his rich American drawl, as Captain Ricky Rafeld. The girl's name was Georgina Grayson and she told Rafeld that she worked as an exotic dancer at the Panama Club, in Knightsbridge. Eager to impress, Captain Rafeld confided that he was really a Chicago gangster and he produced a Colt 45 revolver to prove it. Thrilled, Georgina arranged to meet him again that night, and Rafeld picked her up in an army truck. Fascinated by her potential role as a gangster's moll, Georgina declared, 'Let's do something exciting!' The resulting chain of events resembled a lurid Hollywood movie as 'the gangster' and 'the showgirl' rampaged through wartime London.[1]

Rafeld and Georgina spotted their first victim, Violet Hodge, dragging a heavy suitcase towards Paddington Station. Violet was on her way home to Bristol, so Rafeld offered her a lift. They drove as far as Egham in Surrey, then Rafeld stopped the truck, knocked Violet unconscious and tried to strangle her. When this failed, he threw her into the river and drove off. Meanwhile, Georgina went through Violet's belongings and stole her ration book and cash.[2]

Next day, Rafeld and Georgina tried to hold up a car. This ended in disaster when the driver turned out to be an American officer and pulled his gun on them. The same evening, driving around London, Rafeld knocked a female cyclist off her bicycle. As she staggered to her feet, the couple approached her as if coming to her aid. Instead of helping, they stole her handbag and threw her bicycle over a hedge. By this point, Violet Hodge had gone to the police. Far from drowning, she had been revived by the cold water and was ready to press charges.

Meanwhile, Georgina and Rafeld had embarked on their next adventure. Rafeld flagged down a taxi cab in

Hammersmith, within walking distance of Georgina's flat. But by this time, Georgina knew better than to question his actions. The cab, a grey Ford V8 saloon, was driven by George Heath from Ewell in Surrey. Heath, aged thirty-three, had one distinctive feature, a cleft chin. The taxi drove off down the Great West Road, and near Staines, Rafeld ordered the driver to stop. He did so, turning round to open the door for Georgina. As she emerged from the cab, she heard a click. 'Then I heard a shot. There was a flash. I was deafened,' Georgina later told the court at her trial.[3] Rafeld was standing at the door of the cab with his gun in his hand. He told Georgina to go through the driver's pockets, and when she refused, picked up the revolver. 'You heard what I said. I'll do the same to you if you don't go through his pockets.' Heath was still alive as she took £8 in change, a watch and a fountain pen from his pockets. Rafeld drove the cab to Knowle Green, a stretch of common near Staines, dragged the body from the car and rolled it into a ditch. As Georgina handed over the driver's handkerchief so that Rafeld could wipe the blood off his hands, she said: 'He's dead, isn't he? This is cold-blooded murder. Why did you do it?' Rafeld replied, 'People in my profession are used to things like that.' Georgina shook her head. After all, Captain Rafeld was a Chicago gangster, wasn't he?[4]

Rafeld drove the taxi back to Hammersmith and parked in Lurgan Avenue W6, near Georgina's flat. The following day, the couple spent Heath's £8 dog racing, then went 'Up West' to get Georgina a fur coat. This would not be obtained by the conventional method of entering a shop. Instead, Rafeld tried to steal a woman's coat at gunpoint as she was leaving the Berkeley Hotel. When her shrieks of terror brought a hotel doorman to her rescue, Rafeld and Georgina scarpered.[5]

By this time, Heath's body had been discovered, and was quickly identified by his cleft chin. Then the stolen taxi was found in Lurgan Avenue. When Rafeld got into the taxi at nine o'clock that night, he was arrested. Meanwhile, Georgina got drunk and started dropping hints to an old boyfriend that she had done something terrible. Since this ex-boyfriend, Henry Kimberley, was a special constable, he went straight to his superiors and Georgina was quickly arrested.

Once the gangster and the showgirl were in custody, their extraordinary facade of lies was revealed. Handsome 'Captain Rafeld' was really Karl Hulten, a 22-year-old private, who had stolen the captain's identity, along with an army truck, when he went AWOL. Far from being a Chicago gangster, he was a grocery shop assistant from Boston. As for glamorous Georgina Grayson, she was really eighteen-year-old Betty Jones from Neath, the widow of an English paratrooper. Between the two of them, Karl and Betty had created a fantasy world, with terrible consequences for their victim, George Heath.

The US courts waived their rights to court martial Hulten and he went on trial in Britain. Inevitably, each blamed the other for Heath's murder, Hulten maintaining that the gun had gone off accidentally and there had been no intention to kill. Jones was defended by Mrs Ethel Lloyd Lane, the first female barrister to appear for the defence of a prisoner charged with murder. The trial lasted six days and both were sentenced to death. Hulten was hanged on 8 March 1945 but Jones was reprieved, provoking widespread indignation and streams of telegrams to the Home Secretary. 'SHE SHOULD HANG!' was chalked on the walls of Neath, her native town, beside pictures of a figure dangling from a gallows.[6] Among those calling for Jones' execution was the playwright George Bernard Shaw, who declared that Jones was unfit to live in a civilized community.[7] George Orwell, whose essay on *The Decline of the English Murder* was inspired by this case, had a more thoughtful response. Orwell regarded the couple's *folie à deux* as a product of its times, influenced by the false consciousness of American gangster films. 'The whole meaningless story, with its atmosphere of dance-halls, movie-palaces, cheap perfume, false names and stolen cars, provided distraction amid the doodle-bugs and the anxieties of the Battle of France,' he observed. 'Jones and Hulten committed their murder to the tune of V1, and were convicted to the tune of V2.'[8] Betty Jones went to prison for nine years, and was released on licence in 1954.

Jones had a lucky escape. Young and impetuous, she had been transfixed by the glamour of crime and plunged into a fantasy world. Despite public protests, she was spared the gallows. Jones was also spared the grim fate of another regular at the Panama Club, a young woman named Margery Gardner.

On 21 June 1946, Superintendent Reginald Spooner, of the CID F Division was called to Room Four of the Pembridge Court Hotel, Pembridge Gardens, Notting Hill, where he found the body of a woman lying on the bed. With her long legs and luxuriant red hair, she must have been attractive in life. But in death, she was hideously mutilated. Her wrists and ankles had been bound, her face had been whipped with a riding crop, which had left distinctive diamond-shaped marks, one nipple had been bitten off and a poker had been thrust into her vagina, causing a fatal haemorrhage. Home Office pathologist Keith Simpson commented on the marks from the whip, and told the police, 'Find that whip and you've got your man.'[9]

When the crime reporter Duncan Webb heard about the case from a police contact, he guessed the victim's identity at once. Her name was Margery Gardner, and she was a regular at the Nag's Head in Kinnerton Street, a Knightsbridge pub frequented by ex-servicemen, debutantes and would-be bohemians. According to the landlord, Len Cole, Margery was a spirited woman in her thirties who had abandoned her husband and daughter in Sheffield and run away to London to be an artist. While she waited for that dream to come true, Margery worked as a film extra. Recently, Margery had taken up with a man who referred to himself as Lieutenant Colonel Bill Armstrong, a regular at the Nag's Head. With his unforgettable personality and blond good looks, Armstrong was a distinctive figure in the West End, towering over his fellow drinkers and regaling them with tales of his wartime exploits in the South African air force. The previous evening, Armstrong had left the Nag's Head for the Panama Club, where he had been seen drinking with Margery Gardner.[10]

Armstrong was swiftly identified as Neville Heath. Far from being a war hero, Heath was a cashiered RAF officer with a string of convictions for fraud. Dishonourably discharged from the Royal Army Service Corps in 1940, he had eventually joined the South African Air Force and risen to the rank of captain before being court martialled for wearing medals to which he was not entitled. Heath's photograph was circulated in the *Police Gazette* and every station in the country from Inverness to Worthing. There was a systematic hunt of Heath's haunts and, since he held a pilot's licence, a special watch mounted on all airfields. At this point, a woman came forward and told police that she had gone to a hotel room with Heath months earlier. The woman, who did not wish to be identified, had been the victim of a violent attack and owed her life to the hotel detective who burst into the room when he heard her screaming.[11]

Heath had fled to Worthing, and the family home of his fiancée, Miss Yvonne Symmonds. Yvonne's parents had been very impressed with the valiant ex-serviceman until his name appeared in the Sunday papers in connection with the Margery Gardner murder. Despite Yvonne's tearful protests, her parents threw him out.[12] Heath travelled to Bournemouth, where he took a room at the Tollard Royal Hotel under the poetic alias of Group Captain Rupert Brook. On 8 July Armstrong picked up a former WREN, Doreen Marshall, who was staying at the Norfolk Hotel, and they spent a day together.

The following morning, when Doreen had not returned to the Norfolk Hotel, the manager reported her missing, and told police that she had last been seen with Group Captain Brook. The police interviewed Heath, who claimed he had walked Doreen back to her hotel the previous evening. When the police searched his room, they found a horse-whip that corresponded exactly with the whip that had been used on Margery Gardner. At this point, when it became evident that 'Group Captain Brook' was in fact the wanted Neville Heath, Heath was arrested and taken back to London, where he was charged with her murder. During Heath's interview, the corpse of Doreen Marshall had been recovered from Branksome Chine, Bournemouth. Heath's last victim had been tied up, stabbed and horribly mutilated, while she was still alive.[13]

Neville Heath went on trial for the murder of Margery Gardner on 24 September 1946. His counsel, J. D. Casswell KC, told Heath to plead guilty on the grounds of insanity. However, this defence was destroyed by the prosecution who called two doctors to testify that – although Heath was a sexual psychopath – he was not insane and he was well aware of the consequences of his actions when he killed Margery Gardner.[14] Heath was found guilty and sentenced to death. Just before his execution at Pentonville on 16 October 1946, he was offered a glass of whisky. 'Considering the circumstances,' he quipped, 'better make it a double.'[15]

The hangman Albert Pierrepoint later recorded that Heath was the most handsome man he had ever hanged.[16] Pierrepoint also noted in his diary that he had used a special strap of pale calf leather to bind Heath's hands. Pierrepoint used this special strap on only a dozen or so occasions, when he wanted to indicate, he said, 'more than a formal interest in this particular execution'.[17]

When the crime reporter Duncan Webb interviewed Margery Gardner's husband, he encountered a pathetic little man who, far from being heartbroken, was preparing to mount an exhibition of his murdered wife's paintings at a Blackpool fun fair. Webb also traced the final, wretched months of Margery's life as, destitute and homeless, she drifted around Kensington and Chelsea, staying at over thirty different addresses. Eventually, Webb found a room in Earl's Court where Margery had once lived. The walls were covered with her murals, boxes and cupboards overflowed with paintings and sketches, and, most poignant of all, there was an unfinished manuscript. Having given up acting, and art, Margery had turned to writing. The night before she was murdered by Neville Heath, Margery had written, 'She had girl friends, although she got on better with men. She was bold and reckless in those days, finding her feet and her own values – and her mistakes.' She never had the chance to finish writing that novel.[18]

In the chaotic world of post-war London, people lived wherever they could. While the poor camped out in rented rooms, the wealthy took refuge in seedy residential hotels, the stucco mansions that had seen better days and now sheltered a floating population of distressed gentlewomen, choleric colonels, bogus ex-army officers and elderly widows. Such was the scene at the Onslow Court Hotel, just off Old Brompton Road, in 1949. Residents became familiar over the months, as acquaintance deepened into friendship across the separate tables. The older ladies, who sat playing bridge and patience in the lounge, had a particular favourite in Mr John George Haigh, a dapper, well-dressed chap with a neat moustache who referred to himself as an entrepreneur. Haigh got on particularly well with Mrs Olive Durand-Deacon, a colonel's widow of sixty-nine, who had sat next to him at dinner for over three years. Mrs Durand-Deacon had been intrigued by Haigh's proposal to develop an artificial fingernail business, and he invited her to visit his factory in Crawley. On 18 February 1949 Mrs Durand-Deacon left the Onslow Court Hotel to travel to Crawley. She was never seen again.

A day or two later Mrs Durand-Deacon's friend, Mrs Constance Lane, arrived at Chelsea Police Station to report Mrs Durand-Deacon missing. Mrs Lane, who was accompanied by Haigh, said she feared for her friend's safety. Haigh, with his air of polite concern, seemed eager to help, but Woman Police Sergeant Alexandra Lambourne found him deeply suspect. Lambourne reported her misgivings to Chief Inspector Shelley Symes, who sent a request to Scotland Yard. The CID responded with a file on one John George Haigh who had served a prison sentence for fraud. The photograph confirmed that this was the same man who had called at Chelsea Police Station with Mrs Long.[19]

During the course of the investigation it became clear that Mrs Durand-Deacon had travelled to Crawley with Haigh. A fur coat similar to her Persian lamb had been recently pawned in Horsham. At other pawnbrokers' they found pieces of Mrs Durand-Deacon's jewellery. When Haigh was arrested on 1 March 1949, his response was extraordinary. After asking the police what his chances were of escaping from Broadmoor, he agreed to talk, warning them, 'If I tell you the truth, you would not believe it. It sounds too fantastic.'[20]

Then Haigh made his bizarre confession. He told the police that he had taken Mrs Durand-Deacon into his factory and shot her in the back of the head before putting her body in a tank, and filling the tank with sulphuric acid by means of a stirrup-pump. Leaving the acid to do its work, he had popped out to the Ancient Priors tearoom. Before he put the body in the tank, Haigh drained off a glassful of the victim's blood and drank it.

Three days later, there was nothing left of Mrs Durand-Deacon. Her body had been completely destroyed by the sulphuric acid. Only her plastic handbag, a couple of gall-stones and parts of her false teeth had survived. It took several hours to get a full statement out of Haigh. Quite nonchalantly, he told CI Symes that a pile of ration books and other documents discovered in his hotel room 'were concerned with other jobs'. When the details of these 'other jobs' were revealed, they were enough to send case-hardened police officers heading for the pub, in need of a stiff drink. Chatting away, Haigh blithely confessed to the murder of William McSwann in 1944 in the basement of 79 Gloucester Road, SW7. After luring McSwann to his house, Haigh had coshed McSwann and drunk a glass of his blood before disposing of the body in an acid bath. He sold McSwann's valuables, then approached his parents, telling them that McSwann had gone underground to avoid being called up for military service. After befriending the McSwanns, Haigh killed them and disposed of the bodies in the same manner, before passing himself off as William McSwann and gaining control of their assets, worth £4,000. 'The sludge' as Haigh described the remains of this unfortunate family, was disposed of down a manhole in the basement.[21]

Another couple, a Mr and Mrs Henderson, met the same fate after placing an advertisement for their property at 22 Ladbroke Square. Haigh did not buy the house but remained in touch with the couple when they moved to 16 Dawes Road, Fulham. Subsequently, Haigh travelled to Brighton with the pair where they stayed at the Metropole Hotel. He then took Mr Henderson to Crawley and disposed of him there, and subsequently brought Mrs Henderson down to the factory, on the pretext that her husband was ill. 'I shot her in the storeroom and put her in another tank and disposed of her with acid. In each of the last cases I have had my glass of blood as before.'[22] Haigh then obtained the Hendersons' property by forgery. The statement took hours and ran to thousands of words, and Haigh seemed to take a great deal of pleasure in the proceedings, smiling as he told his macabre tale.

Once the press got hold of the story, London was engulfed by a wave of terror. Soon one newspaper was describing Haigh as 'the human vampire', prowling the streets and attacking unsuspecting women, sucking their blood and leaving them to die in the gutters.[23] Female travellers ran the distance home from the Tube and prostitutes became more wary than usual. Meanwhile, Haigh sat in his cell and dreamed of Broadmoor, building up his case for not guilty on the grounds of insanity by drinking his own urine. But Haigh's cunning defence foundered when the prosecution claimed that Haigh was sane and had acted with malice aforethought. Haigh was found guilty within minutes at Lewes Assizes, and hanged by Albert Pierrepoint at Wandsworth prison on 10 August 1949. As he had done with Heath, Pierrepoint used his special leather strap to bind Haigh's wrists.[24]

As Londoners reeled from news stories about these extraordinary pathological killers, there was mounting anxiety about more conventional forms of crime. Far from being smashed by the Blitz, London's gangland flourished. In 1945, the *Daily Express* warned readers:

Crime is on the march in Britain today, boldly and violently. It is double what it was in 1939 and the evil grows by 10,000 cases each month ... within shouting distance of a spot where Eros may soon stand again [Piccadilly Circus], I have seen men pull out fistfuls of pound notes. Guns, revolvers and Tommy guns sold well over the weekend.

There are more guns at the moment than there is ammunition to fit them.[25]

Two years later, in 1947, 10,300 boys in London aged between
fourteen and twenty were convicted members of criminal
gangs.[26] Regular outbursts of moral panic in the popular press
reached a crescendo with the de Antiquis case of 1947.

Just before 2 p.m. on Monday 28 April 1947, three masked
gunmen, Charles Jenkins, 23, Christopher Geraghty, 20, and
Terence Rolt, 17, burst into L. S. Jay's jewellers in Charlotte
Street. In the ensuing confusion, the assistant manager set off
the alarm and a shot was fired, although the staff were
unhurt. The raiders fled empty-handed, jumped into the getaway car then found it had been blocked by a lorry. As they
scattered across Charlotte Street and into Tottenham Street,
a passing motor mechanic, Alec de Antiquis, swung his
motorcycle round and blocked their path, whereupon Chris
Geraghty shot de Antiquis in the head. As de Antiquis lay
dying in the gutter, he said: 'I'm all right. Stop them. I did
my best.' By sheer chance, the executioner Albert Pierrepoint
was walking along Charlotte Street soon afterwards and
glimpsed the crowd that had gathered around de Antiquis'
body.

The robbers were tracked down within less than three
weeks, thanks to diligent policing on the part of the legendary Fabian of the Yard and DCI Bob Higgins. A
Macintosh raincoat, discarded at the scene of the crime, provided a vital clue. The manufacturer's label enabled the
police to trace it to a consignment sold in Deptford High
Street, and ultimately to Charles Jenkins. Soon afterwards,
the gun that had killed de Antiquis was recovered from the
river at Wapping, while a second gun, a fifty-year-old .455
Bulldog revolver, was found near the Thames in
Bermondsey, close by Jenkins' wife's family home. The

Murder in Soho – the scene at Charlotte Street in April 1947 where Alec de Antiquis was gunned down attempting to foil an armed robbery.

remaining bullets in this gun matched the one that had been fired in Jay's.[27]

Although Geraghty had fired the shot that killed de Antiquis, both men were found guilty of murder by joint enterprise. Jenkins and Geraghty were hanged at Pentonville on 19 September 1947. Albert Pierrepoint, who had witnessed the aftermath of the shooting, was chief executioner. Rolt, who was only seventeen, was given a prison sentence and released from gaol in 1956. The de Antiquis case prompted a national outcry about the threat of gun crime and even inspired the film *The Blue Lamp* (1950), in which Dirk Bogarde, as panicky young villain Tom Riley, shoots dead veteran police officer George Dixon. Dixon's character proved so sympathetic that he was resurrected as lead of the much-loved television series *Dixon of Dock Green*.

The de Antiquis case propelled the debate about capital

punishment back into the newspaper headlines. As supporters of the death penalty argued that the execution of Jenkins and Geraghty was justified since it had led to the successful break-up of their gang, the anti-hanging lobby maintained that a hefty prison sentence represented an equally valid deterrent. The anti-hanging contingent had another argument on their side: that of miscarriages of justice. As had been noted as early as 1386, in the judicial error noted by the *Chronicle of the Grey Friars*, the most appalling outcome of the death penalty was the execution of an innocent man. The tragic consequences of such miscarriages are the subject of the following chapter, the first of which concerns the macabre aftermath of one London's most horrific crimes.

WHO BREAKS
A BUTTERFLY
UPON A WHEEL?

*Miscarriages of Justice and the
Abolition of the Death Penalty*

This chapter tells the extraordinary story of three men and one woman whose executions provoked intense public debate about the implications of capital punishment. The executions of Derek Bentley, Ruth Ellis and James Hanratty sent shockwaves throughout Britain, while the case of Timothy Evans changed the public attitude towards capital punishment forever.

Timothy Evans, hanged in 1950 for the murder of his wife and baby daughter, had lived in a shabby terrace in Notting Hill. At the time, this district was not the fashionable quarter that it has become today. Notting Hill consisted of street after street of dilapidated houses, rented to West Indian immigrants by racketeer landlords. Number 10 Rillington Place, its bricks stained black with soot, was a typical example. Three years after Evans was hanged by Albert Pierrepoint, police were once again summoned to Rillington Place after a tenant made a grim discovery.

On the morning of 24 March 1953 an existing tenant, Beresford Brown, went downstairs to clean up the basement flat. He had been offered the basement after a previous incumbent had disappeared without a forwarding address. Determined to investigate the cause of an offensive smell, Brown had discovered what appeared to be two female bodies hidden behind a wall.[1] When Chief Superintendent Peter Beveridge and Chief Inspector Percy Law arrived from Scotland Yard, along with the coroner and a pathologist, the subsequent discoveries were sickening even to hardened officers. The bodies of three naked women, all strangled, were recovered from the kitchen. Following a search, a fourth corpse was discovered beneath the floorboards in the parlour, and two female skeletons were recovered from the garden. A human femur had been used to prop up the fence. More bones were found in flowerbeds and some blackened skull bones with teeth and pieces of a dress turned up in a dustbin. Bones were also found beneath an orange blossom bush, along with a newspaper fragment dated 19 July 1943.[2]

The first three bodies were identified as Hectorina McLennan, 26, Kathleen Maloney, also 26, and Rita Nelson, 25. Rita had been six months pregnant. All three women had worked as prostitutes, and all three had been suffocated with gas diverted from the fire with a rubber tube, and then strangled. Once unconscious, they had been raped and the sexual assaults had continued after death. The fourth body was that of an older woman, Ethel Christie, who had lived in the house since 1938. Ethel had not been sexually assaulted, but she had been strangled in the same fashion. The two bodies in the garden were identified by dental records as Ruth Fuerst, 21, an Austrian refugee who had disappeared in 1943, and Muriel Eady, 32, a factory worker. Ethel's husband, John Christie, was nowhere to be seen.[3]

The discovery of six female murder victims in one house was sensational enough. What intrigued the police more was the fact that at this very same house, four years earlier in 1949, the bodies of Mrs Beryl Evans and her eighteen-month-old baby daughter Geraldine had been found hidden in the wash-house. They had been strangled and wrapped in cloth. Timothy Evans had been charged with the murder of his wife and daughter, although he had gone to the gallows protesting his innocence, and claiming that the killer was in fact John Christie.

The police launched a manhunt and Christie was captured a week later, after an officer spotted a thin bespectacled man with a toothbrush moustache loitering near Putney Bridge. When the policeman asked the man to take off his hat, he did so, to reveal his distinctive domed forehead. It was Christie.[4]

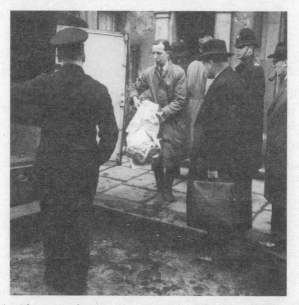

A grisly scene as human remains are removed from 10 Rillington Place, home of the serial killer John Reginald Christie, in 1953.

In custody, Christie confessed to murdering the three women found in the kitchen, the two women buried in the back garden, and Beryl Evans, but he remained adamant that he had not killed baby Geraldine. He claimed that he had gassed the other women accidentally while trying to have sex with them, and that when Ethel had suffered a seizure he had panicked and hidden the body before going on the run. Derek Curtis-Bennett QC, given the impossible job of defending Christie, pleaded diminished responsibility on the grounds of insanity, and argued that Christie had been showing signs of hysteria since developing shell shock in 1918.[5] The murder of his wife, argued Curtis-Bennett, was the final evidence that Christie was 'as mad as a March hare'.[6] After an hour and a half the jury promptly rejected this defence and found Christie guilty. Christie was executed by Albert Pierrepoint at Pentonville on 15 July 1953. Pierrepoint, who had executed over 600 people in the course of his career, later recalled Christie's appalled expression as he stumbled towards the drop. 'It was more than terror,' he wrote. 'At that moment I knew Christie would have given anything in his power to postpone his own death.'[7]

The outcome of Christie's trial immediately led to considerable doubt regarding the conviction of Timothy Evans. The chances of Evans having murdered Beryl and Geraldine when they lived in the same house as a serial killer appeared remote in the extreme. When this argument was combined with the fact that Evans was illiterate and had an IQ of seventy, his execution begins to look like a miscarriage of justice. In the aftermath an appeal committee was formed to clear Evans' name. Influential figures including Sir David Aston, the editor of the *Observer*, and the broadcaster Ludovic Kennedy all campaigned for a posthumous pardon, which was finally granted in October 1966. In 2003, the independent assessor for the Home Office, Lord Brennan QC, accepted that 'the conviction and execution of Timothy Evans for the murder of his child was wrongful and a miscarriage of justice'. In addition, there was no evidence to implicate Evans for the murder of his wife and she was most probably murdered by Christie.[8]

Evans' wrongful conviction was just one of many cases that put miscarriages of justice and capital punishment at the top of the news agenda. An equally controversial case had erupted in November 1952 following a disastrous armed robbery in south London. On 2 November 1952, two young men from Norbury, south-west London, decided to burgle a warehouse. The putative robbers, nineteen-year-old Derek Bentley and sixteen-year-old Christopher Craig, were carrying out an act of bravado, inspired by American gangster movies. Dressed in drape suits and trilby hats, which made them appear older than their years, both carried the weapons that were so easy to come by in post-war London. During a one-day amnesty, the Metropolitan Police had collected 18,500 revolvers, more than 250 machine-guns and over a quarter of a million rounds of ammunition.[9]

Bentley already had a criminal record, and his respectable working-class family were trying to keep him on the straight and narrow, and away from Christopher Craig, an aspiring mobster three years his junior. But Bentley, an epileptic with learning difficulties, was easily led. By 9.15 p.m. on the night of 2 November he was shinning up a drainpipe onto the roof of the Barlow and Parker Confectionary Company, Croydon. Bentley was equipped with a sheath knife and a knuckleduster, while Craig carried a Colt service revolver with the barrel sawn down to fit in the pocket of his drape suit, and several rounds of ammunition, some of which were of the wrong calibre for the weapon, and had to be adjusted to fit into the Colt.

Just as the pair were scrambling up the drainpipe, they were spotted by a nine-year-old girl in a house across the road. The girl quickly informed her father, who telephoned for the police. When the police arrived, Craig and Bentley hid behind the lift-housing, and Craig taunted the police. One of the police officers, Detective Sergeant Frederick Fairfax, climbed the drainpipe onto the roof and grabbed hold of Bentley. Bentley broke free of Fairfax's grasp. What happened then has been a matter of conjecture ever since. According to the police witnesses, Bentley shouted, 'Let him have it, Chris!' to Craig, and Craig fired at DS Fairfax and wounded him in the shoulder. Despite his injury, Fairfax was again able to restrain Bentley. Bentley told Fairfax that Craig was armed with a revolver and had further ammunition for the gun. Bentley had not used either of the weapons that he had in his pockets.[10]

A group of uniformed police officers arrived and was sent onto the roof. The first to reach the roof was PC Sidney Miles, who was immediately killed by a shot to the head. After exhausting his ammunition and being cornered, Craig jumped off the roof and plunged thirty feet onto a greenhouse, fracturing his spine and left wrist.

Bentley and Craig went on trial for murder at the Old Bailey on 9 December 1952. Under the Children and Young Persons Act 1933, sixteen-year-old Craig would be spared the death penalty if found guilty. But Derek Bentley, at nineteen, faced capital punishment. There was no possibility of pleading manslaughter, since the pair were accused of joint enterprise, and 'malicious intent' in attempting to carry out an armed robbery. Bentley's defence was that he had effectively been arrested by DS Fairfax when PC Miles was killed.[11]

The defence claimed there was ambiguity as to how many shots were fired and by whom. A ballistics expert questioned whether Craig could have hit Miles if he had shot at him deliberately. The fatal bullet was never recovered. Craig had used bullets of different under-sized calibres and the sawn-off barrel made it inaccurate to a degree of six feet at the range from which he fired.

Then there was controversy surrounding Bentley's alleged direction: 'Let him have it, Chris!' Craig and Bentley flatly denied that Bentley had said the words, while the police officers maintained that he did say them. Bentley's counsel argued that even if he had said 'Let him have it', it could not be proven that Bentley had intended the words to mean 'Shoot him, Chris,' rather than the literal meaning of 'Give him the gun, Chris.'

The defence's third argument was that Bentley was unfit to stand trial. Dr Hill, a psychiatrist at the Maudsley Hospital, had examined Bentley and reported that he was illiterate, with an IQ of eighty-seven and a mental age of eleven. However, the principal medical officer, Dr Matheson, argued that Bentley was not a 'feeble-minded person' under the Mental Deficiency Acts and was fit to plead and stand trial. The jury took seventy-five minutes to find both Craig and Bentley guilty of PC Miles's murder. Bentley was sentenced to death with a plea for mercy, while Craig was jailed for ten years.

Despite pleas for clemency from the trial jury, 200 Members of Parliament and, most notably of all, Mrs Miles, the widow of the murdered police officer, the Home Secretary David Maxwell Fyfe refused to request a royal pardon. Parliament was not allowed to debate Bentley's death sentence until it had been carried out, and Dr Hill of the Maudsley Hospital was forbidden to publish his report.[12]

Bentley was convinced that he would be reprieved right up until the last minute. But on 28 January 1953, he was hanged at Wandsworth Prison by Albert Pierrepoint. A large crowd gathered outside the prison from early that morning, and some sang the hymn 'Abide With Me' and the Twenty-third Psalm. When it was announced that the execution had been carried out, there were protests and two people were arrested and later fined for damage to property.[13]

Following the execution there was a public sense of unease about the decision and Maxwell Fyfe was criticized for letting the execution go ahead. Convinced that Bentley was innocent, his sister Iris began a long campaign to secure a posthumous pardon for him. In July 1993, Bentley was granted a royal pardon in respect of the sentence of death passed upon him. On 30 July 1998, the Court of Appeal quashed Bentley's conviction for murder on the grounds that the original trial judge was biased against the defendants and misdirected the jury on points of law. Scientific evidence also emerged which proved that the three police officers who testified about Bentley shouting 'Let him have it' had lied under oath. Craig welcomed Bentley's pardon. He has led a law-abiding life ever since the events of 2 November 1952. Tragically, Mr and Mrs Bentley and Derek's sister, Iris, never lived to see the day that Derek Bentley received his posthumous pardon.[14]

Two years after the scenes which had greeted Bentley's hanging at Wandsworth Prison, another angry crowd assembled to protest against an execution. This time, the prison was Holloway, and the demonstrations had been provoked by the decision to hang Ruth Ellis, a nightclub hostess who had been sentenced to death for shooting her lover. On 12 July 1955 the governor of Holloway was forced to call for police reinforcements as 500 people massed outside the prison gates, singing and chanting for hours. Thousands had signed petitions asking for the death penalty to be lifted in this case, including thirty-five members of London County Council who delivered their plea to the House of Commons that night. On the following morning, 13 July, a silent crowd, including women with prams, collected around the prison, waiting for the execution at nine o'clock. Eighteen minutes later, notice of Ellis' death was posted outside and the crowd surged forwards, blocking the road and stopping traffic.[15]

Ruth Ellis had the unenviable distinction of being the last woman to be hanged, a self-destructive butterfly broken upon the wheel of an outdated legal system. To Ellis' supporters, it seemed extraordinary that she should be convicted, thirty years after Madame Fahmy had walked free for killing her abusive husband. But Ellis' story is one of those cases within living memory where details emerge from a fog of speculation and investigation produces more questions than answers.

Ruth Ellis had not always been a victim. Indeed, she appears to have been something of a survivor and, after an abusive childhood and giving birth to a son at seventeen, she had become a hostess at the Little Club in Mayfair. The Little Club, typical of the drinking establishments which had sprung up after the war, was popular with everybody, including King Hussein of Jordan, the film stars Douglas Fairbanks Junior and Burt Lancaster, and Dr Stephen Ward, the society osteopath.[16] Ruth Ellis, with her glittering ash-blonde hair and, in the words of crime reporter Duncan Webb, her 'tinsel-like beauty', was the club's greatest attraction, a good sport, happy to pose nude for the Camera Club when there was no film in the cameras.[17]

In 1950, she had married George Ellis, a wealthy dentist, and moved to the suburbs, but when George Ellis turned out to be a violent alcoholic, Ruth fled back to London with their daughter, Georgina. Leaving both her children with her mother, Ruth returned to work and began a determined course of self-improvement, taking elocution lessons and deportment classes. Impressed by Ruth's ambition, her boss Maurie Conley promoted her to manager of another club, Carroll's. It was here that Ruth first met David Blakely, a tall, handsome young racing driver, and became hopelessly infatuated.[18]

Within weeks Blakely had moved into Ruth's flat above the club and she was bankrolling him. Blakely swiftly proved to be another violent alcoholic, unfaithful to Ruth with women and

Ruth Ellis with her lover, David Blakely, in 1955. After shooting Blakely dead in cold blood, Ruth Ellis was the last woman to be hanged.

men, but Ruth allowed him to run up a tab while Blakely pursued his racing career and returned to his respectable family and his fiancée at weekends. Fuelled by alcohol, the affair was tempestuous, punctuated by terrible rows and violent assaults. On one occasion, Ruth ended up in the Middlesex Hospital with a sprained ankle and a black eye. On another, Blakely assaulted her so severely that she suffered a miscarriage.

It was at such times that Ruth turned to another lover, Desmond Cussens, for comfort. Steady-going, middle-aged Cussens had flown Lancaster bombers during the war and represented stability. Ruth vacillated between both men but events came to a climax at Easter 1955. When Blakely failed to telephone on the evening of Good Friday, Ruth promptly went round to the home of his good friend and mechanic, Seaton Findlater, at Tanza Road, Hampstead. The Findlaters refused to let her in, but she could hear Blakely in the background, laughing with the nanny. Later that evening, the police had to be called. Ruth had smashed all the windows of Blakely's Standard Vanguard car.[19]

There was another doomed expedition the following day, when Cussens had driven Ruth back to Tanza Road to speak to Blakely. Again, the Findlaters refused to let her in. Cussens tried to calm Ruth down with Pernod and tranquilisers, but all she could say was, 'I'd shoot the swine if I had a gun.'[20]

Sunday evening saw the third and final visit to Tanza Road. Driven to the Findlaters' residence by Cussens, Ruth waited in the shadows as Blakely emerged from the house with his friend Clive Gunnell, a car salesman. They drove to the Magdala public house in South Hill Park, and Ruth followed them. The pub was pretty full, with everyone in a bank holiday mood, and Blakely was laughing and drinking along with them. Outside, Ruth watched and waited, taking consolation from the cold steel of the gun between her fingers.[21]

Gunnell left the pub first, and then Blakely followed. He was about to open the car door when Ruth pulled the .38 Smith & Wesson revolver out of her handbag. Blakely glanced round, saw her, and then ignored her. Then Ruth fired at point-blank range. As Blakely fell to the ground she emptied the gun into him. One stray bullet caught a pedestrian, Gladys Yule, wounding her in the hand. Ruth stood motionless and when the gun was empty she said, calmly, 'Call the police.'[22]

When Ruth Ellis appeared before Mr Justice Havers at Number 1 Court of the Old Bailey on 20 June 1955, the crime writer Duncan Webb and his colleagues anticipated a 'long and colourful trial', during which Ruth's defence counsel would put forward all kinds of elaborate pleas 'to justify or mitigate the circumstances'.[23] The public gallery was packed with an enthralled crowd, ranging from East End characters to West End socialites, all agog to see a woman go on trial for shooting her lover.

There was a collective gasp as Ruth entered the witness box. Against the advice of her counsel, Ruth appeared in court wearing an elegant black suit with astrakhan fur lapels and a white silk blouse. As she moved her head, the light glinted on her immaculate ash-blonde coiffure. The governor of Holloway had permitted a hairdresser to visit Ruth in prison, in preparation for her day in court. Far from being the repentant prisoner at the bar, Ruth looked as if she were about to open up Carroll's club for business. The next shock came when Ruth's barrister, Aubrey Melford Stevenson, opened the case for the defence by saying: 'Let me make this abundantly plain: there is no question here but this woman shot this man ... You will not hear one word from me – or from the lady herself – questioning that.'[24]

As the court took in this astonishing approach, the defence pleaded manslaughter and absence of malice. Melford Stevenson's argument was that Ruth had suffered constant and brutal abuse at the hands of David Blakely, 'a most unpleasant person', but had been unable to get away from him, trapped 'in something like an emotional prison guarded by this young man, from which there seemed to be no escape'.[25] A similar defence had been offered for Madame Fahmy. Would a sympathetic jury take the same attitude towards Ruth Ellis, the victim of abuse who had finally turned on her vicious lover?

The prosecution had only one question for Ruth. As the tall, angular figure of Mr Christmas Humphreys, prosecuting, loomed over her, the jury and spectators could have heard a pin drop. Then Humphreys asked his question: 'When you fired that revolver at close range, into the body of David Blakely, what did you intend to do?'[26]

Ruth cast her eyes down to the floor. She pursed her lips. There was a deep hush in court, as if everyone was resisting the impulse to cry out, 'Don't do it! Watch what you say! Be careful!'

'It is obvious,' Ruth replied, in a calm, audible voice. 'When I shot him, I intended to kill him.'

And with that reply Ruth Ellis coolly placed the noose around her own neck.[27] The jury took just fourteen minutes to find Ruth Ellis guilty of murder and she was sentenced to death. The sentence provoked outrage in the press, with the popular columnist 'Cassandra' (William Connor) opining in the *Daily Mirror*, 'The one thing that brings stature and dignity to mankind and raises us above the beasts will have been denied her – pity and the hope of ultimate redemption.'[28] A petition signed by 50,000 people, calling for a reprieve, was rejected by the Home Secretary, while a French reporter, surprised at the lack of a defence of *crime passionnel* in the English legal system reflected that: 'Passion in England, except for cricket and betting, is always regarded as shameful disease.'[29] The crime writer, Raymond Chandler, that expert on *femmes fatales*, described Ruth's sentence as 'the mediaeval savagery of the law' in a letter to the *Evening Standard*, while the judge Cecil Havers filed a personal request for a reprieve.[30] It was ignored.

Two days before she went to the gallows, Ruth Ellis gave a statement to her solicitor, Victor Mischon, and his clerk, Leon Simmons. In it, Ruth stated that Desmond Cussens had given her the gun, got her drunk on Pernod and driven her to Tanza Road. By this action, Cussens had effectively signed her death warrant. Mischon and Simmons took this statement to the Home Office, but it was ignored.[31]

On 13 July 1955, Ruth wrote to Blakely's parents, concluding, 'I have always loved your son, and I will die still loving him.' Then she put her diamante spectacles down on the table, saying, 'I won't need these any more,' and went to her death.[32] Ruth was hanged by Albert Pierrepoint who later said, 'She died as brave as any man and she never spoke a single word.'[33]

A rumour still circulates among the legal profession that this hanging was not one of the highlights of Pierrepoint's career, although the autopsy report gives no indication that anything was amiss. But according to grisly anecdote, Pierrepoint miscalculated the weight of Ruth's petite frame and allocated too much rope to the drop. As a result, when the trapdoor opened beneath her feet, Ruth's head was torn off. Following execution, Ruth was buried within the grounds of Holloway but when the prison was modernized in the 1970s, her remains were reinterred in a private grave in Amersham.

The events of 10 April 1955 continue to inspire speculation to this day, not least the involvement of Desmond Cussens, who appears to have manipulated Ruth into the shooting. Cussens' motivation remains unclear. If Cussens had regarded Blakely as a rival, and wanted him eliminated, he must have been aware that by doing so he stood to lose Ruth to prison, if not the gallows. Another theory, advanced by Ruth's sister, Monica Weller, was that Ruth had close links to Stephen Ward and his shadowy world of blackmail and espionage. In *Ruth Ellis: My Sister's Secret Life,* Monica Weller suggested that, as one of 'Stephen's girls', Ruth had been framed by the security services because she possessed compromising details of respected establishment figures.[34]

In conclusion, my own opinion is that Ruth effectively killed herself when she squeezed the trigger of that Smith & Wesson. By shooting David Blakely, Ruth killed both of them. In the ultimate act of self-destruction, Ruth went bravely to her own death, unable to live with Blakely but unable to live without him. And as with every murder, this case left a painful legacy. In the immediate aftermath, Ruth's estranged husband, George Ellis, hanged himself and their daughter Georgina was adopted. Ruth's son, Andy, had a troubled life. Sir Cecil Havers, the trial judge, sent money every year towards his upkeep. But, in 1982, after smashing up his mother's gravestone, Andy killed himself. Mr Christmas Humphreys paid for his funeral. Georgina died of cancer in 2000. In 2003, the case was referred back to the Court of Appeal by the Criminal Cases Review Commission, but was rejected. Ruth's family continue to campaign for her posthumous pardon.

Although the protests against Ruth Ellis's execution were to no avail, the uproar helped strengthen political support for the end of the death penalty. In March 1956 the Death Penalty (Abolition) Bill was passed by Parliament on its second reading, but subsequently overturned by the House of Lords. The following year, in March 1957, as a half-measure, the Homicide Act was passed. This limited the death sentence to five categories of murder that constituted capital murder. Capital murder was defined as murder committed in the course or furtherance of theft, murder by shooting or explosion, murder whilst resisting arrest or escaping, murder of a police officer or prison officer and two murders committed on different occasions. The defence of diminished responsibility was also incorporated into English law by this Act. Of course these changes came too late for Timothy Evans, Derek Bentley and Ruth Ellis, but it might have spared all three from the gallows – Evans and Bentley on the grounds of mental impairment and Ruth Ellis due to the sustained catalogue of emotional and physical abuse she had suffered at David Blakely's hands.

The grim fates of Timothy Evans, Derek Bentley and Ruth Ellis undermined the case for the death penalty and led to increasing demands for mercy and leniency. But it would take another major trial before the death knell tolled for capital punishment. At the heart of this trial was the vexed question of mistaken identity and the possibility that a man went to the gallows for a terrible crime that he did not commit. The name of that man was James Hanratty, and the case became known as the 'A6 Murder'.

On the evening of 22 August 1961, Michael Gregsten and his girlfriend Valerie Storie were sitting in his car at the edge of a cornfield. This spot, near Dorney Reach, Buckinghamshire, was their regular hideaway, since 36-year-old Gregsten was a married man. The couple had met at the government Road Research Laboratory, where Gregsten was a research scientist and Valerie his laboratory assistant. The affair had endured for months despite departmental reprimands and Mrs Gregsten's attempts to wreck the relationship. As they sat in Gregsten's grey Morris Minor that night, planning their part in a motor rally and discussing their future, the mood was more positive. 'The car seemed so snug and reassuring,' Valerie later wrote, 'a private world.'[35] That world was about to be invaded in the most horrific and terrifying manner.

Darkness had fallen when the couple were startled by a sharp tap on the window. Gregsten wound the driver's window down and found himself staring down the barrel of a gun. Before they could stop him, the smartly suited stranger climbed into the back seat and ordered Gregsten to drive. Over the following six hours, Gregsten drove at gunpoint through Slough and across north-west London. The Morris Minor finally came to a halt off the A6 near Bedford, at a spot called Deadman's Hill. When Gregsten created a diversion by throwing a bag at him, the gunman shot him in the head, killing him instantly. As Valerie screamed in horror, the gunman shouted: 'Be quiet, will you? I'm finking.' Worse was to come. The gunman ordered Valerie to help him drag Gregsten's body out of the Morris Minor. Then he raped her over Gregsten's body, before emptying his gun into her and driving away erratically, with a crashing of gears.[36]

At 6.45 the following morning, the couple were discovered by Sidney Burton, a farm labourer on his way to work. Valerie was taken to Bedford Hospital, where she was found to be *compos mentis* and able to provide a statement to the police.

Valerie had escaped with her life, but she was permanently paralysed as a result of her injuries.[37]

When Valerie described her ordeal to the police, she told them that she had only once seen the gunman clearly, in the lights of a passing car, and admitted that she might not be able to pick him out of an identity parade. The police persevered, however, with the aid of the new technology of the Identikit portrait, and Valerie and another witness, who had seen the driver of the Morris Minor, produced two images. The gunman was described as about five feet eight inches tall, with deep-set brown eyes and a strong East End accent. Two days later, on 24 August, the murder weapon was recovered from under a seat on the top deck of a 36A London bus, fully loaded and wiped clean of prints. It was wrapped in a handkerchief, which was to provide DNA evidence at a later date.[38]

Meanwhile, the police lacked a suspect, let alone a motive, for this appalling crime. It was at this point that Mrs Janet Gregsten entered the drama. On 31 August 1961, eight days after her husband's murder, Mrs Gregsten was standing in the antiques shop in Swiss Cottage owned by her brother, William Ewer. Glancing out of the window, Janet Gregsten caught sight of a young man with black hair walking into a dry cleaner's across the other side of the arcade. Letting out a scream, Janet Gregsten grabbed her brother's arm and said: 'That's him! He fits the description. I have an overpowering feeling that it's him!' Janet Gregsten recognized the killer on account of his 'icy-blue saucer-like eyes'. This was despite the fact that Valerie had described her assailant as brown-eyed.[39]

While William Ewer pursued the mysterious young man in Swiss Cottage, the police were interviewing Peter Alphon, an eccentric loner who eked out a living selling almanacks door to door. Alphon provided an alibi for the night of the murder, saying he had taken a room at the Vienna Hotel in Maida Vale. This was confirmed by the manager, William Nudds. In the meantime, William Ewer had traced the young man from the dry cleaner's. His name was James Ryan, and he was a familiar face in the north London antiques trade. But Ewer claimed that his information was dismissed by the police.[40]

On 11 September William Nudds found two cartridges in the basement room of the Vienna Hotel where Alphon had stayed the night. According to Nudds, another guest had also hired that room on 22 August. (This was not unusual, as the Vienna Hotel was a seedy lodging house where rooms were rented by the hour.) This second man had left the Vienna asking for directions to the number 36 bus, and his name was James Ryan. After Nudds made a second statement implicating Alphon on 21 September, the police announced that Alphon was the suspect and launched a manhunt. That same day, Mrs Gregsten visited Valerie Storie at Guy's Hospital, where she had been transferred for specialist treatment. According to the *Daily Mail*, Valerie had asked Janet to visit, and told her what had happened on that terrible night. The murderer had been in his thirties and respectably dressed, with a Cockney accent and 'blue, staring eyes'.[41]

The same night, Peter Alphon gave himself up at Cannon Row police station, and on 24 September he took part in an identity parade. After Valerie Storie did not identify him as her attacker, he was released without charge. At this point it emerged that James Ryan, the other resident of the basement room at the Vienna Hotel where the cartridges were discovered, was in fact James Hanratty. A professional car thief already wanted in connection with two robberies, Hanratty went on the run and was eventually arrested in Blackpool on 11 October. On 14 October, Valerie Storie attended an identity parade, during which she asked each suspect to repeat the sentence spoken by the killer: 'Be quiet, will you? I'm thinking.' Like the murderer, Hanratty pronounced 'thinking' as 'finking'. Unlike the identikit picture, James Hanratty had bright red hair. But Valerie picked Hanratty out of the parade and he was duly charged with the A6 murder.[42]

Hanratty went on trial at the Bedford Assizes on 22 January 1962 charged with the murder of Michael Gregsten. The trial had originally been scheduled for the Old Bailey, but was changed at the last moment to Bedford, where there was understandable hostility towards the accused. Hanratty's defence rested on the fact that he had no apparent motive. Why would an urban car thief stalk a couple in the middle of the countryside and carry out a random killing? Hanratty had no previous convictions for violence or sexual assault. In addition, as a professional car thief, he was an experienced driver, while the killer had struggled to get the Morris Minor into gear and drive away. While the forensic evidence taken at the scene did show the same blood group as Hanratty, it was a blood group he shared with half the population. Hanratty also had the A6 Defence Committee on his side, a group of witnesses, campaigners and experts assembled by his father, James Hanratty, to prove his innocence. But, given the vicious nature of the crime, popular opinion was against Hanratty and all the sympathy lay with the victim, who appeared in court on a stretcher. Hanratty also lost credibility by changing his alibi halfway through. After claiming that he had spent the night in question with friends in Liverpool, he then changed the alibi and said that he had been in Rhyl, north Wales, instead.

Fuelled by popular outrage, the prosecution steamrollered over Hanratty's defence. Arguing that Hanratty had escalated to violent crime and had been practising 'stick-ups' with a gun at the Vienna Hotel, prosecuting counsel convinced the jury that Hanratty had hijacked Michael Gregsten's car and then raped Valerie after being overcome by lust. A fellow prisoner, Roy Langdale, was produced to give evidence that Hanratty had confessed the crime to him while on remand.[43] Charles France, a small-time crook and a friend of Hanratty's, told the jury that Hanratty had informed him that the back of a bus was a good place to conceal a weapon. France's testimony must have come as a shock to Hanratty. Hitherto, Hanratty had been on good terms with France and had dated France's daughter, Carol. But it was Valerie Storie's identification of Hanratty that convinced the jury. On 17 February, after nine and a half hours, the jury delivered the verdict of guilty and Hanratty was convicted and sentenced to death. Despite a petition signed by more than 90,000 people, an appeal was turned down on 13 March. Three days later, perhaps overcome with remorse, Charles France committed suicide.

On 2 April R. A. Butler, the Home Secretary, refused to issue a reprieve, but Hanratty still maintained his innocence. The day before he was due to be executed he wrote to his family from his cell at Bedford Gaol, saying, 'I'm dying tomorrow but I'm innocent. Clear my name.' On the following morning, 4 April, Hanratty still believed that he might receive a last-minute reprieve. But it was not to be and, with shock and incredulity, he went to the gallows. A month later, Carol France, Charles France's daughter and Hanratty's sometime girlfriend, attempted to take her own life with a drug overdose.

Meanwhile, as if the Hanrattys had not suffered enough, Peter Alphon called at the family home and attempted to offer them 'compensation' for the death of their son. Understandably, the family refused to speak to him. This gesture was just the beginning of an extraordinary sequence of actions by Alphon. In *Queen* magazine in September 1966 Alphon claimed that he was the A6 killer, but then denied his guilt a year later in a *Panorama* television programme. And then, in May 1967, Alphon called a press conference in Paris and confessed to the murder, claiming that someone close to Gregsten had given him £5,000 to 'frighten' the couple. Alphon retracted this confession the following September, and insisted that Hanratty was guilty and had been hired by Mrs Gregsten to break up the relationship.

The investigative journalist Paul Foot took up the Hanratty family's cause, and created a compelling argument for Hanratty's innocence in his outstanding book *Who Killed Hanratty?* (1973). When Foot interviewed Mrs Gregsten shortly before her death in 1995, Mrs Gregsten angrily denied any involvement in the murder of her husband, but no longer seemed convinced of Hanratty's guilt and pointed the finger at Alphon. Alphon lived on, an increasingly frail and eccentric figure. In Bob Woffinden's excellent 1992 television documentary about the case, Alphon makes a final appearance, a spectral, ghoulish figure wearing a flapping raincoat in a windswept underground station. Alphon continued to boast of his involvement in the murder until his death in 2009.

After three Home Office inquiries into the case, the surviving exhibits from the trial were discovered in 1991. Hanratty's relatives donated DNA for forensic testing, hoping that this would exonerate him, but the results from testing in June 1999 were said to be equivocal. On 19 March 1997, the Home Office referred the case to the new Criminal Cases Review Commission. In 2001, Hanratty's body was exhumed in order to extract DNA. This was compared with DNA on the handkerchief wrapped round the gun, and with semen on Valerie's underwear. Although no forensic evidence from the crime scene had been linked to Hanratty previously, DNA samples from both sources matched Hanratty's DNA. At the subsequent appeal hearing, Michael Mansfield QC, acting for the Hanratty family, admitted that if contamination could be excluded the DNA evidence demonstrated that Hanratty had committed the murder and rape. But he added that the evidence may have been contaminated because of lax handling procedures. However, neither sample yielded DNA from any second male source, as would presumably have been expected if another male had committed the crimes and the samples had subsequently been contaminated. The argument for contamination was dismissed as 'fanciful' by the judges, who concluded that 'The DNA evidence, standing alone, is certain proof of guilt.' Hanratty's family and their supporters have continued to contest this conclusion.[44] Paul Foot maintained his belief in Hanratty's innocence until his own death in 2004, despite the results of the DNA tests.[45]

Hanratty was one of the last people to be hanged in the United Kingdom. The last two were Peter Allen and Gwynne Evans, hanged simultaneously on 13 August 1964. In 1965, Sydney Silverman MP introduced a private member's bill to suspend the death penalty. The Murder (Abolition of Death Penalty) Act 1965 suspended the death penalty for five years and substituted it with a mandatory life imprisonment. In 1969, the Act was made permanent. This humane and merciful piece of legislation brought an end to centuries of judicial murder and ensured that never again would an innocent man or woman suffer the ultimate punishment for a crime which they did not commit.

In his memoirs the chief hangman, Albert Pierrepoint, reflected on his own attitude towards capital punishment. 'I have come to the conclusion that executions solve nothing,' he wrote, 'and are only an antiquated relic of a primitive desire for revenge which takes the easy way and hands over the responsibility for revenge to other people. The trouble with the death penalty has always been that nobody wanted it for everybody, but everybody differed about who should get off.'[46]

Latterly, attempts to re-introduce the death penalty have not proved successful. When it was last debated in Parliament in 1998, during the passage of the Human Rights Act, it was rejected by 158 votes.[47]

But in London there remained one pair of men for whom the abolition of the death penalty and indeed the law in general had no relevance. These were hard men who made their own rules and took the law into their own hands. Their names were Ronnie and Reggie Kray.

HARD BASTARDS AND DIAMOND GEEZERS

How the Firm Ruled London

By the 1950s, London's gangland had become a dark and almost mythical realm. Like the subterranean River Tyburn, the underworld rolled on beneath London, populated by legendary 'old faces' such as Billy Hill and Jack 'Spot' Comer, the terrifying Messina family, and intimidating newcomers such as the Kray twins and their 'Firm'. Billy Hill (1911–84) had been the first to build a new empire of crime among the sooty rubble of post-war London. A self-proclaimed hard bastard, he literally carved out his territory, inflicting vicious knife wounds upon the faces of those who offended him, often in the shape of a 'V' for Victory. Hill insisted that 'chivving', as he referred to it, was only used as a last resort. After someone glassed him in a pub, he pulled the glass out of his face with one hand and set about chivving his assailant with the other, wounding with surgical precision. 'I was always careful to draw my knife down on the face, never across or upwards, so that if the knife slips you don't cut an artery. Chivving is chivving, but cutting an artery is usually murder. Only mugs do murder.'[1]

Hill had teamed up with Jack 'Spot' Comer, a Jewish race-course racketeer noted for his flamboyant dress sense and big cigars. Comer was also a self-appointed enforcer to the Jewish community. In 1936 Comer had taken on Oswald Mosley's Blackshirts during the Battle of Cable Street. Together Hill and Comer had set about seizing the Sabini empire from another gangster, Harry White. After the Italian Sabini gang had been interred as enemy aliens during the outset of the Second World War, Harry White had taken over their realm of nightclubs, *spielers* and brothels. Hill and Comer wrested it off him in a showdown forever after known as the Battle of the Stork Club.[2]

In July 1947 Harry White was drinking in the Stork Club in Piccadilly with a racehorse trainer, Tim O'Sullivan, and another man when Comer walked in with ten heavies. Comer accused White of anti-Semitism, and smashed a bottle over his head. As White collapsed in a pool of blood, Comer's men attacked O'Sullivan and the third man. O'Sullivan was beaten unconscious and pushed into an open fire. The third man was slashed with razors and stabbed. According to Comer, White scarpered as soon as he was able. 'You couldn't see the seat of his trousers for dust.' Afterwards Billy Hill crowned himself the 'Bandit King' of London, with Comer in the role of trusted courtier, and masterminded a series of breathtakingly audacious armed robberies.

The first of these was the Eastcastle Street robbery in May 1952, when a team of masked men held up a Royal Mail van just off Oxford Street and escaped with £287,000 (£6,150,000 today). This was a real 'project crime', planned and executed with military precision. The robbers used two cars to sand-wich the van. The first car emerged slowly from a side street causing the van to slow down, the second car then pulled up alongside. The driver and two attendants were dragged out and coshed and the van was stolen. It was later found abandoned near Regents Park. The Prime Minister, Winston Churchill, demanded daily updates, and yet despite the involvement of over 1,000 police officers, nobody was ever caught. Two years later, Hill was behind a £40,000 bullion heist. Again, despite constant suspicion and allegations that Hill was behind the robberies, no one was ever brought to justice.[3]

Meanwhile, Jack Comer, tired of playing second fiddle, was making his own bid for power. Fearing a coup, Hill had Comer and his wife Rita ambushed outside their Hyde Park Mansions flat by 'Mad' Frankie Fraser and his gang of thugs. Rita was knocked to the ground, fortunately unhurt, but Comer was slashed with razors and required seventy-eight stitches and a blood transfusion. Scarred for life, Comer refused to name his attackers, but Rita had no such reservations and Fraser went down for seven years. Comer had learned his lesson, and retired to Ireland. 'I ain't afraid of anyone,' he said, 'but I want a quiet life now.'[4]

While Billy Hill was organizing textbook armed robberies, a sinister family known as the Messinas had seized control of the vice racket. The Messina brothers, Sicilian by way of Alexandria, had arrived in Britain in the 1930s and operated by importing foreign girls, usually from France and Italy, on forged passports, marrying them off to compliant men and setting them to walk the streets of the West End. Anyone who dared stand up to the Messinas was ruthlessly eliminated. Duncan Webb memorably described the 'men and women left lying in pools of blood on the pavements of London'. Hefty backhanders to corrupt Vice Squad officers ensured the gang's immunity from prosecution. Even the Home Secretary, Mr Chuter Ede, confessed in the House of Commons that

Marthe Watts with husband Gino Messina and his brother
Carmelo in 1947. The notorious Messina brothers dominated the
London vice trade in the 1940s.

nothing could be done about the gang, leading Attilio Messina to boast: 'We are more powerful than the British government. We can do as we like in England.' Gino Messina's wife, Marthe Watts, recalled Gino sitting in one of his opulent Mayfair flats like a spider in a web of vice. He invested in property, drove a yellow Rolls-Royce, dressed like a film star and seemed invulnerable. 'London belongs to me!' he bragged to Marthe.[5]

Despite the public outcry, the police did not interfere in these turf wars, which is when Duncan Webb of the *Sunday People* became involved. In true crusading journalistic style, Webb went undercover to investigate the brothers. Posing as a punter, he interviewed dozens of Messina girls on their beats in Shepherd's Market and Bond Street, and was threatened and beaten up for his trouble.

The main barrier to convicting the Messinas was their anonymity. Although Gino was a distinctive figure, with his Jermyn Street suits and handmade shoes, he and his brothers posed as antiques dealers and used a number of English aliases such as 'Charles Maitland' and 'Edward Marshall' to evade detection. The Messinas had a word-of-mouth reputation as a hydra-headed phantom army of villains, who terrorized the London streets with thuggery, violence and corruption. They controlled an army of mythical women, not one of whom could be positively identified, and operated from scores of different addresses. They had corrupt police officers on their side, and excellent lawyers. It proved almost impossible to get a contact to talk. At the mention of the name 'Messina' most interviewees would gulp down their drink and leave. The word carried an atmosphere of fear and horror to the average crook, whispered with hallowed awe and dubious respect.[6]

Despite continual threats of violence, Webb persevered with his investigation. On 3 January 1950, Webb published his exposé of the Messina gang and their empire of vice in the *Sunday People*.[7] Scotland Yard followed up his enquiries and Alfredo Messina went on trial, after a doomed attempt to bribe the arresting officers. The remaining brothers escaped to Europe, where they continued to run a vice racket before being arrested and gaoled. Gino's wife Marthe Watts loyally followed Gino to Belgium, but after a lifetime of hardship she succumbed to a collapsed lung and a nervous breakdown. Marthe left Gino and published her memoirs, *The Men in My Life*, in 1954.[8]

As the underworld ebbed and flowed, old faces were lost to prison and death. Fresh contenders stepped forward, eager to seize power. The most formidable of these was an up-and-coming pair of twins, former boxers who exuded an aura of menace. Their names were Ronnie and Reggie Kray.

Like Bentley and Craig and dozens of other wannabe gangsters before them, the young Krays had been inspired by Hollywood. The first time Ronnie Kray's nemesis, Inspector 'Nipper' Read, clapped eyes on him, in 1964, Ronnie Kray was arriving outside the Grave Maurice pub in Whitechapel like a member of the royal family. Stepping out of a big American car, dressed like a Chicago gangster in a long cashmere coat, with his hair greased and parted, 'he looked like Al Capone without his fedora'.[9]

The Krays' reign of terror was unique. Their gang, known as 'the Firm', gained exceptional domination over London's underworld. Attempts by Scotland Yard to 'collate' or gather evidence against them were met with a wall of silence. Witnesses were intimidated and threatened with death if they talked to the police. Enemies were blatantly murdered. The Kray twins made a profession of violence.

Born on 23 October 1933, the twins initially showed some promise in the boxing ring, but a dishonourable discharge from their National Service and a spell in military prison meant that they could not obtain the licences they needed to turn professional. Instead, the Krays bought the run-down Regal Billiard Club on the Mile End Road. It was here that they established 'the Firm', an impressive organization composed of the twins, their older brother Charlie, Leslie 'Payne the Brain', who acted as a financial advisor, and Freddie 'the Mean Machine' Foreman. Ronnie, openly homosexual despite the dangers of prosecution, had a constant supply of rent boys who doubled as his spies. Enforcement came in the form of violence, through a beating, or murder, but sometimes it took no more than an intimidating stare from 'the Colonel', as Ronnie liked to call himself, to convince a miscreant of the error of his ways.

By the end of the 1950s the twins had made the East End

their empire, thanks to an extensive variety of protection rackets, hijacking, armed robbery and arson. 'If they drove down Commercial Road, everybody waved to them,' recalled Inspector Nipper Read. 'If somebody had a drink with them, it was like having tea with Princess Margaret.'[10]

In February 1960, Peter Rachman, the violent racketeer landlord, offered Ronnie a nightclub called Esmeralda's Barn in Knightsbridge. The Krays were obsessed with show business, and only too delighted to open their own West End club in which they could play host to such luminaries as Barbara Windsor, Diana Dors (the British Marilyn Monroe), Frank Sinatra and Judy Garland.

By the mid 1960s, the Krays controlled half the illegal gambling clubs in London and had friends in high places, including the Tory peer Lord Boothby, and the homosexual Labour MP Tom Driberg, who attended parties given by Ronnie where rent boys were offered round like so many canapés.[11] When the *Sunday Mirror* published allegations of an affair between 'a prominent peer and a West End thug', Boothby sued for libel and accepted damages of £40,000. The police were ordered to drop their enquiries into the case and the newspapers effectively silenced. 'They were the best years of our lives,' Ronnie recollected. 'The Beatles and the Rolling Stones were rulers of pop music, Carnaby Street ruled the fashion world and me and my brother ruled London. We were fucking untouchable.'[12]

While the Krays enjoyed their reign over London, the British public were briefly diverted by the Great Train Robbery, the crime of the century, during which £2,500,000 was stolen from the Royal Mail night train from Glasgow to London. For sheer planning and execution, this job knocked Eastcastle Street and the bullion heist into a cocked hat. With one major difference – Billy Hill's gang never got caught.

Nine months in preparation, the robbery had been devised in London by Bruce Reynolds, an antiques dealer who enjoyed the good life, driving an Aston Martin and staying at the Ritz. Reynolds had selected his men carefully, for brain, brawn and inside knowledge. There were heavies, like Gordon Goody and Jimmy White, a former paratrooper; a train expert, Roger Cordrey; Buster Edwards, a club-owner; Roy James, a racing driver; and Ronnie Biggs, whose critical asset was his friend, a retired train driver, who would play an essential role in the robbery. The plan was to hijack the train with a false signal, steal the mailbags, lie low at Leatherslade Farm, and quietly launder the money.

At 3.03 a.m. on 8 August 1963, Jack Mills was driving the night mail train along the West Coast Main Line towards Euston Station when a red light signal appeared at Sear's Crossing, between Leighton Buzzard and Cheddington. The fireman, David Whitby, climbed out of the cab and went to the telephone at the trackside to find out what had caused the delay. He was seized by Buster Edwards, dragged down the bank and told to keep quiet. When Jack Mills stuck his head out of the cab and asked what was wrong, he was coshed. As the crime reporter Duncan Campbell has noted, this single act of violence marred the robbery in the eyes of many. Subsequently, nobody could ever agree who hit Mills. Biggs' friend, Stan Agate, proved unable to drive the train as he was only familiar with Southern region trains, so the gang patched Mills up, and offered him a cigarette and a share of the takings, which he refused. However he did agree to shunt the train into position at Bridego Bridge so that the robbery could be completed. Mills and Whitby were handcuffed together and told not to move for half an hour while the robbers completed their raid.

Despite the fact that the train was carrying almost £3 million, there were no security guards. The 121 mailbags were removed via a human chain in twenty-five minutes, and the robbers made their getaway to Leatherslade Farm. But the robbers, hitherto so meticulous, had already made a fatal error. In telling Mills and Whitby not to move for half an hour, they had revealed the fact that they had a base nearby. The deserted farmhouse was quickly revealed as their hiding place. Tiny forensic details gave them away. Roy James had fed the farm cats and his prints were all over a bowl. Buster Edwards had left palm prints on a money wrapper. Within five weeks five members of the gang had been arrested, and thirteen men eventually went on trial in 1964 at Aylesbury, chosen because there was less threat of witness intimidation than at the Old Bailey.

While the British public might have been tickled pink by the gang's audacity, the judiciary took a darker view. The judge, Mr Justice Edmund Davies, handed down twenty-five- and thirty-year sentences that sent out a clear message that armed robbery would not be tolerated, and described the robbery as 'a crime of sordid violence inspired by vast greed'.[13]

This represented a tough new approach on the part of the judiciary. The following years would see the Krays and their greatest rival, the scrap metal dealer Charlie Richardson, boss of the Richardson gang, sent down for unprecedented terms.[14]

Like the Krays, the Richardsons had used violence to control their empire, which operated out of Camberwell, south-east London. The Richardson gang was also known as 'the Torture Gang' on account of the tough tactics used on gang members accused of disloyalty. Following a mock trial, gang members were punished with a range of penalties from cigarette burns to whipping and having their teeth pulled out with pliers, the latter being a speciality of 'Mad' Frankie Fraser. When the 'Torture Trial' opened at the Old Bailey in April 1967, witnesses who had turned Queen's Evidence spoke of having toes removed with bolt cutters, being nailed to the floor and urinated upon or punished with the 'black box', an old field telephone with a hand-operated generator which was used to administer electric shocks. Terminals were applied to the nipples and genitalia, and the victim was sometimes immersed in a bath to increase the shock. Richardson, who denied that the black box had ever existed, was sentenced to twenty-five years for grievous bodily harm, with the judge concluding, 'It must be made clear to all those who set themselves up as gang leaders that they will be struck down by the law as you will be struck down.'[15]

While the Krays must have been relieved to have their rival, Charlie Richardson, safely behind bars, they were beginning to lose control. Ronnie's psychopathic outbursts were intensifying, inspired by prodigious quantities of alcohol. He was already taking credit for the shooting of George Cornell in the Blind Beggar pub, and, fuelled by gin and hubris, had forgotten Billy Hill's warning that 'murder is for mugs'. Then there had been the lapse of judgement that had led the twins to help Frank 'the Mad Axeman' Mitchell escape from Dartmoor Prison in December 1966, only to discover that the burly loudmouth with the low IQ was an embarrassment. Mitchell refused to lie low in his safe house and wrote endless letters to the Home Secretary, petitioning for a pardon. According to Albert Donoghue, a Kray heavy, Mitchell was discreetly bundled into a van and shot. Freddie Foreman claimed that the body was disposed of at sea, while other sources state that he was buried in the foundations of a flyover.[16]

Personal tragedy was also taking its toll. Reggie's wife, Frances, died of an overdose in 1967, aged just twenty-three, and in his grief-stricken state Reggie made a final lapse of judgement that was to bring the Krays down once and for all. He accepted Ronnie's request to kill Jack 'the Hat' McVitie, a minor member of the Kray gang who had failed to kill Leslie 'Payne the Brain', despite being paid £1,500 to do so.

A 'Jeckyll and Hyde character', Jack the Hat (it covered his bald spot) was another liability. Constantly drunk and high on amphetamines, McVitie once committed the sartorial outrage of appearing in Bermuda shorts, waving a machete. In Ronnie's immortal phrase, he would 'have to go'.[17]

In October 1967, Tony Lambrianou, one of the Krays' top men, drove McVitie to 'Blonde Carol's' flat in Stoke Newington, promising a 'party, birds and booze'. But when McVitie walked into the basement flat there was no party, just Ronnie and Reggie, waiting for him. Reggie attempted to shoot McVitie in the head, but the gun failed to go off. When McVitie smashed a window, Ronnie brought out the carving knife. Ronnie held McVitie down and Reggie stabbed him in the face and stomach so severely that, according to Lambrianou, McVitie's liver popped out and had to be flushed down the toilet.

Lambrianou, who was convicted of McVitie's murder along with his brother, Chris, had no regrets about McVitie's death, saying that he was a violent man who had once thrown a woman out of a car.[18] McVitie's body was never recovered, but Ronnie enhanced his personal myth by circulating stories that it had been fed to the pigs in Suffolk, burned in the furnaces of Bankside Power Station or buried beneath an office block in the City. John Pearson, the Krays' biographer, met Reggie shortly after this incident and noticed that his hand was bandaged. When Pearson asked what had caused the wound, Reggie commented laconically, 'Gardenin'.'[19]

Despite the wall of silence that made gathering evidence about the Krays well nigh impossible, time was running out for the twins. Chief Inspector Nipper Read contacted Leslie Payne, who had distanced himself from the Krays after they had taken a contract out on him. Payne gave the police a 146-page statement at considerable risk to his life. After his family had been threatened by the Krays, Albert Donoghue agreed to turn Queen's Evidence, as did an American criminal, Alan Cooper.

The Krays and fifteen other members of 'the Firm' were arrested on 9 May 1968, and once they were in custody, witnesses developed the confidence to come forward and give evidence. The trial at the Old Bailey lasted for thirty-nine days, and the twins were sentenced to life imprisonment with a non-parole period of thirty years for the murders of Cornell and McVitie, the longest sentences for murder ever passed at the Old Bailey. Charlie Kray was gaoled for ten years for his part in the murders. Ronnie Kray died in 1995, aged sixty-one, his passing commemorated by a lavish East End funeral. Reggie was released on compassionate grounds in August 2000, suffering from inoperable cancer. He died in his sleep on 22 September 2000 and was buried alongside his twin in Chingford cemetery.

Half a century later, the Kray mythology endures. Even today, East Enders reminisce sentimentally about 'the good old days' when the Krays represented an alternative method of law enforcement, and neighbours could leave their doors unlocked. Defenders of the Krays will tell you that they were devoted to their mother, and they 'only killed their own', as if that somehow justified the brutal gangland executions. The Krays have inspired industrial quantities of books, ranging from lurid memoirs to criminological dissertations, and dozens of movies, novels and television programmes. Ronnie, so hooked on celebrity, must have been deeply gratified when he and Reggie were portrayed by the handsome Kemp brothers, Gary and Martin, in the 1990 film *The Krays*. Cinematic immortality at last, reminiscent of Jimmy Cagney on the roof of the burning warehouse in the closing moments of *White Heat*: 'Made it, Ma! Top of the world!'

Forty years later, the Krays retain their aura as London's most dangerous family. Occasionally other names emerge from the shadows to claim the crown, but their exploits seem a pale imitation of 'the Firm' at the height of its powers. In 1991 the Arif family hit the headlines after a decade of police surveillance. One brother, Dogan, had already been gaoled for an £8.5 million cannabis smuggling plot and the family enjoyed a flamboyant lifestyle, thinking nothing of a £30,000 wedding celebration at the Savoy Hotel with guests including the families of Frankie Fraser and Harry White, plus the notorious north London Adams family.[20] But it was not until an armed robbery went wrong that the police got their men. In November 1990 a gang of armed robbers descended on a Securicor van in Reigate, Surrey. Hoping for an £800,000 haul, the robbers were disguised in Ronald Reagan masks and carrying enough ammunition to start a small war. But armed police were lying in wait and one robber, Kenny Baker, was shot dead. Dennis and Mehmet Arif were gaoled in 1991 for twenty-two and eighteen years respectively, along with their brother-in-law, Tony Downer, who also received eighteen years.[21]

The closing decades of the twentieth century saw two other audacious armed robberies, both of which would have impressed Billy Hill with their daring. On 26 November 1983, six robbers broke into the Brink's-MAT warehouse at Heathrow Airport, intent on stealing £3 million in cash. Brian Robinson had planned the raid with the help of his brother-in-law, Anthony Black, who worked as a security guard at Heathrow. When they arrived, the robbers actually found three tonnes of gold bullion worth £26 million. The gang was swiftly arrested after police discovered the family connection, and Robinson was sentenced to twenty-five years while Black received six. In the meantime, the gold had been disposed of by Kenneth Noye, an associate of the gang, who melted it down and recast it for sale. Noye's involvement was revealed after the Treasury noted large quantities of money moving through his bank account, and Noye was put under surveillance. In 1985, Noye killed a police officer in his garden but was found not guilty on the grounds of self-defence. In 1986, Noye was found guilty of handling the Brink's-MAT gold and sentenced to fourteen years in prison. Most of the gold has never been recovered, and four other men involved in the robbery have never been convicted. According to the BBC, anyone wearing gold jewellery purchased in the United Kingdom after 1983 is probably wearing Brink's-MAT.[22]

The Millennium Dome raid was an equally bold enterprise, one which might have brought a smile to the face of the old highwayman Claude du Vall himself. On 7 November 2000, a gang attempted to steal the flawless Millennium Star diamond, worth over £200 million, from an exhibition at the Millennium Dome. Armed with smoke bombs, ammonia, a sledgehammer and a nail gun, the gang rammed a JCB excavator into the Dome and smashed their way through to the vault. The plan was to snatch the diamond and escape down the Thames on a speedboat. The robbers had no idea they were surrounded and that the diamond had been replaced with a worthless fake the night before. In an operation codenamed 'Operation Magician', 200 police officers, including forty from the specialist firearms unit C019, were in position at the Dome, disguised as cleaners and employees. A further sixty armed Flying Squad officers were stationed around the Thames, with twenty on the river itself. Five of the robbers were caught and received sentences ranging from four to eighteen years.[23]

The failure of the Millenium Diamond heist, foiled by police intelligence work, may account for the fact that armed robbery has been superseded by other modes of crime over the past decade. There is no need for a gang of men in stocking masks to jump out of a Transit van with sawn-off shooters when an individual can empty a bank account at a keystroke. Criminals have always been early adopters and today technology has brought new possibilities in the form of cyber-crime, online fraud and identity theft. The most lucrative form of crime now is drug trafficking or 'narcotics', which has escalated from scare stories of reefer madness and white slavery in the 1920s to an organized, multi-million-dollar industry defying border controls, with links to international criminal gangs including the Italian Mafia and its American and Russian cousins.

The East End underworld has changed, too, under the impact of immigration from the former Eastern Bloc countries. London has always had an Eastern European immigrant community, notably the Ashkenazi Jewish refugees of the Victorian era. A century later, as law and order collapsed in the former Soviet Union, London became a hub for money laundering, drug dealing and gun-running, with weapons from the former Yugoslavia and Afghanistan circulating freely. The old accusations of anarchy and crime once hurled at the Jewish community were now levelled against Albanian, Ukrainian and Polish immigrants in the popular press. When it comes to modern vice, London can claim to be one of the most cosmopolitan crime capitals of the world.

Not all London crime is international and sophisticated, of course. Throughout its long, grim history, London's underworld has always had its local, street-based gangs, from Elizabethan cutpurses to the child pickpockets swarming barefoot through the Victorian capital at twilight. Towards the end of the nineteenth century, the concept of safety in numbers resulted in gangs based on ethnicity, such as the Yiddishers, the Italian and the Irish gangs. And with the rise of organized crime in the post-war years, the family-based gangs – such as the Krays and the Richardsons – combined a lifelong knowledge of their local neighbourhood and its denizens with a formidable code of enforcement that operated as the alternative local police force.

When the Jamaican or 'Yardie' gangs arrived on the scene in the 1980s, their *modus operandi* was recognizably similar. The Yardies (roughly translated as 'from our own back yard') were Jamaican-born gangsters operating in Britain. Like the Yiddishers and the Italians before them, they were bonded by shared ethnicity and family ties. Over the subsequent decade, black-on-black violence in London escalated, with killings worn as a badge of honour in a series of deadly turf wars and impulsive indiscriminate shootings in which innocent bystanders were fatally injured. In 1993, Yardies were blamed for the cold-blooded murder of PC Patrick Dunne, who was on patrol in Clapham when he stumbled across a shooting incident. In 1999, Yardie involvement was suggested in five black-on-black murders in London in just six weeks. In one particularly appalling incident in May 1999, Laverne Forbes, 28, and her partner Patrick Smith, 31, were shot dead in front of their seven-year-old daughter.[24]

A generation later, the term 'Yardie' has dropped from the headlines to be replaced by the phenomenon of home-grown 'postcode' gangs, and an all-pervasive gang culture that is as widespread as it is disturbing. This impossible-to-ignore phenomenon is the stuff of newspaper headlines, television programmes and public outrage. It can be summed up in a few stark words: stabbings, gun crime, turf wars and riots. Gun and knife crime have become commonplace, and every year dozens of young men are killed in what seem to the outsider to be meaningless feuds over 'respect'.

The common perception is that gang culture is associated with the Afro-Caribbean community. In fact, there are as many types of gangs as there are communities, including all-white gangs, African gangs, and Turkish Cypriot, Pakistani and Indian gangs. The so-called 'postcode gangs' of London and other major cities are characterized by the members' fierce attachment to their immediate neighbourhood and hostility to any perceived rivals crossing their turf. In practical terms, this territorial imperative means that youths have to walk a mile out of their way to get to school, and arrive late, or face being attacked.

While gang culture has become more aggressive over the past decade, the most disturbing factor is that the gangsters themselves have become increasingly younger. Just as Fagin groomed his young pickpockets in Dickensian London, today's 'Elders' force or entice their 'Youngers' into a life of crime. Working as a 'shotter' delivering drugs is attractive compared to a life on benefits, and peer pressure is over-whelming. Even children from stable homes find themselves compelled to join a gang just to survive. Much has been said of the perceived glamour of gang culture, but at a more instinc-tive level, it's all about belonging. And the consequences for not belonging can be lethal. While Fagin's gonophs operated in the shadow of the noose, today's child criminals are desen-sitized, brutalized children killing other children, armed with guns and knives. One of the most shocking murders occurred on Valentine's Day 2007, when Billy Cox was shot dead at his home in Clapham, after a dispute about a small amount of cannabis. Popular, 'girly', much-loved Billy had drifted into gang culture and minor crime, but had recently enrolled on a training course in a bid to go legitimate. He was just fifteen years old.[25]

The news that yet another schoolboy has been murdered in gang-related violence has become depressingly familiar. By July 2011, nine young men had already been killed in this way in London. On 26 December 2011 a young man was stabbed to death on Oxford Street during the Boxing Day sales. Eighteen-year-old Seydou Diarrassouba was killed with a single stab wound to the heart in the Foot Locker sports shop, near Bond Street Tube station. His death led to chaotic scenes as officers tried to restrain the crowd that had gathered outside. At the time of writing, a man of twenty has been charged with murder and is awaiting trial.[26]

But there are occasional glimpses of hope. In September 2011, the *Evening Standard* reported the story of Tony Massiah, a young man from Tottenham who has become a pupil barrister after escaping from a life of crime. Massiah, who had been swept up in gang violence as a teenager, re-evaluated his life after being narrowly missed by a bullet during a brawl. After completing his law degree and starting in chambers, Mr Massiah told the newspaper, 'If anyone says that it is impossible, I am proof that it is not. I sympathize with kids drawn into gangs but if I could say anything to them it would be that they are not your real friends if they are asking you to do a crime.' According to the *Standard,* the Bar Council later commented that 'everyone has a right to turn their life around'.[27]

16

LONDON BABYLON

From the Old Bailey to Tyburn

To stand outside the Old Bailey now is to stand in one of the most notable spots in the history of London's underworld. In this place, thousands of prisoners, known and unknown, famous and infamous, pleaded for their lives. In this place, the brigand Blueskin lunged at the thief-taker Jonathan Wild and cut his throat, and it is here that Dr Crippen, Edith Thompson and Ruth Ellis looked on as the judge reached for his black cap and condemned them to death. In this place, old Newgate Gaol was burnt to the ground, rebuilt in its last, grim incarnation and then demolished forever. And in this place the condemned prisoners filed through Dead Man's Walk, across the buried bodies of the former inmates, on their way to the gallows. For those who believe in such things, the Old Bailey must be one of the most haunted places in London, with the legendary Black Dog of Newgate revealing itself to those who are about to die, slithering out of the shadows and draping itself across the walls in a scene of compelling horror.

Turning away from the Old Bailey, the old road to Tyburn

winds its way through Fleet Street. On hanging days, these streets were black with onlookers, crowded onto rooftops, peering out through windows, shouting and chanting their messages of support or derision for the condemned men and women. Before embarking on the last stages of this journey, I will take a detour through St Paul's. In the days of the first Queen Elizabeth, the precincts of St Paul's had become a den of vice, lined with tobacco sellers, pickpockets, conmen and crooks of every variety. In October 2011, the cathedral became host to the Occupy movement, a gathering of young people protesting peacefully against corporate greed and the collapse of the global economy. The fact that London has become more enlightened over the past 200 years was demonstrated by the fact that when the protestors were evicted following a High Court Injunction from the City of London on 28 February 2012, the majority dispersed peacefully, having made their point. Although it was a sad sight to see the peace camp broken up, there were only twenty arrests and at least the event was not marked by a cavalry charge scything through the crowd, as would have been the case two centuries ago.[1]

That is not to say that London has not witnessed disturbing scenes of crowd violence in modern times. London was hit by another, more aggressive form of protest in August 2011 when a series of riots broke out following the shooting of 29-year-old Mark Duggan by police officers in Tottenham. The riots spread to Enfield, Walthamstow and Brixton and resulted in over 100 arrests on the first night. Over the following four nights, rioting continued elsewhere in London and in other major cities, and led to widespread looting and vandalism. While the original riots were sparked by a genuine grievance at the shooting of Mark Duggan, resentment at police 'stop and search' procedures which disproportionately target young black men, and high levels of youth unemployment and social deprivation, there was also an element of greedy opportunism.[2]

While some looters were children in their early teens, guilty of little more than a youthful foolishness, it emerged that 75 per cent of those arrested had previous convictions.[3]

Magistrates sat through the night, just as the Fielding brothers had done two centuries earlier, and were criticized for handing down stiff sentences. But this should be viewed in perspective. The reader will have some idea of how far the English criminal justice system has travelled when they consider that a fine or even a brief custodial sentence for stealing a pair of trainers is merciful compared with the fate of the young Gordon Rioters, around thirty of whom were publically hanged around the city of London.

This is the last stage of the journey, following in the footsteps of so many, up through Fleet Street, past the Royal Courts of Justice, down Oxford Street and so finally into Tyburn. This last trip through London allows me to reflect on the barbaric history of capital punishment and the extraordinary stories I have encountered along the way, some of which stand out so starkly in the memory: Eliza Fenning, accused of poisoning her employer and his family; the dashing highwaymen Plunkett and MacLaine; Maria Manning, the woman who murdered black satin; and the diabolical Wainwright who rounded upon the spectators at his execution with a cry of 'You curs! Come to see a man die, have you!'

To review these old cases, to enquire as to the guilt of one person or the innocence of another, is to engage with the spirit of London's underworld. It is as if the many ghosts encountered during the long journey of this book still crowd around, and retain the power to haunt. In the words of Ford Madox Ford, 'certain corners of certain streets, certain angles of buildings' bring them back again, conjured up with the glamour of memory, the romance of the old days, the recollection of those griefs and those terrors.[4] The shadows of these crimes and their protagonists and victims linger on 'in the wavering reflections of the rain-washed streets'.[5] Now London's underworld is the stuff of tourist trails, with travellers conducted around the back-streets of Whitechapel where Jack the Ripper blazed his trail of terror, or taken for a drink at the Blind Beggar pub where Ronnie Kray shot George Cornell. Crime, in its literary form, has become yet another of London's most famous exports.

Finally, I have come full circle and stand at Tyburn, outside the Roman Catholic oratory that marks the spot where so many martyrs died. Tyburn's historian Alfred Marks urged his readers to remember the thousands of other 'martyrs' who died at this spot and elsewhere, the victims of 'ferocious laws, the innocent, the martyrs to cruel injustice and iniquitous social conditions' who had the life choked out of them.[6]

It seems fitting to pause here for a moment and honour their memory in the knowledge that the barbaric practice of capital punishment has disappeared from Britain forever, and that its victims here at Tyburn and elsewhere did not die in vain.

In memoriam: the plaque that marks the spot where
Tyburn's triple tree once stood.

Bibliography

Babington, Anthony, *A House in Bow Street*, Macdonald, London, 1969

Babington, Anthony, *The English Bastille*, Macdonald, London, 1971

Berresford Ellis, Peter, *A History of the Irish Working Class,* Pluto Press, London 1996

Brandon, David, and Brooke, Alan, *London: The Executioner's City*, Sutton, Stroud, 2007

Brooke, Alan, and Brandon, David, *Tyburn: London's Fatal Tree*, The History Press, Stroud, 2004

Bulwer-Lytton, Edward, *Paul Clifford*, George Routledge & Sons, London, 1877

Burford, E. J., *A Short History of the Clink Prison*, The Clink Prison, London, 1989

Campbell, Duncan, *The Underworld*, BBC Books, 1994

Chesney, Kellow, *The Victorian Underworld*, Temple Smith, London, 1970

Cruikshank, Dan, *The Secret History of Georgian London: How the Wages of Sin Shaped the Capital*, Random House, London, 2009

Defoe, Daniel, *Moll Flanders*, Penguin Classics, Harmondsworth, 1989

De Quincey, Thomas, ed. by Morrison, Robert, *On Murder*, Oxford University Press, Oxford, 2006

Dickens, Charles, *Barnaby Rudge: A Tale of the Riots of Eighty*, Vols 1 & 2, Chapman and Hall, London, 1897

Dickens, Charles, *The Adventures of Oliver Twist*, Chapman & Hall, London, 1897

Fabian, Robert, *London After Dark: An Intimate Record of Night Life in London*, The Naldrett Press, London, 1954

Faller, Lincoln B., *Turned to Account: The Forms and Functions of Criminal Biography in Late Seventeenth- and Early Eighteenth-Century England*, Cambridge University Press, Cambridge, 1987

Fido, Martin, *Murder Guide to London*, Orion Books, London, 1986

Foot, Paul, *Who Killed Hanratty?*, Penguin Books, London, 1988

Foucault, Michel, *Discipline and Punish: The Birth of the Prison*, Penguin, Harmondsworth, 1991

Gatrell, V. A. C., *The Hanging Tree: Execution and the English People 1770–1868*, Oxford University Press, Oxford, 1994

Griffith, Tom (ed.), *The Newgate Calendar*, Wordsworth Editions, Ware, 1997

Grovier, Kelly, *The Gaol: The Story of Newgate, London's Most Notorious Prison*, John Murray, London, 2009

Halliday, Stephen, *Newgate: London's Prototype of Hell*, History Press, Stroud, 2009

Harrison, Brian A., *The Tower of London Prisoner Book: A Complete Chronology of the Persons Known to Have Been Detained*, Royal Armouries, Leeds, 2004

Harrison Ainsworth, William, *The Tower of London*, George Routledge & Sons, London, 1897

Heale, John, *One Blood: Inside Britain's New Street Gangs*, Simon & Schuster, 2008

Herber, Mark D., *Legal London: A Pictorial History*, Phillimore, London, 1999

Hiney, Tom, *Raymond Chandler: A Biography*, Chatto & Windus, London, 1997

Hitchcock, Tim, and Shoemaker, Bob, *Tales from the Hanging*

Court, Bloomsbury, London, 2007

Hodge, James H. (ed.), *Famous Trials 5*, Penguin, 1955

Honeycombe, Gordon, *Murders of the Black Museum*, John Blake, London, 2009

Hooper, W. Eden, *History of Newgate and the Old Bailey*, Underwood Press, London, 1935

Impey, Edward, and Parnell, Geoffrey, *The Tower of London: The Official Illustrated History*, Merrell Publishers Ltd, London, 2000

James, P. D., and Critchley, T. A., *The Maul and the Pear Tree*, Sphere Books, London, 1971

Jonson, Ben, *The Alchemist*, *The Alchemist and Other Plays*, Oxford World's Classics, Oxford University Press, Oxford, 2008

Jonson, Ben, *Bartholomew Fair, The Alchemist and Other Plays*, Oxford World's Classics, Oxford University Press, Oxford, 2008

Kinney, Arthur F., *Rogues, Vagabonds and Sturdy Beggars: A New Gallery of Tudor and Early Stuart Rogue Literature*, University of Massachusetts Press, Massachusetts, 1990

Leeson, B., *Lost London: The Memoirs of an East End Detective*, Stanley Paul & Co Ltd, London, 1934

Linebaugh, Peter, *The London Hanged: Crime and Civil Society in the Eighteenth Century*, Penguin, London, 1993

Linnane, Fergus, *The Encyclopaedia of London Crime and Vice*, Sutton, Stroud, 2005

Darbyshire, Neil, and Hilliard, Brian, *The Flying Squad*, Headline, London, 1993

Madox Ford, Ford, *The Soul of London: A Survey of a Modern City*, Alston Rivers, London, 1905

Majoribanks, Edward, *For the Defence: The Life of Sir Edward Marshall Hall*, Macmillan, London, 1929

Marks, Alfred, *Tyburn Tree: Its History and Annals*, Brown Langham & Co., London, 1908

Mayhew, Henry, *London Labour and the London Poor*; Cassell, London, 1967

Mayhew, Henry (ed.) by Quennell, Peter, *London's Underworld*, Spring Books, London, 1966

Pearsall, Ronald, *The Worm in the Bud: The World of Victorian Sexuality*, Sutton, Stroud, 2003

Pearson, John, *The Profession of Violence*, Harper Collins, London, 1995

Picard, Liza, *Elizabeth's London: Everyday Life in Elizabethan London*, Orion, London, 2004

Pierrepoint, Albert, *Executioner: Pierrepoint*, Harrap, London, 1974

Rivlin, Geoffrey, *Understanding the Law*, Oxford University Press, Oxford, 2009

Salgado, Gamini, *The Elizabethan Underworld*, Sutton, Stroud, 1992

Scott, Sir George Gilbert, *Gleanings from Westminster Abbey*, Parker, Oxford, 1861

Shakespeare, *The Complete Works*, ed. Peter Alexander Collins, London, 1978

Spraggs, Gillian, *Outlaws and Highwaymen*, Pimlico, London, 2001

Stanley, Arthur Penrhyn, *Historical Monuments of Westminster Abbey*, unknown publisher, London, 1868

Stow, John, *A Survey of London Written in the Year 1598*, The History Press, Stroud, 2005

Thomas, Donald Serrell, *The Victorian Underworld*, John Murray, London, 1998

Thompson, Sir Basil, *The Story of Scotland Yard*, The Literary Guild, New York, 1936

Trevelyan, Raleigh, *Sir Walter Raleigh*, Faber and Faber, London, 2010

Watts, Marthe, *The Men in My Life*, Christopher Johnson, London, 1960

Webb, Duncan, *Crime Is My Business*, Frederick Muller Ltd, London, 1953

Webb, Duncan, *Line-up for Crime*, Frederick Muller Ltd, London, 1956

Webster, John, *The White Devil*, ed. F. L. Lucas, Chatto and Windus, London, 1958

Wheen, Francis, *The Sixties*, Ebury, London, 1982

Whitfield, Peter, *London: A Life in Maps*, British Library, London, 2006

Wild, Roland, and Curtis-Bennett, Derek, *'Curtis': The Life of Sir Henry Curtis-Bennett*, Cassell, London, 1937

Wilson, Derek, *The Tower: The Tumultuous History of the Tower of London from 1078*, Scribner, New York, 1979

Yallop, David A., *To Encourage the Others*, W. H. Allen, London, 1971

Young, Filson (ed.), *Trial of Frederick Bywaters and Edith Thompson*, Notable British Trials series, William Hodge, London, 1951

SELECTED WEBSITES

http://eastlondonhistory.com
http://news.bbc.co.uk/onthisday
http://utilitarianism.com
http://www.bailii.org
http://www.british-history.ac.uk
http://www.capitalpunishmentuk.org
http://www.exclassics.com
http://www.lawgazette.co.uk
http://www.met.police.uk/history
http://www.murderpedia.org
http://www.murderuk.com
http://www.nickelinthemachine.com
http://www.oldbaileyonline.org

http://www.outlawsandhighwaymen.com
http://www.thamespolicemuseum.org.uk
http://www.thekrays.co.uk
http://www.trutv.com
http://www.victorianlondon.org

SELECTED NEWSPAPERS AND JOURNALS

Bell's Life in London and Sporting Chronicle
Daily Express
Daily Mail
Daily Telegraph
Evening Standard
Guardian
Independent
Illustrated London News
London Journal
Mist's Weekly Journal
Punch
The Times

Notes

CHAPTER ONE

1 See Webster, *The White Devil*, Act V, Scene 2, line 6
2 See Wilson, *The Tower*, p. 15
3 See Marks, *Tyburn Tree*, p. 62
4 Ibid., p. 28
5 Ibid., p. 80
6 See Stow, *A Survey of London*, p. 35
7 See Marks, op. cit., p. 80
8 Ibid.
9 Ibid., p. 6
10 See http://www.guardian.co.uk/commentisfree/belief/2011/aug/19/church-of-england-capital-punishment
11 See Babington, *The English Bastille*, p. 26
12 See Marks, op. cit., p. 7
13 Ibid., pp. 6–7
14 See Wilson, op. cit., p. 11
15 Ibid.
16 See Marks, op. cit., p. 80
17 Ibid.
18 Ibid., p. 16
19 See Wilson, op. cit., p. 35
20 See Marks, op. cit., p. 96
21 Ibid.
22 See Wilson, op. cit., p. 35
23 See Stanley, *Historical Monuments of Westminster Abbey*, pp. 383–4
24 Ibid.
25 See Marks, op. cit., p. 105

26 See Scott, *Gleanings from Westminster Abbey*, pp. 38–40

27 See Stow, op. cit., pp. 229–30

28 See Marks, op. cit., p. 105

29 Ibid.

30 See Shakespeare, *Henry VI Pt 2*, Act II, Scene 3

31 See Marks, op. cit., p. 124

32 Ibid.

33 Ibid.

34 See Harrison, *The Tower of London Prisoner Book*, p. 523

35 See Marks, op. cit., p. 120

36 Ibid., p. 117

37 Ibid.

38 Ibid., p. 133

39 Ibid., pp. 134–6

CHAPTER TWO

1 See Impey and Parnell, *The Tower of London*, p. 18

2 See Wilson, *The Tower*, p. 11

3 Ibid., p. 5

4 Ibid., pp. 27–8

5 Ibid., pp. 62–3

6 Ibid., p. 64

7 See Impey and Parnell, op. cit., p. 46

8 See Wilson, op. cit., pp. 68–9

9 Ibid., p. 72

10 Ibid., p. 73

11 Ibid.

12 See Harrison Ainsworth, *The Tower of London*, p. 173

13 See Wilson, op. cit., p. 84

14 See Marks, *Tyburn Tree*, p. 121

15 See http://digital.library.upenn.edu/women/yonge/deeds/daughter.html, quoting from Yonge, Charlotte M., *A Book of Golden Deeds*, Blackie & Son Ltd., London, 1864

16 See Wilson, op. cit., p. 96

17 Ibid.

18 Ibid., p. 101

19 See Harrison, *The Tower of London Prisoner Book*, p. 534

20 Ibid., p. 530

21 Ibid., p. 519

22 See Harrison Ainsworth, op. cit., p. 175
23 See Harrison, op. cit., p. 530
24 Ibid., p. 530
25 See Harrison Ainsworth, op. cit., p. 175
26 See Wilson, op. cit., p.109
27 Ibid., p. 110
28 Ibid., p. 110
29 Ibid., p. 110
30 See Harrison Ainsworth, op. cit., p. 323
31 Ibid., p. 511
32 Elizabeth I at the Tower of London during her coronation cere-
    monies, 1559, from *Records of St Giles' Cripplegate* by William Denton,
    G Bell & Son, London, 1883
33 See Harrison, op. cit., p. 260
34 See Trevelyan, *Sir Walter Raleigh*, p. 552
35 See Harrison Ainsworth, op. cit., p. 168
36 Ibid.
37 Ibid., p. 169
38 Ibid.
39 See http://briancatling.com/Site/Tower_2.html

CHAPTER THREE

 1 See Spraggs, *Outlaws and Highwaymen*, p. 68
 2 Ibid.
 3 See Marks, *Tyburn Tree*, p. 137
 4 See Salgado, *The Elizabethan Underworld*, p. 147
 5 Ibid.
 6 Ibid. p. 153
 7 See Hitchcock and Shoemaker, *Tales from the Hanging Court*, p. xi
 8 See Salgado, op. cit., pp. 6–7
 9 See Linnane, *The Encyclopedia of London, Crime and Vice*, p. 6
10 Ibid. p. 192
11 See Salgado, op. cit., p. 33
12 Ibid. p. 11
13 Ibid. p. 15
14 Ibid. p. 11
15 See Picard, *Elizabeth's London*, p. 246
16 See Salgado, op. cit., p. 22
17 See Picard, op. cit., p. 247

18 Ibid.
19 See Salgado, op. cit., p. 19
20 Ibid., p. 17
21 Ibid.
22 Ibid., p. 11
23 See Jonson, *Bartholomew Fair*, Act II, Scene 6, lines 10–15
24 See Kinney, *Rogues, Vagabonds and Sturdy Beggars,* p. 37
25 See Jonson, op. cit., Act III, Scene 2, 35–37
26 See http://www.exclassics.com/foxe/foxe174.htm
27 See Brandon and Brooke, *London*, p. 67
28 Ibid., p. 70
29 See Marks, op. cit., pp. 21–2

CHAPTER FOUR

1   See Hooper, *History of Newgate and the Old Bailey*, p. 26
2   Ibid.
3   Ibid., pp. 74–5
4   See Rivlin, *Understanding the Law*, p. 224
5   Ibid.
6   Ibid.
7   See http://www.usask.ca/english/turne_backe/taylor_bio.html
8   Ibid.
9   Ibid.
10 See http://www.british-history.ac.uk/report.aspx?compid=45054, quoting from Thornbury, Walter, *Old and New London, Volume 1*, 1878
11 See Stow, *A Survey of London*, p. 351
12 See Salgado, *The Elizabethan Underworld*, p. 171
13 Ibid.
14 Ibid.
15 See Herber, *Legal London*, p. 106
16 See Burford, *A Short History of the Clink Prison*, p. 9
17 See Hooper, op. cit., p. 6
18 Ibid., p. 26
19 Ibid., p. 6
20 See Babington, *The English Bastille*, p. 23
21 Ibid., p. 25
22 See Marks, *Tyburn Tree*, p. 104
23 See http://www.british-history.ac.uk/report.aspx?compid=45045
24 See Halliday, *Newgate*, p. 7

25 See Babington, op. cit., p. 24
26 See Hooper, op. cit., p. 35
27 See Babington, op. cit., p. 23
28 Ibid.
29 See http://www.exclassics.com/foxe/foxe174.htm, quoting from Foxe, John, *Book of Martyrs*, 1563
30 See Grovier, *The Gaol*, pp. 66–7

CHAPTER FIVE

 1 See Bulwer-Lytton, *Paul Clifford*, p. 136
 2 See Jonson, *The Alchemist*, Act I, Scene I
 3 See Spraggs, *Outlaws and Highwaymen*, pp. 147–50
 4 See Spraggs, http://www.outlawsandhighwaymen.com/index.htm
 5 See http://www.exclassics.com/newgate/ng2.htm
 6 See Marks, *Tyburn Tree*, p. 194
 7 See http://www.exclassics.com/newgate/ng2.htm
 8 Ibid.
 9 Ibid.
10 See Marks, op. cit., pp. 209–11
11 Ibid., pp. 211–3
12 Ibid., pp. 229–30
13 Ibid.
14 See Spraggs, op. cit., p. 1
15 See Faller, *Turned to Account*, p. 162
16 See Cruikshank, *The Secret History of Georgian London*, p. 335
17 See Spraggs, op. cit., p. 1
18 See Griffith, *The Newgate Calendar*, pp. 183–96
19 See Spraggs, http://www.outlawsandhighwaymen.com/index.htm
20 See Babington, *The English Bastille*, p. 119
21 See Marks, op. cit., pp. 258–9
22 See Bulwer-Lytton, op. cit., p. 147

CHAPTER SIX

 1 See Babington, *The English Bastille*, p. 34
 2 Ibid., p. 19
 3 See Babington, *A House in Bow Street*, p. 15
 4 See Foucault, *Discipline and Punish*, p. 61

5 See Defoe, *Moll Flanders*, pp. 273–4
6 See Babington, *The English Bastille*, p.113
7 Ibid., p.117
8 Ibid., p.115
9 See Griffith, *The Newgate Calendar*, p. 107
10 See Gatrell, *The Hanging Tree*, p. 59
11 See Marks, *Tyburn Tree*, pp. 221–3
12 Ibid., pp. 225–6
13 Ibid.
14 See Griffith, op. cit.
15 Ibid.
16 See *Mist's Weekly Journal*, 2 April 1726
17 Ibid.
18 See *London Journal*, 5 May 1726
19 Ibid.
20 See Marks, op. cit., p. 251
21 See http://www.exclassics.com/newgate/ng186.htm
22 See http://www.capitalpunishmentuk.org/malcolm.html
23 Ibid.
24 Ibid.
25 Ibid.
26 See Gatrell, op. cit., p. 62
27 See Griffith, op. cit.
28 See Marks, op. cit., p. 256
29 Ibid., p. 247
30 Ibid., pp. 260–2
31 Ibid., p. 263
32 Ibid.
33 Ibid.
34 Ibid., pp. 266–7
35 See Babington, *The English Bastille*, p. 147
36 See Marks, op. cit., p. 267

CHAPTER SEVEN

1 See Babington, *A House in Bow Street*, p. 17
2 See Thompson, *The Story of Scotland Yard*, p. 23
3 Ibid., p. 20
4 See Babington, op. cit., pp. 35–7
5 Ibid., p. 58

6 Ibid., p. 57
7 Ibid.
8 Ibid., p. 62
9 See Thompson, op. cit., p. 33
10 Ibid. p.30
11 See Halliday, *Newgate*, p. 138
12 See Thompson, op. cit., pp. 34–5
13 See Babington, op. cit., pp. 159–60
14 Ibid.
15 See Linnane, *Encyclopaedia of London Crime and Vice*, p. 110
16 See Babington, op. cit., p. 164
17 Ibid., p. 179
18 Ibid., pp. 210–11
19 See http://www.thamespolicemuseum.org.uk/h_
   ratcliffehighwaymurders_1.html
20 Ibid.
21 Ibid.
22 See James and Critchley, *The Maul and the Pear Tree*, p. 225
23 See Babington, op. cit., p. 210
24 See Thompson, op. cit., p. 46
25 Ibid.
26 Ibid., p. 51
27 See Gatrell, *The Hanging Tree*, p. 308
28 Ibid.
29 See *The Traveller*, May 1820
30 See Thompson, op. cit., p. 54
31 See 'From the archive, 18 August 1821: Two killed in Queen's funeral procession', *Guardian*, 18 August 2011

CHAPTER EIGHT

1 See Mayhew, *London Labour and the London Poor*, p. 63
2 See *Illustrated London News*, 18 September 1852
3 See Dickens, *Oliver Twist*, p. 69
4 Ibid. p. 77
5 See Chesney, *The Victorian Underworld*, p. 146
6 See Mayhew, *London's Underworld*, p. 291
7 Ibid., p. 293
8 Ibid., p. 196
9 Ibid.

10 Ibid.
11 Ibid., p. 181
12 Ibid., pp. 214–30
13 See Chesney, op. cit., p. 160
14 See Mayhew, op. cit., p. 230
15 See Thomas, *The Victorian Underworld*, pp. 255–6
16 Ibid., pp. 206–29
17 See Babington, *The English Bastille*, p. 191
18 See *Punch*, 31 January 1857
19 See Babington, op. cit., pp. 132–5
20 Ibid., p. 105
21 Ibid., p. 104
22 See http://utilitarianism.com/jeremy-bentham/index.html
23 See Babington, op. cit., p. 199
24 Ibid., p. 210
25 Ibid., p. 213
26 See Herber, *Legal London*, p. 118
27 See Babington, op. cit., p. 210
28 Ibid., p. 197
29 Ibid., p. 210
30 Ibid., p. 191
31 Ibid., p. 199
32 See Thomas, op. cit., p. 268
33 See Babington, op. cit., p. 192
34 Ibid., p. 214
35 Ibid., p. 218
36 Ibid.
37 See Dickens, op. cit., p.500
38 Ibid. p. 504

CHAPTER NINE

1 See Babington, *The English Bastille*, p.146
2 Ibid.
3 See Halliday, *Newgate*, p. 177
4 See Gatrell, *The Hanging Tree*, p. 54
5 See Babington, op. cit., p. 163
6 See http://www.exclassics.com/newgate/ng567.htm
7 See Gatrell, op. cit., p.359
8 Ibid., pp. 363–7

9 Ibid., p. 357

10 Ibid., p. 356

11 See http://www.exclassics.com/newgate/ng567.htm

12 See Gatrell, op. cit., p. 368

13 See Babington, op. cit., p. 163

14 See Gatrell, op. cit., p. 51

15 See http://www.exclassics.com/newgate/ng622.htm

16 See Gatrell, op. cit., p. 69

17 Ibid., p. 39

18 *Weekly Chronicle*, 7 May 1837

19 See Babington, op. cit., p.225

20 Ibid., p. 224

21 See http://www.met.police.uk/history/daniel_good.htm

22 See http://www.capitalpunishmentuk.org/mannings.html

23 See Gatrell, op. cit., p. 605

24 See Babington, op. cit., p. 226

25 See Gatrell, op. cit., p. 606

26 See Babington, op. cit., p. 226

27 See Berresford Ellis, *A History of the Irish Working Class*, p. 140

28 *Daily Telegraph* and *Daily News*, 27 May 1868

CHAPTER TEN

1 See http://www.victorianlondon.org/crime/harrietlane.htm

2 Ibid.

3 See Fido, *Murder Guide to London*, p. 29

4 See http://www.victorianlondon.org/crime/harrietlane.htm

5 See *Bell's Life in London and Sporting Chronicle*, 27 January 1883

6 See http://www.readbookonline.net/readOnLine/2527, quoting
   from Dickens, Charles, 'The Detective Police', London, 1838

7 See Thomson, *The Story of Scotland Yard*, p. ix

8 See http://www.hawthornedvrt.org/Women-and-Domestic-
   Violence.htm

9 See *The Times*, 9 April 1872

10 See Thomas, *The Victorian Underworld*, p. 66

11 See 'Skull found in Sir David Attenborough's garden that solves
    1879 Barnes murder mystery', *Daily Mail*, 26 October 2010

12 See Fido, op. cit., p. 96

13 See Thomas, op. cit., p. 66

14 See http://www.met.police.uk/history/ripper.htm

15 Ibid.

16 Ibid.

17 See Pearsall, *The Worm in the Bud*, p. 310

18 See http://www.met.police.uk/history/ripper.htm

19 Ibid.

20 Ibid.

21 See Thomas, op. cit., p. 66

22 Ibid.

23 Ibid.

24 Ibid.

25 Ibid.

26 Ibid.

CHAPTER ELEVEN

1 See *Daily Mail,* 16 August 1902

2 See Babington, *The English Bastille*, p. 236

3 See Hooper, *History of Newgate and the Old Bailey*, p. 115

4 See http://www.lawgazette.co.uk/news/the-great-defender-sir-edward-marshall-hall

5 Ibid.

6 See http://www.netcharles.com/orwell/essays/decline-of-the-english-murder.htm

7 See http://www.flickr.com/photos/brizzlebornandbred/4803874483/

8 See http://www.met.police.uk/history/dr_crippen.htm

9 See http://www.oldbaileyonline.org/browse.jsp?id=t19101011-74&div=t19101011-74

10 Ibid.

11 See http://en.wikipedia.org/wiki/Hawley_Harvey_Crippen

12 See http://www.nickelinthemachine.com/tag/funeral/

13 See Fido, *Murder Guide to London*, p. 52

14 See http://www.capitalpunishmentuk.org/edith.html

15 See Wild and Curtis-Bennett, *Curtis*, p. 163

16 Ibid., p. 166

17 See Young, *Trial of Fredrick Bywaters and Edith Thompson*, p. 146

18 Ibid., p. 143

19 See http://www.capitalpunishmentuk.org/edith.html

20 See Wild and Curtis-Bennett, op. cit., p. 165

21 Ibid.

22 See http://www.nickelinthemachine.com/tag/egypt/

23 Ibid.
24 See Majoribanks, *For the Defence*, pp. 363–80
25 Ibid.
26 Ibid.
27 Ibid.
28 See http://www.nickelinthemachine.com/tag/egypt/
29 Ibid.
30 See Fido, op. cit., p. 75

CHAPTER TWELVE

1 See http://eastlondonhistory.com/isaac-bogard-and-arthur-harding/
2 See Campbell, *The Underworld*, p. 18
3 See http://eastlondonhistory.com/isaac-bogard-and-arthur-harding/
4 Ibid.
5 See Darbyshire and Hilliard, *The Flying Squad*, p. 25
6 Ibid.
7 See Campbell, op. cit., p. 29
8 Ibid.
9 See Campbell, op. cit., p. 19
10 See http://observer.guardian.co.uk/drugs/story/0,,686503,00.html
11 See http:/www.nickelinthemachine.com/2010/02/sample-post.html/limehouse/
12 Ibid.
13 See http://www.victorianlondon.org/entertainment/opiumsmoking-dens.htm
14 See Campbell, op. cit., pp. 216–7
15 Ibid., p. 214
16 Ibid., p. 215
17 See Fabian, *London After Dark*, p.36
18 Ibid.
19 See http://eastlondonhistory.com/isaac-bogard-and-arthur-harding/
20 See Campbell, op. cit., p. 23
21 See *Daily Express*, 20 November 1922

CHAPTER THIRTEEN

1 See http://www.murderpedia.org/male.H/h/hulten-karl.htm
2 See Webb, *Crime Is My Business*, p.70
3 See Webb, op. cit., p. 73
4 Ibid., p. 73
5 Ibid., p. 71
6 See http://murderpedia.org/male.H/h/hulten-karl.htm
7 Anecdotal
8 See http://www.netcharles.com/orwell/essays/decline-of-the-english-murder.htm
9 See Webb, op. cit., p. 213
10 Ibid., p. 214
11 Ibid., p. 215
12 Ibid., p. 218
13 Ibid., pp. 221–2
14 See Hodge, *Famous Trials 5*, pp. 55–106
15 Ibid.
16 See Honeycombe, *Murders of the Black Museum*, p. 257
17 Ibid., p. 279
18 See Webb, op. cit., p. 222
19 Ibid., p. 79
20 Ibid., p. 80
21 Ibid., p. 84
22 Ibid., p. 85
23 Ibid., p. 87
24 See Honeycombe, op. cit., p. 279
25 See *Daily Express*, 29 April 1945
26 Paul Willetts, via email correspondence with the author
27 Ibid.

CHAPTER FOURTEEN

1 See http://www.trutv.com/library/crime/serial_killers/history/christie/place_7.html
2 Ibid.
3 Ibid.
4 Ibid.
5 See http://news.bbc.co.uk/onthisday/hi/dates/stories/june/25/newsid_3721000/3721267.stm

6 Ibid.

7 See Honeycombe, *Murders of the Black Museum*, p. 314

8 See http://www.bailii.org/ew/cases/EWHC/Admin/2004/2779.html, quoting 'Mary Westlake v Criminal Cases Review Commission', England and Wales High Court, 17 November 2004

9 Paul Willetts, via email correspondence with the author

10 See http://www.murderuk.com/one_off_bentley_craig.html

11 See Yallop, *To Encourage the Others*, p.115

12 Ibid.

13 See http://news.bbc.co.uk/onthisday/hi/dates/stories/january/28/newsid_3393000/3393807.stm

14 Ibid.

15 See http://news.bbc.co.uk/onthisday/hi/dates/stories/july/13/newsid_2745000/2745023.stm

16 See Webb, *Line-Up for Crime*, p. 213

17 See http://www.nickelinthemachine.com/2008/05

18 See Webb, op. cit., p. 213

19 Ibid., p. 216

20 Ibid., p. 217

21 Ibid.

22 Ibid., p. 218

23 Ibid., p. 224

24 Ibid.

25 Ibid.

26 Ibid.

27 Ibid.

28 See http://en.wikipedia.org/wiki/William_Connor

29 See Webb, op. cit., p. 224

30 See Hiney, *Raymond Chandler*, p. 224

31 See 'My sister Ruth', *Guardian*, 27 January 1997

32 See http://www.nickelinthemachine.com/2008/05

33 Ibid.

34 See http://copperknob.wordpress.com/category/albert-pierrepoint/

35 See Foot, *Who Killed Hanratty?*, p.26

36 Ibid., p. 31

37 Ibid., p. 33

38 Ibid., p. 41

39 Ibid., p. 51

40 Ibid., p. 54

41 Ibid., p. 55

42 Ibid., p. 54

43 Ibid., p. 142

44 See 'Hanratty's body is reburied after DNA testing', *Daily Telegraph*, 28 June 2001

45 See 'We will never know the truth about the A6 killer', *Independent*, 7 February 2009

46 See Pierrepoint, *Executioner: Pierrepoint*, p.169

47 See http://www.bbc.co.uk/news/uk-14402195

CHAPTER FIFTEEN

1 See 'When crime grabbed the limelight', *Guardian*, 30 July 2008

2 See Linnane, *The Encyclopaedia of London Crime and Vice*, p. 160

3 See *The Times*, 23 May 1952

4 See Linnane, op., cit. p. 261

5 See Watts, *The Men in My Life*, p. 195

6 See Webb, *Crime Is My Business*, p. 138

7 Ibid.

8 See Watts, op. cit., p. 230

9 See Campbell, *The Underworld*, p. 70

10 Ibid., p. 69

11 See http://www.nickelinthemachine.com/2009/02/no1-eaton-square-lord-boothby-and-ronnie-kray/

12 See http://www.thekrays.co.uk

13 See Campbell, op. cit., p. 130

14 Ibid., p. 134

15 Ibid., p. 104

16 See Pearson, *The Profession of Violence*, pp. 237–9

17 See Campbell, op. cit., pp. 79–81

18 Ibid.

19 See Pearson, op. cit., p. 265

20 See Campbell, op. cit., p. 262

21 Ibid.

22 See http://news.bbc.co.uk/1/hi/uk/714289.stm

23 See 'Dome robbery: how it happened', *Guardian*, 18 February 2002

24 See 'Who are the Yardies?', *BBC News*, 19 June 1999 http://news.bbc.co.uk/1/hi/uk/371604.stm

25 See Heale, *One Blood*, p. 75

26 See 'Man stabbed to death on Oxford Street', *Guardian*, 26 December 2011

27 See 'Ex-street thug becomes trainee barrister', *Evening Standard*, 8 September 2011

CHAPTER SIXTEEN

1 See St Paul's protest: Occupy London Camp evicted 28 February 2012 http://www.bbc.co.uk/news/uk-17187180
2 See http://www.bbc.co.uk/news/uk-england-london-14439970
3 See 'London riots: three-quarters charged over riots had previous criminal convictions', *Guardian*, 15 September 2011
4 See Madox Ford, *The Soul of London*, p. 27
5 Ibid.
6 See Marks, *Tyburn Tree*, p. 268

Illustration Credits

Index

INDEX

Rolling Thunder

The American Strategic
Bombing Campaign Against
North Vietnam 1964 - 68

By

John T Smith

CONTENTS

Rolling
Thunder

by

John T Smith

Air Research Publications

© John T. Smith 1994

First published in 1994 by:

Air Research Publications
P.O. Box 223, Walton on Thames
Surrey, KT12 3YQ
Great Britain

ISBN: 1-871187-20-6

Distributed in the USA by:
Phalanx Publishing Co., Ltd.
1051 Marie Ave. W.
St. Paul, MN 55118-4131 USA

Second Printing, 1995

Printed in the United States of America

Bibliography

Anderton, David, *Republic F-105 Thunderchief*, Osprey Publishing Ltd. London, 1983.

Anderton, David, *North American F-100 Super Sabre*, Osprey Publishing Ltd. London, 1987.

Anthis, Rollin, *Air Power In Vietnam*, (in *Air Force And Space Digest*, August 1967).

Armitage J. and Mason, R. A. *Air Power In The Nuclear Age*, University Of Illinois, Chicago, 1983.

Ashmore, Harry S. Baggs, William C. *Mission To Hanoi*, Putnam and Sons, New York, 1968.

Basil, G.I. *Pak Six*, Associated Creative Writers, La Mesa, California, 1982.

Bearden, Thomas E. *What Really Happened in the Air* Defence *Battle of North Vietnam*, (in *Air Defence Magazine*, April-June 1976, pages 8-15).

Berger, Carl (ed), *The United States Air Force In South East Asia*, Office of Air Force History, Washington D C, 1977.

Berrigan, Daniel, *Night Flight To Hanoi*, Macmillan, New York, 1968.

Berry, F. Clifton, *Strike Aircraft, The Illustrated History of the Vietnam War*, Bantam Books, New York, 1988.

Bonds, Ray, *The Vietnam War*. Salamander Books Ltd, London, 1979

Boyne, Walter J. *Phantom In Combat*, Jane's, London, 1985.

Braybrook, Roy M. *Under Combat Conditions*, (in *Flying Review*, October, 1966).

Brodie, Bernard, *War and Politics*, Cassel, London 1973.

Brooks, Stephen. *Bomber*, Imperial War Museum, London 1983.

Brodie, Bernard, *Why We Were So (Strategically) Wrong* (in *Foreign Policy No. 5*, Winter 1971-72, pages 151-162).

Broughton, Jack, *Going Downtown: The War Against Hanoi and Washington*, Orion Books, New York, 1985.

Broughton, Jack *Thud Ridge*, Bantam Books, New York, 1985.

Brownlow, Cecil, *USAF Boosts North Vietnam ECM Jamming* (in *Aviation* Week *and Space Technology*, February 6 1967, pages 22-24).

Burns, Richard Dean, Leitenburg, Milton, *The Wars In Vietnam, Cambodia and Laos 1945: A Bibliographic Guide*, ABC Information Services, Santa Barbara, California, 1984.

Cagel, Malcolm W. *Task Force 77 In Action off Vietnam* (in *The Naval Review*, US Naval Institute, Annapolis, 1972).

Chant, Christopher, *MiG 21* Haynes Publishing Group, England, 1984.

Chinnery, Phil, *Air War In Vietnam*, Bison Books Ltd. London, 1987.

Chinnery, Phil, *The Air War Over Vietnam*, (in *Aeroplane*, January 1986-October 1986. 10 vols).

Chinnery, Phil D. *Life On The Line: Stories of Vietnam Air Combat*, Blandford Press, London, 1988.

Chodes, John J. *The Myth of America's Military Power*, Branden Press, Boston.

Clark, Wesley K. *Gradualism and American Military Strategy*, (in *Military Review 55*, September 1975, pages 3-13).

Clodfelter, Mark, *The Limits of Air Power*, The Free Press, New York, 1989.

Cole, David K. *The Connies of College Eye*, (in *Airman XVI*, March 1973, pages 4-7).

Collins, John M. *Vietnam: A Senseless Strategy*, (in *Parameters 8*, March 1978, pages 8-14).

Colvin, J. *Hanoi In My Time*, (in *The Washington Quarterly 4*, Spring 1981, pages 138-156).

Coonts, Stephen, *Flight of the Intruder*, Pan Books, London, 1986. (fiction)

Cooper, Chester, *The Lost Crusade, America In Vietnam*, Dodd Mead,New York, 1970.

Cunningham, R. Ethell, J. *Fox Two*, Champlin Fighter Museum, Mesa, Arizona, 1984.

Clausewitz, Carl Von, Translated by Howard Michael and Paret, Peter, *On War*, Princeton University Press, Princeton, New Jersey, 1976. (not directly involving the Vietnam War but great insights on the nature of war in general).

Davis, Larry, *Wild Weasel, The Sam Suppression* Story, Squadron/ Signal Publications, Carrollton, Texas, 1986.

Decornoy, Jacques, *Eye Witness Reports of the Bombing, How the North Survives*, (in *The Observer*, 1st January 1967, page 6).

DeWeerd H. A. *Strategic Decision Making in* Vietnam *65-68*, (in *Yale Review 67*, 1976, pages 481-492).

Donovan, James A. *Militarism USA*, Scribners, New York, 1970.

Dorr, Robert F. *Air War Hanoi*, Blandford Press, London, 1988.

Dorr, Robert F. *Air War South Vietnam*, Arms And Armour Press, London, 1990.

Dorr, Robert F. *F-105 Thunderchief* Arms And Armour Press, London, 1988.

Dorr, Robert F. *McDonnell Douglas F-4 Phantom II*, Osprey Publishing Ltd. London 1984.

Dorr, Robert F, *McDonnell F-101 Voodoo.* Psprey Publishing Ltd. London, 1987

Dorr, Robert F. *Southeast Asian Spad, The Skyraiders War*, (in *Air Enthusiast 36*, May-Aug. 1988).

Dorr, Robert F. *Vietnam, Combat from the Cockpit*, Airlife
Publishing Ltd. England, 1989.
Dorr, Robert F. *Vietnam MiG Killers*, Motor Books International,
Osceola, Wisconsin, USA, 1988.
Douhet, Giulio, *The Command of the Air*, Rivista Aeronautica,
Rome, 1958.
Doyle, Edward, Lipsman, Samuel and Maitland, Terrence. *The North*,
Boston Publishing Company, Boston, 1986.
Drendel, Lou, *The Air War in Vietnam*, Arco, New York, 1968.
Drendel, Lou, *Air War Over Southeast Asia Vol. I* Squadron/Signal
Publications, Texas, 1982.
Drendel, Lou, *Air War Over Southeast Asia Vol. II, Squadron / Signal*
Publications, Texas, 1982.
Drendel, Lou, *...And Kill MiGs* Squadron/Signal Publications,
Texas, 1984.
Drendel, Lou, *USAF Phantoms In Combat*, Squadron/Signal
Publications Inc. Texas, 1987.
Drendel, Lou, *USN Phantoms In Combat*, Squadron/Signal
Publications, Texas, 1988.
Drendel, Lou, *Thud*, Squadron/Signal Publications, Texas, 1986.
Duncan, Scott, *Rolling Thunder*, (in *Airman Vol. 18*, Oct. 1974,
pages 24-28).
Enthoven, Alain C. Smith, K. Wayn, *How Much is Enough*,
Harper and Row, New York, 1971.
Ethel, Jeffrey, Price, Alfred, *One Day In A Long War*, Random House,
New York, 1989.
Fall, Bernard, *Vietnam Witness 1953-66*, Prager, New York, 1966.
Flintham, Victor, *Air Wars and Aircraft*, Arms And Armour Press,
London, 1989.
Francillon, Rene J. *Tonkin Gulf Yacht Club*, Conway Maritime Press,
London, 1988.
Francillon, Rene J. *Vietnam Air Wars*, Temple Press Aerospace,
London 1987.
Fricker, John, *Air Armaments*, (in *Flying Review*, March, 1968,
pages 133-135).
Gallucci, Robert l. *Neither Peace Nor Honour* John Hopkins University
Press, Baltimore, 1975.
Gelb, Leslie H. Betts, Richard K. *The Irony of Vietnam, The System
Worked*, The Brookings Institute, Washington 1979.
Gerassi, John, *North Vietnam a Documentary*, George Allen
and Unwin Ltd. London, 1968.
Giap, General Vo Nguyen, *Peoples War Against US Aero-Naval War*,
Foreign Languages Publishing House, Hanoi, 1975.
Gillcrist, Paul T. *Feet Wet*, Pocket Books, New York, 1990.
Ginsberg, Robert N. *Strategy and Air Power: The Lessons of Southeast
Asia*, (in *Strategic Review I*, Summer 1973, pages 18-24).
Ginsburg, Robert N. *The Tides of War*, (in *Air Force and Space Digest*,
February 1968, pages 46-51).

Gorn, Michael, Gross, Charles, *Published Airforce History Still on the Runway*, (in *Aerospace Historian 31 No.I*, March 1984, pages 30-37).

Goulding, Phil G. *Confirm or Deny, Informing the People on National Security*, Harper And Row, New York. 1970.

Graff, Henry F. *The Tuesday Cabinet*, Prentice-Hall Inc. New Jersey, 1970.

Grant, Zalin, *Over the Beach: Air War in Vietnam*, Norton, New York, 1986.

Greer, Thomas H. *The Development of Air Force Doctrine in the Army Air Arm 1917-1941*, Office of Air Force History, United States Air Force, Washington DC, 1985.

Grindler, Lawrence E. *How They Lost: Doctrines, Strategies and Outcomes of the Vietnam War*, Asian Survey 15, December 1975, pages 1114-32.

Gunston, Bill, *Mikoyan MiG-21*, Osprey, London, 1986.

Gurney, Gene, Vietnam *The War in the Air*, Crown Publishers Inc. New York, 1985.

Halberstam, David, *The Best and the Brightest*, Random House, New York, 1973.

Halberstam, David, *The Programming of Robert McNamara*, (in *Harpers* Magazine, February 1971, pages 37-71).

Harvey, Frank, *Air War Vietnam*, Bantam Books, New York, 1967.

Herman, Edwards S. *Atrocities in Vietnam, Myths and Realities*, Pilgrim Press, Boston, 1970.

Herring, George C. *America's Longest War*, John Wiley And Sons, New York, 1979.

Higham, Robin, *Air Power, A Concise History*, Macdonald, London, 1972.

Hoeffding, Oleg, *Bombing North Vietnam, An Appraisal of Economic and Political Effects*, Rand Corporation, Santa Monica, 1968.

Hoopes, Townsend, *The Limits of Intervention*, David McKay Co. Ltd. New York, 1969.

Hopkins, Charles K. *Linebacker II: A First Hand View*, (in *Aerospace Historian*, September 1976, pages 128-135).

Hopkins, Charles K. *SAC Tanker Operations in the Southeast Asia War*, Office of the Historian, Headquarters Strategic Air Command, 1979.

Janis, Irving L. *Victims of Groupthink*, Haughton Miffin, Boston, 1972.

Johnson, Lyndon B. *The Vantage Point - Perspectives on the Presidency*, Holt, New York, 1971.

Jones, Neville, *The Origins of Strategic Bombing*, William Kimber, London, 1973.

Kasler, J. H. *The Hanoi POL Strike* (in *Air University Review 16*, November-December 1974. pages 19-28).

Kennan, George F. *American Diplomacy*, University of Chicago Press, 1951.

Kennett, Lee, *A History of Strategic Bombing*, Charles Scribner and Sons, New York, 1982.

Kilduff, Peter, *A-4 Skyhawk*, Osprey Publishing, London, 1983.

Kirk, William L. *Gradualism in the Air War Over North Vietnam*, Maxwell Air Force Base, Air University, 1970.

Kohn, Richard H. Harahan, Joseph P. *Air Interdiction in WWII, Korea and* Vietnam, Office of Air Force History, US Air Force, Washington DC, 1986.

Levinson, Jeffrey L. *Alpha Strike Vietnam*, Presidio Press, USA, 1989.

Lane, John J. *Command and Control and Communications Structures in Southeast Asia*, Air War College, Maxwell Air Force Base, Alabama, 1981.

Lavalle, A J C, *The Vietnamese Air Force 1951-1975*. Office of Air Force History, Washington, 1977.

Lewy, Gunther, *America in Vietnam*, Oxford University Press, New York, 1978.

Littaur, R. Uphoff, N. T*he Air War in Indochina*, Beacon Press, Boston, 1972.

Lonie, Frank R. *Interdiction in a Southeast Asian Limited* War, (in *Royal Air Forces Quarterly 9*, Winter, 1969, pages 293-296).

Lowe, James Trapier, *A Philosophy of Air Power*, University Press of America, 1984.

MacIsaac, David, *Voices From the Central Blue: The Air Power Theorists*, (in*Makers of Modern Strategy*, Edited by Paret, Peter, Clarendon Press, Oxford, 1986

McLellan, D. S. *The Myth of Air Power*, in *World View 15*, November 1972, pages 27-34).

Mack, Jerold R. Williams, Richard M. T*he 552nd Airborne Early Warning and Control Wing in Southeast Asia, A Case Study In Airborne Control*, (in *Air University Review XXV*, November-December 1973, pages 70-78).

Maclear, Michael, *Vietnam The Ten Thousand Day War*, Thames Methuen, London 1981.

Marolda, Edward J. *Carrier Operations, The Illustrated History of the Vietnam War*, Bantam Books, New York, 1987.

Marolda, E. J. Et Al. *A Select Bibliography of the United States Navy and the Southeast Asia Conflict 1950-75*, Naval Historical Centre, Washington D C, November 1983.

Marolda, E. J. *A Short History of the United States Navy and the Southeast Asian Conflict 1950-75*, Naval Historical Centre, Department Of The Navy, Washington D C, 1984.

Mason, R. A. *War in the Third Dimension*, Brassey's, London, 1986.

Menault, S. W. B. *The Use of Air Power in Vietnam*, (in *Royal United Service Institute For Defence Studies Journal*, June, 1971, pages 5-15).

Mersky, Peter B. Polmar, Norman, *The Naval Air War In Vietnam*, the Nautical and Aviation Publishing Company of America, Annapolis, 1981.

Middleton, Drew, *Air War Vietnam*, Arms and Armour Press, London, 1978.

Momyer, William W. *Air Power in Three Wars*, Department of the Air Force, Washington, 1978.

Momyer, William W. *The Evolution of Fighter Tactics in Southeast Asia*, (in *Air Force Magazine LVI*, July, 1973, pages 58-62).

Morrocco, John, *Thunder From Above*, Boston Publishing Co. Boston, 1984.

Morrocco, John, *Rain of Fire, Air War 1969-1973*, Boston Publishing Co. Boston, 1985.

Mrozek, Donald J. *Air Power and the Ground War in Vietnam*, Pergamon Brassey's, London, 1989.

Myers, Charles E. *Deep Strike Interdiction*, US Naval Institute Proceedings, Vol 106, Nov. 1980.

Nichols, John B. Tillman, Barrett, *On Yankee Station*, Airlife, England, 1987.

Nordeen, Lon O. *Air Warfare in the Missile Age*, Arms And Armour Press, London, 1985.

Olds, Robin, *Forty-six Years A Fighter Pilot*, (in *American Aviation Historical Society Journal XIII*, Winter 1968, pages 235-238).

Olds, Robin, *How I Got My First MiG*, (in *Air Force and Space Digest*, July, 1967, pages 38-40).

Olds, Robin, *The Lessons of Clobber College*, (in *Flight International*, June 26, 1969, pages 1053-59).

Palmer, David, *Summons of the Trumpet*, Presidio Press, California, 1977.

Palm, Gregory, *The McNamara Strategy and the Vietnam War*, Greenwood Press, Connecticut, 1978.

Parks, W. Hayes, *Rolling Thunder and the Law of War*, (in *Air University Review*, January-February 1982).

Parrish, Noel F. *The Influence of Air Power Upon Historians*, US Air Force Academy, Colorada, 1979.

Pickerill, James H. *Vietnam in the Mud*, Bobbs Merrill, Indianapolis, 1967.

Pisor, Robert, *The End of the Line*, W. W. Norton And Co. 1982.

Price, Dr Alfred. *Instrument of Darkness*, Granada Publishing, London, 1977

Robinson, Daniel, Cummings, Joe, *Vietnam, Laos and Cambodia*, Lonely Planet Publications, Australia, 1991. (a Vietnam guidebook).

Russet, Bruce M. *Vietnam and Restraints on Aerial Warfare*, (in *Ventures Vol 9*, Spring, pages 55-61).

Salisbury, Harrison E. *Behind the Lines: Hanoi Dec. 23 1966-Jan. 7 1967*, Harper and Row, New York, 1967.

Salmon, Malcolm, *North Vietnam: A First Hand Account of the Blitz*, Sydney Tribune, Sydney, Australia, 1969?

Saundby, Robert, *The Ethics of Bombing*, (in *Air Force And Space Digest No. 50*, June, 1967, pages 48-53).

Schandler, Herbert Y. *The Unmaking of a President, Lyndon Johnson and Vietnam*, Princeton University Press, Princeton N.J. 1977.

Schmaltz, Robert E. *The Uncertainty of Predicting Results of an Interdiction Campaign*, (in *Aerospace Historian*, Dec. 17, 1970, pages 150-153).

Schneider, Donald K. *Air Force Heroes in Vietnam Air War College*, Maxwell Air Force Base, Alabama, 1979.

Scutts, Jerry, *Wolf Pack*, Airlife Ltd. England, 1987.

Shaplen, Robert, *The Road From War: Vietnam 1965-70*, Harper and Row, New York, 1970.

Sharp, U. S. Grant, *Airpower Could Have Won in Vietnam*, Air Force Vol. 54, September 1971.

Sharp, U. S. Grant, *Report on the War in Vietnam*, Washington DC GPO, 1968.

Sharp, U. S. Grant, *Strategy For Defeat; Vietnam in Retrospect*, Presido Press, San Rafael, California, 1978.

Smith, John T, *May 10th 1972* (in *Air Enthusiast 45).* Key Publishing Ltd, Stamford, 1992.

Smith, John T, *Operation Bolo* (in *Air Enthusiast 42).* Key Publishing Ltd,Stamford, 1991.

Smith, Melden E. Jr. *The Strategic Bombing Debate*, (in *Journal of Contemporary History Vol. 12*, January 1977).

Sochurek, H. *Air Rescue Behind Enemy Lines*, (in *National Geographic 134*, 1968, pages 346-369).

Staudenmaier, William O. *Vietnam, Mao and Clausewitz*, (in *Parameters,*March 1967, pages 79-89).

Stockdale, Jim, *In Love and War*, Harper and Row, New York, 1984.

Sullivan, Cornelious D. *Air War Against the North, in the Vietnam War: Its Conduct and Higher Direction*, Georgetown University Centre For Strategic Studies, Washington DC, Nov. 1968.

Summers, Harry G. *On Strategy, The Vietnam War in Context*, Strategic Studies Institute, US Army War College, Carlisle Barracks, Pennsylvania, 1981.

Thu, Hai, *North Vietnam Against US Air Force*, Foreign Languages Publishing House, Hanoi, 1967.

Thies, Wallace J. *When Governments Collide: Coercion and Diplomacy in the Vietnam Conflict 1964-68*, Berkley: University Of California. 1980.

Thompson, James C. *Rolling Thunder, Understanding Policy and Program Failure*, Chapel Hill, University Of North Carolina Press, 1980.

Thompson, W. Scott, Frizzel, D. D. *The Lesson of Vietnam*, Crane Russaj and Company, New York.

Tilford, Earl H. *Search and Rescue in Southeast Asia 1961-1975*, Office of Air Force History, Washington DC, 1980.

Tillman, Barrett, *MiG Master: The Story of the F-8 Crusader*, Patrick Stephens Ltd. 1980.

Trotti, John, *Phantom Over Vietnam*, Airlife, England, 1984.

Ulsamer, Edgar, *Air Rescue in Southeast Asia, Right From Hanoi's Own Backyard*, (in *Air Force Magazine 55*, October 1972, pages 30-34).

U.S. Congress, Senate Committee on Foreign Relations, Study No. 5, *Bombing as a Tool in Vietnam: Effectiveness.* 92nd Congress 2nd Session, Washington GPO. 1972.

U.S. Senate, Hearings Before The Preparedness Investigations Subcommittee, Aug. 9th and 10th, 1967.

Van Dyke, Jon M. *North Vietnam's Strategy For Survival*, Pacific Books Publishers, Palo Alto, California, 1972.

Various authors. *Aces and Aerial Victories*, United States Government Printing Office. 1976.

Verrier, Anthony, *Strategic Bombing: The Lessons of World War II and the American Experience in Vietnam*, (in *Journal Of The Royal United Services Institute CXII*, May 1968, pages 157-161).

Vietnam Destruction War Damage, Foreign Languages Publishing House, Hanoi, 1977.

Washington Joint Publications Research, Pro-Communist Eye Witness Reports of US Bombings Of Civilians in North Vietnam, Washington D C, 1967.

Watts, Barry D. *The Foundations of US Air Doctrine, The Problem of Friction in War*, Air University Press, Maxwell Air Force Base, Alabama, December 1984.

Weigley, Russel F. *The American Way of War* Macmillan, New York, 1973.

Weiss, Steve, *Rolling Thunder*, Group Three Games, New York, 1985. (A war simulation).

Welsh, Douglas, *The History of the Vietnam War*. Hamlyn, London, 1981

Witze, Claude, *How Not To Win*, (in *Air Force Magazine 53*, 1970, pages 10-12).

Wolf, Charles, *The Logic of Failure: A Vietnam Lesson*, (in *Journal of Conflict Resolution*, Sept. 1972, pages 397-401).

Wolfe, Tom, *The Truest Sport: Jousting with Sam and Charley,* (in *Mauve Gloves and Madmen*, Clutter and Vine), Farrar, Straus and Giroux, New York, 1976. (fiction)

Yenne, Bill, *The History of the US Air Force*, Hamlyn,

Yudkin, Richard A. *Vietnam: Policy, Strategy and Air Power*, (in *Air Force Magazine 56*, Feb. 1973).

Flight of the Intruder Spectrum Holobyte, Mirrorsoft Ltd. London. (computer air combat simulation)

Makers of Modern Strategy, Edited by Paret, Peter, Clarenden Press, Oxford, 1986.

The Pentagon Papers, The Senator Gravel Edition, Beacon Press, Boston.

The Pentagon Papers, Bantam Books, New York, 1971.

Introduction
The Strategic Bombing Theories

In carrying out the bombing the American military was working within a strategic bombing strategy and doctrine in the belief that it was possible to force an enemy to surrender by bombing alone. These were the theories that were put to the test in Vietnam and there is no doubt that the outcome was not what was expected by their supporters.

Since the early years of the century the protagonists of strategic bombing have claimed that the development of aircraft has given them a special place in the techniques of warfare. This view of aircraft saw their mobility as conferring a unique ability to pass over the heads of naval and ground forces and to strike directly at the enemie's capital city, homeland or centres of power. Taken to extremes, these theories gave air power the ability to win wars by forcing the enemy to surrender without involving ground or naval forces.

The theories of the strategic use of bombing aircraft and the associated nuclear deterrent theories are the only new strategic views of warfare developed during the twentieth century. The American armed forces evolved versions of these theories during the 1920s and 1930s that have survived with few changes, other than technological developments, until today. During the 1930s many young officers supported the idea that the strategic use of aircraft was the primary purpose of military aviation. They used this to campaign for the separation of the Air Force from the army and, by the 1960s had become the core of the Air Force senior staff. There is a continuity in American air power doctrine that has persisted down to today that played a considerable part in what the American military thought could be achieved with the bombing of North Vietnam.

Early statements of the case for strategic bombing were the two Smut's reports produced during the First World War. The

The Italian General Giulio Douhet, whose theories on the use of air power made such a profound impact on military thinking.

Germans had carried out a series of daylight and later night raids on London. Damage caused by the raids compared to Britain's war effort was negligible but the shock caused by the raids affected both the government and the people. The main effect of these raids was on British morale rather than physical damage.

The South African General Jan Smuts, a member of the war cabinet and later Prime Minister of South Africa, was asked to produce a report on British air policy and produced two reports. Together these greatly affected the military use of aviation and most of Smuts' recommendations were put into practice. A separate Air Ministry was created in December 1917 and the Royal Air Force was formed out of the RFC and the RNAS on an equal footing with the Army and Navy in April 1918. An Independent bombing force was also established in France with the specific purpose of attacking targets in Germany. The bulk of the RAF, however, continued to support the army on a day to day basis. The Smuts report stated:

> "As far as can at present be foreseen there is absolutely no limit to the scale of its (air power's) future independent war use. And the day may not be far off when aerial operations with their devastation of enemy lands and the destruction of industrial and populous centres on a vast scale may become the principal operations of war, to which the older forms of military and naval operations may become secondary and subordinate."[1]

Although the RAF had been created there was still little agreement over the correct use of air power as many Army officers still saw the first use of aircraft as direct support of the Army.

Trenchard who had commanded the RFC during most of the First World War had been a supporter of the tactical use of aircraft but he later converted to the idea of strategic bombing, becoming one of its leading advocates. In 1928 he wrote:

"It is not, however, necessary for an air force, in order to defeat the enemy nation, to defeat its armed forces first. Air power can pass over the enemy navies and armies, and penetrate the air defences and attack direct the centres of production, transportation and communications from which the enemy war effort is maintained."[2.]

Trenchard had commanded the Independent Bombing Force and knew that the equipment available for strategic bombing had been only technically marginal. The First World War had shown only the potential of strategic bombing rather than the substance. However the supporters of the theories were left with the argument that the technical developments to make it effective were just around the corner. The weight of the experiences at Verdun and the Somme affected all the military thinking between the wars. The war of attrition, it was thought, would be left behind as aircraft passed over the trenches and rendered them irrelevant. Experiences of World War Two showed that bombing rather than ending the slaughter simply moved it somewhere else.

During the mid-war years the leading air power theorist and the only one to produce a considered and coherent philosophy was the Italian Giulio Douhet. He started his writings on the use of air power as early as 1909 when he said that, '. . . if there are nations that exist untouched by the sea, there are none that exist without the breath of air'. In 1921 Douhet published his main work *Command of the Air* with updated editions in 1927 and 1931. In this he specified that the essential nature of air power is offensive. Any future war would be won by the offensive use of aircraft and any effort diverted to defence would be wasted. The only defence against enemy aircraft would be to destroy them on the ground. War would start with massive bombing attacks by both sides involving the maximum

General Jan Smuts, seen here inspecting a South African labour unit in 1917, produced a report espousing strategic bombing that suggested that future wars would see naval and land forces subordinate to to air forces..

number of aircraft available, as both sides attempted to obtain 'command of the air'.

The idea that there was little or no defence against the bomber gained general acceptance at this time, as shown by the British Prime Minister Stanley Baldwin's statement on defence in 1932, 'the bomber will always get through'. The essence of the theories developed during the inter-war years had emerged as:

> "The fundamental doctrine is that the airplane possesses such ubiquity and such advantages of speed and elevation, as to possess the power of destroying all surface installations and instruments, ashore or afloat, while itself remaining comparatively safe from the ground."[3.]

Aircraft, it was argued, had added a completely new dimension to warfare. Naval and ground forces did not now have to be defeated nor even engaged in battle, but could now be safely ignored while the enemy heartland was destroyed from above.

America's foremost air power theorist was William Mitchell, who had served at the front in France from 1917 to 1918 commanding the combat squadrons of the US Army Air Section. Mitchell had become a fervent, almost fanatical, supporter of air power. During the 1920s he was involved in a series of tests on the effects of bombs on armoured ships. He declared afterwards that the entire defence strategy of the Navy had been disproved. Not surprisingly the Navy disagreed, saying that the tests proved nothing. Mitchell continued campaigning, both vocally and in print, for a separate air force, but he had upset too many people. In 1925 he was court-martialled, for accusing his superiors of incompetency and criminal negligence, forcing him to resign from the Army.

Mitchell agreed with most of Douhet's theories and in 1930 he wrote:

> "The advent of air power which can go straight to the vital centres and entirely neutralise or destroy them has put a completely new complexion on the whole system of making war. It is now realised that the hostile army in the field is a false objective and the real objectives are the vital centres."[4]

The recurring theme had now become 'vital centres' while the enemy army was now 'a false objective'.

These were the ideas behind the bombing of North Vietnam. Sections of the American military thought that they could force the North Vietnamese to stop interfering in the South by bombing their homeland. They believed that the North need not be defeated by a ground war in the South. The doctrine they were working within was that bombing the North was sufficient to cause the North to give way. The *Tet* offensive in 1968, following three years of bombing, showed that *Rolling Thunder* had failed to achieve this. Are there flaws within the strategic bombing theories that meant they could never work, or was the application of the theories to North Vietnam at fault? Was it the practical application of the theories, i.e. the way the bombing was carried out, that was primarily to blame for the failures? These are some questions that it is hoped to address in this book.

Brigadier-General William Mitchell, believed so fervently in the use of the bomber as a strategic weapon that he put his job and reputation on the line. He was court-martialled in 1925 and forced to resign from the army.

(National Archives)

FOOTNOTES

1   Questor, George H. *Deterrence Before Hiroshima*, John Willey and Sons Inc. New York, 1966, page 38.

2   Hastings, Max, *Bomber Command*, Pan Books Ltd. London, 1981, page 46.

3   Warner, Edward, *Douhet, Mitchell, Seversky: Theories of Air Warfare'* in *Makers of Modern Strategy* Edited by Edward Mead Earl, Princeton University Press, Princeton, 1971, page 485.

4   Mitchell, W, *Skyways*, Philadelphia, 1930, page 255.

Chapter One

Countdown to Confrontation

The Military And Political Decision
To Bomb North Vietnam

President Lyndon Baines Johnson ordered the start of the *Rolling Thunder* campaign in early 1965, acting on the advice given by his political and military advisers. It was thought by many senior military figures that North Vietnam would soon be forced to give way under the bombing. The view among the senior Air Force officers was based on Strategic Bombing theories that they had supported all their professional lives. They had based their strategic and tactical ideas on the view of air power that had developed during the early years of the 20th century. However, the American Air Force's experience of bombing had often been at variance with those theories.

The U.S. Army Air Corps Tactical School was at Langley and Maxwell air base From 1920, and especially after William Mitchell had left the Air Force, it had acted as a centre for the development and spreading of the strategic bombing theories. The school developed the concept of a modern industrial state as having a web of production. This involved the idea of interlocking industries, with each part dependant on all the others. This led to the notion that it was not necessary to destroy a nation's industrial capacity to stop its war production, but only to destroy certain industrial bottle necks. It was thought there were 'vital targets' without which a country could not sustain a war.

Just before the entry of America into the Second World War President Franklin D Roosevelt asked for a statement from the Air service of the amounts of equipment needed for victory. This statement became known as AWPD/1 (Air War Plans Division 1) and was a clear exposition of the strategic bombing position. The plan called for the creation of large numbers of long range bombing aircraft and the logistic backup to mount a strategic bombing campaign. The report was drawn up by four Air Force officers, all of whom had been associated with the Air Corps

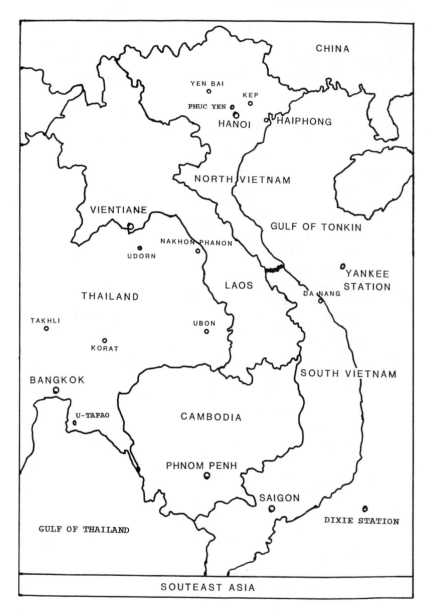

Map 1. Southeast Asia (Peter Edwards RICS and John T. Smith)

Tactical School. The report can be seen as the final development of nearly twenty years work by the school. The numbers of men and aircraft asked for seemed enormous, but were achieved by 1944 and, to a large extent, the plan was implemented. America's Army Air Force was heavily committed to daylight bombing, but their experience of operating from British bases against Germany during WWII was to show the difficulties involved in strategic bombing. The bomber could not always get through. Until the availability of the long range P-51 fighter aircraft in 1944, the existing P-38s and P-47s could not escort the bombing aircraft all the way to the target, on deep penetration raids. The American raids in October 1943, especially the ones on the Schweinfurt factories, suffered such heavy losses that daylight raids were scaled down until fighter escort was available all the way to the target. But once fighter escort was available the U.S. Army Air Force continued with the daylight precision raids and the German fighter force was practically wiped out on the ground and in the air.

The pre-war faith in the effects of strategic bombing were never quite realised in practice. Germany continued to increase its industrial production until very late in the war when for practical purposes the ground war was nearly over. No one can doubt the immense damage caused by the American and British bombing of Germany, but industrial society had proved much more resilient than expected. Vital points, or bottle necks that could close down industrial production, had been hard to find. The Germans as an industrious and resourceful people had reacted to and absorbed the bombing. The idea that a country's morale would break under heavy bombing had proved equally illusory. In China, Britain, Germany and Japan the populations had stoically endured heavy bombing. Morale might have been heavily shaken but nowhere did it break. In fact, the early stages of a bombing campaign seem to have strengthened the population's commitment to a war.

The central points of the American strategic bombing doctrine that had been taught at the Tactical School were hard to justify. Defending fighter aircraft had proved effective; vital points in an economy either did not exist or were very difficult to find and precision bombing was nearly impossible to achieve. Despite this, the accepted doctrine of the U.S. Air Force, that air power was now the decisive factor in war, survived the Second World War intact and was enhanced by the introduction of nuclear weapons. Air Force doctrine also managed to survive the experience of the Korean War. After the first months of the conflict all the major targets in North Korea had been destroyed and all the effort was concentrated on the interdiction campaign to stop supplies moving down from the Chinese border to the front line.

The North Koreans maintained their ground position at the front line, by using manual labour to repair the railways and roads, and if necessary to carry supplies. With enormous effort they kept the supply lines open.

Air power, although it played a considerable part, cannot be seen as having been decisive. Air Chief Marshal John Slessor writing after the Korean War said,

> "The idea that superior air power can in some way be a substitute for hard slogging and professional skill on the ground in this sort of war is beguiling but illusory." [1.]

The US Air Force leadership saw the experience in Korea as a special case with no relevance to general American air policy.

It was thought, after the end of the Korean war, that this type of war would be unlikely to occur again. The view was that the main purpose of the Air Force was nuclear attack upon Russia. The emphasis was on the development of the Strategic Air Command and there was a decline in the tactical use of aircraft. American overall strategy during this period was 'massive retaliation'. There would be no more small wars, if Russia was seen to be behind any aggression, anywhere in the world, the response would be a massive attack on Russia. It is doubtful if this doctrine was ever really valid, especially after the Russians had developed as many nuclear weapons as the Americans. The doctrine for tactical air operations also foresaw the use of small 'tactical' nuclear weapons to support the army. The use of conventional munitions dropped from aircraft was seen as passé. It was also thought that the day of air-to-air combat had passed and little effort was put into the development of 'air superiority' aircraft and tactics.

Colonel Robin Olds, who destroyed four North Vietnamese MiGs during the *Rolling Thunder* bombing campaign, said in a speech he gave on the 4th October 1968:

"…..there was a time not ten years ago, when the suggestion of a need for training in squadron-sized formations, for maintenance of qualifications in delivering conventional ordnance and for keeping current in aerial combat tactics was enough to get one laughed out of the conference room. One was a starry-eyed romanticist, a ghost from the past, The name of the game was nuclear deterrence. Everyone, even fighter pilots, worked at it." [2]

The irony of the *Rolling Thunder* campaign was that the strategic bombing of North Vietnam was carried out using tactical aircraft and the strategic bombers (the B-52s) were mostly used for tactical bombing in South Vietnam. The view of the senior military within the U.S. Armed Forces on air power doctrine remained constant for many years before the start of the Vietnam war. In essence this was that air power was decisive, that precision bombing could be carried out and that countries had 'vital centres'. But in the ten years before the Vietnam war there had been little effort put into either the aircraft or tactics that were used to fight the war.

Having examined the military view of strategic bombing it is necessary to attempt to understand what the political leaders thought could be achieved by bombing. There is no doubt that the American military leaders had strong views on the use of bombing and played a large part in advising the civilian leadership. However, the politicians especially president Johnson ultimately took the decisions that led to the bombing.

One view of the bombing is that it was only the last in a long series of covert actions carried out by America against North Vietnam, or was the point where action against the North changed over from covert to overt action. After America had refused to physically help France at Dien Bien Phu, Vietnam was divided into North and South at the Geneva accords of 1954. Elections to unify the country were to have been held in 1956, but throughout 1954 the CIA, stationed in Saigon, carried out a low level covert sabotage campaign against the North. Many of these actions were trivial in nature, involving the destruction of transport, printing presses and the placing of

The architect of the 'long war' policy, Ho Chi Minh was prepared to allow North Vietnam to take everything that the Americans could throw at it and, by patience and fortitude, win. He had fought the Japanese and the French and, in his view, the US was no different. (IWM)

misinformation about the North's intentions.[3] Although these actions had very little effect they did set the pattern for America's attitude towards the North. During the remainder of the '50s South Vietnam became a major recipient of American aid and, with American backing, President Diem refused the elections that were to have reunified the country. It was thought that Ho Chi Minh was still too popular for the South to risk an election.

President Kennedy issued National Security Action Memorandum 52 on 11th May 1961. This document set out the planned increase in the continuing actions against North Vietnam. The covert program was to include personnel from South Vietnam, Thailand, Nationalist China and America, also mercenaries from other countries. The actual operations were disorganized and achieved very little. The Pentagon Papers says that the insurrection in the South was started in 1957-58 with very little, if any aid, from the North. Although by 1961 the North had become increasingly involved, so the American action against the North dating from 1954 pre-dated the Northern involvement by several years. Although Kennedy had increased the clandestine actions against the North, it made little difference to the war in the South. North Vietnam continued to supply more arms and men to the fighting.

When President Kennedy stated, 'Let every nation know, whether it wishes us well or ill, that we shall pay any price, bear any burden, meet any hardship, support any friend, oppose any foe, in order to assure the survival and success of liberty.' he apparently meant it.

The situation in South Vietnam continued to deteriorate even with increasing American aid. President Diem was removed from office and killed in November 1963. The essence of the American problems was that they never managed to create a stable government in the South that held the support of most of the people. None of the whole series of governments that held control in the South ever had the full backing of the people in the war. During 1964 there were seven military coups and changes of government in Saigon. For much of the time the best of the available troops were stationed in Saigon to support the existing government against possible counter-coups rather than in the countryside fighting the insurrection. As the Americans failed to control the increased fighting in the South, or even the constantly changing South Vietnamese governments, their thinking turned towards forcing the North to end it's support for the insurrection in the South. At this stage of the war it was only support, but included both men and supplies. It was only later that it became a Northern invasion of the South. The Americans turned to a policy of action against the North because of a failure to control the situation in the South.

Following a collapse of confidence in the CIA (after the disastrous 'Bay of Pigs' invasion of Cuba), control of the actions against the North was given to the American military. The American Pacific Command began to draw up a new programme of covert operations against the North in May 1963. This proposed increase was explained as an attempt to raise the costs of North Vietnam's support for the war in the South. The plan that was produced became known as Operation Plan 34A and this was approved by the president in January 1964. OPLAN 34A was intended to last for one year and to apply increasing pressure to the North.

The plan included the use of U-2 aircraft to provide reconnaissance coverage of North Vietnam and twenty 'destructive undertakings'. OPLAN 34A was divided into three segments of four months each and was intended to threaten the North's industrial and economic base. Control of OPLAN 34A

Three men who were to influence the course of the war more than any others. General William C. Westmoreland (left) was appointed to command MACV (Military Aid Commision, Vietnam) in June 1964, becoming supreme commander. Robert McNamara (centre) was Secretary of Defense. Here, the two men discuss the Vietnam situation with President Johnson. (National Archives)

was placed in the hands of the United States Military Command in Vietnam but the 'destructive Undertakings' were to be carried out by South Vietnamese personnel and hired mercenaries. Although not involving Americans directly, General Paul D. Harkins was in command of these operations in Saigon, with the assistance of the CIA. The Pentagon Papers describes this escalation of the war (OPLAN 34A) as, 'A fire break had been crossed'. The plan was put into operation in February 1964.

Another attempt to put pressure on the North Vietnamese had been the creation in Laos of a private air force nominally under the control of the Laotian Government. The aircraft flew bearing Laotian markings but were actually under the control of Leonard Unger, the American Ambassador in Laos. This force operated up to forty obsolescent T-28 fighter-bombers, flown by Laotian, Thai and American (working for Air America, the CIA owned air line) pilots. The force was used against the Pathet Lao forces and in the first of many attempts to stop the infiltration routes from the North to South Vietnam. Targets close to the Northern border were attacked and occasionally villages just over the border into the North were bombed. In the spring of 1964 American aircraft were used for reconnaissance flights over Laos and a number were lost. These flights were outside OPLAN 34A and details of them were released to the press.

The Americans were also using their naval ships to carry out what became known as *DESOTO* patrols in the Gulf of Tonkin. These were carried out in international waters but close to the North Vietnamese coast. Their task was to collect electronic intelligence and particularly to discover the position, type and frequency of any radars used by the North. They were also required to listen in on radio traffic. It was necessary for these patrols to come reasonably close to the Vietnamese coast in order for them to trigger any emergency procedures and then to study them electronically. There is still disagreement over the extent of the co-operation between the OPLAN 34A attacks on the North and the *DESOTO* patrols, but this would have been logical, as the best electronic intelligence would have been obtained when the North was actually under attack.

It is doubtful if anyone thought that the raids on the North carried out under OPLAN 34A would directly force the leadership in Hanoi to stop supporting the war in the South. However but it was believed that the implied threat behind the raids, of what could be done, would force them to reconsider. Walt Rostow, who became Special Adviser to the White House, had put forward what became known as the 'Rostow thesis'. On 13th February 1964 he sent a memo to the Secretary of State in which he said that Ho Chi Minh, 'has an industrial complex to protect: he is no longer a guerilla fighter with nothing to lose'[4]. As early as 1961 Rostow had recommended that contingency planning for air strikes against North Vietnam be carried out. This was set out in a report to Kennedy, but the President had not accepted it.

The hope was that if the implied threat to destroy their industrial base was seen as credible, the North Vietnamese would withdraw their support for the Viet Cong in the South. This is the 'games theory' type of thinking that had become popular during the 1950s, especially from the Rand Corporation.

The stone wall. Pham Van Dong, Prime Minister of North Vietnam. In accordance to the teachings of his mentor, Ho Chi Minh, he never bowed to American pressure, followed the 'long war' strategy to the letter and exploited every American weakness. (via author)

If one sent appropriate signals to the enemy, he would respond in the appropriate way. But how much destruction would be the appropriate signal? It was necessary to 'keep the hostage alive'. If everything was destroyed too quickly, the enemy would have nothing left of value and thus nothing left to threaten. This view stood in complete opposition to standard military thinking which concentrated on war fighting abilities rather than on sending messages. The military think in terms of destroying the enemy's capability to wage war. If force is necessary, to employ all the force available. They did not think in terms of using military action to send signals to the enemy.

In March of 1964 the Secretary of Defence Robert McNamara and General Maxwell Taylor were asked to visit South Vietnam by President Johnson. Their general conclusions were that the situation in Vietnam was deteriorating with the Viet Cong controlling large parts of the countryside. The main recommendation of the report was that the material aid to the South should be continued or increased. The report stated:

"The U.S. at all levels must continue to make it emphatically clear that we are prepared to furnish assistance and support for as long as it takes to bring the insurgency under control." [5.]

However it was also decided to begin contingency planning for the bombing of the North if this was ever felt to be needed.

Shortly after McNamara's return from Vietnam the president approved National Security Action Memorandum 288 (NASAM 288) which was based to a large extent on McNamara's report. The Memorandum set out American aims and objectives in Vietnam in very broad and sweeping terms. It was also the trigger for the Joint Chiefs of Staff to begin the detailed planning of a bombing campaign against the North. The general American strategic thinking in South East Asia at this time was based, to a large extent, on the so called 'domino theory'. The communist threat was perceived as a monolithic force operating throughout the world under central guidance. Therefore, any communist gains in Vietnam would greatly increase their position in Asia and could lead to the downfall of all the countries friendly to America in the area.

NASAM 288 set out a version of the 'domino theory' in clear terms by stating,

> "Unless we can achieve this objective (an independent non-communist Vietnam) in South Vietnam, almost all of Southeast Asia will probably fall under communist dominance." [6.]

The memorandum also spoke of a threat to Burma, Thailand, and even against the Phillipines, India, Australia and Japan. A report from the CIA in June 1964 did not support this view however. Their analysts had, in a series of reports, said that the origin of the insurrection had been in South Vietnam and that the strength of the Viet Cong lay in the countryside. The June report also said that:

> "With the possible exception of Cambodia it is likely that no nation in the area would quickly succumb to communism as a result of the fall of Laos and South Vietnam. Furthermore, a continuation of the spread of communism in the area would not be inexorable." [7.]

This report did little to change the prevailing belief in the 'domino theory'.

Although President Johnson had a strong grasp of domestic American politics he is thought to have been weak on foreign affairs. When he became President, after the murder of President Kennedy, he inherited a very strong team of advisors. He kept this group intact and came to rely implicitly on their views and judgement on international affairs and seems originally to have stood in awe of some of this very intellectually powerful group (Although he later made disparaging remarks about some of them). Johnson appears to have been embarrassed by his own education, inferior when compared with some of the ex-professors by which he was surrounded. It was the

President and this group of advisors who made the decisions in 1964 and 1965 that led to the bombing of the North.

This inner circle of advisors became known as the Tuesday Cabinet because of their habit of meeting every Tuesday at noon. At various times during the Vietnam war this group included, in addition to the President, Robert McNamara as Secretary of Defence, Dean Rusk as Secretary of State, George Ball as Under-secretary of State, McGeorge Bundy and Walt Rostow as Special Advisors and Bill Moyers as Press Secretary. The meetings were also attended by Maxwell Taylor and Earl Wheeler, when they were Heads of the Joint Chiefs of Staff, and the CIA was represented by John McCone (later Richard Helms). Most of these men had known each other for some time and had worked together for several years under Kennedy and Johnson and they became a close knit, cohesive group.

The leading advocate of bombing the North was Walt Rostow, who supported the bombing from the very beginning and continued to support it after many others had turned against it. David Halberstam described Rostow as, 'a total idealogue with a captive President.'[8.] However, Rostow, working in policy planning at the State Department, only became a member of the Tuesday cabinet in 1966. Thus he merely played a supportive role in the decisions to start the bombing.

The most impressive figure among this group of people around Johnson was McNamara. He had been Chairman of Ford Motor Company before he was chosen by Kennedy to be Secretary of Defence. He was heavily involved in organising the Vietnam war, which was christened by the press 'the McNamara war'. In the early years Johnson described him as 'the best Secretary of Defence the nation ever had'. McNamara had completely reorganised the Pentagon and his name is forever associated with the systems analysis approach to cost management. He was known as a clear thinker who could take an enormous amount of information and would clearly grasp the essential points. In some ways his thinking was limited however. He had originally been a teacher of accountancy and seems to have seen the war in terms of profit and loss. He believed that the North Vietnamese would, at some point, realise that the bombing was costing them more than they could hope to gain. He did not see them in terms of revolutionary nationalists who were just as willing as Kennedy to pay any price, bear any burden and meet any hardship to attain their ends.

McGeorge Bundy was Johnson's special advisor on foreign affairs until 1966 and was a supporter of the use of force in foreign policy when he thought it necessary. He had advocated the use of air strikes against Cuba during the missile crisis. James Donovan's view of Bundy was that, 'In fact, Bundy was widely recognised as one of the principal designers of Johnson's Vietnam policies'.[9]

The only one of Johnson's close advisors to remain with him until the very end of his presidency was Dean Rusk, the Secretary of State. Yet another of Kennedy's appointments, Rusk remained loyal to Johnson and continued to support his Vietnam policies to the last.

The only member of Johnson's advisors who consistently spoke out against the bombing was Under-secretary of State George Ball. In October 1964 he produced a memorandum that set out all the arguments against the bombing and it seems certain that he was convinced from the very beginning that the bombing would not work. Ball was opposed to the war in general and to any kind of escalation. He was forced into support for the bombing on the understanding that it would stop or delay the introduction of ground troops. He hoped that the start of the bombing would satisfy the demand for escalation at less cost to America than the use of increasing numbers of ground troops. Ball chose not to resign over the issue and for a period he played the role of 'devils advocate' against the bombing, while staying within the group around Johnson.

Most of these men had been involved in the Cuban crisis. They had seen the limited use of force and the threat of massive force work. It had forced the Russians to back down and to remove the missiles from Cuba and was now seen as a precedent. Bombing, with threats of heavier bombing would, it was believed, force North Vietnam to modify its actions. David Halberstam has said however:

"They forgot that in the Cuban missile crisis it was the Russians, not the Cubans, who had backed down, that the Cubans had been perfectly willing, if imperfectly prepared, to fight. They forgot that this kind of threat of American power had an impact on the Russians who were a compatible society with comparable targets, but little effect on a new agrarian society still involved in it's own revolution." [10.]

Johnson's foreign policy decisions were also affected by internal considerations, as they must be by any democratically elected politician. As increasing effort was put into the American involvement in Vietnam, the more the President's future was dependant on the outcome. Johnson had lived through the politically traumatic 'loss' of China to communism and the effects that this had on Truman's presidency, 'I am not going to be the president who saw Southeast Asia go the way China went'[11.] With one eye on history, Johnson became obsessed with the idea of not being the first president to lose a war. The bombing was one way that Johnson hoped to force the North to let him off the hook.

As stated earlier the situation in the South continued to deteriorate during 1964. The Americans found it progressively difficult to control the Viet Cong and impossible to control the South Vietnamese politicians. The only option that appeared to be open was the use of force against the North, the 'root of the problem', to stop them aiding the insurrection in the South. There had been several intelligence reports that had highlighted the fact that originally the insurrection had been organised and controlled from the South with only marginal help from the North. However in the later stages of the war the North came to play an increasing role in the war and, in 1972 and 1975, carried out conventional invasions of South Vietnam. However in the early years of the war the North was not the primary factor in what was happening in the South.

The Americans seem to have turned to using force against the North because of frustration with their failing policy in the South. Robert L. Gallucci describes the American governments thinking on this point as:

"There was broad agreement in the government that it was in the United States interest that the insurgency in South Viet-Nam fail; the source of support for the insurgents was in the North, and the means were available to exert direct pressure; the decision to exert the pressure was embraced by virtually all participants at the time." [12]

Although there was a clear desire among the American leadership to increase the scale of attacks against the North above that of the OPLAN 34A operations, very little was actually done during 1964. The Joint Chiefs of Staff recommended that action should now be taken against the North, but Johnson refused. He believed that the political base in the South was too weak to withstand the increased pressure (in the South) that could be applied by the North's reaction to the bombing. Paradoxically, this was to be practically the same reason later used to justify the bombing. Also Johnson feared the reaction of Russia and China to increased actions against the North. [13] The memory of the Korean War was still prominent in his mind. In that conflict the Chinese had committed ground forces on a very large scale to oppose what they saw as the American interference in Korea. It would have been a completely different war if the Chinese had intervened in Vietnam. Indeed, in some ways the North's politicians feared the Chinese more than the Americans. Historically the Chinese have been the natural enemies of the Vietnamese and, since the Vietnam war, have clashed militarily in border disputes. The Vietnamese still feel the need to keep over one million men under arms because of what they see as the Chinese threat. But the threat of Chinese intervention appeared real to Johnson and his advisors as they saw the situation in 1964.

America thus tried to increase the pressure on North Vietnam by using OPLAN 34A. They also delivered an ultimatum to Hanoi using the Canadian representative on the control commission, J. Blair Seaborn who, on 18th June 1964, warned them to desist from interfering in the South. In April 1964 the Joint Chiefs of Staff had commenced work to produce a possible list of targets in North Vietnam. This list of 94 targets included bridges, rail targets, military storage areas, oil storage, airfields and the North's few industrial and power plants. The military planning was for this list of targets to be destroyed over a period of two to three weeks. The destruction of this relatively small number of targets in such a short period was probably within the capabilities of the forces available. The plan was consistent with conventional military thinking in the concentrated use of force in the minimum time possible. It would produce a shock effect and deny the enemy time to adapt or reorganise to overcome the effects of the bombing.

The situation in South Vietnam continued to decline even after American covert action and the ultimatum to the North. The covert actions against the North continued. The South Vietnamese, using American- supplied light naval craft, carried out an amphibious raid on the North Vietnamese islands of Hon Me and Hon Nieu on the night of 30th July and the morning of 31st July 1964. These raids used South Vietnamese personnel but were under the command of the Americans in Saigon. Shortly after this attack the American destroyer *Maddox*, carrying out a *DESOTO* intelligence gathering patrol, had steamed into the Gulf of Tonkin. It had orders to stay more than eight miles from the Vietnamese mainland and more than four miles away from any North Vietnamese islands, but its Captain, it is claimed, had not been informed of the raid on the North by the Southern naval forces. On 2nd August the *Maddox* passed the two islands attacked by the Southern naval forces and continued its patrol to the north. After finishing it's patrol and turning south to leave the Gulf it was again passing the general area of the earlier raids when it came under attack from three Vietnamese torpedo boats.

The destroyer was, at this time, twenty-three miles from the coast in international waters and it is assumed that the Vietnamese thought that it had been involved in the raids on Northern territory. The three North Vietnamese boats tried to close with the *Maddox* but there is some doubt about whether the boats actually intended to attack or if they were only investigating a possibly hostile ship close to the site of the recent attack. The *Maddox* opened fire on the three torpedo boats and, helped by aircraft launched from the aircraft carrier *Ticonderoga* that was positioned further south in the Gulf, two boats were damaged and one was left dead in the water. The only damage suffered by the *Maddox* was one hit from a 14.5mm round.

Johnson's reaction to the incident was to refrain from any direct action but to renew the *DESOTO* patrols after increasing the number of destroyers to two. The *Maddox* was joined in the Gulf by the *Turner Joy*. On 3rd August the South Vietnamese navy carried out another raid on the North as part of OPLAN 34A. This time they bombarded the Rhon estuary and other targets at Vinhson and this time the crews of the American destroyers were told that this action had taken place. On the night of 4th August a very confused incident took place and it now appears impossible to determine exactly what did occur. The two destroyers reported that they had intercepted radio traffic from Vietnamese patrol boats planning to attack them. Later that night the destroyers claimed that they had come under attack and at one point two enemy boats were reported sunk.

No visual sightings of the Vietnamese boats were reported but radar and sonar contacts were claimed and the two ships fired over two hundred shells and four depth charges. The two ships continued to manoeuvre for several hours and claimed to have seen and avoided torpedo tracks. The incident took place during darkness and rough seas and it was later considered that it was possible that faulty equipment and inexperienced operators were the cause of the entire incident. The ships were expecting to be attacked after receiving the radio messages and seem to have over-reacted to possible radar contacts. Aircraft were launched from the *Ticonderoga* and the *Constellation* but no Vietnamese boats were seen.

Commander James B. Stockdale from the *Ticonderoga*, who had damaged one of the Vietnamese boats involved in the incident on 2nd August, was also flying on the 4th, he later wrote:

"I had the best seat in the house from which to detect boats-if there were any......but no wakes or dark shapes other than those of the destroyers were ever visible to me." [14.]

Commander Wesley L. McDonald, also launched from the *Ticonderoga*, says:

"(I) didn't see anything that night except the *Maddox* and the *Turner Joy*. And I think the *Maddox*, basically, was in disarray as far as the [Combat Information Center (CIC)] controller was concerned in trying to get us to attack PT boats that were

The large attack carrier USS Constellation (CVA-64) cruising off North Vietnam. On 5th August 1964 the 'Connie' put up 32 A-1 Skyraiders, A-4 Skyhawks and F-4 Phantoms to strike at PT-boat bases on the North Vietnamese coast. Its attack squadrons lost an AD-1 and an A-4. (National Archives)

imaginary. I didn't see any wakes. I didn't see anything." [15.]

The destroyers were so confused that at one stage they ordered three aircraft from the *Constellation* to attack the destroyers themselves. This order was only stopped at the last moment. Lieutenant Commander John Nicholson, who had also been ordered to carry out this attack, wrote:

"I didn't see anything, but we were getting low on fuel and needed to get rid of our ordnance. I thought, the hell with it, let's fire into this general area. That's what we did:" [16.]

Although none of the pilots involved saw anything, it does not appear to have stopped them from firing off large amounts of ammunition and rockets, adding to the general confusion.

When news of these alleged attacks reached Washington, Johnson's reaction was very quick. He agreed to the plan put forward by the JCS, and, on 5th August 1964, strikes on a naval base at Quang Khe and oil storage tanks at Vinh were carried out by sixty-four aircraft from the *Ticonderoga* and the

Constellation operating in the Gulf of Tonkin. The strike, code-named *Pierce Arrow*, resulted in the claimed destruction of 25 patrol boats and ten percent of North Vietnam's fuel oil, but two American aircraft were lost. Because of a delay McNamara had announced the targets while the aircraft were still in the air, thus alerting the defences. One lost American pilot was Lt. E. J. Alvarez, who had flown over the *Maddox* and *Turner Joy* on the 4th. He was captured and spent eight years in North Vietnam prisons, the first of many American pilots.

These strikes were the first overt use of American aircraft against North Vietnam. McNamara had been attempting to obtain more information about the attacks on the American destroyers through the Pacific Command. The report from Captain Herrick in command of the two ships arrived shortly after the air strikes had been launched. Captain Herrick stated that, 'the naval air support did not locate any targets; the *Maddox* scored no known hits and never positively identified an enemy boat as such'.[17.]

President Johnson also announced that considerable reinforcements were being sent to Southeast Asia including fighter-bombers to Vietnam and Thailand and a further build-up in the Philippines. The reaction of the American people to the Tonkin Gulf incident had been one of indignation. Johnson used this to pass the Tonkin Gulf resolution through congress. It had originally been drawn up, in draft form, by the administration several months before in readiness for just such an incident and became the basis for the American position in Vietnam. It gave the President the right to use 'all necessary measures' to 'repel any armed attack' against American forces and was passed, very nearly unanimously, by congress on 7th August 1964.

It has been alleged that the whole incident was manufactured by the administration to pass the resolution through congress. There is no doubt that contingency planing for the reinforcements and the resolution had taken place, allowing them to be implemented very quickly. However, there can be no doubt that the first attack on the *Maddox* actually took place since the North Vietnamese gave medals to some of their naval personnel who took part. It seems unlikely however that the second attack

Ground crew aboard USS Ticonderoga arming an F-8E with five-inch Zuni rockets prior to the strike on 5th August. (US Navy)

ever occurred. The most likely explanation is that confusion on the spot was used by the government to achieve the measures needed to implement their planning for an increase in pressure on the North. It does not appear that there was any 'plot' to create the incident. The North Vietnamese view was that American warships, steaming a short distance from their coast shortly after an attack by American-controlled forces, was a clear provocation.

On 10th August the Americans again used the Canadian Seaborn to pass on an ultimatum to the North Vietnamese, which contained the passage:

> "the events of the past few days should add credibility to the statement made last time, the U.S. public and official patience with North Vietnamese aggression is growing extremely thin," [18.]

Seaborn reported that the response of the Vietnamese Prime Minister, Pham Van Dong, was 'extreme anger'. Pham stated that,

> "We don't hide the fact that the people will have to make sacrifices, but we are in a state of legitimate defence because the war is imposed on us." [19.]

The American hope that the bombing would provide enough

pressure on the North to force them to change their policy was not to be fulfilled and the North Vietnamese escalation would exactly match American escalation. The first infiltration by organised army units from the North was sent into the South in August 1964, leading to further deterioration of the American position in the South.

The American reinforcements, sent to Southeast Asia at the time of the Tonkin Gulf incident, were allowed to stay in place in South Vietnam and Thailand. The American attacks on the North had created an increase in public support for Johnson and there had been only two votes against the Tonkin Gulf resolution in congress.

In political terms the action against the North had been a success and created the feeling that any other attacks on Americans should also lead to bombing against the North. Since 1964 was election year for Johnson, he still wanted to appear in control of the situation in Vietnam, keeping the escalation to a minimum. He also wanted to seem the less bellicose of the two candidates. This was not too difficult as the other candidate was Senator Barry Goldwater, a noted 'hawk'.

After the Tonkin Gulf incident the raids on the North, carried out under OPLAN 34A, continued along with the *DESOTO* patrols, while other pressures on the Northern leadership, including American actions in Laos, were increased. The President ordered contingency plans for further air strikes against the North to be used in retaliation for any further 'spectacular' attacks on the American forces by the Viet Cong or North Vietnamese forces.

By September 1964 there was a consensus among the president's advisers that bombing of the North had become inevitable. Now came a move from purely contingency planning to actual operational planning. Neil Sheehan, in his analysis of the Pentagon Papers, commented:

> "The Johnson Administration reached a 'general consensus' at a White House strategy meeting on Sept. 7th, 1964, that air attacks against North Vietnam would probably have to be launched, a Pentagon study of the Vietnam war states. It was expected that 'these operations would begin early in the new year." [20]

The next major Viet Cong attack on the Americans that could fit into the category of 'spectacular' was the attack on the air base at Bien Hoa on 1st November 1964. A mortar attack killed five Americans, destroyed five B-57s and damaged many others. This was an American air base and it was obviously a deliberate attempt to cause American casualties. There was pressure on Johnson to retaliate against the North for this attack, but it was only two days before the presidential election and Johnson chose not to react. There was no real proof that the North had been involved in the raid on Bien Hoa, but the inability to make any progress in the South had led to the idea of tit-for-tat raids on the North in reprisal.

After the attack on Bien Hoa and before the election Johnson ordered a major policy review, which continued for a month after Johnson was re-elected. The working group, (including William Bundy, John McNaughton and others who had already been involved in formulating the existing policy over the last three years), did not attempt to question the basic American position in Vietnam. Their recommendations amounted to a continuation of the existing policy that had already been in operation for some time.

The main recommendations of this group, all of which included bombing the North, were presented as three options.

Option 'A' included the stepping up of covert actions against the North under OPLAN 34A, further actions against the infiltration routes in Laos and American bombing of the North in retaliation for any major Viet Cong actions.

Option 'B' was an all-out bombing campaign against the North including the destruction of all major targets in as short a time as possible.

Option 'C' was a low-key bombing campaign against the North, starting with the ground routes in Laos, progressing to the Southern half of North Vietnam and working Northwards to include all the country. This 'slow squeeze' approach was intended to place the Northern leadership under increasing pressure to reach agreement with the Americans.

A meeting was held on 1st December, when it seems generally accepted that the final decision was taken to start the bombing campaign. Johnson's reactions to these options was to choose a suggestion put forward by Maxwell Taylor, the Ambassador to

South Vietnam. This involved a combination of options 'A' and 'C'. Under phase one, the covert actions would continue and there would be retaliatory strikes against the North when it was thought necessary. This would continue for thirty days, when phase two would begin. This involved option 'C' and would be carried out by bombing targets up to the 19th parallel in North Vietnam, with a gradually increasing intensity. It was thought that this campaign would last from two to six months. Johnson ordered that phase one should be implemented immediately but he only approved phase two 'provisionally'. This is very close to what actually happened, except that bombing lasted for three and a half years.

This planning was again based on the idea of the graduated use of force to achieve a change of heart by the North Vietnamese leadership. The slowly increasing pressure on the North would give the Americans the option at any point to increase or cease the bombing. The reality was that the Government of the North was prepared to sustain any level of bombing that the Americans were politically prepared to carry out. The bombing was to be a negotiating ploy or bargaining chip to 'signal' America's resolve to support the South and force the North to negotiate. It was not intended to destroy the ability of the North to continue their actions in the South, but to affect the thinking of the North Vietnamese leaders, forcing them to reach a settlement with the Americans.

There is no doubt that the Joint Chiefs of staff had called for the bombing of the North and supported the general aims and objectives of the bombing, but they did not like the bombing campaign they actually got. The idea of a gradual use of force that allows the enemy time to react and develop counter-strategies was anathema to military thinking. The JCS still supported the destruction of the 94 targets on their list in the shortest possible time to achieve the maximum shock effect. President Johnson was worried by the effect of the bombing on world opinion, but the view of the JCS was that the gradual approach was the worst of both worlds. Bombing could lower America's international standing in some quarters, but it was not going to be carried out in a way that would hit the Vietnamese hard enough to force them to change their policies.

Where the buck stopped. Lyndon B. Johnson in the Oval Office at the White House. (National Archives)

The view of Johnson's advisors on the graduated strategy was that it gave them the initiative to increase or decrease the bombing as they saw fit, dependant on Vietnamese reactions. In reality the initiative was given to the North Vietnamese. While they were prepared to withstand the level of the bombing, they were controlling the situation. They could make use of the American desire to end the bombing by using even the faintest hint of talks to create bombing pauses and reductions. Once the 'slow squeeze' was adopted, to force the Vietnamese leadership to Change its support for the war in the South, the Americans were tied into a policy in which the initiative for ending that policy, was in the hands of their enemy.

Johnson's advisors had reached a consensus on their advice to the President, though they may have had different reasons to support the bombing and different views on the type of bombing to be used, especially the military. However Johnson stresses in his book *The Vantage Point* the unanimous nature of the advice given to him. Henry F. Graff interviewed the Secretary of State Dean Rusk and quotes him as saying, 'He (Dean Rusk) was at pains to say that the advice to the President on the air attacks had been unanimous.' [21].

The American attack on North Vietnam after the Tonkin Gulf incident and the American ultimatums to the North had undoubtedly alerted the North to the possible vulnerability of their positions. The North's Premier, Pham Van Dong, had visited Russia in November 1964 to ask for increased aid and - especially - a modern anti-aircraft system. Eventually Russia responded and created one of the most intensive air defence systems ever seen. It is thought that Dong waited until after Khrushchev was deposed before he visited Moscow because he considered he would gain more support from Khrushchev's successors.

The first action in the policy of graduated response was the starting of the *Barrel Roll* operations in Laos. These started on 14th December 1964. The bombing was intended to stop the infiltration from the North to the South along the Ho Chi Min trail and to disrupt the operations of the Pathet Lao anti-government forces. American Air Force and Navy aircraft were involved in this bombing, operating with the permission of the Laotian Premier. The idea was that the aircraft were to attack any 'targets of opportunity' that presented themselves as the aircraft patrolled over the Laotian Panhandle. The use of American aircraft in this way became known in January 1965 after the loss of two aircraft to ground fire.

America had hoped to strengthen the South politically before starting to bomb the North, but the uncertainty of the situation in the South forced them to delay. As it became obvious that the situation in the South was not going to improve, the weakness of the South became not a reason for delay but one reason for carrying out the bombing. On this point Richard N. Goodwin has written:

> "...early in 1965, the President was advised that morale in South Vietnam could be revived only if we bombed military targets in North Vietnam. This would assure Saigon of our determination to stay the course." [22].

A series of war games had taken place in the Pentagon to judge the effects of the bombing of North Vietnam. These war games, known under the code name *Sigma II*, had been a high level exercise and had included people like Curtis LeMay, Chief of the Air Force, and John McNaughton, General Earl Wheeler, William Bundy and Marshal Green. The course of these exercises seem to have followed the actual pattern of bombing that was to take place over the coming years. As the American side in the exercise stepped up the bombing, the North increased it's infiltration to the South, which forced the Americans to increase the numbers of their ground troops in the South. While bombing was kept on a limited level (no area bombing of the cities or the irrigation system) the North could accept the destruction of its industry and disperse its military establishment to frustrate the raiders' intentions. The outcome of the games was not what most of the participants wanted to learn and the results were generally ignored.

There was a major attack on American personnel at Christmas 1964, the Brinks raid, but the President decided against retaliation. As the situation in the South continued to deteriorate the President came under pressure to initiate phase two of the campaign against the North as had been decided earlier. The Americans were now waiting for an incident in the South large enough to justify the start of the bombing. This is what McGeorge Bundy meant when he described the attack at Pleiku as being like a streetcar, if you wait there will always be one along presently. *DESOTO* patrols were continued in February 1965 and it was thought that this might provoke a reaction from the North. The United States now had the forces in place to carry out the bombing and the plans had been drawn up to use these forces. There were Air Force units in Thailand and South Vietnam, plus aircraft carriers in the Gulf of Tonkin. All these forces were only waiting for the order to be given to begin the bombing.

It was thought that the beginning of the bombing could be made to appear only retaliatory in natured by waiting for major attacks by the Viet Cong, before reacting against the North. Even after bombing began, an initial attempt was made to link raids on the North to specific attacks in the South but, as the tempo of the raids built up, this specific linkage was quietly dropped. After the first raids Johnson described the attacks as reacting, 'not to isolated incidents but to the whole pattern of aggression and terrorism which Hanoi had been carrying out...'[23]

The incident that finally started the bombing campaign against the North was the Viet Cong attack on the barracks at Pleiku, in the central highlands, on 7th February 1965. Mortar and machine-gun fire killed eight Americans and wounded over a hundred more. This, the most serious attack on the American forces thus far, was a deliberate attempt to kill American personnel. McGeorge Bundy presented another report to the president calling for the start of the bombing and the President sent him to Vietnam to report on the situation. Bundy visited Pleiku and telephoned the President to advise him to retaliate and to begin the phase two bombing. In a meeting in the White House on the evening of 6th February 1965 (Washington dates are one day behind Vietnamese dates because of the international date line) Johnson and his principal advisors, plus House Speaker McCormack and Senator Mansfield, reached the decision to retaliate against the North. The one voice to speak against the decision was Senator Mansfield who had fears about the involvement of China and Russia.

At the time of the attack on Pleiku the Russian premier Kosygin was in Hanoi along with economic aid experts, the Russian Minister of Aviation and the Chief of Staff of the Air Force, possibly discussing the air defence requirements requested by the North Vietnamese. It is possible that the Viet Cong chose that particular time for the attack on Pleiku, because they thought that the Americans would not react while the Russian delegation was in Hanoi. Kosygin was infuriated by the bombing and it is possible that this increased the chances of the Russians supplying more aid to the North,

On 10th February, three days after the attack on Pleiku, the Viet Cong struck at the American barracks at Qui Nhon. This time the number of Americans killed was twenty-three, the largest number killed in one day, up to that time. This again triggered an American response against the North in the form of air attacks.

February 1965. Johnson's special adviser McGeorge Bundy visits the scene of the attack at Pleiku with General Nguyen Khanh. Within days, Rolling Thunder had started.
(US Army)

The American air raid against the North for the attack on Pleiku was code named *Flaming Dart I* and the air raids after Qui Nhon, *Flaming Dart II. Flaming Dart I* employed aircraft from the aircraft carriers *Coral Sea, Hancock* and *Ranger.* Their targets were military barracks and storage areas for infiltration to the South. Johnson authorised four targets to be attacked but only one was struck. This was the barracks at Dong Hoi, just north of the border between the North and the South. The other three targets were obscured by bad weather, which prevented the aircraft from finding them. On the following day, 8th February, the South Vietnamese Air Force took part in the strikes, allowing the Americans to say they were only helping the South Vietnamese. The South Vietnamese strike was led by General Ky, later to be President, with twenty-four A-1 Skyraiders. The South Vietnamese chose to attack the head-quarters of an anti-aircraft regiment, losing two Skyraiders to ground fire, while every one of the returning aircraft was damaged. The Americans also lost one aircraft and pilot.

Flaming Dart II was carried out on 11th February by Navy and Air Force aircraft, which attacked barracks at Chang Hoa and Vit Thu Lu situated just North of the De-Militarised Zone. The weather was again bad and the attack on Chang Hoa was only partially successful. Three aircraft and one pilot were lost.

Once the North had been attacked as retaliation, the decision to bomb the North on a regular basis was taken on 13th February 1965. The President later described this as, '...we would carry out measured and limited air actions jointly with the GVN against military targets in the North below the 19th parallel'. [24.]

This new program of air strikes against the North was known as *Rolling Thunder*, planned to last only a few weeks or months but would be carried out with increasing intensity for three and a half years. The first four air strikes in the *Rolling Thunder* series were cancelled because of bad weather, the political situation in the South and the chance of negotiations. The first strike to go ahead was *Rolling Thunder 5* on 2nd March 1965, and the second on 15th March. 'The policy of gradual but steady reprisal against North Vietnam for its continuing aggression in the South had been put into action'.[25.]

The first targets bombed under the Rolling Thunder programme were below the 19th parallel and mostly military objectives or targets involved in the transportation system; bridges, roads and storage areas. Each raid was individually nominated and organised on specific days, but very soon the *Rolling Thunder* raids were re-organised on a weekly basis, which gave the military more leeway in scheduling the raids, during periods of bad weather.

The targets for the bombing were chosen by the Tuesday Cabinet, having been suggested by the Pacific Command and by an intelligence group for the Joint Chiefs of Staff. The JCS then decided which proposals were to be sent to the President to be discussed by his advisors, each individual target being given a grading by each individual advisor and then the grading was averaged out. This cumbersome system even involved the President discussing the suitability of individual buildings as targets. The numbers of aircraft involved, types of ordnance and the frequency of the strikes were also controlled from the very top, leaving very little flexibility to the local commanders.

As the original thinking behind the bombing - the idea that a demonstration of American resolve would affect the North's policy towards the South - became less likely to happen, the reasons put forward for the bombing began to change. The explanations expounded in public by McNamara, Taylor and others at various times usually included three points.

(1.) To make it clear to the North that they must pay a price for their actions in the South.

The 24 South Vietnamese A-1 Skyraiders taking part in 'Flaming Arrow I' were led by General Ky, who would soon lead a successful coup to overthrow the government. Thus he became the new leader of South Vietnam.
(via Author)

(2.) To reduce the flow of men and supplies to the South or to increase the cost of this flow.

(3.) To raise the morale of the South Vietnamese people.

As the bombing developed the reasons given for the bombing were altered. The original attempt to influence thinking or to send messages was seen to fail and so the bombing campaign became an attempt to influence the military position. Although it was still hoped to influence the North, now it was to be through force, not the threat of force. Messages were not enough. Johnson was now forced to walk the tightrope between the level of force that was thought to be needed and the degree of force that the American public would support. As the amounts of force were increased so the level of support by the public declined.

The Joint Chiefs of Staff had always supported the bombing, but their view had been that it should be as heavy as possible. Thus they criticised the limited nature of the campaign. The military chiefs had nearly all served in the Second World War and still thought in terms of unconditional surrender. An enemy should be put under such pressure that he is forced to surrender, or until he can no longer be a military threat. The economic, military and morale base of an enemy should be destroyed in the shortest possible time. Yet in a limited war with limited objectives this is not always possible. The military did not want to be drawn into a Korean situation. This would allow the enemy sanctuaries and the American military forces would be controlled with what they saw as artificial restrictions. It was not the military's job to be directly concerned with politics, but it was Johnson's. He had a clearer view, at the start of the bombing campaign, of what was politically possible; of what the American public would accept.

The Pentagon Papers makes it clear that the American intelligence community had also criticised the strategy behind the bombing. The three major intelligence agencies were the Central Intelligence Agency, the Defence Intelligence Agency and the State Department's Bureau of Intelligence. These together, 'did not concede very strong chances for breaking the will of Hanoi'.[26.] Their view was that the North Vietnamese did not think that the Americans would carry out unrestricted bombing and that in sum were prepared to lose what industry it had. It was essentially an agricultural country and the true economic base lay in large numbers of agricultural communes. It would thus have required huge amounts of bombing to affect these self-sufficient units. It was thought possible to destroy the North's industry and interdict the transport system, reducing the ability of the North to help the Viet Cong. The general view of the intelligence community however did not believe that it would be possible to stop or dramatically to reduce this help by the use of bombing. However the head of the CIA, John McCone, was more in line with the Chiefs of Staff in supporting the bombing while thinking that it should be carried out at a much heavier rate.

The Air Force Chiefs had supported the introduction of the bombing. Indeed, its whole existence as a separate service was based on the theories of strategic bombing. Vietnam was not the ideal place to attempt to prove the strategic bombing theories and this fact was fully appreciated, but they had very little choice in the matter. After years of saying what air power could achieve, they could not now refuse to support the start of the bombing. They could only hope that they would be allowed to carry out the type of bombing they thought necessary. The U.S. Navy was in much the same position. The aircraft carrier had become the conventional capital ship and a heavy slice of their appropriations had been spent on aircraft. The Navy leaders now needed to prove their theories on the use of naval air power as much as those of the the Air Force needed to prove theirs. It is thought that the Army supported the bombing to see it fail. This, it was believed, would lead to the introduction of more ground troops, which the army saw as necessary to win the war on the ground.

The small group of people who actually made the decisions to begin bombing undoubtedly had an over-optimistic view of what could be achieved. They appear to have lost sight of America's long term aims in Southeast Asia and how to relate these aims to the means of achieving them. If the maintenance of a non-communist South Vietnam was the long term aim, then the creation of a stable democratic government, acceptable to the majority of the people in the South, was the first priority.

The number of choices given to President Johnson was always limited. All the options presented to Johnson, at the series of meetings before the decision to begin the bombing, included increased pressure on the North. Intelligence reports, questioning the basis of the 'domino theory' and the possible affects of bombing, were ignored. It seems that some of these were not even shown to the President. The over-optimism was about what could be physically achieve by bombing and about the reaction of the North Vietnamese to it. The aim was to apply pressure to the North but initially the bombing was restricted and hedged around with such artificial constraints as to actually reduce its effect. In reality it was assumed that the threat of the bombing, and the threat of what could be bombed, would be enough. The bombing would be a 'signal' to show that the full weight of American power could be used if necessary.

The reaction of the North Vietnamese was considerably more stoic than was thought likely, at the time the decision to start bombing was taken. They seemed prepared to accept the highest level of bombing that was politically possible for the Americans. They absorbed the bombing and called the American's bluff on the level of further bombing. The group of decision makers around Johnson never seem to have considered the depth of resilience shown by the North Vietnamese to be possible.

The Tuesday Cabinet became a close knit cohesive group with a very narrow view of the options available to them. Henry F. Graff describes this as:

> "The men of the Tuesday Cabinet were loyal to each other, with a devotion compounded of mutual respect and common adversity. They soon learned, as all congenial committeemen learn, to listen selectively and to talk harmoniously even when in disagreement."[27.]

In this atmosphere it became increasingly difficult for any them to deviate from the norms of group thinking. The ethos that developed within the group restricted the number of choices available to the President, who always stressed the unanimous nature of the advice given to him, but the group did not re-examine any of the decisions that had already been taken. The closeness of the group was not conducive to any kind of objective discussion of either the long term aims or the choices available other than bombing.

FOOTNOTES

1   Slessor, John, quoted in *Air Power In the Missile Age*, by Armstrong J. and Mason R. A, University of Illinois Press, page 45.

2   Olds, Robin, *Forty-six Years a Fighter Pilot*, American Aviation Historical Society Journal, XIII (winter 1968), page 237.

3   Sheehan, Neal, *The Pentagon Papers*, Bantam Books, 1972, New York, page 16-18.

4   Sheehan, Neal, *The Pentagon Papers*, Bantam Books, New York, 1972, page 241.

5   Johnson, Lyndon Baines, *The Vantage Point*, Holt, Rinehart and Winston, 1971, page 66.

6   Halberstam, David, *The Best and the Brightest*, Random House, New York, 1969, page 354.

7   Sheehan, Neal, *The Pentagon Papers*, Bantam Books, 1971, page 254.

8   Halberstam, David, *The Very Expensive Education of McGeorge Bundy'*, Harper's Magazine, July, 1969.

9   Donovan, James A. Militarism U.S.A. Charles Scrivener's Sons, New York, 1970 page 121.

10   Halberstam, David, *The Programming of Robert McNamara*, Harper's Magazine, Feb 1971, page 68.

11   Wicker, Tom, *JFK and LBJ*, William Morrow, New York, 1968, page 244.

12   Gallucci, Robert L. *Neither Peace Nor Honour*, The John Hopkins University Press, Baltimore, 1975, page 35.

13   Johnson, Lyndon Baines, *The Vantage Point*, Holt Rinehart and Winston, New York, 1971, page 66-7.

14   Stockdale, Jim and Sybil, *In Love and War*, Harper and Row, New York, 1984, page 19.

15   Levinson, Jeffrey L. *Alpha Strike Vietnam*, Presidio Press, 1989, page 13.

16   Levinson, Jeffrey L. *Alpha Strike Vietnam*, Presidio Press, 1989, page 15.

17   Donovan, James A. *Militarism U.S.A.*, Charles Scrivener's Sons, New York, 1970, page 106.

18   Palmer, Gregory, *The McNamara Strategy and The Vietnam War* Greenwood Press, 1978, page 110.

19   Maclear, Michael, *Vietnam. The Ten Thousand Day War*, Thames Methuen, London, 1981, page 163.

20   Sheehan, Neal, *The Pentagon Papers*, Bantam Books, New York, 1972, page 307.

21   Graff, Henry F. *The Tuesday Cabinet*, Prentice-Hall Inc. New Jersey. 1970, page 39.

22   Goodwin, Richard N. *Triumph or Tragedy: Reflections On Vietnam*, Vintage Books, New York, 1966, page 31.

23   Johnson, Lyndon Baines, *The Vantage Point*, Holt, Rinehardt and Winston, 1971, page 129.

24   Johnson, Lyndon Baines, *The Vantage Point*, Holt, Rinehart and Winston, New York, 1971, page 130.

25   Johnson, Lyndon Baines, *The Vantage Point*, Holt, Rinhart and Winston, New York, 1971, page 132.

26   Sheehan, Neal, *The Pentagon Papers*, Bantam Books, New York, page 331.

27   Graff, Henry F. *The Tuesday Cabinet*, Prentice-Hall Inc. New Jersey, 1970. page 6.

Chapter Two
1965: 'A Few Isolated Thunderclaps'

The first strikes in the *Rolling Thunder* campaign were carried out on 2nd March 1965. These were known as *Rolling Thunder 5*, the first four having been cancelled because of delays. At this stage each series of raids was programmed for one day and the targets could not be returned to if they were not fully destroyed by the first attack. These initial attacks on 2nd March were carried out by F-105 Thunderchiefs from Thailand, plus B-57 Canberras and F-100 Super Sabres from South Vietnam. There were also seventeen South Vietnamese Air Force aircraft involved in the raid, since co-operation by the South Vietnamese was one restriction placed on the attacks by President Johnson. However, this restraint was soon allowed to lapse. The target was an ammunition depot at Xom Bong 35 miles north of the De-Militarised Zone. The raid on Xom Bong led to the loss of five American aircraft in return for only limited success, while the first Air Force prisoner of war, Captain Hayden J. Lockhart, was taken. The strength of the North Vietnamese defences and the aircraft losses came as something of a shock to the Air Force.

On 15th March, after a delay of nearly two weeks, *Rolling Thunder 6* was carried out. This was a series of raids on ammunition depots and barracks in the Southern part of North Vietnam and was the first Navy participation in the *Rolling Thunder* campaign, carried out by aircraft from the aircraft carriers *Ranger* and *Hancock*. One Douglas A-1 Skyraider was lost. Naval aircraft had been flying tactical reconnaissance missions over North Vietnam since 2nd March under the code name *Blue Tree*.

Maxwell Taylor, the American ambassador to South Vietnam, had called the *Rolling Thunder* campaign 'a few isolated thunder claps' and asked Johnson to increase the tempo of the bombing. Thus on 15th March the President changed the time

An F-100D Super Sabre accelerating downhill and about to ruin someones entire day. The 'Hun' took part in the first Rolling Thunder strikes, but its limited range and inedequate performance made it more suitable for close support work in the South. The 'Hun' was to fly more combat sorties in southeast Asia than any other front line type. (USAF)

scale allowed for each series of raids from a one day to a one week basis. This gave more flexibility to the commanders on the spot in the timing of the raids to allow for bad weather. Authorisation was also given to attack secondary targets without specific permission from the government.

Meanwhile the first American combat troops, from the 9th Marine Expeditionary Brigade, had landed at Da Nang on 8th March, while a squadron of Marine F-4 Phantoms moved into this base on 10th April followed by other Marine squadrons to form a Marine wing. These squadrons were mainly to be used over South Vietnam, but would also take part in *Rolling Thunder* raids over the Southern part of North Vietnam. One Marine Squadron, flying F-8 Crusaders, would also take part in raids on the North. These would operate from the aircraft carrier *Oriskany* during 1965.

The shortage of authorised targets over the North increased the traditional rivalry between the Air Force and the Navy for the right to strike the targets available. Although both the Navy and the Air Force came under the control of the Pacific Command there was insufficient liaison and communication between the two services in the early days of the *Rolling Thunder* campaign. This led to duplication of effort and confusion over what targets would be struck. The first solution to this problem was to divide each day into three-hour 'slots', alternating control of the airspace over North Vietnam between the two services to avoid any overlap of effort. In practice this system proved cumbersome. Any delay caused by bad weather could still cause confusion between the two services operating over the same targets.

The day-to-day control of the armed reconnaissance part of the campaign was given to the commander of the 2nd Air Division in Saigon and to the commander of Task Force 77. The *Rolling Thunder* Armed Reconnaissance Coordinating Committee (RTARCC, later RTCC) was also established in an attempt to co-ordinate the efforts of the Navy and Air Force

By November 1965 this committee had divided North Vietnam into six Route Packages in an attempt to avoid any overlap, these packages alternating between the services on a weekly basis. Later each of them was given control of a specific area of North Vietnam.

Route Package 1 was the area just North of the De-Militarised Zone and came under the control of General Westmoreland in Saigon. This was because it was considered as directly affecting the fighting in the South and was thought of as part of the 'extended battlefield'. Route Packages 2, 3 and 4 were under the control of the Navy and RP 5 was the responsibility of the Air Force. Many Air Force aircraft were operating from Thailand and it was easier for them to reach the Western part of North Vietnam. The North East part of North Vietnam was designated RP 6, which was divided into two sectors, the line of demarcation being the northeast rail line into China. The Western part was controlled by the Air Force and the Eastern part by the Navy. Route Package 6 (Pak 6) contained both Hanoi and Haiphong, also most of the other major targets, therefore the bulk of the Vietnamese air defence organisation was deployed there. Most of the American aircraft lost during *Rolling Thunder* would be shot down while operating over Pak 6.

The choice of targets in the North was decided during President Johnson's Tuesday luncheon meetings with his close advisers. During the first few months of the campaign most of

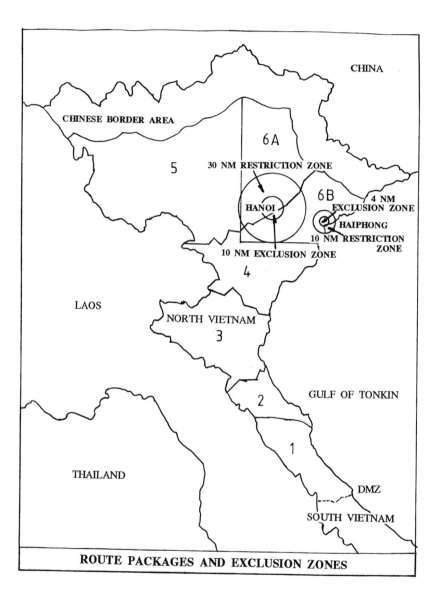

Map 2. The Route Packages and Exclusion Zones
(Peter Edwards RICS and John T. Smith)

the targets were of a military character such as barracks and ammunition dumps. Very few targets on the GCS 94 target list were attacked until much later in the campaign. The GCS list had been drawn up with the intention of destroying North Vietnam's ability to continue the war. Johnson's original intention for the bombing however, was to apply sufficient pressure and the threat of further pressure on the North's leadership. Admiral Sharp described this early part of the campaign as:

> "It does not seek to inflict maximum damage on the enemy. Instead, it is a precise application of military pressure for the specific purpose of halting aggression in South Vietnam." [1]

While it is correct that political leaders should maintain overall control, such control should not extend to the level that Johnson attempted to carry it. The Tuesday Cabinet at the start of the bombing specified not only the targets but the types of ordinance, fuses, height, direction and the timing of attacks. These are the sort of operational decisions best left to experienced commanders 'on the spot' and in daily contact with the airmen carrying out the raids.

While the first few targets were allocated by the Tuesday group on a one-day basis and later a weekly basis, they were finally extended to cover longer periods. How long each numbered series of *Rolling Thunder* raids was to last was specified and the number of sorties were allocated. The number of sorties was based on the number thought to be necessary to cause 80 per cent destruction. Strict Rules of Engagement (RoE) were also clearly laid down for the pilots involved. Only primary and secondary targets could be hit and any unused bombs could be jettisoned only into the sea. There was no pre-strike reconnaissance and bomb damage photographic coverage aircraft were to accompany the strike or to follow immediately after, operating at medium altitude without fighter cover. The North Vietnamese quickly learned to expect reconnaissance aircraft immediately after a raid and many were lost in this way. The armed reconnaissance raids were only permitted to attack military trucks that were moving along the roads and not stationary or travelling through a village. This was later relaxed

The North Vietnamese soon became adept at camouflage. This shot, taken by a low-flying RF-101C Voodoo, shows a train barely distinguishable from the surrounding countryside.

(National Archives)

to allow trucks up to a certain distance off the road to be attacked - at first 100 metres later increased to 300 metres.

The area of North Vietnam available to be attacked under *Rolling Thunder* slowly expanded northwards after the bombing had begun. This movement of the bombing towards the capital of Hanoi had been part of the original planning to pressurise the Vietnamese government, but it had been thought that the American objectives would have been achieved before the bombing had reached that far. The first raids were below the 19th parallel and it was 22nd May 1965 before a target north of the 20th parallel was struck, the barracks at Quang Soui. It would be July 1966 before all of North Vietnam was released for attack, apart from exclusion zones which remained in operation until the end of *Rolling Thunder. 1,* of thirty nautical miles along the Chinese border, was excluded to reduce the chance of American aircraft flying into Chinese airspace, although this happened occasionally. There were also zones of ten miles radius around the centre of Hanoi and four miles around Haiphong inside which American aircraft needed specific permission to attack any target. This permission was rarely given. Within a radius of thirty nautical miles of Hanoi and ten miles around Haiphong aircraft could only retaliate against anti-aircraft batteries if they were fired on first.

At this early stage of the war the Air Force aircraft in Vietnam were under the control of the 2nd Air Division commanded by Major General Joseph H. Moore. This was subordinated to the MACV (Military Assistance Command Vietnam) in Saigon, under general Westmoreland, for the operations in South Vietnam. It was also subordinated to the 13th Air Force in the Phillipines for operations in Laos, Cambodia and North Vietnam. This division of responsibilities led at times to conflicting requests being placed on the 2nd Air Division. Both the Navy and Air Force units in Vietnam came under the control of the Pacific Command in Hawaii under Admiral U.S.G. Sharp.

The Naval ships in the Gulf of Tonkin were under control of Task Force 77 through the 7th fleet. This normally operated between one and five aircraft carriers for use in *Rolling Thunder*, with large numbers of support ships. The fighting ships were backed up by the supply ships of Task Force 73 that kept the aircraft carriers supplied at sea with fuel and munitions. The carriers and their escorts were positioned in the Gulf of Tonkin at *Yankee Station*. This was a geographical position about one hundred miles East of Da Nang and was occasionally moved further North. The Gulf of Tonkin is dominated by the Chinese Island of Hainan so the carriers in Task Force 77 were not only under possible threat from the North Vietnamese but also from the Chinese, who maintained a force of MiG-17s and MiG-19s on Hainan, which occasionally harassed the naval aircraft operating over the Gulf. In May 1965 General Westmoreland requested further naval air support. Accordingly another carrier was placed off South Vietnam at *Dixie Station*, about one hundred miles southeast of Cam Ranh Bay. The aircraft from the carrier at *Dixie Station* operated over South Vietnam and the Navy placed newly arrived carriers at *Dixie Station* to 'work up' before moving up to the more demanding environment over North Vietnam.

After the start of *Rolling Thunder* the Air Force continued to increase the size of its forces in Thailand, from where the majority of Air Force sorties over North Vietnam were to be mounted. The Air Force controlled six major airfields in Thailand. The main ones were Ubon, Korat, Udorn and Takhli, where the capacity and facilities were greatly increased to support the campaign.

*The mighty F-105D Thunderchief. This huge fighter-bomber, nickna-
med the 'Thud', was to bear the brunt of bombing operations over the
North and was also to take most of the losses. (USAF)*

The Air Force commitment in Thailand increased from eighty
aircraft and one thousand personnel in early 1965, to six
hundred aircraft and 35,000 men when *Rolling Thunder* ended
in 1968. The main weight of the Air Force bombing campaign
against the North was carried by the F-105 Thunderchief force
stationed in Thailand. The F-105 was originally designed for
delivering nuclear weapons and it's long range and heavy bomb
load made it the best aircraft available for use over the North.

Two wings of F-105s were eventually stationed in Thailand,
the 355th Tactical Fighter Wing at Takhli and the 388th
Tactical Fighter Wing at Korat. These had about 72 aircraft
each, at full complement, which was rarely achieved, and
carried out 75 per cent of the Air Force strike missions over
North Vietnam during *Rolling Thunder*. Over three hundred
F-105Ds and Fs were to be lost over North Vietnam, nearly half
the number of these types produced.

The airfields in Thailand were over four hundred miles from
the targets in the northeastern part of Vietnam. F-105s and F-4
Phantoms could operate at this range but not with an effective
bomb load, nor could they 'loiter' in the target area for any
length of time. To overcome these difficulties, air-to-air refuelling became standard for strikes over the North. This aerial
refuelling was carried out using KC-135s of Strategic Air
Command from Thailand. The limiting factor in the size of air

strikes was often not the availability of strike aircraft but the availability of air refuelling aircraft.

The type of campaign that was possible over the North was to some extent controlled by the extremes of the weather patterns over the North. During the summer months, May until September, the weather is fixed by the southwest monsoon. This gives rise to heavy rain showers and thunderstorms with restricted visibility during the early morning and late afternoon. This was considered the good weather period and most of the bombing was carried out during the summer. The period between November and April is the northeast monsoon. Cooler air from central Asia meets the warmer air from the South China Sea, which creates heavy rain, low continuous cloud cover and very restricted visibility. There were very few days when visual bombing was possible during this period and thus many raids were cancelled.

After the start of *Rolling Thunder* in early March 1965, the first weekly package was *Rolling Thunder 7*. This was carried between 19th - 25th March and was the first package to allow, besides listed targets, armed reconnaissance of specified roads and rail lines rather than individual targets. Only military targets on the roads could be attacked, if positively identified. *Rolling Thunder 8* was between 26th March and 1st April. At the insistence of Admiral Sharp, attacks on nine radar sites below the 19th parallel were also included. These had been used for tracking incoming American raids. The North Vietnamese had been causing heavier losses to the Americans than had been expected and it was hoped that the destruction of the radar stations would weaken the air defence system. The nine radar sites were destroyed but proved hard targets to eliminate. One in particular was on the island of Bach Long Vi, 75 miles off the coast of North Vietnam in the Gulf of Tonkin, from where it provided clear coverage of Task Force 77 aircraft. Two seventy-aircraft strikes were needed to destroy it, at a cost of several Naval aircraft to anti-aircraft fire.

The bombing continued to expand. During April a total of fifteen hundred sorties were flown over North Vietnam, split approximately evenly between Naval and Air Force aircraft. All the targets were below the 20th parallel and were mostly

All things to all men. The McDonnell-Douglas F-4B Phantom first arrived in Vietnam as part of the Marine Air component at Da Nang. This aircraft is from VMA-122, the second squadron deployed by the USMC. Although it was designed to hunt long-range bombers, it became the work-horse in Vietnam. It operated in long-range strike, photo-reconnaissance, bomber protection and close support rôles as well as becoming the most proficient MiG killer. It did everything.
(USMC)

transportation routes thought to carry men and equipment to the South. The number of armed reconnaissance sorties was also increased to 24 per day. The rail line running south from Vinh carried a considerable load. It was believed that the destruction of two bridges, one a road and rail bridge at Dong Thuong and the bridge at Than Hoa (of which we will hear more later), would trap a large amount of rolling stock south of Hanoi. The bridge at Dong Phuong Thong was bombed and the centre section destroyed on 3rd April. However the Than Hoa bridge survived these attempts to destroy it and would continue to do so for many years. The U.S. Air Force carried out several major raids on the Than Hoa bridge but the standard Air Force munitions, *Bullpup* missiles and 500 up to 2,000 lb bombs, were simply not big enough to destroy such a large target. It was constructed on large concrete abutments on either bank and, while the approaches to the bridge and parts of the road way and rail line across the bridge were damaged, the structural part of the bridge remained intact. When North Vietnam was divided into Route Packages the bridge at Than Hoa was in RP 4, becoming the responsibility of the Navy. During the course of *Rolling Thunder* Naval aircraft continued to attack the bridge with as little success as the Air Force. The bridge was even attacked by C-130 cargo aircraft, dropping 5,000 lb mines into the Song Ma river above the bridge. The Than Hoa bridge, a major target in the North, was still standing when the *Rolling Thunder* campaign came to a close in 1968. However, by the end of April 1965 large numbers of trucks and rolling stock had been destroyed along with 26 other bridges.

The first contact between the North Vietnamese Air Force and American aircraft occurred on the 3rd of April. Three MiG-17s attacked and damaged an F-8 Crusader during an attack on the bridge at Dong Phuong Thong. The F-8 was damaged but managed to return safely. The first American aircraft shot down by North Vietnamese aircraft were two F-105s on 4th April. The Thunderchiefs, from the 355th Tactical Fighter Wing, were part of a flight of four waiting their turn to bomb the Than Hoa bridge. Two MiG-17s appeared without warning behind the American aircraft and shot down the two F-105s using cannon fire. The MiGs were chased out of the area by F-100 Super Sabres, flying *MiGCAP* to the strike forces. One F-100 pilot fired a *Sidewinder* missile at the MiGs without success and the MiGs left the area without loss.

On 9th April a flight of F-4Bs from the carrier *Ranger* became involved with four MiG-17s of the Chinese Air Force, operating from the island of Hainan. The Phantoms were flying a *BarCAP* mission to protect the fleet from any interference by North Vietnamese aircraft. The Chinese aircraft headed towards the American ships and the F-4s moved in to cut them off. The Americans claimed one Chinese aircraft probably destroyed but one American aircraft was shot down. The Chinese however claimed that the lost Phantom was hit by a AIM-7 *Sparrow* missile fired by another American aircraft. During the course of the war there would be other examples of missiles hitting the wrong aircraft, so the Chinese claim could have been true.

The North Vietnamese slowly built up their Air Force with aid from Russia and China. They fully realised that they could never match the Americans in numbers or quality and always used their aircraft carefully. Whenever they suffered heavy casualties they usually pulled back to re-train and re-equip rather than allowing themselves to be fought to a standstill.

On one of the first sorties to the area northwest of Hanoi, four F-105Ds from Takhli left their calling card on the Lang Met highway bridge, 45 miles from the capital. (National Archives)

This would have been the result had they attempted to meet the American attack head on. The Vietnamese fighters were used to disrupt raids by forcing the American aircraft to drop their bombs before they reached their targets. The Vietnamese under tight ground control would attempt one high speed attack on the American formations and then break away. By the middle of 1965 they had about 70 MiG-17s available to them.

In early 1965 it was estimated that the North Vietnamese had between fourteen hundred and two thousand anti-aircraft guns in use. Most of these were thought to be 37mm or 57mm weapons, light and medium guns. The 57 mm was effective up to about 15,000 feet using optical sights. By the end of 1968 the total of guns available had increased to eight thousand including radar guided 85mm and 100mm guns. The 85mm guns were effective up to 25,000 feet and the 100mm up to 40,000 feet. Most American aircraft losses throughout *Rolling*

Thunder were caused by anti-aircraft guns, even after the introduction of surface-to-air missiles and MiG-21 interceptors.

The North Vietnamese built up an integrated air defence system involving hundreds of radars to control aircraft, guns and missiles. The quantity of long range early warning radars, code-named *Moon Cone* by NATO, increased from 22 in late 1964 to 47 at the end of 1965 and 144 by 1966. Fire control radars for the anti-aircraft guns also increased to at least 250 by 1967. This system was based on the Russian model, which employs many more radars than the western equivalent, and was set up with Russian aid.

With so many radars available to the North Vietnamese it was nearly impossible for American aircraft to penetrate North Vietnamese airspace undetected. Even after the introduction of radar jamming aircraft and equipment it was impossible for the Americans to jam all the radars. Also, the mere fact of jamming warned the North Vietnamese that something was happening. The Chinese also had radars mounted on Hainan island covering the Gulf of Tonkin with the resulting information passed to the North Vietnamese by radio. The American carriers in the Gulf were shadowed by Russian intelligence ships who also reported the numbers of aircraft taking of and landing to the North Vietnamese. Given these facts it was nearly impossible for the Americans to achieve surprise with any raids on the North. The North Vietnamese air defence system controllers may not have known the exact target of a raid but usually knew the general area.

The North Vietnamese interceptors were used under very tight Ground Controlled Intercept (GCI) techniques, again using the Russian system. From take-off to landing the ground controller, at one of the three major GCI centres at Phuc Yen, Bac Mai, and Kep, dictated the actions of the aircraft. Using the radar coverage the MiGs were brought into what was hoped was tactically favourable positions to attack the American strike aircraft. General W W Momyer described this as:

> "Controllers vectored the MiGs into position for attack with surprisingly detailed instructions, even to the point of telling an individual pilot when to arm his weapon and when he was 'cleared for attack.' If the situation didn't look favourable, the controller would direct the pilot out of the area of the potential engagement." [2]

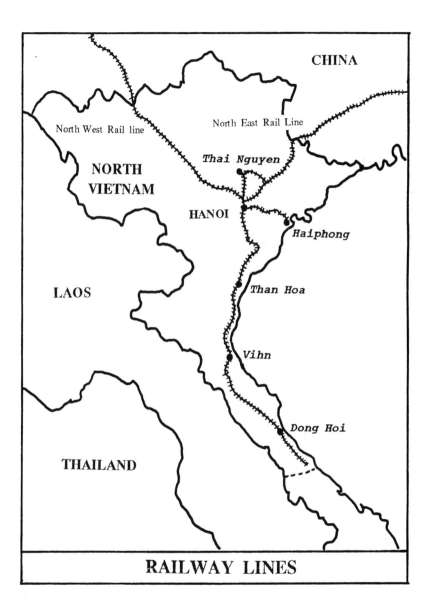

Map 3. Transportation and Railway Lines
(Peter Edwards RICS and John T. Smith)

Although both individual anti-aircraft gun sites and aircraft actually in the air could be attacked, a political decision was taken not to attack the air defence system itself, the control centres, airfields, aircraft on the ground, etc. until much later in the campaign.

On 5th April a reconnaissance RF-8A, operating from the carrier *Coral Sea* on a *Blue Tree* photographic mission, brought back pictures of the first SA-2 surface-to-air missile site. This was fifteen miles southeast of Hanoi. By the end of the year 56 sites had been identified in North Vietnam. The North Vietnamese constructed large numbers of sites, moving the semi-mobile SA-2 missile batteries around between the available sites as required. The missile batteries could be moved and ready for use in three to four hours, which meant that the Americans were never sure which sites were active until the SAM tracking radar was turned on. When the first site was detected both the Air Force and Navy requested permission to attack the site before it could be completed. The right to attack the site was refused by the political leaders in Washington. One reason for this was that Russian advisers were thought to be working on the site. The possibility that Russians might be killed was something to be avoided.

Some civilian leaders seem to have considered the missiles to have only been a propaganda move by the North Vietnamese. General Westmoreland said that he was told by John T. McNaughton, Assistant Secretary of Defence that, 'You don't think the North Vietnamese are going to use them…putting them in is just a political ploy by the Russians to appease Hanoi.'[3.] Therefore none of the sites under construction were attacked until after the first aircraft had been shot down. The first missile sites were built around Hanoi. Later, more were constructed around Haiphong and along the northeast rail line into China.

The Vietnamese did not use their SA-2s until July, when on the 24th an F-4C Phantom of the 47th Tactical Fighter Squadron based at Ubon was shot down. The pilot, Captain Richard P. Keirn, had been a prisoner of war in World War II. He now became a prisoner in another war after ejecting successfully. The shot down aircraft had been part of a

Raising the stakes. The North Vietnamese began to retaliate in 1965 when the first SA-2 'Guideline' missile sites were installed. They were not attacked until the first US aircraft was shot down by a missile. Then the 'Wild Weasels' were formed to hunt them down, 'close up and personal', by deliberately exposing themselves to the missiles.
(National Archives)

four-aircraft flight on *MiGCAP* to an F-105 strike northwest of Hanoi. The Phantom had been flying over dense cloud cover when the missile had risen through the clouds and exploded without warning, destroying Keirn's aircraft and damaging the other three. The first Naval aircraft shot down by a missile was an A-4 Skyhawk flown by Lieutenant (jg) Donald H. Brown Jr. during the night of 11/12th August 1965.

Once the SA-2s were established as a direct threat the military leaders were given permission to attack the missile sites. On 12th August 124 aircraft from the carriers *Coral Sea* and *Midway* attempted to find missile sites and destroy them but, without the specialised equipment that later became available, no active sites were found. Over the next two days seven aircraft were damaged and five shot down by anti-aircraft guns as they attempted to find the missile sites.

The Air Force response to the surface-to-air missiles was the development of specialised aircraft to deal with them. These aircraft became known as *Wild Weasels*. The first of these were four specially adapted two seat F-100F Super Sabre aircraft that arrived at Korat in Thailand on 26th November 1965 after first being tested in Florida. There had been great difficulty in discovering where, among the large number of possible sites, the missiles were actually positioned. The mobility of the missiles was another problem. By the time that photographic reconnaissance information had been distributed the missiles could have been moved to a different site, where they could become active again after only a few hours.

The first *Wild Weasel* aircraft were equipped with RHAW (radar homing and warning) equipment that could detect the radar emissions from the *Fan Song* radar used by the SA-2s. This equipment also allowed the aircraft to home in on the radar and mark the site for bomb-carrying attack aircraft. As soon as the North Vietnamese turned on the SA-2s radar they became liable to attack. This type of mission against the air defence system became known as *Iron Hand* missions.

The Naval response to the missile threat was to develop the equipment for their normal attack aircraft to carry out the *Iron Hand* missions rather than to employ specialised *Wild Weasel* aircraft. After the Russians had introduced the SA-2s Strategic Air Command had designed electronic equipment to counter the missiles for their B-52s, to allow them to penetrate the Russian defences. Designed specifically for the B-52, this equipment was too bulky for use in much smaller strike aircraft. However in Operation *Shoe Horn*, electronic counter measure equipment was developed to fit into the tiny A-4 Skyhawks and the other strike aircraft used by the Navy. This included chaff dispensers used to disrupt radar coverage. The Navy had also backed the development of the *Shrike* missile with a guidance system that could home on to the SA-2's radar. Once launched the *Shrike* would home in on and destroy the missile system's radar, which was normally housed in a trailer to aid mobility. The obvious Vietnamese response to this was to turn off the radar. However, the attacking aircraft had thus suppressed the defences long enough for the strike aircraft to carry out their mission. All major strikes on the North were accompanied by *Iron Hand* aircraft, briefed to either destroy or suppress the surface-to-air

By Vietnam standards, the Douglas Skywarrior possessed a somewhat mediocre performance as an attack bomber. However, both the USAF and the US Navy employed as an ECM aircraft as the EB-66 and the EA-3B respectively. This example is an EA-3B from VQ-1, landing aboard USS Hancock. Note the belly pack containing the ECM intelligence and jamming equipment. (US Navy)

missiles for long enough to allow the main strike force through to the intended target.

The number of aircraft lost to SA-2s was never more than a small proportion of the total numbers lost, but the very existence of the missile threat forced the American commanders to change their tactics. Operating procedures were revised from what were thought of as the optimum, to those necessary to minimise the missile danger. Large numbers of aircraft were also diverted from the main strike forces into the *Iron Hand* mission to attempt to suppress the missiles.

The preferred height for operating the strike forces over North Vietnam was over 20,000 feet, above the effective range of most of the *Flak*. Since this was also the most effective height for the SA-2s the operating height was forced down to around 12,000-15,000 feet. This was a compromise, for the missiles were still effective at this height but the aircraft were above the range of most of the light anti-aircraft guns.

The Americans also used several specialist aircraft in an attempt to defeat the Vietnamese air defence system. In 1965 the Air Force used EB-66Cs to accompany the strike forces into North Vietnam. These were equipped with the electronic means of detecting and analysing any radars being used by the North Vietnamese, both the long range detection radar and the shorter range missile homing radars. Once these radars had been located, the EB-66Cs could jam them. The voice link between the North Vietnamese ground controllers and the Vietnamese MiGs was also vulnerable to jamming. Large and relatively slow aircraft, the EB-66Cs could not penetrate into the most heavily defended areas of the North, but orbited as close to the target areas as possible to protect the strike aircraft.

At the start of *Rolling Thunder* the Navy found itself without an equivalent to the EB-66 other than the four-seat version of the A-1 Skyraider, the EA-1F. This was an obsolescent propeller driven aircraft, but was the only type available to provide ECM escort for Naval strike aircraft. The Marine Corps had adapted the first jet aircraft to enter service with the Navy in 1950, the F-3, to provide themselves with a radar jamming (ECM) aircraft. These elderly aircraft, known as the EF-10B, proved effective and were in demand from the Navy and Air Force before adequate numbers of their own ECM aircraft became available. The Marines had ten EF-10Bs, stationed at Da Nang, where they remained in service until 1969.

It had been part of the original plan that the *Rolling Thunder* raids should move slowly North and East to increase the pressure on North Vietnam. It was also part of the original intention that there should be bombing halts or pauses to allow the North Vietnamese to come to terms with the Americans. Thus they were attempting to use a 'carrot and stick' approach on the North Vietnamese. The bombing was the 'stick' and the bombing halts were the 'carrot'. The halt in the bombing would be continued if the North Vietnamese reached an acceptable agreement with the Americans. Over the three and a half years of the bombing there were many bombing halts, ranging from 24 hours to 36 days. Of all the American strategies in Vietnam the use of the bombing pause, as an aid to diplomacy, was one of the weakest. The North Vietnamese leadership never showed the least interest in reaching an agreement to stop a resumption of the bombing during the course of *Rolling Thunder*. They were never prepared to change their policy in the South.

USAF F-4C Phantoms en route for the North. The standard grey colour scheme would not last long. By late 1965 most USAF and Marine combat aircraft would be re-painted in camouflage colours.

The first bombing halt was started on 12th May 1965 and lasted until 18th May, but the North Vietnamese ignored American diplomatic moves and refused to move from their original negotiating position. The American ambassador in Russia, Foy Kohler, asked the Russians to pass a message to the North Vietnamese but this was refused. A hand delivered message to the North Vietnamese embassy in Moscow was returned unopened. The North Vietnamese always made use of bombing halts to move as much materials and men as possible while they could do so without fear of attack. They also used the halts to try to repair damaged bridges, roads and railway lines.

After the resumption of operations on 18th May other targets in the North were released for bombing during the following months. These included targets along the northwest rail line between Hanoi and China. The first North Vietnamese MiGs shot down over the North occurred on 17th June, when two Navy F-4B crews from the carrier *Midway* were acting as fighter escort for yet another strike against the Than Hoa bridge, detected four MiG-17s heading towards the strike force.

The Phantoms closed to visual range, as the Rules of Engagement stipulated, then both aircraft fired AIM-7 *Sparrow* missiles. Two MiGs were destroyed, the first by Commander Louis C Page and his radio operator Lieutenant John C Smith. The second was credited to Lieutenants Jack E Bateson and Robert B Doremus.

The first MiGs destroyed by the U.S. Air Force were shot down on 10th July. A pattern had developed when North Vietnamese aircraft intercepted American strike forces and now the Air Force attempted to exploit this pattern to their own advantage. The MiGs habitually waited until late in the course of an American strike, attempting to catch the strike aircraft and their fighter cover low on fuel as they left the target area. On 10th July four F-4Cs, from the 45th Tactical Fighter Squadron stationed at Ubon in Thailand, entered North Vietnam fifteen minutes behind the main strike force. These Phantoms flew the same routes and speed as the big F-105 fighter-bombers, trying to appear on the Vietnamese radar screens as bomb carrying strike aircraft rather than fighters. The flight of F-4s was attacked by four MiG-17s of which two were shot down by *Sidewinder* missiles. The successful American crews were Captains Tom S Roberts and Ron C. Anderson in one F-4 and Captains Ken E Holcombe and Arthur C Clark in the other. At this time the U.S. Air Force classed both of the crew members of the F-4 as pilots. Later, the 'back-seat' man was classified as Weapons System Officer, or 'WISO'.

After the loss of the first American aircraft to North Vietnamese MiGs in April the EC-121 Airborne Early Warning aircraft was introduced into the Tan Son Nhut air base in South Vietnam. This was a large four-engined aircraft, developed from the Lockheed Constellation airliner. It was originally designed to provide early warning to the continental United States and carried a large long-range radar. By circling over the Gulf of Tonkin and over Laos it could give radar coverage over North Vietnam, although coverage at low level was restricted. The purpose of this was primarily to give warning to the American aircraft operating over the North of the activities of the North Vietnamese fighter aircraft. At this early stage in the war warnings to American strike aircraft were given using a colour

The first MiG killers. Cdr Louis C. Page Jr and Lt John Smith flying a VF-21 Phantom, destroyed a MiG-17, using a Sparrow missile. They were operating from the carrier USS Midway.
(US Navy)

code. A yellow warning meant that there were Vietnamese fighter aircraft airborne and a red warning meant that the MiGs were approaching the American aircraft.

During 1965 Task Force 77 maintained two or three aircraft carriers at Yankee station in the Gulf of Tonkin. This formed the basis of their operations in the bombing campaign over the North, although some Navy aircraft operated from the Marine airfield at Da Nang. The carriers based on the West coast of America or Hawaii were used in cruises of up to six months.

Squadrons attached to a Carrier Air Wing trained together at the naval base NAS Fallon in Nevada and were then embarked as the carrier left for Vietnam. When the carrier joined Task Force 77 off Vietnam it would usually be assigned initially to *Dixie Station*, for a working up period in the less demanding air space over South Vietnam, before heading north. When it joined *Yankee Station* for operations over the North it was theoretically placed 'on line' for periods of about thirty days, but longer periods were known to occur. Between periods spent on line the carriers moved back to Subic Bay in the Phillipines or to Hong Kong for periods of rest and relaxation. While it was 'on line', it was involved in launching and recovering aircraft for up to 24 hours a day, although in practice twelve to fourteen was the norm. When operating their aircraft at full stretch carriers would use their full stock of munitions in only a few days, when they would withdraw for re-supply at sea by the support ships of Task Force 73.

The intensive use of the carriers in this way meant that the Navy was forced to transfer aircraft carriers from the Atlantic Fleet to the Pacific Fleet to make up the numbers needed. The four carriers of the Western Pacific Fleet were joined by the *Independence*, which first went into action from *Dixie Station* on 27th June 1965 before transferring to *Yankee Station* on 2nd July. Operations from the carriers were basically of two types, cyclic operations or maximum effort strikes, which became known as *Alpha Strikes*. Cyclic operations were the day-to-day missions, mainly armed reconnaissance sorties involving small numbers of aircraft or small scale raids against named targets. Most bombing strikes during 1965 were carried out by A-4 Skyhawks or A-1 Skyraiders. Besides strike missions, the carriers also launched fighter aircraft to cover the strike aircraft from the Vietnamese MiGs (*MiGCAP*) and other fighter aircraft to cover the carriers from possible attack (*BaRCAP*). Other carrier aircraft carried out photographic reconnaissance, *Iron Hand* defence suppression, electronic countermeasures, aerial refuelling and helicopter rescue missions.

The maximum effort *Alpha Strikes* involved one or more of the carriers mounting a maximum effort against one target. Targets for cyclic operations were usually selected by the Naval commanders on the spot, from the list of targets or areas for armed reconnaissance available to them. Targets for *Alpha Strikes* however were usually decided in Washington. When a new target was added to the list of *Rolling Thunder* targets a maximum effort strike could be mounted against it, if the importance of the target justified it. It was possible for the carriers to mount up to three *Alpha Strikes* a day with around an hour between the return of one strike and the launch of the next.

Thirsty work. A flight of F-105D Thunderchiefs rendezvous with a KC-135 tanker en route to North Vietnam in late 1965. The big Thud was powered by a single Pratt and Whitney J-75 turbojet that drank fuel at an alarming rate, particularly on full afterburner. When chased by MiGs, pilots frequently dropped to tree-top height, hit the 'burner and 'came out of the North with the speed of light'. (USAF)

In 1965 America had available sixteen attack carriers and ten anti-submarine carriers. Some anti-submarine carriers operated off Vietnam as limited attack carriers on occasions. These carriers were stationed all over the world and a certain number were undergoing refit at any one time. The main types were the *Essex* and *Midway* classes dating from the Second World War and just post-war, and the *Forrestal* and improved *Forrestal* classes. The *Essex* class had a standard displacement of around 33,000 tons and the *Forrestal* class a displacement of 63,000 tons. There was also one example of the *Enterprise* class nuclear powered carrier with a standard displacement of 75,000 tons.

Both these major classes of carriers operated around seventy aircraft, but the *Essex* class tended to operate lighter and smaller types of aircraft. The smaller carriers operated F-8 Crusaders as fighter aircraft while larger carriers flew F-4 Phantoms. The standard strike aircraft on the *Essex* type carriers were A-4s and A-1s, the larger carriers employing A-4s and A-6 Intruders in the strike rôle. The photo reconnaissance rôle was carried out on the *Forrestal* class by the A-5 Vigilante - the largest combat aircraft to be used aboard American, or indeed any, carriers - and on the *Essex* class by the RF-8s. The larger of these ships carried a crew of over four thousand men and have often been compared to small floating towns with their own bakeries, laundries, hospitals, canteens and churches. When the carriers were 'on line' and their aircraft were being operated to the maximum, the whole organisation of the ship was working 24 hours a day to keep the aircraft flying.

The aircraft made up the Carrier Air Wing comprised two fighter squadrons (VF numbers), Two light attack squadrons (VA numbers) and one medium attack squadron. There were also detachments of support aircraft in less than squadron strength. These included photo reconnaissance, ECM, tankers and AEW aircraft in addition to helicopters.

During 1965, as the amount of bombing carried out over the North increased, the Air Force increased the numbers of squadrons available. By the end of the year the USAF had eighteen squadrons of jet fighters for use in *Rolling Thunder*, the majority of bombs delivered over the North being carried by the two F-105 Thunderchief wings in Thailand. The 333rd, 354th and the 334th Tactical Fighter Squadrons formed the 355th Tactical Fighter Wing at Takhli airbase in Thailand, while the 388th Wing at Korat was made up of the 421st and 469th Tactical Fighter Squadrons. There were six squadrons of F-4C Phantoms. Two were stationed Ubon in Thailand, the 433rd and 497th Tactical Fighter Squadrons, while another was based at Da Nang and three more at Cam Ranh Bay in South Vietnam. The F-4s were dual rôle aircraft but, at this early stage of the campaign, they were used primarily as bombing aircraft. However, the increased use of MiGs by the North forced their use as fighter escorts, usually for F-105s. Over South Vietnam, with the greatly reduced chance of encountering any of the North's MiGs, the F-4s were normally used as fighter-bombers.

There were four squadrons of F-100 Super Sabres, one squadron of F-5 Freedom Fighters and one squadron of B-57s (a variant of the English Electric Canberra, licence-built by Martin) stationed in South Vietnam. There was also one

When not involved with Rolling Thunder missions, Navy fighter-bombers were on call for the 'in-country' war, flying close support missions within South Vietnam. Here an F-4 of VF-21, operating from USS Midway, releases its load of iron bombs on a VC position, 24th October 1965. (National Archives)

squadron of F-102 Delta Dagger interceptors broken down into detachments stationed in Thailand and South Vietnam to guard against the possibility of an air attack from the North. As the bombing campaign developed, the North Vietnamese strengthened their defences. It was soon discovered that the F-100s and B-57s were too slow and the F-5s and F-104 Starfighters (when they were introduced) were too short-ranged to be used effectively over the North. Thus F-105s and F-4s became the main Air Force aircraft to be used over North Vietnam.

After their initial successes against American strike aircraft in the early part of the year, the North Vietnamese Air Force began to come under increasing pressure from American fighters. By late summer they had lost six MiGs to American aircraft. The North Vietnamese had been forced to create their air defence system practically from scratch, with massive aid from the Russians and Chinese. They simply did not have the experienced pilots, radar operators or GCI (ground controlled intercept) controllers to make the system work under the intensity of the American attack. In August 1965 the North Vietnamese decided to withdraw most of their air force into Southern China to carry out an intensive training campaign to make the system work, for many technicians and pilots had very little experience or technical education.

American pilots often complained that they were forced to habitually use 'stereotyped tactics'. To some extent this was forced on them by the weather, which tended to be very cloudy especially during the northeast monsoon. The best flying weather was normally late morning or early afternoon, when most of the raids over North Vietnam took place. The political restrictions and the Rules of Engagement forced the American crews to use certain routes for entry into Vietnamese air space. Sometimes even the direction of attack was specified for a target by the political leadership in Washington. Usually this was to reduce the possibility of civilian casualties but the Vietnamese were quick to capitalise on any predictability in American tactics. The anti-aircraft guns used by the North were easily moved and re-positioned to cover expected routes and targets. The way that new targets were released piecemeal by the political leadership in Washington meant that, when a new target or new set of targets was bombed, the Northern leadership could expect the same target or types of target to continue to be attacked for the succeeding few weeks. This gave them the chance to concentrate their defences on the predicted targets and routes.

Anti-aircraft guns claimed most of the American aircraft losses, even though most American jets were capable of 600 mph. It had originally been thought that this speed would give some immunity from anti-aircraft guns. However, when the

The Douglas Skyraider was one of the unsung heroes of the Vietnam war. While it lacked the glamour of the fast jets, its enormous bomb load and impressive loiter time made it ideal both close support work, carrying out attacks with a precision that the 'fast movers' were seldom able to achieve. Fondly nicknamed 'Sandy', it also provided cover and close support for helicopter rescue sorties. This aircraft, an A-1H from VA-115, served aboard the USS Kitty Hawk in 1965/66.
(via author)

enemy could predict routes and targets, defences could be concentrated to give very large volumes of fire. The usual way of attacking a target was to dive towards the target from 12,000 to 15,000 feet and to release the bombs at 3,000 to 4,000 feet before pulling away out of the dive. Many heavy guns were radar directed and very accurate but the lighter guns were trained by hand. It was not a question of the guns being aimed at the aircraft or using deflection to be aimed at where the aircraft would be when the shell reached it. If the attack routes could be predicted or the aircraft could be seen to be starting their dive towards the target the guns simply fired into a predetermined block of airspace that the aircraft would have to fly through to reach the target. The aircraft then had to pass through this section of airspace filled with anti-aircraft fire to have any chance of reaching the target. John B Nichols, who flew 350 missions over the North for the U.S. Navy, wrote:

> "Gunners didn't have to track a jet. All they had to do was draw a straight line between the airplane's roll-in point and its target, then fill that portion of the sky with as much steel as possible. Regardless of its speed, the jet had to fly through that box. At that point probability theory takes over. It becomes a crapshoot."[4.]

The first major strike against an industrial target came late in December 1965. Until then most of the targets had been either military, (barracks and storage depots) the transportation system or the air defence system. President Johnson decided to call a bombing halt over Christmas 1965 lasting into the new year. However, it was thought that a demonstration of the fact that America could increase the pressure of the bombing still further would influence the North Vietnamese to use the bombing halt to reach an agreement.

The target chosen for this demonstration was the thermal power station at Uong Bi, which was believed to produce twenty-five per cent of the North's electrical power. It was situated to the north of Haiphong, across the Red River estuary, in Route Package 6B controlled by the Navy. In late December Task Force 77 had three aircraft carriers, *Enterprise*, *Kitty Hawk* and *Ticonderoga*, on *Yankee Station*. On 22nd December, 110 aircraft from the three carriers attacked the power station from three different directions at thirty minute intervals, losing two A-4Cs from the *Enterprise* to *Flak* in the first wave of aircraft. The power station was reported as having been left in flames and covered in oily black smoke. It was indeed substantially damaged and produced no electrical power for several months thereafter.

After the original isolated raids over the North in March 1965 the total of Navy and Air Force *Rolling Thunder* sorties had been 1,500 in April, this increasing to 4,000 in October. The sortie rate then declined slightly due to the northeast monsoon that had caused a deterioration in flying conditions. The Navy aircraft carriers had flown more than 56,000 sorties over North and South Vietnam, Cambodia and Laos during 1965, while the Air Force had dropped a considerable tonnage of bombs during 10,570 sorties over North Vietnam. The Air force had also been dropping propaganda leaflets since April 1965, using C-130 cargo aircraft. By the end of the year hundreds of millions of leaflets had been dropped over the North. However, despite the increasing rate of the bombing during 1965, the North Vietnamese had shown no indication that they were willing to change their policy towards the war in the South.

On 24th December 1965 President Johnson ordered a cease-fire in the bombing for the Christmas period, this extending into a 37-day bombing pause. Secretary of State Dean Rusk said that he hoped that peace negotiations could take place if the North Vietnamese did not exploit the situation. North Vietnam refused to acknowledge the American efforts and did not see the bombing halt as any kind of concession by America.

FOOTNOTES

1. Cagel, Malcolm W *Task Force 77 In Action Off Vietnam*, The Navy Review, United States Naval Institute, Anapolis, 1972, page 74.
2. Momyer, General W W *Air Power in Three Wars*, U.S. Government Printing Office, Washington D C 1978, page 119.
3. Westmoreland, William C *A Soldier Reports*, Doubleday and Co. New York, 1976, page 85.
4   Nichols. John B and Tillman, Barrett, *On Yankee Station*, Airlife Publications Ltd. England, 1987, page 50.

Chapter Three
1966: MiGs, SAMs and Flak

The North Vietnamese did not attempt to enter negotiations with the Americans during the Christmas truce. They merely used the bombing pause to rebuild as much of their transport system as possible and many bridges that had been destroyed were again carrying traffic. The North Vietnamese knew that the bombing halt was not likely to last; thus they attempted to rush as many supplies to the South as possible while it was in force. American reconnaissance aircraft reported that the roads were crowded day and night with trucks rather than just at night, as before. The North's air defence system was also strengthened during this period with new radars being installed and 29 new missile sites being constructed. Writing in The Naval Review in 1972 Malcolm W Cagel stated concerning the bombing halt,

"Photographic reconnaissance during the pause showed the enemy reconstructing and improving his roads and bridges, improving and increasing the air defence of important areas, digging his POL system underground and into caves, dispersing his military support base, and pushing large numbers of loaded trucks towards the DMZ and the infiltration routes which fed the Ho Chi Minh trail."[1.]

The Americans attempted to negotiate with the North Vietnamese through the United Nations and by using diplomats from several different countries. The Vietnamese however stated flatly that they would not be bound by any resolutions of the United Nations and would not give up their support for the war in the South. President Johnson was now under pressure from some sections of the American public, from many countries at the United Nations and from America's allies in NATO not to resume the bombing. However, the fighting in the South was continuing unabated. President Johnson now faced the dilemma of American troops being killed in the South with weapons and

Any time, any weather. The Grumman A-6A Inruder looked a little less than sleek, but its on-board avionics enabled it to make pin-point attacks by day and night and in all weather conditions. It was later developed for use in Iron Hand missions and was responsible for mining the rivers and estuaries, paralyzing North Vietnam's sea traffic. This aircraft is from VA-65, aboard USS Independence.

(US Navy)

ammunition that were being transported down from the North with impunity while the bombing pause continued.

Bombing was resumed on 31st January 1966 with *Rolling Thunder 48*. The attacks were again restricted to the southern part of North Vietnam and concentrated on the transport system. Besides being restricted in area *Rolling Thunder 48* was also limited to 300 sorties a day for both the Navy and the Air Force. The weather during the early months of 1966 was particularly bad over the North, which also restricted the number of sorties flown. The northeast monsoon created poor visibility, low cloud and heavy rain. Haze and cloud often completely covered the ground up to 14,000 feet. Under these conditions, 'it can be understood why bombing aircraft usually could locate their targets over North Vietnam less than one-third-of the time'.[2] Although they were only operating in the Southern part of North Vietnam where the air defences were weaker than the Hanoi area both the Air Force and the Navy continued to suffer casualties, the Air Force losing one of their EB-66Cs on 25th February 1966.

In March McNamara, the Secretary of Defence, stated that American troops in South Vietnam now totalled 215,000 and that further reinforcements were being despatched. President Johnson and President Thieu of South Vietnam had met for a conference in Hawaii on 7th February, when they agreed that the American build up in the South should continue and that the *Rolling Thunder* bombing of the North should also continue.

On 26th March the estuaries of the Song Ca river at Vinh and the Song Giang river were mined to stop the use of these waterways by cargo carrying barges. The mines were dropped by A-6A Intruders operating from the American carriers. The military had always wanted to mine the approaches to Haiphong harbour, through which came 85% of North Vietnam's imports. Johnson never allowed this to take place for fear of the reaction of the Russians and Chinese and thus it was not until 1972 that Haiphong harbour was eventually mined.

As the American commitment of aircraft to the area continued, the status of the Second Air Division was upgraded to become the Seventh Air Force on 1st April 1966, controlling most of the Air Force aircraft based in Thailand and South Vietnam. Previously, The Second Air Division had been under the command of the Thirteenth Air Force in the Philippines. Now however, the Seventh Air Force reported direct to the Pacific command in Hawaii for most things involving the bombing of the North but reported to General Westmoreland for matters involving the war in the South. This division of authority would continue for most of the war. The Commanding Officer of the Second Air Division, Lieutenant General Joseph H. Moore, became the head of the Seventh Air Force, with his headquarters at Tan Son Nhut airfield near Saigon.

Also on 1st April 1966 *Rolling Thunder 50* began. North Vietnam was now completely open to bombing except for the specific exclusion areas around Hanoi, Haiphong and along the Chinese border. Target lists were still provided from Washington but most of the country was now open to armed reconnaissance sorties against the transport system. 1st April was also the date of the changeover of the Route Package system from a 'time share' basis with the Air Force and Navy alternating the packages on a weekly basis, to the permanent division of the

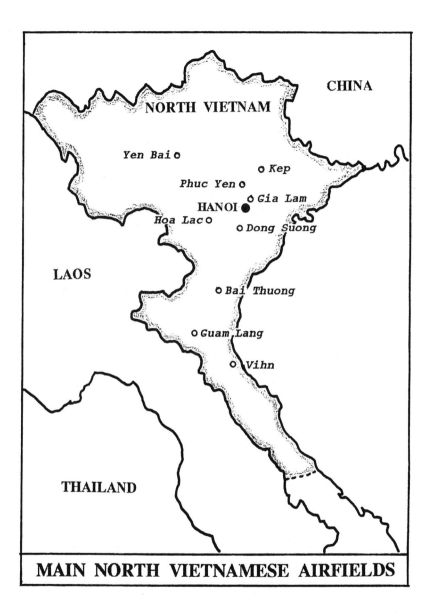

Map 4. The main North Vietnamese airfields
(Peter Edwards RICS and John T. Smith)

packages. The Navy was given Route Packages 2, 3, 4 and 6B, while the Air force concentrated on 1, 5 and 6A. Strikes against targets in RP 1 were carried out by both the Air Force and the Marine Corps aircraft stationed at Da Nang in South Vietnam. The air defences in RP 1 were only relatively weaker than the massive defences around Hanoi and Haiphong.

American pilots, operating from Thailand, were expected to fly 100 missions over the North as their tour of duty before they were transferred out of the war zone. The first missions flown by new pilots were, when possible, in the less dangerous RP 1 to introduce them to combat conditions. The Marine pilots flying in RP 1 were operating from bases close to their targets and their missions were often completed in less than one hour. Occasionally they completed as many as four missions in one day, but the Marine Corps aircrew did not return home after 100 missions. After the division of the Route Packages between the Air Force and Navy there was a reduction in aircraft losses for both services. This was credited to the fact that pilots became more familiar with specific areas of North Vietnam. With pilots flying over the same areas on a day to day basis they came to know them well and any significant changes could be noted and reported. They learned the best directions for attacking and leaving targets and where the heaviest defences were situated.

During April 1966 the position of *Yankee Station* was moved further northwards, closer to the bombing targets. From a position East of Da Nang *Yankee Station* was moved east of Dong Hoi between the coast of Vietnam and Hainan Island (17°30N - 108°30E). The actual position of *Yankee Station* was never more than nominal and the carriers were constantly on the move. At times of major strikes the carriers moved even further north and once in 1972 were within 70 miles of Haiphong. The American ships were constantly tracked by Russian intelligence gathering ships that counted all aircraft launches, attempted to determine the ordnance carried and informed the North Vietnamese accordingly.

The effect of *Rolling Thunder 50* was to release what the military thought of as more significant targets. The rail line and road transport system from Haiphong was dependant on two major bridges, one at Hai Duong, half way to Hanoi, and the

The B-52F of Strategic Air Command was used briefly over the North in 1966, but the risks were high. The aircraft shown here is from the 320th SBW, equipped with underwing racks and carrying out an Arc Light mission over South Vietnam, where it was principally used in tactical operations. (USAF)

other just outside Haiphong. Both these bridges spanned over one thousand feet and crossed the channels that made up the Red River delta. On 13th April the Haiphong bridge was badly damaged by aircraft from the carrier *Ticonderoga* that destroyed five of the bridges 21 spans. Later in the month the Hai Duong bridge was also put out of action by Naval aircraft. The Uong Bi power station had been partially repaired after the December 1965 raid and this was again attacked on the night of 18th April by two A-6 Intruders from the carrier *Kitty Hawk*, each carrying thirteen 1,000 lb bombs. All 26 bombs landed in the power station, again putting it out of action. This attack displayed the precision all-weather capabilities of the A-6 in the right circumstances. The port at Cam Pha North of Haiphong, normally used for exporting coal, was also attacked within ninety minutes of it being added to the list of targets.

The huge B-52s, based on Guam in the Pacific, were used over North Vietnam for the first time on 11th April. They had operated over South Vietnam before, but their first target over the North was the Mu Gia pass, the main crossing point over the mountains between Laos and North Vietnam. Several passes through the mountains were used to feed supplies into the Ho Chi Minh trail but the Mu Gai pass was most heavily utilised. It was attacked by thirty aircraft dropping 600 tons of bombs on the narrowest part of the pass. The raid cost $21,000,000 and reports showed that the pass had been closed. However only two days later trucks were again running through the pass, requiring further strikes by the fighter-bombers. B-52s were used only sparingly over the North during *Rolling Thunder* and then only over the southern part of North Vietnam to avoid the heaviest air defences. The destruction of a B-52 by the North Vietnamese would have been a propaganda victory for them and sometimes they moved small numbers of SA-2s to the southern part of North Vietnam in an attempt to shoot one down. None were lost until the *Linebacker II* raids in 1972.

The MiG-21 was first introduced into combat by the North Vietnamese in March 1966. These were supplied by the Russians, who were also training the North Vietnamese pilots in Russia to fly the new fighter. The early model MiG-21s were clear-weather, short-ranged interceptors, but were manoeuvrable and much faster than the MiG-17s already in service. The quantity of MIG-21s supplied at this stage of the war was never very large but, with their cannon armament and Russian *Atoll* missiles, they posed a severe threat to the American strike forces. The first MIG-21 was seen over the North on 23rd April and the first combat took place on 26th when two MiGs attacked two F-4C Phantoms that were covering an EB-66 near Hanoi.

F-4C Phantoms used by the Air Force at this stage of the war had no cannon armament and their *Sparrow* and *Sidewinder* missiles had a minimum range. Thus they were at a disadvantage in close combat with cannon-armed fighters. One Phantom flown by Major Paul T Gilmore and Lieutenant William T Smith fired three *Sidewinders* at one MiG, the pilot was seen to eject and the aircraft exploded. A *Sidewinder* was also fired at another MiG-21 but the range was too short and the missile failed to guide.

The MiGs continued to oppose the American strike forces when they thought they had the advantage. June was especially active for the MiGs with twelve combats taking place over the North. During these engagements three MiG-17s were shot down by the Navy and one more was destroyed by an Air Force F-105D.

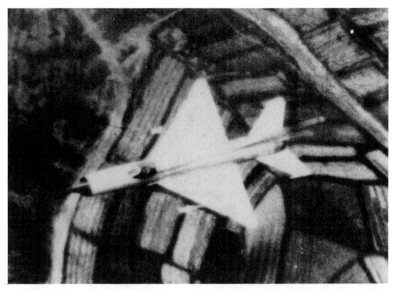

A rare photo of a NVAF MiG-21 in combat. An Atoll heat-seeking missile can be seen beneath each wing. The North Vietnamese operated only a small number of this type, but its performance and manouevreability made it a dangerous opponent, particularly when using 'hit and run' tactics against F-105 strikes. (National Archives)

During May and June the attack on the transport system continued. There were specific targets that were cleared for attack but most of the sorties continued to be armed reconnaissance sorties against roads, railways and river transport. During this period the carriers *Ranger*, *Hancock* and *Kitty Hawk* were on station in the Gulf of Tonkin.

As the air war against North Vietnam continued to escalate, a rising number of shortages now became apparent; ships, aircraft, munitions and pilots were in short supply. Both the Navy and Air Force found themselves with less pilots than required. It takes at least eighteen months to train a combat pilot to the level of being ready for war conditions. It cost $100,000 to train a Navy pilot and $75,000 to train an Air Force pilot and both services were forced to train the extra pilots they needed. This became a booming time for civil aviation, since to avoid the war numbers of pilots from both services left for well-paid jobs with the air lines. It was estimated that the Navy was short of 1,660 pilots and the Marine Corps 600 pilots. Navy pilots could fly up to thirty combat sorties a month over the North, although fifteen to twenty was a more common figure. While the Air Force tour of duty was one hundred missions, Navy pilots flew for the length of time the aircraft carrier cruise lasted. This was normally five to nine months with short periods 'off line'. The first Navy pilots to finish a cruise in 1965 were expected, because of the shortages, to start a second cruise after only three months back in the United States. However it was finally decided that pilots should not be expected to take part in more than two cruises in a fourteen-month period. One Navy pilot, Denis Weichman, completed five cruises and 625 missions over North Vietnam during the full course of the war to 1972.

The Air Force decided that it would not force pilots to complete more than one tour of 100 missions until all its pilots had completed one tour, although they could volunteer. This was very fair but it did make the shortage of pilots worse. Steve Ritchie was the leading Air Force fighter pilot, with the destruction of five MiGs to his credit. He wrote:

"Air Force policy during the war meant that no-one would be required to serve twice until everyone had been once. As a result, many who had never flown fighters or even knew the tactical mission, and many who had not flown for years, were suddenly rushed through five to six months of combat crew training and sent to South-east Asia. Quite often, on account of their rank, these men found themselves in combat leadership roles for which they were unqualified." [3.]

The tempo of the bombing increased and the pressure on the pilots built up. The increasing numbers of casualties and prisoners in the hands of the North Vietnamese brought on a slump in the morale of some Navy and Air Force pilots. The legendary test pilot Chuck Yeager described how he was asked by General Hunter Harris, who was Chief of the Pacific Air Forces in Hawaii, to visit the fighter wings in South East Asia to try to improve the commitment of some pilots. He quotes General Harris as saying:

"I want you to give a talk to each of our fighter wings. We're having trouble getting those men to do any good over there. They're releasing their bombs too high and pulling out, missing a target by five miles." [4.]

As the political opposition to the war continued to build up back

'Last of the Gunfighters'. The F-8 Crusader was the standard carrier-borne fighter until supplemented by the Phantom. Its on-board 20mm cannon armament gave it the capability to fight MiGs in a way that the F-4s were denied, close-in dogfighting. Here, an F-8D of VF-111, 'The Sundowners' streams wing-tip vortices in a high-G pull-out during a strike on the North. (National Archives)

in the United States, many pilots became disillusioned with the war. The Rules of Engagement were bitterly resented by the pilots and many books written after the war by pilots stress the hatred of the RoEs. The pilots seem to have thought of themselves as trying to fight with one arm tied behind their backs. Rightly or wrongly the feeling among the pilots was that the Rules of Engagement were responsible for many deaths and for many pilots being captured. This should be viewed against the backdrop of declining support for the war among the civilian population in America. Although morale may have declined, the American pilots - who were a professional all-volunteer force - maintained the bombing until it was stopped by a political decision in 1968.

The massive amounts of munitions being dropped on Laos, Cambodia, South Vietnam besides North Vietnam in 1966 also created a shortage of bombs. McNamara denied that there was any bomb shortage and there was considerable controversy in the U.S. media concerning this. The American government had sold thousands of old bombs as scrap to the West Germans in the early 1960s. The selling price had been $1.70 each, but now they were being forced to buy them back for $21.00 each. Despite denials, aircraft were now being sent on missions with less than the ideal load of weapons. One reporter saw an F-100 Super Sabre take off from a base in South Vietnam with a bomb on one wing and a block of concrete on the other to balance the load. Pilots were expected to risk their lives carrying nominal bomb loads. One Naval pilot Donald D Smith wrote:

> "I can vividly remember reading the paper, and Defence Secretary McNamara saying there 'is no bomb shortage, there are plenty of bombs.' At the time, I literally had been catapulted off the front end (of an aircraft carrier) with a single World War II 500-pounder on the centre line. In all honesty that didn't happen very often, but we did drop a lot of the World War II inventory until it ran out." [5.]

The bomb shortage was over by the end of 1966 although some shortages occurred again in 1968.

The continuing shortage of aircraft carriers put continued pressure on the carriers that were available and carriers were still being transferred from the Atlantic fleet. The carrier *Midway* made one cruise to Vietnam in 1965 and was then put into dock receiving a major refit until 1970. McNamara said that the Navy needed a force of fifteen attack aircraft carriers on active service, but this was never achieved. It continued to be the stated aim of the navy during the Reagan years, but seems to have been finally abandoned with the thaw in East West relations in 1990.

The command of the Seventh Air Force passed to General William W. Momyer on 1st June 1966. Momyer later complained about the divided nature of the command that he had in Saigon. For raids over the North he was responsible to the Pacific Air Force Commander General Hunter Harris, and later to General John Ryan in Hawaii. For aircraft sorties in South Vietnam he was under the command of General Westmoreland in Saigon. For raids in Laos he was nominally under the command of the American ambassador in Laos. Targets could only be chosen from the list drawn up by Johnson during the Tuesday lunches. Targets could be requested, but these needed the backing of the Pacific Air Force and then the Joint Chiefs of Staff before they were placed in front of the president and his advisers. The B-52 Stratofortress operations were the responsibility of Strategic Air Command even when operating over the North. The availability

The thunder rolled on. The Thai Nguyen rail yards were visited several times by F-105Ds during 1966. This reconnaissance photo taken by an RF-101C Voodoo pilot shows the results. Fifteen wagons wrecked, twelve rail lines cut and a number of large craters, the typical calling card of the F-105. (National Archives)

of air refuelling was often the limiting factor in the size of strike forces during *Rolling Thunder* but the KC-135 tanker aircraft were also under command of Strategic Air Command and remained so. There was liaison between the Navy and the Air Force but although they were both bombing North Vietnam there was no overall commander closer to the fighting than Admiral Sharp in Hawaii. Momyer thought that there should have been one overall commander of all the air assets in the area:

"Airpower has great flexibility to perform many tasks in war, and its ability to respond with varying levels of firepower to a variety of targets has led Army and Navy commanders to seek control of air power as part of their forces. But to give in to these undesirable wishes of surface commanders is to destroy the very thing that gives airpower its strength - the ability to focus quickly upon whatever situation has the most potential for victory or for defeat. Airmen know the centralised control of airpower in a theatre of war can best serve armies and navies: to fragment airpower is to court defeat." [6.]

This is a clear statement of the U.S. Air Force strategic air power doctrine that air power correctly used is uniquely capable of decisive action in war. However, command of *Rolling Thunder* remained divided until the end.

In a major change of policy the Americans started a sustained attack on the North Vietnamese Petrol, Oil and Lubricants (POL) storage system on 29th June 1966. There had been considerable discussion in the American media over the desirability of destroying the North Vietnamese oil stocks since *Rolling Thunder* had begun and the North Vietnamese had put enormous effort into dispersing their stocks throughout the countryside. Since North Vietnam had no oil fields and no refining capability, all their stocks were imported. Most came through Haiphong, which was the only port with bulk handling capabilities, but a small amount came down the rail link with China. It was estimated that 32,000 tons of oil were required to run the North Vietnamese economy each year. The total capacity of the Vietnamese storage system was put at 179,000 metric tons by the American Defence Intelligence Agency. The two oil storage areas at Haiphong were thought to hold 72,000 tons and the Hanoi storage area 34,000 tons. In 1965 the North Vietnamese had imported 170,000 tons of oil so it was believed that the storage system was full to capacity.

As the North Vietnamese slowly built up their regular forces in the South and continued to supply the Viet Cong they became more dependant on the supplies brought down the Ho Chi Minh trail. The amount brought down the trail became dependant on thousands of trucks to move these supplies.

These trucks in turn were dependant on fuel supplies. American pilots had been requesting, from the start of the bombing campaign, permission to bomb the POL targets. On 29th June the Hanoi oil storage was attacked by Thailand-based F-105s of the 355th and 388th Tactical Fighter Wing from Takhli and Korat respectively. The raid was a complete success. The storage was annihilated for the loss of only one aircraft.

Major James H Kasler led sixteen Thunderchiefs from the 355th as part of this strike force. Crossing into Vietnam north of Hanoi, they flew south towards Hanoi on the east side of Thud Ridge. This was a 5,000 high mountain range formed from limestone karst that ran Northwest of Hanoi, ending about 25 miles from Hanoi. The strike aircraft in that area often used the mountains for cover as they were too rough and steep for

Bombing was not the sole task for the F-105s. Here, an F-105D salvoes rockets at a target in North Vietnam.
(USAF)

anti-aircraft guns to be stationed on the sides of the mountains. The height of the range also masked the aircraft, to some extent from the Vietnamese radar, since the strike force hugged the mountainsides. The F-105 Thunderchief had been nicknamed 'Thunderthud', more usually shortened to the very apt 'Thud' and this range of mountains thus became known as Thud Ridge. Later in the war the Vietnamese sited guns on Thud Ridge using helicopters.

After approaching Hanoi from the Northwest along Thud Ridge the strike force had to fly over Hanoi to approach the target from the south. Major Kasler described the reason for this as,

> "The operations order had also directed that all attacks would be executed on a south-to-north heading to preclude tossing a hung up bomb into the city of Hanoi. Approaching from the north, we had to make a 180-degree pop-up manoeuvre to strike the target as ordered. What the attack order meant was that every aircraft would be rolling into the bomb run at approximately the same spot, heading in the same direction. Not too smart from the pilot's viewpoint, but in the interest of protecting civilian populations, such orders were commonplace in Vietnam. Ideally, attacks should be on divergent headings to confuse the gunners and thus prevent them from zeroing in on one spot." [7.]

While the USAF was attacking the storage farms at Hanoi, Navy aircraft attacked Haiphong and Do Son. Twenty-eight aircraft from the carrier *Ranger* attacked Haiphong without loss and aircraft from the *Constellation* attacked Do Son, ten miles

*Over the North, SAMs were becoming an increasing problem.
Avoiding action could be taken if the missile was spotted in time,
otherwise the mach 2.5 rocket could 'take out' aircraft flying at up to
60,000 feet. This launch was recorded by the pilot of an RF-101
Voodoo near Hanoi. (USAF)*

southeast of Haiphong on the same peninsula of land. The
strikes were successful and the storage facilities were destroyed.
More than 50% of North Vietnam's fuel storage had been
destroyed in one day for the loss of only one aircraft. Major Fred
L Tacey flying, an F-105, shot down a MiG-17 using the F-105s
20 mm cannon during the raids on the 29th June. The attacks
on the POL targets continued during July and all the major
above-ground tanks were struck. No Soviet tankers entered
Haiphong during July and, when they subsequently began
supplying fuel again, they did so 55 gallon tanks. Foreign ships
in Haiphong were still inviolate, but Vietnamese lighters
carrying fuel ashore in tanks, after the pumping and storage
facilities had been destroyed, had no such immunity. These
lighters were moored next to foreign ships during the day and
at night attempted to work during the hours of darkness, but
four of the ten available barges were sunk during night attacks.

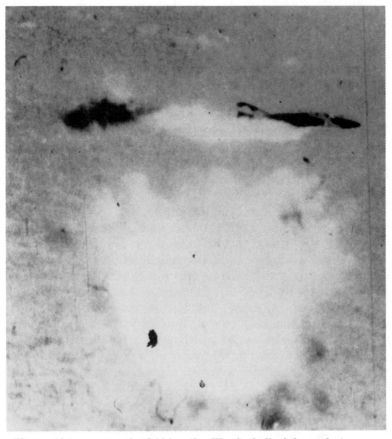

The terrifying power of a SAM strike. The fireball of the explosion can be seen below this RF-4D, instantly on fire. For this crew, if they survived, the war was over. (National Archives)

Rolling Thunder 51 commenced early in July. The monthly total of sorties was increased from 8,100 to 10,100 with the oil targets given priority. The use of a carrier at *Dixie Station* ceased in August since more airbases had been constructed in South Vietnam for the aircraft operating in the South. The carrier moved to *Yankee Station,* ensuring that three or four carriers were now on *Yankee Station* at all times. When it became obvious that the oil system had been targeted, the Vietnamese concentrated the mobile parts of their air defence system around these targets. The Americans lost 43 aircraft during July, the highest monthly total since the start of *Rolling Thunder*. North Vietnam had long expected an attack on their oil storage system and considerable effort had gone into the construction of small underground storage tanks. These were dispersed throughout the country along the main routes where it was thought they would be needed. It was an inefficient way of storing oil compared with the large over-ground tanks, but the North Vietnamese had built enough of these to maintain their needs. Sometimes the new Russian 55 gallon fuel tanks were simply left at the side of the road in small amounts, too small to be worth attacking.

By the end of August practically all of North Vietnam's pre-war over-ground large scale oil storage facilities had been destroyed but the dispersed system and the underground facilities still contained large amounts of oil. At the start of the campaign against the POL targets the North Vietnamese had over five years worth of oil in storage. Although much had now been destroyed, American intelligence estimated that there were still sixty thousand tons of oil in North Vietnam at the end of 1966. It was also estimated that the trucks on the Ho Chi Minh trail only needed 1,600 tons of oil a year to keep running. It was obvious that the campaign against the POL system had failed.

The command and control of the strike aircraft over North Vietnam was made possible through the establishment of a Positive Identified Radar Advisory Zone (PIRAZ) which was based on a series of American radars. An American cruiser, working under the code-name *Red Crown*, was stationed in the Gulf of Tonkin off Haiphong, its radar scanning up the Red River valley. The information from *Red Crown* was passed to the Combat Information Centre on board a carrier at *Yankee Station*, which controlled the aircraft. The USAF operated a Lockheed EC-121 airborne command and control centre over either the Gulf or Laos, operating under the code-name *Big Eye* and then later *College Eye*. There were also ground based radars in Northern Thailand and at Dong Ha in Northern South Vietnam. Raids were under the command of the Mission Commander who was flying as part of, and leading, the strike.

USS Kitty Hawk (CVA-63) left Yankee Station on 13th June 1966 and returned on 17th November 1966, carrying Phantoms, Skyhawks, Vigilantes and Skywarriors. During its three cruises during Rolling Thunder, Phantom crews shot down four North Vietnamese aircraft, but combat losses amounted to 38 aircraft over the North and three more over Laos. Here, the forward catapult hurls an A-3B Sywarrior off the bows. (National Archives)

The information from the radar stations was only advisory and only the Mission Commander could cancel a strike.

During 1966 the North Vietnamese continued to increase their air defence network. At the start of the year they had approximately two thousand anti-aircraft guns placed around four hundred sites. Fifty-six missile sites had also been located and photographed by reconnaissance aircraft, but some were inactive. By the end of 1966 the Vietnamese had increased these totals to around 4,400 guns plus twenty to twenty-five active missile battalions distributed around 150 missile sites. Admiral Sharp, the American commander in the Pacific, described the Vietnamese defences in 1966 by saying:

"Throughout 1966 the proliferation of SAM sites continued, and continuous SAM coverage extended from Yen Bai to Haiphong in the North to about Ha Tinh in the South....Observed expenditures in 1966 totalled almost nine times the number of SAM's expended in 1965 and the effectiveness statistically of the SAM defences dropped to an average of about 33 missiles required per aircraft shot down....The total number of radar sites at the end of 1966 numbered over 100, consisted of a well balanced inventory of early warning, GCI, AAA fire control, and SAM associated equipment." [8.]

American pilots who had flown over Germany in the Second World War compared the defences around Hanoi with those in the Ruhr in Germany. Although German defences were spread over a considerably larger area, the North Vietnamese anti-aircraft defences, concentrated in a relatively small area around Hanoi, have been called the heaviest ever encountered by pilots anywhere.

The North Vietnamese Air Force also continued to expand. During the second half the year, under pressure from the American raids, North Vietnamese MiGs were attacking American strike aircraft on average twelve times a month. By the end of the year eleven American aircraft had been shot down by MiG pilots. The North Vietnamese aircraft ground controllers had now become experienced in the understanding of American tactics, types of aircraft, routes into and out of North Vietnam and the types of target attacked. The MiG-17s were normally kept at low level, where their lack of speed was less marked and the American radar coverage was poor. They were then directed onto the American strike aircraft from astern and below. The MiG-17s were more manoeuvrable than the F-105s and the Phantoms and used this advantage to good effect. The first Phantom shot down in air-to-air combat was lost to three MiG-17s on 21st September. This was an F-4C of the 433rd Tactical Fighter Squadron attached to the 8th Tactical Fighter Wing. Although the MiG pilots clearly wanted to shoot American aircraft down, their main tactic was to disrupt the raids by forcing the strike aircraft to jettison their bombs to escape. During late 1966, these tactics were forcing many strike aircraft to drop their ordnance and turn back. The MiG-21s were used at higher altitude, where they were nearly as fast as the F-4s and considerably more manoeuvrable. By the end of 1966 The North Vietnamese Air Force was estimated to number about 70 aircraft, fifteen MiG-21s and 55 MiG-17s. They were also expanding the airfields capable of taking jet aircraft (Phuc Yen and Kep were the main bases) with revetments, bunkered fuel storage and were also building new airfields. The airfields used by MiGs were not yet on the list of targets that could be attacked and American fighter pilots were forced to watch the MiGs taking off and landing from Phuc Yen with impunity.

Out of reach. For several years the fighter bases operating MiGs remained inviolate, in direct contravention of the accepted strategy that dictates that the enemy air force be eliminated immediately. Thus MiGs could be seen on airfields, waiting for the scramble order that would probably lead to the loss of American crews. The anger and frustration felt by American aircrews can readily be understood. Here, a pair of MiG-17s photographed by an RF-101C at Kep airfield remain immune from attack. (National Archives)

As the defence system continued to grow in quality and quantity American strikes began to include less bombing aircraft and an increasing number of support aircraft to counter the anti-aircraft system. Commander John B Nichols describes the make up of a Naval strike as.

"A maximum effort from an *Essex*-class air wing typically involved twenty bombers - sixteen A-4s and four F-8s with two A-4 *Iron Hands* and their Crusader escorts on either side of the strike birds. A two or four-plane *TarCAP* took station on the side most likely to encounter MiGs, while four F-8 flak suppressors flew opposite. A *MiGCAP* section or division brought up the rear. In addition, an EA-1 or EA-3 remained offshore to provide electronic support. a pair of KA-3s, and frequently a section of A-4s with 'buddy packs', also stood by to provide airborne fuel. And two helos awaited at the northern SAR station." [9.]

The make-up of Air Force strikes was much the same. However less than half the aircraft involved were involved in the actual bombing, the rest were countering the defence system.

As the numbers of aircraft shot down by the Vietnamese continued to grow the American forces began to develop a system of combat search and rescue to bring home the aircrew from crashed aircraft. Damaged aircraft were forced down in Laos, Cambodia, South Vietnam, Thailand, the Gulf of Tonkin as well as over North Vietnam. Apart from any humanitarian considerations, aircrew were considerably more valuable than the aircraft they were flying. It takes eighteen months to train even a inexperienced pilot. Although numbers of aircraft shot down were a constant drain on American morale, the knowledge that every effort would be made to bring back shot-down pilots was a comforting thought for the American aircrew. The USAF used HH-3E helicopters stationed in Thailand to rescue aircrew in combat areas including North Vietnam. These 'Jolly Green Giants' were protected and escorted by A-1 Skyraiders - nicknamed 'Sandys' - to suppress the defences in the pick-up areas. The rescue services monitored the strike aircraft radio frequencies and, when any aircraft were lost, the search and rescue services were called in immediately. The HH-3 helicopters could fly at 140 mph and often penetrated deep into North Vietnam. HU-16 amphibian aircraft were used by the Air Force over the Gulf of Tonkin. The US Navy also developed their SAR services for pilots downed over the Gulf. The Gulf of Tonkin was divided into North and South sections, each of which had destroyers covering it. These were equipped with UH-2 helicopters for recovering aircrew from the sea or from North Vietnam. Longer ranged SH-3 Sea King helicopters were also operated from the aircraft carriers at *Yankee Station*.

In September the 8th Tactical Fighter Wing (the Wolf Pack) came under the control of Colonel Robin Olds. During the Second World War Olds had destroyed 24 German aircraft (thirteen plus one damaged air-to-air, while flying P-38s and P-51s with the 434th Fighter Squadron). The 8th were flying F-4Cs and over the next year Olds led his wing on fighter

Colonel Robin Olds (left) proved that experience mattered more than reflexes. His dynamic and fiercely aggressive leadership made the 8th TFW 'Wolf Pack' the most successful fighter unit in southeast Asia.
(USAF)

sweeps and bombing missions over the North. During the *Rolling Thunder* campaign Olds was to become the leading air-to-air pilot, with the destruction of four MiGs over North Vietnam. The 8th was to destroy more MiGs than any other Air Force wing, which led Bob Hope to call it the 'leading MiG parts distributor in Asia'.

The first MiG-21 shot down by a US Navy aircraft was on 9th October 1966 by Commander Richard Bellinger, Commanding Officer of VF-162, from the carrier *Oriskany*. Bellinger had been shot down in July by a MiG-17 using cannon fire and was rescued after ejecting safely into the Gulf. He was leading a flight of four F-8 Crusaders on 9th October, escorting attack aircraft from the carrier *Intrepid*, one of the converted anti-submarine carriers without fighter aircraft of its own. An E-1 naval radar aircraft picked up a flight of MiGs and Bellinger's Crusaders were vectored onto them. The MiG-21s were found at 3,000 feet and Bellinger led the F-8s underneath before climbing from behind to attack. He fired two *Sidewinders* at one MiG and destroyed it.

On 26th October the *Oriskany* suffered an horrific fire shortly after a strike had been cancelled due to bad weather. The munitions had to be removed from the aircraft and returned to the magazines but, during this operation, a magnesium flare ignited and set fire to others causing an enormous blaze. For a time it seemed that the fire would get completely out of control and destroy the vessel but, after several hours, the blaze was brought under control. Over three hundred bombs had been hauled out of the flames and dumped overboard and several aircraft were also damaged and pushed over the side. The flames trapped large numbers of the crew below decks, killing many in their cabins. When the fire was out 44 people were dead including 25 aircrew, while many more were injured. The carrier was pulled off line and managed to reach Subic Bay in the Philippines. It later returned to the west coast of America.

As the conflict developed the USAF and U.S.Navy F-4 Phantom became the primary American air-to-air fighter. It was armed only with missiles and no gun armament, but later models of USAF Phantoms carried gun pods and later still the F-4E mounted an internal gun. The Naval F-8 Crusader (known to its pilots as 'the last of the gunfighters') and the Air Force and Navy strike aircraft carried guns but again, not the F-4. The two missiles normally carried by the Phantom were the radar-guided *Sparrow* and the heat-seeking *Sidewinder*. Both were found to be less effective than expected since their prime purpose had been the destruction of Russian heavy bombers and not small highly maneouvrable fighters. The *Sparrow* had a nominal range of about 30 miles but the Rules of Engagement, requiring visual identification of enemy aircraft, usually negated this advantage. Early models of the *Sidewinder* used in Vietnam were not usable from the front hemisphere of the target i.e. 'head-on', but only from the rear where the missile seeker head could track the hot jet exhausts. They could also not reliably be used if the target was aligned anywhere near the sun as this was a more attractive target than jet exhaust. Both missiles had minimum ranges and once the North Vietnamese aircraft were within this minimum range they were safe. Large

Two Presidents better than one? Lyndon Johnson with Dwight D.Eisenhower aboard Air Force One at March AFB, California. As Supreme Commander in Europe 1944-45, Eisenhower could certainly have given Johnson's advisers lessons in the correct use of air power. From left: Johnson, Walt Rostow, William Bundy, Cyrus Vance, Eisenhower and General Earl Wheeler. (National Archives)

numbers of both missiles were launched for each MiG destroyed. Both American services had great hopes for air-to-air missiles, but were to be largely disappointed.

The main tactics of the strike forces were still to penetrate into North Vietnamese airspace at an altitude of around 15,000 feet. F-105s from Thailand had now been supplied with adequate numbers of ECM pods by late 1966 and these helped to disrupt the SA-2 surface-to-air missiles. As the strike forces flew into North Vietnam they accelerated to 480 knots (564mph) and, as they entered the most heavily defended areas, accelerated again to 540 knots (635mph). General Momyer the commander of the Seventh Air Force described the tactics thus:

"Our strike forces delivering conventional ordnance had to start their dive towards the target at about 12,000 feet and pull out above 4,500 feet. During the moments of stable flight between roll-in and pull-out, our aircraft were the most predictable and therefore the most vulnerable. And it was during these moments that the enemy would open up with everything they had."[10.]

The ECM pods were not perfect and pilots had to rely on the RHAW (Radar Homing and Warning) equipment, after this had been fitted, to tell them when missiles had been launched at them and from which direction the missile was coming. The RHAW could also tell them when missiles were being prepared to fire and when the guidance radars were turned on. In the Hanoi area, where there were many missile sites, the RHAW equipment tended to be swamped with warnings. When missiles were launched and guiding it was essential for the pilots to observe the missiles visually. Once the missiles, often described as 'flying telegraph poles', had been seen, it was possible to out-manoeuvre them. The SA-2s had a slow reacting guidance system and if the aircraft manoeuvred violently the missile could not follow. When the SA-2 was seen it was necessary to turn towards it. (if the aircraft turned away the missile followed) and then, at the right moment, turn away as hard as possible at high Gs. The missile's guidance system was incapable of reacting fast enough to follow and it would become 'blind'.

Dean Cramer, who flew 397 missions over the North while in the U.S. Navy, described dodging missiles by saying:

"Something told me the only way to handle the SAMs was to play 'chicken' with them, let the missiles get as close as possible, make a violent manoeuvre, and cause it to miss by a couple of hundred feet. On this day one of the missiles was luckily ahead of the other. The first one came, I waited, waited and evaded. Here came the other one, and I evaded again."[11.]

Rolling Thunder 52 began on 12th November 1966, the bombing generally shifting away from the series of attacks on the POL system, which was now seen to have failed. The numbers of sorties authorised was again raised from 10,100 monthly to 13,200 sorties monthly and the areas open for armed reconnaissance remained as before with the same prohibited areas. The listed targets under *Rolling Thunder 52* included some POL targets but also included industrial targets including power plants, steel and cement plants, i.e. targets intended to destroy

As the strikes intensified, so did the AAA, SAMs and MiGs - and inevitably, the losses rose. An HH-53 Super Jolly Green hovers over a downed airmen, just visible in the large clump of bushes lower centre. Even with a Skyraider escort, it took nerve to fly such a slow and vulnerable machine into North Vietnam. (National Archives)

the North's economy. However, since there was a chance of negotiations with the North through a Polish diplomat, President Johnson limited some targets listed under *Rolling Thunder 52*. These negotiations came to nothing when the North Vietnamese refused to limit their infiltration into the South and Johnson reintroduced these targets in 1967.

The worst day so far in the war for the destruction of American aircraft occurred on 2nd December 1966. At this time there were five aircraft carriers 'on line' at *Yankee Station*; *Coral Sea*, *Ticonderoga*, *Kitty Hawk*, *Franklin D Roosevelt* and *Enterprise*. Aircraft from *Franklin D Roosevelt* and *Ticonderoga* co-operated with aircraft from the USAF to mount a major attack on a truck park at Van Dien. The raid on Van Dien was carried out without loss for the Naval aircraft but, during the day, an F-4B and two A-4Cs from the *Coral Sea* were lost. The North Vietnamese missile sites had a successful day as the USAF lost three F-4Cs to SAMs on this date, while an F-105D fell to a missile while attacking POL storage near Phuc Yen airfield. Finally an RF-4C was later shot down by anti-aircraft guns while trying to photograph the results of the raid on Phuc Yen. The loss of eight aircraft on one day to the North Vietnamese defence system was hard for the American pilots to accept when, under the Rules of Engagement, large parts of that system were immune from attack.

With the introduction of *Rolling Thunder 52* in November the sortie rate had again been increased and the idea of the 'sortie rate' came in some ways to dominate the conduct of the air war. McNamara had introduced quantifiable accounting and control methods into his management of the Pentagon and this had included expected sortie rates for each of the different types of aircraft in service. In the search for a quantifiable measure of success or failure of the bombing the sortie rate seems to have been chosen because of the lack of other criteria. McNamara, with his accountancy background, seems to have needed to produce figures that could be reduced to statistics for use in evaluation reports. This kind of thinking produced the 'body counts' in the ground war in the South. In reality success or failure in war cannot be reduced to such simplistic terms and the imposition of this type of measurement produced some peculiar thinking by the American leadership.

Once the sortie rate had become the measure of success, careers and reputations became dependant on this criterion. The bomb shortage had produced the situation where six aircraft were being sent out with only one bomb each, when one aircraft could carry six bombs, simply to keep up the sortie rate.

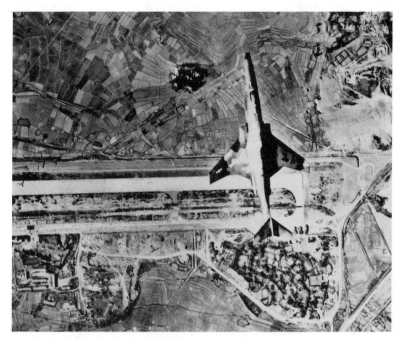

Even though MiG airfields were immune from attack, it was still necessary to maintain a close watch on them to monitor movements and re-deployments of the MiG units. The RF-101 pilots of the USAF visited them regularly. Photographed by a second Voodoo, this RF-101 is seen high over Kep with what appears to be a fighter (far left) on the runway below. (National Archives)

The normal, healthy competition between the Air Force and the Navy was exacerbated by the desire for each service to produce a higher sortie rate than the other, to look good on paper in Washington. If the civilian analysts in the defence department could produce statistics to show that one service was better than the other, using the limited criterion of sortie rates, the apparently 'inferior' service could lose out in the next round of appropriations. This situation forced the service chiefs to make sure that the commanders in the field flew all the sorties allocated to them, even in marginal weather and when no real targets were available. If a strike was launched and then through bad weather was forced to attack a secondary target this counted in the sortie rate calculations. Because of the limitations on the targets that could be struck there were times when no worthwhile targets remained to be attacked. Therefore if unused sorties remained, they were flown as armed reconnaissance sorties even if not strictly necessary.

The Deputy Commander of the Seventh Air Force between April 1965 and August 1966 General Gilbert L Meyers stated before the Senate Preparedness Investigating Subcommittee that:

> "If the weather was bad, we were always concerned about the repercussions as a result of not flying the sorties that had been allocated to us. Obviously if you do not fly them, you can make a case that you did not really need that many anyway. On that basis, sortie allocations could be reduced in the future." [12.]

With the use of the sortie rate as the criterion for success and the restrictive Rules of Engagement a dichotomy developed between the people who were fighting the war and those directing it from thousands of miles away. In any war the aims and objectives must be kept clearly in mind along with how they are to be achieved. The obsession with statistics rather than the real outcome of the bombing was unfair - to say the least - on the aircrews.

It had been intended from the beginning that the air war against the North should gradually increase. This is what happened, but each development and increase in the bombing had thus far failed to cause any change in the North Vietnamese objectives. McNamara had originally been a supporter of the bombing but he seems to have moved slowly against the bombing as the lack of any decisive outcome became apparent. The failure of the POL campaign seems to have been the final turning point. From McNamara's point of view the military had, from the very beginning of the covert action against the North in the early 1960s, continually promised more than they could deliver. The military had promised that the destruction of the Vietnamese POL system would greatly limit the infiltration of men and supplies from the North to the South, but this did not happen. Although the attacks on the North were tactical successes, in that the American pilots could and did destroy the targets they were given, the strategic outcomes of these tactical successes had never lived up to expectations. The main critic of the bombing in Johnson's

Bombed-up and heading out. This F-4D has empty outer pylon on the port wing and no Sidewinders, but carries a pair of long-range Sparrow missiles in front of the long-range tank beneath the fuselage.
(National Archives)

Tuesday Cabinet, George Ball, left during the summer of 1966. However Ball's position came increasingly to be taken by McNamara as he began to turn against the bombing.

On 29th August 1966 a committee of scientists from the Jason Division of the Institute for Defence Analysis submitted a report that became known as the Jason Report. This committee was made up of 47 independent scientists who had very high credibility with the government as they had in the past worked on several government weapon systems. The Pentagon Papers called these scientists 'the cream of the scholarly community in technical fields.' The Jason Report stated:

"As of July 1966 the U.S. bombing of North Vietnam (NVN) had no measurable direct effect on Hanoi's ability to mount and support military operations in the South at the current level. Although the political constraints seem clearly to have reduced the effectiveness of the bombing program, its limited effect on Hanoi's ability to provide such support cannot be explained solely on that basis....Since the initiation of the *Rolling Thunder* program the damage to facilities and equipment in North Vietnam has been more than offset by the increased flow of military and economic aid, largely from the USSR and Communist China."[13.]

It was the Jason Report that finally disenchanted McNamara

Another guest for the 'Hanoi Hilton'. This photograph - almost certainly carefully staged for propaganda purposes - show a very dejected American airman under guard, surrounded by the wreckage of his aircraft. Note the symbolic position of the guard's left foot.

(via author)

with the results that could be achieved by bombing.

There was a bombing pause during Christmas 1966 (24th - 26th December) and over New Year 1967. During the year American fighter bombers had carried out 79,000 sorties over North Vietnam and B-52 strikes added another 280 sorties. During these sorties over 100,000 tons of bombs had been dropped. American aircraft losses from action over the North during 1965 and 1966 had now reached 451, the highest loss rate being sustained by the F-105s from Thailand. All told 126 F-105s were lost in 1966, 111 of failing to return from sorties against the North. This was over 15 per cent of the total number of F-105s manufactured by the Republic company. By the end of 1966 the Americans had in place an enormous number of Naval and USAF aircraft and the infrastructure and supply lines to support them. The North Vietnamese had developed a modern effective air defence system and were taking a steady toll of the attacking American aircraft. There had yet been no decision reached in the air war and the two sides were both ready to fight it out to reach a decision in the air over North Vietnam.

FOOTNOTES

1. Cagel, Malcolm W *Task Force 77 In Action Off Vietnam*, Frank Uhlig, ed. The Naval   Review, United States Naval Institute, Anapolis, 1972, page 78-79.
2. Ibid, page 94.
3. Boyne, Walter J *Phantom In Combat*, Jane's Publishing Company, London, 1985, page 6.
4. Yeager, Chuck, *Yeager*, Arrow Books, London, 1986, page 382.
5. Levinson, Jeffrey L *Alpha Strike Vietnam*, Presido Press, California, 1989, page 72.
6. Momyer, William W *Air Power In Three Wars*, U.S. Government Printing Office, Washington, 1978, page 107-8.
7. Kasler, James H *The Hanoi POL Strike*, in The Air Force University Review XXVI, Nov.-Dec. 1974, page 24.
8. Sharp, U S G *Report On The War In Vietnam*, Washington, 1968, page 26-27.
9. Nichols, John B and Tillman, Barret, *On Yankee Station*, Airlife Publishing Ltd. England, 1987, page 103.
10. Momyer, William W Ibid.
11. Levinson, Jeffrey L Ibid.
12. United States Senate, Armed Services Committee, Preparedness Investigation Subcommittee, Air War Against Vietnam: Hearings, U.S. Government Printing Office, Washington, Page 479.
13. *The Pentagon Papers*: The Defence Department History Of United States Decision-Making On Vietnam, Vol. IV, Beacon Press, Boston, 1971, page 116.

Chapter Four

1967: Hanoi, 'The Centre of Hell'

North Vietnamese MiGs had become more effective during 1966, but their airfields were still not on the target list. Therefore, a plan was devised to lure them up, under favourable tactical conditions to the Americans, to destroy them in the air. Missile-armed F-4s would fly the routes and use the same call signs as bomb-carrying F-105s. When the North Vietnamese reacted to this raid, they would not find the expected vulnerable fighter-bombers but Phantoms waiting for them. This mission was code-named *Operatiuon Bolo* and, as the Vietnamese had in the past reacted strongly after a bombing halt, it was decided to carry out this operation after the New Year two day truce. It was to be a major operation involving over one hundred USAF aircraft from Thailand and South Vietnam. The main part of the plan However involved the 8th Tactical Fighter Wing - The Wolfpack - commanded by Colonel Robin Olds.

The weather on 2nd January 1967 had been forecast as good, but in fact proved marginal and, although the operation was delayed, it still took place above complete cloud cover at 10,000 to 12,000 feet. The 8th had used the New Year stand-down to carry out training and a series of briefings. Most of its pilots' experience had been in bombing missions and this training was aimed at improving their air combat capabilities. The wing took off in flights of four at five minute intervals, the first led by Colonel Olds. The plan called for the American aircraft to pass over the top of Phuc Yen, one of the main MiG bases, and then head towards Hanoi. The North Vietnamese were slow to react but the first three flights of F-4s were attacked by MiG-21s and seven were shot down without loss to the Americans. Colonel Olds shot down one MiG, the first of the four that he was eventually to destroy. Two days later two more MiG-21s were shot down. It was thought that the Vietnamese had only about fifteen MiG-21s available before *Operation Bolo*, so the loss of

Aircrews of the 8th TFW. From left: Captain Francis Gullick, 1st Lieutenant William D.Lafever, Captain Richard M.Pascoe, Colonel Robin Olds, Major Thomas M.Hirsch, Captain Norman Wells and Major Everett J.Raspberry. During 1967, all would become MiG killers. (USAF)

over half their force of MiG-21s forced them to curtail their fighter activities until they had regrouped and re-equipped. This led to a decline in North Vietnamese fighter activity in the early part of the year.

In January Admiral U.S.G. Sharp, the Commanding Officer in the Pacific, put forward a plan to attack six categories of target in North Vietnam thought to be essential to the North's war making capacity. These were the air defence system, the remaining POL targets, power generation plants, the transport system, military bases and essential industrial plants. It was hoped to get permission to strike these targets without restriction. This plan came to nothing. Johnson had again kept the final choice of targets to the politicians in Washington and the sanctuary areas still applied, although the list of possible targets continued to expand.

By January 1967 the number of American troops inside South Vietnam had risen to over 380,000. Bad weather caused by the monsoon had caused a reduction in the number of sorties flown during the autumn and winter of 1966 and, when *Rolling Thunder 53* started on 24th January, it incorporated attacks on several industrial targets near to Hanoi as well as continuing the level of armed reconnaissance missions.

Control of the USAF in the Pacific passed from General Hunter Harris to General John D. Ryan on the 1st February 1967. Although it was a strategic campaign, the air war against North Vietnam was now being carried out by fighter-bombers undertaking missions they had not been designed for. F-105s had been designed to drop tactical nuclear weapons while the F-4s had originally been designed to carry out fleet air defence against bombers. The background of General Ryan (Three Fingered Jack) was in bombers and in Strategic Air Command. After the Second World War the major effort in the US Air Force had been in the build-up of the strategic bombing force and most of the high level leadership within the Air Force had a bomber background. It was strategic bombing theories that had led to the formation of the Air Force after the Second World War. Now however the giant B-52 Stratofortresses were being used in a tactical rôle, dropping thirty tons of conventional bombs a time on to the jungles of South Vietnam, while the fighter-bombers undertook strategic bombing in the North.

The pilots operating the aircraft from Thailand thought that the stereotyped tactics laid down by Air Force Headquarters in Hawaii were not the best approach to the air war over the North. General Ryan and his staff attempted to control the formations, routes, altitudes, speeds and types of ordnance carried by the strike aircraft. Col Jack Broughton, second in command of the F-105 wing at Takhli and who flew 102 missions over the North, wrote about General Ryan that:

> "He did not know the mechanics of flying and fighting our war and perhaps he was lost without his SAC umbrella. He projected himself as the demonic, all-knowing, one and only personal ruler of all. His personality could be most kindly described as gruff and antagonistic. He was another general who enjoyed hollering and yelling obscenities as a method of leadership and he very definitely led by fear and intimidation....Nobody wanted to talk to General Ryan....we felt that anything we accomplished was in spite of General Ryan and his immediate staff....I have been personally castigated in front of my own people by General Ryan for espousing combat theories we

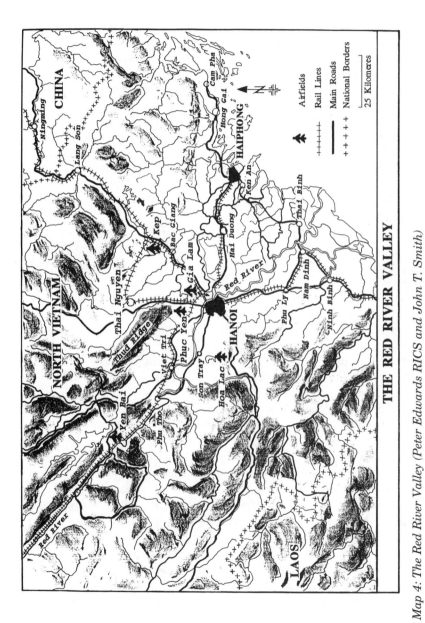

Map 4: The Red River Valley (Peter Edwards RICS and John T. Smith)

learned over Hanoi at the risk of our lives and in which we firmly believed."[1]

Broughton's view of General Ryan may be extreme - he was later court-martialled by Ryan - but it reflects the view of the pilots fighting the war about their leadership four thousand miles away. The pilots were suffering heavy losses but they felt that one hand was being held behind them by the Rules of Engagement and that they were being criticised by their own leadership for failings that were not of their making. By this stage of the war every level of the military and political leadership had become frustrated by the lack of obvious success. Truly enormous amounts of equipment, men and money had been committed to *Rolling Thunder* but the North Vietnamese still appeared firmly dedicated to their support of the war in the South.

There was another truce over the Vietnamese new year, the *Tet* holiday. This truce lasted for four days (8th - 12th February 1966) and The North Vietnamese again used the truce to rush supplies through their transport system, the roads solid with traffic 24 hours a day. American photo reconnaissance aircraft continued to fly and brought back the evidence that the supplies were still moving along the Ho Chi Minh trail. As usual the Vietnamese had ignored the truce. They had never agreed to negotiate or felt themselves to be under any kind of obligation to the U.S. and thus viewed the bomb pauses in a completely different way to the Americans.

Air raids had put heavy pressure on the roads and railways in North Vietnam during 1966. Therefore the Vietnamese increased their use of the inland water ways and coastal waters, as much as fifty per cent of their logistics were at one time travelling by water. It was decided that the best way to slow this movement of supplies was to mine the estuaries of five rivers with mines. On 26th February 1967 six A-6 Intruders from the carrier *Enterprise* mined the estuaries of the Ca and Giang rivers. The mines were laid at night by the Intruders flying radar courses to place the mines in exact patterns. The main Vietnamese ports of Haiphong, Cam Pha and Hon Gai were not included in the mining programme, although that is where mining would have had most effect. During March another three minefields were laid in the estuaries of the Kieng

A flight of F-105Ds heading for the North. Two of the aircraft are carrying Bullpup optically-guided missiles. These were accurate and effective against 'soft' targets, but without the explosive power necessary to destroy structures like the Than Hoa bridge, which was hit several times by Bullpups but refused to fall. (USAF)

Giang, Song Ma and Cua Sot rivers. The North Vietnamese made some attempts to sweep the mines but with little effect. Movement of boats in these areas was soon restricted and several sunken boats were observed in the Song Giang estuary.

A Harris poll, carried out during early February and published on the 13th of that month, showed that there was still support for *Rolling Thunder*, Sixty-seven per cent of the American public continuing to back the President's policy. Johnson met with his civilian advisers on the 21st. At this meeting it was decided to add more industrial plants to the list of approved targets. These included the steel works at Thai Nguyen, the Haiphong cement works and more of the power supply stations outside Hanoi and Haiphong. Accordingly, *Rolling Thunder 54* opened on 23rd. The bombing of these major targets was, however, delayed by the continuing bad weather caused by the northeast monsoon.

On 9th March the Thai government finally admitted that the Americans were using their air bases for raids over North

The Thai Nguyen Power Station, following an F-105 strike in March 1967. (USAF)

Vietnam. It was, of course, common knowledge, but the Thai government had maintained the fiction that the American presence was only defensive. On 13th March the Thai Prime Minister also admitted that the newly built base at U-Tapao was for B-52 operations.

When the bad weather lifted on the 10th March the iron and steel plant at Thai Nguyen was attacked for the first time. This complex, situated in a valley on the East side of Thud Ridge and about forty miles north of Hanoi, had its own rail line running south into Hanoi. Thai Nguyen was estimated to produce 300,000 tons of pig iron a year and was the only plant in the North that could produce the prefabricated pontoon and bridge sections used in the repair of the many bombed bridges in the North. The steel works also produced coke and sections for the

Congressional Medal of Honor

Aircrews flying the Wild Weasel missions against SAM sites usually caught everything, from automatic Flak to rifle fire. Captain Merlyn H.Dethlefsen (left) won the CMH on 10th March and Major Leo K.Thorsness was awarded the decoration for a mission on 19th April.
(via Author)

oil storage tanks that had been used to disperse the POL storage throughout the country. Both the Air Force and the Navy continued to bomb Thai Nguyen during March and although most of the plant was destroyed, production was never quite stopped. The North Vietnamese reply to this was simply to import more steel products from Russia and China.

On the same day that the steel plant at Thai Nguyen was first bombed, 10th March, Captain Merlyn Hans Dethlefsen of the 355th Tactical Fighter Wing was awarded The Congressional Medal of Honor, the highest American award for bravery. The Thai Nguyen site, one of the most important targets in the North, was protected by guns, missiles and aircraft. Captain Dethlefsen was flying a F-105F two seat *Wild Weasel*, part of a four aircraft defence suppression mission that arrived in the target area five minutes before the main strike forces, F-105Ds from Takhli in Thailand. The four *Wild Weasels* at once attacked the surface-to-air missile sites to clear the way for the fighter-bombers. The flight leader was shot down by Flak, but the three remaining SAM suppression aircraft destroyed the missile site while avoiding both anti-aircraft fire and attacks by several MiG-21s. They returned to base, but all three aircraft suffered damage.

Also on 10th March Captain Max C Brestel became the first USAF American pilot to shoot down two North Vietnamese aircraft in one day. He was also part of the strike on Thai Nguyen, flying an F-105D from Takhli. After pulling off the target and heading south, the flight leader, Colonel Philip C Gast, spotted a flight of four MiG-17s followed by four more. The MiGs were a lower altitude heading north and the two Thunderchief pilots turned down behind them. Brestel, using full afterburner, closed in fast and shot down two of them using the F-105s internal 20 mm cannon.

A new development in war technology occurred on 11th March. This was the introduction into combat of the first of the 'new generation' of "smart weapons" as opposed to the old 'dumb' iron bombs. This was the *Walleye* glide bomb. This weapon was designed to be released outside a targets anti-aircraft defences and would then glide on its stub wings the remainder of the way to the target. The guidance system was based on a camera in the nose of the missile that provided a picture on the screen in the aircraft cockpit. The pilot specified a point on this picture and a computer in the missile, which could differentiate a particular pattern of light and shade, would guide the missile exactly on to the specified point. The *Walleye* was a true 'fire and forget' missile since once it was launched the aircraft could turn away and leave the area. The first use of the *Walleye* was by Commander Thomas J Walker, flying an A-4 Skyhawk, from the carrier *Bon Homme Richard*. The target was a barracks at Sam Son and the missile was observed to hit a window in the barracks and explode inside. On 12th March three *Walleyes*, launched against the Thanh Hoa bridge, all hit the target. However the 850 lb warhead was not powerful enough to cause serious damage.

The size of the Sparrow missile can be appreciated as ground crew prepare a USAF Phantom for MiGCAP at Cam Ranh Bay. From left: Airman 1st Class Gary P.Mincer, Sergeant Vernon E.Kisinger, Airman 1st Class Lonnie J.Hartfield and Sergeant Phineas T.Berry.
(USAF)

The *Wild Weasel* and *Iron Hand* missions were among the most dangerous flown by the pilots over the North. Following Captain Dethlefsen's award of the Medal of Honour while flying a *Wild Weasel* mission in March, two more Medals of Honour were awarded in April, both to pilots flying defence suppression aircraft. On 19th April Major Leo K. Thorsness was flying an F-105F from Takhli on a *Wild Weasel* mission protecting a raid on a barracks at Xuan Mai, thirty miles south of Hanoi, when his wingman's aircraft was shot down by anti-aircraft fire. He twice refuelled in the air while organising the rescue of the shot-down crew, then returned to the spot where his comrades had landed, to protect and direct the rescue aircraft. The A-1 'Sandy' rescue aircraft then came under attack by MiG-17s and Thorsness shot one down using the 20 mm cannon. However the gallant rescue attempt proved to be a failure and the two downed aircrew were taken prisoner. While flying an A-4E from the *Ticonderoga* Lieutenant Commander Michael J Estocin on both 20th and 26th April carried out attacks on SAM sites using *Shrike* missiles On the latter mission he was shot down and killed and was awarded the Medal of Honour posthumously.

After the losses in early January the North Vietnamese Air Force had reduced their combat operations, while the northeast monsoon had also curtailed all American activity in the air over North Vietnam. In April and May 1967 the North Vietnamese Air Force returned, again attempting to disrupt the *Rolling Thunder* campaign. The addition to the target list of the industrial targets in the area around Hanoi and Haiphong, forced them to react against the American strike forces. There were fifty engagements between MiGs and American aircraft in April and seventy-two in May, the highest monthly total for the whole of the three and a half years of *Rolling Thunder*. The mission on 19th of April, on which Major Thorsness had shot down a MiG-17 and been awarded the Medal of Honour, had also seen three other F-105 pilots from the 355th Tactical Fighter Wing shoot down MiG-17s. The USAF destroyed nine North Vietnamese aircraft during April while the US Navy shot down two more. During the heavy fighting in May the USAF destroyed twenty of the North's MiGs including seven on the 13th and six on the 20th, the US Navy adding six more to this total. The Commanding Officer of the 8th Tactical Fighter Wing, Colonel Robin Olds, shot down three of the MiGs destroyed during May. The attacks on the industrial targets that could affect the North's capacity to continue the war had forced their Air Force to react against the bombing and they had thus lost 37 aircraft in two months. The North Vietnamese Air Force had relearned the lesson that they could not win a stand up fight against the greater numbers, better training and greater experience of the Americans. North Vietnamese fighters were better used as part of the overall air defence system operating under ground control to disrupt the American air strikes before they entered the target area when possible. They were better used in attempting to pick off any stragglers or isolated aircraft, when they could pick the time and place to their own advantage.

President Johnson had included North Vietnamese electrical generation plants in the targets released for attack during April

Colonel Robin Olds, commanding the 8th TFW, destroyed three MiGs in May to bring his score to four, the only USAF pilot to do so. Since the Phantom back-seat WSOs also received victory credits, this total was to be exceeded by Chuck de Bellvue who, flying back-seat to more than one pilot, was credited with six and became the only USAF 'ace'.
(USAF)

and May. After several delays due to weather the US Navy carried out major air strikes against the two thermal plants in Haiphong causing heavy damage on 20th April. Further attacks on the power stations at Uong Bi and at Bac Giang were carried out by Naval aircraft during May. The main power station for Hanoi was inside the city and the weather again delayed the attack on this target until 19th May. To reduce the chances of civilian deaths likely to be caused by attacking the power station inside Hanoi, it was decided to use the *Walleye* glide bomb that was now establishing a reputation for accuracy.

The attack was carried out by two A-4 Skyhawks led by Commander Homer Smith and was protected by six F-8E Crusaders as air cover and *Flak* suppression. Flying in low over Hanoi the A-4s pulled up to get a clear view and released the *Walleyes*, both of which hit the 32,000 kilowatt power station. Two of the escorting F-8s were shot down by *Flak* but the other four Crusader pilots engaged and shot down three MiG-17s as they left the Hanoi area. John Colvin, the British consul in Hanoi, saw the American aircraft coming in, heard the sounds of the raid and noted that his electric fan stopped moments after the raid. Colvin later visited the power station and saw that the main building had been damaged and two chimneys brought down. The disruption did not last long however. Electric power supplies were restored in Hanoi the following day either by diesel generators or by another power station feeding into the grid.

The power stations had been attacked under *Rolling Thunder 55*, which had started on 23rd April. The numbers of armed reconnaissance sorties had remained constant but new fixed targets had been added to the list including power stations, cement works, rail repair yards and storage areas. American pilots operating over the North had long sought permission to attack the North Vietnamese fighter airfields, which had long been safe havens from which MiGs could attack the American raids at times and places of their own choosing. Under *Rolling Thunder 55* their pleas were finally accepted. Two airfields, at Hoa Lac and Kep, were now released for attack. The first airfield attacks took place on 24th April 1967 when eight F-105Ds from Thailand carried out a raid on Hoa Lac, twenty-four miles west of Hanoi and claimed the destruction of fourteen MiGs on the ground. On the same day the Navy attacked Kep, thirty-eight miles northeast of Hanoi and originally built by the Japanese during the Second World War. Aircraft from the carrier *Kitty Hawk* managed to damage the runway and several aircraft on the ground. Later in the day

Aerial view of Udorn Air Base, Thailand, home of the 8th TFW 'Wolfpack'. More than a hundred aircraft are parked here, showing the massive American commitment during the height of Rolling Thunder. (USAF)

129

aircraft from the *Bon Homme Richard* also bombed the Kep runway. During the raids Naval aircraft shot down two MiGs that had taken off.

The North Vietnamese had seven airfields with jet capacity and expanded this number to fifteen by building new ones and expanding existing ones. They also had access to airfields in Southern China. The main fighter base used by the North was at Phuc Yen, which was not bombed until October. All the bases in North Vietnam were eventually bombed except Gia Lam, situated only three miles outside the capital, which was the North's international airport. This airfield was used by the International Control Commission, set up by the Geneva accords, for its twice-weekly flights into Hanoi and by the Russians and Chinese. Although it was used by MiGs, it was never bombed. The bombing of the fighter bases was strictly controlled and was only intermittently carried out.

Rolling Thunder 56 commenced on 2nd May 1967 and included ten new fixed targets. The northeast monsoon had finished in April and the good weather over the North now allowed an increase in bombing. The main effort was again directed against the transport system, attempting to cut the road and rail lines of communication down from China. Admiral Sharp described *Rolling Thunder 56* by writing:

"This pattern of air attacks continued throughout 1967 with the overall purpose of isolating Haiphong from Hanoi, and Hanoi and Haiphong from the rest of the country, especially those LOCs radiating southward to Laos and the De-Militarized Zone." [2]

May also saw the first use of the new version of the F-4 Phantom, the F-4D, when the type entered service with the 555th Tactical Fighter Squadron at Ubon air base in Thailand on 28th May. The F-4D still had no internal gun but the 20 mm M61 A1 Vulcan cannon in an external pod was introduced in May. This was known as the SUU-16A and its use on the central pylon meant that the Phantom could not carry the fuel tank normally carried on this stores hardpoint. The gun pod weighed 1,615 lbs and the loss of the centre-line fuel tank reduced the range at which the Phantom could operate. The six-barrelled Vulcan cannon could fire 6,000 rounds a minute and greatly improved the Phantom's air-to- air capabilities. The

Throughout 1967, the Air Force and Navy pounded away until there was little feft to bomb. Top, rail trucks bombed and burned near the infamous Than Hoa bridge. Bottom, a POL target in flames at Haiphong. (via Author)

minimum range of the missiles used by the F-4s meant that in close combat they would be at a disadvantage. The introduction of the gun pod helped to overcome this disadvantage, although movement in the pylon the gun pod was attached to tended to degrade the accuracy.

On 2nd June a flight of F-105s from Takhli, returning from a strike mission over North Vietnam, passed over the North Vietnamese port of Cam Pha. As they passed overhead they came under fire from anti-aircraft batteries in the port and also, they later claimed, they were fired on by one of the ships in the port. The Thunderchief pilots responded by strafing the guns with their 20 mm cannon, hitting guns on the land and on the ship. Under the Rules of Engagement the American aircraft were banned from attacking harbours unless specifically targeted and were prohibited from attacking foreign shipping. President Johnson had always kept a tight control of the bombing because of his fear of the Chinese and Russians becoming involved directly in the fighting, which understandably he did not want to happen.

The ship involved turned out to be the Soviet ship *Turkestan*. The Russians protested that one crew member had been killed and several injured by the attack. The port of Cam Pha had been bombed that day by other F-105s who, it was proved, had not been involved in the attack on the *Turkestan*. In these circumstances the Americans denied that their aircraft had been involved. The aircraft that attacked the ship had been on a strike against the Bac Giang rail yard and had only passed over Cam Pha on their way home. Three weeks after the incident took place the Russian Premier Aleksei Kosygin, holding talks with Johnson in Glassboro, New Jersey, produced an American 20 mm cannon shell taken from the hull of the *Turkestan*. This forced the American military to investigate the incident more thoroughly and it was then established that two pilots from Takhli had been involved. Meanwhile Colonel Jack Broughton, second in command of Takhli Wing, had destroyed camera gun film showing the attack on the *Turkestan* in an attempt to support his men. Colonel Broughton and the other two pilots were court-martialled. The two pilots, Major Tollman and Major Ferguson were acquitted, but Colonel Broughton was found guilty of destroying the camera gun film. Although he only received the minimum possible sentence, his career was finished

The tiny Douglas A-4 Skyhawk operated from the very beginning of Rolling Thunder. It was used as a fighter-bomber, tanker, 'Iron Hand' SAM suppressor and ECM aircraft. Although it was supplemented by the A-7 Corsair, it kept going until the end. Here, a flight from VA-155, the 'Silver Foxes', which operated from USS Coral Sea from July 1967. (National Archives)

in the Air Force. The pilots risking their lives flying over the North came to hate the Rules of Engagement that said they could bomb some things but not others.

Rolling Thunder 57 began on 20th July 1967 and included sixteen new fixed targets. The weather during July was good and there was a maximum effort in the attempt to cut of Haiphong and Hanoi. During August another thirty fixed targets were authorised under *Rolling Thunder 57*. These were mostly targets associated with the transport system, storage areas, bridges and rail lines. There was another Harris poll in America during July, on the popularity of the bombing, which showed that 72 per cent of the public still supported the bombing of North Vietnam, 40 per cent of the population wanting an increase in the bombing.

Another major aircraft carrier fire occurred on 29th July when the *Forrestal* was preparing to launch a strike from *Yankee Station*. The deck of the carrier was covered in aircraft waiting to be launched, all carrying bombs, rockets and fuel tanks. An air-to-ground rocket was accidentally fired by an F-4B, which hit the fuel tank of an A-4. The tank exploded, covering the deck in blazing fuel that ignited other aircraft and their stores. Aircraft and munitions exploded, adding to the blaze on the flight deck. The deck crew fought through the flames to dump as much of the remaining ordnance over the side as possible. Fire quickly spread below decks asphyxiating crew members trapped in the smoke. The *Forrestal's* crew fought the blaze as best they could with the help of the other ships from Task Force 77 but, when the fire was finally out 134 of the crew had died and 62 had been injured. The ship had also lost twenty-one aircraft destroyed and 43 badly damaged. *Forrestal* returned to America under her own power, after a halt at the Philippines, and never returned to Vietnam.

The fact that McNamara was becoming disillusioned with the effects of the bombing was now becoming apparent to the military high command. The military leaders came to think that McNamara favoured a reduction in the bombing or a complete halt, and believed that air power had never been given a real chance to show what could be achieved. The Air Force officers in particular had devoted their lives to the idea of the unique ability of air power to win wars. If the bombing was now scaled down they thought that this would show that air power had failed. They considered that the targeting policy, forced on them by the political leadership in Washington, had stopped the bombing offensive from producing results. If the bombing was now seen as a failure it would be seen also as a failure of the military leadership. In their view however they had never been given a chance to succeed with the bombing because of political limitations. If air power was seen as a failure then both the Air Force and the Navy could expect a cut in future roles and budgets.

In an attempt to pre-empt any move to cut the bombing or to show that the bombing had failed, the high-level military leaders turned to their friends among the political leadership.

If a pilot saw a SAM in time, he could evade it. He could never out-run it. An SA-2, photographed in July 1967, by a reconnaissance aircraft, streaks over Phuc Yen airfield, near Hanoi. For obvious reasons, they were known as 'flying telegraph poles'. (USAF)

135

The Senate Armed Services Committee Preparedness Subcommittee and its chairman Senator John Stennis were essentially supporters of the war and air power. The Pentagon Papers says of the committee:

> "The subcommittee had unquestionably set out to defeat Mr. McNamara. It's members, Senator Stennis...(and others) were well known for their hard line views and military sympathies. They were defenders of 'air power' and aligned themselves with the 'professional military experts' against what they considered 'unskilled civilian amateurs.' They viewed the restraints on bombing as irrational, the shackling of a major instrument which could help win victory." [3.]

The hearings involved eleven military leaders, who had played a part in the *Rolling Thunder* campaign, testifying before the committee with McNamara as the only civilian. Through the way they were structured the hearings allowed the military leaders to pour out their complaints before the committee and then McNamara was forced to justify the political decisions.

The first military commander to testify was Admiral Sharp, commander in the Pacific, who stated that there were large numbers of targets in North Vietnam that he considered it necessary to attack but had never been allowed to. He thought that bombing had reduced the infiltration into the South and that a reduction in the bombing would lead to an increase in the fighting and the casualties occurring in the South. The military leadership, including the Joint Chiefs of Staff, then appeared one after the other before the committee and said that the bombing would have succeeded if it was not for the artificial restrictions placed on it by the political leadership. McNamara had by this time lost much of his original faith in what could be achieved with the bombing and does not seem to have felt the need to justify the bombing to the committee.

After listening to the military the committee adopted an aggressive stance towards McNamara and the political limitations placed on the military running of the war. McNamara's argument was that the bombing had not materially affected the war in the South. He said that the amount of supplies needed by the North Vietnamese and the Vietcong forces in the South was so small that no achievable level of bombing could stop it. With the aid from China and Russia the supply was practically limitless. McNamara also suggested that the destruction of a

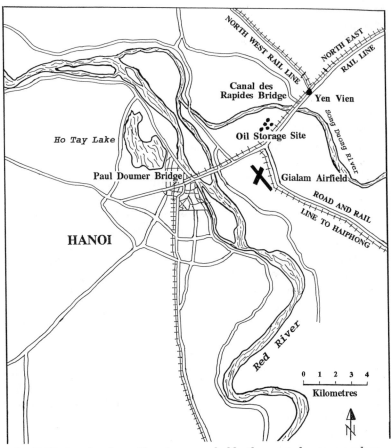

In 1967, the sky above Hanoi was probably the most dangerous place on earth. The Paul Doumer bridge, right in the centre of the city, was bombed for the first time on 11th August 1967. The raid caused severe damage, keeping it out of action until October. (Author)

large amount of North Vietnam's industry, POL storage and power generation had been achieved, with no noticeable reduction in the North's support for the war in the south. Although the bombing had raised the cost of the war to the North they seemed prepared to pay this cost. McNamara did not support an increase in the bombing. He told the commission that:

"I am convinced, however, that the final decision in this conflict will not come until we and our allies prove to North Vietnam that she cannot win in the south, The tragic and long drawn out character of that conflict in the south makes very tempting the prospect of replacing it with some new kind of air campaign against the north. But however tempting, such an alternative seems to me completely illusory." [4.]

This is a statement against the concept of strategic bombing and was anathema to the military supporters of air power. The committee forced Johnson to react and sixteen extra targets had been added to the list two days before the committee had started its work.

With McNamara attacking the bombing campaign in public, Johnson now seemed to have finally lost faith in him, the man who had originally advised him on the bombing at every stage during the escalation of the campaign. If the original purpose of the bombing was an attempt to force the North Vietnamese Government to change its policy towards the war in the south, McNamara had now told the North quite clearly it was not going to work and was unlikely to be increased. If Johnson was playing a game of poker with the North's political leaders McNamara had now told the North what cards Johnson held and had revealed his bluff. It did not help the morale of the pilots risking their lives over the North to hear that they were wasting their time and effort. The hearings forced Johnson to add to the target list, but they were McNamara's swan song as the Secretary of Defence and he seems to have lost his influence with Johnson after this date.

The primary target for the transport system raids was the Paul Doumer bridge on the Northern outskirts of Hanoi. This carried both the rail line from China and the rail line from Haiphong across the Red River. An average of 26 trains a day crossed the bridge carrying over 5,000 tons of supplies. Besides the rail line the bridge also carried roadways on either side of the rail track. The American military leaders and the pilots had frequently asked to be allowed to bomb the bridge but its closeness to Hanoi had thus far saved it. Now, two days before the Congressional hearings, Johnson gave permission to bomb the bridge in an attempt to pre-empt the committee. This permission took the leadership of the Seventh Air Force headquarters in Saigon by surprise and it was decided to mount

With wingtip vortices streaming, an F-4 rolls into a high-G turn as the North Vietnamese target comes into view. (USAF)

an operation against the bridge the same day, 11th August, before permission could be revoked. F-105Ds from the 355th Tactical Fighter Wing at Takhli had already been given targets for that day and the bombed-up aircraft were waiting for take-off. Previous experience gained from attacks on the Than Hoa bridge, which had resisted the combined attacks of the Air Force and the Navy for two years, was that the heaviest possible bombs should be used. This meant that the F-105s needed to be re-armed with one 3,000 lb. bomb, rather than the load of 750 lb. bombs with which they had been loaded that morning. Colonel Giraudo, the Wing leader, was forced to relax safety regulations to allow aircraft to be armed and fuelled simultaneously to meet the take-off deadline at 2:18 pm (14.18 hours).

The strike also included aircraft from the 388th Tactical Fighter Wing with F-105s from Korat, while Colonel Olds 8th Tactical Fighter Wing F-4 Phantoms were to provide fighter cover and *Flak* suppression. Because of the importance of the target only the most experienced pilots were chosen. The mission commander for the 355th Tactical Fighter Wing was Colonel Bob White, the Wing Deputy Commander. As the strike force crossed into North Vietnam the lead aircraft were four F-105F *Wild Weasels* led by Lieutenant Colonel James F McInerney. During the raid this flight attacked two missile sites and forced four others to close down their radar coverage. The main strike force crossed the Red River north of Thud Ridge and flew south towards Hanoi close to the eastern side of Thud Ridge. The main MiG base in the North was Phuc Yen just to the west of Thud Ridge and the bomb-carrying F-105Ds had to pass within sight of it. Although MiGs took of from the airfield they passed underneath the F-105s heading north and did not attempt to attack the American aircraft.

The attacking force passed the southern end of Thud Ridge heading towards Hanoi at 600 knots (690 mph) with the four *Wild Weasels* and four *Flak* suppression aircraft leading. These latter were the first into the target area. The weather over Hanoi was clear with no clouds and the bridge, over a mile long, could be seen clearly from a considerable distance. But the attacking aircraft could also be seen clearly by the defences. The bridge, one of the most important targets in the country and the Hanoi area generally, was surrounded by hundreds if not thousands of anti-aircraft guns.

As the aircraft approached the target area they came under heavy anti-aircraft fire. When the bridge was in sight the strike force climbed to 13,000 feet then dived at an angle of 45 degrees towards it. This dive had to be maintained at a constant angle towards the bridge and was the most vulnerable time for the attackers, although it only lasted around seven seconds. The F-105s released their bombs at between 7,000 and 8,000 feet and continued their dive to low level to leave the area to the East. The attack by the 355th Tactical Fighter Wing aircraft was followed by the 8th and the 388th Tactical Fighter Wing aircraft.

Altogether thirty-six aircraft, supported by fighter cover and defence suppression aircraft, dropped nearly a hundred tons of bombs, the target proving to be less heavily constructed than the Than Hoa bridge. One span of the rail line and two spans of

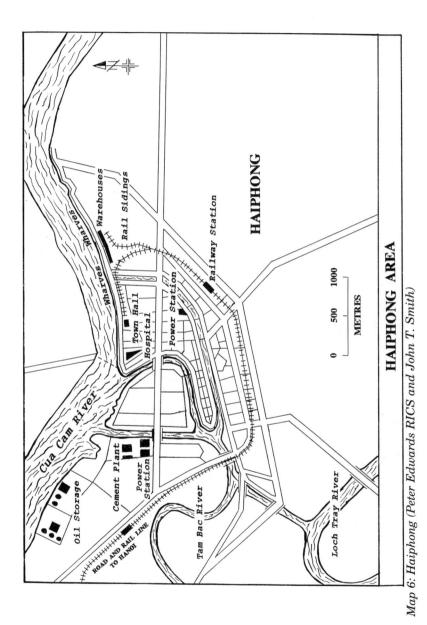

Map 6: Haiphong (Peter Edwards RICS and John T. Smith)

141

the road part of the bridge were destroyed by the 3,000 lb bombs. Only two of the attacking aircraft had been damaged. The Vietnamese began to repair the bridge immediately, finding that the only way to get rail traffic across the Red River in the meantime was a rail ferry four miles downstream from the bridge, or by putting railcars on to barges. The Paul Doumer bridge was in operation again by October and was bombed again on 25th of that month, when several more spans were destroyed. Again it was repaired and in December was again attacked. By April 1968 the North Vietnamese had constructed a pontoon rail bridge five miles downstream from the bridge.

The leader of the *Wild Weasels* involved in the initial raid, Lieutenant Colonel McInerney and his radar operator Captain Fred Shannon, were both awarded the Air Force Cross for their work during the attack.

During the preceding months the F-105F *Wild Weasels* commanded by McInerney had been used for night attack duties besides their normal anti-SAM duties. The Navy had the A-6 Intruder, which had an all-weather and night attack capability but no Air Force aircraft possessed a real night attack capability. To overcome this, the radar equipped F-105Fs had been used for a mission that had never been envisaged. However this had given the Air Force some limited capability to continue bombing the North at night.

Naval A-6s could achieve spectacular accuracy by night. On 30th October 1967 one single Intruder from VA-196, flying from the carrier *Constellation,* attacked the slipway of the railway ferry brought into use after the bombing of the Paul Doumer bridge. Lieutenant Commander Charles B. Hunter and Lieutenant Lyle F. Bull were the crew of the A-6 and managed to avoid eighteen SA-2 missiles fired at their aircraft as they approached the target. Flying at low level at 450 knots without visual reference to the ground, the crew used the aircraft's radar set to navigate and to carry out the bombing attack. The crew successfully dropped eighteen 500 lb bombs onto the railway ferry slipway putting it out of action. Although they had an excellent all-weather avionics navigation and attack system, the A-6s were relatively large and slowish aircraft, and were better employed during bad weather at night, as they tended to be

more vulnerable to fighter aircraft than some other Naval aircraft. Two A-6s were shot down by Chinese MiG-19s on 21st August when they crossed into Chinese air space by mistake after bombing the rail yard at Duc Noi, close to the border.

Rolling Thunder reached its highest level of intensity during the late summer of 1967, before the bad weather of the northeast monsoon in September forced a reduction in the bombing. During those late summer months both sides committed huge amounts of effort including men, materials and money into the fight to win or loose the bombing campaign. The North Vietnamese continued to increase their defences and, by August 1967, had two hundred missile sites with twenty-five active missile batteries moving between them so the Americans never knew which sites were active. The missile system coverage had now expanded to the northeast of Hanoi and to the southern part of the country. Missiles were fired at B-52s in October and in December without success. They had also reorganised their Ground Controlled Interception (GCI) system and now had about eighty interceptors available to them. In 1966 only 3 per cent of the American aircraft losses had been to the North Vietnamese fighter force but during 1967 8 per cent of losses (twenty-five aircraft) were caused by the MiG force. Jack Broughton described the war over the North at this stage as:

> "The desperate assault and parry over the frighteningly beautiful, green-carpeted mountains leading down into the flat delta of the Red River. The center of Hell with Hanoi as its hub. The area that was defended with three times the force and vigor that protected Berlin during World War II." [5.]

Attempts to cut Haiphong off from the rest of the country continued during late 1967. In August the four major bridges on the route between Haiphong and Hanoi were bombed in the hope that the 85 per cent of the North's imports that came in through Haiphong would be isolated from the transport net that led to the battlefronts in the South. Although the North Vietnamese put considerable effort into rebuilding the bridges the Navy continued to bomb them to keep them out of use. The Navy also attacked the dredgers needed to stop the channel connecting Haiphong harbour with the sea from silting up. The facilities for building barges and small boats used for unloading ships around Haiphong were also raided during October. Admiral Sharp described Haiphong during October by saying:

> "The attacks caused a bottleneck at Haiphong where the inability to effectively move goods inland from the port resulted in congestion on the docks and a slowdown in unloading ships. By October road and rail interdictions had reduced the transportation clearance capacity at Haiphong to about 2,500 tons per day. An average of 4,000 tons per day of imports had arrived in Haiphong during the year." [6.]

Movement of supplies was reduced and warehouses in and around Haiphong filled up. By October there were 200,000 tons of supplies stacked in the open. The North Vietnamese placed these supply dumps within built up districts and in the port

Conference in the White House. Maxwell Taylor, Ambassador to North Vietnam, Dean Rusk, President Johnson and Robert MacNamara discuss policy. By late 1967, MacNamara had become disillusioned with the war and would soon be replaced as Secretary of Defense.
(National Archives)

areas where self-imposed restrictions by the Americans kept them safe. American bombing slowed the process of unloading ships in Haiphong, the time taken to unload individual ships increasing from thirteen days to over a month. Shipbuilding and maintenance facilities were rebuilt in residential areas where they were safe from the bombing.

Permission was finally given to attack the main North Vietnamese air base at Phuc Yen on 24th October and General Momyer decided to carry out the attack the same day. The raids scheduled for that afternoon were cancelled, which involved reloading aircraft with different ordnance and re-briefing the pilots. The permission to attack Phuc Yen included instructions on the timing of attacks, numbers of aircraft involved, directions of attack and types of bombs to use. These detailed orders limited the scope of the commanders on the spot. Both the Navy and the Air Force carried out attacks on Phuc Yen and Cat Bi airfields over a three-day period. The airfields were put out of action with twenty aircraft being claimed as destroyed on the ground. Under this combined attack the North Vietnamese Air

Force moved some aircraft into Southern China to keep them safe and to re-equip.

In South Vietnam an all-weather bombing capability had now been established using ground based radar. Aircraft flying in formation at high level were ordered to drop their bombs by the radar operators, who positioned them exactly over the target. By this means it was possible to achieve an accuracy of 400 to 500 feet.

A radar station was constructed in Laos during 1967 in an attempt to use the same system over the North. This was positioned on top of a mountain in the territory controlled by communist Pathet Lao forces. The radar station could only be set up and serviced by using helicopters to lift in the men and materials and was positioned 160 miles west of Hanoi to cover North Vietnam. Bombing could now be carried out over the North during bad weather, the flights being usually led by EB-66Es. However when aircraft were operating over cloud cover SA-2 missiles could come up through the cloud without warning, too late for evasive action to be taken. It was also necessary for aircraft to fly straight and level for thirty miles before dropping their bombs, which made them vulnerable to the Vietnamese air defence system.

The accuracy achieved by this high level radar bombing was never sufficient for the type of targets attacked over the North. With a 500-foot accuracy the system could not find bridges, trucks or rail lines, although marshalling yards and large storage areas could be hit - but not near residential areas. In reality the USAF had no all weather-bombing capability to match the Navy's low level radar system in the A-6, even using the F-105F *Wild Weasels*.

After the Stennis hearings the military continued to press President Johnson to expand the bombing. McNamara however could not support any expansion. At this stage Johnson still maintained his backing for the original NASAM 288 that had led America into the war. Because McNamara had lost faith in the bombing and believed that nothing more could be achieved by it he advised against any further escalation. As he felt that

The LTV A-7 Corsair II. This fighter-bomber, a direct development of the F-8 Crusader, went from first flight (27.9.65) to service with Task Force 77 off North Vietnam in just two years. VA-147 arrived aboard USS Ranger in November 1967 and was to prove a worthy bearer of a famous name. The aircraft depicted is an A-7E from VA-146, about to catapult from USS Ranger, later in the war. (US Navy)

his position had become untenable McNamara resigned as Secretary of Defence in November to take a job as President of the World Bank. Clark Clifford, who was thought to hold more 'hawkish' views than McNamara, became Secretary of Defence in February 1968.

At McNamara's instigation, the Jason group of scientists met again in late 1967 to discuss the bombing of North Vietnam. The group was again briefed by the intelligence agencies, had access to government documents and presented its report in December 1967. It gave the remarkable conclusion that, in the group's opinion, the bombing campaign had actually increased the North's ability to continue the war in the South: 'As of October 1967, the U.S. bombing of North Vietnam has had no measurable effect on Hanoi's ability to mount and support military operations in the South.'7.

The transport system in the north had been reorganised to give redundancy of routes and remove bottlenecks, while the bombing had increased the aid given by Russia and China. This more than balanced the losses due to the bombing. The study concluded that they could not devise any type of bombing campaign that could stop or substantially reduce the flow of supplies into South Vietnam.

In November the Joint Chiefs of Staff requested a renewed bombing campaign involving twenty-four further targets, while the President had created a special senior advisory group to counsel him on the course of the war. The advice given to him by this group was that bombing would force the North to negotiate on American terms. Johnson chose to follow the advice given to him by both the Chiefs of Staff and the advisory group. Ten of the targets requested by the Chiefs of Staff were released for bombing in December, but the second Jason Report was not acted upon.

December 1967 saw the introduction of the A-7 Corsair into Naval service on board the *USS Ranger*, with the first combat operation taking place on the 17th. During 1967 eleven aircraft carriers had taken part in the bombing at various times for losses of 133 Navy aircraft over the North, although a third of the crews had been recovered. Seventeen North Vietnamese aircraft were claimed as destroyed by the Navy in 1967. The combined Air Force and Navy fixed wing aircraft losses had now risen from 171 in 1965, 280 in 1966 to 326 in 1967. The Air Force type that had suffered the heaviest losses was again the F-105s with 113 destroyed, but Thunderchief pilots had claimed 22 of the 59 Vietnamese MiGs credited as destroyed by the Air Force in 1967.

It was planned that the bombing halt for Christmas 1967 would only last for 24 hours and the New Year stand down for 36 hours. The Joint Chiefs of Staff had insisted that any bombing cease fire should last for less than 48 hours to limit the amount of materials that could be moved free from attack. American reconnaissance aircraft flying over the North had recorded an average of 170 trucks a day in the Southern half

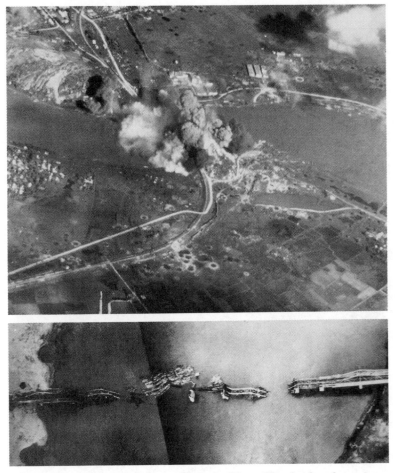

Some dropped, some did not. Top, the Than Hoa bridge, known as 'The Dragon's Jaw', under attack in November, remained standing. Bottom, the Paul Doumer bridge in the centre of Hanoi, photographed after the attack on 17th December. (USAF)

North Vietnam during December 1967. On Christmas day 1,300 trucks were counted and 1,700 during the New Year stand down.

FOOTNOTES

1. Broughton, Jack, *Going Downtown*, Orion Books, New York, 1988, page 104-5.
2. Sharp, Admiral U.S.G. *Report on the War In Vietnam*, U.S. Pacific Command, Washington DC: GPO, 1968, page 32-3.
3. *The Pentagon Papers, The Senator Gravel Edition*, Vol. IV, Beacon Press. Boston. 1971, page 197.
4. United States Senate Armed Services Committee Preparedness Investigating Subcommittee, Air War Against North Vietnam: Hearings, 90th Cong. 1st Sess. US Government Printing Office, Washington, 1967, Vol. IV page 282.
5. Broughton, Jack, Ibid.
6. Sharp, U.S.G. Ibid.
7. The Pentagon Papers, Ibid.

Chapter five

1968: The Thunder Wanes

The North Vietnamese made the most of the 36-hour truce over the New year holiday, reconnaissance pilots reporting that the coastal road was 'carrying as much traffic as one of the New Jersey turnpikes'. The number of American troops inside South Vietnam had now grown to over 400,000. and there was now a certain amount of cynicism among some of the public and the military over the conduct of the war. However, large numbers still believed that it was still possible to win the war at this stage.

At the start of 1968 *Rolling Thunder 57* was still in force, continuing until June. Nine new targets had been added to the list, seven actually being attacked before bombing was stopped. The attention of the American military was diverted away from Vietnam momentarily when, on the 23rd of January, the North Koreans captured the American vessel USS *Pueblo* while she was steaming in international waters. The *Pueblo* had been on an electronic intelligence gathering operation against North Korea but had never entered Korean waters. Two aircraft carriers earmarked for Vietnam were diverted to the Sea of Japan and, for a time, it looked as if another war against North Korea was possible.

The bombing of North Vietnam still concentrated upon isolating the port of Haiphong from Hanoi and the transport system to the south. The North Vietnamese were putting considerable effort into building a redundant capability into their transport net. Multiple roads were built running between the same centres and, where possible, several bridges were constructed over the same river. Bypass routes were prepared around any bottleneck points to avoid congestion. The bombing during the late summer of 1967 had stretched the North Vietnamese to the utmost, but they were learning to live with the bombing. Aid from other countries continued to pour into

Robert McNamara's waning enthusiasm for the war resulted in his being replaced as Secretary of Defence on 1st March 1968. His successor was Clark M. Clifford, who was believed to hold more belligerent views.
(National Archives)

the country to make good any losses. Admiral Sharp described this period by saying:

"Distribution problems for Hanoi were further aggravated by the arrival of a near-record number of foreign ships in Haiphong in January and again in March when over forty ships arrived each month for off-loading. The port of Hon Gai was used in February as an off-loading point for a Soviet and a British ship, probably in an effort to reduce the pressure on Haiphong." [1.]

While they could still import goods to make good losses and distribute them even with severe difficulties, the North Vietnamese would still not bow to the bombing.

The level of bombing that had been sustained during summer and early autumn 1967 was reduced by the weather brought on by the northeast monsoon. Conditions during the first three months of 1968 were very bad and February was the worst month for bad flying conditions during whole of the *Rolling Thunder* campaign. In January, February and March there was only an average of three days a month when visual bombing conditions were possible. Heavy rain, storm clouds and low level cloud blanketed most of the northern part of North Vietnam covering most of the targets that had been repeatedly bombed in 1967. Air Force conventional aircraft continued to bomb the North during the few clear days available and used radar

Despite the almost non-stop air attacks, the North Vietnamese refused to give in, using any methods to survive and continue the war. This reconnaissance photo shows a cultural centre at Haiphong, built in the centre of a lake and containing fifty camouflaged trucks. Large quantities of boxed stores are located both on the island and around the perimeter of the lake. (National Archives)

bombing techniques for some larger targets during the bad weather. Blind bombing operations by Navy A-6s, the only aircraft with a proven all-weather capability and the ability to find and bomb small targets during the bad weather, were restricted by their rather limited numbers.

The infamous Than Hoa bridge again came under attack in January 1968. This enormously strong structure had now been on the receiving end of a whole series of raids by the Air Force, the Navy and the Marine Corps, who had attacked and hit the bridge for nearly three years with minimal results. The superstructure had often been damaged, but the basic structure had withstood hits from bombs of up to 2,000 lbs, while the approaches were built directly into the solid rock at the edge of the Song Ma river. By this stage of the war the Vietnamese had organised several bypass routes to the Thanh Hoa bridge and it had lost some of its practical importance, becoming mainly symbolic. The inability to destroy the bridge had given it a mythical status among the *Rolling Thunder* pilots. It had now come to stand as a metaphor for the inability of the bombing to force the Vietnamese leadership to bend to the American will. Navy aircraft from the *Coral Sea* and Air Force aircraft carried out attacks on the bridge on the 28th January 1968, during a break in the bad weather. In total 44 aircraft attacked the bridge dropping 2,000 lb. bombs but, although damage was caused to the Southern approach and upper part of the bridge, including the road and rail line, the bridge was back in use on the 8th of February 1968.

The 30th of January was the eve of the *Tet* Holiday. This had always been regarded a truce period by both sides. However on this occasion the Viet Cong and North Vietnamese forces in the South violated the truce by launching what became known as the *Tet* Offensive. The Americans had known for some time that a major communist offensive was imminent but the timing and scale of the attack took them by surprise. It was later estimated that 70,000 (some estimates say double this figure) communist troops had attempted to take thirty-six provincial capitals in the South, including Saigon. The Viet Cong wrongly hoped that the offensive would spark a general revolution throughout the South. After being taken by surprise the South Vietnamese and the Americans reacted quickly. The Americans had always wanted to face the Viet Cong in a stand up fight and, using their superior equipment and firepower, the *Tet* Offensive was crushed with massive losses to the Viet Cong and the North Vietnamese. The Americans had always claimed that the Viet Cong was controlled by the North Vietnamese but, up to the *Tet* Offensive, this had not really been true. Although the North supplied, helped organise and strongly influenecd them, the VC was mainly composed of southerners, although some North Vietnamese units were involved. The losses suffered during the *Tet* Offensive destroyed the structure of the Viet Cong as a separate force. After *Tet*, the Americans and South Vietnamese

While the Rolling Thunder attacks decreased during 1968, the defences grew stronger, offset by improved American counter-measures. A SAM, launched during a US Navy attack upon Kep airfield, dives into the ground due to ECM jamming of the radar guidance system. (US Navy)

Looking for trouble. An Air Force F-4C Phantom heads for the North.
(USAF)

(ARVN) forces found themselves fighting the North Vietnamese regular army units (NVA) that infiltrated into the South.

While the *Tet* Offensive had been a tactical disaster for North Vietnam, it had, in the long run, been an overwhelming strategic success. They had lost on the ground but had won in the psychological effect they had on the minds of the American public and leadership. Before *Tet* many of the public and military had been cynical about the possibility of success in the war, but the media and the military leadership created the impression that the communists were on the run. Most of the American public believed that the war was as good as over. Now, after seeing the size, scope and ferocity of the *Tet* offensive, especially the capture of the American embassy compound in Saigon on television, the American public could not believe the war was anywhere near being won.

Although there were members of the American military who thought that the war could still be won, nobody thought it would be either easy or quick. There was now no doubt that the bombing of the North had not stopped or even limited in any meaningful way the flow of supplies from the North to the South. Most of the logistics used to mount and sustain the *Tet* Offensive had come down the Ho Chi Minh trail from the North. It was also obvious that the bombing had failed to break the will of the Northern Government to continue to support the war in the south.

Immediately after the *Tet* Offensive a major attack was mounted against the US Marine base at Khe Sanh in South Vietnam, near to the De-militarized zone. In a 71-day siege the Americans again inflicted a major defeat on the communist forces causing thousands of casualties. Every time the North Vietnamese faced the Americans in conventional large scale ground fighting they were defeated. However, the siege at Khe Sanh reinforced the ideas planted by the *Tet* Offensive that, after three years of large scale fighting, the war was still nowhere near being won. The communists could still mount large scale operations. Both the *Tet* Offensive and the siege at Khe Sanh diverted aircraft from the *Rolling Thunder* campaign to a tactical support role during the increased ground fighting in the South. This, combined with the bad weather over the North, during this period, led to a reduction in the number of *Rolling Thunder* sorties flown over the North.

With the massive amount of aid available from the Russians the North Vietnamese continued to improve their air defence system in 1968. It was estimated that the Vietnamese now had 8,000 anti-aircraft guns in use in North Vietnam. The numbers

During 1968, USS Coral Sea (CVA-43) had ninety days 'on line' at Yankee Station in two separate combat cruises. While no enemy aircraft were destroyed, only three aircraft were lost in strikes against the North and a fourth due to an accident. (National Archives)

of radars in use also continued to expand and the radar coverage was now effective in tracking aircraft flying as low as 1,500 - 2,000 feet and, by April, 350 radars were in use in the North. This made it impossible for the American aircraft to jam or avoid all the radars in the multiple redundancy of the radar system. The MiGs were less active during the first part of 1968 with Phuc Yen and Gia Lam airfields still the main bases. The USAF is credited with the destruction of eight MiGs during January and February 1968 and they were the last North Vietnamese aircraft to be shot down by the U.S. Air Force until February 1972. One of these was a MiG-21 shot down by Captain Robert B Hill and Lieutenant Bruce V Huneke on 5th February while flying an F-4D. This was shot down using a *Falcon* AIM-4D missile, one of the few examples of the successful use of this weapon. The US Navy managed to shoot down seven MiGs between June and September 1968, these being the last North Vietnamese aircraft shot down by the Navy until March 1970.

Secretary of Defence McNamara finally left office on 1st March 1968. He was replaced by Clark Clifford, a friend of President Johnson. McNamara, a brilliant manager, was said to be near to a mental breakdown when he eventually stepped down because of the frustration caused by his inability to achieve the objectives he had set himself. He had always supported the war and the bombing but he had finally been forced to admit that he had not achieved the results he had hoped for.

March saw the debut of the General Dynamics F-111A into Thailand for operations over North Vietnam. Six moved into Takhli air base under the code-name *Operation Combat Lancer.* The F-111 had been intended for use by the USAF and the US Navy but only the Air Force finally accepted the aircraft into service. It was a large 'swing-wing' all-weather attack aircraft, which was believed to match the capability of the Navy A-6 Intruder and would fill this need by the USAF. Its terrain following radar and radar bombing system gave the ability to fly at very low level at high speed without visual reference to the ground being flown over. This was a highly complicated and advanced system and the Air Forces need for this type of aircraft led to the introduction of the F-111 into combat before all the inevitable teething troubles had been eradicated. By the end of March two of the F-111s had been lost on bombing missions over the North and a third was reported missing on 22nd April. All succumbed to technical failures rather than to North Vietnamese defences. It was later assumed that they suffered failures in the structure of the tailplane at a welded joint. After these losses the F-111 was withdrawn from combat. However, 51 low-level missions had been flown successfully, proving its combat capability, when the teething troubles were overcome. The F-111 later became the backbone of the USAF long range strike force for the next twenty years.

In its search for an all weather capability the Air Force introduced the use of *LORAN* (LOng RAnge Navigation) radio aids for bombing over North Vietnam in March 1968. *LORAN* was a navigation aid rather than a bombing system, but its accuracy was judged sufficient for use in this role. It was similar in concept to the *GEE* navigation and bombing system devised in World War Two for Royal Air Force Bomber Command night operations. The time difference between pulses transmitted by a master station and one or more slave stations is used to

In March 1968, the F-111 was deployed for the first time. It showed its potential, but was soon withdrawn following several losses due to technical failure. Twenty-four years later, in the Gulf War, it was still hitting targets with phenomenal accuracy, day or night and in all weathers. (USAF)

The Douglas A-1 Skyraider flew its last combat missions against the North in April and was henceforth relegated to the 'in-country' war in the South as well as flying cover to helicopter search-and-rescue missions. In the jet age, it was an anachronism, yet the Americans could not have done without it. This photograph depicts an A-1E, loaded up with the deadly napalm canisters. (National Archives)

159

calculate the position of the receiving aircraft. It was claimed that aircraft using *LORAN* could bomb from high altitude with an accuracy of 500 feet. This level of accuracy meant that pinpoint targets could still not be attacked with any real hope of success during bad weather. Range limitations with the ground stations meant that some areas of North Vietnam were still out of range of the system.

March 1968 also saw the introduction of the Standard ARM anti-radiation missile. This was intended to be used by the Air Force specialist *Wild Weasel* aircraft, now the F-105F, against the North Vietnamese air defence system. The earlier *Shrike* had proved to be less than effective in attacking SA-2 air-defence missile batteries but the Standard ARM, originally equipped with the homing head from the *Shrike*, could lock on on to the *Fan Song* radar used by the SA-2s from a much longer range and had a larger warhead. As with the earlier weapon, if the North Vietnamese realised that a missile had been launched against them they closed down and the Standard ARM no longer homed, but the SA-2 battery would now be ineffective. The Navy also adapted the Standard Arm for use by their defence suppression A-4 Skyhawks and A-7 Corsairs.

Clark Clifford had originally been known as a supporter of the Presidents strong position on Vietnam, before he became Secretary of Defence. From this position as a 'hawk' he was forced, from practical considerations, to move to the position that the war was as good as unwinnable in any pragmatic view. After the *Tet* Offensive the JCS, Admiral Sharp and General Westmoreland asked for another 200,000 men and thirteen more fighter squadrons to be sent to Vietnam. Yet even with these reinforcements it was admitted that the war could last another four or five years; there was no more talk of an early end to the war. There was little chance of America finding these reinforcements without calling up the reserves and going onto a full war footing and, with the build-up of anti-war feeling among the population, this would have been hard to achieve.

In response to this request for more aircraft and troops Clifford created a inter-agency task force to consider the situation. Although large sections of the military still thought the war could be won, most of the political and civil leadership

The new F-4J Phantom arrived in Vietnam during April. It equipped VF-33, 'The Tarsiers', aboard USS America. Although its performance was slightly inferior to earlier models of the Phantom, it had improved electronics and bombing capability. Even so, despite the combat experience of the previous years, it still carried no on-board gun. (via author)

saw only deadlock and political suicide. After taking part in the discussions and reading all the relevant documents Clifford was forced to change his stand. A former supporter of the war, he now accepted the position that there seemed little chance of winning the war in the short term without an enormous increase in resources and with no guarantee of success.

In an attempt to influence President Johnson to change his thinking on the war Clifford asked for a meeting of the 'wise men', the Presidents senior informal advisory group on Vietnam. This group, which included Dean Acheson and McGeorge Bundy, had earlier backed a strong policy on the war, but Clifford now believed that this had changed. The group met with the President on 26th March 1968 and the overall feeling was that, with the existing policy, there was no military end to the war in sight. Most, but not all, of his advisors now advised a de-escalation. Faced with this, Johnson again decided to try for negotiations with the North Vietnamese by offering a reduction in bombing in return for negotiations and a reduction in the North's actions in the South. The military commanders agreed that a reduction in the bombing during April, when the weather was still bad over the North, would be acceptable to them.

Johnson had been elected in 1964 so 1968 was an election year. As the incumbent President, he would, under normal circumstances, have expected to have been given the automatic backing of his own party for another term of office. However, as the feeling against the war continued to build up in America generally, opposition in the Democratic party to Johnson continued to increase. In the New Hampshire Democratic Presidential Primary in March Johnson only just managed to beat the 'anti-war' Senator Eugene McCarthy. The results of this primary had signalled to Johnson that he was in deep trouble politically. He knew that he had a good chance of beating McCarthy, but when Robert Kennedy also declared his candidacy, he realised that he was facing the possibility of a humiliating defeat. Johnson broadcast to the American people on 31st March, a major speech that admitted the failure of *Rolling Thunder* and announced his own political destiny. He told the world that bombing of North Vietnam would now be limited to south of the 20th parallel in the hope that the Vietnamese would also limit their actions in the South and enter negotiations to end the war. He also announced that he would not be seeking re-election as President.

The 'bomb line' accordingly was moved south to the 19th parallel on 4th April and the North Vietnamese agreed to the talks that had been requested. These began in Paris on 13th May and continued during the following months, achieving very little. Most of the time was taken up with procedural wrangles and arguments over whom should be included in the meetings. The North Vietnamese strategy had all along been a 'long war' strategy and their view was that this was finally paying off. Since the Paris talks had brought a reduction in the bombing so it was now in their interests for talks to continue. They were not prepared to make any major concessions however, so the longer the talk dragged along with little progress the better.

HANOI RR/HWY BR OV RED RIVER

27 MAY 68

FLOATING CRANE

REPLACED SPANS

As fast as the Americans knocked them down, so the North Vietnamese rebuilt. A reconnaissance photo shows the Red River road and rail bridge under repair, 27th May 1968. (National Archives)

During this period they made no attempt to limit their military actions in the South or to limit the amounts of material moving down the Ho Chi Minh trail. They could sense American resolve beginning to crack and could see no reason to change their long term policy. It has been said that the bombing forced the Vietnamese to the negotiating table, but the American negotiators were hardly faced with a cowed enemy ready to agree to American terms. It was just the reverse. The North Vietnamese could now see the Americans need to get themselves 'off the hook'.

The stopping of the bombing north of the 19th parallel released more aircraft to carry out bombing in Laos and the area below the 19th parallel and North of the De-Militarised Zone, where bombing increased. Attacks upon North Vietnam were now almost entirely concentrated on lines of communication, as there were few other worthwhile targets in the area to

A Talos ship-launched missile. On 23rd May, a MiG-21 was shot down by one of this weapons as it attempted to bounce American aircraft operating in Route Package Two. (National Archives)

which bombing was now restricted. Another major new weapon system was introduced in May, This was the laser-guided or 'smart bomb'. These weapons were ordinary bombs with a special homing head and steerable fins. F-4D Phantoms had been provided with the necessary on-board systems to operate the weapons. In operation, the launch aircraft marked the target with a laser designator, carried in a pod, and the head of the bomb homed onto the laser energy reflected from the target. The bombs proved highly accurate when they operated correctly but one drawback was that the launch aircraft needed to continue 'illuminating' the target until the bombs impacted. This meant that the attacking aircraft might have to spend longer within range of anti-aircraft defences than would be the case with conventional bombs.

Bombing was now limited to route packages 1, 2, and the lower part of Pak 3. This freed the area around Hanoi and Haiphong from the constant bombing they had suffered in the past. The North Vietnamese re-built and improved their infrastructure. Damaged roads and bridges were repaired and road traffic could now move both by day and night. Massive

The storm is over. President Johnson (right) announces the end of the Rolling Thunder campaign to Walt Rostow, Secretary of Defense Clark Clifford and General Earl Wheeler, Chairman of the Joint Chiefs of Staff. The place is the Oval Office and the date is 31st October 1968. (UPI)

stockpiles of material and equipment that had accumulated around the dock area in Haiphong were now slowly distributed around the country. They also improved their air defence system and attempted to move their missile coverage as far south as possible by establishing missile sites as close to the bomb line as they thought safe. All major MiG airfields were now out of range of the bombing and were safe from attack. On 23rd May a MiG-21, attempting to attack American aircraft operating in RP 2, was shot down by a US Navy ship using a *Talos* surface-to-air missile.

This restricted bombing continued throughout the summer of 1968. Meanwhile the delegates continued to argue at the meetings in Paris. It was finally agreed that the main conference would take place between North Vietnam, South Vietnam, the National Liberation Front and the U.S. President Johnson believed that he had reached other agreements with the North Vietnamese and that they would, 'join us in de-escalating the war and moving seriously towards peace.' It was hoped that the peace talks would lead to a general cease fire and halt to the bombing, but the North Vietnamese view saw the talks merely as another step in the process of removing the Americans from Vietnam. On 31st October 1968 President Johnson stated that all bombing of the North would end at 08.00 am Washington time on 1st November. Major Frank C Lenahan, of the 8th Tactical Fighter Wing, is credited with carrying out the last bombing mission of *Rolling Thunder* when, flying an F-4D, he attacked a target near Dong Hoi only an hour and a half before the President made his announcement.

The *Rolling Thunder* campaign was over. Far from the original 'few weeks or months' it ended after three years and eight months sustained bombing of North Vietnam. Nearly 300,000 sorties had been flown over North Vietnam, with more than 600,000 tons of bombs dropped. The North Vietnamese had destroyed over 900 of the attacking aircraft and helicopters. It was estimated that 382 pilots and 289 aircrew had been killed and 702 were listed as missing, many of whom were held prisoner. America had devoted an enormous amount of effort, time, men and resources to *Rolling Thunder* to either destroy North Vietnam's capability to affect the war in the South, or to break their will to continue the war, neither of which were achieved.

NOTES

1. Sharp, U.S.G. *Report On The War In Vietnam*, US Government Printing Office, Washington, 1968, page 44.

Chapter Six
The View From The North

North Vietnam originally ran from approximately the 23rd parallel in the North to the 17th parallel in the south. It was bordered to the east by the Gulf of Tonkin, to the north by China and to the west by Laos. The land area was 62,000 square miles and, in 1964 the population was estimated at 18.4 million. For a period of over three and a half years between 1965 and 1968, apart from short respites, North Vietnam was bombed practically every day by American aircraft, on average more than 500 tons of bombs being dropped every day during this period. If the main aim of the bombing was to force the North to cease its aid to the insurrection in the South, there is no doubt that it failed. How was it possible for the North Vietnamese government to maintain it's objectives under such a powerful and sustained attack?

Vietnam has a long history of armed conflict against powerful neighbours to maintain its existence. The Vietnamese claim to have fought more than twenty wars against foreign invaders. For most of its history Vietnam has been under the nominal control of China but, over the centuries, the two countries have often clashed. This has left Vietnam with a fear of its Northern neighbour. China attempted a punitive invasion of Vietnam in 1980. It achieved little and both countries are still in dispute over the Paracel and Spratley islands in the South China Sea, which has led to small scale armed conflict between them. In 1288 the Vietnamese defeated an invading army of 300,000 Mongols, under the command of Gengis Khan's grandson. The Vietnamese have always been prepared to defend their independence both before and after the American bombing. In the last century the French gained control of Indochina in a series of campaigns between 1840 and 1883. However the Vietnamese date the start of the Indochina wars from 1883, when guerrilla warfare started against the French. The Vietnamese fought to regain their independence from the French, then During the Second World War against the Japanese (with American assistance) and then against the French again.

The French were finally forced to admit defeat after their disaster at Dien Bien Phu in 1954 and the Vietnamese took to heart the lesson that they could defeat a major power. North Vietnam was created out of the settlement with the French, the Geneva Accords of 1954. There were to have been elections in the South, on the creation of one country in 1956, but these were never allowed to take place. This was because Ho Chi Minh was believed to be sufficiently popular throughout the country to have won. The Americans, who replaced the French in South Vietnam, did not consider themselves bound by the Geneva Accords. The effect of Dien Bien Phu on Vietnamese thinking would be hard to overstress. At Dien Bien Phu the French only lost one battle, and could have continued the war if they had so desired. Actually Dien Bien Phu had broken the French spirit rather than completely defeated them militarily. The Vietnamese came to feel that if they waited long enough the Americans would go the same way as the French and eventually were proved right

The North Vietnamese planned from the very beginning for a long war against America. They saw the war as only the latest phase of their struggle against imperialism dating back to 1883. They expected the war to be destructive, would last for a considerable time and based their planning on these premises. Before the bombing started the population had been warned to expect it and to expect severe destruction. Nobody had any illusions over America's ability to carry out and maintain the bombing.

The leadership of North Vietnam was made up of guerrilla fighters who had defeated the French and many of them had spent all their adult lives in organising a people's war to free their country from foreign domination. The troops sent South into South Vietnam from the North were told to expect a war lasting up to twenty years. President Ho Chi Minh, in his appeal to the Vietnamese people and army on 17th July 1966, said:

"The war may last another five, ten, twenty years or longer. Hanoi,

Haiphong and other cities may be destroyed, but the Vietnamese people will not be intimidated. Nothing is more precious than independence and freedom." [1.]

He understood the power of the Americans and knew that the only way to defeat them was the 'long war' strategy. He accepted that America could destroy their industry and their cities, but even before the bombing started the North Vietnamese leadership had psychologically prepared the population to be ready for, and even to expect such bombing.

The North Vietnamese Prime Minister Pham Van Dong's view of the Americans was that:

"Americans do not like long, inconclusive wars......thus we are sure to win in the end." [2.]

The Vietnamese realised correctly that they had little chance of beating the military might of the Americans in any stand-up fight. However, if they could be drawn into a long drawn-out war, costly in lives and money, the American temperament would not accept it. By warning their population to expect the destruction before it occurred and even to exaggerate the expected levels of destruction, the North Vietnamese leadership stayed one jump ahead of the Americans. As the Americans expanded the bombing throughout the North, the people now expected it. In fact the level of the bombing never reached that predicted (area bombing of the cities) and in some ways was even an anticlimax after the many warnings issued by their Government. George H. Questor speaking of the British public's reaction to bombing in the First and Second World Wars stated:

"A psychologically prepared population......will feel that the threat is predictable and manageable, when it notices the failure of assaults to exceed authoritatively predicted levels of damage." [3.]

The North Vietnamese authorities had even told their population to expect an American land invasion of the North (as requested by American 'hawks') and to prepare for guerrilla warfare in the countryside. The bombing devastated large areas of the country and destroyed North Vietnamese industry, but from the very beginning this had been accepted as the price they would have to pay, the people expecting even worse conditions than actually occurred. Their definition of victory was for the Americans to stop bombing and to leave Vietnam.

Therefore they reorganised their society to achieve this. They intended to outwait the Americans and to force up the costs to America of continuing the war to as high a level as possible.

The Government of North Vietnam was strongly communist, Ho Chi Minh was a life-long communist supporter and most of the vast amounts of aid received by the North came from the communist block, Russia, China and Eastern Europe. However, it would be wrong to view the Vietnamese as belonging to some kind of monolithic communist world movement. They were primarily patriotic nationalists whose relations with both Russia and China were never very warm, even when they became dependent on their aid. Their relations with China especially were always cool, both before and after the war.

Most foreign visitors to Hanoi during the *Rolling Thunder* campaign were taken to the Museum of the Revolution, a museum devoted to Vietnamese history going back to the Stone Age. The Vietnamese were fond of quoting the fact that Vietnamese history stretched back thousands of years before Columbus had set sail for America. Their strong sense of cultural identity was, in some respects, even strengthened by the bombing. Ho Chi Minh is quoted as saying:

> "We have learned the lesson, we have been taught to be nationalists by two thousand years of our history. We are reasonable people, and we want an end to this war. But the freedom and independence of Vietnam will never again be negotiable." [4.]

The North Vietnamese could never hope to match the Americans on a technological level but the chief Vietnamese asset was the Vietnamese people. The leadership, having fought and won a people's war against the French, rightly or wrongly saw themselves fighting the same kind of war in the South. This view of war considers the will of the people and their belief in their cause as the major factors for victory rather than modern weapons or technology, although effective weapons are not to be ignored. (The use of modern artillery at Dien Bien Phu had been the decisive factor.) The 'long war' strategy, along with a population who had been prepared for the worst and had a deep

Opoosite page, the main bridges in the North. All were repeatedly attacked during Rolling Thunder.

170

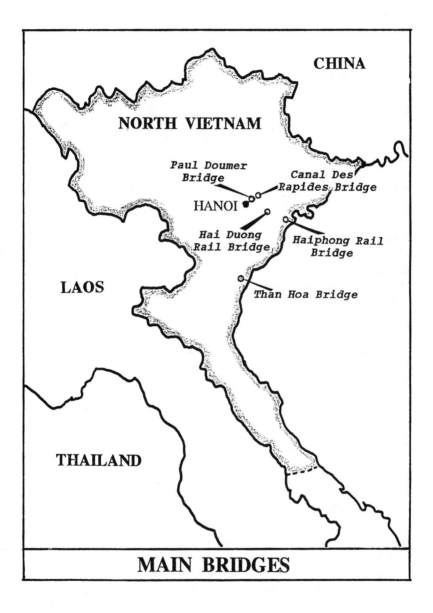

Map 6: Main bridges (Peter Edwards RICS and John T. Smith)

nationalist pride and belief in the justness of their cause, was the basis of the Vietnamese defence against the bombing.

During this period of the war (1965-8) the Vietnamese were insisting on the Americans accepting four points before they would agree to negotiations. These were: (1) Recognition of the integrity of Vietnam and the removal of all American troops. (2) Respect of the Geneva Accords. (3) Settlement of the situation in the South in accordance with the programme of the National Liberation Front. (4) Peaceful reunification of the North and South without foreign intervention.

Not surprisingly the Americans saw these conditions as establishing the outcome of any talks before they had started. One of the unstated aims of the bombing had been to attempt to force the Vietnamese leadership to modify their stance, but there was very little movement in their position. When talks began in Paris in May 1968 the North Vietnamese position was that they were only meeting to obtain, 'unconditional cessation of US bombing raids and all other acts of war so that talks may start.'[5.]

Before 1965 the aid given to the South had comprised mostly supplies. The personnel involved had been Southerners, who had fled to the North after 1954, who returned to the South to help the Viet Cong. After 1965 an increasing number of North Vietnamese regular army troops were infiltrated into the South. According to American estimates the numbers involved were 35,000 in 1965, 89,000 in 1966, up to 90,000 in 1967 and 150,000 in 1968. Even McNamara was forced to admit that the number of trucks moving South was twice as high in 1966 as it had been in 1965, when bombing had started. If bombing had been intended to stop the infiltration, it had not succeeded. If it had been intended to raise the costs of the infiltration, it had succeeded. However, the North had been prepared to meet those costs. McNamara stated in 1968 that he thought it was difficult to conceive of any interdiction campaign that could have stopped the movement of supplies to the South.

The amount of materials needed by the Viet Cong and the North Vietnamese Army in the South was relatively small. McNamara went on record as saying:

"Intelligence estimates suggest that the quantity of externally supplied material, other than food, required to support the VC/NVA forces in South Vietnam at about their current level of combat activity is very, very small. This reported figure is fifteen tons per day, but even if the quantity were five times that amount it could be transported by only a few trucks." [6.]

Although other estimates suggest a larger figure than fifteen tons the amounts involved are still relatively modest during the period we are dealing with. Later, in 1972 and 1975 when North Vietnam carried out conventional invasions of the South, the amounts of supplies involved were much higher. With the Viet Cong holding the initiative in the South they could also increase or scale down their actions to match the amounts of materials available. '...the enemy was able to disengage many units and to seek refuge in sanctuaries in Laos, Cambodia, and North Vietnam, where our ground forces were not permitted to strike him. This permitted him to establish the pace of the ground war to his advantage,'[7.] The figure of fifteen tons could be carried in five medium sized trucks and, with the entire effort of the North involved, it is impossible to see how these amounts could have been stopped.

The main routes into North Vietnam for military supplies were through the port of Haiphong and along the two railway lines from China. The supplies were then transported down the length of the country by road, waterway or rail, with smaller amounts going by sea. Most of the personnel going into the South seem to have walked. American interrogation of prisoners captured in the South disclosed, 'Ten to twenty per cent of the personnel dispatched to the South.....never reached the battle area.'[8.] Most of these casualties were caused by malaria and only two per cent by bombing. The Annamite range of mountains runs down the Eastern border of North Vietnam, restricting the crossing points into Laos to a few passes. These include the Ban Karai and Na Pe passes, the main one being the Mu Gia pass. Small amounts of supplies were sent across the De-Militarised Zone into the South but the main routes for men and supplies crossed over into Laos and then either into South Vietnam, or down into Cambodia and then into the South.

Mu Gia pass is about seventy miles north of the De-Militarised Zone and runs from North Vietnam into Laos. A high percentage of the supplies going south came through this pass and, during the three and a half years of *Rolling Thunder*, the Mu Gia pass attracted thousands of tons of bombs. This 'choke point' proved very difficult, if not impossible, to close. The pass is only about two and a half miles wide by twenty-one miles long and it was claimed that as many as 150,000 people were involved in repairing the roads and keeping the traffic flowing through. The pass was heavily bombed by B-52s on 12th April 1966, but trucks were rolling through it only two days later.

After crossing into Laos the supply route became a mass of interlocking paths and roadways, known as the infamous Ho Chi Minh trail. This was an ever expanding network of tracks, (some were only earth roads, while others were surfaced with crushed rock), heading down to the South. Numerous North Vietnamese regular troops and civilian workers were employed in guarding the track, creating new roads and maintaining the existing ones. At short intervals along the tracks there were many truck parks and rest areas. Great effort was put into keeping these as small and dispersed as possible. Each section of the track had its own repair and maintenance crew constantly renewing any damage to trucks or to the roadway. A large amount of food needed by the Viet Cong came from South Vietnam or from Cambodia and did not need to come down the Trail, so it was mainly only military equipment and personnel that needed to make the journey from the North.

One of the few undoubted American successes was the stopping of the sea route to the South. Before the start of the bombing most of the supplies going to the South went by sea, using large numbers of small boats. American ships and aircraft sank thousands of barges and small craft off the coast of North and South Vietnam in an operation code-named *Market Time*. Although this route was never completely closed, for practical purposes the land route came to carry the bulk of the traffic. The port of Sihanoukville in neutral Cambodia was also used for some supplies.

The North was visited by foreign observers during the period of the bombing and they nearly all spoke of the North's transport system coming to life in the evening. The country

Bombs rain down upon the unloading and storage facilities at Haiphong harbour. (via author)

moved by night to avoid the bombing. Jacques Decornoy, who visited the North in 1966, stated:

"At six o'clock in the evening Vietnam starts to move. It pedals, drags, digs, patches up, clears away, rebuilds. The way this people moves into action again every night is astonishing.......I saw the lines of lorries that leave the main towns at night. They are countless, in spite of the destruction of convoys. Their headlights are kept on as far as Than Hoa. Then farther towards the South, the journey goes on slowly, obstinately, in the dark." [9.]

Harry S. Ashmore and William C. Braggs commented:

"We saw one concentration of about 30 big fuel tank trucks gathered under trees near the road, presumably halted until dark." [10.]

During *Rolling Thunder* little night bombing occurred around the Hanoi area. However in the southern area of North Vietnam, where most of the bombing took place, the transport lines were attacked day and night. Aircraft worked in pairs, one dropping flares, while the other attempted to interdict the supply lines. In the Northern part of the country the trucks kept their lights on during the relatively safe night time (neither Hanoi or Haiphong were blacked out during *Rolling Thunder*), but further South the blackout was complete. Harrison E. Salisbury who visited the country in late 1966 describes this as:

"The trucks formed up in convoys in Hanoi in the late afternoon. During the day they were scattered about, but towards dusk they collected at loading points and then began to roll out of the city as darkness fell. There was little or no movement of trucks of supplies southward except after dark. But once night came the highways bustled with movement which continued, so far as I could see, until dawn." [11.]

In late 1967 American intelligence estimated of the numbers of trucks used by the North was 10 - 12,000 ('You must remember that they are operating only somewhere between 10,000 and 12,000 trucks.'[12.]) These operated on an estimated 5,800 miles of road in North Vietnam, only just over 1,000 usable in all weathers. The drivers seem to have been a very hardy breed. Not only were they expected to be on the road for up to 120 days, but also had to load and unload their trucks. There were shortages of spare parts for the transport fleet and the drivers were expected to repair and maintain their own trucks as best they could. They were also expected to help in any repairs to the roads that were holding them up. When roads were blocked drivers were told to find their own detours if possible. They were also expected to be responsible for camouflaging their vehicles. Once the trucks had left the Hanoi area they were liable to attack at any time and constant efforts were made to hide them from above, both on the road and when they had halted during the day. The trucks were camouflaged with netting and the branches or leaves of any available trees. On this point Harrison E. Salisbury said:

"We fell into a long line of truck traffic, mostly big military two-and-a-half-ton trucks turned out by the Likhachev factory of Moscow....They moved down the highway steadily with a variety of burdens-I could not make out exactly what because of the murk and because each truck was carefully camouflaged with a canopy of boughs and tropical leaves. This, I was to learn, was the constant dress of motor vehicles outside Hanoi.." [13.]

Even cars and jeeps were covered in leaves and pontoon bridges that were broken down during daylight hours were camouflaged with foliage. How effective this was from the air is very hard to determine.

Although trucks provided the basis of the transport system there were also other elements. The famous Vietnamese bicycles contributed to the total of goods moved. It has been claimed that using bicycles the Vietnamese could move 150lbs of materials up to 25 miles a night. If the bicycle was converted with a bamboo frame, up to 600 lbs of goods could be transported by wheeling it by hand for up to ten miles a night. The cyclists worked in teams to help each other push the loads up any inclines they encountered. John Gerassi, who visited the country in early 1967, describes seeing the bicycles in action:

> "..the roads were mostly crammed with bicycles (mainly Chinese-made), each lugging so much material that only the wheels were visible. We were told that each bike could carry as much as one ton (sic). True or not, they did in fact seem to transport everything from sacks of rice and logs of bamboo to bricks and sections of rails." [14.]

If we ignore one ton as too much of an exaggeration even McNamara is quoted as saying that bicycles could carry 500lbs ('Even bicycles capable of carrying 500-pound loads to move goods over this network.'[15.]) If these figures are correct it is hard to see what level of bombing could have stopped this type of transport system. If we also accept the figure of fifteen tons of supplies needed in the South per day, this total could have been delivered by something like 60 bicycles a day. With the entire effort of North Vietnam involved the bombing needed to stop this would have to have been enormous.

The railways in Vietnam are a legacy of French colonial rule. The main lines include two running North from Hanoi into China, one to the northwest and one to the northeast. Another forty mile line ran from Haiphong into Hanoi. The other main line had run from Hanoi south to Saigon but during this period it stopped North of the De-Militarised Zone. The North Vietnamese put considerable effort into keeping this rail network in operation and several rail bridges became primary targets of the entire bombing campaign. Railways were an easier target than the road system and were more difficult to repair, but the North Vietnamese kept their trains running. Harrison Salisbury thought that the Vietnamese valued the railways so highly because they did not run on oil or petrol, but on wood and coal. If at any time their supply of oil was cut off they still had the railways to fall back on. Jon M. Van Dyke considered that the main reason that the system was kept open was that the rail lines provided the major access route from China. Part of the Chinese railway system ran through North

Vietnam and the Chinese provided 50,000 troops to maintain the system north of Hanoi.

Large amounts of materials were also transported on the inland waterway system. There were many navigable rivers and canals in the north, especially in the Red River delta. These had always been used to transport goods around the country. American aircraft came to attack any type of river craft seen in the North and even small boat building yards were attacked. After most of the bridges in the country had been destroyed, they were replaced by pontoon bridges built on small boats that were broken down and hidden each day. The areas building these pontoons were also attacked.

In reaction to the bombing the North Vietnamese built up both an active and a passive defence. They created an air defence system using large numbers of radars to control air defence missiles, aircraft and anti-aircraft guns, that cost the American pilots dear. They also created a passive defence to the bombing; a civil defence system, air raid shelters, dispersal of population and industry, rationing and decentralisation of control to the regions. Taken together these measures allowed the Vietnamese to contain the bombing and to continue to operate in spite of it, while simultaneously forcing the Americans to pay a considerable cost in aircraft destroyed and lost aircrew.

The active part of the Vietnamese defence was based on the air defence system supplied mostly by the Russians and to a lesser extent the Chinese. This system was base on many overlapping radars. These were both long range search radars and short range tracking radars, backed up by a network of ground observers who reported any aircraft movement by land lines to control centres. The radar system and reporting network was used to control an anti-aircraft system that included fighter aircraft, surface-to-air missiles plus heavy and light anti-aircraft guns. During *Rolling Thunder* the Vietnamese continued to increase and upgrade their anti-aircraft system and, over a period of three and a half years, their defence system destroyed over 900 American aircraft.

The Vietnamese Air Force came to include both MiG-17s and 21s, pilots received training in both China and Russia. Thus

With the ending of Rolling Thunder, reconstruction work in the North proceeded quickly. Here, work on the the Canal des Rapides bridge, east of Hanoi, is nearly complete. (USAF)

they built up their Air Force from practically nothing to a respectable force, credited with the destruction of 55 American aircraft. They were never a real match for the American Air Force but, by choosing their own time and place, could destroy American aircraft. The surface-to-air missile used by the Vietnamese was the SA-2 or SAM-2 (NATO code-name *Guideline*). This was the type of missile that had shot down Gary Powers in his U-2 over Russia on 1st May 1960, the first successful use of a surface-to-air missile in combat. The missiles, radars and guidance systems were supplied by Russia, along with the necessary technicians, but the day to day running of the missile sites were in the hands of the Vietnamese. Bechir Ben Yahmed commented on the use of missiles in 1967 by saying,

"...the operators of the surface-to-air missiles are Vietnamese. The Russian technicians criticize the way in which the Vietnamese, too quickly trained, use them. ("As if they were machine guns". commented one Russian) but cannot move in except for maintenance visits or big repairs." [16.]

The missiles functioned by radio command guidance and were much more effective at higher attitude. During *Rolling Thunder* they were responsible for 101 American aircraft destroyed. The North Vietnamese constructed large numbers of missile sites and moved the missile units around between the sites. A complete unit could move in four hours, thus the Americans were never sure which sites were active.

Most of the American aircraft destroyed were in fact shot down by the anti-aircraft guns (*Flak*). They were mostly Russian 23mm, 37mm, 57mm, 85mm and 100mm or Chinese and Eastern European copies, some 85 and 100mm guns being radar directed. In 1965 the Americans estimated that North Vietnam had about 1,500 AA guns and by 1968 this had grown to a total of around 8,000. Not only the quantity of guns had increased but also the quality with a larger proportion being of the heavier calibres and more were directed by radar. It was estimated that in 1967 these guns were firing 25,000 tons of ammunition a month at American aircraft.

North Vietnam was also one of the few countries in history to have accepted the responsibility of fully arming it's population. Visitors to the North speak of people working in the fields with rifles on their backs and people in factories with their rifles hanging on the wall next to their machines. A significant minority of American losses were to small arms fire. The population was encouraged to fire on any American aircraft within range. In built-up areas groups of people were positioned on roof tops to give themselves a clear field of fire at any attacking aircraft. Most of this was futile, but gave the people a chance to feel that they were fighting back against the Americans. Anybody who participated in the destruction of an aircraft was hailed as a hero. Harrison Salisbury described this when he said:

"Everybody had a sense of participation in the battle because so many people had been issued rifles and actually shot back at the American aircraft." [17.]

The North Vietnamese managed to destroy American aircraft

throughout North Vietnam (and in South Vietnam, Laos and Cambodia), but most were brought down in the Hanoi and Haiphong areas (Pak 6). Most of the air defence system was concentrated in this area as was most of the population and industry. The loss rate in the Hanoi area was fifteen times higher than for the rest of the country.

The radar and reporting organisation was used to trigger an alarm system for the population. When aircraft were within thirty kilometres a system of air raid sirens and warnings was given over the radio. As the raid came nearer the air raid wardens used bamboo drums or even metal containers to warn the people. Out in the countryside at night there was a system of yellow and red lights. The system appears to have been primitive but to have worked quite efficiently. Bechir Ben Yahmed commented, 'I never experienced an alert without bombing, or bombing without an alarm. The system works perfectly, it seems.'[18.]

The passive side of the Vietnamese reaction to the bombing was to organise a network of shelters throughout the country and to evacuate and disperse their population and industry. During *Rolling Thunder* the Vietnamese claim to have constructed 21 million air raid shelters, which varied from concrete and steel structures in Hanoi and Haiphong to covered trenches in the country districts. Every able-bodied person in the country was supposed to be involved in the shelter building programme and to ensure that they were provided with a shelter at home and another one at their work place. The slogan was 'The shelter is your second home'. In the southern part of the country, where the bombing was heaviest, whole communities moved underground. Living quarters, schools, hospitals and workshops were constructed in underground tunnels to avoid air raids.

In Hanoi and Haiphong all major streets were lined with the famous individual shelters. These were constructed of concrete cylinders, about five feet long and two and a half feet wide, buried into the pavements and were covered over with a loose concrete lid. Thousands of these shelters were available for use by people caught out in the open by a bombing raid.

After the bombing had continued for some time, some people, especially those in areas that were not heavily bombed, became blase about the shelters and neglected their construction, repair and cleaning. This forced the government to make it a responsibility of all citizens to ensure they were not injured. Non-productive people would become a drain on the state. Malcolm Salmon, who had visited the country, said:

> "The significance attached to the sheltering of non-combatants during air raids has to be seen to be believed. In North Vietnam today, it seems that only the poorest of types is unaware that the protection of one's life is a social as well as an individual responsibility." [19.]

North Vietnam's population in the cities and large towns was, where possible, dispersed throughout the countryside as was the small but significant industry. Hanoi had a population of around one million and large numbers of non-essential people were evacuated from the city. This plan was never fully carried through since many people did not want to leave their homes and others returned to their homes where possible. Not only industry but also markets, that would attract large numbers of people, were dispersed to lessen the chance of heavy casualties. Before the attacks began the government had drawn up plans for people to be moved out of the heavily populated Red River area to less crowded areas.

Heavy industry like the iron foundry at Thai Nguyen and the cement factory in Haiphong could not be evacuated because of the large size of the industrial plant they used, but much of the lighter industry was dispersed. Small factories were broken down into smaller units and distributed into small villages. Sometimes the factories were reduced to such an extent that each individual machine was in a different location. This obviously caused a reduction in the amount produced but kept some production going. The Americans attacked the Vietnamese oil storage facilities in 1966, destroying nearly all the fixed oil plants, but the Vietnamese reaction to this was to distribute the oil storage throughout the country. Oil was stored in 55 gallon tanks in fields and along the major road routes in small amounts and in a random pattern that did not provide any targets worthy of bombing. As with the distribution of the industry, this was an inefficient method of organising the fuel supply but it allowed the system to continue to operate.

The government of North Vietnam had been heavily centralised and the industry had been built up under centralised control. With the decision to move the industry into the provinces they also found it necessary to devolve a large amount of decision-making to the regions. The North Vietnamese Government had been preparing for the possibility of an American invasion and it may have been necessary for the government to abandon the area of the Red River Delta, which was the most likely area for such an invasion. Jacques Decornoy stated, 'The decentralisation of the economy and the administration, on the pattern of the petrol drums, has robbed the planes of big targets'.[20.] The decentralisation also helped the transport situation by reducing the amount of traffic in and out of the Hanoi area. The reduction of the population in Hanoi also reduced the amount of food that needed to be transported into the city.

For a centralised communist state, the decision to decentralise some government functions to the regions was not taken lightly. To maintain the control of the party, the number of party workers was increased after the start of the bombing. These party workers were the government officials, the leadership in the communes, the supervisory staff in the factories and the school teachers. Party workers were given some privileges and higher rations but, in return for this, were expected to devote themselves to the party. By increasing the numbers of party workers the government hoped to maintain their tight control, even after increasing the power of the regional administration.

The North Vietnamese also carried out dispersal of nearly all schools and education institutions from their cities. This involved a major relocation of people and equipment into the countryside. Although this must have affected standards the Vietnamese claimed that they were providing schooling for four million students in 1968-69. Visitors to North Vietnam who were shown schools noted that they were well provided with shelters and trenches, while the buildings were surrounded with earth banks. Many schools in the south of the country spent years completely underground, working in tunnels. The party vice-chairman Ton Duc Thang stated that it was more important for the children to protect themselves from the bombing than to continue their studies. It was thought that in reality many children travelled back every weekend, to visit their parents, risking their lives on the heavily bombed transport system. Many visitors also described the school children as wearing plaited straw hats that were supposed to be protection against bomb fragments and the shrapnel from cluster bombs.

Concerning the morale of the people, we can speak only in general terms. We only have information from visitors who spent a short time in North Vietnam, (apart from propaganda published by the North). However, the morale of the population appeared to have remained reasonably high throughout the bombing. There was considerable suffering and damage, but the bombing never reached a level where it could break the spirit of the Vietnamese people. The bombing also allowed the North Vietnamese government to convince their population that the Americans were more than just political opponents, but were evil colonialists seeking to dominate the South. The attacks motivated the population in the direction the government wanted, but never reached a level capable of breaking the people's morale. Malcolm Salmon speaking about the North Vietnamese morale stated:

> "Suffering constant civilian losses as they do, with their industries and communication lines, cities and villages subject to constant attack, the Vietnamese nevertheless have superb morale. Englishmen I met in Hanoi constantly recalled the spirit of London during the blitz as the only thing they could compare with North Vietnam today." [21.]

The Vietnamese seem a hardy and stoic people who refused to be overawed by the bombing and tried to continue their lives in as normal a way as possible. Hai Thu said, 'the strategists of the Pentagon left out an essential element in their calculations: the Vietnamese people's moral strength.'[22.] Many visitors to North

Opposite page. The Ho Chi Minh trail began in the North, but proceeded through Laos and Cambodia. It was not a single road, but thousands of jungle trails leading into the South. The Americans attacked the three main passes many times, but never succeeded in closing this major supply route.

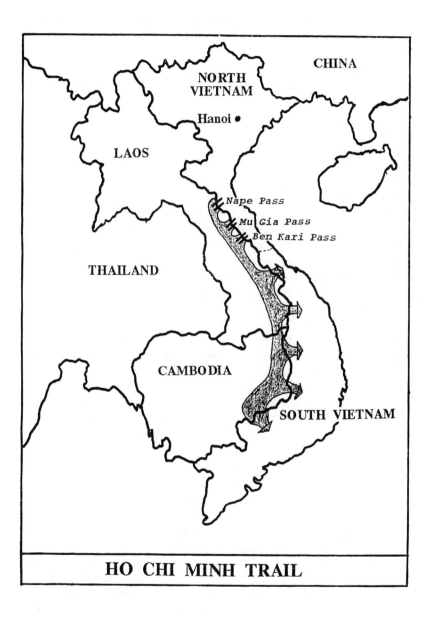

Map 7: The Ho Chi Minh trail.
(Peter Edwards RICS and John T. Smith)

Vietnam described the way the Vietnamese adapted their way of living to cancel out the effects of the bombing and to continue their daily lives where possible. It must be borne in mind however that many of these visitors were Vietnamese supporters. After his trip to the North John Gerassi described the Vietnamese morale by saying:

"They won't crack, these people. They are firm. resolute, brave, disciplined. They go about their business, produce goods, build up their communities ......Our courage (American) is individual. Theirs is collective. It is taken for granted, it is the courage of a whole people." [23.]

During the three and a half years of *Rolling Thunder* the Americans dropped 1.9 billion leaflets on North Vietnam in an attempt to give their side of the bombing and to attempt to influence North Vietnamese morale. The people were ordered to pick up the leaflets and to turn them over to party officials. They are not known to have had any influence on the North Vietnamese will to continue the war. The level of bombing it would have taken to break the morale of the Vietnamese people will never be known, but whatever that level was the Americans never reached it.

The bombing created shortages of many basic materials. Harrison Salisbury speaks of shortages of matches, cigarettes, soap and salt. Other things in short supply were sugar, paraffin, shoes and bicycles for private use. The food supply suffered from shortages at various times, but this was to a large extent made up by imports from China, Russia and eastern Europe. The rice ration in 1967 was said to be fifteen kilograms a month for office workers and twenty-two kilograms for manual workers. Russia supplied cereals to Vietnam but these were not as popular as rice with the people. Meat was scarce and the ration was ten ounces a month. This was not always available and was sometimes supplied as lard. Fresh fish was scarce but dried and salted fish was in reasonable supply. In the open market vegetables and fruit could easily be bought but meat and chicken were expensive. Things like cloth were supplied through a person's work place and were rationed at between four and six yards a year. John M. Van Dyke quotes the average daily intake of calories for a city-dweller as between 1,700 and 1,900 calories. While this seems inadequate by western standards it compares reasonably well with the pre-war totals in Vietnam. Although there was hunger at times in North Vietnam there was never any starvation.

The health care standards in North Vietnam had been improved after the end of the war with the French, but were still generally very low even before the bombing. Hospitals were evacuated to the countryside and located among the towns and villages. Although many local medical facilities were very rudimentary, in some ways medical care became easier for the people to obtain because it was available through local units. A large number of medical personnel were sent to the South however, which compounded the shortage in the North.

North Vietnamese agriculture was mainly run by farming co-operatives, state run farms and a few privately owned farms (less than 10 per cent of the total). After they had won the war against the French, the Vietnamese had redistributed the land to the peasants. Later there had been pressure on the people to join farming communes, the majority complying. Although the country had a small industrial base, it was still overwhelmingly agricultural in nature. The numbers of people employed in agriculture provided the reservoir for the enormous numbers of men taken into the army and the people working to keep the transport system operating. It was thought that there were large numbers of people underemployed in agriculture. These were drawn off to work in projects necessary to overcome the effects of the bombing. Oleg Hoeffding, in a report written for the Rand Corporation, stated:

> "..where removal of manpower from the village is involved, as by military moblilization and recruiting, the adverse impact on the farm labour force is reinforced by the fact that such drafts fall mainly on its most able bodied and relatively best educated male members, who often also exercise leadership functions in the cooperatives." [24.]

Many communes were also expected to undertake projects for the government besides their farming tasks.

Before the *Rolling Thunder* campaign, the farming cooperatives had failed to provide the required food production. Thus the bombing provided the Vietnamese with a ready made excuse for the shortfall in food. The bombing also allowed the government to extend its plans to reduce the numbers of private farms as the government controlled the supply of everything the farmers needed, tools, fertiliser, etc. This forced many to join the local cooperatives to obtain needed supplies.

The primary Vietnamese crop was rice, which requires the use and control of large quantities of water. North Vietnam is crisscrossed with thousands of dykes to control the water supply. The area of the Red River Delta, which includes Hanoi and Haiphong and contains much of the country's population, was originally low-lying marsh land. Indeed, Hanoi is about twenty feet below the river level during the rainy season. To control water levels the river banks were raised and a system of canals and dykes was constructed to drain off surplus water. In 1945 between one and two million people were killed when the dykes were destroyed by heavy rains and by the Japanese. This shows the extent to which the Red River delta is vulnerable to flooding. John Gerassi described this as, 'If a hydrogen bomb were dropped on Vietnam's Red River delta fewer people would die from the explosion than from the destruction of the dykes.'[25.]

The Vietnamese continually claimed that the Americans deliberately tried to bomb the system of dykes, but the Americans have always denied this. The Vietnamese used the dykes for positioning anti-aircraft guns, because in some areas the dykes were the only ground high enough to give a clear field of fire. They also stored fuel and other supplies along the length of the dykes. There is no doubt that the Americans on occasions caused damage to the dykes. Also they continually attacked all traffic on the inland waterways, which must have caused damage, while considerable amounts of ordnance was used against the anti-aircraft network. It is doubtful that there was a serious effort made to destroy the dykes, simply because of the lack of serious damage that actually occurred. The dyke system could easily have been destroyed had the Americans wished to.

The majority of bombs dropped by the Americans over North Vietnam were used against the transport infrastructure, causing heavy damage. The roads, rail lines, canals and bridges were frequently attacked, especially in the southern part of North Vietnam. One American pilot described parts of the country near the De-Militarised Zone as resembling the surface of the moon. Whole communities were forced to live and work underground in tunnels. Most American sorties over the North were armed reconnaissance missions, which were primarily directed against the transport network.

During the war with the Japanese, and later the French, the entire railway system, with its hundreds of bridges and thousands of miles of track, had been destroyed. The North Vietnamese Government had taken over a ruined transport system in 1954 and the system had still not been completely restored when the bombing started in 1965. The Vietnamese had years of experience of working with a transport system that was barely functional and had considerable practice in repairing roads and continuing to operate with a minimum system, although nothing had prepared them for the destruction the Americans caused.

There can be little doubt that the bombing caused enormous damage to the transport system. All the visitors to North Vietnam speak of the scope of the damage. John Gerassi describes one journey in the following terms:

"Continuing on Route No.1 from Phu Ly to Nam Dinh, we were struck by the extent of bomb damage along the open countryside. Almost every farm house near the road had been demolished or damaged or was surrounded by bomb craters. Every bridge.... had been knocked out, and repaired. In our relatively short ride, we must have crossed almost a hundred." [26.]

As the bombing progressed, the Vietnamese created an organisation capable of carrying out repairs to keep the system operating.

The North Koreans had faced the same problems during the Korean war and provided expertise to the Vietnamese during the early days of the bombing. However the Vietnamese soon developed their own ways of dealing with the bomb damage. Along every road and rail line materials were stored for carrying out repairs. Every few hundred yards were to be found supplies of the necessary tools, equipment and materials to keep the transport moving after any bombing. Jacques Delcornoy described how, 'Detour routes are prepared in advance. Everywhere there are mounds of earth and stones, sleepers and rails waiting to be used.'[27.] Repairs to damaged roads often took only hours to complete. Many roads were only composed of a surface of crushed rock, thus repairs were only a matter of filling in the holes and re-surfacing with the crushed rock.

The rail system was a lighter gauge system than either European or American railways and was easier to repair than either of these. It still required considerable effort to keep it running however. The Vietnamese claimed to have distributed enough sleepers, ties and track along the 700 miles of tracks to build up to three times the entire length of rail line. As stated earlier the Chinese provided 50,000 construction troops to keep the railways running in the north of the country, since this line also served southern China.

The most vulnerable part of the transport network were the bridges. As the area of North Vietnam that was open for bombing moved north, the major bridges were among the first targets in newly released areas to be attacked. Despite this the North Vietnamese built up an amazing expertise in repairing and building bridges. All the smaller rivers were surveyed and all possible fording sites were noted. If stone or steel bridges were only damaged they were repaired with wooden sections if feasible. If bridges were destroyed the Vietnamese developed several ways of building new ones. The wider rivers or canals were crossed by pontoon bridges; flat bottomed boats or barges were placed side by side across the river and a roadway laid across the top. During daylight hours the bridge was broken down and the pieces hidden along the banks of the river to be replaced every night.

It was also possible to cross wider rivers by using a barge or an old boat as a ferry. This would not need to be powered but could be pulled across the river by a system of pulleys on either bank. Here again the ferry would be hidden and camouflaged during the day. On more important crossing points larger powered ferries were used. Although ferries could only handle a few trucks at a time, it kept the traffic flowing.

Narrower waterways could be bridged by using lightweight cable suspension bridges. The North Vietnamese also became expert in constructing bridges out of bamboo, which were compared favourably with British steel Bailey bridges. Bridges could quickly be constructed from bamboo, lashed together with ropes. John Gerassi describes how on a journey to Haiphong a road bridge in front of them had been destroyed:

"I looked at it (the bridge): it was completely destroyed. I was certain we'd be stuck for the night. Less than two hours later, however the officer returned. 'You may cross now,' he said. A whole new bridge, forty feet long, had been built - out of bamboo. And it was sturdy enough for two loaded trucks which were ahead of us." [28.]

All high risk bridges had repair materials stored close at hand. Another Vietnamese tactic was, where water conditions permitted, to construct bridges under water just shallow enough for trucks to cross but deep enough for it to be difficult to spot on reconnaissance photographs.

The primary target on the transport system was the Paul Doumer or Long Bien bridge, carrying the rail line from the north of the country and from Haiphong across the Red River into Hanoi. One of the targets on the Chief of Staffs original 94 target list, this bridge was named after a former French governor, and was the main crossing point of the Red River. It had nineteen spans and was 5,532 feet long and 38 feet wide, the centre of the bridge carried the rail line and there was a ten-foot wide roadway on either side of the rail track. The southern end of the bridge ran into Hanoi and the Northern end started in the Gai Lam area. For a long time the Americans were prevented from bombing the bridge because of its proximity to Hanoi. All visitors to Hanoi landed at Gia Lam airfield, then travelled across the Paul Doumer bridge into Hanoi and all confirm the amount of traffic carried by the bridge. The bridge was hit on 11th August 1967 by F-105s carrying 3,000lb bombs and put out of service for several months. However the North Vietnamese had, by this time, prepared another pontoon bridge downstream to carry the traffic.

The second most important target in the transport network was probably the bridge over the Song Ma river at Than Hoa one hundred miles south of Hanoi. This was a very strongly built road and rail crossing built in the 1950s. It was 540 feet long and 56 feet wide and was supported on concrete piers. First attacked on 3rd April 1965, it was hit by several bombs but this was to be only the first of many such raids. The structure proved to be too strong for the standard American 500 lb and 750 lb 'iron bombs' and, although the bridge was often damaged, it defied all efforts to bring it down. A later generation of weapons was necessary to destroy it during the *Linebacker* raids in 1972.

The port facilities at Haiphong became increasingly important as the war continued, since an increasing proportion of Vietnam's imports arrived there. These supplies were then moved by road or rail through Hanoi and into the transport system. The link between Haiphong and Hanoi was about sixty miles long and involved several bridges. Although the North Vietnamese were forced to travel by night the average journey time was only about four hours and roads and bridges were usually repaired within hours of any bombing.

To keep it's transport moving the North Vietnamese built up several organisations dedicated to repairing and developing the system. By 1967 The Americans estimated that large numbers of Vietnamese were involved in keeping the transport moving:

"There are 97,000 full-time people that are diverted to coping with the air campaign....The balance, somewhere between 370,000 and another 500,000 that are part time are involved in war-related tasks." [29].

These figures ignore Chinese construction troops keeping the rail lines running in the North of the country. The number of people involved in the repairs was indeed immense, but the Vietnamese were prepared to commit the people needed to keep the supplies moving.

Army engineers co-ordinated the groups involved in repairs and large numbers of army personnel were also involved. In 1965 the government created the 'Youth Shock Brigade Against The Americans For National Salvation' as a specialised repair organization. Young people were enlisted in this force, which specialised in road repairs. Most were women, since most of the men were already in the army. The Vietnamese claimed that there were 50,000 members of this organisation, formed into small groups along all the major transport routes, ready to carry put repairs when necessary. If they were permanently stationed in one area these 'Youth Brigades' were also expected to grow a percentage of their own food. They were also required to help the local farming communes if there was no bomb damage to repair.

Other organisations were also involved in keeping the transport moving. The local Militia were expected to help in their own areas and the self defence forces formed at people's work places were used. Another group was the 'peoples engineering units' also organised on a local basis. The farming communes were used to provide a reservoir of labour for the repair work and people were expected to give several days a month to working on the roads and rail lines in their own areas.

The Vietnamese claimed to have developed a bomb disposal organisation capable of dealing with unexploded bombs and delayed action bombs, dropped to hamper immediate repairs. If it was not known when a bomb is going to explode, repairs cannot be started until the bomb has either gone off, or has been defused.

"Delayed-action bombs dropped wantonly on communication lines, are another source of disappointment for the men in the Pentagon. Each village in hard-hit zones has at least a few persons capable of unpriming the most complex delayed-action bombs." [30.]

There is no doubt that the bombing forced the Vietnamese to divert large numbers of people into non-productive tasks such as shelter building and road repairs. However, the under-productive agricultural industry provided the work force for the numbers of people needed. Although this affected agricultural production it was not decisive since they could still import food to make up any shortfall. Oleg Hoeffding estimated the total numbers of North Vietnamese diverted by the war as:

"The total scale of manpower diversion at the peak of this effort can only be crudely guessed at. Somewhere between one and 1.5 million men and women (including military) seems as good a guess as any. This would amount to something like 10 to 15 percent of the total more or less adult and more or less able-bodied population." [31.]

Although they were never critically short of manpower the Vietnamese were as short of skilled workers, as they were before the bombing started. They claim to have trained large numbers of people to become the political and technical cadres to make good the people needed by the evacuation to the countryside, but numbers quoted by the Vietnamese were either very quickly trained or exaggerated. The closing down of some industrial enterprises by the bombing released some skilled labour for redeployment.

What labour shortages there were in the North were to a large extent made up by increasing the use of women both in the economy and in positions of authority. By 1967 about half the farm labour was provided by women, who also head many of the cooperatives. The use of women in industrial and textile jobs also increased during the bombing. North Vietnam had tried to improve the position of women after the successful war with France. Ho Chi Minh is quoted as saying, 'unless we liberate women we will not be liberating one half of mankind. Unless we liberate women we will be building socialism half-way.' The war in some ways allowed the party to overcome the prejudice against taking women out of the home and they were able to implement this policy.

By 1967 the armed forces of North Vietnam numbered about 400,000, the vast majority being in the army. This ignores the large numbers in the militia and local defence forces. The numbers of troops sent to the south steadily increased and very few of them ever returned during the *Rolling Thunder* campaign. The Americans estimated that there were only 2,000 North Vietnamese troops in South Vietnam in 1964 but, by 1968, this estimate had increased to 100,000. It was also thought that there were 40,000 North Vietnamese in Cambodia. There were about 190,000 men reaching the age of 18 in North Vietnam each year of which around 120,000 were actually conscripted. Despite this, the numbers were insufficient thus the conscription was expanded to take sixteen to forty-five year-old people in 1967. Although Vietnam's manpower was stretched, the shortages never reached a critical position.

American bombing destroyed the small industrial base as it existed before the bombing. The Vietnamese had a small but developing industry that included power plants, thermal power plants and steel works. They also had factories producing soap, tyres, tobacco, ceramics and textiles. In 1965 Vietnamese industry employed only 20 per cent of the population, but produced more than 50 per cent of the Gross National Product. The value of Vietnam's industrial production before the bombing was estimated at $1 billion. At the beginning of *Rolling Thunder* the Americans were restricted in the targets they could attack but, by the end of the campaign in 1968, practically all

Architect of American defeat. Ho Chi Minh's 'long war' strategy clearly proved superior to American firepower, but he did not live to enjoy his nation's triumph. (UPI)

the fixed Vietnamese industrial targets had been destroyed. In late 1967 McNamara estimated that the value of all the facilities destroyed in North Vietnam was about $320 million of which about $44 million was included for the value of industrial plant destroyed. McNamara also stated:

"I think it is generally agreed all of the major industrial capacity in the North has been Destroyed, $44 million representing the value of 85 percent of the power system, the entire cement production capacity, the entire pig iron capacity, and the entire explosive capacity." [32.]

The Americans made the true claim to have destroyed nearly all the North Vietnamese heavy and fixed industry. However North Vietnam still managed to produce on a small scale the bare minimum necessary to keep the country viable and to import the shortfall.

There was originally to have been a five-year plan of industrial development intended for 1966-70 but this had to be abandoned. Instead a two-year plan was instigated to move investment from large scale heavy industry to small scale localised industry. The aim was to move manufacturing into the villages and into small units, hard to find and hard to bomb. The manufactured products were also changed to reflect the emphasis now placed on regionalised agriculture. Small-hand powered agricultural machinery became one of the manufacturing priorities, as this type of product could be produced on a handicraft basis in village workshops.

Most of North Vietnam's iron and steel production was concentrated at the Thai Nguyen steel works situated about thirty-five miles north of Hanoi. Before the bombing started, the Vietnamese were exporting increasing amounts of pig iron to Japan, the value of these exports being $2,650,000 in 1965. Iron was also exported to Hong Kong. Because of the large size of the plant involved it proved, in practice, impossible to evacuate the steel works. The plant was kept going as long as possible but, by late 1967, it had been attacked many times and was out of production for the rest of *Rolling Thunder*.

Many power plants had been destroyed and machine tools had been distributed over wide areas, although the evacuation of factories was not carried out 100 per cent. Thus there was still a need for electrical power, now required over a wide area. This problem was met by importing large numbers of small diesel generators from Russia. Each small workshop had its own generator to provide electrical power for the machines available. In very remote areas where even generators were not available work was continued using hand power on a handicraft basis.

Another major Vietnamese production facility before the bombing was the cement works in Haiphong. This was another French legacy to the Vietnamese and, by 1965, was producing half a million tons each year. The position of the plant close to the docks at Haiphong had helped the Vietnamese to become exporters of cement to the rest of Asia, But after the plant had been bombed they were forced to import cement. They had created other factories to use the cement to produce building products and were now forced to import cement in an attempt to keep these industries going and to provide the necessary building materials to maintain the transport system.

The Vietnamese textile industry had also been developing before the start of the war. There were several large textile factories in production in the North. The breaking down of these factories and the evacuation of the machines to the country side caused severe disruption. The army and other government services took large amounts of cloth for uniforms, which restricted the amount available for civilian clothing. The industry also had difficulty in obtaining raw materials such as bleach, dyes, cotton and synthetic fibres. The Americans bombed textile targets where there were still substantial targets left after evacuation. The textile factory in Nam Dinh was damaged, but there is some disagreement over whether the factory was in fact the intended target.

Before the war North Vietnam stored most of its oil in several large storage dumps near to Hanoi and Haiphong. They required 32,000 tons of oil a year to supply their needs. Even before the bombing started they were constructing large numbers of small oil tanks scattered throughout the country. These tanks, which held between 2,000 and 3,000 gallons, were built underground along the major roads. During 1965, as the bombing continued, the Vietnamese expected their oil storage to be bombed and continued to build the system of storage in smaller amounts. In the summer of 1966 the Americans carried out a series of attacks on the Vietnamese POL (petrol, oil and lubricants) system. All the major installations outside populated areas were hit.

By late 1966 the Americans were claiming that 80 per cent of the Vietnamese oil storage had been destroyed along with the oil unloading facilities at Haiphong harbour. To overcome these difficulties the Vietnamese increased their oil imports and began to use their dispersed storage system. By the end of 1966 the Vietnamese had 60,000 tons of dispersed oil, enough stocks for nearly two years use. They also began to store oil in 55 gallon tanks and simply left these in small amounts, out in the open, along the road system where they would be needed. With the port at Haiphong unable to unload the oil they unloaded the tankers outside the port and carried the oil ashore in lighters and barges. It was then distributed around the country by road. Since the Americans were reluctant to bomb foreign ships, there was little they could do about this. McNamara was forced to admit in late 1967 that the Vietnamese had at least 120 days supply of oil in storage inside the country.

Early in 1967 the Americans mounted a series of attacks on the Vietnamese power stations, claiming to have destroyed 87 percent of the electrical generation capacity. Here again the effect of this on the Vietnamese was considerably less than the Americans had expected. The Vietnamese simply reorganised themselves and rolled with the punches.

The Vietnamese had a thriving coal industry before the bombing began. In 1965 the mines produced about 4.3 million tons but after the bombing was pursued in earnest this dropped to two million tons a year. The Japanese were importing one million tons of Vietnamese coal, which was cut to only 500,000 tons by the bombing. It had been hoped to replace some oil consumption by using extra coal, which had been in good supply, but the availability of coal became as difficult as oil. The difficulties with the power system meant that miners could be trapped underground by power cuts. Many miners had also been conscripted into the armed forces and there were also difficulties with transporting the coal because it is a bulky commodity. However the Vietnamese managed to keep the mines producing, although at a reduced rate.

Conditions in Hanoi were never as bad as in some other parts of the country. Although efforts had been made to evacuate large numbers of the population there were still considerable numbers left and many of those who had been evacuated later returned. They had originally expected their capital to be wiped out and had contingency plans ready for this emergency. In the early part of the bombing the Americans avoided Hanoi but individual targets in the city were subsequently bombed. Johnson kept a specific veto on any target within Hanoi, his approval being needed before any such target could be attacked. Although the Americans claimed to be bombing only identified targets in Hanoi, some damage was done to residential areas, and civilian casualties were caused. In several periods during 1967 targets in Hanoi were struck hard. The city's power station, the Gia Lam railway complex, the Paul Doumer bridge and the Canal des Rapides bridge were all attacked, but for most of the time there was no night blackout in Hanoi.

The Americans usually seem to have bombed Hanoi during the late morning or early afternoon and the working day was rearranged around this. Bechir Ben Yahmed wrote:

> "Waking-up time in Hanoi is 5.00 am Since the bombing began the town has kept to an odd timetable. Work is done from 6.00 to 10.30 am and from 2.30 to 5.00 pm when bombing is least likely. The shops open at midday and late in the evening." [33.]

Many American pilots complained that they were too rigid in the timing of their raids, which allowed the Vietnamese to organise themselves around the bombing.

Haiphong was Vietnam's second city and the country's major port, besides being an important industrial area. Like Hanoi, Haiphong had originally been spared bombing but, like Hanoi, was later bombed at the American President's discretion, limited to specific targets. During 1965 North Vietnam imported by sea about 700,000 tons the vast majority coming through Haiphong. By 1968 this total was up to over 1.5 million tons. The percentage of Vietnam's imports coming by sea was given as 85 per cent, including most of the heavy equipment. These facts were vital to the ability of the Vietnamese to withstand the bombing. They not only kept open their main importation route but managed to more than double the amount of these imports during the bombing.

During the 1950s the Vietnamese increased the size of the docks at Haiphong to include ships of more than 10,000 tons and, by 1965, the unloading wharves could take seven ships of 12,000 tons at a time. The docks were inland from the sea, on a channel of the Red River, the Cua Cam, which tended to suffer from silting up and required regular dredging. The Americans did not bomb the actual dock area because of the presence of foreign ships especially Russian and Chinese ships. The massive increase in imports through Haiphong meant that the port was taking more ships than it could really handle. At one stage, ships were held up outside the docks for up to a month waiting for a berth. In January and March 1968 forty ships a month arrived to be unloaded. There was more cargo unloaded at the docks than there was warehouse space available and there were delays with the transport system. Therefore goods were stored out in the open all round the port area. While they remained in the immediate area of the port these supplies were safe from attack.

The third largest city in North Vietnam was Nam Dinh, situated about 50 miles south from Hanoi and about 25 miles inland from the coast. The original population was 90,000 but this was greatly reduced by evacuation. The two main cities of Hanoi and Haiphong had been protected by Presidential decree during the early part of the bombing, but Nam Dinh and similar cities were heavily bombed from early in the campaign. Nam Dinh's main industry had been textiles and 13,000 people had been employed in the mills before the war. The Americans carried out a series of raids during 1966 destroying large numbers of buildings in the city. However, most of the textile making machinery had already been moved out into the countryside into smaller units.

Most visitors to North Vietnam in 1967 were taken to view the damage at Nam Dinh. It would appear that the Vietnamese thought of the destruction as particularly wanton and wanted their view of it to be accepted by world opinion. Jacques Decornoy described the damage by saying:

> "In the centre of the town near the cathedral, a whole district, 240 houses, they say, has been razed to the ground. What remains upright stands unsteadily among piles of rubbish yards high...The railway line along the river had, of course, been attacked and since repaired. The skeletons of camouflaged trucks and engines remain from the raids." [34.]

What remained of the textile mills had also been bombed and the buildings severely damaged. Some government offices continued to work in the city however and it was never completely evacuated.

Another large industrial town in North Vietnam was Viet Tri. This is situated about 35 miles north west of Hanoi on the main rail line into China. There is an important rail bridge in Viet Tri that was the target for several American raids. The bridge was destroyed on 14th June 1966 but was replaced by a pontoon bridge. The population of 40,000 was cut to less than 20,000 by evacuation.

Than Hoa, which is 80 miles south of Hanoi on the main route to the south of the country, was also heavily bombed. The mayor is quoted as saying that the city had ceased to exist and half the population had left. Conditions in Vinh, in the south of the country, were even worse. The southern part of the country was the first to be bombed and always suffered the heaviest raids. It had a population of around 70,000 before the war started but during 1965 and 1966 the city was all but destroyed. The surrounding area was used as a major staging area for the Mu Gia pass and the transport route into South Vietnam. By 1967 it was claimed that between 80 and 90 per cent of the buildings in the town had been destroyed.

Another smaller town that suffered very heavily from the bombing was Phu Ly just south of Hanoi. Harry S. Ashmore and William C. Braggs described the destruction there:

"Whatever military targets had been in Phu Ly, a rail and road junction town 59 Kilometres south of Hanoi, had been destroyed along with everything else - including the dwellings of a now vanished population of 7,700." [35.]

The Americans claimed that the town contained a number of military targets including storage areas, a barracks, a rail bridge, railway sidings and port facilities on the stretch of river nearby. These were just a few of the many areas in Vietnam that were very heavily bombed.

The one vital fact in North Vietnam's ability to almost ignore the bombing was their ability to obtain almost limitless supplies from abroad together with financial aid from their supporters, Russia, China and Eastern Europe. For their own political reasons both Russia and China gave enormous amounts of military and civilian assistance. The Americans estimated that the Vietnamese obtained $420 million aid from abroad in 1965, $730 million in 1966 and $1 billion in 1967. It was thought that Russia provided 60 per cent of this total and China 30 per cent. The Chinese also supplied large quantities of food and much of the small arms, anti-aircraft guns and ammunition used by the North Vietnamese. Most of the more sophisticated weapons and the MiG-17 and 21 aircraft along with the SA-2 surface-to-air missiles were supplied by Russia. The Russian aid was either shipped in by sea from Europe or Vladivostock, or sent overland through China by rail. There are reports of the Chinese interfering with Vietnamese aid passing through China and the Russians made more use of the sea routes later in the war.

The fact that Vietnam's allies were prepared to supply these amounts of aid and gave assurances that they would continue to do so, underpinned Vietnamese confidence that they could mount and survive a long war strategy against the Americans. The Vietnamese also thought that the aid would still be available after the war to enable them to rebuild their industry and commerce. They could never have financed the war without this aid from abroad, nor was there any question of repayment from their own resources. This constant, increasing supply of aid from abroad allowed them to mount a war that was completely beyond their own resources and allowed them to withstand the destruction of their industry and many of their cities. If they had been forced to buy arms, equipment and food on the open market for hard currency they would not have sustained the type of resistance to the bombing that took place.

This was the period of strained relations between Russia and China, with Vietnam managing to walk the tightrope between the two. She received aid from both while managing not to alienate either one. By accepting aid from many sources the Vietnamese maintained their independence of action. The Chinese, North Korean and Cubans all offered to send combat troops to North Vietnam but, while they were prepared to take technical help, they were not prepared to accept foreign troops. Even technicians were only accepted when they were thought to be absolutely necessary, for example the Russian surface-to-air missile technicians. Although they accepted large amounts of aid from Russia and China, both were kept at arms length to maintain their independence. They were determined, as they saw it, to win their freedom from colonialism by their own efforts, without feeling obligated or indebted to anyone. Bechir Ben Yahmed described the Vietnamese feeling towards the Russians and Chinese as:

"Chinese and Russians, whether diplomats or journalists, are subject to the same laws as other foreigners, need the same permits, and complain of the same difficulties. The Sino-Soviet dispute, the cultural revolution, dealings between Russian and Chinese diplomats are not admitted in Vietnam." [36.]

The Vietnamese saw themselves as in the vanguard of the world socialist struggle against American imperialism and thought it was the duty of all other socialists to support them. In their struggle to maintain their sovereignty they were however, only willing to give grudging thanks for this help. North Vietnam was not dominated by, or a puppet of, either Russia or China in any way, although they were totally dependant on them to continue the war in the way that they did.

During the early part of the bombing the Americans claimed that they were only bombing military targets and using surgical precision in their attacks. However the definition of military targets in this kind of war is 'as long as a piece of elastic' and can be stretched to cover practically anything. The idea that tens or even hundreds of thousands of tons of bombs can be dropped over a period of months or years with precision is untenable. If a factory is bombed there is a strong likelihood that the people who work in the factory will live around the factory. Therefore 'co-lateral damage' (the killing of noncombatants) is inevitable. When a road junction was bombed there is a high probability that people using those roads or living in the immediate area will be killed. The Americans never denied that civilians were being killed but they created the impression that civilian damage was minimal and that all targets were military (arms factories or barracks). The impression created was that the bombs only destroyed concrete and brick targets and most of the American public believed this impression.

When Harrison Salisbury, a reporter for the New York Times, sent back his reports from North Vietnam in January 1967, they caused a furore in America. Salisbury described the destruction at Nam Dinh, in the suburbs of Hanoi and at other places in North Vietnam. He also quoted as to the extent of civilian casualties (from figures provided by the North Vietnamese). These came as a shock to many Americans who had believed the gloss the Government had placed on the bombing. This led to a build up of popular feeling against the bombing, increasing pressure on the government to abandon the campaign. The American military were wrong to allow the impression that it was possible to carry out a bombing campaign against 'military targets' with little or no civilian casualties to gain such credence. When it was disproved there was a collapse in support among the public.

North Vietnam always claimed that the Americans deliberately tried to kill civilians and saturation bombed their cities, but this was untrue. American politicians and high ranking military leaders tried to miniminise civilian casualties and many pilots died because of approach tracks and timing that had been chosen for this reason. The mounting of a strategic bombing campaign must involve large numbers of people being killed and all the ramifications of this should be faced when the decision to under take such a campaign is taken. There are no available reliable figures for the numbers of North Vietnamese casualties caused by the bombing, but these must be in the tens of thousands. One American estimate puts the figure at 52,000 killed over three and a half years. During the Second World War RAF Bomber Command killed 50,000 Germans in one night in Hamburg and over 100,000 in Dresden on another, even though the Germans had an efficient experienced civil defence organisation. The Americans killed up to 100,000 Japanese in one night in Tokyo. The North Vietnamese suffered horrific casualties in the bombing but there is no doubt that the Americans, had they wanted to, could have killed ten times as many Vietnamese as actually perished. Although more bombs were dropped on North Vietnam, there were less casualties than in the bombing of North Korea.

The idea of precision when thousands of tons of bombs are involved is a mistake. Even in South Vietnam American aircraft never guaranteed anything like surgical precision and there was nothing like the northern anti-aircraft fire to worry about. This does not mean that the American pilots could not achieve accurate results, they could, but this could not be assured, some bombs will always go astray. Because of pilot error, equipment faults and the thousand and one things that can go wrong. (Clausewitz's friction) Accurately delivering ordnance from an aircraft travelling at 600 miles an hour, while avoiding enemy aircraft, missiles and anti-aircraft guns, was extremely difficult.

The Americans at various times restricted the bombing of the Haiphong and Hanoi areas and avoided some built up areas. The Vietnamese understood these restrictions and attempted to use them to their own advantage by storing military supplies and setting up truck parks in residential areas. They also stored materials and guns on the dykes as these were supposed to be off limits to American attack. The Americans seemed to view these actions as somehow underhand or unsporting, but the Vietnamese view was that they were locked in a life or death struggle with the most powerful country on earth who had caused the deaths of thousands of their citizens. W. Hays Parks has stated:

> "In addition to parking military convoys in civilian residential areas and storing military supplies in such places as the Haiphong cultural centre, normally a civilian object protected from attack, the North Vietnamese maximised for military purposes their use of objects enjoying special protection under the law of war." [37.]

Air Force colonel Jack Broughton who was involved in a raid on Viet Tri in 1967 describes the Vietnamese use of civilian positions:

> "They had one large complex of buildings just north of the town that was billed as a hospital, and was naturally off limits. If it was in fact a hospital, it must have been a hospital for sick flak gunners, because every time we looked at it from a run on the railhead, it was one mass of spluttering flashing gun barrels. Like I said, there is no sporting blood up there." [38.]

North Vietnam saw itself as involved in a total war in which anything that improved their position was acceptable. The Vietnamese also exploited the many bombing halts and pauses by moving supplies quickly through their system, and by repairing bridges and roads.

The bombing stretched North Vietnam's resources to the extreme, affecting the industry, agriculture, transport and commerce and forced an extensive diversion of labour into war related tasks. However they were prepared to accept these disastrous affects on their economy and stoicly continue their war effort. They overcame the American technological superiority and survived the bombing by using determination and ingenuity. Marc Riboud, who visited the country in 1969, explains Vietnam's ability to withstand the bombing by saying:

> "Poverty linked with an incredible will has forced them all, from the leaders to the peasants and students, to develop to the extreme human limit their intelligence, their ingenuity, their patience, in order to compensate for their lack of technical means. These things enable a nation of poor peasants to

stay alive and to withstand the most advanced technology of the most powerful nation and army on earth." [39].

There is evidence that the bombing actually strengthened the resolve of the Vietnamese Government and people. The measures the government took to control the effects of the bombing also improved the government's position to allow it to effectively carry out its policies. The German bombing of Britain and the American and British bombing of Germany strengthened, to a certain extent, the resolve of the country under attack. The Vietnamese writer Hai Thu describes the Vietnamese reaction to the bombing by saying, 'The day they dropped their first bomb on North Vietnam the Americans in fact welded the nation into a single, indestructible bloc.'[40]. While allowing for a certain amount of hyperbole in this statement, in what was essentially a propaganda publication, it suggests the reaction to the bombing.

The bombing seems to have enhanced the government's position in several ways. Oleg Hoeffding stated that:

> "Military and paramilitary mobilization will have greatly strengthened the internal security apparatus. The National emergency enables the regime to resort to coercion where in peacetime it might be constrained to persuasion. It also makes the population more dependant on the Government for essential goods and services, and the ability to supply or withhold them becomes a potent instrument for control." [41].

The development of the militia and peoples defence forces strengthened the ability of the government to know what was going on and to extend their control down to village level. Government training of large numbers of extra cadres, with known allegiances to the party, was made necessary by the de-centralisation to the regions forced by the bombing. This also gave the government more control at the local level.

For years the Americans had sent saboteurs and spies into the North, never very successfully. This activity was used to create local organisations dedicated to catching 'foreign spies'. The Vietnamese government used these organisations to increase their control of the population at the local village level. The government could also, under the emergency conditions created by the bombing, move groups of people around the country simply by revoking their ration cards in a particular area. It was the government that was receiving the food aid from abroad and it was the government that was distributing it, giving them a powerful means of social control.

Harry S. Ashmore and William C. Braggs who visited the country in 1968 quoted one Vietnamese who claimed that the bombing had allowed the government to increase it's control over the education system:

> "In the face of the strong Oriental family tradition, no one had previously dared undertake the separation of children from their peasant and bourgeois parents in order to provide a school system on the Russian model, and thereby guarantee that their revolutionary education would be uncorrupted by any carry over from the decadent past. Now American bombing of the cities and towns has made such segregation of school children not only possible but mandatory, and even the youngest see their parents only on weekend visits." [42.]

Rolling Thunder also made it easier for the government to motivate the people to support the war in the south. People in the north were not faced with some abstract enemy in the distant south but an enemy who was bombing their homes on a daily basis. The number of deaths and destruction caused by the bombing forced the ordinary North Vietnamese citizen to face the reality of the war and increased the support for the war against the Americans in the south.

From the very beginning *Rolling Thunder* took the gradual approach. A slowly increasing amount of bombing moving steadily north towards Hanoi. This gave the Vietnamese time to develop their passive and active defences to the bombing. It also allowed them time to gain the necessary skills and experience in keeping their transport system running. The organisations needed to keep the traffic moving were therefore in place before the bombing reached it's heaviest level. They were allowed to change their air-defence system from practically nothing to what was described as one of the most effective ever seen. They were also given time to distribute their industry into the countryside and to evacuate their urban population.

The breaking up of industry into smaller units and moving it into the countryside may have made it much more inefficient but kept some kind of production going. By taking one factory with twenty machines and splitting it into twenty small units each with one machine, they may have created a nightmare supply problem. However, they effectively placed the machines out of the reach of American air power using any practical level of bombing. North Vietnam was essentially an agricultural country and its strength lay in the countryside and in the Vietnamese people. While it could continue to import to meet it's needs the partial destruction of the Vietnamese industry was irrelevant.

By moving its industry and people back into the countryside Vietnam was returning to its roots and giving itself a strong base to work from. The fact that North Vietnam was a third world poor underdeveloped country (although it was one the strongest countries in it's own region) was the basis of the Vietnamese defence. The fact that there were very few vital industrial targets within the country gave Vietnam a certain immunity to the type of bombing campaign mounted by the Americans. The factories producing arms and equipment used by the Vietnamese lay safe from the Americans in Russia and China. General Momyer was forced to admit that it was impossible to interdict enough of the supplies to count. 'To reduce the flow through an enemy's supply line to zero is virtually impossible so long as he is willing and able to pay an extravagant price in lost men and supplies.'[43.]

The Americans were fighting a limited war with limited objectives. They wanted the North Vietnamese to stop their aid for the war in the south. They found themselves locked into a process of escalation, but there were still limits to the men and resources they were prepared to commit to the fighting. The Vietnamese on the other hand were fighting a total war, with no limit to the extent of their commitment. They never, at any time during the bombing, envisaged stopping their support for the war in South Vietnam. Although there must have been some level of bombing that would have forced the Vietnamese to agree to the American wishes, the bombing never achieved that end. The Americans never understood the Vietnamese thinking on the war and they never understood the extent of the commitment to the fighting in the south by the Vietnamese leadership.

By attacking economic and communication targets in North Vietnam the Americans were hoping the North Vietnamese Government would either collapse in some way or be forced to accept American demands. This is an entirely deterministic view since there is no logical necessity in the connection between economic collapse and political surrender. In any case economic collapse was never achieved. Any shortfall in production caused by the bombing was made good by imports, given as aid, from abroad. If economic collapse had been achieved there is no causal link between this and political collapse. The amounts of supplies needed in the south to maintain the war were so small that even an under developed country like Vietnam could still have supplied these amounts without too much difficulty.

NOTES

1.   Hai Thu, *North Vietnam Against US Air Force*, Foreign Languages
      Publishing House, Hanoi, 1967, page 9.
2.   Van Dyke, Jon M. *North Vietnam's Strategy For Survival*. Pacific Books,
      Publishers, California, 1972, page 30-1.
3.   Questor, George H. *Deterrence Before Hiroshoma*, John Wiley and Sons,
      New York, 1966, page 177.
4.   Ashmore, Harry S. and Braggs, William C. *Mission To Hanoi*, Putnam's Sons,
      New York, 1968, page 43.
5.   Heering, George C. *America's Longest War*, John Wiley and Sons, New York,
      1979, page 207.
6.   Senate Preparedness Subcommittee, *Air War Hearings*, 1967, page 277.
7.   Sharp, U.S. Grant, *Report On The War In Vietnam*, U.S. Printing Office,
      Washington, 1969, page 7.
8.   Senate Preparedness Subcommittee, *Air War Hearings*, 1967, page 280.
9.   Decornoy, Jacques, *Eye Witness Report Of The Bombing, How North Vietnam
      Survives*, The Observer, 1 January 1967, page 6.
10.   Ashmore, Harry S. and Braggs, William C. Ibid. page 134.
11.   Salisbury, Harrison E. *Behind The Lines: Hanoi* Dec. 23 1966-Jan. 7 1967",
      Seeker and Warburg, London, page 84.
12.   Senate Preparedness Subcommittee *Air War Hearings* Ibid.
13.   Salisbury, Harrison E. page 83 Ibid.
14.   Gerassi, John, *North Vietnam, A Documentary*. George Allen and Unwin Ltd.
      London, 1968, page 35.
15.   Senate Preparedness Subcommittee, *Air War Hearings*, 1967, page 277.
16.   Yahmed, Bechir Ben, *Report From North Vietnam'*, Times, 17 April 1967,
      page 9.
17.   Salisbury, Harrison E. Ibid, page 139.
18.   Yahmed, Bechir Ben, Ibid, page 9
19.   Salmon, Malcolm, *North Vietnam: A First Hand Account Of The Blitz*,
      The Sydney Tribune, Sydney, Australia, 1969? page 8.
20.   Decornoy, Jacques, Ibid, page 6.
21.   Salmon, Malcolm, Ibid, page 6

22. Thu, Hai, *North Vietnam Against US Air Force*, Foreign Languages Publishing House, Hanoi, 1967, page 55.
23. Gerassi, John, Ibid, page 41.
24. Hoeffding, Oleg, *Bombing North Vietnam. An Appraisal of Economic and Political Effects*, The Rand Corporation, California, Dec. 1966, page 9-10.
25. Gerassi, John, Ibid, page 121.
26. Gerassi, John, Ibid, page 76.
27. Decoroy, Jacques, Ibid, page 6.
28. Gerassi, John, Ibid, page 86.
29. Senate Preparedness Subcommittee, Ibid, page 425.
30. Thu, Hai, Ibid, page 29.
31. Hoeffding, Oleg, Ibid, page 7.
32. Senate Preparedness Subcommittee, Ibid, page 283.
33. Yahmed, Bechir Ben, Ibid, page 9.
34. Decornoy, Jacques, Ibid, page 6.
35. Ashmore, Harry S. Ibid, page 22.
36. Yahmed, Bechir Ben, Ibid, page 9.
37. Parks, W. Hays, *Rolling Thunder and the Law of War*, Air University Review, Jan-Feb 1982, page 20.
38. Broughton, Jack, *Thud Ridge*, Bantam Books, New York, 1985, page 236.
39. Riboud, Mark, *Life In the Land of Uncle Ho*, Sunday Times Magazine, 2nd Feb. 1969, page 18.
40. Thu, Hai, Ibid, page 50-1.
41. Hoeffding, Oleg, Ibid, page vi.
42. Ashmore, Harry S. and Baggs, William C. Ibid, page 32-3.
43. Momyer, William W. *Air Power In Three Wars*, U.S. Government Printing Office, Washington, 1978, page 338.

Chapter Seven
Conclusions

The *Rolling Thunder* campaign had started as a series of individual specific raids directed at named targets in the southern portion of North Vietnam. It developed into a continuous strategic bombing campaign covering almost the entire country. The original raids had been intended as a threat to the North to show the leadership what was possible if they did not change their approach to the war in the South. The plan was to gradually increase the scope and intensity of the bombing until the Northern Government stopped supporting the Viet Cong. It had been thought that the level of bombing necessary to achieve this would soon be reached. In fact over the three and a half years of the bombing the number of sorties and the tonnage of bombs dropped continued to increase substantially each year, except short-term declines during bad flying weather caused by the monsoon. Even after this enormous effort the North Vietnamese still refused to change their policy towards the war.

Rolling Thunder appeared to follow the original plan, which was slowly to increase the area and weight of the bombing until the North Vietnamese backed down. Nobody involved in the initial decision-making envisaged the campaign that actually occurred.

The idea that the bombing would last for three and a half years, would involve the dropping of hundreds of thousands of tons of bombs and see the loss of over 900 American aircraft over North Vietnam had never been considered. Although the campaign superficially resembled the 'slow squeeze' originally planned, it was thought at the time that within weeks or months the North Vietnamese would have had enough. The way the campaign developed was in reality the outcome of a series of decisions taken in reaction to the North's refusal to change their basic policy towards the war in the South. It did not follow a carefully designed course but simply developed out of the impotent rage that the American leadership felt at the refusal of the North Vietnamese to give way under the bombing. Dropping hundreds of thousands of tons of bombs may be seen to be a positive act, but the North Vietnamese actually held the initiative throughout the period of *Rolling Thunder*, the Americans only reacting to the decisions taken by the North.

The weight of the bombing developed from 25,000 sorties dropping 63,000 tons of bombs in 1965, 79,000 sorties dropping 136,000 tons of bombs in 1966, 108,000 sorties dropping 226,000 tons of bombs in 1967 to 82,000 sorties dropping 180,000 tons of bombs in 1968. Of this total less than 5 per cent of the sorties were directed against fixed specified targets. The vast majority of sorties carried out against the North were armed reconnaissance missions mainly directed against the transport system. In essence, *Rolling Thunder* developed into a long range interdiction campaign to stop the transport of men and supplies to the South. In addition, most North Vietnamese industry -electrical supply, oil storage and infrastructure - were also destroyed in an attempt to end the North's ability to continue the war.

During *Rolling Thunder* there was no consistent set of reasons or objectives for the bombing given by the decision makers involved and those reasons that were given tended to change. The same can be said for America's involvement in the Vietnam war in general. Hugh M.Arnold examined the official justifications for American involvement in South East Asia and found that between 1949 and 1967 there had been twenty-two different reasons given for this involvement.

The clearest rationale for the bombing, and what it was thought would be achieved by it, was given by President Johnson and Robert McNamara. Johnson, in a speech in March 1967, said that the bombing had been intended to support the Americans fighting in the South. Also to penalise the North Vietnamese for breaking the Geneva Accords and to limit, or increase the costs of, the movement of men and materials from the North to the South. Robert McNamara, during Congressional Testimony in June 1966, gave reasons not entirely the same, but very similar. To reduce the flow or increase the costs of the infiltration of men and supplies from the North. To make it clear that the North Vietnamese would have to pay a price for their policy in the South. It was also said that the bombing was intended to raise the morale of the South Vietnamese people. General Maxwell Taylor said 'The overall purpose was to apply limited force with limited means to gain limited results.'[1] Other reasons given for the bombing at various times included direct retaliation for Viet Cong attacks on American personnel in the South, as punishment for the North, to demonstrate to the North the depth of American commitment in South East Asia, to break the will of the North's leadership, to make up for the weakness and corruption in the South and as a bargaining device to be traded in at the negotiating table. There seems little doubt that *Rolling Thunder* was not a carefully thought out or planned campaign but an *ad hoc* programme that developed as America sought to apply more and more pressure to North Vietnam, as the bombing failed to produce tangible results.

Whatever reasons are accepted, the *Tet* Offensive in 1968 proved that *Rolling Thunder*, on any reasonable criterion, had failed. The North Vietnamese delivered sufficient materials for the Viet Cong and the North Vietnamese regular forces in the South to launch a major offensive throughout the country. The vast majority of materiel used in the *Tet* offensive had been carried down from the Chinese border, or the port at Haiphong, through North Vietnam and along the Ho Chi Minh trail and into the South. Most of the bombing sorties carried out over the North had been aimed at the transport system but this had not stopped the transport of men and materials from North to South. On this point there can be no doubt that the bombing totally failed. There can also be little doubt that the bombing increased enormously the costs of moving these forces to the South, but whatever those costs were the Vietnamese were clearly prepared to pay them. They were ready to devote their entire national effort to the war in the South and to overcome the effects of the bombing. To keep the supplies moving they reorganised their society to withstand the bombing so they could continue their support. The *Tet* Offensive also showed that after three years of bombing their political will had not been broken. They had shown that they were prepared to endure necessary hardships and suffering that their chosen policy entailed and were prepared to continue with it.

If the *Tet* Offensive proved that *Rolling Thunder*, with its massive expenditure of effort, had failed, then why had it been allowed to continue for three years? *Rolling Thunder* in fact achieved some of it's aims, at least partially. The morale in South Vietnam was boosted in 1965 when the first attacks took place, but once the programme was established it became the norm and any help that it had on Southern morale became discounted. The second Jason study, reporting on the bombing in 1967 said that:

> "There had been an appreciable improvement in South Vietnamese morale immediately after the bombing began and subsequent buoyancy always accompanied major new escalations of the air war. The effect was always transient however, fading as a particular pattern of attack became a part of the war. There was no indication that bombing could ever form a permanent support for south Vietnamese morale if the situation in the South itself was adverse." [2.]

The American political leadership then decided that, while the bombing campaign could further improve morale, to end the campaign would have the opposite effect by lowering morale. The start of the bombing had provided a temporary respite, but morale among the people in South Vietnam suffered a long slow decline after 1965. As the ground war continued in the South the morale of the people bearing the brunt suffered because of it. In 1966 only one in seven of the conscripted South Vietnamese troops (ARVN) actually registered for service. As the level of fighting in the South increased the South Vietnamese Army was suffering 20 per cent desertions every year. The ARVN forces lost 568,500 people to desertion between 1967 and 1971. The term used by McNamara was that the bombing would 'raise' the morale of the South Vietnamese. The word 'raise' is relative and it is possible to imagine that, while morale in South Vietnam could have been lower, nobody could say that it was high.

The military leadership had advised against the gradual application of force against North Vietnam. The essence of air power is mobility, concentration and surprise and the gradualist approach loses at least two of these advantages. Following the end of the Vietnam War the military have put forward this misuse of air power, in the gradualist manner, as a main cause of the failure of *Rolling Thunder*. The political leadership chose to apply a steadily increasing amount of bombing to the North because they never really considered the possibility that the Vietnamese could resist them. The war was fully intended to be limited and the chances of forcing the Russians or the Chinese to enter the war were to be kept to a minimum. The easiest way of finding the lowest level of bombing that would force the North to stop backing the war in the South would be to start low and increase until this level was reached. After three and a half years, dropping hundreds of thousands of tons of bombs and with the loss of tens of thousands of lives this level was never attained.

This gradualist approach degenerated into a war of attrition between attacking American aircraft and the North Vietnamese air defence system. This meant that the attacking forces were obliged to devote many aircraft to air defence countermeasures rather than bombing their primary targets. This view ignored the dichotomy between the American view of the war as essentially limited and the Vietnamese view of the war as total. The level of bombing that would have forced the North Vietnamese out of the war in the South would have been achieved when it became physically impossible for them to continue. The bombing never achieved this level of destruction and the politically imposed limitations on American air operations would not have allowed this level of destruction to take place. The North Vietnamese leadership had always planned for a long war and the gradual approach played into their hands. They felt that the longer the war lasted, their chances of eventual victory increased. The US leaders, operating in a democratic country, had ultimately to carry public support and opinion polls showed that the public continued their support to a certain extent. However, the longer the war continued the greater became the opposition to it. It would have been in America's interests to have ended the war as fast as possible, rather than to be drawn into a war of attrition in both the South and over the North.

A sudden massive attack on the original 94 targets suggested by the Joint Chiefs of Staff would undoubtably have been a more logical application of air power. It would have been within the capabilities of the forces available in South East Asia to have carried this plan out over a period of two or three weeks. The destruction of the targets, before the North had created an efficient air defence system, could have been achieved without too many losses. If such attacks had taken place in early 1965, the North could not have evacuated all the likely targets and could not have created a distributed oil and petroleum system. The shock effect of such a concentrated campaign on the Vietnamese leadership could have been salutary. However, it is doubtful whether attacks even on this scale would have been enough to change the views of the North's leaders. The idea that the entire Vietnam war could have been won by such a series of attacks cannot be sustained.

To explain the failure of *Rolling Thunder* the leaders of the American military air power produced a variation of the 'stab in the back theory'. After the First World War the German army chiefs claimed that they had never been beaten in battle but had been stabbed in the back by their own politicians and civilians who had let the army down by insisting on a peace settlement. The American variation of this theory was that the civilian leaders had never allowed air power to show what it could do. The gradualist approach had been forced on the Air Force and the Navy. The bombing, it was said, was surrounded with restrictive Rules of Engagement and the best targets were always 'off limits' within Hanoi and Haiphong. They have also been very critical of the way that targets were allocated. The fact that targets for most of *Rolling Thunder* were selected by Johnson and his advisors and only released in dribs and drabs, often ignoring the recommendations of the military on the spot, is listed as one of the reasons for failure. The image of the President of America choosing individual targets in Vietnam 12,000 miles away and even aircraft types, bomb loads and directions of attack, over the heads of the leaders directly involved, appears somehow absurd.

These arguments carry a great deal of weight and few could now deny that air power was not used to its best advantage in Vietnam. Admiral Sharp. Commander of American forces in the Pacific during *Rolling Thunder*. has written, in an article revealingly titled *Airpower Could Have Won in Vietnam* (He also wrote another article called *We Could Have Won in Vietnam Long Ago*):

> "I want to comment on the air war over North Vietnam because as Commander in Chief, Pacific, I was running the air war, with not much help from certain sectors in Washington. I believe that the air war was the most misunderstood part of our whole engagement. It was especially misunderstood by the civilians in the Pentagon who were making the broad decisions and many of the smaller decisions of the air war. The severe restrictions under which our Air Force operated resulted in markedly decreased effectiveness of the tremendous power we had available and resulted in wide misunderstanding of the effectiveness of airpower when properly used." [3.]

The military leaders sincerely believed that air power had been used incorrectly. Thus they had been prevented from winning the war in the North by civilian interference. General McConnell, the Air Force chief, after a Pentagon briefing in 1967 sat with his head in his hands and said, 'I can't tell you how I feel...I'm so sick of it...I have never been so goddamn frustrated by it all...I'm so sick of it...'[4.] It was felt that the artificial restrictions imposed on the bombing campaign had exposed the pilots involved to all the dangers of carrying out the bombing but had held them back from really applying the full weight of air power.

The military leaders used the Senate Preparedness Subcommittee Hearings in 1967 in an attempt to force this view onto the civilian leaders. The Subcommittee, assembled from supporters of the war, wanted to show their support for the military view of the restrictions on the bombing by using the hearings to pressurise McNamara into changing the civilian control. Witnesses, testifying before the committee, included most military leaders involved in *Rolling Thunder* and they made it clear that they considered that civilian control of the bombing had been responsible for the lack of tangible results. The hearings forced President Johnson to release additional targets for the bombing. By this time however, McNamara had become disillusioned with what could be attained by the bombing and the civilian control remained in place.

The argument that air power could have been used better in Vietnam is hard to resist but the idea that the failure of *Rolling Thunder* was because of political restrictions or the gradualist approach are also difficult to prove. The sudden concentrated application of air power in 1965 would have had more of an impact on the North Vietnamese, but there is no evidence that this would have been decisive. They proved their strength of purpose, their ability to bear hardships for their political beliefs and their total commitment to the war. Whether this sudden application of force would have forced a climb down, rather than the growing sustained application of force, can only remain conjecture. The controls on *Rolling Thunder* were, at the start of the campaign, very restrictive. Later, during the course of the campaign, most restrictions on types of target and areas open for bombing were lifted. The areas 'out of bounds' remained the buffer zone along the Chinese border, Haiphong and Hanoi, although specific targets in these areas were sometimes authorised for attack. The number of major targets excluded from attack was thus quite small.

During the late summer of 1967 the bombing campaign reached its peak with few real restrictions. On this point the Pentagon Papers state:

> "Thus, except for the port of Haiphong and a few others, virtually all of the economic and military targets in NVN that could be considered even remotely significant had been hit. Except for simply keeping it up, almost everything bombing could do to pressurise NVN had been done." [5.]

The military argument that heavier or more concentrated bombing would have had more effect on North Vietnam is merely a truism. Whether this would have had the desired effect is doubtful and can never be proven.

The original view of the bombing had been that a small amount of bombing, plus the threat of more, would be enough to frighten the North Vietnamese into line. Many military and the civilian leaders thought that the threat behind the earlier raids would be enough to accomplish the objectives of the campaign. America was undoubtedly the most powerful country in the world. Its leaders considered that even the threat of the bombing attacks, backed up by small scale attacks to show they were not bluffing, would be all that was required to force a small third world country to give way. The initial plan for *Rolling Thunder* had therefore contained a large measure of this threat. The Vietnamese however never gave way under the bombing and the Americans were forced to apply increasing force into the bombing campaign. They had found that threats alone were not enough. As more and more of the targets in the North were destroyed the threat factor thus decreased. Once the worst had happened, there was nothing of any value left to threaten. Some Pentagon civilian advisers had originally viewed *Rolling Thunder* as an exercise in sending signals to the North Vietnamese. It would show what could happen if they continued their policy in the South. But it is necessary to 'keep the Hostage alive' if one is going to threaten to kill it. If the hostage is known to be dead then the threat losses all meaning. It was no good threatening to destroy the North Vietnamese industry, economy and transport system when this had already been done, without success.

The vast majority of air attacks on the North were directed not directed against their economy but against the transport system, but the *Tet* Offensive proved that this part of *Rolling Thunder* had also failed. The transport system had proved a very unrewarding target for the attackers since the system itself was very rudimentary and basic. This meant that repairs were easily carried out, especially after the Vietnamese had organised hundreds of thousands of people into conducting these repairs. The whole of the national effort seems to have been directed into keeping the supplies moving. There was also massive redundancy within the transport system and the Vietnamese were continually constructing new routes, bridges and bypasses. It was estimated that only 15 per cent of the capacity of the Vietnamese road system was in use at any one time.

The small amounts of supplies needed by the Viet Cong and Northern forces in the South meant that the amounts moving along the transport system were relatively small. The gradualist approach had given the initiative in the war to the North Vietnamese, while the Viet Cong held the initiative in the ground fighting in the South. They could choose both the time and place of most of the fighting. While the communist forces used only small amounts of material in the south, and held the initiative, the interdiction bombing campaign was doomed to fail. Writing about the interdiction campaign in Korea, David Macisaac said:

> "...the lessons of 1944-5 in Italy had to be learned all over again: essentially, that for the aerial interdiction of the enemy's battlefield supplies to be successful, one's own surface forces had to be in control of the tactical initiative, so as to force the enemy to expend supplies in amounts and at rates he could not plan against. Without such pressure being applied to the enemy on the ground, aircraft could harass, delay, irritate - no more." [6.]

This is equally applicable to the Vietnam war. The amount of munitions being used in South Vietnam by the Communist forces before 1972 never reached the level of that in Korea and the air attacks in Korea never stopped supplies reaching the front line. The communist forces in the South could scale their actions up or down to suit the level of supplies available. The American ground forces could never pin down the Viet Cong and could not force up the amount of necessary supplies used to a higher level than could be brought down the Ho Chi Minh trail. Thus the interdiction was bound to fail.

The Korean War also provided the example of Chinese intervention that coloured American thinking during the Vietnam war. President Johnson often said that he did not want a wider war in Vietnam. When it looked like the United Nations forces were going to win in Korea the Chinese sent hundreds of thousands of troops into the war to prevent it. The constant fear of Chinese intervention in Vietnam provided a constraint on the Americans, who never understood that the North Vietnamese would never have allowed foreign troops to take part in the war. The existence of the Chinese threat thus limited the actions that the American political leadership thought were available to them.

To a large extent the Vietnam war had been forced upon Johnson. That does not absolve him from any decisions that he took about the war but, throughout his political career, his main interests had always been in the field of domestic American politics. His main aim was the 'Great Society' he wanted to create in America. He wanted to end the war as quickly and as cheaply as possible, but did not want go down in history as the man who lost Vietnam alongside Truman and Acheson, the men who 'lost' China to the communists. Thus he became committed to at least not losing in Vietnam and was forced to commit increasing amounts of men and materials into the war. He finally realised that the amounts of money that the war was finally costing together with the anti-war campaigns throughout the country, much of it directed personally at himself, (Hey! Hey! LBJ! How many kids did you kill today?) had destroyed any chance of creating his 'Great Society'. He did not stand for nomination from the Democrats in 1968 once he understood that this could have lead to a humiliating defeat.

As Johnson became disillusioned with his inability to reach a solution to the war, he turned more to his inner circle of advisers. He had always relied on the group of people he had inherited from President Kennedy, especially in foreign affairs. As the situation in Vietnam worsened and his personal popularity with the United States deteriorated, this group became more exclusive and the decision making more central-ised. The Tuesday lunch group became the forum for decisions on the Vietnam war and the range of opinion available was limited to known supporters of the war, apart from George Ball.

Any member who began to doubt the wisdom of the administration policy on Vietnam was either isolated or forced to leave. Even McNamara, the chief architect of policy on Vietnam, was eventually driven to leave when he became disillusioned by the bombing. The small number of people in the group around Johnson limited the extent of the discussion of the major topics, any dissenters being excluded from the process. Townsend Hoopes, Under Secretary of the Air Force, described the decision making by this group as:

> "...the climate of cozy, implicit agreement on fundamentals which had for so long characterised discussions within the inner circle on Vietnam, where never was heard a disparaging word." [7.]

One of the reasons that the bombing continued for as long as it did, was that Johnson had restricted his options. He was now only asssociating with people who had taken part in the original decision to start bombing the North and who were committed to its continuance.

A large amount of the information Johnson received was also coloured and shaded by the bureaucratic process of intelligence gathering. It is physically impossible for someone in Johnson's position to read all the raw intelligence data on any topic. Every level of intelligence analysis, in both the military and political system, tended to stress the aspects of intelligence material supporting government policy. Typically the reports coming from Vietnam were highly optimistic of the results of the bombing. Junior staff do not want to be the ones to tell superiors that their policy is not working. Nobody ever got promoted by proving a superior's policy to have been wrong and to have continued being wrong for several years. By the time information was reaching Johnson it had been processed by the system to a large extent to endorse government programmes. Townsend Hoopes also wrote on this particular point of Walt Rostow's:

"Selective briefings - the time-honoured technique of underlining, within a mass of material, those particular elements that one wishes to draw to the special attention of a busy chief." [8.]

In 1968 the Senior Advisory Group told Johnson that, in their view, the bombing was unlikely to achieve anything more and advised de-escalation. Johnson demanded to know what else they had been told that he had not. It was not that anyone had lied to Johnson. Rather that information reaching him was the end product of a system that had an overly sanguine bias. He had also surrounded himself with people who were heavily committed to the bombing and tended to discount any evidence contrary to their views.

Much information given to Johnson was very optimistic, but some specific intelligence agencies produced reports that were highly critical of the outcome of the bombing. The CIA produced a monthly appraisal on the bombing of North Vietnam and, although these reports listed the damage done by the bombing, they noted that the bombing did not appear to be having any effect on the North Vietnamese leadership. The CIA report for 1966 stated:

"The evidence available does not suggest that *Rolling Thunder* to date has contributed materially to the achievement of the two primary objectives of the air attack-reduction of the flow of supplies to VC NVA forces in the South or weakened the will of North Vietnam to continue the insurgency.......There may be some degree of escalation which would force the regime to re-examine its position, but we believe that as far as pressure from air attack is concerned the regime would be prepared to continue the insurection indefinitely in the face of the current level and type of bombing programme." [9.]

Although written in 1966 this was an accurate description of the bombing and a correct assessment of what bombing could achieved in the future.

What became known as the Jason Group presented a report on 29th August 1966. This group was made up of forty-seven scientists and twenty experts from the Institute of Defence Analysis, the full tile being the Jason Summer Study Group. Most of the scientists were independent of the government and together comprised a very prestigious company. They were not only looking into the bombing but had been asked to give their opinion on a barrier or fence across the De-Militarised Zone to stop enemy infiltration. Their conclusions stated unequivocally, 'As of July 1966 the U. S. bombing of North Vietnam (NVN) had had no measurable effect on Hanoi's ability to mount and support military operations in the South at the current level'. [10.] This restricted-circulation report seems to have played little part in the thinking of either the military or President Johnson. But, coming as it did after the failure of the oil campaign, it appears to have been part of the process of disillusionment with the results of the bombing that had come to dominate Robert McNamara's thinking.

The Jason Group produced a second report in December 1967. This considered the outcome of the bombing in the light of its aims and objectives given by McNamara in 1966 and reiterated in Congressional testimony in August 1967. Regarding the first objective - reducing the flow of men and materials to the South and/or increasing the cost of this flow - it repeated the 1966 findings that, 'As of October 1967, the U.S. bombing of North Vietnam has had no measurable effect on Hanoi's ability to mount and support military operations in the South.' [11.] The second objective given by McNamara was the raising of morale in the South. The report said that the bombing had raised morale transiently. The third objective given by McNamara was to force the North Vietnamese leadership to pay a price for their support of the war in the South. On this point the report stated, 'The bombing campaign against NVN has not discernibly weakened the determination of the North Vietnamese leaders to continue to direct and support the insurgency in the South'. [12.]

Johnson had been given a considerable amount of over-sanguine intelligence on the achievements of *Rolling Thunder*, but there were other authoritative voices criticizing the success of the bombing. These were generally ignored.

The Air Force doctrine of the primacy of strategic bombing was still deeply held by most of the Air Force High Command. The doctrine that strategic bombers could attack enemy 'vital centres' to destroy an enemy's ability and will to continue a war had been the basis of American strategy during the Second World War. Now, in the 1960s, airmen who had taken part in the bombing campaigns against Germany and Japan were in positions of command. The doctrine that the use of air power had rendered partially obsolete ground and naval forces was deeply ingrained in Air Force thinking. The development of Strategic Air Command had dominated Air Force policy during the 1950s and early 60s. Many American Air Force Chiefs had dedicated their professional lives to the putting into practice the doctrine of strategic bombing. Once evidence began to accumulate that *Rolling Thunder* was unsuccessful, they could only view this through the doctrine of strategic bombing theory. They were working within the paradigm of air power being the decisive factor in warfare and could not accept the view that it was failing. Their first reaction was that not enough effort was being put into the campaign. This led to a continual increase in the numbers of sorties flown and the tonnage of bombs dropped. When this still failed to produce results, they tried to emphasise both the choice of targets and the restrictions placed on certain targets as being at fault. The doctrine had stressed the destruction of 'vital targets' and Douhet had practically reduced strategy to the choice of the correct targets. It became very hard for the military leadership to admit that the bombing was failing. An assistant secretary of state Phil G Goulding described this by saying:

> "Within the Department of Defence emotion overcame logic on discussions of the role and importance of air power and the specific missions of air power in Vietnam. Somehow the bombing of Vietnam became the symbol of the importance of air power, which was both tragic and illogical." [13.]

Since the end of the war, apologists for the failure of *Rolling Thunder* have pointed to the bombing restrictions and the choice of the wrong targets as the main cause of that failure. However, by the end of 1967 there were very few targets left in North Vietnam of any significant value.

The US Navy was also heavily committed to strategic bombing. The Air Force, while it was still part of the Army, had been in conflict with the Navy since before the Second World War over who should control strategic bombing. The Navy, heavily committed to the construction and use of aircraft carriers for the tactical and strategic use of air power, planned to use carrier-launched aircraft armed with nuclear weapons against Russia if the necessity arose. Its leaders found it as difficult as those of the Air Force to admit that *Rolling Thunder* was failing due to their own commitment to bombing doctrine. This was also the period when the Navy was trying to obtain funding for a new generation of large nuclear aircraft carriers that, with their Air Wings were among the most expensive and complex organisations ever devised. If sea-based air power could not deliver the goods against North Vietnam, how could it be expected to succeed against the Warsaw Pact and Russia? The Navy could not admit the failure of *Rolling Thunder* without having to face the fact that the type of Navy created after the Second World War, and that which it hoped to create in the future, was based on a faulty premise.

Throughout the war the Navy and the Air Force were in competition about which one would appear the most effective in their use of air power. When it was created in the 1940s, the Air Force had attempted to control as much of the air operations as possible. This had created friction with the Navy who wanted the same thing. The Army also recreated its own air wing to replace the Air Force it had lost. It was thought that the future allocation of government funds would depend on the perceived performance of the different services in their use of air power during the war. Both services attempted to provide more sorties over North Vietnam than the other, even when suitable targets or ordnance were not available. The overwhelming majority of missions were armed reconnaissance sorties over areas that had already been picked clean with limited chances of fresh success. Once a criterion had been established officers attempted to achieve results measured by this criterion. This occurred even when it meant losing sight of the overall results. The real objective was to defeat North Vietnam, not necessarily to provide more sorties. About the sorties Captain Clarence S. Vaught, who flew two tours over Vietnam, said:

> "We were playing sortie games, and that's one of the elements that made flag out of the ships CO's. How many sorties the ship got off. It didn't make a shit what you did over there, as long as the aircraft got off the ship." [14.]

When new targets were released to the bombing campaign both services attempted to obtain what were seen as the best targets for themselves.

One essential of a military campaign is unity of command, but there was never any one single commander of *Rolling Thunder*. It appeared that the lessons of the Korean War were ignored and that Navy and Air Force operations remained under separate control. The Seventh Air force in South Vietnam and Thailand was under the authority of the Pacific Command in Hawaii through the military command in Saigon, but the aircraft used by the Seventh Air Force were under the administrative control of the Thirteenth Air Force in the Philippines. Task Force 77 was under the control of the Pacific Fleet and the Pacific Command.

The small numbers of B-52s used over the North were under the direction of Strategic Air Command, responsible directly to the Joint Chiefs of Staff. There was also the added complication that air operations in Route Package 1 were under the authority of the army headquarters in Saigon. The dividing of North Vietnam into Route Packages can only be described as a compromise solution to the problem of unified command. Some of the main advantages of air power are it's flexibility and it's ability to concentrate en masse on individual targets. The dividing of North Vietnam into separate areas and the division of command merely had the effect of limiting the flexibility of air power. Both the Air Force and the Navy recognised this problem and supported the idea of a single command provided it was someone from their own service. However, neither would have welcomed surrendering command to the other. General William W. Momyer, commander of the Seventh Air Force wrote, 'Airmen know the centralized control of airpower in a theatre of war can best serve armies and navies, to fragment airpower is to court defeat."[15.]

The extraordinary targeting system developed for *Rolling Thunder* can only have added to the command problems. The President and his immediate advisers were those involved in choosing individual targets, bomb types, direction of attack, timing and numbers of aircraft involved in raids, i.e. people least qualified to do so. This targeting system removed initiative from the people involved in actually flying the bombing raids. Experience is the hardest won thing in war and the targeting system devised by the political leaders ignored the experience of the people who were daily risking their lives over the North.

The rigidity of the targeting system forced the Navy and the Air force into what has been called stereotyped tactics. The slow release of new targets to the bombing campaign meant that when new targets were made available they became the focus for a series of attacks. The North Vietnamese could move their mobile defences to cover new targets when it became obvious that the American forces were going to focus on them. The American aircraft carriers mounting major strikes (*Alpha Strikes*) could launch three strikes a day. To achieve this, the carriers launched strikes at approximately the same times every day. Charles E.Myers speaking of the Navy and Air Force has said:

> "Little ingenuity is displayed in the conduct of deep-strike operations. Missions against North Vietnam were launched on a 'Dr. Pepper' schedule (10, 2, and 4) to fly established routes into heavily defended areas to attack targets where the alerted enemy had concentrated anti aircraft artillery." [16.]

Many higher ranking Air Force officers had been bomber aircrew during the Second World War. Some of these attempted to impose Second World tactics on crews attacking the North without considering the fact that the war against North Vietnam was in the main being carried out by unsuitable tactical aircraft. There is no doubt that many aircraft shot down over the North were lost because of this. The overall strategy of wars should be left to higher command, but day-to-day tactics should be left to the commanders on the spot. The pilots who flew into combat on a daily basis were the best judges of tactics.

Robert McNamara, the Secretary of Defence, had introduced the systems analysis approach to the control, especially the financial control, of the American military before the Vietnam war. The essence of this approach was the idea of 'how much is enough'. While this can be an effective way of planning for the buying of military equipment, or even the planning for war, it is not the most effective way of fighting a war. Military leaders always want overwhelming superiority if possible. General Slim's famous dictum was that, 'The more you use the less you lose'. The idea of having 'just enough' is anathema to the military mind. Each type of aircraft had been allocated an expected daily sortie rate by systems analysis and this was one reason that sortie rates came to dominate the Naval and Air force approach to the war. Both services went to great lengths to maintain the nominated sortie rates but pressure was applied by the Service chiefs for the units not to exceed these. In thinking about long term planning goals the service chiefs had to consider the fact that, if more than the laid down sorties could be flown, the services would need less aircraft. Thus McNamara's Planning, Programming and Budgeting System became something of a liability in the actual fighting of the Vietnam war. The great German writer on war Clausewitz describes this wish to reduce war to easily quantifiable factors as one of the recurring human desires in dealing with war by saying:

> "..the conduct of war branches out in almost all directions and has no definite limits; while any system, any model, has the finite nature of a synthesis. An irreconcilable conflict exists between this type of theory and actual practice.....As in the science concerning preparations for war, they wanted to reach a set of sure and positive conclusions, and for that reason considered only factors that could be mathematically calculated." [17.]

The conduct of war is so infinitely complex that any simple and measurable system is bound to fail.

The Air Force had chosen a very unprofitable arena in which to prove the validity of their doctrine on strategic bombing. It was based on the premise that only industrialised countries would be involved in high intensity warfare. A country must contain industrial targets that the country needs to maintain their war effort for bombing to destroy that country's ability to continue fighting. Although North Vietnam had a small manufacturing industry, its economy was based upon subsistence agriculture. For the bombing theories to work the level of the war needed to be of a high intensity. The amount of industrial production being used in a war needed to be consistently high, therefore only a country producing and using a large amount of military supplies on a daily basis could be susceptible to bombing stopping its capability to produce those supplies. The small amounts of materials used in the basically guerilla war in the South did not justify the scale of the bombing.

The strategic bombing theories were also based on the premise of warfare between advanced western industrialised nations with highly developed and closely organised economies. For it to be possible for strategic bombing to bring a country to its knees it is necessary for that country to have a highly organised infrastructure to attack. The transport system, industry and agricultural base of North Vietnam was considerably less vulnerable to disruption by bombing than any industrialised western nation. It was a basic flaw in *Rolling Thunder* that North Vietnam was a very poor target for a strategic bombing campaign.

It is theoretically possible to pinpoint vital targets in a highly industrialised country. These would include synthetic oil plants, aircraft engine manufacturers and power generation systems. The doctrine was based on the idea that it was not necessary to destroy a nation's industry completely. With careful analysis it should be feasible to pinpoint and destroy certain targets that would bring the rest of the economy to a halt. With a highly organised industrialised economy it is possible to envisage 'bottle necks' or sections of industry, the destruction of which could affect all the others. It has been argued that ingenuity and resourcefulness can avoid this. Despite massive destruction, the Germany economy continued to increase its production of military equipment until the last few months of the Second World War. While it may be possible to visualise such targets in an industrialised country there were very few 'vital targets' in North Vietnam.

One of the most heavily bombed targets in North Vietnam was the Than Hoa bridge. This was often attacked during

Rolling Thunder, involving enormous effort and the loss of many pilots and aircraft. Despite the attempts to destroy the bridge during *Rolling Thunder*, it was not until 1972, during *Linebacker I*, that it finally fell. Even so the North Vietnamese had already prepared for the loss of the bridge. Pontoon sections were ready and waiting and rail ferries were available to keep the traffic flowing. In any case there was an accessible ford within five miles. A considerable amount of the American air power was directed against this target but it could never be described as a vital target in the sense that it's destruction would have won the war. The loss of the bridge would merely have added to the problems faced by the North Vietnamese. The idea of vital targets was indeed deeply ingrained in American air power doctrine. Even after the end of the Vietnam War General Momyer, Commander of the Seventh Air Force, wrote as one of his conclusions on the war that 'Airpower can be strategically decisive if its application is intense, continuous, and focused on the enemy's vital systems.'[18.] There were few such truly vital targets in North Vietnam.

The overwhelming majority of military supplies used by North Vietnam were produced in Russia, China or Eastern Europe and were imported into the country. As America had no intention of bombing Russia or China the factories producing the equipment needed by the North were completely safe. While they could continue to import into the North the necessary supplies, the North Vietnamese leadership had no need to worry about the destruction of their own small limited industrial production. There were no industrial production facilities in the North that the northern leadership were not prepared to do without, provided that outside aid continued.

Besides being based on war between industrialised western countries the strategic bombing theories were also based on the idea of total war. The original theories had grown out of the stalemate of the western front in the First World War. That stalemate had seen the opposing sides mobilise their whole populations, their total industrial production and their entire societies in a war of attrition for what they saw as their very survival as independent states. When a country's very existence is at stake and practically their entire population is involved in one way or another in a war, they will be prepared to go to any lengths to achieve victory. It was against this background of total commitment and mass destruction that the original strategic bombing theories were formulated.

For the Americans the Vietnam War was never anything but a limited action, in area, in scope and in objectives. The American reserves were never called into action and war was never declared against the North. In the Second World War the Americans and the British were prepared to carry out area bombing (under various names) against the populations of Germany and Japan, killing over 550,000 Germans. During *Rolling Thunder* the Americans made a genuine attempt to limit civilian casualties. They never had the necessary commitment to the bombing to make the strategic bombing theories work. Whether any amount of commitment would have made the bombing successful is another argument.

The costs of *Rolling Thunder* were higher for the Americans than for the North Vietnamese. A CIA report produced in 1967 estimated that in the 1965 bombing each dollar's worth of damage caused to North Vietnam had cost America $6.60, but in 1966 each dollar's worth of damage had cost $9.60. Only a superpower could mount a campaign against an enemy that was costing nearly ten times as much to organise as the damage it was causing. During the three and a half years of *Rolling Thunder* It was also estimated that the total cost of the bomb damage to North Vietnam was $600 million during the three and a half years of the campaign. This figure comprised destroyed industrial plant, military facilities and lost production. After the war it was calculated that the cost of the American aircraft lost in the bombing was $6 billion. The monetary costs of *Rolling Thunder*, ignoring the human costs, may have been enormous, but the Americans would have paid gladly had *Rolling Thunder* succeeded.

During the same period North Vietnam had received over $2,000 million in aid from their allies Russia and China. For every dollar's worth of damage caused by *Rolling Thunder* the North had received $3.33 in outside aid. During 1965, including aid from abroad, its Gross National Product had actually risen by six per cent, despite the bombing. This was during the period of strained Sino-Soviet relations but the bombing brought them together to supply whatever North Vietnam needed to continue the war. In the years just before the start of the bombing, Russia had supplied practically nothing to the North but *Rolling Thunder* forced them to compete with the Chinese or loose all influence in that part of the world. Both Russia, China and the rest of the communist bloc were dedicated to anti-American activities and the bombing provided the ideal circumstances to build up world wide propaganda against the Americans. The Russians were willing to 'put their money where their mouth was' by supplying the North Vietnamese with practically everything they could possibly need. The bombing had disrupted conditions within the North and this, along with their limited infrastructure, reduced the amount of aid that could be absorbed. But for this limitation the North's allies would have supplied even more aid. There was no chance of North Vietnam ever paying back other than a nominal amount of the aid they had received and, in reality, it had been a gift. The North had access to all the aid they could require from abroad, indeed considerably more supplies than was being destroyed by bombing. Therefore there was little chance of the bombing forcing the Vietnamese leadership to back down. The fact that the North Vietnamese were allowed to import into the country more than the bombing was destroying was a major flaw in American strategy during *Rolling Thunder*. American desires to limit the extent of the war and to ensure the exclusion of China placed heavy restrictions on the chances of the bombing succeeding.

Although strategic bombing theory was based the idea of 'vital targets' the real target was the will of the North Vietnamese political leadership. An American definition of success in the bombing was for North Vietnam to end it's support for the war in the South. Cornelius D. Sullivan said:

> "Since the political objective in Vietnam was to compel the Hanoi regime to cease it's aggression against South Vietnam, the logical military target was the will of the Hanoi leadership to continue this aggression." [19.]

The American aim of not expanding the war to include China and limiting the war, in area and scope, gave the North Vietnamese the advantage of being prepared to enlarge the area of the fighting. They could raise the degree of the war above the level the Americans were prepared to accept. Throughout *Rolling Thunder* there were zones around Hanoi, Haiphong and along the Chinese border were the bombing was severely limited. These self-imposed lines of demarcation and commitment gave the North Vietnamese what has been called 'escalation dominance'. If one is willing to expand the war and give total commitment, they will always have an advantage over an opponent that has clearly marked out it's limited obligations and commitments.

President Johnson clearly stated on several occasions that the object of the war was not to remove the North Vietnamese leadership or to change the regime in the North. This was clearly showing to the North the limited nature of the American commitment by letting them know that the bombing would not be pressed to the extreme destruction of the society in the North. The view of Von Clausewitz on pressurising an enemy was expressed clearly in *On War* written 170 years ago:

> "If the enemy is to be coerced you must put him in a situation that is even more unpleasant than the sacrifice you call on him to make. The hardships of that situation must not of course be merely transient - at least not in appearance. Otherwise the enemy would not give in but would wait for things to improve. Any change that might be brought about by continuing hostilities must then, at least in theory, be of a kind to bring the enemy still greater disadvantage." [20].

This seems to be what America clearly failed to achieve with *Rolling Thunder*. The North Vietnamese never felt that the situation was worse than losing the war. They were prepared to wait for things to improve.

The main target of the bombing was the will of the North's political leadership, but the bombing was never clearly focused on this. Among the signals sent to the North Vietnamese leaders by the bombing campaign was that there was a definite limit to American commitment to the war, and that the Americans were not prepared to risk a war with China or Russia. Therefore the North Vietnamese could see what was and was not possible in the war. Some sections of the American military and politicians were talking about 'bombing North Vietnam back into the Stone Age'. However, statements by other military and political leaders, plus the evident political unrest within America caused by the war, made it clear that this was not realistically possible. If the will of the Northern leadership was the main target of the bombing, the signals sent by the bombing were never clear and unambiguous.

The various bombing halts that occurred during *Rolling Thunder* were intended to give the North Vietnamese a chance to enter negotiations. They never showed the slightest interest in accepting this ploy until 1968, merely using the bombing halts to re-establish their communication systems and to move supplies quickly to the South. The signal sent by the bombing halts to the North Vietnamese was that the Americans were looking for an end to the bombing and that they, the Americans, did not want the total destruction of North Vietnam. To use Clausewitz's phrase the situation the Americans had placed the North Vietnamese in was not more unpleasant that giving up their policy in the South would have been. It was also a situation that seemed only transitory.

McNamara, speaking before the Senate Foreign Relations Committee in May 1966, said:

"Our air operations have been very closely controlled to assure that we do not inadvertently widen the war. We are doing everything that we can to make clear to the North Vietnamese and to Communist China the limited character of our political objectives. I think great restraint has been shown in the application of our airpower." [21.]

The Americans put considerable effort into trying to reduce civilian casualties through bombing even where this affected the success of a raid. Large numbers of civilians were, however, unintentionally killed. This humanitarian approach to strategic bombing is, to a certain extent, self-defeating as the attack on civilian morale was a central part of all the early bombing theories. No government should ever be criticised for being too humanitarian but these considerations should be taken into account before a war is started. If humanitarian views are paramount then war should be avoided. Once the decision to go to war is taken the war should be prosecuted to the full extent. It is wrong to ask one's own armed forces to risk their own lives to save the lives of citizens of an armed enemy nation. The essence of war is death and destruction. A country not prepared to accept this should not go to war. There is no humanitarian way to wage war, as war should only be entered into when humanitarian means of ending conflicts have been exhausted. Writing on this point Clausewitz stated:

> "Kind-hearted people might of course think there was some ingenious way to disarm or defeat an enemy without too much bloodshed, and might imagine this the true goal of the art of war. Pleasant as it sounds, it is a fallacy that must be exposed: war is such a dangerous business that the mistakes which come from kindness are the very worst. The maximum use of force is in no way incompatible with the simultaneous use of the intellect."[22]

There was a basic flaw in the original *Rolling Thunder* strategy, which lay in the concept of slowly increasing the intensity of the bombing until the North Vietnamese agreed to end their support for the war in the South. The flaw lay in the fact that the Americans were not prepared to increase the level of the bombing to the point were the Northern leadership were forced to give way. This meant that ultimately the North Vietnamese were prepared to withstand a higher level of bombing than the Americans were prepared to deliver. The Americans entered a process of escalation and the North Vietnamese were prepared to see the escalation continue to a higher level than their enemies.

Rolling Thunder did not take place in a vacuum, but was part of the overall American strategy in the war. Although it was a major part of the war in Vietnam, it was still only part of the wider military operations that included bombing in Laos, Cambodia and South Vietnam together with the ground actions in the South, which was eventually to involve 550,000 American troops.

Rolling Thunder was a failure. However, had it been successful it is doubtful that it would have compensated for the failure of the overall strategy of the war in the South. The central part of the war was the ground war in South Vietnam. If America and its allies could have won this war, there would have been no need for the bombing campaign.

The crucial failure in the Vietnam War was failure of the strategy adopted by America to achieve their overall aims and objectives in the war. In fact one writer on the war, Colonel Harry G. Summers, has said that, '..our so-called strategy was never a strategy at all. At best it could be called a kind of grand tactics.'[23]

The war in the South was a political conflict. The original American commitment had been to give breathing space to the Government in South Vietnam to create a stable society, capable of sustaining it's own defence. Unfortunately the population in the South never showed any real faith or belief in the various Governments that held power over them. Indeed, a large section of the population genuinely supported Ho Chi Minh, especially in the early years of the war. The various Governments in South Vietnam during the 1950s, 1960s and early 1970s were a collection of undemocratic authoritarian and military Governments all supported by the Americans. None had the loyalty or support of a large section of the population. All American actions in Vietnam were doomed to failure while most of the people were not prepared to back what they saw as corrupt Governments that had no relevance to their everyday lives. One American writer on the war has stated that, 'Eradicating rebel causes should have been our key goal in Vietnam. Instead, we wrestled with symptoms.'[24.] As the failure of the successive and unrepresentative Governments in the South became increasingly obvious, the Americans were forced to pour more and more resources into Vietnam to hold them in place. All the other failures in Vietnam stem from this failure to create a popular Government in South Vietnam. Lawrence E. Grindler, writing in the Asian Survey has said that:

> "At heart it was a problem of socio-political relevance, of mobilizing, protecting and involving a population to fight on behalf of a nation. Saigon lost the war because it could not build a political community in South Vietnam." [25.]

By ignoring the political dimension of the war the Americans ensured that whatever strategy they adopted for the military side of the war, including *Rolling Thunder*, had little chance of success.

South Vietnam could never be mobilised to the extent achieved by the North because of lack of support and corruption. This forced the Americans steadily to increase their commitment to the war to make good the lack of effort from South Vietnam. It was no longer a struggle between North and South Vietnam, with some American aid to the South. It became a war between America and North Vietnam. America took on the full burden of the war but simultaneously assured the Government in the North that it was only prepared to fight a limited war and did not want to change the type of government in the North. While America was being drawn further and further into its commitment to the war, it was giving pledges to the North that the war would not be carried to its logical conclusion.

The ultimate flaw in American strategy was the political situation in the South. The southern part of the country could not be mobilised sufficiently to carry the major burden of the war. Bombing the North was not enough to offset this basic policy defect. Harvey A. DeWeerd described this weakness in American planning by saying:

> "North Vietnam always had more well-trained, well-disciplined, highly-motivated soldiers than it needed to frustrate American efforts in South Vietnam. These soldiers were willing to fight and die for their cause, and the soldiers of a corrupt regime in Saigon were not. North Vietnam could send reinforcements into South Vietnam faster and in greater numbers than the United States could." [26.]

Total war for the North Vietnamese and limited war for the Americans led to the position that throughout the war the North Vietnamese overall strategy was offensive and the American strategy defensive. The North Vietnamese aims and objectives in the war were positive in that they wished to gain control of the South and the American aims were negative in that they wanted the North to stop interfering in the South. Although they adopted an offensive position on the strategic level, the North Vietnamese were tactically defensive for most of the war. The exceptions to this were the *Tet* offensive in 1968 and the ground offensives in 1972 and 1975. On the tactical level the Americans spent most of the war attacking, in both the ground war in the south, and the air war. *Rolling Thunder* was undoubtedly an offensive bombing campaign, but was part of the overall strategic defensive policy adopted by the Americans. The aims of the campaign were negative in that the campaign was intended to force the North Vietnamese to stop their support for the war in the South. There were many faults in the organisation and operation of *Rolling Thunder* but no matter how effective the bombing by itself could have been, while it was part of the defective overall strategy, it could not be successful.

The American adoption of what was basically a defensive strategy meant that they had handed over to their enemy the initiative in the war. To be on the defensive contains the idea that at some point in the future the situation or conditions will have improved. At some point it will be necessary to go over to the offensive to achieve the aims of the war. On this idea of the defensive in war Clausewitz has written:

> "But we must insist that defence without an active purpose is self-contradictory both in strategy and in tactics, and in consequence we must repeat that within the limits of his strength a defender must always seek to change over to the attack as soon as he has gained the benefits of the defence." [27.]

This is a description of how the North Vietnamese acted during the war on the tactical level. They only moved on to the offensive when they thought, not always correctly, that they could succeed. The Americans however maintained their defensive posture, on the strategic level, throughout the war.

The North Vietnamese 'long war' strategy, spending most of the war on the tactical defensive, eventually paid off for them. As early as December 1965 one American intelligence agency reported that, 'They continue to believe that time is their ally and that their own staying power is superior.'[28.] The North Vietnamese always believed that in the end they would outlast the Americans who gave them assurances that their war aims were only limited. By adopting a tactically defensive position the North Vietnamese were willing to wait until things improved, but they never wavered from their offensive position on the strategic level. Speaking about the defensive doctrine Clausewitz wrote that:

> "...the aim of the defence must embody the idea of waiting - which is after all its leading feature. The idea implies moreover, that the situation can develop, that in itself it may improve, which is to say that if improvements cannot be effected from within - that is by sheer resistance - it can only come from without: and an improvement from without implies a change in the political situation. Either additional allies come to the defender's help or allies begin to desert his enemy." [29.]

The real enemy of North Vietnam in the war was the Government in South Vietnam. The North waited until the political situation changed and the South was deserted by its ally America.

The flawed American strategy meant that any part of that strategy was doomed to fail, including *Rolling Thunder*, no matter how successful it may have been on the tactical level. The American leaders misunderstood the true nature of the war from the beginning choosing to view the war as something it was not. Clausewitz wrote:

> "The first, the supreme, the most far-reaching act of judgement that the statesman and commander have to make is to establish by that test (war as an instrument of policy)the kind of war on which they are embarking; neither mistaking it for, nor trying to turn it into, something that is alien to its nature, This is the first of all strategic questions and the most comprehensive." [30.]

The war in South Vietnam was essentially a political conflict but the Americans only saw it as a military problem with a military solution. The only real answer to the war in the South was the creation of a Government that held support from most of the people. It may have been impossible to create that Government, in which case the war was unwinnable from the very beginning. Very little effort was put into trying to create such a Government and America chose to look for a military result to the problem from the start, misunderstanding the kind of war they had embarked upon.

By choosing to fight a ground war in South Vietnam America made the defeat of the Viet Cong and North Vietnamese forces the central part of their strategy. Sun Tzu, the Chinese strategist, writing more than 2,000 years ago, stated, 'Thus, what is of supreme importance in war is to attack the enemy's strategy.'[31.] The Americans chose not to attack the enemy's strategy but to attack the small proportion of the North Vietnamese armed forces in the South. Clausewitz put forward the idea of a 'centre of gravity' that should be 'The point against which all our energies should be directed.' As Harry G. Summers pointed out in his book *On Strategy: The Vietnam War in Context* the Americans directed their energies against the wrong centre of gravity, or even against something that was not a centre of gravity. The largest part of the North Vietnamese army was throughout the war kept in North Vietnam were it was safe from the American army. The Americans chose to concentrate on the military side of the war in Vietnam, but chose a centre of gravity that they could not attack directly because of their own doctrine of not invading North Vietnam.

The stated aim of the war was to establish an independent Government in South Vietnam. In this case the aim of the war should have also been the strategy followed, to establish a Government that could command a consensus among the people in the South. This would have obviously have involved fighting the Viet Cong and the North Vietnamese, but this should have been seen as only a means to an end and not the end itself. On the relationship between war and its political objective Clausewitz wrote:

> "It is clear, consequently, that war is not a mere act of policy but a true political instrument, a continuation of political activity by other means...The political objective is the goal, war is the means of reaching it, and means can never be considered in isolation from their purpose." [32.]

The war, to ensure the continuing existence of an independent South Vietnam, was strategically mistaken from the start.

The Americans, who seem to have been drawn into the war piecemeal from the beginning, also appear to have underestimated the abilities and resolve of the North Vietnamese to match every increase in the American commitment to the war. To quote Clausewitz again:

> "No one starts a war - or rather, no one in his senses ought to do so -without first being clear in his mind what he intends to achieve by that war and how he intends to conduct it. The former is its political purpose; the latter its operational objective. This is the governing principle which will set its course, prescribe the scale of means and effort which is required and make its influence felt throughout down to the smallest operational detail." [33.]

The American leadership clung to the overall strategy they had developed at the start of the war. They maintained it through a whole series of escalatory stages, without anybody realising the level of commitment that would be required to achieve the operational objective. They underestimated their opponents and never had a clear view of how they intended to achieve their objectives. They never realised that the level of commitment required to reach their military objectives was politically, if not physically, beyond their abilities to achieve.

The American decision to remain on the tactically offensive and strategically defensive throughout the war, meant that tactical successes in the South and those that they achieved with *Rolling Thunder* would not directly influence the outcome of the war. They were never able to engage more than a small portion of the Northern army in the South. They had also told the Northern leadership that they did not want to change the North Vietnamese government. The amount of bombing required to destroy Northern involvement in the South would risk involving China and Russia and probably would have been politically impossible for the Americans to realise. In these circumstances their many tactical achievements could not bring strategic success. 'The original means of strategy is victory - that is tactical success; its ends in the final analysis, are those objects which will lead directly to peace.'[34.] was Clausewitz's view on the relation between ends and means in war. In the Vietnam war the means, tactical victories were not directly related to the ends, the political objectives of the war. Neither American troops in the South or airmen over the North were ever tactically defeated by the North Vietnamese but this did not win the war for the Americans.

The North Vietnamese, with their 'long war' strategy, seem to have chosen as their 'centre of gravity' the political opinion inside America and the alliance between South Vietnam and America. To the North Vietnamese the Americans were the strongest member of that alliance and that, if the war could be dragged on long enough, the political situation in America would force the Americans to withdraw, leaving them to face only the South Vietnamese. If the casualty rate could be forced high enough, America, with it's limited view of the war, would not generate the amount of commitment to the war necessary to carry it to a successful conclusion. Clausewitz's view on this point was:

> "Since war is not an act of senseless passion but is controlled by its political object, the value of this object must determine the sacrifices to be made for it in magnitude and also in duration. Once the expenditure of effort exceeds the value of the political object, the object must be renounced and peace must follow." [35.]

The North Vietnamese raised the costs until the Americans could no longer politically afford to pay them.

The North Vietnamese knew that they could never physically defeat the American forces in any campaign. The Americans also knew this and this led them into being grossly overconfident in their approach to the war. The North Vietnamese chose to attempt to split America from South Vietnam by waiting until America was sick of the war. North Vietnamese long term military planning was directed towards the political side of the war rather than the military. To quote Clausewitz again:

> "It is possible to increase the likelihood of success without defeating the enemy's forces. I refer to operations that have direct political repercussions, that are designed in the first place to disrupt the opposing alliance, or to paralyze it, that gain us new allies, favourably affect the political scene, etc. If such operations are possible it is obvious that they can greatly improve our prospects and that they can form a much shorter route to the goal than the destruction of the opposing armies." [36.]

The North Vietnamese managed to disrupt the opposing alliance and waited until the political scene inside America was favourable towards them. This offered them a much shorter route than the impossible task of destroying all American forces.

America's democratic system needs a measure of popular support for any war to be carried to its conclusion. At the beginning of the Vietnam war there was backing for the American support of South Vietnam but, as the costs and deaths increased, support declined. There were no American central interests involved in Vietnam and many people in America came to believe that the war was just not worth the costs involved. After the Japanese attack on Pearl Harbour in 1941 there was no doubt that primary American interests were under threat. Support for the war against Japan was massive and was maintained after many setbacks and enormous costs. In the Vietnam conflict however, the American public came to see Indo-China as only peripheral to the country's real concerns and the steady escalation of costs, both human and financial, as a tragic mistake. When the North Vietnamese decided that they could outwait the Aericans they were correct. President Johnson was never prepared to call up the Armed Forces reserves or the National Guard and the American economy was never put on a war footing. Colonel Harry G. Summers quotes a conversation he had with a North Vietnamese Colonel in Hanoi during 1975:

'You know you never defeated us on the battlefield,' said the American colonel. The North Vietnamese colonel pondered this remark a moment. 'That may be so' he replied, 'but it is also irrelevant.'[37.] The American airmen were never defeated in the air over North Vietnam either but this was also irrelevant to the course of the war.

The American's have always turned towards a technological solution for all problems, especially military problems. President Johnson attempted to keep the impact of the Vietnam War on America as small as possible, but found himself on the horns of a dilemma by having constantly to escalate the numbers of troops and the size of the American commitment. Finally the war destroyed his political career. As a democracy it has been essential for the American political leadership to keep their casualties to a minimum, (although that is an unfair comment as American pilots were killed attempting to keep North Vietnamese casualties as low as possible). It was therefore natural for the Americans to turn to technological solutions to minimise their combat losses. They thought that the strategic bombing campaign would apply the maximum pressure to the Northern leadership, with least American casualties. This did not work out in practice as the air campaign followed the same course of escalation as did the ground campaign in the South. Air Marshal John Slessor wrote in an essay *Air Power and World Strategy* published in 1954:

> "We must expect to be faced with other Koreas... The idea that superior air power can in some way be a substitute for hard slogging and professional skill on the ground in this sort of war is beguiling but illusory... All this is cold comfort for anyone who hopes that air power will provide some kind of short cut to victory." [38.]

There is little doubt that the American leaders believed that the bombing of the North would have provided a short cut to victory in the South. There is also little doubt that the bombing failed to provide this kind of short cut and became part of the general problems of the war.

The North was seen as the source of the war in the South. Therefore, it would have been nearly impossible for the Americans to have mounted a major land campaign in the South without attacking the North. If American troops were fighting and dying in the South the American public would not have been prepared to see North Vietnam left unpunished. The bombing campaign started before the major commitment of American ground troops took place. In some ways this was a political necessity. The American leadership needed to be seen to be doing everything possible, before large numbers of American ground troops were sent to Vietnam. If we accept this view of *Rolling Thunder*, the fact that it was seen to be failing from the beginning was used to justify the American escalation in the war on the ground in South Vietnam. Taking this view, *Rolling Thunder* was a political success simply by existing and being seen to fail on the practical level. In reality this is much too cynical a view. In 1965 America possessed the most powerful Air Force in the World and there was no chance that America would become involved in a massive war without this Air Force being used to the fullest extent.

They assumed that there was a level of bombing that would force the North Vietnamese to give up their policy towards the South. They also assumed that the destruction of the industry and transport system in the North would achieve this. They believed that the North Vietnamese had a 'profit and loss' view of the war. As the weight of the attack was gradually increased and when the losses became large enough, they believed the North would abandon their support for the war. But the Northern leadership had dedicated their lives to the unification of their country and viewed the war in a completely different light. The Americans thought they were dealing with reasonable people but were dealing with fanatics. There undoubtedly was a level of bombing that would have crushed the North but this was beyond the political and practical level that the Americans were prepared to go.

There has been an underlying, if unstated, hope in most bombing campaigns that at some stage the morale of the people under bombardment would crack or collapse. There are few examples of a civilian community completely breaking down under air attack however. It has been said that bombing has occasionally strengthened the resolve or increased the morale of people being bombed. The truth is that although people might not actually break under air attack their morale is usually weakened. The German air raids on London in the First World War affected the people involved and production. During the Blitz on London in the Second World War the bombing had more of a general effect on the population than was admitted at the time or since. Massive Allied bombing of Germany produced a decline in morale, as is shown by American and British bombing surveys. Bombing focuses peoples hatred towards their attackers, but morale does, in general, decline under sustained bombardment with an adverse effect on war production and commitment.

Although there is a documented history of bombing reducing morale there are few examples of complete breakdown. Bombing may affect people's feelings but it has less effect on their actual behaviour. Germany had a highly organised central government with many types of social control available to it, but the population continued to go to work every day and do most of the things that were asked of it. With an efficient police force and secret police force plus Government control of food supplies, the ordinary people, most of whom would have had some kind of family, had little choice. People undergoing heavy bombing may develop feelings of despair and apathy but there is little they can do about it. Winston Churchill wrote about civilian morale in October 1917 that:

> "It is not reasonable to speak of an air offensive as if it were going to finish the war by itself. It is improbable that any terrorization of the civil population which could be achieved by air attack could compel the Government of a great nation to surrender. Familiarity with bombardment, a good system of dug-outs and shelters, a strong control by police and military authorities, should be sufficient to preserve the national fighting power unimpaired." [39.]

This appears a prophetic description of the course of *Rolling Thunder* and the consequent reaction of the North Vietnamese.

Not only did the bombing not break the North Vietnamese morale but it gave a focus to the North Vietnamese war effort. The war for the people in the North was not some abstract battle for the principle of Vietnam being one country. It was a war that was brought home to them on an almost daily basis by air attacks. The death and destruction caused by the raids allowed the Northern government to mobilise the population largely behind the war in the South. The war ended in 1975 and the North no longer had this as an excuse for the hardships the population were being forced to endure. They now had considerably more difficulty in motivating the population. When the external threat was removed the people expected things to improve and were less willing to endure the continuing vicissitudes. This was the start of the period when thousands of the 'boat people' left the country.

The strategic bombing doctrine adopted by America from the 1930s was flawed in several respects when applied to a third world conflict. The doctrine was predicated on the existence of 'vital targets' and on the ability to destroy these targets. In North Vietnam there were very few installations that the Vietnamese themselves viewed as vital compared with their commitment to the war in the South. In some ways the lack of development in North Vietnam placed the country beyond the amount of bombing that the Americans were prepared to use. The doctrine also had a rigid deterministic view of war, but war as Clausewitz has pointed out operates mainly in the area of chance. There are no guarantees in any war, whatever theory is being followed. Few military plans survive contact with the enemy. To quote Clausewitz yet again:

> "...war is not an exercise of the will directed at inanimate matter, as is the case with the mechanical arts, or at matter which is animate but passive and yielding, as is the case with the human mind and emotions in the fine arts. In war, the will is directed at an animate object that reacts." [40.]

There is no doubt that the North Vietnamese were forced to react to *Rolling Thunder* by devoting considerable time and energy to overcome the effects of the bombing. The American will was directed against the North Vietnamese and they reacted to this and to a large extent they prevailed, although at great cost.

The strategic bombing theories had remained unproven into the 1960s and the start of *Rolling Thunder*. They had developed from the experiences of the First World War but, before the start of the Second World War, the strategic bombing theories were essentially a priori as there was no major experience to base them on. After the massive strategic bombing campaign of the Second World War there was still no consensus on how effective this bombing had been. This disagreement continues to this day. Leaders of the Allied bombing campaigns claimed that it was bombing that had won the war. Another view was that, especially in Britain, the amount of national resources devoted to the strategic bombing of Germany, cost Britain more than it cost Germany. The bombing surveys carried out by America and

Britain after the war came to the conclusion that the bombing theories were neither substantiated nor disproved, but still unproven. The supporters of air power again hoped to prove the bombing doctrine in the Korean War but the true effect of the bombing was again hard to quantify.

At the start of the Vietnam War the proponents of 'victory through air power alone', again saw their chance to prove their theories, on which the existence of the American Air Force as a separate service was based. In the final analysis *Rolling Thunder* was a failure in that it did not force the North Vietnamese to stop their support for the war in South Vietnam. The adherents to air power doctrine have again said that the test was unfair. Some of the factors in the use of air power against North Vietnam mitigated against it being a true test of the effectiveness of air power as a war winner on it's own. America limited the amount of bombing it was prepared to sustain, but the North Vietnamese reorganised their country so that the amount of bombing needed to force a solution would have been enormous. The costs of the bombing were in the end bearable to the Vietnamese but the economic, political and morale costs were not acceptable to the Americans. North Vietnam adapted to the effects of the bombing and learned to live with it.

NOTES

1. Taylor, Maxwell D. *Swords And Plowshares*, W.W. Norton and Company Inc. New York, 1972, page 403.

2 U.S. Congress, Senate Committee On Foreign Relations Study No.5, Bombing As A Policy Tool In Vietnam: Effectiveness, 92nd Congress 2nd Session, Washington G.P.O. 1972.

3 Sharp, U.S. Grant, *Airpower Could Have Won In Vietnam*, Air Force Magazine Vol. 54, (Sept. 1971), page 82-83.

4 Halberstam, David, *The Best And The Brightest*, Random House, New York, 1969, page 647-7.

5 *The Pentagon Papers, The Senator Gravel Edition*, Vol. 4, Beacon Press, Boston, 1971, page 216.

6 Mason R. A. (Editor), War In The Third Dimension, Brasseys Defence Publishers, London, 1986, page 16.

7. Hoopes, Townsend, *The Limits Of Intervention*, David McKay Company Inc. New York, 1969, page 218.

8. Hoopes, Townsend, Ibid, page 218

9. *The Pentagon Papers*, Ibid, page 137.

10. *The Pentagon Papers*, Ibid, page 116.

11. *The Pentagon Papers*, Ibid, page 223.

12. *The Pentagon Papers*, Ibid, page 224.
13. Goulding, Phil G. *Confirm Or Deny*, Harper and Row, New York, 1970, page 178-9.
14. Levinson, Jeffrey L. *Alpha Strike Vietnam*, Presidio Press, California, 1989, page 241.
15. Momyer, William W. *Air Power In Three Wars*, U.S. Government Printing Office, Washington, 1978, pages 107-8.
16. Myers, Charles E. *Deep Strike Interdiction*, Proceedings - United States Naval Institute, Vol. 106, November 1980, page 47-52.
17. Clausewitz, Carl Von, *On War*, Edited and Translated By Howard, Michael and Paret, Peter, Princeton University Press, Princeton, New Jersey, 1976, page 134.
18. Momyer, William W. Ibid, page 339.
19. Sullivan, Cornelious D. *The Vietnam War: Its Conduct And Higher Direction*, The Centre For Strategic Studies, Georgetown University, Washington D.C. 1968, page 111.
20. Clausewitz, Carl Von, Ibid, page 77.
21. McNamara, Robert, *Foreign Assistance*, 1966, Hearings Before The Committee On Foreign Relations, US Senate, 89th Congress, 2nd Session, Washington GPO, page 679-80.
22. Clausewitz, Carl Von, Ibid, page 75.
23. Summers, Harry G. *On Strategy: The Vietnam War In Context*, Strategic Studies Institute, US Army War College, Carlisle Barracks, Pennsylvania, 1981, page 56.
24. Collins, John M. *Vietnam Postmortem: A Senseless Strategy*, Parameters, Vol. 8, March 1968, page 9.
25. Grindler, Lawrence E. *How They Lost: Doctrines, Strategies And Outcomes Of The Vietnam War*, Asian Survey 15, Dec. 1975, page 117.
26. DeWeerd, Harvey A. *Strategic Decision Making: Vietnam, 1965-1968*, The Yale Review, Vol. 67, June 1978, page 485-6.
27. Clausewitz, Carl Von, Ibid, page 600.
28. U.S. Congress, Senate Committee On Foreign Relations, Ibid.
29. Clausewitz, Carl Von, Ibid, page 613.
30. Clausewitz, Carl Von, Ibid, page 88-9.
31. Tzu, Sun, *The Art of War*, Translated By Griffith, Samuel B. Oxford University Press, 1971, page 77.
32. Clausewitz, Carl Von, Ibid, page 87.
33. Clausewitz, Carl Von, Ibid, page 579.
34. Clausewitz, Carl Von, Ibid, page 143.
35. Clausewitz, Carl Von, Ibid, page 92.
36. Clausewitz, Carl Von, Ibid, page 92-3.
37. Summers, Harry G. *On Strategy*, US Army College Pennsylvania, 1981, page 1.
38. Quoted in, Armitage, M.J. and Mason, R.A. *Air Power in the Nuclear Age*, University of Illinois Press, Chicago, 1983, page 45.
39. Quoted in, Fuller, Major General J.F.C. *The Conduct Of War 1789-1961*, Eyre Methuen, London, 1972, page 279.
40. Clausewitz, Carl Von, Ibid, page 149.

Epilogue

After the ending of the *Rolling Thunder* campaign in 1968 the bombing of North Vietnam continued sporadically for over four years until finally ending in early 1973. Richard Nixon had become President in January 1969, continuing Johnson's policy of suspending the raids on the North. Peace talks had started in Paris on 13th May 1968, but little progress had been made. The North Vietnamese had always maintained that they would never negotiate under the threat of bombing. Even after the limitation of bombing to south of the 20th parallel and the later ending of bombing completely, no serious negotiations had taken place. The stumbling block was the position of the Viet Cong vis a vis the Government in the south. Even the seating arrangements took months to discuss.

As part of the policy on ending the bombing the Americans believed that an agreement existed with the North Vietnamese to allow reconnaissance flights to continue over the North unmolested. These flights operated under the code name *Blue Tree* but many aircraft involved in these sorties were fired on by the North Vietnamese defences. An F-105 was shot down in January 1969 while accompanying a reconnaissance aircraft and a rescue HH-53 helicopter was shot down by a MiG over Laos while attempting to rescue the crew. In early 1970, following the shooting down of several such unarmed reconnaissance aircraft, Nixon authorised 'protective reaction strikes' against any anti-aircraft sites firing on reconnaissance aircraft.

Blue Tree reconnaissance flights began with single unarmed photographic aircraft, but the missions soon developed into complex operations over the North. Fighters were included to cover MiG airfields, *Wild Weasel*s blocked the defensive radar and strike aircraft were used to attack anti-aircraft sites. Thus, large numbers of aircraft continued to operate over North Vietnam.

Apart from the obvious dangers when operating fast jets from carriers, other perils existed, even outside the war zone. An accident with a rocket caused this fire aboard USS Enterprise (CVAN-65) while off Hawaii, en route for Yankee Station in 1969. Fifteen aircraft were destroyed and 371 casualties were sustained, 27 of them fatal. (via author)

The bombing of Laos continued and, with the release of extra aircraft, increased after the ending of *Rolling Thunder*. During the course of the war over three million tons of bombs were dropped on Laos. This was more than three times the number dropped on the North. Indeed, parts of the Ho Chi Minh trail became some of the most bombed places in history.

Tactical reconnaissance of the North was carried out by the ageing F-101 Voodoo and the more modern RF-4C Phantom for the Air Force. The SR-71 and the U-2 were responsible for strategic reconnaissance. The Navy was forced to put the RA-5 Vigilante back into production for use over the North, as it, with the RF-8 Crusader, was the mainstay of Navy reconnaissance forces.

In March 1969 the secret bombing of Cambodia was started in the *Menu* series of raids by B-52 bombers. Even the aircrew were not supposed to know the position of the targets when

An A-7E Corsair II of VA-147, 'The Argonauts'. This attack unit operated Corsairs during five combat cruises aboard USS Ranger (2), USS America and USS Constellation, finally leaving the Vietnam conflict on 11th October 1973. (National Archives)

bombing by radar guidance from the ground. When these missions finally became public knowledge in March 1970 the US had carried out 3,630 sorties over Cambodia and had dropped more than 100,000 tons of bombs.

An RF-4C was shot down while on a flight over North Vietnam on the 5th June 1969 and came down in the Gulf of Tonkin. Nixon ordered a series of reprisal raids by the Air Force and Navy on the associated anti-aircraft batteries, radar sites and covering missile sites.

By the end of 1969 779 attack and reconnaissance sorties had been carried out over North Vietnam by the United Stated Air Force. Ho Chi Minh had died in September 1969. His long war strategy had meant that he would not live to see the conclusion of his life's work.

In November 1970 a rescue mission was mounted to attempt to bring back some American prisoners of war held by North Vietnam. It was thought that up to fifty prisoners were held in a camp at Son Tay north west of Hanoi. The raiding force comprised five HH-53 helicopters and one HH-3 helicopter carrying American special forces, supported by two C-130Es. The single HH-3 was used because it was small enough to crash-land inside the prison compound carrying a group of the American commandos. Phantoms flew MiGCAP, *Wild Weasel* F-105s were on hand to suppress the defences, while the Navy mounted a major night attack on Haiphong and Hanoi to distract the defence network. One of the raiding helicopters missed its target and attacked a nearby barracks before moving on to the prison camp, which was quickly captured. It was then discovered that the American prisoners had been removed weeks before. The force then withdrew back to the base in Thailand. This was the only time during the war that American ground forces had fought a major engagement inside North Vietnam.

At this stage of the war the American public had become deeply dissatisfied with the war in Vietnam and demonstrations against the war involving hundreds of thousands of people became commonplace. In a democracy public opinion cannot be permanently ignored by any politician. Nixon said that he wanted 'peace with honour' but this option was never a real possibility. The general strategy chosen by Nixon was 'Vietnamization', i.e. the strengthening of the South Vietnamese forces to such a point where they could carry the full weight of the war with only minimal American support. Nixon began the rundown of American ground forces and, to a lesser extent, the air forces in the region. It was hoped that air power would hold the communists at bay until the South Vietnamese were strong enough to accept the responsibility. The tens of thousands of deaths among the American ground forces meant that the form of support shown hitherto was no longer acceptable to the American public, as Ho Chi Minh had always known it would be. In the end Vietnamization failed because no government in South Vietnam had the full support of most of the people.

The first MiG shot down since the end of *Rolling Thunder* was destroyed on 28th March 1970 by an F-4J from the USS *Constellation* during protective reaction strikes against the defences in the North. The ending of continuous bombing had

Five HH-53 'Super Jolly Greens' took part in the attempted rescue of American PoWs from their camp at Son Tay in November 1970. The siezure of the camp went to plan, but the prisoners had already been moved away. (National Archives)

given the North the opportunity to move their anti-aircraft defences south to threaten US aircraft attacking Laos. Mobile SA-2s were also moved south in an attempt to destroy a B-52. In February 1971 a reconnaissance aircraft was tracked by North Vietnamese radar from a SAM site. In retaliation for this, a raid involving 67 sorties was mounted in the area around the Ban Carai pass inside North Vietnam.

Air power was meant to hold the line but, as the numbers of ground troops declined, the numbers of aircraft in South East Asia also decreased. By the end of 1971 the total number of land-based aircraft available had diminished to less than five hundred, stationed in Thailand and South Vietnam. Reconnaissance over the North had revealed a buildup of forces in the southern area of North Vietnam, which seemed to suggest that a major ground campaign was planned for 1972. On 26th December 1971, Operation *Proud Deep Alpha* began, a five-day bombing campaign intended to disrupt this buildup. The raids, all south of the 20th parallel, were made up of 1025 sorties including over 400 from the carriers *Constellation* and *Coral Sea*. The targets were the SAM sites that had been moved south plus selected anti-aircraft sites. Logistic targets, truck parks, POL storage and supply dumps were also hit.

Navy pilots had scored no successes against MiGs since March 1970. However, on 19th January 1972 Lieutenant Randy Cunningham of VF-96 based on the *Constellation* escorted a Vigilante on a reconnaissance mission to the airfield at Quang Lang. MiGs were launched from Bai-Thiong airfield, one of these being brought down by Cunningham and his back seat radar operator Lieutenant (jg) William Driscoll, using a *Sidewinder*. Cunningham would go on to become the first 'ace' of the Vietnam War. On 21st February 1972 Air Force Major Robert Lodge shot down a MiG-21 over Laos, while flying a Udorn-based F-4D. The first North Vietnamese aircraft shot down by the Air Force in four years. Two other MiGs were shot down during March as the tempo of the fighting started to increase.

The commander of the Seventh Air Force in early 1972 was General John D. Lavelle, but he was removed from command in April for falsifying reports of attacks on reconnaissance aircraft. This was done so that protective reaction strikes could be launched even when aircraft had not been attacked. Lavelle had authorised somewhere between twenty and thirty strikes on North Vietnamese targets, including airfields and air defence targets, which he considered a threat to the aircraft and aircrews under his command.

By early 1972 the North Vietnamese had increased the size and quality of their air defence network and extended the coverage in the southern part of their country. The defence system operators now had years of experience behind them, while the North Vietnamese Air Force had increased to around 250 aircraft including MiG-17s, 19s and 21s. The number of jet-capable airfields had also increased. The American capabilities had also improved since the end of *Rolling Thunder*. The F-4 Phantom was now the standard fighter in both the Navy and the Air Force. F-105s had previously been retired from the bomber squadrons, but the F-105G was still the standard *Wild Weasel*.

More accurate 'smart weapons' were now being used than the old 'dumb bombs'. These included laser-guided bombs and electro-optically guided weapons. The use of chaff to jam the North's radar network had also started, based on the Second World War *Window* jamming device and consisting of light weight tin foil cut into long sections. It was released into the air in large quantities and was light enough to continue floating in the air for a considerable time. On the radar screen the chaff appeared as a large blip that obscured any aircraft in the area. The Americans had also developed a device that allowed the Russian developed IFF (Identification Friend or Foe) used by the North's MiGs to be triggered. This device (code-named *Combat Tree*) allowed them to know when the MiGs were airborne and their approximate position.

The technological advances were largely offset by a general decline in the level of Air Force combat experience since pilots who had flown in World War Two, Korea and *Rolling Thunder* had started to retire. The policy of no compulsory second tour in South East Asia also meant that there was now a significant number of relatively inexperienced pilots being introduced to operations. The Navy had reacted to the relatively low level of the ratio of air to air combat successes during *Rolling Thunder* (it was claimed to have been ten to one in favour of the Americans during the Korean War) by starting the Navy Fighter Weapons School at Miramar Air Base, soon better known by its more popular name 'Top Gun'. The school specialised in air combat manoeuvring and produced pilots of the calibre of Randy Cunningham and several other Navy pilots who were to shoot down MiGs in 1972. This development distributed this needed expertise throughout the fleet. The Air Force *Red Baron* survey, *Red Flag* exercises and 'Aggressor Squadrons' came too late to affect the war.

The numbers of aircraft available continued to decline until in 1972 there were only between seventy and eighty aircraft in four squadrons available in South Vietnam, three F-4 squadrons and one A-37 squadron. The number of fighter aircraft in Thailand was down to just under 120 plus a wing of B-52s. The number of carriers on station in the Gulf was two. Although the South Vietnamese Air Force had been massively increased, it had not yet had time to absorb the number of aircraft available.

The North Vietnamese began a major conventional invasion of the South on 29th March 1972. It was on three fronts, across the De-Militarized Zone, in the central highlands and from Cambodia close to Saigon and comprised the twelve regular divisions that formed the bulk of the North Vietnamese army. The North had received supplies of Russian made SA-7 shoulder-launched, infrared homing, anti-aircraft missile and these brought down several American aircraft in South Vietnam. Their existence now forced strike aircraft to operate at a higher altitude.

On 5th April President Nixon ordered the bombing of the North to be resumed in response to the invasion. The main aim was to disrupt the movement of men and equipment supporting the main force NVA invading the south. The first strikes were limited to south of the 19th parallel, but this restriction was moved northwards. By the end of the month the 'bomb line' had been moved north to 20 degrees 25 minutes, while several individual strikes above this line were authorised. On 15th and 16th April *Freedom Porch Bravo* saw B-52s attacking POL storage areas in the Hanoi and Haiphong areas, seventeen of which were destroyed. Over two hundred SA-2 missiles were launched at the B-52s but only one was badly damaged.

As the bombing increased the aircraft needed increased proportionally. A massive redeployment of aircraft to Thailand and South Vietnam then took place. In a series of operations known as *Constant Guard I* to *IV*, the numbers of available aircraft grew to over one thousand, the B-52 strength at U Tapao in Thailand and at Guam being increased to 210.

After *Rolling Thunder* ended in late 1968 the North Vietnamese had increased the capacity of land routes into China by building extra road and rail lines. However, the harbour at Haiphong was still the entry point for most of their supplies from Russia and the eastern European countries. One failing of

Linebacker I began on 10th May 1972. The MiGs rose in force to oppose the attacks on Hanoi and sustained heavy losses. Top, Lt. John Markle, Capt Stephen Eaves, Capt. Chuck DeBellvue and Capt. Steve Ritchie of Oyster Flight, 8th TFW. Both crews brought down MiG-21s on 10th May. Left, 'Oyster One', crewed by Maj. Bob Lodge and Capt Roger Locher, was shot down. Locher survived 23 days on the run before being rescued by a 'Super Jolly Green', backed up by Skyraiders, while Phantoms strafed the nearby airfield at Yen Bai. The relief on his face as he leaves the helicopter needs no further comment

(National Archives)

Rolling Thunder had been that the port had never been closed to shipping. To intensify pressure on the North to stop their invasion of the South, Nixon ordered the mining of the harbour at Haiphong, carried out on 8th May 1972 when Navy A-6s and A-7s mined the river channel downstream from Haiphong. Other harbours at Cam Pha, Hon Gai, Vinh and Than Hoa were also mined in the following days. By the end of the year 11,000 mines had been sown in the waters off North Vietnam. The mines were programmed to arm after three days, to allow Russian ships to leave Vietnamese waters. After this period the mines were fully effective and no ships entered or left Haiphong until they were removed.

Nixon now found himself in the same position as his predecessor Lyndon Johnson; the North Vietnamese would still not negotiate with him in any meaningful way. He had already said that American forces were leaving Vietnam and was now forced to turn to air power to pressurise the North Vietnamese into scaling down their invasion of the South, which continued. On 10th May Nixon ordered the start of *Linebacker I*. He had said 'the bastards have not been bombed like they are going to be bombed this time'. Now he told the military to carry out the type of campaign they had always asked for; one with minimal restraints.

On the first day of the campaign the Paul Doumer bridge was heavily damaged and eleven MiGs were shot down, including three by Randy Cunningham to bring his total to five. On the way back to the carrier Cunningham and Driscoll's Phantom was shot down by an SA-2 missile, forcing them down in the Gulf to be quickly rescued by helicopter. The bridge at Than Hoa had become almost mythical to the pilots involved in attacking it during *Rolling Thunder*. It had resisted all attacks for three and a half years but, on 13th May it fell to laser-guided 2,000 and 3,000 lb bombs launched by Phantoms from the 8th fighter wing based at Ubon. By the end of May all major bridges on the transport system were down and, by the end of June over four hundred bridges - practically every crossing in the system - had been destroyed. The amount of supplies entering the country had been cut from 160,000 to 30,000 tons a month by the end of June. By late summer major

Top: A little bedraggled, but otherwise unharmed, Randy Cunningham and William Driscoll safe aboard USS Constellation after
destroying three MiGs, then ejecting into the Gulf following a SAM
hit. Cunningham credited his success to the training he received at
the 'Top Gun' Navy Fighter Weapons School at Miramar.

(National Archives)

Bottom: F-4J Phantom '100' of VF-96, crewed by Cunningham and
Driscoll on 10th May, from which they subsequently ejected.

(National Archives)

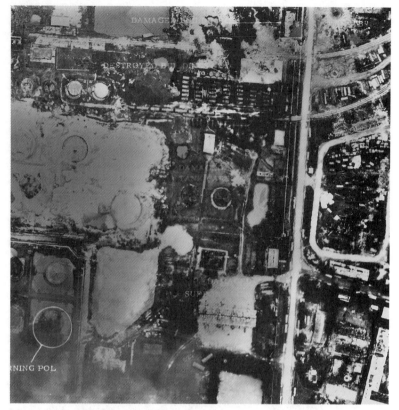

On 18th May 1972, F-4 Phantoms of the 8th TFW attacked the Hanoi POL storage facility with laser-guided bombs, causing extensive damage and destroying an estimated 5.5 million gallons of petroleum products. (National Archives)

targets with any military significance had been hit, including POL storage, power generation, storage and rail yards.

Linebacker I proved more effective in some ways than *Rolling Thunder*, but this was because the North Vietnamese had launched a major conventional invasion of the South. The amount of supplies needed for twelve divisions with artillery and tanks was considerably more than needed for the earlier, basically guerrilla, war needing minimal supplies. This tied the North Vietnamese more closely to their lines of communications and rendered them more vulnerable.

With Sparrow missiles beneath their fuselages and laser-guided bombs on the pylons, F-4Ds of the 4th TFW head toward North Vietnam, September 1972. (National Archives)

Linebacker I was an overwhelming tactical success. With new weapons and the removal of political limitations all targets listed were destroyed, yet again the bombing was not a strategic success. The bombing certainly cut off a large part of the supplies from the North to their army in the South and the invasion of the South ground to a halt because of this. The South Vietnamese army, however, proved incapable of driving out the Northerners. The North Vietnamese troops, having waited until practically all the American ground forces had gone, now found that they could maintain most of their gains in the South. The North Vietnamese resumed their 'long war strategy', dug in and waited for the Americans to leave.

On 22nd October 1972 the bombing was again restricted to south of the 20th parallel, as most of the targets in the North had been hit and the level of the fighting in the south had waned. From the start of 1972 until the end of the *Linebacker I* campaign, the Navy lost 61 aircraft over the North, while the Air Force lost 46 aircraft

between 10th May and 22nd October. During *Linebacker I* 155,548 tons of bombs had been dropped. During some periods of *Linebacker I* there had been six aircraft carriers on station and 23,652 sorties had been flown during the campaign by the Navy. September had seen the highest monthly total of sorties with 4,819 flown by Navy aircraft.

One reason for stopping *Linebacker I* was that it was thought that a break through had been reached at the Paris talks and that a settlement was likely, Henry Kissinger saying 'Peace is at hand'. However, bombing continued south of the 20th parallel at a reduced rate. On 22nd November 1972 the first B-52 to be brought down by the North Vietnamese crashed in Thailand on the way back to U-Tapao, after being hit by a SAM. The North Vietnamese yet again used the reduction in bombing to rebuild roads and railways. With the pressure now relaxed, the North Vietnamese again started to prevaricate in the Paris talks, which broke down on the 13th December 1972. Nixon was so enraged by this that he ordered the military to mount a maximum effort attack on the Hanoi and Haiphong areas. The only limitation was to keep civilian casualties to an acceptable minimum.

This became known as the *Linebacker II* campaign. The Haiphong area had thirteen targets, while sixteen more had been listed around Hanoi. Attacks started on 18th December 1972 with 129 B-52s bombing airfields close to Hanoi and the storage area at Yen Vien, losing three B-52s to SA-2 missiles. Bombing continued until 29th December with a break on Christmas day. In this period B-52s flew 729 sorties against 34 targets in the Red River valley area, during which 15,237 tons of bombs were dropped.

The North Vietnamese missile defences launched 1,293 missiles at the attacking aircraft, but managed to destroy only fifteen of the attacking B-52s. The first raid had been carried out with all the attacking aircraft approaching from the same direction over a five-hour period, which led to several losses. Later attacks were made from up to five different directions and were carried out in a fifteen-minute period. This helped to swamp the defence and reduce the losses. A large part of the defence system was destroyed, also helping to reduce losses. The Air Force and Navy had also flown large numbers of covering operations in support of the B-52s and this included the

Epitomising Linebacker II, the B-52D of Strategic Air Command. Fifteen of these huge aircraft were lost to ground defences during the campaign. (USAF)

dropping of chaff and flying *Wild Weasel* operations against the defences. Bombing was again reduced to south of the 20th parallel when *Linebacker II* ended.

Peace talks resumed in Paris on 2nd January 1973, with the main talks scheduled for the 8th. American public reaction to the Christmas bombing had weakened the position of the Americans in the talks and agreement was soon reached. The Americans forced the South Vietnamese to accept the terms of the settlement although they were loath to do so; North Vietnamese troops in the South were allowed to stay in place. The agreement came into force on the 27th January.

It has since been said that *Linebacker II* bombed the North Vietnamese back to the negotiating table and this is essentially true. However the settlement was one that would have been available to the Americans years earlier had they been prepared

15th January 1973. A-6 Intruders of VA-145, 'The Swordsmen', dropping some of the last bombs on North Vietnam. When they returned to USS Ranger, the shooting war in the North was over and all offensive operations were suspended. Eight days later, on 23rd January, the cease-fire was signed. (National Archives)

to accept it. The bombing had not changed the resolve of the North Vietnamese politicians to achieve their long term goals.

The last MiG shot down by the US Air Force was shot down on 8th January and the last one destroyed by the Navy was on the 12th, by an F-4 Phantom flown by Lieutenants Victor Kovaleski and James Wise, Co-incidentally, Kovaleski, with Ensign D H Plautz became the last crew to be shot down by the North when their Phantom was brought down two days later. They were safely rescued from the Gulf by helicopter. The final bombing missions over North and South Vietnam took place on 15th January 1973 and all reconnaissance missions were stopped on the 27th. South Vietnam was left to fend for itself.

The first American prisoners were released on 12th February and they were all home by the 29th March. Meanwhile the American bombing operations over Laos and Cambodia not only continued, but increased as more aircraft became available. On 15th August 1973 the American Congress ordered the stopping of all action in Southeast Asia, which brought to an end the American participation in the war. The South Vietnamese managed to hang on for another two years until 1975, before the North Vietnamese took over the entire country.

Between 1962 and 1973 the Americans dropped more than 6.2 million tons of bombs on Southeast Asia including Laos, Cambodia and all of Vietnam. America dropped considerably more bombs on the country of their ally, South Vietnam, than on their enemy North Vietnam. More than 3.5 million fixed-wing combat sorties were flown and the total number of aircraft lost in this period was 3,720 fixed-wing aircraft and 4,868 helicopters. In the final analysis this enormous effort did not achieve it's intended results. The misuse of air power could not balance the lack of a credible strategy.

Air-To-Air Refuelling

There had been experiments and stunts with air-to-air refuelling during the 1920s and 30s. A DH-4 had remained airborne for 37 hours in 1923, operated by the United States Army, but it was only after the Second World War that air refuelling became a practical proposition. At the end of February 1949 Strategic Air Command flew a Boeing B-50 Superfortress around the World nonstop, refuelling it in the air along the way. There was a small amount of air refuelling used during the Korean War but not regularly. During *Rolling Thunder* the use of air refuelling became the norm and the availability of tanker aircraft rather than the availability of strike aircraft was, for a time, the limiting factor on the size of the air strikes over North Vietnam. The bombing campaign could not have been carried out in the way it was without the use of air refuelling.

Hanoi was over 400 miles away from the main airfields in Thailand. While most of the aircraft involved could fly these distances, they could only have done it with extremely light loads and at optimum cruising speeds, with no reserves. When carrying heavy loads the use of afterburners was necessity for take-off. Afterburner was also used for high speed in the target area and to increase speed in any contacts with enemy aircraft. They use an enormous amount of fuel and are an inefficient way of increasing thrust. The types of afterburners in use by the F-105s and F-4s used about 10% of internal fuel per minute so their use increased the aircraft's speed but reduced the range considerably. The only way that combat aircraft could have bombed the Hanoi area from Thailand, with a reasonable bomb load was by using air-to-air refuelling.

There were two systems of air refuelling used during the Vietnam War. The earlier of these two systems was the probe and drogue method developed (and still used) by the British. This method utilises a flexible cone, fixed on the end of the fuel

The Flying Boom system. A KC-135 Stratotanker refuels a flight of thirsty F-105Ds en route to North Vietnam in January 1966. The blister beneath the rear fuselage of the tanker is the crew compartment for the boom operator, who was responsible for 'finding' the fuel inlet in the nose of the fighter. (USAF)

line towed behind the aircraft and known as the drogue. The receiving aircraft is equipped with a rigid metal probe forward of the pilot's field of view. The pilot of the aircraft receiving the fuel guides the aircraft to force the probe into the conical drogue. When contact has been made, fuel is pumped into the receiving aircraft. This system was used by the US Air Force during the 50s and early 60s and is still the system used by the US Navy. The system that replaced the probe and drogue method in Air Force use was the flying boom method. A telescopic boom is attached to the rear of the tanker aircraft, which can be moved from side to side and up or down. The boom is under the control of a specialist operator in the rear of the tanker. Receiving aircraft are equipped with a receptacle built into the airframe. To receive fuel the pilot has only to position the aircraft behind and below the tanker and the boom operator does the rest by manoeuvring the boom into the receptacle and pumping the fuel.

Aircraft in use with the Air Force for air refuelling in 1964 were the KC-97, derived from the Boeing C-97 Stratofreighter, which was still in use with Strategic Air Command in limited numbers, and the KB-50, a version of the Second World War B-29 Superfortress fitted with two extra turbojet engines for more speed. The KB-50 used the probe and drogue system and could refuel three aircraft simultaneously, but had trouble keeping up with F-105s and F-4s. Although obsolescent, it was still in use in 1964 with the Tactical Air Command and the Pacific Air Forces. Following the crash of a KB-50 at Takhli Air Base, Thailand, in October 1964, this type was phased out of service, leaving all air to air refuelling to the more modern KC-135. This latter was a close relative of the Boeing 707 and was capable of carrying more fuel at a much higher speed than the other tankers. It used the flying boom system, but could be modified to use the probe and drogue. However this modification could only be carried out before take-off, which meant that careful pre-mission planning was called for, to enable the tanker and the combat aircraft to be 'matched'. During the early part of the war some aircraft such as the F-100, F-104 and early F-105s were equipped with probes, but were later standardised to the flying boom system. The KC-135 was more efficient than earlier tankers and was in great demand from all branches of the Air Force, but it was decided that all KC-135s should be placed under control of Strategic Air Command. Thus for most of *Rolling Thunder*, the tactical strike aircraft were totally dependant upon SAC's KC-135 fleet.

As the American buildup progressed through 1964, it was admitted that photographic reconnaissance flights had been taking place. Several had been damaged by communist gunfire, and the first to be shot down, a Navy RF-8E Crusader, fell on 6th June. The US Air Force retaliated on 9th with strikes against Pathet Lao forces, using F-100 Super Sabres refuelled by SAC KC-135 tankers operating from Clark Field, in the Phillippines. Six had been transferred there from Guam for this operation. The official history of SAC air refuelling said, 'The Yankee Team KC-135s flew their first refuelling mission over southern Laos on 9th June 1964 and thus began the history of SAC aerial refuelling in the employment phase of operations.'[1]

The Navy way. A KA-3B of VAH-2 'The Royal Rampants' refuels an F-4B of VF-96 using the probe and drogue system developed by the British. The responsibility for this type of operation lay with the fighter pilot, who was required to 'fly' the probe into the trailing cone. The photo was taken in 1968, when both units were aboard USS Enterprise. (US Navy)

Following the Gulf of Tonkin incident in August, the American forces in southeast Asia continued to increase and the 4252nd Wing was activated at Kadena Air Force Base on Okinawa on 12th January 1965 to provide air refuelling support in the theatre. It was intended to base some aircraft at Don Muang airport near Bangkok, from where the 4252nd Wing flew their first combat refuelling on 25th January. Following the opening of *Rolling Thunder* in March, the number of bombing sorties began to escalate, requiring increased KC-135 aircraft to support them. Thus many tankers became stationed in Thailand, by October 1967 35 were based at Kadena, 32 at U Tapao and eight at Takhli. During the entire air war (1964 - 1973) KC-135s flew 194,685 tanking missions, carrying out 813,878 air-to-air refuellings.

KC-135 refuelling areas were established over Thailand and the Gulf of Tonkin. Later, refuelling patterns were established over Laos, but the American Ambassador insisted that these were well away from the Laotian capital. Occasionally tanking aircraft even went into the border areas of North Vietnam to refuel aircraft in trouble and short of fuel. The tanking aircraft normally flew around a 'race track' pattern at specific points in the air, with inbound strike aircraft taking on between 8,000 lbs. and 12,000 lbs. of fuel. On their way home, strike aircraft again refuelled taking on around 5,000 lbs of fuel to provide a reserve in case of delays in landing caused by weather or damaged aircraft crashing on runways. The average amount of fuel off-loaded on one refuelling flight by the KC-135s was around 55,000 lbs, refuelling seven aircraft.

The preferred height for refuelling was about 26,000 feet but the heavily laden F-105s could not reach more than around 15,000 feet and refuelling took place at this height. Tankers were not supposed to descend bellow 15,000 feet but if damaged aircraft could nor reach this height the tankers were forced to join them at whatever height they could reach.

A major strike could involve sixty strike aircraft and fifteen tankers, who had to rendezvous at just the right place and time. Both strike aircraft and tankers were under control of radars based in Thailand, South Vietnam, in aircraft over Laos and in ships in the Tonkin Gulf. This ground control was so good that aircraft could be operating in the same airspace with as little as 500 feet vertical separation between them.

In very general terms Navy aircraft did not have to fly quite the ranges of Air Force aircraft, since *Yankee Station* was closer to Hanoi than most airfields in Thailand. Most Air Force strike aircraft operating over the North were equipped with afterburners (F-105s and F-4s) and, while this increases speed, it takes large amounts of fuel. The Navy need for air refuelling was probably marginally less than for the Air Force. While some of their aircraft used afterburners (F-4s and F-8s) most strike aircraft did not (A-4s, A-6s and A-7s), which reduced their need for fuel. The US Navy used the drogue and probe system (and still does) throughout the war. At the start of the Rolling Thunder campaign the main carrier-borne tanker aircraft was a version of the Douglas A-3, a large twin-engined aircraft intended as a long range nuclear bomber and was also used for photographic reconnaissance and electronic countermeasures.

Later in the war the main Naval tanking aircraft became the KA-6, a version of the A-6 developed for this purpose. They also used the 'buddy-buddy' system of refuelling. With this method ordinary strike aircraft (A-4s, A-6s or A-7s) were equipped with external fuel tanks and a pod containing pumps and a drogue attached to a length of hose. In flight the aircraft could deploy the drogue and another aircraft could take on fuel through the drogue from the lead aircraft's tanks. Obviously the amount of fuel that could be transferred was strictly limited as the tanking aircraft had to keep enough fuel for its own needs. This method also reduced the number of strike aircraft available to carry bombs, but did give flexibility by allowing any type of strike aircraft to be temporarily used as tanker aircraft.

Before the start of *Rolling Thunder* it was thought that for tactical aircraft air refuelling was only to be used for allowing aircraft to be deployed overseas, especially across the Pacific. However, it would have been impossible to mount raids on North Vietnam without air refuelling. Tankers also saved many strike aircraft, who had lost fuel through being damaged in combat, or had used more fuel than planned and could not reach base otherwise. On the 5th July 1966 a KC-135 refuelled a flight of four F-105s, none of whom had enough fuel left to have reached their own bases, after burning an unexpected amount of fuel in an engagement with North Vietnamese MiGs. It was estimated that KC-135 tankers had saved 76 aircraft for the Air Force up to July 1967, and the Navy credited its A-3 tankers with saving 380 aircraft during 1966-67.

FOOTNOTES

1.   Hopkins, Charles K. *SAC Tanker Operations in the Southeast Asia War.* Office of the Historian, Headquarters, Strategic Air Command, Page 2.

Appendix II
Radar Command, Control and Communications

During the early 1960s ever increasing numbers of American aircraft were committed to Southeast Asia. The need arose for increased air traffic control facilities to monitor the movements of these aircraft and, by 1964, radar sites had been established at Saigon, Da Nang and Pleiku in South Vietnam. With the massive increase in activity in 1965 other radar sites had to be established at other places in the South and were also established in Thailand at Udorn, Nakhon Phanom, Mukdahan and Ubon. These facilities were originally intended to control the aircraft flying over Thailand and South Vietnam and to give air defence against any attacking aircraft from the North. However, after the start of *Rolling Thunder* in 1965 the northernmost of these radars were used to provide control of the strike forces heading into North Vietnam.

The ground based radars in South Vietnam and Thailand had only limited ranges and could only give high altitude coverage over the Southern part of North Vietnam. The curvature of the Earth and the fact that radar beams only travel in straight lines meant that at long range a large portion of the airspace close to the ground was below the radar horizon. With the increase in the tempo of *Rolling Thunder* there was a need for further coverage over the Hanoi area. To meet this need it was decided to introduce airborne command and control aircraft into the radar system. This was the Lockheed EC-121 Warning Star, a developed version of the Lockheed Super Constellation. It was a large four-engined aircraft with a crew of up to thirty. A long-range aircraft, the EC-121 had an endurance of eighteen hours and was capable of twelve hours on station. Two large radars were fitted, one below the fuselage and one in a large fin like dorsal structure. The aircraft had been originally designed as radar pickets to increase the range of the continental radar system in the United States and the radar was designed

'College Eye'. An EC-121R Command and Control aircraft orbits above the Gulf of Tonkin. This model differed from the EC-121 Warning Eye aircraft in not having the bulbous radome on the upper fuselage. (USAF)

primarily for use over water. This presented some difficulties when used over land.

EC-121s were operated by the 552nd Airborne Warning and Control Squadron originally using the code-name *Big Eye* and were based at Tainan in Formosa, while using Tan Son Nhut airfield outside Saigon as a forward operating base. They flew patrol patterns over the Gulf of Tonkin or over Laos. With the quality of radar then in use it was very difficult for radars to look down at the ground as returns from aircraft at low level were swamped by radar signals bounced back from the ground terrain. In practice this meant that if the radar carrying aircraft flew higher it increased the radar range but it was difficult to detect low flying aircraft. If the aircraft flew lower this decreased the range of the radar but made it possible to detect aircraft flying at a lower level, as these were now seen against the back ground of the sky rather than lost in the ground returns. On occasions two radar aircraft were used, one at low level and one at a higher level, but low level radar coverage was never very clear and aircraft flying low could usually avoid detection.

The Naval part of the radar net over North Vietnam was made up of two parts. These comprised radar-carrying aircraft based on the carriers at *Yankee Station* and an American

One of the mainstays of the US Navy warning system was the E-2A Hawkeye, which replaced the earlier E-1 Tracer. These aircraft are from VAW-122, pictured in 1969. (US Navy)

cruiser positioned off the North Vietnamese coast with its radars looking up the Red River valley towards Hanoi. The cruisers chosen for this were equipped with high quality radar and communications equipment and with anti-aircraft weapons. The code-name for these ships was *Red Crown* and they formed an essential part of the Navy's *PIRAZ* (Positive Identification Radar Advisory Zone) used to control the aircraft operating over North Vietnam. At the start of the war the standard ship-borne radar aircraft was the Grumman E-1B Tracer, a development of the Grumman S-2 Tracker anti-submarine aircraft. This carried the radar above the fuselage and was an old aircraft with only limited range and endurance, but continued to be used for several years, especially on the smaller carriers. The replacement for the Tracer was the Grumman E-2 Hawkeye, a larger, more modern aircraft with better equipment and range. It first flew in 1960 and was just entering service in 1965. The first deployment of the Hawkeye to Vietnam was in November 1965

'Red Crown', one of the cruisers permanently located off the mouth of the Red River, with radar constantly monitoring the Red River valley area and broadcasting warnings of SAM and MiG activity to attacking American aircraft on the 'guard' radio frequency. These cruisers, a vital part of the Rolling Thunder campaign, were never seriously threatened by North Vietnamese naval or air forces.

(National Archives)

aboard the *Kitty Hawk*. The Hawkeye's radar was carried in a 26 feet diameter disk above the fuselage containing the antenna, which revolved at six times per minute.

Air Force EC-121s flew their first mission on 17th April 1965, after the first American aircraft had been shot down by North Vietnamese MiGs. The idea was that the EC-121s would provide airborne early warning, by extending the radar net to cover North Vietnam and provide advanced warning of MiGs to American aircraft over the North. During the early part of *Rolling Thunder* the 552nd Squadron EC-121s used the radio call sign *Disco*, issuing warnings to strike aircraft over the North by using a colour code. A Yellow Warning meant that there were MiGs in the air and a Red Warning indicated that MiGs were within ten minutes flying time of American aircraft. EC-121s broadcast this information on the 'guard' radio channel (243.0 MHz), not directly to individual aircraft at this early stage of the war but instead gave general warnings. Due to the restricted low level radar coverage, EC-121s also gained information on the movement of North Vietnamese aircraft by monitoring their communications. The MiGs operated under the

Russian method of tight ground control. Thus by monitoring the communications between MiGs and their controllers it was possible to tell when the fighters were in the air. Later in the war the Americans developed the equipment necessary to trigger the Russian supplied *IFF* (Identification Friend or Foe) system in use on the North's MiGs. This allowed them to be detected even at low level, but this was after the close of the *Rolling Thunder* campaign.

Besides providing warnings of the presence of enemy aircraft the EC-121s also provided control facilities for strike aircraft. There was an exclusion zone thirty miles wide along the border with China and American aircraft could only enter this area under specific instructions. Any aircraft approaching this area was provided with warnings to prevent any accidental penetration of Chinese airspace. With their long endurance the EC-121s could remain on station and co-ordinate search and rescue missions that were organised to recover any aircrew that had been shot down. With the large numbers of aircraft that were at times in the air over North Vietnam, American aircraft were obliged to carry out visual recognition of targets before firing any missiles. *Sparrow* missiles had a theoretical maximum range of thirty miles they could not be fired using radar contacts alone without visual recognition, because of the possibility of hitting other American aircraft. The only exception to this was when the EC-121s or the Navy's *Red Crown* could guarantee that there were no other American aircraft in the vicinity and could authorise the use of missiles beyond visual range. *Big Eye* aircraft also passed information to the strike aircraft on any changes in the weather, anti-aircraft missile warnings and provided vectors for tankers and aircraft needing fuel or any other information the strike formations could need.

In February 1967 the 552nd Squadron moved to Udorn in Thailand and in March their code name was changed to *College Eye*. In October the EC-121s were moved again, now to Korat air base. A newly developed version of the EC-121, the EC-121M, was evaluated from July 1967 until December. It had a higher quality radar and could issue more accurate warnings of MiG activity.

To help to pull together the different elements of the radar control system it was found necessary to have dedicated radio relay aircraft to improve communications between disparate parts of the system. Several variants of the KC-135 were used for this rôle equipped with extra communications equipment, also examples of the EC-135L normally operated by SAC. By using ground, sea and air-based radars and communications aircraft the 7th Air Force headquarters could follow and communicate with a strike over North Vietnam from take-off to landing. The setting up of this system meant that a considerable amount of control and communications was available, but this was essentially advisory in nature as the overall command of a strike was still in the hands of the mission commander, who was normally flying in the lead strike aircraft.

The Wild Weasel
and Iron Hand Missions

The introduction of the SA-2 *Guideline* surface-to-air missiles by the North Vietnamese was something of a traumatic experience for the Americans. While they were never very effective in destroying American aircraft, the American reaction involved developing new types of aircraft and missions to mitigate their effects. The Air Force and the Navy had watched the development of the missile sites in North Vietnam but had been stopped from attacking them for political reasons. The first aircraft lost to the missiles was an F-4C Phantom on 24th July 1965. A major strike was mounted three days later against the site it was thought had fired the missile. This strike was carried out by forty-six F-105s but three were shot down over the target and two others crashed on the way back. The general reaction to the missiles was for all strike aircraft to operate at a lower altitude to restrict the operational envelope of the missiles. This forced aircraft down into the range of large numbers of anti-aircraft guns, which were to shoot down most American aircraft lost during the Vietnam War. The second aircraft lost to an SA-2 missile was a Navy A-4 Skyhawk on the night of 11/12th August. During the following two days (12th and 13th) the Navy launched 124 aircraft in a massive attempt to attack the missile launching sites. Many missile sites had been constructed, the mobile missile launchers being constantly moved between them. The Navy aircraft, flying at low level searching for the missile sites, failed to find a even one and six aircraft were shot down and seven more were damaged by anti-aircraft fire. This hasty reaction to the missiles became known as "Black Friday".

The electronic equipment necessary to locate the missile sites had already been developed, known as the Radar Homing and Warning system (RHAW). It could both detect the *Fan Song* guidance radar used by the SA-2 and show the direction of the

The first specialised Wild Weasel was the two-seat F-100F Super Sabre. (via author)

radar signals. The *Fan Song* operated in the S band, but changed to the L band when missile firing was imminent and this change could also be detected by the RHAW equipment. In time, all strike aircraft were fitted with this equipment. While the Navy chose to fit this equipment into standard examples of their attack aircraft, the A-4s, the Air Force decided to create a new specialised type of aircraft to operate against the missile sites. This type of specialism became known by the code name *Wild Weasel*, a system never adopted by the Navy. The missions to attack missile sites were given the code-name *Iron Hand*.

The first *Wild Weasel* was a development of the two seat F-100F Super Sabre, four arriving at Korat air base in Thailand in November 1965. The second cockpit was used for the EWO (Electronic Warfare Officers), who were transferred from Strategic Air Command, to operate the new equipment. The F-100 was already obsolescent and never really had the range to operate over North Vietnam with an adequate bomb load. F-100Fs were intended to operate in teams with F-105Ds. The idea was that these hunter-killer teams of aircraft would fly in front of the strike formation and enter the target area before the strike aircraft arrived. The F-100F would detect any signals from the *Fan Song* radars and then turn and fly towards the missile sites until the site was detected visually and identified for the F-105s to destroy.

Wild Weasel aircraft normally carried two enormous 355 gallon fuel tanks and two pods of twenty-four rockets. After using their electronic equipment to show the direction of the missile sites and when they were detected visually the F-100s attacked with rockets and 20 mm cannon. The F-105s flying behind the F-100Fs followed up the rocket attack with bombs and cluster bomb units. By attacking any missile sites that posed a threat to the main bombing force the *Wild Weasels* allowed the strike aircraft to approach the target area at a higher altitude above the main anti-aircraft gun threat. *Iron Hand* flights had to be the first aircraft into the target area and the last to leave which made the missions extremely dangerous. The RHAW equipment released the aircraft tasked with attacking the missile sites from the need to search blindly for them at low level. It showed the attacking aircraft which sites were a threat to the strike forces and gave the general position of these sites. The first missile site was destroyed by *Wild Weasels* on the 22nd December 1965.

During the early 1960s the US Navy had developed the *Shrike* missile at it's China Lake Weapons Centre. Originally intended for use against Soviet defences, the *Shrike* could detect the frequencies that Russian missile systems worked on, using a passive homing head designed by Texas Instruments. It could then 'fly down the radar beam' and destroy the tracking and guidance radar, normally housed in a caravan type vehicle. The *Shrike* was 10 feet long and weighed 400 lbs. including a 145lbs. warhead. The fuse was both impact and proximity and the warhead used a fragmentation charge that could rip apart radar antenna, even if a direct hit was not achieved. If the radar was turned off during the attack however, the *Shrike* could not continue homing as the missile had no way of memorising the position of the radar.

The F-100Fs had received three replacement aircraft but had also suffered the loss of three aircraft by March 1966. *Shrike* missiles were issued to the *Wild Weasel* detachment in Thailand

The ultimate Wild Weasel was the F-105G, replacing the earlier 'F' model. The use of the Shrike anti-radiation missile improved its capability by forcing the Fan Song radar sites to shut down. SAMs already launched could no longer guide. The Standard ARM missile, introduced in 1968 had greater range and striking power.

(National Archives)

in March and the first was fired on 18th April 1966. The *Shrike*, with a range of about five miles, gave the F-100s the advantage of attacking missile sites without having to overfly them and risk the surrounding anti-aircraft guns. However the F-105Ds that accompanied the *Weasels*, as the killer part of the hunter-killer team, still had to attack the site with conventional ordnance. The *Shrike* did not need the specialised equipment used by the F-100Fs, as the seeker head on the *Shrike* could detect the required radar emissions. The Navy used the *Shrike* mounted on standard A-4s and A-7s, modified to carry the missile.

F-100s lacked the performance to be truly effective in the SAM suppression role and the Air Force decided to use the two-seat F-105F as the next version of the *Wild Weasel* to enter service. It had a longer range and could carry a heavier load but used the same electronic equipment as the F-100F and performed the same task. The first F-105Fs were deployed to Korat in May 1966 as part of the 13th Tactical Fighter Squadron of the 388th Tactical Fighter Wing and flew their first mission on the 3rd June, still operating as a part of an hunter killer team and normally paired with an F-105D. As more *Wild Weasel* aircraft became available it became standard practice for all strikes on the North to be escorted by F-105Fs to suppress the missile defences. As the North Vietnamese missile operators came to recognise the threat from *Wild Weasels* and the Shrikes they began to turn their radars off if they thought missiles had been launched against them. By forcing the missile sites to close down the *Wild Weasels* were achieving their main objective of protecting the main strike forces and allowing them to carry out the bombing attacks without interference from the SA-2 missiles. It became a game of 'chicken' between the *Wild Weasel* operators and the SA-2 missile operators as they each attempted to destroy the other without themselves being destroyed.

By the end of 1967 F-105F *Wild Weasels* had been credited with the destruction of eighty-nine missile sites, although usually they achieved their objective by forcing the missile radars off the air. The *Wild Weasel* mission had proved to be one of the most dangerous missions flown by the Air Force and many *Wild Weasels* were shot down. The North Vietnamese, once they had recognised the way the *Wild Weasels* worked, began to use bogus missile sites by employing equipment that produced a signal that appeared the same as that produced by the *Fan Song* radar. These bogus sites were surrounded by anti-aircraft guns in the hope of luring *Wild Weasels* into attacking them. Two of the twelve awards of the Medal of Honour made to Air Force personnel during the Vietnam War 1965-73 were made to *Wild Weasel* pilots. Captain Merlyn H. Dethlefsen was awarded the medal for a mission on 10th March 1967 flown to protect a major strike on the steel mill at Thai Nguyen, to the North of Hanoi. Dethlefsen, after avoiding North Vietnamese MiG-21s and intense anti-aircraft fire that had shot down another member of his flight, managed to destroy a missile site guarding the complex at Thai Nguyen. Major Leo K. Thorsness was awarded the medal for a mission flown on 19th

April 1967. Besides attacking missiles in the target area Thorsness and his back-seater shot down a MiG-17.

The Navy *Iron Hand* missions were carried out by standard strike aircraft, a major Naval *Alpha Strike* involving four or eight *Iron Hand* aircraft. A-4s carrying Shrike missiles would be given specific missile sites to attack where it was known these sites were active and close to the route of the main strike force. They could be paired with F-8s to provide protection and to add weight to the attack on the missile sites.

The Air Force continued to develop the *Wild Weasel* idea and the third type to enter service was another mark of the F-105, the F-105G, equipped with internal ECM (Electronic Counter Measures) equipment and improved RHAW and missile capabilities. They were deployed to Thailand in April 1968 when *Rolling Thunder* had been restricted to the Southern part of North Vietnam, restricting the targets available. A new type of missile was also introduced in 1968. This was the Standard ARM, much larger than the *Shrike*. It worked in the same way in that it homed onto the radar emissions used by the SA-2 but had a much longer range and heavier warhead. The first firing in a combat situation took place on 10th March 1968 when several were launched from F-105Fs over North Vietnam.

Wild Weasels came to play an essential part in all the major Air Force raids during *Rolling Thunder* by suppressing or destroying the North Vietnamese missile defences. The enormous number of missiles and radar equipment supplied by the Russians meant that they never managed to achieve the upper hand over the missile system but they reduced the threat and allowed strike aircraft to operate. The tactics evolved by *Wild Weasels* in Vietnam during *Rolling Thunder* became the standard tactics used for defence suppression aircraft in the Air Force, and still form the basis of the tactics used to this day.

Appendix IV
Combat Search and Rescue

During the build up of American military aircraft in South East Asia during the early 1960s the Air Force had only two types of aircraft available for the rescue service. These were the HH-43B Husky helicopter and the HU-16 Albatross, a fixed wing amphibian. The Husky was a short-range rescue helicopter for use close to air bases. In peacetime most aircraft crashes occur when aircraft are either landing or taking off, thus the Husky was intended to lift rescue personnel and fire fighters, and their equipment, to the site of crashes that had occurred close to base. As the air war began to develop in southeast Asia, so the numbers of aircraft shot down or forced to crash through battle damage increased. With aircraft operating over North Vietnam, Cambodia and Laos it was inevitable that aircraft would be forced down in these countries.

Any pilot coming down over North Vietnam and large areas of Cambodia and Laos would be lucky if they were only take prisoner as numbers of shot-down American aircrew were murdered, especially in Laos. The type of aircraft needed to mount rescue operations over enemy-held territory was one with a good range and endurance, able to protect itself to a reasonable extent and strong enough to withstand some battle damage. In 1964 there was no such aircraft available, so as a temporary measure, the HH-43B was developed into the HH-43F with a larger engine, more fuel, 800 lbs. of armour plate and machine guns for self defence. But even this version did not have the performance to venture far into North Vietnam. In late 1964 there were 13 HH-43B/Fs based at various airfields in Thailand and South Vietnam.

The HU-16 Albatross was an amphibian intended for rescue operations over water. The Gulf of Tonkin stretches down the Eastern coast of North and South Vietnam and aircraft damaged over the North found that generally, the fastest way

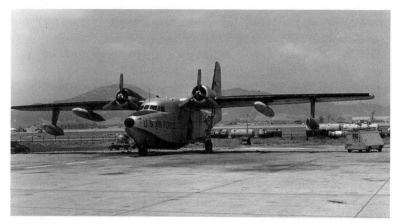

One of the earliest rescue aircraft to be employed by the US forces was the Grumman HU-16 Albatross amphibian. It was an excellent aircraft for hauling airmen out of the Gulf of Tonkin, but its use was limited by sea conditions. It could not land in a heavy swell.

(National Archives)

out of enemy airspace was to fly out over the Gulf. Thus many aircrew ended up floating in the sea. The ability of the Albatross to land on water gave it the task of rescuing these aircrew and, if weather conditions were too bad for a landing the Albatross could drop life rafts and survival equipment to the aircrew in the water. The Albatross continued in service until 30th September 1967, by which time it had taken part in the rescue of 26 Air Force personnel and 21 Naval fliers.

Some rescues carried out by Albatross aircraft were very close to the Vietnamese coast and thus highly dangerous. On 18th March 1966 an Albatross landed within two miles of the North Vietnamese coast while trying to rescue the crew of a shot-down Phantom. It was destroyed by artillery fire and two of the crew killed.

With the increase that took place in the numbers of aircraft and ships involved in rescue work there was a need for a command and control function on the spot to co-ordinate all the forces involved. Two HU-16s were equipped with extra communications equipment to carry out this mission but this was only a temporary measure as they did not have the endurance to be fully effective and they were thought of as crowded and cold aircraft.

The position of the Americans in Laos was peculiar; while it was well known that they operated inside Laos, it was not admitted publicly. The CIA-run airline *Air America* operated in Laos and provided the cover for clandestine supply of friendly forces and also took part in actions against the Pathet Lao communist forces. Additionally, *Air America* helicopters provided most of the rescue effort for American aircrew forced down inside Laos. The *Air America* pilots had been flying over Laos for years and had the best available local knowledge for carrying out this work. In the period between June 1964 and June 1965 the Air Force rescued five aircrew from inside Laos and Air America recovered twenty-one.

The rescue services expanded throughout the region, carrying out rescues using slow vulnerable helicopters over areas of North Vietnam and Laos, where they frequently came under heavy anti-aircraft fire. Therefore it became necessary to escort and protect them. It was also necessary to isolate and protect the survivor on the ground from North Vietnamese ground forces attempting to capture them. The ideal aircraft for these missions was the Douglas A-1 Skyraider, originally used as a carrier-borne attack aircraft. It was a propeller driven aircraft in an age of jets, but since helicopters cruised at about 120 miles an hour, jet aircraft would have had great difficulty keeping in contact with them. It also had an excellent range, could carry up to 7,000 lbs. of ordnance and had four wing-mounted 20mm cannon. The big radial piston engine used by the Skyraider proved very reliable and rugged, like the rest of the aircraft. Using the call sign 'Sandy', the mission of the A-1s was to find the downed aircrew, guide the helicopters to them and to suppress any enemy ground defences in the area. There is no doubt that the Sandy missions along with the *Wild Weasel* missions were among the most dangerous. During *Rolling Thunder* the A-1 Skyraiders had the highest loss rate of any aircraft operating over North Vietnam, averaging 6.2 per 1,000 sorties. When they arrived in an area where a pilot was down the only way they could find out if there were any ground defences was to fly over the area and wait to be shot at. Once

The Lockheed C-130 Hercules was one of the truly great aircraft of modern times. Apart from its use as a transport, it also served as a gunship and (pictured) as an airborne rescue command and control aircraft designated HC-130. (National Archives)

they had pinpointed any troops or anti-aircraft guns in the area they would attack them with bombs, rockets and cannon fire, before the helicopters could move in to pick up the downed aircrew.

The HU-16s were never really adequate as command and control aircraft and were replaced in this role by the Douglas SC-54 Rescuemaster, although they continued flying sea rescue missions. The SC-54 was a version of the C-54 Skymaster, in it's turn a version of the DC-4 cargo aircraft and was fitted with extra fuel tanks to give an endurance of up to eighteen hours and equipped with the necessary communications equipment. These aircraft were necessary to control and co-ordinate the increasing numbers of aircraft, ships and ground forces dedicated to rescue missions. They only remained in service for six months when they were replaced by a version of the ubiquitous Lockheed C-130 Hercules, the HC-130, fitted with the latest radios and communications equipment.

A rescue control centre at Udorn in Thailand was responsible for controlling rescue operations in North Vietnam and Laos. For operations in Laos permission had to be gained from the American Ambassador to Laos. It was found that the first thirty minutes after a crew had been shot down were vital. After this time it became increasingly difficult to effect a rescue. The longer the North Vietnamese or the communists in Laos had to organise a search for the shot down airmen the less chance of rescue they had. The short range of the helicopters and the desire to cut down the reaction time, meant that for operations over North Vietnam and Northern Laos the helicopters had to use temporary landing grounds inside Laos to position them nearer to their operating areas. These landing grounds were known as *Lima* sites and were sometimes inside territory held by the communist Pathet Lao forces. The most Northern site, *Lima Site 36*, was just over 170 miles from Hanoi. The Lima sites were run either by the CIA or by non communist Laotian guerrilla forces.

At the start of the war the Navy was in the same position as the Air Force in that they had no real combat rescue helicopter. The UH-2 was the standard carrier-based helicopter used to rescue crews of aircraft crashing into the sea close to the carriers, but did not have the range or self protection capability required for combat rescue operations. Since it was one of the only two types available it was used in this role. The other helicopter available to the Navy was the Sikorsky SH-3A Sea King anti-submarine machine. This was a specialised submarine hunter-killer, but was pressed into service, with local modifications of extra armour, fuel and machine guns, in the rescue role. There was no dedicated Naval rescue squadron until HC-7 (Helicopter Combat Support Squadron 7), was established in September 1967.

The Navy established a northern and a southern search and rescue zone in the Gulf of Tonkin. At each of these two stations, a destroyer was positioned and, when bombing raids were being carried out, helicopters were moved onto the landing pads of these destroyers in readiness to pick up aircrew shot down over North Vietnam or the Gulf. A system was also developed to extend their endurance, by allowing them to refuel from ships

The HH-53 'Super Jolly Green Giant', answer to a shot-down airmans prayer. It first appeared in late 1967. (National Archives)

without a landing pad by lowering down a fuel line to the ship, while hovering over it. In the early part of the war the Navy, like the Air Force, used the A-1 Skyraider to escort the rescue helicopters.

The Air Force introduced the Sikorsky CH-3C helicopter into service in Thailand as a rescue helicopter in July 1965. This was a version of the Navy Sea King helicopter and had a considerably better range and load carrying capacity than the HH-43. The CH-3 was also a twin-engined aircraft that gave better safety when operating over enemy territory. The HH-3, introduced in November, was the developed version for specialised use as a search and rescue helicopter with heavier armour, self sealing fuel tanks and heavy armament. Because of their large size and green and brown camouflage the HH-3s quickly beacame known as the 'Jolly Green Giants'.

By the end of 1966 the Air Force had taken part in saving 37 aircrew from inside North Vietnam and 51 from inside Laos. The Navy rescue forces had saved eleven people from inside North Vietnam, eleven more from Laos and had also picked up 19 flyers from the waters of the Gulf while the Air Force had rescued 26 from the sea. The numbers of aircraft and men dedicated to search rescue continued to rise as the war escalated. In January 1967 the Air Force had fifty aircraft involved in rescue duties, most still HU-43s but there were ten HH-3Es and more were becoming available.

As more of the longer ranged helicopters became available the standard procedure was for the rescue helicopters from the Air Force to be in the air during bombing raids over the North, to cut down the time aircrew would have to spend on the ground. There were four orbits that the helicopters would fly in, one over Laos West of Hanoi, one over Laos West of Vinh, one over the Gulf of Tonkin and one near the border between North and South Vietnam. The helicopters were in position before the strike aircraft flew into the North and remained in position until the last aircraft had safely returned. If any aircraft were shot down the helicopters would immediately move into position to pick them up, if remotely possible.

The crews of the strike aircraft operating over the North carried with them at least one, if not more, small rescue radios, the quality of which improved as the war continued. With these radios it was possible for the downed aircrew to contact the aircraft searching for them and if possible guide them to their location. The North Vietnamese used captured radios to impersonate shot-down Americans and lure rescue aircraft into elaborate traps using large numbers of anti-aircraft guns. To eliminate this each person who flew over the North had on file three questions and answers that only they could know. If the shot-down pilot could not answer the questions the rescue services were not supposed to respond. But they still picked up the pilot who, in the heat of the moment, could not remember his wife's Christian name!

It had originally been thought that it was not a practical proposition to refuel helicopters in the air. However, to extend the range of rescue services this capability was indeed developed. The command and control HC-130Ps were also equipped to be used as tanker aircraft to refuel rescue helicopters. This enabled the helicopters to maintain orbits close to the North Vietnamese border while the strike aircraft were in action. The first experimental refuelling of a helicopter by a HC-130P occurred in December 1966 and the first combat refuelling was in June 1967. This ability to refuel greatly increased the reach of the rescuers.

The definitive rescue helicopter introduced during the Vietnam War was the HH-53B, known as the 'Super Jolly Green

Object of the exercise. A downed airman is winched to safety. Apart from the relatively simple rescues from the Gulf, shot-down airmen stood a very good chance of being picked up from deep inside North Vietnam. (National Archives)

Giant'. It was nearly three times the weight of an HH-43 and twice the weight of the HH-3. Its introduction meant that the rescue service finally had a helicopter of a size that could carry an adequate amount of armour, armament and fuel at a good speed with twin-engined safety. It was armed with three mini-guns, with the combined fire power of over ten normal machine guns and were first deployed to southeast Asia on 8th September 1967.

By the end of *Rolling Thunder* in 1968 the combat rescue services had expanded into enormous organisations using large numbers of different types of aircraft to attempt to bring back shot-down aircrew. The fact that there was a good chance of recovery, as long as the unfortunate flyer did not land in 'Down Town Hanoi', was undoubtedly a boost for the morale of the aircrew involved in raids over North Vietnam. There were times during the war when hundreds of aircraft became involved in rescue missions lasting several days, as rescue missions normally had precedence over normal *Rolling Thunder* operations and, at times, other lives were lost attempting to bring back shot-down crewmen.

The Electronic
Counter-measures War

Electonic Counter Measures (ECM) are the use of electronic equipment to degrade or cancel the use of electronic equipment used by the enemy. The North Vietnamese adopted both Russian equipment and method of air defence. Both the radars and the radio equipment used by the North were targets for American electronic counter-measures. There were a number of different types of radar in use for many differing tasks; long range surveillance, height finding, tracking and guidance for the SA-2s and gun laying for the heavy anti-aircraft guns. Strategic Air Command had developed ECM for use in their long-range bombers to penetrate Russian airspace in case of war. However, in the 1950s and early 1960s little work had been done on ECM for tactical aircraft and the equipment used by SAC was too bulky to be fitted in tactical aircraft.

One of the first uses of ECM equipment in Vietnam was by F-101 Voodoo reconnaissance aircraft, carrying early model ECM pods to accompany F-105 strike aircraft, on 29th March 1965. These early support missions were not successful and soon discontinued. The first specialised aircraft available in any numbers was the Douglas EF-10B Skyknight, based on the twin-jet naval fighter that had entered service in 1950 and was clearly obsolescent. EF-10Bs were in service with the Marine Corps and, after being deployed on several carriers in the Gulf, were redeployed to Da Nang on 10th April 1965. They were part of composite Marine squadron VMCJ-1 and were sometimes used to accompany both Naval and Air Force strikes over the North.

The objective of ECM aircraft flying with fighter-bombers was to jam the enemy tracking radar, which operates by sending out a signal that 'bounces back' from any aircraft in range and is then shown on a screen. Jamming aircraft work by sending out large amounts of signals on the same frequency as a detecting radar, swamping the receiver and radar screen with false echoes. The real radar returns from any aircraft are lost in the resulting screen clutter. EF-10Bs were used in this way and also for Electronic Intelligence Gathering (ELINT). To jam radar effectively it is necessary to know what radars an enemy has and on what frequencies they operate. When they were over or close to North Vietnam ELINT equipped aircraft could scan the electronic spectrum for any radar or radio signals, recording their type and location. With this information it would be known what frequency of jamming would be needed and the best position for the jamming aircraft. The Skyknights, despite their age, remained in service in Vietnam until 1969. In the four years they were in service three EF-10s were lost over South Vietnam and one was shot down over the North.

The Air Force had only one type of aircraft available to carry out the ECM mission, the EB-66. This was a version of the Navy A-3, further developed for use by the Air Force who used it as a bomber, the B-66 Skywarrior. Although it was another obsolescent aircraft, it was the only one available. It was a large twin-jet that could carry four electronic equipment operators. The C version of the EB-66 carried four radar receivers and nine radar jammers. Six EB-66Cs were moved to South Vietnam in May 1965 and in September 1965 five EB-66Bs equipped with twenty-three jammers were sent to Takhli airbase in Thailand, where those based in South Vietnam joined them.

EB-66s were used to provide cover for major Air Force raids over North Vietnam. General Momyer describes their use by saying:

"EB-66s were positioned on the outer limit of the 30-mile restricted area (around Hanoi) to cover the approach to the target and the withdrawal route. By being so close to the major target area, these EB-66s could provide effective blocking of acquisition radars. Two EB-66s in the northwest quadrant and two in the southeast quadrant provided, in effect, a jamming beam into and out of Hanoi for the F-105s." [1]

The EB-66 was a large and relatively slow aircraft and, as the North Vietnamese improved their defences, it became necessary because of their vulnerability to move EB-66 operations further and further away from the target area. With the jamming aircraft now forced to operate over Laos or the Gulf they were not as effective. One EB-66 was shot down on 24th February

The EB-66, used by the USAF, practically identical to the EA-3 of the US Navy, was an early ECM aircraft. It proved very effective initially, but as the defences improved, several losses occurred. This resulted in the EB-66s operating further from the target area and consequent reduction of jamming cover. (National Archives)

1966 near Vinh in North Vietnam by an SA-2 missile and another EB-66 was lost later in the year. By that stage of the war however, most strike aircraft were now carrying their own ECM pod.

The Navy had as its main jamming aircraft an even more obsolete aircraft, the Douglas EA-1F, a four-seat version of the A-1 strike aircraft. The same aircraft, with practically the same equipment, had operated in the Korean War. The jamming equipment carried was vacuum tube based and required very skilful handling by the operators. The usual load carried was two jammers, two detectors and sometimes two chaff dispensors. They cruised at only about 140 knots and had to be launched well before any of the strike aircraft they were protecting. They normally operated in pairs flying at around 5,000 feet just offshore from the North Vietnamese coastline, covering the route followed by the strike aircraft entering and leaving the North. When a radar was detected the EA-1 turned towards it and jammed. The fact that the aircraft had to turn to face the radar to jam it, then fly towards it over the Vietnamese coast, in a very slow aircraft, made them very vulnerable, but only one EA-1 was lost to enemy action in several years of intensive use.

The Navy also had a few EA-3Bs equipped as ECM aircraft. These large twin-engined aircraft had a crew of three plus four electronic equipment operators. These were among the largest aircraft operated by the Navy from aircraft carriers and there was never room for more than a few. They were considered too valuable to risk being shot down over the North and were employed mainly for gathering electronic intelligence by cruising close to the borders of North Vietnam. The EKA-3B was introduced in 1968 and was a combination of tanker and ECM aircraft, but since there was never enough tanking capability available the primary use of the EKA-3B was in this role. The Navy also used the four-engined EC-121 from bases in Thailand to carry out ELINT missions along the North's borders to detect what equipment the North was using.

The radio link between the MiGs and their ground based controllers was also a weak link in the defensive system. The MiGs were under tight control from the ground controllers who used information from ground-based radars to position the MiGs to attack the American strike formations. The MiG pilots were given little room for initiative and tended to be lost if the radio link with the ground was jammed. ELINT aircraft could also tell when MiGs were airborne by monitoring Vietnamese radio frequencies, although at times the Vietnamese played tape recordings on some frequencies, while operating on others.

One of the simplest ways of jamming radar is by using 'chaff'. This was developed from what was known in the Second World War as *Window*. This was first used in 1943, by the RAF to swamp the German radar during a major raid on Hamburg, which caused the deaths of at least 50,000 people. Chaff was originally aluminium strips but the more modern variety is glass fibre or nylon strips, cut about half the length of the

The remarkable A-6 Intruder was developed by both the US Navy and Marine Corps into a very effective ECM aircraft, the AE-6A Prowler. It entered service too late to operate in the Rolling Thunder campaign. A further development, the EA-6B, was a four-seat version that operated off-shore during the Linebacker operations and proved very effective.
(USMC)

wavelength of the radar it is hoped to jam. Bundles of chaff are dispensed into the atmosphere and each individual piece reflects radar returns to the receiver, creating hundreds of false 'blips' on the screen. Being very light, chaff continues to float in the air for a considerable time. It was used over the North during *Rolling Thunder* but not to the extent that it was during the later bombing of the North during *Linebacker I* and *II*.

There were never enough specialised ECM aircraft available and they tended to be to expensive to operate in high risk areas, so the obvious answer was to equip each strike aircraft with it's own ECM equipment. The Air Force view was that ECM equipment should be fitted in pods mounted on store-carrying pylons or 'stations' outside the strike aircraft. The ECM equipment tended to be heavy and bulky, and fitting it inside the aircraft meant that the aircraft was permanently carrying extra weight that might not be needed in some situations. Carrying ECM equipment in a pod was considered a more flexible approach. The US Navy on the other hand tried to fit

ECM equipment permanently inside the A-4, their most widely used attack aircraft. The industrial project to install this equipment was called *Project Shoe Horn* because of the small amount of space available and an extra fairing had to be fitted on the A-4 to cover some of it, giving the aircraft a 'hunch backed' look. The Navy also used ECM equipment in pods to give extra coverage when necessary.

The US Air Force in Thailand began to receive the first of the ALQ-71 jamming pods in September 1966 and first started to use them in October 1966. They carried noise jammers, operating on the L S and C bands, to jam the *Fan Song* radar used by SA-2s and gun-laying radar used by the heavy anti-aircraft guns. After a series of test flights they went into general use with F-105s. The pods allowed the attacking aircraft to go back to operating at a height of around 15,000 feet, above the height of most of the AAA fire. With ECM pods blocking the SA-2s radar guidance, the F-105s could now operate at their preferred altitude.

A single pod was not powerful enough effectively to jam the radars in use on its own and it was normally the tactic to operate aircraft in flights of four, giving the necessary power and coverage. They maintained a stepped-up 'V' pattern, keeping the correct spacing for the pods to give the maximum coverage. When there was enough pods for all strike aircraft to carry one the capabilities of the SA-2 surface-to-air missiles and gun-laying radars were seriously degraded.

The Radar Homing and Warning (RHAW) equipment, when it had been first available in limited numbers, had been used by the Air Force to equip the specialised *Wild Weasel* aircraft. When the sets became available in quantity all strike aircraft were so equipped. General Momyer felt the RHAW sets were so important to aircraft survival against the North Vietnamese air defence system that, once the equipment was readily available, he would not allow aircraft to fly over the North without an operational set. The RHAW sets gave an indication in the aircraft's cockpit that the aircraft had been picked up on radar and by what type of radar and in what direction. Colonel Jack Broughton described the use of the equipment:

"Among other things ours would tell you if it were SAM or the guns or both

An interesting development of the ECM war. The AP-2H Neptune, operated by VAH-21 of the US Navy, operated over the Ho Chi Minh trail, dropping sensors to detect movement, body heat and even odours. Immediate air and artillery strikes followed. (US Navy)

of them that were looking at you. It also had a visual screen and an aural tone that buzzed you just like a rattlesnake. If Sam or the big Guns had a weak contact on you, a small, dim and intermittent green circle would glow in the middle of the screen (one ringer) and the snake would rattle mildly to get your attention. If the contact was pretty good you would get a larger circle glowing steadily (two ringer) and the rattle would become irritating. If Sam or the big guns locked on with a good contact and were ready to launch or fire at you, you would get a still larger green ring that would shine brightly (three ringer) and it would sound like that big rattler was coiled in your flying suit pocket." [2]

The electronic war over North Vietnam fluctuated from one side to the other as did the war in general. America developed a whole range of electronic devices to counter the North Vietnamese defences, but the many radars available to the Vietnamese meant that the American's never totally dominated the Vietnamese air defence system.

FOOTNOTES

1. Momyer, William W. *Air Power in Three Wars*, Department Of The Air Force, Washington, 1978, page 220-2.
2. Broughton, Jack, *Thud Ridge*, Bantam Books, New York, 1985, page 52.

Reconnaissance

Knowing exactly what an enemy is doing and what his capabilities are are two major factors in any military campaign. The Chinese strategist Sun Tzu writing more than two thousand years ago said 'Know the enemy, Know yourself: your victory will never be endangered'.[1] For *Rolling Thunder* to operate effectively it was necessary for the Americans to know where the major industrial targets were situated, where bottle necks in the transport system were situated and where major military installations where located. Once the bombing campaign was under way it was also necessary to know how effective individual bombing raids had been. Had a target been destroyed, or would it need to be attacked again? If a bridge had been destroyed it was necessary to know when it had been repaired and put back into use. All these factors made it imperative for the reconnaissance effort over North Vietnam to be carried out both before and after *Rolling Thunder* began.

The first major reconnaissance aircraft in the area were RF-101C Voodoos from the 15th Tactical Reconnaissance Squadron stationed at Don Muang airfield in Thailand during 1961, which were originally intended to give coverage of South Vietnam and Laos. These were single seat aircraft and usually only carried photographic equipment.

In December 1963 examples of the infamous U-2 from the 4080th Strategic Reconnaissance Wing were stationed at Bien Hoa, intended to operate over Laos and North Vietnam under the code-name *Dragon Lady*. In the early months of 1964 the American High Command began to develop a series of plans for covert action against North Vietnam under the code name OPLAN 34A. U-2s were now flying over North Vietnam providing information for these plans, which were also an intelligence gathering exercise to provide as much information about the North as possible. The destroyer USS *Turner Joy* was

The RF-101C Voodoo first arrived in southeast Asia in 1961 with the 15th TRS, 'The Cotton Pickers'. They were well named. Their missions involved high-speed photo runs 'down on the deck', requiring both nerve and skill. of the 31 combat losses, seven pilots were rescued and eight were captured. (USAF)

on a *DESOTO* Electronic Intelligence gathering mission against the North when it was fired on by North Vietnamese vessels. The 94 target list, part of the General Staff plan for a three-week bombing campaign against the North, was based on information from these U-2 flights that pinpointed the main militarily significant targets.

Information was also available from satellites throughout this period covering all of South East Asia. However the quality of the photographs obtained from space had not yet reached the quality achieved later. While satellite photographs were useful they did not remove the need for photographic coverage from aircraft. Their main use was to provide weather coverage over North Vietnam. During the northeast monsoon there was extensive cloud cover over North Vietnam for long periods and satellite pictures gave information on any likely breaks in this cloud cover over the target areas.

After the introduction of *Rolling Thunder*, RF-101s started to operate over North Vietnam on a regular basis. Where possible it became standard practice for reconnaissance aircraft to fly missions over targets that had been bombed within a couple of hours, to provide bomb damage assessments for the air commanders. This became a regular pattern. Thus the Vietnamese defences were always waiting for these unarmed recon-

naissance aircraft and these missions became extremely dangerous. The first RF-101 was lost on 3rd April 1965. The main
Naval reconnaissance aircraft early in the war was the RF-8, an
unarmed variant of the standard F-8 fighter, the first loss
occurring over Laos on 6th June 1964.

The Air Force introduced the RF-4C, the specialised version of
the Phantom optimised for reconnaissance work, into South
East Asia on 30th October 1965. They operated first from Tan
Son Nhut air base at Saigon with the 16th Tactical Reconnaissance Squadron. The nose of the RF-4 was equipped with optical
cameras and infra-red sensors, with the ability for in-flight
developing of the film. Some were also equipped with a
sideways-looking radar that gave a radar picture of the target
area. It was faster and better equipped than the RF-101, but
the earlier aircraft was to remain in service throughout the
Rolling Thunder campaign. The Navy heavy reconnaissance
aircraft was the RA-5C Vigilante, a version of the unsuccessful
A-5 carrier strike aircraft, modified by the addition of a ventral
reconnaissance pack. It was a large fast aircraft, indeed too
large to operate from anything except the larger 'big deck'
carriers and was even faster than a Phantom if it was carrying
any kind of external load.

By the end of 1966 the Air Force had one wing of
reconnaissance aircraft stationed at Tan Son Nhut in South
Vietnam close to Saigon, the 460th Tactical Reconnaissance
Wing operating both RF-4s and RF-101s. The 432nd Tactical
Reconnaissance Wing was stationed at Ubon in Thailand, but
although nominally a reconnaissance wing, only one squadron
was equipped with reconnaissance RF-4 aircraft. The SR-71
Blackbirds of the 9th Strategic Reconnaissance Wing, also used
for reconnaissance over North Vietnam, were based on
Okinawa, at the Kadena airbase. These were under the control
of Strategic Air Command and flew missions over China and
North Korea, as well as North Vietnam. It is also believed that
the A-12 (the CIA version of this aircraft) was also used over
North Vietnam, but very little is known on this.

Reconnaissance aircraft operating over North Vietnam and
Laos suffered heavy losses during the war. From November
1966 to January 1967 six RF-4s and three RF-101s were shot

The RF-4C supplanted the RF-101 as the main USAF tactical reconnaissance aircraft. It was faster and more manoeuvreable, but the older Voodoo continued operating until mid-1968. (USAF)

down. From 1965 to 1968 thirty-one RF-101s and fifty-one RF-4s were lost to enemy action. The Navy and Marine Corps had nineteen RF-8s and fourteen RA-5s shot down. Flying unarmed reconnaissance aircraft over North Vietnam remained a dangerous occupation. The Americans realised the dangers inherent in reconnaissance missions and developed a range of remotely piloted vehicles for use in dangerous or difficult areas. These were small pilotless aircraft based on the Ryan Q-2 target drone. The Ryan 147 RPV (remotely piloted vehicle) became operational in July 1963 and were deployed to South East Asia in August 1964. There were several different types of the Ryan 147 used for electronic intelligence, photographic reconnaissance, decoy work and for 'real time' television coverage. In appearance the RPVs looked like a small conventional aircraft with wings, tailplane and a rudder. The propulsion unit was a small Continental jet engine fixed under the body of the aircraft and the wing span varied depending on if the drone was meant for high or low altitude work.

The Ryan 147s were carried to the launch position beneath the wings of specially modified DC-130 Hercules aircraft from which they were released at the appropriate moment. While the drones normally used a pre-programmed inertial guidance system, they could also be controlled from other aircraft or from ground stations. At the end of a mission a drone was recovered by directing it to a recovery area, land or sea, where a

The two main types of reconnaissance aircraft operated by the US Navy were the RA-5 Vigilante, the largest jet to be operated from American carriers, and the RF-8 Crusader. (US Navy)

parachute was deployed bringing it safely down. It was then picked up by waiting recovery units. A second recovery method was for the drone to be recovered in mid-air after parachute deployment, using specially equipped helicopters. Drones were intended to be reused and the average was 7.3 missions, before it was lost. There were several hundred drones lost over North Vietnam (the North Vietnamese claimed to have shot down large numbers) but in general the Ryan 147 was very successful.

Another type of reconnaissance over North Vietnam was weather reconnaissance. The weather was one controlling factor during *Rolling Thunder* and there were long periods when bad weather covered most of the North and precluded any strikes. The strike forces had very little bad weather capability and the vast majority of the bombing was visual, thus accurate weather reports and forecasts became very important. Before any strike was carried out, weather reconnaissance aircraft were sent into the general target area two or three hours before the strikes were launched to provide weather information.

By 1967 some strike aircraft had been equipped with rearward facing cameras to give coverage of individual bombing attacks. These were triggered as the aircraft pulled away after dropping their bombs, to photograph the effects of these bombs on the target. The quality of the photographs produced could not match that of the specialist reconnaissance aircraft, but could give fast results. The cameras could also be used to check on the bombing accuracy of individual pilots. The idea was that the cameras were only to increase the amount of information available and were not intended to replace specialised reconnaissance aircraft that flew coverage of each bombing raid.

FOOTNOTES

1. Tzu, Sun, *The Art Of War*, Translated By Griffith, Samuel B. Oxford University Press, 1982, page 129.

Appendix VII
The Air-to-Air War

During the Korean War the Air Force and the Navy had learned that the basic lessons of air-to-air combat were still the same as they had been since the First World War. Fighter aircraft needed to be fast, with a good climb rate, good manoeuvrability and powerful armament. During the 1950s and the early 1960s however, top speeds of fighter aircraft had reached over one thousand miles per hour. This fact, together with the development of missiles and radar, produced the theory that, in the future, it was unlikely that fighter aircraft would have to be involved in close contact dog fighting. The main thrust in development for the Air Force during the 1950s was in the field of nuclear weapons delivery. Strategic Air Command came to dominate the Air Force and even on the tactical level the emphasis was placed on delivery systems for nuclear weapons.

Fighters developed during this period were either interceptors, intended to stop long range Russian nuclear bombers from reaching America, or strike aircraft intended to carry nuclear bombs. Even the superlative F-86 Sabre air superiority fighter was converted to carry nuclear weapons during the 1950s. Thus, with the start of *Rolling Thunder* in 1965 the US Air Force had no classic air superiority aircraft available. The US Navy had followed much the same route but still had one dedicated fighter aircraft available to it in 1965, the F-8 Crusader, a single-seat, single-engined aircraft with good manoeuvrability plus a gun and missile armament. The concentration on nuclear weapons meant that many younger fighter pilots had not concentrated their training on the traditional air-to-air skills. The most successful fighter pilots during *Rolling Thunder* tended to be the older pilots who had fought in the Second World War or the Korean War. Colonel Robin Olds, the leading pilot during *Rolling Thunder* with four North Vietnamese aircraft destroyed

*The F-8 Crusader was the only US Navy air superiority fighter
equipped with an on-board gun. Its four 20mm cannon, Sidewinder
missile armament and manoeuvreability gave it an advantage denied
to the later F-4s. It could dogfight MiGs close-in. (via author)
Speed: 1,120 at 40,000 feet. Combat radius 600 miles.*

in the air, had also destroyed 24 and a half German aircraft
during the Second World War.

The North Vietnamese had very few combat aircraft before
1964 but preparations had been taking place, some of their
pilots receiving training in Russia and China. After the first
American bombing raids in 1964 the North Vietnamese Air
Force was considerably reinforced. On 7th August 1964, two
days after raids on patrol boat bases as retaliation for the Gulf
of Tonkin incident (the *Pierce Arrow* raids), between thirty and
forty MiG-17s were flown into Phuc Yen airfield from China.
This base, situated just North West of Hanoi at the Southern
end of Thud Ridge, became one of Vietnam's major bases
throughout the war.

The MiG-17 had entered service in the Russian Air Force in
the early 1950s. It was a small fighter aircraft that could only
operate during the day and clear weather. It was only about a
quarter of the weight of its principal adversaries the F-105 and
the F-4 and proved a difficult target to hit. Although it was
slower than all American air-to-air fighters it was highly
manoeuvrable and had a powerful close-in armament of three
cannon.

*Designed at a point-interceptor, the McDonnell-Douglas F-4 Phantom
did it all. Fleet defence, escort, fighter-bomber, photo-reconnaissance
were all performed superbly. (National Archives)
Maximum speed 1,485 mph at 48,000 feet. Combat radius 800 miles.*

On 4th April 1965 the first two American aircraft were shot
down by North Vietnamese MiG-17s. During one of the many
raids on the Than Hoa bridge, four F-105Ds were orbiting south
of the target waiting for their turn to attack. The first two
aircraft in the flight were attacked by two MiGs diving on them
from above, and were shot down. The MiGCAP F-100s were not
positioned to be able to respond to the attack and the MiGs
escaped. The top speed of the MiGs was less than the top speed
of the American attack aircraft but usually exceeded the
cruising speed of the attacking aircraft especially when they
were laden with bombs and external fuel tanks. The North
Vietnamese GCI, when it was operating correctly, could position
the MiGs to their best advantage. The American aircraft could
out run them if they received enough warning, by dropping their
bombs and going into afterburner. It became a standard tactic of
the Vietnamese to make feint attacks on the bomber formations
to force then to drop their bombs before they reached their
targets.

The American Air-to-Air Missiles

The Sparrow missile was intended to bring down bombers at long range. Its main advantage was therefore negated in Vietnam by the need to viasually acquire and identify targets under the Rules of Engagement. These were amended later, when it became possible to identify MiGs by 'triggering' their radar transponders.

(National Archives)

Great hopes had been pinned on the AIM-9 Sidewinder, but the success rate was relatively low. (National Archives)

Earliest and most numerous opponent for the USAF forces was the MiG-17. It was small, highly manouevreable and was armed with three 23mm on-board cannon. Later, four AA-1 missiles were carried. Although obsolete by world standards, the MiG-17 proved itself to be a tough opponent in combat.
Maximum Speed 710 mph at 10,000 feet. Combat Radius 360 miles.

When F-4s were first used, shortage of aerial refuelling capacity meant that they were used to carry bombs as part of the bombing formations. It was intended that if the bombing formations were attacked the F-4s would drop their bombs and engage the MiGs. During World War Two, the Germans had learned in the Battle of Britain and the USAAF over Germany, that it does not pay to tie fighter escorts too closely to the bombing force. Now, in Vietnam, the lesson had to be re-learned. Fighter aircraft are more effective if they are allowed to sweep ahead of and to the flank of bombing formations and the F-4s were later allowed to fly specific MiGCAP operations.

The first MiG-17s were shot down on 17th June 1965 when two Naval F-4Bs from the carrier USS *Midway* shot down two, using *Sparrow* missiles. Three days later, on 20th June, another fell to two propeller-driven A-1Hs using 20mm cannon fire. The A-1 was one of the few aircraft involved in the conflict that had a smaller turning circle than the MIG-17. The first two MiGs

*'The Mig Killers'. Colonel Robin Olds, CO of the 8th TFW 'Wolfpack'
adds the 19th, 20th and 21st MiGs to the Wing scoreboard on 20th
May 1967. The successful crews are from left, Major Philip P.
Combies, 1st Lieutenant Daniel L. Lafferty, Major John R. Pardoe,
1st Lieutenant Seempen B. Croker and 1st Lieutenant Stephen A.
Wayne. (National Archives)*

shot down by the Air Force were on 10th July by F-4Cs of the
45th Tactical Fighter Squadron using *Sidewinder* missiles.

The number of aircraft available to the North Vietnamese
grew to about seventy by the end of 1965. This increased to a

hundred by mid-1967. There were times when the North suffered heavy losses of aircraft. Nine MiGs were lost in early January 1967 and forty-two were shot down from April to June 67, but losses of MiGs were replaced from stocks held in China and pilots were trained in both Russia and China. When they suffered heavy losses the North Vietnamese Air Force stood down for periods of up to several months while they re-equipped and developed new tactics. They carried out a programme of airfield building and increased the number of jet capable airfields from two early in 1964 (Cat Bi and Gia Lam, Hanoi's international airport), to nine by the end of 1968. The American policy of not attacking the airfields until 1967 meant that, for most of *Rolling Thunder*, North Vietnamese airfields were safe havens for the MiGs. The two major airfields used for the North Vietnamese MiGs throughout the war were Phuc Yen, which was finished in late 1964, and Kep, northeast of Hanoi.

The MiG-21 was first introduced into North Vietnam in early 1966. This was a more modern aircraft than the MiG-17, but never completely replaced it. It had a high top speed, a good climb rate and was highly manoeuvrable but, compared with the American aircraft, was very short ranged and had a poor radar and fire control system. Even with these defects the Mig-21 was an effective point defence fighter. Its armament was two cannon and two *Atoll* missiles. The *Atoll* was a less effective copy of the American infra red homing *Sidewinder*. The first MiG-21 was shot down on the 26th April 1966 by a F-4C using a *Sidewinder*.

MiGs operated as part of an integrated air defence system based on many long range radars, used to control the movements of the MiGs under the Russian system of tight Ground Control. Even with American jamming the large numbers of radars used meant that the North Vietnamese could still follow the progress of the American raids. General Momyer said:

"There were about 200 radars in the North Vietnamese air defence system with three major ground control intercept (GCI) sites: Bac Mai, Phuc Yen and Kep. Bac Mai and Phuc Yen normally controlled most of the air defence missions, although for missions staged into the southern portion of North Vietnam, a subordinate control unit was established at Vinh. This site could not handle large numbers of aircraft." [1.]

Ground controllers informed MiG pilots which way to turn,

The lightweight MiG-21, equipped with twin 23mm on-board cannon and Atoll heat-seeking missiles, was the most modern combat aircraft to equip the NVAF. (via author)
Maximum Speed 1,386 mph at 36,000 feet. Combat Radius 375 miles.

when to climb and descend and when to use their afterburners. When it worked correctly it was possible to position aircraft in just the right place to carry out attacks.

The North Vietnamese knew that they would be bound to lose any all-out fight with the American forces. Throughout the war the basic tactic used by the North Vietnamese Air Force was the 'hit and run' attack. The North Vietnamese needed to husband their limited resources of pilots and aircraft for what they knew would be a long war. When American aircraft entered North Vietnamese airspace, they were followed from either behind or to the side by Vietnamese aircraft. When the ground controllers thought they had the advantage the MiGs would carry out high speed attacks making only one firing run and then leave the area at top speed. It was possible to disrupt the raids by only feigning an attack and forcing the bombers to drop their ordnance. Another tactic was to attack the last formation of

American bombing aircraft to leave the target area when the covering fighter aircraft were low on fuel.

The main fighter aircraft used by both the US Air Force and the Navy was the McDonnell Douglas F-4 Phantom, a large powerful aircraft with an effective radar and fire control system. The Air Force had used the North American F-100 Super Sabre in early 1965, as a counterbalance to the North Vietnamese MiGs, but it had not been successful. They also used the Convair F-102 Delta Dagger, the F-5 Freedom Fighter and the Lockheed F-104 Starfighters over the North but these were only used in small numbers. The Republic F-105 Thunderchief was essentially a bombing aircraft, not very manoeuvrable but very fast at low level. It could certainly look after itself against MiGs, since F-105 pilots shot down twenty-five North Vietnamese aircraft using 20mm cannon fire and sidewinder missiles. The Navy also used the Chance-Vought F-8 Crusader as a fighter aircraft, which proved to be an effective aircraft in the early years of *Rolling Thunder*, but the major fighter aircraft was the Phantom. Although the Phantom was not as manoeuvrable as the MiG-17 or 21 it was powerful and was effective in the vertical plane because of its high thrust-to-weight ratio. This went some way to redressing the advantage of the tight turning circle of the MiGs, as the North Vietnamese pilots tended to avoid vertical manoeuvring. The MiG-17 especially had a climb rate of only about one third of the Phantom. The lack of an internal gun in the Phantom for close combat was partially removed by the introduction of gun pods in 1967. The main armament of the F-4 was four *Sparrow* missiles and four *Sidewinder* missiles.

The *Sparrow*, a radar guided missile, uses the radar in the aircraft to 'illuminate' the target and homes onto this reflected radar energy. One drawback with this is that the aircraft needs to keep the radar set pointing at the target while the missile is homing. The *Sparrow* could be fired at aircraft approaching from head on however, unlike the *Sidewinder* that needed to be able to 'see' the heat from the target's exhaust and would home onto the infra-red signal produced. Occasionally however, they were used to attack trains by homing on the heat of the steam engine. The *Sidewinder* is a smaller missile than the *Sparrow* and has a shorter range. Early models of the Sidewinder had the drawback that they tended to wander off target and home onto hot spots on the ground, the heat of the sun or reflections of the sun on clouds.

One major drawback with both missiles was the minimum range before the missiles started guiding. If a MiG could stay close to a Phantom, inside the minimum range of the missiles, then the fact that the Phantom did not have an internal gun made the MiG immune from attack. (This was remedied later with the provision of a Vulcan cannon, mounted in an external pod). The *Sidewinder* had a slightly better success ratio than the *Sparrow*. Approximately one out of eight *Sidewinders* fired hit the target. With *Sparrows* the ratio was approximately one in ten. Between 1965 and 1968 twenty-nine North Vietnamese aircraft were shot down by *Sparrows* and forty-six by *Sidewinders*, not counting aircraft shot down by both missiles and cannon fire.

The standard Air Force fighter formation during this period was still a variation of the Second World War finger-four made up of two elements of two aircraft. Each element comprising a leader and a wingman, with the lead alternating between the two as the situation dictated. The standard Navy formation was the 'loose deuce', two aircraft flying abeam of each other at about one mile distance. In this position both pilots could cover the others rear quarter, or 'six o'clock' visually. If one aircraft turned to meet an attack the other aircraft could turn behind the lead aircraft or turn to be abreast of it covering it from attack from another direction.

During *Rolling Thunder 118* North Vietnamese aircraft were shot down by American fighters. In the same period 56 American aircraft were shot down by North Vietnamese aircraft. This is a loss ratio of just over 2:1 to the American fighters. The North Vietnamese Air Force improved during the course of the campaign. The loss ratio for the Americans declined from 4:1 during the early part of the campaign to around 1:1 during the last year. The loss ratio during the Korean War had been somewhere between 7:1 and 14:1, although there still is some disagreement on the figures.

The US Navy felt that the loss ratio during *Rolling Thunder*, as compared with the Korean War was not acceptable. They started an inquiry into what were the reasons for the comparatively poor showing of the American fighters. It was headed by Captain Frank Ault, who had commanded a carrier stationed on *Yankee Station* during *Rolling Thunder*. The conclusions were presented in 1968 and gave three main proposals for improvement. They recommended that the standards of the missile armament should be improved, that more effort should be spent on air combat manoeuvring training and advised the setting up of a high level centre to study the needs of air combat. This centre became the Navy Fighter Weapons School at Miramar Air Base, San Diego and quickly became known as the 'top gun' course.

The Air Force attempted to analyse air combat over North Vietnam in a study with the project name *Red Baron*, started in 1972 too late to affect the course of the war. This showed that the more flying hours a pilot had the more likely they were to shoot down enemy aircraft. On the other hand the number of hours flown had no relation to the likelihood of being shot down. Both experienced and inexperienced pilots were shot down by the North Vietnamese fighters. The North Vietnamese Air Force was never large enough to be a major threat to *Rolling Thunder* but continued to exact a toll of American aircraft shot down. Colonel Robin Olds described the North Vietnamese Air Force by saying:

> "When you think in terms of the enemy, maybe he only has ten or twelve airplanes airborne, whereas there are up to forty-eight of you, but he has the complete advantage. You are just sitting there, and he can come in on you whenever he chooses. Once the enemy has the advantage of altitude and speed, you are completely on the defensive....I don't care if there are a thousand of you! He can pick away at you." [2]

By using the correct defensive tactics the North Vietnamese Air Force remained a credible threat to the American aircraft throughout *Rolling Thunder*.

FOOTNOTES

1. Momyer, William W. *Air Power In Three Wars*, US Government Printing Office, Washington, 1978, page 118-9.
2. Drendle, Lou, *USAF Phantoms In Combat*, Squadron/Signal Publications, Texas, 1987, page 6.

American and South Vietnamese Units Involved in Rolling Thunder

Large numbers of American Units were committed to the war in South East Asia without being involved in Rolling Thunder. The following is a list of only those units that can be thought to have played a part in the Rolling Thunder Campaign. Only units in the theatre of operations between March 1965 and October 1968 are included. Detachments are marked thus: (D).

US Air Force

Tactical Fighter Wings

3rd Tactical Fighter Wing

90TFS	F-100D	Bien Hoa	Oct 65-Jan 69
307TFS	F-100D	Bien Hoa	Oct 65-Jan 67
308TFS	F-100D	Bien Hoa	Oct 65-Jan 66
510TFS	F-100D	Bien Hoa	Oct 65-Jan 69
531TFS	F-100D	Bien Hoa	Oct 65-Jan 67
4503TFS	F-5A	Bien Hoa	Oct 65-Feb 66*

Operation Skoshi Tiger

8th Tactical Fighter Wing

25TFS	F-4D/C	Ubon	Dec 65-Nov 72
433TFS	F-4C/D	Ubon	Dec 65-Jan 74
435TFS	F-4D	Ubon	Jan 68-Jan 74
497TFS	F-4C/D	Ubon	Jan 65-Jan 74
555TFS	F-4D	Ubon	Jan 68-Jan 73
555TFS	F-4C/D	Ubon	May 67-Jan 68

12th Tactical Fighter Wing

43TFS	F-4C	Cam Ranh Bay	Nov 65-Jan 68
45TFS	F-4C	Ubon	Apr 65-Jan 68
557TFS	F-4C	{Cam Ranh Bay {Udorn	Nov 65-Jan 68
558TFS	F-4C	Cam Ranh Bay	Nov 65-Jan 68
559TFS	F-4C	Cam Ranh Bay	Nov 65-Jan 68

18th Tactical Fighter Wing

67TFS	F-105D	Korat	Aug 64-May 65
44TFS	F-105D	Korat	Aug 64-May 65

23rd Tactical Fighter Wing

563TFS	F-105D	Da Nang	Apr 65-Jan 66

31st Tactical Fighter Wing

136TFS	F-100D/F	Tuy Hoa	May 68-Jun 69
188TFS	F-100D/F	Tuy Hoa	May 68-Jun 69
306TFS	F-100D/F	Tuy Hoa	Jan 66-Jan 70
308FTS	F-100D/F	Tuy Hoa	Jan 66-Jan 70
309TFS	F-100D/F	Tuy Hoa	Jan 66-Jan 70
355TFS	F-100D/F	Tuy Hoa	Jan 66-Jan 67
416TFS	F-100D/F	Tuy Hoa	Jan 66-Jan 67

35th Tactical Fighter Wing

120TFS	F-100D/F	Phan Rang	May 68-Apr 69
352TFS	F-100D/F	Phan Rang	Jun 66-Jun 71
612TFS	F-100D/F	Phan Rang	Aug 64-Jun 71
614TFS	F-100D/F	Phan Rang	Aug 64-Jun 71.
615TFS	F-100D/F	Phan Rang	Aug 64-Jun 71
8TBS	B-57	Da Nang	Jun 66-Oct 69*
13TBS	B-57	Da Nang	Jun 66-Jan 68*

* Tactical Bomber Squadrons

37th Tactical Fighter Wing

174TFS	F-100D/F	Phu Cat	May 68-May 69
355TFS	F-100D/F	Phu Cat	Jan 67-Jan 69
416TFS	F-100D/F	Phu Cat	Jan 67-Jan 69

347th Tactical Fighter Wing

556RS	RB-57E	Yokota	June 67-Jan. 70*

*Recce unit only

355th Tactical Fighter Wing

333TFS	F105D/F	Takhli	Nov 65-Oct 70
334TFS	F-105D	Takhli	Nov 65-Oct 70
335TFS	F-105D	Takhli	Nov 65-Oct 70
357TFS	F105D/F	Takhli	Nov 65-Oct 70
428TFS	F-111	Takhli	Mar 68-Oct 68
6460TRS	RB-66B	Takhli	Sep 65-Jan 68*

* ECM

366th Tactical Fighter Wing

389TFS	F-4C/D	Phan Rang	Mar 66-Jan 70
390TFS	F-4C/D	Phan Rang	Mar 66-Jan 72
480TFS	F-4C/D	Phan Rang	Mar 66-Jan 70

388th Tactical Fighter Wing

12TFS	F-105D/F	Korat	Jan 68-Jan 69
13TFS	F-105D	Korat	Nov 65- 1966
44TFS	F-105F	Korat	Jan 68-Oct 69
421TFS	F-105D	Korat	Nov 65-Sep 68
469TFS	F-105D/F	Korat	Mar 66-Jan 73
561TFS	{F-100D	Korat	Mar 66-Jan 71
	{F-105F		

474th Tactical Fighter Wing

429TFS	F-100D	Bien Hoa	Jun 65-Dec 65
481TFS	F-100D	Tan Son Nhut	Jun 65-Nov 65

479th Tactical Fighter Wing

435TFS	F-104C	Da Nang	Jul 66-Jul 67
476TFS	F-104C	Da Nang	Jul 66-Jul 67

Strategic Bomber Wings

3960th Strategic Wing

B-52	Anderson	Apr 55-Feb 66

4133rd Bombardment Wing

B-52	Anderson	Feb. 66-April 70

4252nd Strategic Wing

B-52	Kadena	Jan. 68-April 70

4258th Strategic Wing

B-52	U-Tapao	June 66-April 70

Reconnaissance Wings

432nd Tactical Reconnaissance Wing

11TRS	RF-4C	Udorn	Jan 66-Jul 67
14TRS	RF-4C	Udorn	Nov 67-Jan 73
15TRS	F-4C	Udorn	Sep 67-Aug 71
13TFS	F-4D	Udorn	Jan 67-Aug 73*
7ACCS	C-130E	Udorn	Jan 65-Jan 75**

Fighter squadron
**Early Warning and Control unit*

460th Tactical Reconnaissance Wing

12TRS	RF-101C	Tan Son Nhut	Jan 66-Aug 71
15TRS	RF-101C	Udorn	Apr 65-Apr 67
16TRS	RF-4C	Tan Son Nhut	Oct 65-Aug 70
20TRS	RF-101C	Tan Son Nhut	Dec 65-Oct 67
33TG	RB-57E	Tan Son Nhut	May 63-Aug 71
45TRS	RF-101C	Tan Son Nhut	Feb 65-Nov 70
6461TRS	RF-4C	Udorn	Jul 65-Jan 66

Independent Reconnaisance Squadrons

556RS	RC-130A	Don Muang	Jul 64-Jan 71 (D)
6091RS	RB-57D	Don Muang	Jul 64-Jun 67

Strategic Reconnaissance Wings

6th Strategic Reconnaissance Wing

RC-135D	Kadena	Jan 67-Jan 74

55th Strategic Reconnaissance Wing

RB-47H	Kadena	Sep 64-Jan 67

100th Strategic Reconnaissance Wing

350SRS	DC-130A/E	Bien Hoa	Feb. 66-April75

4080th Strategic Reconnaissance Wing

	U-2A/C	Bien Hoa	Jan 63-Feb 66
4025RS	DC-130A	Bien Hoa	Aug 64-Feb 66
4028SRS	U-2A/C	Bien Hoa	Dec 63-Nov 66

Strategic Reconnaissance Squadrons

1SRS	SR-71A	Kadena	Apr 68-Jan 75
82SRS	RC-135M/U	Kadena	Sep 67-Jan 74
349SRS	U-2C/F	Bien Hoa	Feb 66-Mar 76

Search and Rescue Units

14SOW

1SOS	A-1E/G	Bien Hoa	Feb 64-Jan 68
6SOS	A-1E/H	Pleiku	May 69-Jan 72
604SOS	A-37A/B	Bien Hoa	Aug 68-Jan 71

56SOW

1SOS	A-1E	Nakhon Phanom	Jan 68-Dec 72
602SOS	A-1E	Nakhon Phanom	Nov 64-Dec 70

3ARRG

33ARRS	HH-43B/CH-3C HU-16B	Various	Jun 64-Sep 67
37ARRS	HH-43B/F, HH-3, HH-53B/C, HU-16B	Udorn	Aug 64-Jun 73
38ARRS	HH-43, HH-3E HC-54, HC-130H	Various	Dec 65-Aug 73
39ARRS	HC-130P	Tuy Hoa	Sep 67-Jan 73
40ARRS	HH-43, HH-3 HH-53	Udorn	Nov 67-Jan 73

Air Refuelling Units

KC-135 tanker aircraft remained under SAC and a large number of squadrons were placed on temporary duty. The holding units for these squadrons were as follows

43rd Strategic Wing

KC-135	Anderson

307th Strategic Wing

KC-135	Takhli, U-Tapao, Korat

376th Strategic Wing

KC-135	Clark

3960th Strategic Wing

KC-135	Anderson

4220th Strategic Wing

KC-135	Ching Chang Kang

4252nd Strategic Wing
    KC-135   Kadena, Ching Chang Kang
4258th Strategic Wing
    KC-135   Takhli, U-Tapao, Korat

Electronic Counter-measures Units

363rd Tactical Reconnaissance Wing

41TRS	RB-66B/C	Tan Son Nhut	Apr 65-Jan 68*

* ECM

355th Tactical Reconnaissance Wing

41TEWS	EB-66C	Takhli	Jan 68-Nov 70*
42TEWS	EB-66B	Takhli	Jan 68-Nov 70*

* ECM

Early Warning and Control Units

522AEWCW	EC-121D/M	Various	April 65-June74

United States Navy

Aircraft Carriers in Vietnam Service

The dates are the time the carriers left their home ports to when they returned. The carriers were not on line, ie launching strikes, for all the time they spent in Vietnamese waters.

CVW-6	*USS America*	Apr 68 to Dec 68
CVS-20	*USS Bennington*	Jul 65 to Sep 65
		Dec 66 to Apr 67
		Jun 68 to Oct 68
CVW-19	*USS Bon Homme Richard*	Apr 65 to Jan 66
		Jan 67 to Aug 67
		Jan 68 to Oct 68
CVW-15	*USS Constellation*	May 66 to Dec 66
		Apr 67 to Dec 67
		May 68 to Jan 69
CVW-15	*USS Coral Sea*	Oct 64 to May 65
		Jul 66 to Feb 67
		Aug 67 to Mar 68
		Sep 68 to Mar 69
CVW-9	*USS Enterprise*	Oct 65 to May 66
		Dec 66 to Jul 67
		Jan 68 to Jul 68
CVW-17	*USS Forrestal*	Jun 67 to Sep 67
CVW-1	*USS Franklin D Roosevelt*	Jun 66 to Feb 67
CVW-21	*USS Hancock*	Nov 64 to May 65
		Dec 65 to Aug 66
		Jan 67 to Jul 67
		Jul 68 to Mar 69
CVS-12	*USS Hornet*	Oct 65 to Feb 66
		May 67 to Oct 67

CVW-7	*USS Independence*	May 65 to Dec 65
CVW-10	*USS Intrepid*	Apr 66 to Nov 66
		May 67 to Dec 67
		Jun 68 to Feb 69
CVS-33	*USS Kearsarge*	Aug 66 to Nov 66
		Oct 67 to Feb 68
CVW-11	*USS Kitty Hawk*	Nov 65 to Jun 66
		Nov 66 to Jun 67
		Dec 67 to Aug 68
		Dec 68 to Jul 69
CVW-2	*USS Midway*	Mar 65 to Nov 65
CVW-16	*USS Oriskany*	May 65 to Dec 65
		May 66 to Nov 66
		Jul 67 to Jan 68
CVW-9	*USS Ranger*	Aug 64 to May 65
		Dec 65 to Aug 66
		Nov 67 to May 68
		Oct 68 to May 69
CVW-5	*USS Ticonderoga*	Sep 65 to May 66
		Oct 66 to May 67
		Dec 67 to Jul 68
CVS-10	*USS Yorktown*	Feb 65 to Apr 65
		Feb 66 to Jul 66
		Mar 68 to Jun 68

Fighter Squadrons

VF-11	F-4B	*USS Forrestal*	Jun 67 to Sep 67
VF-14	F-4B	*USS Franklin D Roosevelt*	Jun 66 to Feb 67
VF-21	F-4B	*USS Midway*	Mar 65 to Nov 65
	F-4B	*USS Coral Sea*	Jul 66 to Feb 67
	F-4B	*USS Ranger*	Nov 67 to May 68
	F-4J	*USS Ranger*	Oct 68 to May 69
VF-24	F-8C	*USS Hancock*	Nov 64 to May 65
	F-8C	*USS Bon Homme Richard*	Dec 65 to Aug 66
	F-8C	*USS Hancock*	Jan 67 to Aug 67
	F-8H	*USS Hancock*	Jul 68 to Mar 69
VF-32	F-4B	*USS Franklin D Roosevelt*	Jun 66 to Feb 67
VF-33	F-4J	*USS America*	Apr 68 to Dec 68
VF-41	F-4B	*USS Independence*	May 65 to Nov 65
VF-51	F-8E	*USS Ticonderoga*	Sep 65 to May 66
	F-8E	*USS Ticonderoga*	Jan 67 to Jul 67
	F-8H	*USS Hancock*	Jan 68 to Oct 68
VF-53	F-8E	*USS Ticonderoga*	Sep 65 to May 66
	F-8E	*USS Ticonderoga*	Jan 67 to Jul 67
	F-8E	*USS Hancock*	Jan 68 to Oct 68
VF-74	F-4B	*USS Forrestal*	Jun 67 to Sep 67
VF-84	F-4B	*USS Independence*	May 65 to Nov 65

VF-92	F-4B	*USS Ranger*	Aug 64 to May 65
	F-4B	*USS Enterprise*	Oct 65 to Jun 66
	F-4B	*USS Enterprise*	Nov 66 to Jul 67
	F-4B	*USS Enterprise*	Jan 68 to Jul 68
VF-96	F-4B	*USS Ranger*	Aug 64 to May 65
	F-4B	*USS Enterprise*	Oct 65 to Jun 66
	F-4B	*USS Enterprise*	Dec 66 to Jul 67
	F-4B	*USS Enterprise*	Jan 68 to Jul 68
VF-102	F-4J	*USS America*	Apr 68 to Dec 68
VF-111	F-8C	*USS Midway*	Mar 65 to Nov 65
	F-8E	*USS Oriskany*	May 66 to Nov 66
	F-8C	*USS Intrepid* (det)	May 67 to Dec 67
	F-8C	*USS Oriskany*	Jun 67 to Jan 68
	F-8C	*USS Intrepid* (det)	Jun 68 to Feb 69
VF-114	F-4B	*USS Kitty Hawk*	Nov 65 to Jun 66
	F-4B	*USS Kitty Hawk*	Nov 66 to Jun 67
	F-4B	*USS Kitty Hawk*	Dec 67 to Aug 68
	F-4B	*USS Kitty Hawk*	Dec 68 to Sep 69
VF-142	F-4B	*USS Constellation*	Dec 65 to Aug 66
	F-4B	*USS Ranger*	Apr 67 to Dec 67
	F-4B	*USS Constellation*	May 68 to Jan 69
VF-143	F-4B	*USS Constellation*	Dec 65 to Aug 66
	F-4B	*USS Ranger*	Apr 67 to Dec 67
	F-4B	*USS Constellation*	May 68 to Jan 69
VF-151	F-4B	*USS Coral Sea*	Oct 64 to May 65
	F-4B	*USS Constellation*	May 66 to Dec 66
	F-4B	*USS Coral Sea*	Aug 67 to Mar 68
	F-4B	*USS Coral Sea*	Sep 68 to Apr 69
VF-154	F-4B	*USS Coral Sea*	Jul 66 to Feb 67
	F-4B	*USS Ranger*	Jan 67 to May 68
	F-4J	*USS Ranger*	Oct 68 to May 69
VF-161	F-4B	*USS Constellation*	May 66 to Dec 66
	F-4B	*USS Coral Sea*	Aug 67 to Mar 68
	F-4B	*USS Coral Sea*	Sep 68 to Apr 69
VF-162	F-8E	*USS Oriskany*	Apr 65 to Nov 65
	F-8E	*USS Oriskany*	May 66 to Nov 66
	F-8E	*USS Oriskany*	Jun 67 to Jan 68
VF-191	F-8E	*USS Bon Homme Richard*	Apr 65 to Jan 66
	F-8B	*USS Ticonderoga*	Oct 66 to May 67
	F-8E	*USS Ticonderoga*	Dec 67 to Jul 68
VF-194	F-8E	*USS Bon Homme Richard*	Apr 65 to Jan 66
	F-8E	*USS Ticonderoga*	Oct 66 to May 67
	F-8E	*USS Ticonderoga*	Dec 67 to Jul 68
VF-211	F-8E	*USS Hancock*	Nov 64 to May 65
	F-8E	*USS Hancock*	Dec 65 to Aug 66
	F-8E	*USS Bon Homme Richard*	Jan 67 to Aug 67
	F-8J	*USS Hancock*	Jan 68 to Mar 69

VF-213	F-4B	*USS Kitty Hawk*	Nov 65 to Jun 66
	F-4B	*USS Kitty Hawk*	Nov 66 to Jun 67
	F-4B	*USS Kitty Hawk*	Dec 67 to Aug 68
	F-4B	*USS Kitty Hawk*	Dec 68 to Sep 69

Attack Squadrons

VA-12	A-4E	*USS Franklin D Roosevelt*	Jun 66 to Feb 67
VA-15	A-4B	*USS Intrepid*	Apr 66 to Nov 66
	A-4C	*USS Intrepid*	May 67 to Dec 67
VA-22	A-4C	*USS Midway*	Mar 65 to Nov 65
	A-4C	*USS Coral Sea*	Jul 66 to Feb 67
	A-4C	*USS Ranger*	Nov 67 to May 68
VA-23	A-4E	*USS Midway*	Mar 65 to Jan 65
	A-4E	*USS Coral Sea*	Jul 66 to Feb 67
	A-4F	*USS Ticonderoga*	Dec 67 to Jul 68
VA-25	A-1H	*USS Midway*	Mar 65 to Nov 65
	A-1H	*USS Coral Sea*	Jul 66 to Feb 67
	A-1H/J	*USS Coral Sea*	Aug 67 to Mar 68
VA-27	A-7A	*USS Contellation*	May 69 to Jan 69
VA-34	A-4C	*USS Intrepid*	May 67 to Dec 67
VA-35	A-6A	*USS Enterprise*	Dec 66 to Jul 67
	A-6A	*USS Enterprise*	Jan 68 to Jul 68
VA-36	A-4C	*USS Interprise*	Oct 65 to Jun 66
	A-4C	*USS Intrepid*	Jun 68 to Feb 69
VA-46	A-4E	*USS Forrestal*	Jun 67 to Sep 67
VA-52	A-1H/J	*USS Ticonderoga*	Sep 65 to May 66
	A-1H/J	*USS Ticonderoga*	Oct 66 to May 67
	A-6A	*USS Coral Sea*	Sep 68 to Apr 69
VA-55	A-4E	*USS Ranger*	Dec 65 to Aug 66
	A-4E	*USS Constellation*	Apr 67 to Dec 67
	A-4F	*USS Hancock*	Jul 68 to Mar 69
VA-56	A-4E	*USS Ticonderoga*	Sep 65 to May 66
	A-4C	*USS Enterprise*	Dec 66 to Jul 67
	A-4E	*USS Enterprise*	Jan 68 to Jul 68
VA-65	A-6A	*USS Constellation*	May 66 to Dec 66
	A-6A	*USS Forrestal*	Jun 67 to Sep 67
VA-66	A-4C	*USS Intrepid*	Jun 68 to Feb 69
VA-72	A-4E	*USS Independence*	May 65 to Nov 65
	A-4E	*USS Franklin D Roosevelt*	Jun 66 to Feb 67
VA-75	A-6A	*USS Independence*	May 65 to Nov 65
	A-6A/B	*USS Kitty Hawk*	Dec 67 to Aug 68
VA-76	A-4C	*USS Bon Homme Richard*	Oct 65 to Jun 66
	A-4C	*USS Enterprise*	Jan 67 to Aug 67
VA-82	A-7A	*USS America*	Apr 68 to Dec 68
VA-85	A-6A	*USS Kitty Hawk*	Nov 65 to Jun 66
	A-6A	*USS Kitty Hawk*	Nov 66 to Jun 67
	A-6A/B	*USS America*	Apr 68 to Dec 68

VA-86	A-4E	*USS Independence*	May 65 to Nov 65
	A-7A	*USS America*	Apr 68 to Dec 68
VA-93	A-4C	*USS Ranger*	Aug 64 to May 65
	A-4C	*USS Enterprise*	Oct 65 to Jun 66
	A-4E	*USS Hancock*	Jan 67 to Jul 67
	A-4F	*USS Bon Homme Richard*	Jan 68 to Oct 68
VA-94	A-4C	*USS Ranger*	Aug 64 to May 65
	A-4C	*USS Enterprise*	Oct 65 to Jun 66
	A-4C	*USS Hancock*	Jan 67 to Jul 67
	A-4E	*USS Bon Homme Richard*	Jan 68 to Oct 68
VA-95	A-1H/J	*USS Ranger*	Aug 64 to May 65
	A-4B	*USS Intrepid*	Apr 66 to Nov 66
VA-97	A-7A	*USS Constellation*	May 68 to Jan 69
VA-106	A-4E	*USS Forrestal*	Jun 67 to Sep 67
	A-4E	*USS Intrepid*	Jun 68 to Feb 69
VA-112	A-4C	*USS Kitty Hawk*	Nov 66 to Jun 67
	A-4C	*USS Kitty Hawk*	Dec 67 to Aug 68
VA-113	A-4C	*USS Kitty Hawk*	Nov 65 to Jun 66
	A-4C	*USS Enterprise*	Dec 66 to Jul 67
	A-4F	*USS Enterprise*	Jan 68 to Jul 68
VA-115	A-1H/J	*USS Kitty Hawk*	Nov 65 to Jun 66
	A-1H/J	*USS Hancock*	Jan 67 to Jul 67
VA-144	A-4C	*USS Ticonderoga*	Sep 65 to May 66
	A-4C	*USS Kitty Hawk*	Nov 66 to Jun 67
	A-4E	*USS Kitty Hawk*	Dec 67 to Aug 68
VA-145	A-1H/J	*USS Ranger*	Dec 65 to Aug 66
	A-1H/J	*USS Intrepid*	May 67 to Dec 67
VA-146	A-4C	*USS Ranger*	Dec 65 to Aug 66
	A-4C	*USS Constellation*	Apr 67 to Dec 67
VA-147	A-7A	*USS Ranger*	Nov 67 to May 68
	A-7A	*USS Ranger*	Oct 68 to May 69
VA-152	A-1H/J	*USS Oriskany*	May 65 to Nov 65
	A-1H/J	*USS Oriskany*	May 66 to Nov 66
	A-1H/J	*USS Oriskany*	Jul 67 to Jan 68
VA-153	A-4C	*USS Coral Sea*	Oct 64 to May 65
	A-4C	*USS Constellation*	May 66 to Dec 66
	A-4C	*USS Coral Sea*	Aug 67 to Mar 68
	A-4F	*USS Coral Sea*	Sep 68 to Apr 69
VA-155	A-4E	*USS Coral Sea*	Oct 64 to May 65
	A-4E	*USS Constellation*	May 66 to Dec 66
	A-4E	*USS Coral Sea*	Aug 67 to Mar 68
	A-4E	*USS Coral Sea*	Oct 68 to May 69
VA-163	A-4E	*USS Oriskany*	May 65 to Nov 65
	A-4E	*USS Oriskany*	May 66 to Nov 66
	A-4E	*USS Oriskany*	Jul 67 to Jan 68
	A-4E	*USS Hancock*	Jul 68 to Mar 69

VA-164	A-4E	*USS Oriskany*	May 65 to Nov 65
	A-4E	*USS Oriskany*	May 66 to Nov 66
	A-4E	*USS Oriskany*	Jul 67 to Jan 68
	A-4E	*USS Hancock*	Jul 68 to Mar 69
VA-165	A-1H/J	*USS Coral Sea*	Oct 64 to May 65
	A-1H/J	*USS Intrepid*	Apr 66 to Nov 66
	A-6A	*USS Ranger*	Nov 67 to May 68
	A-6A	*USS Ranger*	Oct 68 to May 69
VA-172	A-4C	*USS Franklin D Roosevelt*	Jun 66 to Feb 67
VA-176	A-1H/J	*USS Intrepid*	Apr 66 to Nov 66
VA-192	A-4C	*USS Bon Homme Richard*	Mar 65 to Jan 66
	A-4E	*USS Ticonderoga*	Oct 66 to May 67
	A-4E	*USS Ticonderoga*	Dec 67 to Jul 68
VA-195	A-4C	*USS Bon Homme Richard*	Mar 65 to Jan 66
	A-4C	*USS Ticonderoga*	Oct 66 to May 67
	A-4C	*USS Ticonderoga*	Dec 67 to Jul 68
VA-196	A-1H/J	*USS Bon Homme Richard*	Mar 65 to Jan 66
	A-6A	*USS Constellation*	Apr 67 to Dec 67
	A-6A/B	*USS Constellation*	May 68 to Jan 69
VA-212	A-4C	*USS Hancock*	Nov 64 to May 65
	A-4E	*USS Hancock*	Dec 65 to Aug 66
	A-4E	*USS Bon Homme Richard*	Jan 67 to Aug 67
	A-4F	*USS Bon Homme Richard*	Jan 68 to Oct 68
VA-215	A-1H	*USS Hancock*	Nov 64 to May 65
	A-1H/J	*USS Hancock*	Dec 65 to Aug 66
	A-1H/J	*USS Bon Homme Richard*	Jan 67 to Aug 67
VA-216	A-4C	*USS Hancock*	Nov 64 to May 65
	A-4C	*USS Hancock*	Dec 65 to Aug 66
	A-4C	*USS Coral Sea*	Sep 68 to Apr 69

Reconnaissance Units

RVAH-1	RA-5C	*USS Indepemdence*	May 65 to Nov 65
	RA-5C	*USS Enterprise*	Jan 68 to Jul 68
RVAH-5	RA-5C	*USS Ranger*	Aug 64 to May 65
	RA-5C	*USS Constellation*	May 68 to Jan 69
RVAH-6	RA-5C	*USS Constellation*	May 65 to Dec 66
	RA-5C	*USS Ranger*	Nov 67 TO May 68
RVAH-7	RA-5C	*USS Enterprise*	Oct 65 to Jun 66
	RA-5C	*USS Enterprise*	Dec 66 to Jul 67
RVAH-9	RA-5C	*USS Ranger*	Dec 65 to Aug 66
	RA-5C	*USS Ranger*	Oct 68 to May 69
RVAH-11	RA-5C	*USS Forrestal*	Jun 67 to Sep 67
	RA-5C	*USS Kitty Hawk*	Dec 67 to Aug 68
	RA-5C	*USS Kitty Hawk*	Dec 68 to Sep 69
RVAH-12	RA-5C	*USS Constellation*	Apr 67 to Dec 67
RVAH-13	RA-5C	*USS Kitty Hawk*	Nov 65 to Jun 66
	RA-5C	*USS Kitty Hawk*	Nov 66 to Jun 67
	RA-5C	*USS America*	Apr 68 to Dec 68

VFP-62	RF-8G	*USS Franklin D Roosevelt*	Jun 66 to Feb 67 (D)
VPF-63	RF-8A	*USS Ranger*	Aug 64 to May 65 (D)
	RF-8A	*USS Hancock*	Oct 64 to May 65 (D)
	RF-8A	*USS Coral Sea*	Dec 64 to Nov 65 (D)
	RF-8A	*USS Midway*	Mar 65 to Nov 65 (D)
	RF-8A	USS Oriskany	Apr 65 to Dec 65 (D)
	RF-8A	*USS Bon Homme Richard*	Apr 65 to Jan 66 (D)
	RF-8G	*USS Ticonderoga*	Sep 65 to May 66 (D)
	RF-8G	*USS Hancock*	Nov 65 to Aug 66 (D)
	RF-8G	*USS Oriskany*	May 66 to Nov 66 (D)
	RF-8G	*USS Coral Sea*	Jul 66 to Feb 67 (D)
	RF-8G	*USS Ticonderoga*	Oct 66 to May 67 (D)
	RF-8G	*USS Hancock*	Jan 67 to Jul 67 (D)
	RF-8G	*USS Bon Homme Richard*	Jan 67 to Aug 67 (D)
	RF-8G	*USS Intrepid*	May 67 to Dec 67 (D)
	RF-8G	*USS Oriskany*	Jun 67 to Jan 68 (D)
	RF-8G	*USS Coral Sea*	Jul 67 to Apr 68 (D)
	RF-8G	*USS Ticonderoga*	Dec 67 to Aug 68 (D)
	RF-8G	*USS Bon Homme Richard*	Jan 68 to Oct 68 (D)
	RF-8G	*USS Intrepid*	Apr 68 to Feb 69 (D)
	RF-8G	*USS Hancock*	Jul 68 to Mar 69 (D)
	RF-8G	*USS Coral Sea*	Jul 68 to Apr 69 (D)

Helicopter Units

HC-1	UH-2A/B	*USS Coral Sea*	Jul 65 to Nov 65 (D)
	UH-2A	*USS Midway*	Jul 65 to Nov 65 (D)
	UH-2A/B	*USS Oriskany*	Jul 65 to Dec 65 (D)
	UH-2A/B	*USS Bon Homme Richard*	Jul 65 to Jan 66 (D)
	UH-2A/B	*USS Ticonderoga*	Sep 65 to May 66 (D)
	UH-2A/B	*USS Kitty Hawk*	Oct 65 to Mar 66 (D)
	UH-2A/B	*USS Enterprise*	Oct 65 to Jun 66 (D)
	UH-2A/B	*USS Hancock*	Nov 65 to Aug 66 (D)
	UH-2A/B	*USS Ranger*	Dec 65 to Aug 66 (D)
	Uh-2A/B	*USS Constellation*	May 66 to Dec 66 (D)
	UH-2A/B	*USS Oriskany*	May 66 to Nov 66 (D)
	UH-2A/B	*USS Coral Sea*	Jul 66 to Feb 67 (D)
	UH-2A/B	*USS Ticonderoga*	Oct 66 to May 67 (D)
	UH-2A/B	*USS Kitty Hawk*	Nov 66 to Jun 67 (D)
	UH-2A/B	*USS Enterprise*	Nov 66 to Jun 67 (D)
	UH-2A/B	*USS Hancock*	Jan 67 to Jul 67 (D)
	UH-2B	*USS Bon Homme Richard*	Jan 67 to Aug 67 (D)
	UH-2A/B	*USS Constellation*	Apr 67 to Dec 67 (D)
	UH-2A/B	*USS Oriskany*	Jun 67 to Jan 68 (D)
	UH-2A	*USS Coral Sea*	Jul 67 to Apr 68 (D)
	UH-2A/C	*USS Ranger*	Nov 67 to May 68 (D)
	UH-2C	*USS Kitty Hawk*	Nov 67 to May 68 (D)
	UH-2B	*USS Ticonderoga*	Dec 67 to Aug 68 (D)

	UH-2C	*USS Enterprise*	Jan 68 to Jul 68 (D)
	UH-2C	*USS Bon Homme Richard*	Jan 68 to Oct 68 (D)
	UH-2C	*USS Constellation*	May 68 to Jan 69 (D)
	UH-2C	*USS Hancock*	Jul 68 to Mar 69 (D)
	UH-2C	*USS Coral Sea*	Sep 68 to Apr 69 (D)
	UH-2C	*USS Ranger*	Oct 68 to May 69 (D)
HC-2	UH-2A	*USS Independence*	Jul 65 to Dec 65 (D)
	UH-2A/B	*USS Intrepid*	Apr 66 to Nov 66 (D)
	UH-2A/B	*USS Franklin D Roosevelt*	Jun 66 to Feb 67 (D)
	UH-2A/B	*USS Intrepid*	May 67 to Dec 67 (D)
	UH-2A/B	*USS Forrestal*	Jun 67 to Sep 67 (D)
	UH-2A/B	*USS America*	Apr 68 to Dec 68 (D)
	UH-2A/B	*USS Intrepid*	Jun 68 to Feb 69 (D)
HU-1	UH-2A	*USS Ranger*	Aug 64 to May 65 (D)
	UH-2A	*USS Hancock*	Oct 64 to May 65 (D)
	UH-2A/B	*USS Coral Sea*	Dec 64 to Jun 65 (D)
	UH-2A	*USS Midway*	Mar 65 to Jun 65 (D)
	UH-2A/B	*USS Oriskany*	Apr 65 to Jun 65 (D)
	UH-2A/B	*USS Bon Homme Richard*	Apr 65 to Jun 65 (D)
HU-2	UH-2A	USS Independence	May 65 to Jun 65 (D)
HC-7	SH-3A		
	/HH-3A	Various	Sep 67 onwards
HS-2	SH-3A	*USS Hornet*	Aug 65 to Mar 66
	SH-3A	*USS Hornet*	Mar 67 to Oct 67
	SH-3A	*USS Hornet*	Sep 68 to May 69
HS-4	SH-3A	*USS Yorktown*	Oct 64 to May 65
	SH-3A	*USS Yorktown*	Jan 66 to Jul 66
	SH-3A	*USS Yorktown*	Dec 67 to Jul 68
HS-6	SH-3A	*USS Kearsarge*	Jun 66 to Dec 66
	SH-3A	*USS Kearsarge*	Aug 67 to Apr 68
HS-7	SH-3A	*USS Bennington*	Mar 65 to Oct 65
	SH-3A	*USS Bennington*	Nov 66 to May 67
	SH-3A	*USS Bennington*	May 68 to Nov 68

Airborne Tanker Units

VAH-2	A-3B	*USS Ranger*	Aug 64 to May 65 (D)
	A-3B	USS *USS Coral Sea*	Dec 64 to Nov 65
	A-3B	*USS Ranger*	Dec 65 to Aug 66 (D)
	A-3B	*USS Coral Sea*	Jul 66 to Feb 67 (D)
	A-3B	*USS Enterprise*	Nov 66 to Jul 67 (D)
	KA-3B	*USS Coral Sea*	Jul 67 to Apr 68 (D)
	KA-3B	*USS Ranger*	Nov 67 to May 68 (D)
	KA-3B	*USS Enterprise*	Jan 68 to Jul 68 (D)
	Ka-3B	*USS Constellation*	May 68 to Oct 68 (D)
VAH-4	A-3B	*USS Hancock*	Oct 64 to May 65 (D)
	A-3B	*USS Oriskany*	Apr 65 to Dec 65 (D)
	A-3B	*USS Independence*	May 65 to Dec 65 (D)

	A-3B	*USS Ticonderoga*	Sep 65 to May 66 (D)
	A-3B	*USS Kitty Hawk*	Oct 65 to Jun 66 (D)
	A-3B	*USS Enterprise*	Oct 65 to Jun 66 (D)
	A-3B	*USS Oriskany*	May 66 to Nov 66 (D)
	A-3B	*USS Ticonderoga*	Oct 66 to May 67 (D)
	A-3B	*USS Kitty Hawk*	Nov 66 to Jun 67 (D)
	A-3B	*USS Hancock*	Jan 67 to Jul 67 (D)
	A-3B	*USS Bon Homme Richard*	Jan 67 to Aug 67 (D)
	KA-3B	*USS Oriskany*	Jun 67 to Jan 68 (D)
	KA-3B	*USS Ticonderoga*	Dec 67 to Aug 68 (D)
VAH-8	A-3B	*USS Midway*	Mar 65 to Nov 65
	A-3B	*USS Constellation*	May 65 to Dec 66
	KA-3B	*USS Constellation*	Apr 67 to Dec 67
VAH-10	A-3B	*USS Franklin D Roosevelt*	Jun 66 to Feb 67 (D)
	KA-3B	*USS Forrestal*	Jun 67 to Sep 67 (D)
	KA-3B	*USS America*	Apr 68 to Dec 68 (D)
	KA-3B	*USS Coral Sea*	Sep 68 to Apr 69 (D)
	KA-3B	*USS Ranger*	Oct 68 to May 69 (D)

Early Warning and Counter-measures Units

	EA-1E	*USS Yorktown*	Oct 64 to May 65 (D)
VAW-11	EA-1E	*USS Yorktown*	Oct 64 to May 65 (D)
	E-1B	*USS Ranger*	Aug 64 to May 65 (D)
	E-1B	*USS Hancock*	Oct 64 to May 65 (D)
	E-1B	*USS Coral Sea*	Dec 64 to Nov 65(D)
	E-1B	*USS Midway*	Mar 65 to Nov 65 (D)
	E-1B	*USS Bennington*	Mar 65 to Oct 65 (D)
	E-1B	*USS Oriskany*	Apr 65 to Dec 65 (D)
	E-1B	*USS Bon Homme Richard*	Apr 65 to Jan 66 (D)
	E-1B	*USS Hornet*	Aug 65 to Mar 66 (D)
	E-1B	*USS Ticonderoga*	Sep 65 to May 66 (D)
	E-1B	*USS Enterprise*	Oct 65 to Jun 66 (D)
	E-1B	*USS Hancock*	Nov 65 to Aug 66 (D)
	E-1B	*USS Yorktown*	Jan 66 to Jul 66 (D)
	E-1B	*USS Oriskany*	May 66 to Nov 66 (D)
	E-1B	*USS Kearsarge*	Jun 66 to Dec 66 (D)
	E-1B	*USS Ticonderoga*	Oct 66 to Apr 67 (D)
	E-1B	*USS Bennington*	Nov 66 to Apr 67 (D)
	E-1B	*USS Hancock*	Jan 67 to Apr 67 (D)
	E-1B	*USS Bon Homme Richard*	Jan 67 to Apr 67 (D)
	E-1B	*USS Hornet*	Mar 67 to Apr 67 (D)
	E-2A	*USS Kitty Hawk*	Oct 65 to Jun 66 (D)
	E-2A	*USS Ranger*	Dec 65 to Aug 66 (D)
	E-2A	*USS Constellation*	May 66 to Dec 66 (D)
	E-2A	*USS Coral Sea*	Jul 66 to Feb 67 (D)
	E-2A	*USS Kitty Hawk*	Nov 66 to Apr 67 (D)
	E-2A	*USS Enterprise*	Nov 66 to Apr 67 (D)
VAW-12	E-1B	*USS Independence*	May 65 to Dec 65 (D)
	E-1B	*USS Franklin D Roosevelt*	Jun 66 to Feb 67 (D)

VAW-13	EKA-3B	*USS Ranger*	Nov 67 to May 68 (D)
	EKA-3B	*USS Enterprise*	Jan 68 to Jul 68 (D)
	EKA-3B	*USS Bon Homme Richard*	Jan 68 to Sep 68 (D)
	EKA-3B	*USS America*	Apr 68 to Sep 68 (D)
	EKA-3B	*USS Constellation*	May 68 to Sep 68 (D)
	EKA-3B	*USS Hancock*	Jul 68 to Sep 68 (D)
	EKA-3B	*USS Coral Sea*	Sep 68 to Apr 69 (D)
VAQW-33	EA-1F	*USS Ticonderoga*	Dec 67 to Aug 68 (D)
	EA-1F	*USS Intrepid*	Jun 67 to Feb 68 (D)
VAW-111	E-1B	*USS Bennington*	Apr 67 to May 67 (D)
	E-1B	*USS Ticonderoga*	Apr 66 to May 67 (D)
	E-1B	*USS Hancock*	Apr 67 to Jul 67 (D)
	E-1B	*USS Hornet*	Apr 67 to Oct 67 (D)
	E-1B	*USS Bon Homme Richard*	Apr 67 to Aug 67 (D)
	E-1B	*USS Oriskany*	Jun 67 to Jan 68 (D)
	E-1B	*USS Kearsarge*	Aug 67 to Apr 68 (D)
	E-1B	*USS Ticonderoga*	Dec 67 to Aug 68 (D)
	E-1B	*USS Yorktown*	Dec 67 to Jul 68 (D)
	E-1B	*USS Bon Homme Richard*	Jan 68 to Nov 68 (D)
	E-1B	*USS Bennington*	May 68 to Nov 68 (D)
	E-1B	*USS Hancock*	Jul 68 to Mar 69 (D)
	E-1B	*USS Hornet*	Sep 68 to May 69 (D)
VAW-112	E-2A	*USS Enterprise*	Apr 67 to Jul 67
	E-2A	*USS Enterprise*	Jan 68 to Jul 68
VAW-113	E-2A	*USS Constellation*	Apr 67 to Dec 67
	E-2A	*USS Constellation*	May 68 to Jan 69
VAW-114	E-2A	*USS Kitty Hawk*	Apr 67 to Jun 67
	E-2A	*USS Kitty Hawk*	Nov 67 to Jun 68
VAW-115	E-2A	*USS Ranger*	Nov 67 to May 68
	E-2A	*USS Ranger*	Oct 68 to May 69
VAW-116	E-2A	*USS Coral Sea*	Jul 67 to Apr 68
	E-2A	*USS Coral Sea*	Sep 68 to Apr 69
VAW-121	E-1B	*USS Intrepid*	May 67 to Dec 67 (D)
	E-1B	*USS Intrepid*	Jun 68 to Feb 69 (D)
VAW-122	E-2A	*USS America*	Apr 68 to Dec 68
VAW-123	E-2A	*USS Forrestal*	Jun 67 to Sep 67
VAW-124	E-2A	*USS America*	Apr 68 to Dec 68
VAQ-130	EKA-3B	*USS Bon Homme Richard*	Jan 68 toOct 68 (D)
	EKA-3B	*USS America*	Oct 68 to Dec 68 (D)
	EKA-3B	*USS Constellation*	Oct 68 to Jan 69 (D)
	EKA-3B	*USS Hancock*	Oct 68 to Mar 69 (D)
	EKA-3B	*USS Coral Sea*	Oct 68 to Apr 69 (D)
	EKA-3B	*USS Ranger*	Oct 68 to May 69 (D)
VS-21	S-2E	*USS Kearsarge*	Jun 66 to Dec 66
	S-2E	*USS Kearsarge*	Aug 67 to Apr 68
VS-23	S-2E	*USS Yorktown*	Oct 64 to May 65
	S-2E	*USS Yorktown*	Jan 66 to Jul 66
	S-2E	*USS Yorktown*	Dec 67 to Jul 68

VS-25	S-2E	*USS Yorktown*	Oct 64 to May 65
	S-2E	*USS Yorktown*	Jan 66 to Jul 66
	S-2E	*USS Yorktown*	Dec 67 to Jul 68
VS-29	S-2E	*USS Kearsarge*	Jun 66 to Dec 66
	S-2E	*USS Kearsarge*	Aug 67 to Apr 68
VS-33	S-2E	*USS Bennington*	Mar 65 to Oct 65
	S-2E	*USS Bennington*	Nov 66 to May 67
	S-2E	*USS Bennington*	May 68 to Nov 68
VS-35	S-2D/E	*USS Hornet*	Aug 65 to Mar 66
	S-2E	*USS Hornet*	Mar 67 to Oct 67
	S-2E	*USS Hornet*	Sep 68 to May 69
VS-37	S-2E	*USS Hornet*	Aug 65 to Mar 66
	S-2E	*USS Hornet*	Mar 67 to Oct 67
	S-2E	*USS Hornet*	Sep 68 to May 69
VS-38	S-2E	*USS Bennington*	Mar 65 to Oct 65
	S-2E	*USS Bennington*	Nov 66 to May 67
	S-2E	*USS Bennington*	May 68 to Nov 68

Antisubmarine Units

VSF-3	A-4B	*USS Intrepid*	May 67 to Dec 67

SHORE BASED SQUADRONS

VW-1	EC-121K Da Nang		Sep 64 onwards
VQ-1	EC-121K		
	\EKA-3B Da Nang		Aug 64 onwards
VAP-61	RA-3B	Da Nang	?
VAP-62	RA-3B	Don Muang	?

United States Marine Corps Units

Tactical Fighter Units

Marine Air Group 11

VMF234	F-8E	Da Nang	Jan 65-May 68
VMFA531	F-4B	Da Nang	Apr 65-Jan 66
VMFA542	F-4B	Da Nang	Mar 65-Feb 70
VMA242	A-6A	Da Nang	Nov 66-Sep 70*
HMS11	TF-9J	Da Nang	Jan 65-Jun 71**

* attack unit
** Reconnaissance unit

Marine Air Group 13

VMFA115	F-4B	Chu Lai	Jan 68-Jul 70
VMF232	F-8E	Da Nang	Dec 66-Sep 67
	F-4J	Chu Lai	Mar 68-Jan 69
VMFA323	F-4B	Chu Lai	Jan 66-Jan 69

Carrier-borne Unit

VMFA-212 F-8E	USS Oriskany	May 65 to Nov 65

331

Attack Units

Marine Air Group 12

VMA121	A-4E	Chu Lai	Nov 66 - Oct 68
VMA211	A-4E	Chu Lai	Dec 65 - Dec 70
VMA214	A-4C	Chu Lai	Jun 65 - Apr 70
VMA223	A-4E	Chu Lai	Dec 65 - Jan 70
VMA224	A-4C	Chu Lai	Jan 65 - Jan 66
VMA225	A-4C	Chu Lai	Jun 65 - Jan 66
VMA311	A-4E	Chu Lai	Jun 65 - Jul 70
VMA533	A-6A	Chu Lai	Apr 67 - Dec 69

Reconnaissance Units

HMS13	TF-9J	Chu Lai	Sep 66 - Oct 69
HMS17	TF-9J	Da Nang	Jan 67 - Jan 70

Electronic Counter-Measures Units

VMCJ1	EF-10B		
	\EA-6A	Da Nang	Apr 65 - Jan 73

Air Refuelling Units

VMGR152	KC-130F	Da Nang	Jun 64-Mar 65
VMGR352	KC-130F	Da Nang	Jan 66 - May 70

Vietnamese Air Force Units

23rd Tactical Wing

514FS	A-1H	Bien Hoa	Jan 65-Apr 75
518FS	A-1H	Bien Hoa	Oct 63-Apr 75
522FS	F-5A/B	Bien Hoa	Jun 67-Apr 75

33rd Tactical Wing

715RS	RF-5A	Tan Son Nhut	Jul 66-Apr 75*

* Reconnaissance unit

41st Tactical Wing

516FS	A-1H	{Nha Trang	Jan 63-Jan 68
	A-1H	{Da Nang	
615 Flt	B-57B	Da Nang	Aug 65-Apr 66

62nd Tactical Wing

524FS	A-1H	Nha Trang	Sep 65-Dec 67

74th Tactical Wing

520FS	A-1H	Nha Trang	Jun 64-Mar 75

83rd Survey and Observation Group

522FS	A-1H	Tan Son Nut	Apr 65-Sep 75

Appendix IX
Operations Over
North Vietnam 1964-1968

1964

PIERCE ARROW 5/8/64 Was an attack on North Vietnamese patrol boat bases and oil storage by aircraft from the carriers *Ticonderoga* and *Constellation*.

1965

FLAMING DART I 8/2/65 Aircraft from the carriers *Hancock* and *Coral Sea* attacked the barracks at Dong Hoi together with aircraft from the South Vietnamese Air Force.

FLAMING DART II 11/2/65 Strikes by 99 aircraft from the *Ranger*, *Coral Sea* and *Hancock* on North Vietnamese installations at Chanh Hoa.

ROLLING THUNDER 1 20/2/65 Cancelled because of political unrest in South Vietnam. It was to have been an attack on a naval base and barracks in the southern part of North Vietnam.

ROLLING THUNDER 2, **3 and 4** Also cancelled.

ROLLING THUNDER 5 2/3/65 Attacks on an ammunition depot at Xom Bong and Quang Khe naval base. At this stage the attacks were specified to be carried out on a particular day and could not be re-attacked later. The target was clearly stated with only a limited number of alternates if bad weather covered the primary target. The involvement of the South Vietnamese Air Force was also a condition of the strikes being carried out. Five US Air Force aircraft were lost.

ROLLING THUNDER 6 15/3/65 This involved a series of attacks on targets in the Southern part of North Vietnam, including an ammunition depot at Phu Qui and a radar installation on Tiger island, a small island 20 miles off the Vietnamese coast. The strikes were carried out by one hundred

US Air Force and Navy aircraft. The use of napalm was authorised for the first time during *Rolling Thunder 6* but only against specific military targets away from civilians.

ROLLING THUNDER 7 19-25/3/65 For the first time targets were released in weekly packages and the participation of the VNAF was no longer required. *Rolling Thunder 7* also introduced armed reconnaissance missions. Five targets and alternates were listed to be attacked, including Vu Con barracks and various radar sites. One US Air Force and two VNAF armed reconnaissance missions were included.

ROLLING THUNDER 8 26/3/65-1/4/65 The targets included in this package were nine radar sites and the VNAF was authorised to strike an army barracks. There were also three armed reconnaissance missions allowed. All the targets were below the 20th parallel except for a radar station on the island of Bach Long Vi which was 75 miles off the North Vietnamese coast and gave good radar coverage of strikes mounted from the American carriers. On the 26th March 70 Naval aircraft attacked the island but the destruction was not complete and the island was attacked again on the 29th, when four aircraft were lost.

ROLLING THUNDER 9 2-8/4/65 The targets in this package concentrated on lines of communication in the Southern part of North Vietnam and included attacks on the Than Hoa and Dong Phuong bridges. The first attack, of many, on the Than Hoa bridge was on the 3/4/65. The bridge was attacked again on the 4th and two F-105Ds were shot down by MiG-17s, the first losses to North Vietnamese aircraft. The first photograph of a North Vietnamese SA-2 surface to air missile site, 15 miles Southeast of Hanoi, was obtained on the 5th.

ROLLING THUNDER 10 9-16/4/65 The targets in this package again concentrated on transport targets including the bridges at Qui Vinh and Khe Khien. The number of armed reconnaissance sorties was increased to not more than 24 in any 24 hour period.

ROLLING THUNDER 11 - 14 17/4/65 to 12/5/65 The targets were still released in weekly packages. The total of sorties flown in April 1965 was 3,600. The main targets were still transport and army bases below 20 degrees.

BOMBING PAUSE 12/5/65 to 18/5/65 5 days and 20 hours.

ROLLING THUNDER 15 18-24/5/65 The bombing was re-started after the pause and specific areas were named for the armed reconnaissance for the first time. There was one raid allowed above the 20 degree parallel, which was on the barracks at Quang Suoi.

ROLLING THUNDER 16 25-31/5/65 The number of armed reconnaissance sorties was increased to 40 per day with no more than 200 during the package. The total number of strikes during May had increased to 4,000.

ROLLING THUNDER 17 1-7/6/65 In this package the total of armed recon. sorties was again increased to 260.

ROLLING THUNDER 18 - 47 8/6/65 to 24/12/65 The area and scope of the Rolling Thunder campaign continued to slowly expand in scope and area. A small number of targets in the northern part of North Vietnam were authorised but the restricted areas around Hanoi, Haiphong and along the Chinese border were established. The first strikes in Route Package VI were in September. The main targets were still transport and military. The total number of sorties for 1965 was 25.000.

BOMBING PAUSE 24/12/65 to 31/1/66 36 days and 15 hours.

1966

ROLLING THUNDER 48 31/1/66 to 28/2/66 The re-start of the bombing campaign saw the re-imposition of several of the restrictions on the bombing. The armed reconnaissance sorties were again restricted to below 21 degrees north. The weather was particularly bad during February limiting the carrying out of the package.

ROLLING THUNDER 49 1/3/66 to 31/3/66 The area covered by the raids was again extended to cover most of North Vietnam. The number of sorties in March was 8,000. The weather was still causing a number of mission cancellations.

ROLLING THUNDER 50 1/4/66 to 8/7/66 This package allowed armed reconnaissance of all North Vietnam including Route Package VI except for specific restricted areas. The number of sorties in April went up to 10,000. Four new bridges were included on the list of targets. The leaders of the air campaign were warned to prepare for attacks on several important targets in the North including the petrol, oil and lubricants storage (POL) but were told that they would have to wait for permission to be given for the raids to take place. The first B-52 raids over the North took place on the 11 april when 30 of the bombers struck the Mu Gia pass. The POL raids finally started on the 29th June and included attacks on targets in Hanoi and Haiphong.

ROLLING THUNDER 51 9/7/66 to 11/11/66 The target package for *Rolling Thunder 51* only included the existing targets with the addition of a small number of new bridge targets and one bypass. The armed recon. missions on the north east rail line into Hanoi forced the closure of the line for most of September and October.

ROLLING THUNDER 52 12/11/66 to 23/1/67 The monthly total of sorties in *Rolling Thunder 52* was increased to 13.200. The target list was expanded to include power stations, cement plants and steel works but these were removed from the list before they could be attacked. There were 79,000 *Rolling Thunder* sorties during 1966.

BOMBING PAUSE 24/12/66 to 26/12/66 2 days.

BOMBING PAUSE 31/12/66 to 2/1/67 2 days.

1967

ROLLING THUNDER 53 24/1/67 to 22/2/67 The existing target list was continued with only minor changes. The bad weather during the monsoon season restricted some missions.

ROLLING THUNDER 54 23/2/67 to 22/4/67 The targets included in this package were the steel works at Thai Nguyen north of Hanoi, which was bombed on the 10/3/67, and the Haiphong cement works. Power stations were also added to the list. Estuaries and inland waterways up to the 20 parallel were listed as being candidates for mining. The weather improved over North Vietnam after the early part of April and all the major targets in the package had been struck by the 22nd.

BOMBING PAUSE 8/2/67 to 12/2/67 5 days 18 hours.

ROLLING THUNDER 55 23/4/67 to 1/5/67 This included attacks on the MiG airfields at Kep and Hoa Lac for the first time. The power transformer in the centre of Hanoi and other targets in the restricted areas were allowed. Other targets included the Hanoi rail repair yards, three extra bridges and POL storage areas.

ROLLING THUNDER 56 2/5/67 to 19/7/67 The good weather over the north during this period meant that the bombing campaign was pursued to the full. Ten new targets were added to the list including the thermal power station in the centre of Hanoi, which was bombed on 19th May. A major effort was made to cut the lines of communications into Hanoi from China and Haiphong.

BOMBING PAUSE 23/5/67 to 24/5/67 1 day.

ROLLING THUNDER 57 25/5/67 to 1/6/68 Sixteen fixed targets in Route Package VI were authorised and in a political move to prempt the Stennis Hearings in Congress President Johnson added 20 more targets to the list in August. The summer of 1967 saw the heaviest period of the bombing of the north during *Rolling Thunder*. The main effort continued to be to cut off the transport system into Hanoi. On 11th August the Paul Doumer bridge in Hanoi was bombed for the first time. The Chinese Air Force shot down two F-4s that strayed across the border on the 21/8/67 while attacking the north west rail line. The sortie total for August was 11,634. During September 17 new fixed targets were added to the list. In October eight more targets were again added. The first strike on the port at Cam Pha close to Haiphong was 8th October. The airfield at Phuc Yen was bombed on 25th October. More targets were again added during November but the deterioration in the weather slowed down the rate of attacks. No new targets were added during December but the targets on the existing list were attacked again if it was thought necessary. Airfields, transport targets plus the Canal Des Rapides and Paul Doumer bridges were struck again. The total number of sorties carried out during 1967 was 108.000. But only 9,740 of these had been against the fixed targets on the authorised list.

BOMBING PAUSE 24/12/67 to 25/12/67 1 day.

BOMBING PAUSE 31/12/67 to 2/1/68 1 day and 12 hours.

1968

ROLLING THUNDER 57 (continued) The weather during the first three months of 1968 was very poor limiting the bombing campaign. February's weather was the worst of any month during the course of *Rolling Thunder*. On only three days, on average, each month was the weather good enough to make large scale raids possible. There were eight more targets placed on the bombing list during the early months of 1968. President Johnson announced the cut back in the bombing on 31st March. The bombing was restricted to bellow the 19th parallel and was concentrated on the transport system.

BOMBING LIMITATION 1/4/68 to 1/11/68 limited below 20th parallel. After the 4/4/68 the limit was bellow the 19th parallel.

ROLLING THUNDER 58 2/7/68 to 1/11/68 The sortie rate continued at approximately the same rate as before but was restricted to a much smaller area, Route Packages I, II and the southern part of III. This concentration of effort into a smaller area meant that the bombing was extremely heavy in this area. The focus of the bombing was again the transport system which was very badly hit. Johnson brought the *Rolling Thunder* campaign to an end with his announcement of a halt to the bombing of the North on 1st November 1968.

Air-to-Air Victories Claimed By US Fighter Crews During Rolling Thunder.

No 'official' list of air-to-air combat successes has been published. The listing below has been taken from information supplied to the membership of the now defunct *Cassidy Group* of fighter researchers by Barrett Tillman and supplemented by information already published, notably the listings to be found in *The Tonkin Gulf Yacht Club* by Rene J Francillion and *"..and kill MiGs"* by Lou Drendle.

Date	Svce/Unit		Type	Crew	Credit	Notes
9.4.65	USN	VF-96	F-4B	Lt(jg)TMMurphy /EnsRJFegan	MiG-17	1.
17.6.65	USN	VF-21	F-4B	CdrLPage /LtJCSmithJr	MiG-17	
	USN	VF-21	F-4B	LtJEDBatesonJr /LtRBDoremus	MiG-17	
20.6.65	USN	VA-25	A-1H	{LtCBJohnson	MiG-17	
	USN	VA-25	A-1H	{Lt(jg)CHartman		
10.7.65	USAF	45TFS	F-4C	CaptKEHolcombe /CaptACClark	MiG-17	
	USAF	45TFS	F-4C	CaptTSRoberts /CaptRCAnderson	MiG-17	
6.10.65	USN	VF-151	F-4B	LtCdrDMcIntyre /Lt(jg)AJohnson	MiG-17	
23.4.66	USAF	555TFS	F-4C	CaptREBlake /1LtSWGeorge	MiG-17	
	USAF	555TFS	F-4C	CaptMFCameron /1LtREEvans	MiG-17	
26.4.66	USAF	480TFS	F-4C	MajPTGilmore /1LtWTSmith	MiG-21	
29.4.66	USAF	555TFS	F-4C	CaptWBDDowell /1LtHEGossard	MiG-17	
	USAF	555TFS	F-4C	CaptLRKeith /1LtRABleakley	MiG-17	
30.4.66	USAF	555TFS	F-4C	CaptRHGolberg /1LtGDHardgrave	MiG-17	
12.5.66	USAF	390TFS	F-4C	MajWRDudley /1LtIKringelis	MiG-17	2.

Date	Svce/Unit		Type	Crew	Credit	Notes
12.6.66	USN	VF-211	F-8E	Cdr H.L.Marr	MiG-17	
21.6.66	USN	VF-211	F-8	Lt E.J.Chancy	MiG-17	
	USN	VF-211	F-8E	Lt(jg)P.V.Vampatella	MiG-17	
29.6.66	USAF	388TFW	F-105D	Maj F L Tacey	MiG-17	
13.7.66	USN	VF-161	F-4B	Lt B McGuigan /Lt(jg)B Fowler	MiG-17	
14.7.66	USAF	480TFS	F-4C	Capt W J Swendner /1Lt D A Buttell Jr.	MiG-21	
	USAF	480TFS	F-4C	1Lt R G Martin /1Lt R N Krieps	MiG-21	
18.8.66	USAF	334TFS	F-105D	Maj K T Blank	MiG-17	
16.9.66	USAF	555TFS	F-4C	1Lt J W Jameson /1Lt D B Rose	MiG-17	
21.9.66	USAF	421TFS	F-105D	1Lt K W Richter	MiG-17	
	USAF	333TFS	F-105D	1Lt F A Wilson Jr	MiG-17	
9.10.66	USN	VA-176	A-1H	Lt(jg)W T Patton	MiG-17	
	USN	VF-162	F-8E	Cdr R.M.Bellinger	MiG-17	
5.11.66	USAF	480TFS	F-4C	Maj J E Tuck /1Lt J J Rabeni Jr	MiG-21	
	USAF	480TFS	F-4C	1Lt W J Latham Jr /1Lt K J Klause	MiG-21	
4.12.66	USAF	469TFS	F-105D	Maj R S Dickey	MiG-17	
20.12.66	USN	VF-114	F-4B	Lt H.D.Wisely /Lt(jg)D.L.Jordan	An-2	
	USN	VF-213	F-4B	Lt D.McCrae /Ens D.Nichols	An-2	
2.1.67	USAF	555TFS	F-4C	Col R Olds /1Lt C C Clifton	MiG-21	
	USAF	555TFS	F-4C	Capt W S Radeker III /1Lt J E Murray III	MiG-21	
	USAF	555TFS	F-4C	Capt E T Raspberry Jr /1Lt R W Western	MiG-21	
	USAF	555TFS	F-4C	1Lt R F Wetterhahn /1Lt J K Sharp	MiG-21	
	USAF	433TFS	F-4C	Maj P P Combies /1Lt L R Dutton	MiG-21	
	USAF	433TFS	F-4C	Capt J B Stone /1Lt C P Dunnegan Jr	MiG-21	
	USAF	433TFS	F-4C	1Lt L J Glynn Jr /1Lt L E Cary	MiG-21	
6.1.67	USAF	555TFS	F-4C	Maj T M Hirsch /1Lt R J Strasswimmer	MiG-21	
	USAF	555TFS	F-4C	Capt R M Pascoe /1Lt N E Wells	MiG-21	
10.3.67	USAF	354TFS	F-105D	Capt M C Brestel	MiG-17	
	USAF	354TFS	F-105D	Capt M C Brestel	MiG-17	

Date	Svce/Unit		Type	Crew	Credit	Notes
26.3.67	USAF	333 TFS	F-105D	Col R R Scott	MiG-17	
19.4.67	USAF	354 TFS	F-105D	Maj J J Hunt	MiG-17	3.
	USAF	357 TFS	F-105F	Maj L K Thorsness /Capt H E Johnson	MiG-17	
	USAF	354 TFS	F-105D	Maj F G Tolman	MiG-17	
	USAF	354 TFS	F-105D	Capt W E Eskew	MiG-17	
23.4.67	USAF	389 TFS	F-4C	Maj R C Anderson /Capt F D Kjer	MiG-21	
24.4.67	USN	VF-114	F-4	Lt H.D. Wisely /Lt(jg) G.L. Anderson	MiG-17	
	USN	VF-114	F-4B	Lt C.E. Southwick /Ens J.W. Laing	MiG-17	
26.4.67	USAF	389 TFS	F-4C	Maj R W Moore Jr /1Lt J F Sears	MiG-21	
28.4.67	USAF	357 TFS	F-105D	Lt Col A F Dennis	MiG-17	
	USAF	357 TFS	F-105D	Maj H E Higgins	MiG-17	
30.4.67	USAF	333 TFS	F-105D	Capt T C Lesan	MiG-17	
1.5.67	USAF	390 TFS	F-4C	Maj R G Dilger /1Lt M Thies	MiG-17	4.
	USN	VF-211	F-8E	Lt Cdr M O Wright	MiG-17	
	USN	VA-76	A-4C	Lt Cdr T Schwartz	MiG-17	5.
4.5.67	USAF	555 TFS	F-4C	Col R Olds /1Lt W D Lafever	MiG-21	
12.5.67	USAF	333 TFS	F-105D	Capt J A Suzanne	MiG-17	
13.5.67	USAF	433 TFS	F-4C	Maj W L Kirk /1Lt S A Wayne	MiG-17	
	USAF	433 TFS	F-4C	Lt Col F A Haeffner /1Lt M R Bever	MiG-17	
	USAF	354 TFS	F-105D	Lt Col P C Gast	MiG-17	
	USAF	333 TFS	F-105D	Maj C D Osborne	MiG-17	
	USAF	333 TFS	F-105D	Maj R G Rilling	MiG-17	
	USAF	44 TFS	F-105D	Maj M E Seaver Jr	MiG-17	
	USAF	354 TFS	F-105D	Capt C W Couch	MiG-17	
14.5.67	USAF	480 TFS	F-4C	Maj S O Bakke /Capt R W Lambert	MiG-17	
	USAF	480 TFS	F-4C	Maj J A Hargrove Jr /1Lt S H Demuth	MiG-17	
	USAF	480 TFS	F-4C	Capt J T Craig Jr /1Lt J T Talley	MiG-17	
19.5.67	USN	VF-211	F-8E	Cdr P H Speer	MiG-17	
	USN	VF-211	F-8E	Lt(jg) J M Shea	MiG-17	
	USN	VF-24	F-8C	Lt Cdr B C Lee	MiG-17	
	USN	VF-24	F-8C	Lt P R Wood	MiG-17	
	USN	?????	F-8	Unknown pilot	MiG-17	6.

341

Date	Svce/Unit		Type	Crew	Credit	Notes
20.5.67	USAF	389 TFS	F-4C	Maj R D Janca /1Lt W E Roberts Jr	MiG-21	
	USAF	389 TFS	F-4C	Lt Col R F Titus /1Lt M Zimer	MiG-21	
	USAF	433 TFS	F-4	Maj J R Pardo /1Lt S A Wayne	MiG-17	
	USAF	433 TFS	F-4C	Col R Olds /1Lt S B Croker	MiG-17	
	USAF	433 TFS	F-4C	Col R Olds /1Lt S B Croker	MiG-17	7.
	USAF	433 TFS	F-4C	Maj P P Combies /Lt D L Lafferty	MiG-17	
22.5.67	USAF	389 TFS	F-4C	Lt Col R F Titus /1Lt M Zimer	MiG-21	
	USAF	389 TFS	F-4C	Lt Col R F Titus /1Lt M Zimer	MiG-21	
3.6.67	USAF	13 TFS	F-105D	Maj R L Kuster Jr	MiG-17	
	USAF	469 TFS	F-105D	Capt L D Wiggins	MiG-17	
5.6.67	USAF	480 TFS	F-4C	Maj D K Priester /Capt J E Pankhurst	MiG-17	
	USAF	555 TFS	F-4C	Maj R M Pascoe /Capt N E Wells	MiG-17	
	USAF	555 TFS	F-4C	Maj E T Raspberry Jr /Capt F M Gullick	MiG-17	
21.7.67	USN	VF-24	F-8C	Lt Cdr M H Isaacks	MiG-17	
	USN	VF-24	F-8C	Lt Cdr R L Kirkwood	MiG-17	
	USN	VF-211	F-8E	Lt Cdr R G Hubbard	MiG-17	
	USN	VF-24	F-8C	Lt(jg) P Dempewolf	MiG-17	
10.8.67	USN	VF-142	F-4B	Lt G H Freeborn /Lt(jg) R A Elliot	MiG-21	
	USN	VF-142	F-4B	Lt Cdr R C Davis /Lt Cdr G O Elie	MiG-21	
23.8.67	USAF	334 TFS	F-105D	1Lt D B Waldrop III	MiG-17	
	USAF	334 TFS	F-105D	1Lt D B Waldrop III	MiG-17	
	USAF	??? TFS	F-105D	Maj B R Givens	MiG-17	
18.10.67	USAF	333 TFS	F-105D	Maj D M Russell	MiG-17	
24.10.67	USAF	433 TFS	F-4D	Maj W L Kirk /1Lt T R Bongartz	MiG-21	
26.10.67	USAF	555 TFS	F-4D	Capt L D Cobb /Capt A A Lavoy	MiG-17	
	USAF	555 TFS	F-4D	Capt W S Gordon III /Lt J H Monsees	MiG-17	
	USAF	555 TFS	F-4D	Capt J D Logeman Jr /1Lt F E McCoy II	MiG-17	
	USN	VF-143	F-4B	Lt(jg) R.P.Hickey /Lt(jg) J.G.Morris	MiG-21	

Date	Svce/Unit		Type	Crew	Credit	Notes
27.10.67	USAF	354 TFS	F-105D	Capt G I Basel	MiG-17	
30.10.67	USN	VF-142	F-4B	Lt Cdr E.P.Lund /Lt(jg)J.R.Borst	MiG-17	8.
6.11.67	USAF	435 TFS	F-4D	Capt D H Simmonds /1Lt G H McKinney Jr	MiG-17	
	USAF	435 TFS	F-4D	Capt D H Simmonds /1Lt G H McKinney Jr	MiG-17	
14.12.67	USN	VF-162	F-8E	Lt R.E.Wyman	MiG-17	
17.12.67	USAF	13 TFS	F-4D	Capt D D Baker (USMC) /1Lt J D Ryan Jr	MiG-17	
19.12.67	USAF	357 TFS	F-105F	Capt P M Drew /Maj W H Wheeler	MiG-17	
	USAF	333 TFS	F-105F	Maj W M Dalton /Maj J L Graham	MiG-17	9.
	USAF	435 TFS	F-4D	Maj J D Moore /1Lt G H McKinney Jr	E/A	10.
3.1.68	USAF	435 TFS	F-4D	Lt Col C K Squier /1Lt M D Muldoon	MiG-17	10.
	USAF	433 TFS	F-4D	Maj B J Bogoslofski /Capt R L Huskey	MiG-17	11.
17.1.68	USAF	??? TFS	F-4C	Unknown crew	MiG-21	12.
18.1.68	USAF	435 TFS	F-4C	Maj K A Simonet /1Lt W O Smith	MiG-17	
5.2.68	USAF	13 TFS	F-4D	Capt R G Hill /1Lt B V Huneke	MiG-21	13.
6.2.68	USAF	433 TFS	F-4D	Capt R H Boles /1Lt R B Battista	MiG-21	
12.2.68	USAF	435 TFS	F-4D	Lt Col A E Lang Jr /1Lt R P Moss	MiG-21	
14.2.68	USAF	435 TFS	F-4D	Col D O Williams Jr /1Lt J P Feighny Jr	MiG-17	
	USAF	555 TFS	F-4D	Maj R D Howerton /1Lt T L Voight II	MiG-17	
9.5.68	USN	VF-96	F-4B	Maj J.P.Hefferman (USAF) /Lt(jg)F.A.Schumacher	MiG-21	
26.6.68	USN	VF-51	F-8H	Cdr L R Myers	MiG-21	
9.7.68	USN	VF-191	F-8E	Lt Cdr J.B.Nichols	MiG-17	
10.7.68	USN	VF-33	F-4J	Lt R Cash /Lt(jg)J E Kain Jr	MiG-21	
29.7.68	USN	VF-53	F-8E	Cdr G Cane	MiG-17	
1.8.68	USN	VF-51	F-8H	{Lt N K McCoy	MiG-21	14.
	USN	VF-51	F-8H	{Lt G E Heise		

Date	Svce/Unit		Type	Crew	Credit	Notes
19.9.68	USN	VF-111	F-8C	Lt A.J.Nargi	MiG-21	

Notes:

1. This crew failed to return and were originally credited with a 'probable', later upgraded to confirmed.
2. Chinese Air Force
3. Possibly a 'probable' rather than confirmed.
4. Forced to crash, not hit by missile.
5. Hit by Zuni air-to-ground rocket
6. Upgraded from 'probable'
7. Upgraded from 'probable'
8. During this engagement the crew was shot down by one of their own Sidewinder missiles and were later rescued.
9. There is some doubt as to whether this claim was subsequently confirmed.
10. Combat occurred between 19th December 1967 and 3rd January 1968.
10. Upgraded from 'probable'
11. Upgraded from 'probable'
12. Upgraded from 'probable'
13. Using AIM-4D Falcon
14. Shared credit

Index

People - American

People, mentioned in the text, who were directly involved in the political or military prosecution of Rolling Thunder

People - Vietnamese

People - Others

Not directly involved in Rolling Thunder

Units - USAF, USN, USMC

37th ARRS	320
37th TFW,	318
38th ARRS	320
39th ARRS	320
40th ARRS	320
41st TEWS	321
41st TRS	321
41st TEWS	321
43rd SW	320
43rd TFS,	317
44th TFS,	317, 318, 341
45th TFS	74, 311, 317, 339
45th TRS	319
47th TFS	68
55th RS	319
55th SOW	320
55th SRW	319
67th TFS,	317
82nd SRS	320
90th TFS,	317
100th SRW	320
120th TFS,	318
136th TFS,	318
174th TFS,	318
188th TFS,	318
306th TFS,	318
307th SW	320
307th TFS,	317
308th TFS,	318
309th TFS,	318
320th SBW	89
333rd TFS	78, 318, 340, 341, 342, 343
334th TFS	78, 318, 340, 342
335th TFS	318
347th TFW	318
349th SRS	320
350th SRS	320
352nd TFS	318
354th TFS	78, 340, 341, 343
355th TFS	318
355th TFW	61, 64, 78, 96, 126, 139, 140, 318
355th TRW	321
357th TFS	318, 341, 343
363rd TRS	321
366th TFW	318

376th SW	320
388th TFW	61, 78, 96, 139, 140, 282, 318, 340
389th TFS	318, 341, 342
390th TFS	318, 339, 341
416th TFS	318
421st TFS	78, 318, 340
428th TFS	318
429th TFS	319
432nd TRW	301, 319
433rd TFS	78, 102, 317, 340, 341, 342, 343
434th FS	104
435th TFS	317, 319, 343
460th TRW	301, 319
469th TFS	78, 318, 340, 342
474th TFW	319
476th TFS	319
479th TFW	319
480th TFS	318, 339, 340, 341, 342
481st TFS	319
497th TFS	78, 317
510th TFS	317
522nd AEWCW	321
531st TFS	317
552nd AWW Wing	273, 276
555th TFS	130, 317, 339, 340, 341, 342, 343
556th RS	318
557th TFS	317
558th TFS	317
559th TFS	317
561st TFS	318
563rd TFS	318
602nd SOS	320
604th SOS	320
612th TFS,	318
614th TFS,	318
615th TFS,	318
3960th SW	319, 320
4025th RS	320
4028th SRS	320
4080th SRW	300, 320
4133rd SW	319
4220th SW	320
4252nd SW	269, 319, 321

VAW-111	330	VF-213	324, 340
VAW-112	330	VMA-121	332
VAW-113	330	VMA-122	63
VAW-114	330	VMA-211	332
VAW-115	330	VMA-214	332
VAW-116	330	VMA-223	332
VAW-121	330	VMA-224	332
VAW-122	274, 330	VMA-225	332
VAW-123	330	VMA-242	331
VAW-124	330	VMA-311	332
VF-11	322	VMA-533	332
VF-14	322	VMCJ-1	293, 332
VF-21	75, 322, 339	VMF-232	331
VF-24	322, 341, 342	VMF-234	331
VF-32	322	VMFA-115	331
VF-33	161, 322, 343	VMFA-212	331
VF-41	322	VMFA-323	331
VF-51	322, 343	VMFA-531	331
VF-53	322, 343	VMFA-542	331
VF-74	322	VMGR-152	332
VF-84	322	VMGR-352	332
VF-92	323	VPF-62	327
VF-96	254, 259, 269, 323,	VPF-63	327
	339, 343	VQ-1	71, 331
VF-102	323	VS-21	330
VF-111	93, 323, 344	VS-23	330
VF-114	323, 340, 341	VS-25	331
VF-142	323, 342, 343	VS-29	331
VF-143	323, 342	VS-33	331
VF-151	323, 339	VS-35	331
VF-154	323	VS-37	331
VF-161	323, 340	VS-38	331
VF-162	105, 323, 340, 343	VSF-3	331
VF-191	323, 343	VW-1	331
VF-194	323	Western Pacific Fleet, USN 76	
VF-211	323, 340, 341, 342		

Units - South Vietnamese Air Force

23rd TW	332	518th FS	332
41st TW	332	520th FS	332
62nd TW	332	522nd FS	332
83rd SOG	332	524th FS	332
514th FS	332	615 Flt	332
516th FS	332	715th RS	332

Ships

Places

Aircraft - American

356

Aircraft - North Vietnamese and Chinese

Aircraft - Others

Miscellaneous